Sudanese Arabic—English
English—Sudanese Arabic

A Concise Dictionary

SIL International®
Publications in Linguistics
150

Publications in Linguistics are published by SIL International®. The series is a venue for works covering a broad range of topics in linguistics, especially the analytical treatment of minority languages from all parts of the world.

Series Editor
Mike Cahill

Volume Editor
Julia Anne McCord

Production Staff
Bonnie Brown, Managing Editor
Judy Benjamin, Compositor
Barbara Alber, Cover design

Cover Photograph
Ola Ahmed Diab, Sudanese journalist

Sudanese Arabic—English
English—Sudanese Arabic

A Concise Dictionary

edited by

Rianne Tamis

Janet Persson

SIL International®
2013

Library of Congress Catalog No: 2012950424
ISBN: 978-1-55671-272-2
ISSN: 1040-0850

Printed in the United States of America

Copies of this and other publications of SIL International® may be obtained from:

SIL International Publications
7500 W. Camp Wisdom Road
Dallas, TX 75236-5629

Voice: 972-708-7404
Fax: 972-708-7363
publications_intl@sil.org
www.ethnologue.com/bookstore.asp

Acknowledgements

The idea of composing a basic dictionary of Sudanese Arabic came into being when the management of Catholic Language Institute of Khartoum (CLIK) undertook to update the content of the *Spoken Arabic of Khartoum* (2005) course initiated by the Comboni Fathers. This book contained a glossary, but included only words used in the book itself. So there was a dire need for 'something more complete'. Andrew and Janet Persson of SIL, authors of *Sudanese Colloquial Arabic for Beginners* (2003), were also feeling the same need, so it was decided to work together. One dictionary already existed, *Sudan Arabic: English-Arabic Vocabulary*, compiled by S. Hillelson and published in London in 1925. Though we did make use of this work, many entries were obsolete and of course we wanted to have an Arabic-English part.

We are most indebted to Rianne Tamis, who coordinated the project at CLIK and did the editing of the Arabic-English part. Together with Awadia Yousuf and Ahmed Abdelmukarram, she was mainly responsible for the compilation and, with Mohammed Aljazouli Alsanhouri, for most of the corrections. Furthermore, we are very grateful to Janet and Andrew Persson for their valuable advice, and particularly to Janet for her corrections of the English in both parts and the editing of the English-Arabic part.

Already having a vast experience in compiling dictionaries, SIL International provided us with a computer tool, the database program *Shoebox*, conceived to develop dictionaries and wordlists. The name itself reminds us of the heroic time when filing cards had to be in such a box. We are grateful to the 'two Matthews' whose contributions were essential for the technical side of the story: Matthew Burdon, whose presence in Khartoum was sponsored and facilitated by Emmanuel Prinz of Partner Aid International, not only installed and introduced the database, but also helped in entering the glossary we already had. Some stages later, Mathieu Diserens not only 'saved' the program when it got stuck with problems due to the Arabic script, but improved the complete layout, in particular the English-Arabic part, according to our wishes. In this regard, we should also express a special thanks to Henk Pel, Peter Kahrel, John Duerksen and Vinton Goff, who assisted us with their valuable technical advice, and in particular to Bev Cope for coming to our rescue in the final stages.

Santurlino Lado patiently typed all the entries in Arabic. We also thank Ismail Abu Garga, Hamdan Elagib and Jihad Yousuf for their corrections of the pre-final version, Leoma Gilley for her helpful critique, Paul Hannon for the proofreading, and last but not least, Yves Lecocq for the overall coordination.

And beyond them all, we remember the many Sudanese we met in daily life, who helped us, sometimes without knowing it, to deepen our knowledge of the colourful Sudanese colloquial. We wish to express to them our deep gratitude.

Etienne Renaud
Director of CLIK (2002–2005)

Introduction

This dictionary seeks to present the basic vocabulary of the Sudanese Arabic language as it is spoken in Greater Khartoum. This vocabulary, however, is far from standardized. Contrary to the spoken language of other Arabic-speaking countries, where mass media have played an important role in the standardization of the country's main colloquial (generally that of the capital), the spoken language of Khartoum has developed along divergent lines since the 1980s. Before that time, Radio Omdurman, the only radio station then operating, was broadcasting to parts of Northern Sudan, and the spoken Arabic of the population of Omdurman took precedence.

This colloquial, however, has been affected by large waves of migrants from all regions of the country during the last decades. Until the 1970s, most of the migrants were bilingual or Arabic-speaking migrants from the northern states. During the seventies the first non-Arabic-speaking Sudanese from the Nuba Mountains came in search of work and education. Then, from the 1980s onwards, unprecedented waves of migrants seeking refuge from civil war in the South, drought in the West or sheer poverty in the East, arrived in Khartoum. The capital's population increased from 250,000 in 1956 to an estimated 2,831,000 in 1993. This figure would double and reach an officially estimated 4.5 million (unofficial estimates speak of six to seven million) by 2005. Large groups of these newcomers spoke a non-Arabic language; others were bilingual, and some spoke another Sudanese colloquial. With the passing of time, varieties of Arabic developed within and between these groups. Gradually, these varieties became the settlers' first language and have now become part of the group of colloquials that form the 'spoken Arabic of Khartoum'.

This 'spoken Arabic of Khartoum' has also been influenced, in particular since the 1990s, by an increase of popular Arabic 'soaps' on national television, in which the more prestigious Egyptian and Syrian colloquial languages are spoken. Also, with the appearance of Arabic satellite channels and the return of Sudanese expatriates from Saudi Arabia and the Gulf, vocabulary from these countries has, to a lesser extent, entered everyday language.

For these reasons, compiling the vocabulary for this dictionary has been challenging. The guiding principle has been to meet the wishes of foreigners for a basic dictionary as a tool to communicate with inhabitants of Greater Khartoum and its surroundings. For this purpose, too, the dictionary contains a number of Modern Standard Arabic words and phrases, such as medical, legal or political terminology. The Arabic-English section also contains a number of slang words and examples of the usage of words and expressions. The English-Arabic section is more concise. It has not listed slang words and gives examples of usage only to clarify ambiguous words or phrases.

The corpus of the colloquial is based on vocabulary still in use found in S. Hillelson's *Sudan Arabic: English-Arabic Vocabulary* (1925), Dr. Awn ash-Shariif Qaasim's *qaamuus al-lahja al-'aammiyya fi s-suudaan* (Khartoum, 1972), and the glossaries in *Spoken Arabic of Khartoum,* edited by Orlando Dal Cason, Muhammed Mabrouk and Shahinaz Muhammed. (Khartoum, 1991). It has been supplemented by words collected during daily conversations. Needless to say, the vocabulary is by no means complete.

Transcription

Roman	Arabic	Name	Pronunciation
ʿ	ع	ʿeyn	a strong guttural sound
'	ء	hamza	glottal stop ('short cutting of the breath')
a		fatḥa	as in English 'bud'
aa	ا	aalif	as in English 'father'
b	ب	baa'	as in English
d	د	daal	as in English
ḍ	ض	ḍaad	emphatic d
e			as in English 'wet'
ee	ي	yaa'	as in English 'eight'
f	ف	faa'	as in English
g	ق	qaaf	as in English 'got'
gh	غ	gheyn	like the French r
h	ه	haa'	as in English
ḥ	ح	ḥaa'	a very strongly aspirated h
i		kasra	as in English 'sip'
ii	ي	yaa'	as in English 'sheet'

j	ج	jiim	like the English j but softer
k	ك	kaaf	as in English
kh	خ	khaa'	like the ch of German 'Bach'/Scots 'loch'
l	ل	laam	as in English
m	م	miim	as in English
n	ن	nuun	as in English
o			as in English 'hot'
oo	و	waaw	similar to the vowel in English 'floor'
q	ق	qaaf	usually pronounced as gh
r	ر	raa'	a rolled r as in Italian 'rosa'
s	س	siin	as in English
ṣ	ص	ṣaad	emphatic s
sh	ش	shiin	as in English 'ship'
t	ت	taa'	as in English
ṭ	ط	ṭaa'	emphatic t
u		ḍamma	as in English 'put'
uu	و	waaw	as in English 'soothe'
w	و	waaw	as in English
y	ي	yaa'	as in English 'yet'
z	ز	zaa'	as in English
ẓ	ظ	ẓaa'	emphatic z
a	ة	taa' marbuuṭa	-a/-at in construction

Pronunciation and spelling

Since spoken Arabic is not normally written, it has no fixed spelling rules. Both the roman script and the Arabic script used here represent the *actual Sudanese Arabic pronunciation* of a word. However, words imported from other languages are transcribed according to the pronunciation in roman script only, e.g. **diblomaasi**. The Arabic script follows the rules of Modern Standard Arabic: ديبلوماسي .

The Classical Arabic suffix **-an,** for the accusative case-ending appearing 'fossilized' in some Sudanese Arabic words, like **tabʿan** or **shukran,** is represented in Arabic script by an **aalif,** following the Classical Arabic.

Note that the Arabic script is only given with the main words. Compound words, phrases, expressions, etc. are not followed by the Arabic script.

salad salaṭa سلطة ; **mixed salad** salaṭa ḥamra
ḥaaris حارس *n* (*pl* **ḥurraas**) guard, doorman; **ḥaaris al-marma** goalkeeper

Consonants

The Classical Arabic **qaaf,** a 'k-sound' produced in the back of the throat, is generally pronounced as **g.** The **qaaf** in words borrowed from Modern Standard Arabic is mostly pronounced as **gh.** Both **g** and **gh** are represented by the **qaaf** in Arabic script.

Vowels

The Classical Arabic diphthong **aw** has generally become **ow, oo** or **uu** in Sudanese Arabic, e.g. **yowṭa, yooḍaḥ, yuujaᶜ,** while the Classical Arabic diphthong **ay** is generally pronounced **ey, ee** or **ii** in Sudanese Arabic, e.g. **meydaani, sheekh, meedaan/miidaan**. Note, too, that the **ii** and **ee** are generally interchangeable, e.g. **jiiraan/jeeraan.**

In particular the pronunciation of the short vocals varies between groups of speakers. The main variations are:

Dictionary	Variation(s)	Examples
a	**e**	The definite article: **el-** for **al-**; **jebel** for **jabal.**
i	**a**	**shihaada** for **shahaada; wisaakha** for **wasaakha.**
u	**a**	In particular in participles: **maᶜawwag** for **muᶜawwag.** In a few cases the **u** variable has disappeared, e.g. in **mamaḥḥan.**
u	**i**	Plurals or verbal nouns of the **u-uu** pattern, like **guruush** or **zuhuur,** are often pronounced as **giruush** or **zihuur.** Other instances occur in nouns like **zikma** for **zukma** or in diminutives like **giṣayyir** for **guṣayyir.**

Arrangement of entries

Headwords

Headwords of the same form but not related are entered separately.

ᶜabar عبر *vt* (**i, ᶜabir**) to measure (e.g. grain)
ᶜabar عبر *vt* (**i, ᶜabra, ᶜubuur**) to cross, pass (street, bridge)

tease haẓẓar maᶜa هظّر (hiẓaar); kaawa كاوى (-i, mukaawaa); shaaghal (fi) شاغل (mushaaghala)
tease (**wool, cotton**) nafash نفش (u, nafish)

In the Arabic-English section a headword may only exist in compound version. It then immediately follows the part of speech or the verbal noun:
shihheeg شهيق *n* **abu sh-shihheeg** hiccup
intahaz انتهز *vt* (**intihaaz**) **intahaz al-furṣa** to take the opportunity

Part of speech

The part of speech refers to the headword in both Arabic-English and English-Arabic sections. The order in which different parts of speech appear after a headword varies according to its main usage. In the Arabic-English section the part of speech is always given. In the English-Arabic section it is only given when the headword refers to more than one part of speech.
smell *n* riiḥa ريحة (*pl* aryaaḥ, rawaayiḥ); **bad smell** ᶜafaana عفانة ; (of body) ṣunaan صنان • *vt* shamma شمّ (i, shamm) • *vi* ṭallaᶜ riiḥa

Verbs

In Arabic the citation form for a verb is always the third person singular masculine of the perfect (past) tense, which is what appears as the headword for each verb.

For the so-called basic verb form, the vowel of the imperfect (present) tense is given between brackets, followed by the verbal noun(s).
marag مرق *vi* (**u, muruug**) - the **u** represents the vowel in the present tense: **yamrug**.
nisa نسى *vt* (**-a, nasayaan**) - the **-a** represents the end vowel in the present tense: **yansa**.

For the derived forms that have standard vowels for the present tense, the vowel is only given with the verbs that end with a yaa' (**i/a**).
faḍḍa فضّى (**-i, fiḍḍeey, tafḍiya**) - the **-i** represents the vowel in the imperfect tense: **yafaḍḍi**.

If a verb is both used with or without a preposition, the preposition is put between brackets.
najaḥ نجح *vi* (**a, najaaḥ**) (**fi**) to succeed, be successful; to pass (an exam)
admit iᶜtaraf (be-) إعترف (iᶜtiraaf); garra (be-) قرّ (i, igraar)

In the case of fixed phrases, the preposition is put directly after the verb or part of speech.

gaḍa قضى (**-i, gaḍiya, gaḍayaan**) *vt* to finish • *vi* ʿ**ala** to finish with, terminate; to eliminate

herd *v* raʿa رعى (-a, raʿi); saraḥ be- سرح (a, sariḥ)

Active and passive participles

Active and passive participles have been listed only when they are very commonly used, or if they have an extra or different meaning from the verb they are related to, or if they consist of a compound phrase.

maktuub مكتوب *adj* **1** written **2** predestined, decreed by God

possessed ʿind-o zaar

Nouns

Nouns in the singular are followed by the plural between brackets. The plural is only given in the case of broken plurals. When both a regular and a broken plural exist, both are given.

faas فاس *n* (*pl* **fu'uus**) axe, hatchet

kettle kafateera كفتيرة (*pl* -aat, kafaatiir)

Plurals of the **-yyiin** and **-yya** pattern are both given.

intihaazi إنتهازي *adj* (*pl* **-yyiin**) opportunist

electrician kahrabji كهربجي (*pl* -yya)

Where an English noun is given with an attached **(s)**, it represents an Arabic collective noun. The unitary noun is given if it differs from the regular pattern of an added **a**. When both a regular and a non-regular unitary noun exist, both are given.

ant's namil نمل (*unit n* namla)

suksuk سكسك *coll n* (*unit n* **suksuka, suksukaaya**) bead(s)

Reading signs

A slash refers to both possibilities of usage.

naḍam نضم *vi* (**u, naḍim**) (**fi**/ʿ**an**) to talk, speak (about)

cheer *v* hataf هتف (u, hutaaf); **to cheer up** *vt/vi* farfash فرفش (firfeesh, farfasha)

A comma refers to different functions or meanings, except in the case of verbal nouns where it indicates that both are current.

kaḍḍab كضّب *vi* (**kiḍib**) (ʿ**ala, fi**) to lie (to, about)

tingle nammal نمّل (nimmeel, tanmiil)

Gender

It is only for practical reasons that the male form has been used for verbs, active and passive participles, as well as in expressions.

Abbreviations

adj adjective
adj invar invariable adjective
adv adverb
affirm affirmative
agr agricultural
anat anatomical
arith arithmetic
art article
chem chemical
Chr Christian
coll n collective noun
conj conjunction
def definite
dem pron demonstrative pronoun
dual dualis
elec electrical
excl exclamatory
f feminine
fig figurative
fin financial
geog geographical
geom geometry
gram grammatical
imp imperative
indef indefinite
instr instrument
interj interjection
interrog interrogative
Isl Islamic
leg legal
lit literal
m masculine
mech mechanical
med medical
mil military
n noun
neg negative
num numeral
o.s. oneself
part particle
pej pejorative
phys physics
pl plural
pol political
prep preposition
pron pronoun
prop n proper noun
rel pron relative pronoun
sg singular
s.o. someone
sth. something
trad traditional
unit n unitary noun
v verb
vi intransitive verb
vn verbal noun
vt transitive verb
zool zoological

Sudanese Arabic—English

ع - ʿ

ʿaab عاب *vt* (**i, ʿeeb**) to blame
ʿaada عادى *vt* **1** (**-i, muʿaadaa**) to be hostile to **2** (**-i, ʿadwa**) to infect
ʿaada عادة *n* (*pl* **-aat, ʿawaayid**) custom, habit; **al-ʿaada** menstruation
ʿaadal عادل *vt* (**muʿaadala**) to counterbalance
ʿaadatan عادة *adv* usually
ʿaadi عادي *adj* normal, usual, ordinary, common, customary
ʿaadil عادل *adj* just, fair
ʿaadim عادم *n* (*pl* **ʿawaadim**) exhaust pipe
ʿaaf عاف *vt* (**i, ʿuwaafa**) to loathe
ʿaafa عافى *vi* (**-i, ʿafu**) **min** to be happy with, proud of • *vt* (**-i, muʿaafaa**) (of God) to cure, heal
ʿaafya عافية *n* (*pl* **ʿawaafi**) good health, vigour; **Allah yaddii-k al-ʿaafya** may God give you good health; **ʿaafya ʿann-ak** (*of mother to her son*) I am proud of you; **be-l-ʿaafya** by force
ʿaagiba عاقبة *n* (*pl* **ʿawaagib**) negative consequence or outcome
ʿaagil عاقل *adj* sensible, wise, prudent
ʿaagir عاقر *adj* barren, sterile
ʿaaj عاج *n* ivory
ʿaajil عاجل *adj* urgent
ʿaajiz عاجز *adj* weak, powerless, incapable, impotent
ʿaakas عاكس *vt* (**muʿaakasa**) to contradict, oppose
ʿaakis عاكس *n* (*pl* **ʿawaakis**) reflector; sun reflector (e.g. for in car)
ʿaal عال *vt* (**u, iʿaala**) to support, provide for, sustain
ʿaalaj عالج *vt* (**ʿilaaj, muʿaalaja**) to treat medically, cure, heal
ʿaalam عالم *n* (*pl* **ʿawaalim**) world
ʿaalami عالمي *adj* international
ʿaali عالي *adj* **1** high **2** loud
ʿaalim عالم (*pl* **ʿulama**) *adj* learned • *n* scholar, scientist
ʿaam عام *vi* (**u, ʿoom, ʿuwaama**) to swim
ʿaam عام *n* (*pl* **aʿwaam**) year; **ʿaam an-awwal** last year
ʿaamal عامل *vt* (**muʿaamala**) to behave towards, treat
ʿaamil عامل *adj m* doing; **ʿaamil keef** how are you doing? • *n* (*m*) **1** (*pl* **ʿummaal**) worker, labourer **2** employee **3** (*pl* **ʿawaamil**) factor
ʿaamila عاملة *adj f* doing; **ʿaamla keef** how are you doing • *n* (*f*) **1** worker, labourer **2** employee
ʿaamm عامّ *adj* common, general, public; **be-shakil ʿaamm** in general
ʿaammiyya عامّية *n* (**al-lugha**) **al-ʿaammiyya** the colloquial language, spoken Arabic
ʿaana عانى *vi* (**-i, muʿaanaa**) to suffer
ʿaanad عاند *vi* (**muʿaanada**) to be stubborn, obstinate
ʿaanis عانس *n* (*pl* **ʿawaanis**) elderly unmarried woman
ʿaaqab عاقب *vt* (**ʿiqaab, muʿaaqaba**) to punish
ʿaaraḍ عارض *vt* (**muʿaaraḍa**) to oppose
ʿaariḍ عارض *n* (*pl* **ʿawaariḍ**) **1** obstacle, obstruction **2** misfortune
ʿaariḍ عارض *vt* (**muʿaaraḍa**) to contradict, oppose

ʿaariyya عاريّة *n* loan
ʿaas عاس *vt* (**u, ʿuwaasa**) to make **kisra**
ʿaaṣi عاصي *adj* (*pl* **-yyiin**) disobedient
ʿaaṣifa عاصفة *n* (*pl* **ʿawaaṣif**) storm
ʿaaṣima عاصمة *n* (*pl* **ʿawaaṣim**) capital city
ʿaash عاش *vi* (**i, ʿeesh, ʿeesha**) to live, be alive
ʿaashar عاشر *vt* (**ʿushra**) to live together for a certain period of time
ʿaashig عاشق *n* lover; **ʿaashig maʿshuug** hinge
ʿaashir عاشر *num* tenth
ʿaatab عاتب *vt* (**ʿitaab, muʿaataba**) to reproach
ʿaati عاتي *adj* (*pl* **ʿaatiin**) big, huge
ʿaaṭifa عاطفة *n* (*pl* **ʿawaaṭif**) emotion
ʿaaṭifi عاطفي *adj* emotional
ʿaaṭil عاطل *adj* idle; jobless, unemployed
ʿaawan عاون *vt* (**muʿaawana**) to help, assist, support
ʿaawiz عاوز *adj* (*used for*) to want; to need; **hi ʿaawza shinu** what does she want?; **ʿaawziin ʿarabiyya** do you need a car?; **zayy ma (inta) ʿaawiz** as you like
ʿaayan عاين *vt* (**ʿiyyeen, muʿaayana**) (**le-**) to look (at)
ʿaayash عايش *vt* (**muʿaayasha**) to live during, witness; **ʿaayash zaman ar-riqq** he lived during the era of slavery
ʿaayid عايد *n* (*pl* **-aat, ʿaa'idaat**) revenue
ʿaayish عايش *adj* alive
ʿaayiz عايز *adj* (*used for*) to want; to need; **hi ʿaayza shinu** what does she want?; **ʿaayziin ʿarabiyya** do you need a car?; **zayy ma (inta) ʿaayiz** as you like
ʿaaz عاز *vt* (**u, ʿooza**) to want
ʿaazil عازل *n* (*pl* **ʿawaazil**) insulator, non-conductor
ʿabaaṭa عباطة *n* stupidity, foolishness
ʿabad عبد *vt* (**u, ʿibaada**) to worship
ʿabar عبر *vt* (**i, ʿabir**) to measure (e.g. grain)
ʿabar عبر *vt* (**i, ʿabra, ʿubuur**) to cross, pass (street, bridge)
ʿabba عبّى *vt* (**-i, ʿibbeey, taʿbiya**) to fill
ʿabba عبّا *vt* (**-i, taʿbiya**) to mobilize
ʿabbar عبّر *vt* (**taʿbiir**) **ʿan** to express, be expressive of
ʿabda عبدة *n* (*f*) slave
ʿabid عبد *n* (*m*) (*pl* **ʿabiid**) slave
ʿabiiṭ عبيط (*pl* **ʿubaṭa**) *adj* stupid, foolish • *n* fool
ʿabra عبرة *n* (*also fig*) lump (in throat)
ʿada عدا *prep*; **ma ʿada** except
ʿadaala عدالة *n* justice
ʿadaawa عداوة *n* hostility, aggression
ʿadad عدد *n* (*pl* **aʿdaad**) number, amount; **ʿadad al-muntaẓiriin** waiting list; **ʿadad as-sukkaan** number of inhabitants, population
ʿadadiyya عدديّة *n* number, amount
ʿadal عدل *n* **1** s.o./sth. exactly suitable or fitting **2** reinfibulation of circumcised women
ʿadal عدل *vt* (**i, ʿadil**) to mend; to adjust
ʿadala عدلة *n* right side of a piece of cloth, the side with the pattern
ʿadam عدم *n* **1** non-existence, absence (of things); **ʿadam al-ʿirfa ḍalaam** absence of knowledge

means darkness **2** extreme poverty, destitution
ʿadas عدس *coll n* (*unit n* **ʿadasa, ʿadasaaya**) lentil(s)
ʿadasa عدسة *n* lens
ʿadda عدّ *vt* (**i, ʿadd**) to count
ʿadda عدّى (**-i, ʿiddeey**) *vi* **ʿala** to call in at, pass by at • *vt* **1** to pass, go past, overtake **2** to cross, pass (street, bridge) **3** to last, take time; **ash-shughul ʿadda maʿaa-na khamsa shuhuur** the work took us five months
ʿaddaad عدّاد *n* (*pl* **-aat**) meter (e.g. for electricity)
ʿaddal عدّل *vt* (**taʿdiil**) to straighten, adjust
ʿadiil عديل *n* sister-in-law's husband
ʿadiil عديل *adj* **1** straight **2** balancing (of loads) • *adv* straight ahead
ʿadiila عديلة *interj* all right
ʿadl عدل *n* justice
ʿadmaan عدمان *adj* extremely poor
ʿadu عدو *n* (*pl* **aʿdaa**) enemy
ʿaḍala عضلة *n* muscle; **shadd fi l-ʿaḍala/shadd ʿaḍali** muscle cramp
ʿaḍḍa عضّ *vt* (**u, ʿaḍḍ, ʿaḍḍa**) to bite; to sting (scorpion)
ʿaḍiir عضير *adj* handicapped
ʿaḍu عضو *n* (*pl* **aʿḍaa**) **1** limb **2** member
ʿaḍum عضم *n* (*pl* **ʿuḍaam**) **1** bone; **ʿaḍum aḍ-ḍahar** spine, backbone; **ʿaḍum ash-sheeṭaan** ankle **2** stone (of fruit)
ʿafa عفى (**-i, ʿafu**) *vi* **le-/ʿan** to forgive; **ʿafeet lee-ho ghalaṭ-o maʿaa-y** I have forgiven him for offending me • *vt* to forgive; **ʿafeet-o** I have forgiven him
ʿafaana عفانة *n* bad smell
ʿafaarim عفارم *interj* **ʿafaarim ʿalee-k** well done!
ʿafan عفن *n* stench
ʿafaṣ عفص *vt* (**a, ʿafiṣ, ʿafṣa**) to dent
ʿafash عفش *n* **1** luggage, baggage **2** furniture
ʿaffan عفّن *vi* (**ʿiffeen**) to stink; to rot, decay
ʿaffaṣ عفّص *vt* (**ʿiffeeṣ**) to dent
ʿaffash عفّش *vt* (**ʿiffeesh, taʿfiish**) to furnish
ʿafiif عفيف *adj* modest
ʿafin عفن *adj* nasty (of smell), stinking; **ʿamal ḥaaja ʿafna** he did a nasty thing
ʿafrat عفرت *vt* (**ʿifreet, ʿafrata**) to jack up (e.g. a car)
ʿafriit عفريت *n* (*pl* **ʿafaariit**) ghost; dust devil
ʿafriita عفريتة *n* (*pl* **-aat, ʿafaariit**) **1** car jack; (hydraulic) lifting ramp **2** overalls, boiler suit **3** negative of a film
ʿafṣa عفّصة *n* dent
ʿafu عفو *n* forgiveness; amnesty, pardon; **al-ʿafu** I beg your pardon
ʿafwan عفواً *interj* (*reply to thanks*) don't mention it; you're welcome!
ʿagaab عقاب *n* **1** end; **baji fi ʿagaab al-yoom** I'll come at the end of the day **2** family (household); offspring, descendants; **al-ʿagaab keef** how's your family?
ʿagab عقب *vt* (**i, ʿagib**) to succeed (come after)
ʿagaba عقبة *n* mountain pass
ʿagad عقد *vi* (**i, ʿagid**) to make up a contract • *vt* **ʿagad ijtimaaʿ** to fix a meeting
ʿagga عقّ *vt* (**u, ʿuguug**) to be disrespectful towards elders
ʿaggad عقّد *vt* (**taʿgiid**) to complicate

ʿagid عقد *n* (*pl* **ʿuguud**) contract
ʿagid عقد *n* **1** construction supporting the roof of a house **2** roof covered by cement
ʿagiid عقيد *n* (*pl* **ʿugada**) colonel
ʿaglaani عقلاني *adj* (*pl* **-yyiin**) rational
ʿagli عقلي *adj* mental
ʿagrab عقرب *n* (*pl* **ʿagaarib**) scorpion
ʿagul عقل *n* (*pl* **ʿuguul**) mind; reason
ʿahd عهد *n* (*pl* **ʿuhuud**) **1** pledge, vow **2** covenant; **al-ʿahd al-gadiim** the Old Testament; **al-ʿahd aj-jadiid** the New Testament
ʿajaaj عجاج *n* **1** dust **2** sandstorm
ʿajab عجب *vt* (**i, ʿajab**) to delight, please; **ʿajab-ni kalaam-ak** I liked your speech • *n* amazement
ʿajala عجلة *n* **1** wheel, tyre **2** bicycle **3** haste, rush; **ʿajala ʿajala** very quickly
ʿajan عجن *vt* (**i, ʿajin**) **1** to knead **2** to do (a job) badly
ʿajiib عجيب *adj* strange, weird, odd
ʿajiiba عجيبة *n* (*pl* **ʿajaayib**) a strange or amazing thing
ʿajiin عجين *n* leavened **kisra** batter; **ʿajiin khammaar** sourdough
ʿajiina عجينة *n* dough, batter
ʿajjaali عجّالي *adj* pertaining to calves; veal
ʿajjal عجّل *vt* (**ʿijjeel, ʿajala**) to hasten
ʿajjan عجّن *vt* (**ʿijjeen, ʿajan**) **1** to knead **2** to spoil (a child)
ʿajjaz عجّز *vi* (**ʿijjeez**) to grow old
ʿajjuur عجّور *coll n* ridge cucumber(s)
ʿajlaan عجلان *adj* in a hurry
ʿajuuz عجوز *adj* (*pl* **ʿajaayiz, ʿajaza**) old (humans) • *n* old person
ʿajz عجز *n* shortage, deficiency
ʿajzaan عجزان *adj* weak, powerless
ʿakas عكس *vt* (**i, ʿakis**) **1** to reflect light **2** (*sports*) to centre the ball
ʿakk عكّ *n* mess, muddle
ʿakka عكّ *vt* (**u, ʿakk**) to muddle, make a mess of
ʿakkar عكّر *vt* (**ʿikkeer, taʿkiir**) to muddy (water); **da ʿakkar mazaaj-i** that put me in a bad mood
ʿaknan عكنن *vt* (**ʿaknana**); **da ʿaknan mazaaj-i** that put me in a bad mood
ʿakraan عكران *adj* muddy; **washsh ʿakraan** looking troubled; **mazaaj ʿakraan** a bad mood
ʿaks عكس *n* opposite, reverse; **be-l-ʿaks** on the contrary
ʿala على *prep* **1** on, upon; **ʿala l-ʿalee-h** on top of this, in addition to this; **ʿalee-k Allah a** please (requesting) **b** well I never! **2** to, towards; **ʿala ween** where to? **3** for; **ʿala mada usbuuʿeen** for (the period of) two weeks; **ʿala shinu** what for? **4** (*used for*) to have to, must; **ash-shaghala di ʿala Aḥmad** Ahmed has to do this job; **ʿalee-k takhalliṣ ash-shughul hassaʿ** you must finish the work now
ʿalaaga علاقة *n* (**be-**) connection, relation (with); **al-ʿalaagaat al-ʿaamma** public relations
ʿalaama علامة *n* mark, sign **ʿalaamat istifhaam** question mark; **ʿalaamat taʿajjub** exclamation mark
ʿalaawa علاوة *n* pay rise
ʿalaf علف *vt* (**i, ʿalaf**) to feed animals • *n* (*pl* **aʿlaaf**) fodder

ʿalag علق *vi* (**a, ʿalga**) to get stuck (of a car in sand or mud); to run aground (of ships)
ʿalam علم *n* (*pl* **aʿlaam**) flag, banner
ʿaliiga عليقة *n* (*pl* **ʿalaayig**) fodder
ʿalla علّى *vt* (**-i, ʿilleey, taʿliya**) to raise
ʿallaaga علاقة *n* any hook, cord, string or ring to hang sth. on/ with; peg, clothes hook, clothes rail; key ring
ʿallag علّق *vt* (**ʿilleeg, taʿliig**) to hang • *vi* (**ʿilleeg, ʿalga**) to get stuck (e.g. of car horn); to freeze (e.g. of computer screen)
ʿallam علّم *vt* **1** (**taʿliim**) to teach, instruct; to educate **2** (**ʿalaama**) to mark, tick
ʿallaq علّق (**taʿliiq**) *vt* to suspend • *vi* (**ʿala**) to comment (on), to note
ʿamaara عمارة *n* building of more than one storey
ʿamal عمل *n* **1** (*pl* **aʿmaal**) deed **2** (*pl* **aʿmaal**) work, labour **3** (*no pl*) category of diagnosis used by a **faki** **4** (*no pl*) (black) magic
ʿamal عمل *vt* (**a/i, ʿamal**) **1** to do; **ʿamal ʿamaayil** to do something incredibly good or bad; **ʿamal ʿamaliyya** to operate; **aʿmal ḥisaab-ak** take care **2** to make **3** to work; **ʿamal (lee-ho) ʿarabiyya** he (worked and) got himself a car **4** to take care of (a matter)
ʿamali عملي *adj* practical
ʿamaliyya عمليّة *n* operation, process; medical operation
ʿamaliyyan عمليّا *adv* practically
ʿambalook عمبلوك *n* (*pl* **-aat**) young he-goat, kid
ʿambar عمبر *n* ambergris
ʿamiid عميد *n* (*pl* **ʿumada**) **1** dean **2** (*mil*) colonel
ʿamiiq عميق *adj* deep
ʿamm عم *n* (*pl* **aʿmaam**) **1** paternal uncle **2** *used to address s.o. in a familiar way*: **ya ʿamm** mate, buddy; **ʿamm-o** 'uncle'
ʿamma عمّة *n* paternal aunt
ʿammad عمّد *vt* (**taʿmiid**) (*Chr*) to baptize
ʿammam عمّم *vt* (**taʿmiim**) to generalize
ʿammar عمّر (**taʿmiir**) *vi* to last, stay in good condition, to reach an old age • *vt* **1** to build **2** to service, replace (parts) (e.g. of an engine) **3** to load (a gun)
ʿamra عمرة *n* **1** full service (e.g. of an engine) **2** loading of a gun
ʿamuud عمود *n* (*pl* **ʿawaamiid, aʿmida**) **1** pole, post, pillar; **ʿamuud an-nuur** lamp post; **ʿamuud al-ʿajala** hub (of wheel); **al-ʿamuud al-faqri** the spinal column **ʿamuud al-akil** tiered set of saucepans, used to transport food **2** newspaper column
ʿamyaan عميان *adj* blind
ʿan عن *prep* about
ʿana عنى *vt* (**-i, ʿanayaan**) to mean; **yaʿni** that's to say, that is, it means
ʿanbar عنبر *n* (*pl* **ʿanaabir**) **1** barrack room **2** ward (of hospital, prison)
ʿangara عنقرة *n* (*pl* **anaagir**) nape
ʿangareeb عنقريب *n* (*pl* **ʿanaagriib**) bed with wooden frame, strung with rope or hide
ʿanguud عنقود *n* (*pl* **ʿanaagiid**) bunch of grapes; **aakhir al-ʿanguud** the last one (son/girl) of the bunch

ʿaniid عنيد *adj* obstinate, stubborn

ʿaniif عنيف *adj* violent, vehement, fierce, rough, tough; **yoom ʿaniif** a tough day

ʿankabuut عنكبوت *n* (*pl* **ʿanaakib**) spider

ʿankooliib عنكوليب *n* a variety of sorghum

ʿantat عنتت *n pl* weevils; **ʿantat al-ḥubuub** corn weevils

ʿanz عنز *coll n* goat(s)

ʿaqiida عقيدة *n* (*pl* **ʿaqaayid**) belief, creed, conviction

ʿaqiim عقيم *adj* sterile (man)

ʿaqqam عقّم *vt* (**taʿqiim**) to sterilize

ʿarab عرب *coll n* **1** Arabs; those having an Arab ancestor **2** nomads; **ʿarab sayyaara** nomads; **ʿarab al-khala** desert Arabs (*used disparagingly by townspeople*)

ʿarabi عربي *adj* Arabic, pertaining to the Arabs • *unit n* (*pl* **ʿarab**) **1** Arab **2** nomad

ʿarabiyya عربيّة *n* (*pl* **-aat, ʿarabaat**) car; **ʿarabiyya ṣaaloon** estate car, station wagon **ʿarabiyya mallaaki** private car; **ʿarabiyyat isʿaaf** ambulance; **ʿarabiyyat al-maṭaafi** fire engine; **ʿarabiyyat nagil** truck, lorry; **ʿarabiyyat ujra** hired car

ʿaradeeb عرديب *n* tamarind

ʿaraḍ عرض (**i, ʿariḍ, ʿarḍ**) *vt* to show, exhibit, display • *vi* **le-** to make an offer, offer (e.g. a job)

ʿarag عرق *n* sweat, perspiration

ʿaragi عرقي *n* arak, araki, home-made spirits distilled from dates, fruit or sorghum

ʿaraj عرج *vi* (**i, ʿaraj, ʿarja**) to be(come) lame, crippled; to limp

ʿarash عرش *vt* (**i, ʿarish**) to thatch

ʿarbaji عربجي *n* (*pl* **-iyya**) cart driver

ʿarbuun عربون *n* (*pl* **ʿaraabiin**) down payment, deposit

ʿarḍa عرضة *n* military parade

ʿarḍaḥaal عرضحال *n* application or petition to a court

ʿargaan عرقان *adj* sweating

ʿargal عرقل *vt* (**ʿargala**) to hinder, impede

ʿarguub عرقوب *n* (*pl* **ʿaraagiib**) ankle

ʿariḍ عرض *n* (*pl* **ʿuruuḍ**) **1** breadth; width **2** presentation, display, performance, show(ing) **3** offer

ʿariiḍ عريض *adj* broad

ʿariiḍa عريضة *n* (*pl* **ʿaraayiḍ**) petition; **ʿariiḍat istirḥaam** petition for mercy

ʿariif عريف *n* (*pl* **ʿurafa**) (*mil*) corporal

ʿariiq عريق *adj* deep-rooted; **ʿeela ʿariiqa** an old, respectable family

ʿariis عريس *n* (*pl* **ʿirsaan**) bridegroom

ʿarish عرش *n* (*pl* **ʿuruush**) roof; ceiling

ʿarraaḍ عرّاض *n* (*pl* **-aat**) cross-piece (e.g. of a bed), crossbeam

ʿarraaḍa عرّاضة *n* crossbeam (e.g. of a roof); crossbar (of goalpost)

ʿarraagi عرّاقي *n* (*pl* **ʿaraariig**) light undershirt worn under a jellabia

ʿarrad عرّد *vi* (**ʿirreed, ʿarda**) to rear and kick (donkey)

ʿarraḍ عرّض *vt* **1** (**taʿriiḍ**) to broaden **2** (**ʿariḍ**) to expose

ʿarraf عرّف *vt* (**taʿriif**) **be-** to introduce (a person) to (another person)

ʿarraj عرّج *vi* (**ʿirreej, taʿriij**) **ʿala** to call in at; **lamma tamshi s-suug, ʿarrij ʿala beet-i** when you go to the market, call in at my house

ʿarras عرّس *vt* (**ʿiris**) to marry
ʿarrash عرّش *vi* (**ʿirreesh, taʿriish**) to form a natural roof or sun shelter (of trees)
ʿarsh عرش *n* (*pl* **ʿuruush**) throne
ʿaruuḍ عروض *n* any drink or food offered to a guest; **ʿadam al-ʿaruuḍ jafa** failure to offer a guest refreshments is rude
ʿaruus عروس *n* (*pl* **ʿaraayis**) bride
ʿaruusa عروسة *n* (*pl* **ʿaraayis**) doll, puppet
ʿaryaan عريان *adj* naked, bare
ʿasal عسل *n* honey; **ʿasal an-naḥal** honey; **ʿasal gaṣab** molasses, treacle; **ʿasal sukkar** sugar syrup
ʿasaliyya عسليّة *n* a light variety of millet beer
ʿaskar عسكر *n* **ʿaskar u ḥaraamiyya** hide-and-seek
ʿaskari عسكري *adj* military; martial • *n* (*pl* **ʿasaakir**) **1** military; soldier; **ʿaskari nafar** private soldier **2** policeman
ʿassal عسّل *vi* (**ʿisseel**) to go or to be on honeymoon
ʿaṣa عصى *vt* (**-i, ʿiṣyaan**) to disobey
ʿaṣa عصا *n* (*pl* **ʿiṣi**) stick
ʿaṣaaba عصابة *n* gang
ʿaṣaaya عصاية *n* (*pl* **ʿiṣi**) stick
ʿaṣab عصب *n* (*pl* **aʿṣaab**) **1** nerve; **fagad aʿṣaab-o** he went berserk **2** sinew; tendon
ʿaṣabi عصبي *adj* nervous; neurotic
ʿaṣabiyya عصبيّة *n* **1** kinship ties **2** tribalism; chauvinism **3** nervousness; irritability
ʿaṣar عصر *vt* (**i, ʿaṣir**) to squeeze; to press (oil, etc.); **ʿaṣar banziin** to accelerate
ʿaṣbaji عصبجي *n* (*pl* **-yya**) outlaw
ʿaṣfuur عصفور *coll n* (*pl* **ʿaṣaafiir**) **1** any type of small coloured bird(s) **2** sparrow(s); **ʿaṣfuur aj-janna** swallow(s)
ʿaṣiida عصيدة *n* stiff porridge made with sorghum or millet flour, sourdough and water
ʿaṣiir عصير *n* (*pl* **ʿaṣaayir**) juice
ʿaṣriyya عصريّة *n* late afternoon
ʿaṣṣaara عصّارة *n* **1** press (e.g. for oil) **2** juicer, lemon-squeezer
ʿaṣṣar عصّر *vt* (**ʿiṣṣeer**) to massage
ʿaṣur عصر *n* late afternoon
ʿasha عشا *n* evening meal, supper
ʿashaan عشان *conj* **1** because **2** so that, in order to
ʿashaan عشان *prep* **1** for, for the sake of; **ʿashaan shinu** why? what for? for what? **2** because of; **ʿashaan kida/kadi** because of this, therefore
ʿasham عشم *n* hope; **ʿasham ibliis fi j-janna** (*lit* the hope of the devil to enter heaven) an utterly unrealistic hope
ʿashara عشرة *num* ten
ʿashiira عشيرة *n* (*pl* **ʿashaayir**) clan
ʿashiyya عشيّة *n* evening
ʿashmaan عشمان *adj* hopeful
ʿashoosha عشوشة *n* female sparrow
ʿashsha عشّى *vt* (**i, ʿasha**) to give supper to
ʿashshar عشّر *vt* (**ʿishsheer, taʿshiir**) to mate
ʿashshash عشّش *vi* (**ʿishsheesh**) to build a nest
ʿashwaa'i عشوائي *adj* haphazard; **aḥyaa ʿashwaa'iyya** unplanned, illegal settlements; shanty towns • *adv* haphazardly
ʿatab عتب *n sg/pl* lintel(s)

ʿatab عتب *vi* (**i, ʿatib**) to limp, stumble, totter

ʿataba عتبة *n* doorstep, threshold

ʿatala عتلة *n* crowbar

ʿatra عترة *n* stumbling; **al-ʿatra bitṣalliḥ al-mashiya** with stumbling one learns to walk

ʿattaab عتّاب *coll n* young locust(s), hopper(s)

ʿattaali عتّالي *n* (*pl* **ʿattaaliin, ʿattaala**) porter

ʿattal عتّل *v* (**ʿittaala**) to work as a porter

ʿattat عتّت *vi* (**ʿitteet**) to be(come) infested with weevils

ʿattat عتت *n pl* weevils; **ʿattat al-ḥubuub** corn weevils

ʿatuud عتود *n* (*pl* **ʿittaan**) young he-goat, kid

ʿaṭaa عطا *n* (*pl* **ʿaṭaa'aat**) tender, bid

ʿaṭaala عطالة *n* idleness, unemployment

ʿaṭaf عطف *vi* (**i, ʿaṭf**) **ʿala** to be kind to

ʿaṭan عطن *vt* (**i, ʿaṭin**) to soak, steep

ʿaṭas عطس *vi* (**a, ʿaṭis**) to sneeze

ʿaṭash عطش *n* thirst; drought

ʿaṭiyya عطيّة *n* (*pl* **ʿaṭaaya**) gift, donation present

ʿaṭlaan عطلان *adj* out of order, defective, broken down (e.g. a car)

ʿaṭruun عطرون *n* natron

ʿaṭshaan عطشان *adj* thirsty; **al-bildaat ʿaṭshaana** the fields are suffering from drought

ʿaṭṭaar عطّار *n* seller of ingredients for homemade cosmetics, perfume and incense

ʿaṭṭaay عطّاي *adj* generous

ʿaṭṭal عطّل *vt* (**taʿṭiil**) to hold up, hinder

ʿaṭṭar عطّر *vt* (**ʿiṭṭeer, taʿṭiir**) to perfume; to flavour with perfume

ʿaṭṭas عطّس *vt* (**ʿiṭṭees**) to cause to sneeze

ʿaṭuuf عطوف *adj* kind, friendly

ʿawaafi عوافي *interj* hello; **ʿawaafi ʿalee-kum** hello

ʿawaara عوارة *n* folly, stupidity

ʿawaayid عوايد *n pl* **1** traditional customs **2** property taxes

ʿawaḍ عوض *prep* **ʿan** instead of

ʿawaj عوج *vt* (**i, ʿawaj**) to make crooked, bend

ʿawaja عوجة *n* problem; **ma fii ʿawaja** there's no problem, there's no harm done, all is well

ʿawda عودة *n* return

ʿawiin عوين *n pl* women

ʿawiir عوير (*pl* **ʿuwara**) *adj* stupid, foolish, silly • *n* fool

ʿawja عوجة *n* curve, bend (in road; materials)

ʿawlama عولمة *n* globalisation globalism

ʿawwa عوّى *vi* (**-i, ʿiwweey, ʿawwa**) **1** to howl **2** to wail

ʿawwaam عوّام *n* a good swimmer; **ibn al-wizz ʿawwaam** (*lit* the son of a goose swims well) like father, like son

ʿawwaama عوّامة *n* ballcock, float (e.g. of lavatory cistern)

ʿawwad عوّد *vt* (**taʿwiid**) **ʿala** to accustom s.o. to

ʿawwaḍ عوّض *vt* (**taʿwiiḍ**) to compensate

ʿawwag عوّق *vt* (**ʿiwweeg, taʿwiig**) to injure

ʿawwaj عوّج *vt* (**ʿiwweej, taʿwiij**) to make crooked, bend (materials)

ʿawwar عوّر *vt* (**ʿiwweer, taʿwiir**) to injure, wound

ʿaya عيا *n* illness
ʿayna عينة *n* sample, specimen
ʿayyaan عيّان *adj* ill; sick
ʿayyab عيّب *vt* (**ʿeeb**) (**ʿala**) to blame (for); to point (to defects)
ʿayyad عيّد *vi* (**ʿiyyeed**) (**ʿala**) to celebrate a (religious) feast
ʿayyan عيّن *vt* (**taʿyiin**) to appoint
ʿayyar عيّر *vt* (**ʿiyyeer**) to abuse verbally
ʿayyash عيّش *vt* (**iʿaasha**) to sustain, support financially
ʿazaab عزاب *n* suffering, vexation
ʿazaba عزبة *n* a woman without a man (widow or a divorced woman)
ʿazaf عزف *vt* (**i, ʿazif**) to play (a musical instrument)
ʿazal عزل *vt* (**i, ʿazil**) **1** to choose, select **2** to dismiss (from military service) **3** to isolate
ʿazam عزم *vt* (**i, ʿazuuma**) to invite
ʿazam عزم *vi* (**i, ʿaziima**) (**ʿala**) to be determined
ʿazam عزم *vt* (**i, ʿaziima**) to charm, heal by incantation
ʿazar عزر *vt* (**i, ʿuzur**) to excuse
ʿaziima عزيمة *n* (*pl* **ʿazaayim**) **1** strong will, determination **2** healing by incantation
ʿaziiz عزيز *adj* (*pl* **aʿizzaa**) dear, beloved
ʿazraa عزرا *n* (*pl* **ʿazaara**) virgin
ʿazuuma عزومة *n* (*pl* **-aat, ʿawaaziim**) invitation
ʿazza عزّى *vt* (**-i, ʿaza, taʿziya**) to condole
ʿazzaabi عزّابي *n* (*pl* **ʿazzaaba**) bachelor
ʿazzab عزّب *vt* **1** (**ʿazaab**) to make s.o. suffer **2** (**ʿizzeeb, taʿziib**) to torture
ʿazzaz عزّز *vt* (**taʿziiz**) to strengthen, enhance, foster
ʿaẓama عظمة *n* greatness, grandness
ʿaẓiim عظيم *adj* (*pl* **ʿuẓama**) great, grand, magnificent
ʿeeb عيب *n* **1** shame; shameful behaviour; **ʿeeb ʿalee-k** shame on you **2** (*pl* **ʿiyuub**) defect
ʿeela عيلة *n* (*pl* **ʿaayilaat, ʿawaayil**) extended family, kin group
ʿeen عين *n* (*pl* **ʿiyuun**) **1** eye; **al-ʿeen** the evil eye, the capacity for harming people by regarding them enviously; **ʿeen-o ḥaarra** he has the evil eye; **ʿeen as-samak** corn on foot; **be-ʿeen-** (the very self) same; **yaa-ho ar-raajil be-ʿeen-o** this is the same man **2** knot (in wood) **3** well, spring **4** eighteenth letter of the Arabic alphabet
ʿeesh عيش *coll n* **1** (*pl* **ʿiyuush**) sorghum; millet; **ʿeesh riif** corn, maize **2** bread
ʿeesha عيشة *unit n* loaf of bread
ʿibaada عبادة *n* worship
ʿibaara عبارة *n* expression (phrase)
ʿibaaya عباية *n* cloak
ʿibra عبرة *n* (*pl* **ʿibar**) example (warning), lesson
ʿidda عدّة *n* (*pl* **ʿidad**) **1** (set of) utensils/tools, gear, equipment **2** dishes **3** luggage **4** a number of items or persons; several; **ʿiddat naas** several people
ʿideelaat عديلات *n pl* **abu ʿideelaat** mumps
ʿiffa عفّة *n* modesty
ʿigid عقد *n* (*pl* **ʿuguud**) necklace
ʿiid عيد *n* (*pl* **aʿyaad**) feast, celebration **ʿiid miilaad** birthday;

ʿ**iid miilaad-i bukra** my birthday is tomorrow; ʿ**iid al-fiṭr** the Feast of Breaking the Fast (end of Ramadan); ʿ**iid al-aḍḥa**/ʿ**iid aḍ-ḍaḥiyya** the Feast of the Sacrifice, Eid al Adha; ʿ**iid miilaad al-masiiḥ** Christmas; ʿ**iid al-fiṣḥ**/ʿ**iid al-giyaama** Easter; ʿ**iid al-ʿansara**/ʿ**iid al-khamsiin** Pentecost; ʿ**iid aṣ-ṣuʿuud** Ascension

ʿ**iisha** عيشة *n* mode of living, livelihood

ʿ**ijil** عجل *coll n* (*unit n* ʿ**ijla**) Nile perch

ʿ**ijil** عجل *n* (*pl* ʿ**ujuul**) calf, heifer

ʿ**ijla** عجلة *n* calf

ʿ**ilaaj** علاج *n* (*pl* **-aat**) medical treatment

ʿ**ilba** علبة *n* (*pl* ʿ**ilab**) small box; tin can ʿ**ilbat at-turuus** gearbox; ʿ**ilbat al-karanki** crankcase

ʿ**ilim** علم *n* (*pl* ʿ**uluum**) **1** knowledge **2** science; ʿ**ilm an-nafs** psychology; ʿ**ilm al-ijtimaa**ʿ sociology

ʿ**ilim** علم *vi* (**a,** ʿ**ilim**) **be-** to know

ʿ**ima** عمى *vi* (**-a,** ʿ**ama**) to be(come) blind

ʿ**imma** عمّة *n* (*pl* ʿ**imam**) turban

ʿ**inaad** عناد *n* obstinacy

ʿ**inaaya** عناية *n* care; ʿ**inaaya mukassafa/murakkaza** intensive care

ʿ**inab** عنب *coll n* grape(s)

ʿ**ind** عند *prep* **1** at (a place) **2** (*used for*) to have; ʿ**ind-ak kam guruush** how much money do you have?; ʿ**ind-i lee-ho miit alif** I owe him a hundred thousand

ʿ**inya** عنية *n* **min duun** ʿ**inya** unintentionally

ʿ**iqaab** عقاب *n* punishment

ʿ**iraaq** عراق *prop n* **al-**ʿ**iraaq** Iraq

ʿ**iraaqi** عراقي (*pl* **-yyiin**) *adj* Iraqi • *n* an Iraqi

ʿ**irḍ** عرض *n* honour

ʿ**irfa** عرفة *n* knowledge

ʿ**irgi** عرقي *adj* ethnic

ʿ**irif** عرف *vt* (**a, ma**ʿ**rifa**) to know; to recognize

ʿ**irig** عرق *vi* (**a,** ʿ**arag**) to sweat

ʿ**irig** عرق *n* (*pl* ʿ**uruug**) **1** root; ʿ**irig abyaḍ** ginger; ʿ**irig aḥmar** ginger-like, reddish root, used in stews, *also called* **ghurunjaal** **2** crushed or ground root or any other substance, used for magic **3** vein, blood-vessel **4** breeding, descent; race, ethnicity; **fii-ho** ʿ**irig/fii-ho** ʿ**irig murr** he is of a bad origin

ʿ**iris** عرس *n* (*pl* **a**ʿ**raas**) wedding

ʿ**irraaf** عرّاف *n* a person who tells the future by consultation of jinns

ʿ**irreef** عرّيف *n* **abu l-**ʿ**irreef** know-all

ʿ**irreeja** عرّيجة *n* diversion, digression; **inta maashi** ʿ**ala ṭuul wala** ʿ**ind-ak** ʿ**irreeja** are you going straight there or or will you go somewhere else first

ʿ**irriif** عرّيف *n* title of a person to be consulted by authorities about (e.g. names, sex, age, etc., of) people living in the same neighbourhood or area (required due to the absence of a population register)

ʿ**irwa** عروة *n* (*pl* ʿ**araawi,** ʿ**arraaw**) buttonhole

ʿ**iṣyaan** عصيان *n* (*pl* **-aat**) disobedience

ʿ**ishig** عشق *n* ardent love, passion

ʿ**ishim** عشم *vi* (**a,** ʿ**asham**) to hope

ʿ**ishriin** عشرين *num* twenty

ʿ**ishsha** عشّة *n* (*pl* ʿ**ishash**) hut

ʿitaab عتاب *n* reproach
ʿitir عتر *vi* (**a, ʿatir, ʿatra**) (**fi**) to stumble (at/over), trip (at/over); (**ʿala**) to stumble (across/on)
ʿitta عتّة *n pl* weevils
ʿiṭir عطر *n* (*pl* **ʿuṭuur**) perfume
ʿiṭish عطش *vi* (**a, ʿaṭash**) to be(come) thirsty
ʿiya عيى *vi* (**-a, ʿaya**) to be(come) sick, ill
ʿiyaada عيادة *n* clinic
ʿiyaal عيال *n pl* children
ʿiyaar عيار *n* carat (gold)
ʿizza عزّة *n* dignity
ʿooʿa عوعى *vi* (**-i, ʿooʿaay**) to crow
ʿooma عومة *n* a swim
ʿoon عون *n* help, aid; **rabba-na yakuun fi ʿoon-ak** may God help you
ʿudwaani عدواني *adj* (*pl* **-yyiin**) hostile; aggressive • *n* aggressor
ʿuḍwiyya عضويّة *n* membership
ʿufuuna عفونة *n* stench
ʿugaal عقال *n* (*pl* **-aat**) **1** foot rope, hobble **2** headband
ʿugbaal عقبال *interj* **ʿugbaal-ak** may the same happen to you (*reply to congratulations or wishes*)
ʿugda عقدة *n* (*pl* **ʿugad**) **1** knot (e.g. in a rope) **2** complex (psychological)
ʿugub عقب *n* offspring, descendants • *prep* after
ʿuguug عقوق *n* disrespect towards elders
ʿuhda عهدة *n* (*pl* **ʿuhad**) charge, custody, guardianship
ʿukkaaz عكّاز *n* (*pl* **ʿakaakiiz**) **1** club (stick) **2** crutch
ʿuluum علوم *n pl* (*sg* **ʿilim**) sciences
ʿulya عليا *adj f* (*m* **aʿla**) upper; superior
ʿumda عمدة *n* (*pl* **ʿumad**) chief, tribal leader, clan leader; magistrate of a village or district
ʿumla عملة *n* currency; **ʿumla ṣaʿba** hard currency
ʿumq عمق *n* depth
ʿumra عمرة *n* the minor pilgrimage to Mecca
ʿumur عمر *n* (*pl* **aʿmaar**) age; **ʿumr-ak kam** how old are you? what's your age?; **ʿumr-i ma shuft-o** I've never seen him/it in my life
ʿumuula عمولة *n* commission (payment)
ʿumuum عموم *n* generality; **ʿala l-ʿumuum** generally, in general
ʿumuuman عموما *adv* generally, in general
ʿumuumi عمومي *adj* general, public
ʿunf عنف *n* violence
ʿunq عنق *n* **ʿunq ar-riḥim** cervix, neck of the womb
ʿunṣur عنصر *n* (*pl* **ʿanaaṣir**) element
ʿunwaan عنوان *n* (*pl* **ʿanaawiin**) **1** address **2** title (e.g. of a book, film)
ʿuquuba عقوبة *n* punishment, sanction
ʿurf عرف *n* (*pl* **aʿraaf**) **1** cockscomb, crest **2** mane
ʿurf عرف *n* (*leg*) custom, practice
ʿurfi عرفي *adj* traditional, customary
ʿuruḍ عرض *n* breadth; width (materials)
ʿuṣaar عصار *n* (*pl* **-aat**) hurricane, tornado, whirlwind
ʿushar عشر *coll n* Sodom apple
ʿushba عشبة *unit n* (*coll n* **ʿushub**) a sprig (of a herb)
ʿushra عشرة *n* close friendship as a result of living or working together for a period of time

ʿushsh عش *n* (*pl* **ʿashaash**) nest
ʿushub عشب *coll n* (*unit n* **ʿushba**) plants, herbage
ʿuṭla عطلة *n* holiday
ʿuṭul عطل *n* breakdown (e.g. of a car)
ʿuud عود *n* (*Isl*) (*pl* **aʿwaad**) share of inheritance
ʿuud عود *n* **1** (*pl* **ʿeedaan, aʿwaad**) stick; piece of wood **2** (*pl* **aʿwaad**) lute
ʿuwwaara عوّارة *n* (*pl* **-aat, ʿawaawiir**) wound; sore
ʿuzla عزلة *n* isolation
ʿuzur عزر *n* (*pl* **aʿzaar**) excuse

a – ا

aʿdam أعدم *vt* (**iʿdaam**) to execute s.o.
aʿgaab عقب *n pl* offspring, descendants
aʿla أعلى *adj* (*f* **ʿulya**) (**min**) higher (than); upper, superior; senior; **al-aʿla** the highest
aʿlan أعلن *vi* (**yuʿlin, iʿlaan**) (**ʿan**) to announce
aʿma أعمى *adj* (*f* **ʿamya**, *pl* **ʿamaaya**) blind
aʿma أعمى *vt* (**-i, ʿamiya, ʿama**) to blind
aʿmaal أعمال *n pl* (*sg* **ʿamal**) business; **raajil aʿmaal** businessman
aʿmash أعمش *adj* (*f* **ʿamsha, ʿamshaana**, *pl* **ʿumush**) half blind; suffering from night blindness
aʿraj أعرج *adj* (*f* **ʿarja**, *pl* **ʿuruj**) lame, crippled
aʿsar أعسر *adj* (*f* **ʿasra**, *pl* **ʿusur**) left-handed
aʿshaab أعشاب *n pl* herbs
aʿwaj أعوج *adj* (*f* **ʿawja**, *pl* **ʿuwuj**) crooked
aʿwar أعور *adj* (*f* **ʿawra**, *pl* **ʿuwur**) one-eyed
aʿyaan أعيان *n pl* prominent people
aʿzab اعزب *n* (*pl* **ʿazzaaba**) bachelor
a- ا *interj* **a-ho** here he/it is
aabanuus آبنوس *n* ebony
aabree آبري *n* homemade drink consumed at breakfast during Ramadan, *also called* **ḥilu murr**
aadaab آداب *n pl* (*sg* **adab**) literature, belles lettres; **kulliyyat al-aadaab** faculty of arts
aakhar آخر *adj m* (*f* **ukhra**) other, another
aakuul آكول *n* (*pl* **akuuliin**) glutton
aakhir آخر *adj invar* (*before indef n*) last; **aakhir waaḥid/waaḥda** the last one; **ila aakhiri-hi** et cetera
aakhra اخرة *n* **al-aakhra** the hereafter
aala آلة *n* instrument; **aala kaatba** typewriter; **aala ṭaabiʿa** printer, printing machine; **aalat taṣwiir** photocopier
aaliyya آليّة *n* mechanism
aaman آمن *vt* (**ya'aamin, mu'aamana**) to trust
aaman آمن *vi* (**yu'min, iimaan**) **be-** to believe in
aamiin آمين *interj* amen
aamin آمن *adj* safe, secure
aasaar آسار *n pl* (*sg* **asar**) antiquities
aasiya آسيا *prop n* Asia
aasiyawi آسيوي (*pl* **-yyiin**) *adj* Asian • *n* an Asian
aasif آسف *adj* sorry; (**niḥna**) **aasfiin jiddan** we're very sorry

aay آي *interj* yes

aaya آية *n* Koranic or Bible verse

aba أبى *vi* (**biyaaba, abayaan**) to refuse (*the past tense can also refer to the present tense; often used with the neg part* **ma**); **aba ma yaakul** he refuses/refused to eat

abaaliis اباليس *n pl* (*sg* **ibliis**) little devils, naughty children

abaaṭ أباط *n* (*pl* **-aat**) armpit; **abaaṭ-o wa n-najim** (*lit* his armpit and the stars) he is extremely poor

abad أبد *n* **le-l-abad** forever

abadan أبدا *adv* **1** (*with neg part*) never, at all; **ma shuftaa-ho abadan** I've never seen him/it **2** never, certainly not!

abadi أبدي *adj* eternal

abadiyya ابديّة *n* **al-abadiyya** eternity

abajuura أبجورة *n* table lamp

abarool ابرول *n* (*pl* **-aat**) overalls

abayaan أبيان *n* refusal

abbaali ابّالي *n* (*pl* **abbaala**) camel owner; camel driver

abdaᶜ ابدع *vt* (**yubdiᶜ, ibdaaᶜ**) to create (of humans)

abkam أبكم *adj* (*f* **bakma**, *pl* **bukum, bukama**) dumb, mute

ablah أبله *adj* (*f* **balha**, *pl* **buluh**) mentally retarded; idiot

ablam أبلم *adj* (*f* **balma**, *pl* **bulum, bulama**) **1** dumb, dumbfounded **2** stupid

abrag أبرق *adj* (*f* **barga**, *pl* **burug, buraga**) speckled, spotted, freckled; **wadd abrag** (male) sparrow

abraṣ أبرص *adj* (*f* **barṣa**, *pl* **buruṣ**) afflicted with vitiligo

abrashiyya أبرشيّة *n* diocese

abriil أبريل *n* April

abu أبو *n* **1** (*pl* **abbahaat, abawaat**) father; **abuu-y** my father, dad, daddy; **abu awlaad-i** my husband **2** (*pl* **abaa'**) priest, father; **abuu-na** form of address to a priest or monk; **al-abaa' al-biiḍ** the White Fathers, the Carmelites **3** (*denotes a distinguishing feature, for instance:*) **abu n-naḍḍaara** the man wearing spectacles; **galam abu khamsiin** a pen costing fifty (piastres); **abu d-dardaag** dung beetle

abyaḍ أبيض *adj* (*f* **beeḍa**, *pl* **buyuḍ**) white

adaa ادا *n* performance (in job)

adaa اداة *n* (*pl* **adawaat**) tool

adaan أدان *vt* (**i, idaana**) to condemn to, convict

adaar أدار *vt* (**yudiir, idaara**) to administer, manage, direct

adab أدب *n* **1** good manners, decency; **galiil al-adab** impolite, rude **2** (*pl* **aadaab**) literature

adabkhaana ادبخانة *n* lavatory, toilet; latrine

adabtar أدبتر *n* (*pl* **-aat**) adaptor

adawaat أدوات *n pl* tools, utensils; **adawaat maktabiyya** stationery

adbakhaana أدبخانة *n* lavatory, toilet; latrine

adda أدّى *vt* **1** (**ya'addi, iddeey**) to give, provide (with); to pass, hand; **adda bas/baas** to pass the football **2** (**ya'addi, adaa**) to carry out, implement; to perform (job); to fulfil; **adda l-ᶜalee-ho** he fulfilled his obligations

addab أدّب *vt* (**ta'diib**) to teach manners, discipline

adman أدمن *vi* (**i, idmaan**) (**ᶜala**) to be(come) addicted (to)

adna أدنى *adj* (*f* **dunya**) (**min**) lower (than), inferior (to); **le-l-ḥadd al-adna** minimum

adruuj أدروج *adj* (*pl* **adaariij**) beardless

aḍaaf اضاف *vt* (**yuḍiif, iḍaafa**) to add

aḍaan أضان *n* (*pl* **iḍneen**) ear (organ of hearing)

aḍrab أضرب *vi* (**i, iḍraab**) to go on strike

afḍal أفضل *adj* (**min**) more preferable (than), better (than); **al-afḍal** the most preferable, the best

afraj أفرج *vt* (**i, ifraaj**) (**ʿala**) to release (e.g. from prison)

afranji افرنجي (*pl* **-yya**) *adj* European

afriiqi افريقي (*pl* **-yyiin**) *adj* African • *n* an African

afsad أفسد *vt* (**i, ifsaad**) to corrupt s.o.

afta افتى *vi* (**-i, iftaa**) (*Isl*) to issue a legal opinion

afṭas أفطس *adj* (*f* **faṭsa**, *pl* **fuṭus**) flat-nosed

afyuun أفيون *n* opium

agʿudaak اقعداك *imp* let's sit down here

agaarib أقارب *n pl* (*sg* **gariib**) relatives; **al-agaarib ʿagaarib** relatives are scorpions

agall أقل *adj*; **agalla** (**min**) less (than); inferior; **ʿala l-agall, agall-o/agall-a, agalla shi/ḥaaja** at least, minimal

agalliyya أقلّيّة *n* minority

agdam أقدم *adj* (**min**) older (than); **al-agdam** the oldest

agdamiyya أقدميّة *n* seniority

agiif أقيف *imp* (*v* **wagaf**) stop!

aghbash أغبش *adj* (*f* **ghabsha**, *pl* **ghubush**) covered or polluted with dust or mud

aghlabiyya أغلبيّة *n* majority

aghlaf أغلف *adj* (*f* **ghalfa**, *pl* **ghuluf**) uncircumcised

aghosṭos أغسطس *n* August

aghra أغرى *vt* (**-i, ighraa**) to tempt

aghziya اغزية *n pl* (*sg* **ghiza**) foodstuffs

ahaan أهان *vt* (**i, ihaana**) to humiliate

ahal أهل *n* (*pl* **ahaali**) kin, (nuclear) family; relatives; people; **ahl al-beet** family; women folk; **ahl al-beet keef** how's your wife?; how are your wives?; how are your relatives?; **ahl al-balad** indigenous people

ahamm أهم *adj* (**min**) more important (than); **ahamma ḥaaja/shii** the most important thing

ahbal أهبل *adj* (*f* **habla**, *pl* **hubul**) stupid, silly

ahhal اهّل *vt* (**yu'ahhil, ta'hiil**) to qualify

ahlan أهلا *interj* welcome; hi, hello; **ahlan wa sahlan** welcome

ahli أهلي *adj* **1** privately owned **2** national

aḥbaṭ احبط *vt* (**i, iḥbaaṭ**) to frustrate

aḥdab أحدب *adj* (*f* **ḥadba**, *pl* **ḥudub**) hunchbacked

aḥfaad أحفاد *n pl* (*sg* **ḥafiid**) grandchildren

aḥmaq أحمق (*f* **ḥamqa**, *pl* **ḥumuq**) *adj* quick to take offense

aḥmar أحمر *adj* (*f* **ḥamra**, *pl* **ḥumur**) red; **aḥmar shafaayif** lipstick

aḥraj احرج *vt* (**i, iḥraaj**) to embarrass

aḥsan أحسن *adj* (**min**) better (than); **al-aḥsan** the best

aḥwal أحول *adj* (*f* **ḥawla**, *pl* **ḥuwul**) cross-eyed, squint-eyed

aḥwaṣ أحوص *adj* (*f* **ḥawṣa**, *pl* **ḥuwuṣ**) cross-eyed, squint-eyed

aḥyaanan أحياناً *adv* sometimes, occasionally

ajaawiid أجاويد *n pl* (*sg* **ajwaad**) (*trad*) council of elders, mediation and arbitration council (between tribes)

ajal أجل *n* (*pl* **aajaal**) appointed span of lifetime; **ajal gheer musamma** unspecified period of time

ajdaad أجداد *n pl* ancestors

ajhaḍ اجهض (**i, ijhaaḍ**) *vt* to abort (a pregnancy) • *vi* to miscarry, abort

ajii اجي *interj* (*used by women only*) how strange!

ajinda أجندة *n* **1** agenda (of a meeting) **2** pocket diary, day planner

ajjal أجل *vt* (**ya'ajjil, ta'jiil**) to postpone, adjourn, suspend

ajjar أجّر *vt* (**ta'jiir**) **1** to rent, hire, lease **2** to let (for rent)

ajl اجل *n* **le-ajl, min ajl** for the sake of

ajnabi أجنبى (*pl* **ajaanib**) *adj* foreign • *n* foreigner

ajr أجر *n* reward; **ajr-ak ʿala Allah** God will reward you

ajur أجر *n* reward; **ajur wa ḥasana** (*lit* a reward and a good deed) *expression used when sth. bad has happened or when s.o. is ill*

ajwaad اجواد *adj* (*pl* **ahl juud**) generous

ajwaf أجوف *adj* (*f* **jawfaa**) hollow

ajzakhaana أجزخانة *n* pharmacy

akʿab أكعب *adj* (**min**) worse (than); **akʿab ḥaaja** the worst thing

akal أكل *vt* **1** (**biyaakul, akil**) to eat; **akalat-o an-naar** it is burnt **2** (**biyaakul, akalaan, akuula**) to itch; **jild-i biyaakul-ni** my skin itches

akbar أكبر *adj* (*f* **kubra**) (**min**) greater, larger (than); older (than); **al-akbar** the greatest; **Allahu akbar** God is the greatest one

akiid أكيد *adj* sure, certain • *adv* surely, certainly

akiila أكيلة *n* itch(ing)

akil أكل *n* food

akkad اكّد (**ya'akkid, ta'kiid**) *vi* **le-** to assure, reassure, confirm • *vt* to verify sth.

akkal أكّل *vt* (**ya'akkil, ikkeel**) to feed

akla أكلة *n* meal

akram اكرم *vt* (**i, karam, ikraam**) to be generous to • *adj* (**min**) more generous (than); (*reply to* **ramaḍaan kariim:**) **wa Allahu akram** God is more generous

aktar أكتر *adj* (**min**) more (than); **al-aktar** the most

akuula اكولة *n* itch(ing)

akziima اكزيما *n* eczema

akhad أخد *vt* (**biyaakhud, akhid**) **1** to take; to pick up (a person); **akhad dush** to take a shower; **akhad taar** to take revenge (blood feud); **akhad tajruba** to gain experience; **al-fariig akhad khamsa (ahdaaf)** the team lost with five (goals) against **2** to marry (of men) **3 le-** to buy

akhawaat اخوات *n* (*sg* **ukhut**) sisters

akhbaar أخبار *n pl* (*sg* **khabar**); **al-akhbaar** the news (in the media)

akhḍar أخضر *adj* (*f* **khaḍra**, *pl* **khuḍur**) **1** green **2** dark brown (of skin)

akheer أخير *adj* (**min**) (it's) better (than)

akhiir أخير *adj* last
akhiiran أخيرا *adv* finally
akhiṣṣaa'i أخصّائي *n* (*pl* **-yyiin**) medical specialist; **akhiṣṣaa'i takhdiir** anaesthetist
akhkhar أخّر *vt* (**ya'akhkhir, ta'khiir**) to make late, delay, adjourn
akhlaaq أخلاق *n pl* morals; **akhlaaq faasda** bad morals
akhlaṣ أخلص *vi* (**i, ikhlaaṣ**) to be faithful, devoted, loyal
akhraani أخراني *adj* last
akhu أخو *n* (*pl* **akhwaan**) brother; **akhu fi r-riḍaaʿa** foster brother; **akhu akhwaan** a gentle and generous person; **al-akhwaan al-muslimiin** the Muslim Brothers
al- الـ *art* the • *rel pron* who, whom; which, that; where
alam ألم *n* (*pl* **aalaam**) pain
alfaaẓ الفاظ *n pl* (*sg* **lafẓa**) words, phrases, expressions; **haasib alfaaẓ-ak** watch what you say!
alif ألف *num* (*pl* **aalaaf; uuluuf**) thousand; **khamsa alif, khamsa aalaaf** five thousand; **alif u tusʿumiyya sitta wa khamsiin** 1956; **uuluuf min an-naas** thousands of people
aliif أليف *adj* tame, domesticated
aljan ألجن *adj* (*f* **lajna**, *pl* **lujun**) having a speech defect; replacing a letter with another letter (for example *l* instead of *r*)
alkaʿ ألكع *imp* get a move on!
allaf ألّف *vt* (**ya'allif, ta'liif**) **1** to compose (e.g. a song, a poem), to write (a story, a book) **2** to concoct, make up (a story) • *vi* to concoct, make up a story
Allah الله *n* (*and* **Allaah**) God; **in sha/shaa Allah** God willing, Deo volente; **ma sha/shaa Allah** well I never!; **wa llaahi/be-llaahi** by God, really?
allam ألّم *vt* (**ya'allim, illeem, alam**) to hurt
almaan المان *coll n* Germans
almaani الماني *adj* (*pl* **almaan**) German • *unit n* a German
almaanya المانيا *prop n* Germany
amaan أمان *n* safety; security
amaana أمانة *n* **1** **ʿind-o amaana** he's reliable, trustworthy **2** deposit (sth. held in safekeeping)
amal أمل *n* (*pl* **aamaal**) hope
amar أمر *vt* (**ya'mur, amir**) (**be-**) to order, command
ambuuba أمبوبة *n* (*pl* **anaabiib**) tube; cylinder; **ambuubat ghaaz** gas cylinder; **khaṭṭ anaabiib** pipeline
amhal أمهل *vt* (**i, imhaal**) respite
amiin آمين *interj* amen
amiin امين *adj* faithful, sincere • *n* (*m*) (*pl* **umana**) trustee; **amiin khazna** treasurer; **amiin maktaba** librarian
amiina أمينة *n* (*f*) **amiinat khazna** treasurer; **amiinat maktaba** librarian
amiina أمينة *n* (*pl* **amaayin**) house post
amiir أمير *n* (*pl* **umara**) prince
amiira أميرة *n* princess
amis أمس *adv* yesterday; **awwal amis** the day before yesterday
amjaad أمجاد *n* (*pl* **-aat**) type of small minibus
amlas أملس *adj* (*f* **malsa**, *pl* **mulus**) smooth, soft

ammal أمّل *vi* (**ya'ammil, amal**) (**fi**) to hope (for)

amman أمّن *vt* (**ya'ammin, amaana**) **1** to secure, render safe (also of firearms) **2** to entrust; **ammant-o sirr-i** I entrusted my secret to him • *vi* (**ya'ammin, ta'miin**) **ʿala** to insure

amn أمن *n* security; **al-amn** the security services

amr أمر (*and* **amur**) *n* **1** (*pl* **awaamir**) order, command; **tiḥit amr-ak** at your orders, at your service!; **amr gabiḍ** arrest warrant **2** (*pl* **umuur**) issue, matter; **amr waagiʿ** fait accompli

amriika أمريكا *prop n* America; **amriika al-laaṭiiniyya** Latin America

amriiki امريكي (*pl* **amriikaan**) *adj* American • *n* an American

amrikaan امريكان *coll n* Americans

amrikaani امريكاني *adj* (*pl* **amriikaan**) American • *unit n* an American

amshi امشي *imp* go away!, move off!

amur أمر (*and* **amr**) *n* **1** (*pl* **awaamir**) order, command **2** (*pl* **umuur**) issue, matter

ana أنا *pron sg m/f* I

anaani أناني (*pl* **-yyiin**) *adj* selfish, egoistic • *n* egoist

anaaniyya أنانيّة *n* selfishness, egoism

ananaas اناناس *n* pineapple

anbuuba أنبوبة *n* (*pl* **anaabiib**) tube; cylinder; **anbuubat ghaaz** gas cylinder; **khaṭṭ anaabiib** pipeline

andaaya اندابة *n* (*pl* **anaadi**) local drinking bar (inside a house)

anfaq أنفق *vt* (**yunfiq, infaaq**) **ʿala** to support s.o. financially, sustain

anjaz أنجز *vt* (**i, injaaz**) to achieve, accomplish

ankar انكر *vt* (**u, inkaar**) to deny

ann- أنّ *conj* that

anno أنو *conj* that

anṣaar أنصار *n pl* **1** early supporters of the Prophet Mohammed; **anṣaar as-sunna** those who live according to the Sunna, i.e. the customs and usages of the Prophet Mohammed **2** followers of the Mahdi

anṣaari انصاري *n* (*pl* **anṣaar**) follower of the Mahdi

antaj انتج *vt* (**yuntij, intaaj**) to produce

antiika انتيكة *n* (*pl* **anaatiik**) **1** antique **2** handmade ornaments (e.g. wooden statues) • *adj invar* old-fashioned

anzar أنزر *vt* (**yunzir, inzaar**) (**min**) to give a warning to (not to do sth.); **anzart-ak min al-kiḍib** I warned you not to lie

aqnaʿ أقنع *vt* (**yuqniʿ, iqnaaʿ**) to convince, persuade

aqsam أقسم *vi* (**i, qasam**) **1** to swear an oath **2** (**be-**) to swear (on/by)

aqṣa أقصى *adj* more extreme; **al-aqṣa** the most extreme; **aqṣa ḥaaja, aqṣa shi; al-ḥadd al-aqṣa** maximum

araajooz اراجوز *n* (*pl* **-aat**) **1** hand puppet **2** fool

araak أراك *n* tree (*Salvadora persica*) from which toothpicks are made

araḥ أرح *interj* let's go; **araḥ-ka/ araḥ-kaka** let's go!

arbaʿa أربعة *num* four; **umm arbaʿa w arbaʿiin** centipede
arbaʿiin أربعين *num* forty; **arbaʿiin yoom** forty-day period of seclusion following e.g. a birth
arbaʿṭaashar أربعطاشر *num* fourteen
ardab أردب *n* (*pl* **araadib**) ardeb, dry measure (189 kg approx.)
arḍa ارضة *coll n* termites, white ants; **al-arḍa jarrabat al-ḥajar** (*lit* the termites tried to break down a stone) nothing is impossible
arḍiyya أرضيّة *n* charge on stored goods
arḍiyya أرضيّة *n* (*pl* **araaḍi**) piece of land, plot
argaṭ أرقط *adj* (*f* **ragṭa**, *pl* **ruguṭ**) piebald
arhab أرهب *vt* (**i, irhaab**) to terrorize
arhaq ارهق *vt* (**yurhiq, irhaaq**) to tire
ariḍ أرض *n* (*pl* **araaḍi**) land; earth; soil; ground; **giṭʿat ariḍ/ḥittat ariḍ** a piece of land, plot; **al-araaḍi al-munkhafiḍa** the Netherlands
ariyal أريل *n* (*pl* **araayil**) aerial
armal أرمل *n* (*pl* **araamil**) widower
armala أرملة *n* widow
arnab أرنب *n* (*pl* **araanib**) hare; rabbit
arrakh أرّخ *vt* (**ya'arrikh, ta'riikh**) **1** to put a date on, to date **2** to record
arshad أرشد *vt* (**i, irshaad**) to guide
arshiif ارشيف *n* (*pl* **-aat**) archive
arwash أروش *adj* (*f* **rawsha**, *pl* **ruush**) **1** scatterbrained **2** clumsy
aryaaḥ ارياح *n pl* winds
asaa اسا *vt* (**yusii, isaa'a**) **le-** affront, offend, wrong
asaas أساس *n* **1** (*pl* **usus**) foundation, basis **2** (*pl* **-aat**) furniture
asaasi أساسي *adj* basic; fundamental
asad أسد *n* (*pl* **usuud**) lion
asaf أسف *n* regret; **le-l-asaf** it is regrettable; unfortunately
asar أسر *n* (*pl* **aasaar**) trace; footprint; track; **asar jariḥ** scar
asar أسر *vt* (**i, asr**) to take prisoner
asbaan اسبان *coll n* Spaniards
asbaani اسباني *adj* (*pl* **asbaan**) Spanish • *unit n* a Spaniard
asbaanya اسبانيا *prop n* Spain
asbat أسبت *vt* (**yusbit, isbaat**) to prove; to confirm
asfal أسفل *prep* under
asfal أسفل *adj* (*f* **sufla**) (**min**) lower (than)
asgaṭ أسقط *vt* (**yusgit, isgaaṭ**) **1** to cause to fall, let fall **2** to abort a pregnancy
asiir أسير *n* (*pl* **usara**) prisoner of war
aslam أسلم *vi* (**i, islaam**) to convert to Islam
asmant اسمنت *n* cement; **asmant musallaḥ** reinforced concrete, ferroconcrete
asmar أسمر *adj* (*f* **samra**, *pl* **sumur**) brown skinned
asriʿ اسرع *imp* hurry (up)
assa اسّا *adv* now
assar أسّر *vt* (**ya'assir, ta'siir**) **ʿala/fi** to affect; to influence
assas أسّس *vt* (**ya'assis, ta'siis**) to found
aswa أسوا *adj* (**min**) worse (than); **al-aswa** the worst
aswad أسود *adj* (*f* **sooda**, *pl* **suud**) black • *n* eggplant, aubergine
aṣala أصلة *n* python
aṣarra أصرّ *vi* (**yuṣirr, iṣraar**) (**ʿala**) **1** to insist (on) **2** to persist

aṣbaᶜ أصبع *n* (*pl* **aṣaabiᶜ, aṣaabᶜeen**) finger; **al-aṣbaᶜ al-kabiir** thumb; **aṣbaᶜ ar-rijil** toe; **foog raas al-aṣaabiᶜ** on tiptoe

aṣbaḥ أصبح *vi* (**i, ṣabaaḥ**) **1** (of day) to dawn **2** to wake up in the morning; **aṣbaḥta keef** (*in the morning:*) how are you doing; **taṣbaḥ ᶜala kheer** good night

aṣdar أصدر *vt* (**i, iṣdaar**) to promulgate (e.g. instructions); to issue; to publish

aṣfar أصفر *adj* (*f* **ṣafra**, *pl* **ṣufur**) yellow

aṣiil أصيل *adj* **1** original **2** (*pl* **-iin, uṣala**) honourable; correct (of conduct)

aṣiiṣ أصيص *n* (*pl* **aṣaayiṣ**) plant pot, flowerpot

aṣil أصل *n* (*pl* **uṣuul**) origin, root, source; descent; **ᶜind-o aṣil** he comes from a respectable family; he is a respectable person

aṣlaḥ اصلح *vi* (**yuṣliḥ, ṣuluḥ**) **been** to make peace between, reconcile

aṣlan أصلا *adv* in fact, actually

aṣli أصلي *adj* genuine; original; **nuskha aṣliyya** original

aṣliḥa اسلحة *n pl* weapon(s), firearms; **asliḥa beeḍa** weapons such as knives, bayonets

aṣlo أصلو *adv* in fact, actually

ashaada أشاد *vi* (**yushiid, ishaada**) **be-** to praise, speak in glowing terms of

ashiᶜᶜa أشعة *n pl* (*sg* **shuᶜaaᶜ**) X-rays

ashraf اشرف *vi* (**i, ishraaf**) (**ᶜala**) to supervise

ashshar أشّر (**ya'ashshir, ishsheer, ta'shiir**) *vi* (**ᶜala/le-**) to indicate, signal; to point (at) • *vt* **1** to mark **2** to issue a visa or travel permit

ashtar أشتر *adj* (*f* **shatra**, *pl* **shutur**) **1** clumsy **2** not having a sense for rhythm; unable to sing in tune

ashwal أشول *adj* (*f* **shawla**, *pl* **shuwul**) left-handed

atᶜaab اتعاب *n pl* fees (for a lawyer)

ataawa اتاوة *n* protection money (paid to gangsters)

atar أتر *n* (*no pl*) trace; track; footprint; rut

aṭfaal أطفال *n pl* (*sg* **ṭifil**) children, infants

aṭibba أطبّا *n* (*sg* **ṭabiib**) medical doctors, physicians

aṭlag أطلق *vt* (**i, iṭlaag**); **aṭlag saraaḥ-o** he was released (e.g. from prison)

aṭrash أطرش *adj* (*f* **ṭarsha**, *pl* **ṭurush**) **1** deaf **2** stupid

aw أو *conj* or

awᶜa اوعى *imp invar* let it not be that, don't; **awᶜa tamshi** don't go!; **awᶜaa-k...** don't you...!; **awᶜaa-k takoorik** don't shout!

awdaᶜ أودع *vt* (**i, wadiiᶜa**) to entrust sth. to; **awdaᶜt-o guruush-i** I entrusted my money to him

awlaad أولاد *n pl* (*sg* **walad, wad**) children; sons, boys; **keef al-awlaad** how are your wife and children?

awlawiyya أولويّة *n* priority

awliya اوليا *n pl* (*sg* **wali**) (*Isl*) holy men, saints

awsaṭ أوسط *adj* (*f* **wusṭa**) middle; **ash-sharq al-awsaṭ** the Middle East; **al-quruun al-wusṭa** the Middle Ages

awwal أوّل *adj* (*f* **uula**) first; **be-l-awwal; fi l-awwal** firstly, first of all; **awwal ma** as soon as;

awwal umbaariḥ the day before yesterday
awwalaani أوّلاني *adj* first
awwalan أوّلا *adv* firstly, first of all
ayskriim أيسكريم *n* ice cream
aywa أيوا *interj* yes
ayyad أيّد *vt* (**ya'ayyid, ta'yiid**) to support
ayyi أي *adj invar* any; **ayyi ḥaaja/shi** anything; **ayyi waaḥid** anybody; **fi ayyi ḥaal/ḥaala** in any case
azʿaj أزعج *vt* (**i, izʿaaj**) to annoy, disturb, vex
azaal ازال *vt* (**yuziil, izaala**) to remove
azan أزن *vi* (**ya'zin, izin**) **le-** to permit, allow
aziyya أزيّة *n* one who brings harm to others
azma أزمة *n* asthma
azma أزمة *n* (*pl* **-aat, izam**) **1** crisis; **azma galbiyya** heart attack, heart failure **2** shortage (of goods at market)
azma ازمة *n* (*pl* **izam**) pickaxe; mattock; **azma abu raaseen** two-headed pickaxe
azrag أزرق *adj* (*f* **zarga**, *pl* **zurug**) **1** black **2** blue
azwaaj أزواج *n pl* (*sg* **zooj**) married couple
azzaan أزان *n* (*pl* **-aat**) (*Isl*) call to prayer
azzan أزّن *vi* (**ta'ziin, azzaan**) (*Isl*) to call to prayer

b – ب

baʿʿaati بعاتي *n* (*pl* **baʿaaʿiit**) zombie
baʿad بعد *prep* after; **al-baʿd-o** the next one, the following one; **baʿad bukra** the day after tomorrow; **baʿd kida** then, after that; **baʿad ma** after; **ma baʿad** beyond
baʿaḍ بعض *n* **1** some **2** each other; **maʿa baʿaḍ** together
baʿar بعر *coll n* droppings (e.g. of goats, rabbits)
baʿbuuṣ بعبوص *n* (*pl* **baʿaabiiṣ**) a worthless thing or person; **addaani baʿbuuṣ** he gave me 'a pig in a poke'; **gaaʿid lee-hum baʿbuuṣ** he was not of any use to them
baʿdaak بعداك *adv* then, after that; afterwards
baʿdeen بعدين *adv* **1** later (short time, e.g. some hours) **2** then, after that; afterwards
baʿiid بعيد *adj* (*pl* **buʿaad**) (**min**) far (from), far away (from); distant; **ma baʿiid** not far; around
baʿshoom بعشوم *n* (**baʿaashiim**) jackal
baʿzaag بعزاق *n* (*pl* **baʿaaziig**) squanderer
baʿzag بعزق *vt* (**baʿzaga**) to squander, waste (money)
baaʿ باع *vt* (**i, beeʿ**) **1** to sell; **baaʿ be-khasaara** to sell at a loss **2** to buy
baaʿuuḍ باعوض *coll n* mosquito(es)
baa'is بائس *adj* (*pl* **-iin, bu'asa**) miserable
baab باب *n* **1** (*pl* **beebaan, abwaab**) door **2** (*pl* **abwaab**) chapter of book
baaba بابا *n* dad, daddy; **al-baaba** the pope

baabaay بابای *coll n* pawpaw, papaya
baabanuus بابنوس *n* ebony
baabooy بابوی *n* baby (boy)
baabooya بابوية *n* baby (girl)
baabuunj بابونج *n* camomile, chamomile
baabuur بابور *n* (*pl* **-aat, bawaabiir**) **1** pump; **baabuur mooya** irrigation pump **2** engine; **baabuur baḥar** steamboat, steamer; **baabuur al-gaṭar** railway engine **3** generator
baadal بادل *vt* (**mubaadala**) to exchange, swap
baadiya بادية *n* (*pl* **bawaadi**) area traditionally belonging to a particular tribe of nomads
baagi باقي *adj* lasting; **baagi lee-y** I think that • *n* (*pl* **bawaagi**) **1** rest, remnant, remainder **2** change from a payment; balance of an account
baagha باغة *n* jerrycan
baahit باهت *adj* pale, faded
baaḥ باح *vi* (**u, booḥ**) **be-** to disclose one's feelings, bare one's soul
baaḥis باحس *n* researcher; surveyor
baako باكو *n* (*pl* **baakwaat, bawaaki**) packet
baakriyya باكرية *n* early morning
baakhat باخت *vt* (**mubaakhata**) to congratulate
baal بال *vi* (**u, bool**) to urinate
baal بال *n* mind; **baal-o mashghuul** he's worried; **baal-o murtaaḥ** he doesn't have to worry; **baal-o ṭawiil** he is a patient person; **khalli baal-ak** take care!; **ʿala baal ma** by the time that
baala بالة *n* bale (of cotton)
baalagh بالغ *vi* (**mubaalagha**) to exaggerate
baaligh بالغ *adj* mature, adult
baaloona بالونة *n* balloon
baambey بامبي *n* sweet potato(es), yam
baamya بامية *n* okra, ladies' fingers
baar بار *vi* (**u, boora**) **1** to be fallow **2** to be unsold
baara بارا *vt* (**-i, mabaaraa**) to follow; **baara d-darib** to track, follow a track
baarak بارك (**mubaaraka**) *vi* **1 fi** to bless; **baarak Allahu fii-k/Allah yabaarik fii-k** God bless you, thank you **2 le-** to congratulate • *vt* to bless
baarid بارد *adj* **1** cold, cool (of things); **ḥaaja baarda** soft drink **2** insensitive
baaruud بارود *n* gunpowder
baaruuka باروكة *n* wig
baas باس *vt* (**u, boos**) to kiss
baaṣṣ باص *n* (*pl* **baṣṣaat**) large bus; **baaṣṣ safari** long distance bus; **baaṣṣ daa'iri** circular bus
baaṣta باسطة *n* sweet pastries
baasha باشا *n* pasha
baashkaatib باشكاتب *n* head clerk
baashmuhandis باشمهندس *n* **1** chief engineer **2** term of address to any skilled or professional person
baat بات *vi* (**i, beeta, bayataan**) to spend the night; **baat al-gawa** to spend the night without having had supper
baaṭil باطل *adj* impotent, ineffectual, good-for-nothing
baaṭini باطني *adj* internal; **ṭibb baaṭini** internal medicine; **diktoor baaṭini** physician

baayiᶜ بايع *n* seller, vendor
baayikh بايخ *adj* **1** silly; tedious; annoying **2** smutty (e.g. of jokes)
baayin باين *adj* clear, evident • *adv* apparently
baayir باير *adj* fallow; unsold
baayit بايت *adj* **1** spending the night **2** stale **3** repeating a school year
baayiẓ بايظ *adj* **1** rotten, spoiled **2** out of order
baazinjaan بازنجان *n* eggplant, aubergine
baaẓ باظ *vi* (**u, bawaẓaan, booẓ**) **1** to be(come) spoiled or useless **2** to rot, decay
bada بدا *vi* (**-a, bidaaya**) (**be-**) to begin, start (with) • *vt* to begin, start with
badal بدل *n* (*pl* **-aat**) **1** substitute; **jaab badal-o** he replaced him/it; **badal min/ᶜan/ma** instead of **2** exchange, barter, swap **3** allowance; **badal safariyya** travel allowance
baddaal بدّال *n* (*pl* **-aat**) pedal
baddaala بدّالة *n* switchboard
baddal بدّل *vt* (**biddeel, tabdiil**) to barter, replace, swap, substitute
badiil بديل *adj* alternative, substitute • *n* (*pl* **badaayil**) alternative, replacement, substitute
badla بدلة *n* (*pl* **bidal**) suit; **badla kaamla** full suit
badri بدرى *adv* early
badur بدر *n* (*pl* **buduur**) full moon
bafra بفرة *n* cassava
bafta بفتة *n* calico
bagaaya بقايا *n pl* (*sg* **bagiyya**) remains, remnants
bagar بقر *n* cow(s); **bagar al-waḥsh** oryx(es)
bagari بقري *adj* pertaining to cows; **laḥam bagari** beef; **damm-o tagi-il, bagari bass** he is a real bore
bagduunis بقدونس *n* parsley
bagg بق *coll n* bugs; bedbugs
bagga بقّ *vt* (**u, bagga**) to sip, take a sip of
baggaari بقّاري *n* (*pl* **baggaara**) cattle owner
baggag بقّق *vt* (**biggeeg**) to cause to blister
bagiyya بقيّة *n* (*pl* **bagaaya**) rest, remnant, remainder
baghal بغل *n* (*pl* **bighaal**) mule
baghbaghaan بغبغان *n* (*pl* **-aat**) parrot (generic); parakeet, budgerigar
bahaayim بهايم *n pl* (*sg* **bahiima**) livestock; domesticated animals
bahag بهق *n* skin disease that discolours parts of the skin, pityriasis alba; vitiligo
bahat بهت *vi* (**a, bahta, bahataan**) to fade
bahdal بهدل *vt* (**bahdala**) to treat disrespectfully
bahiima بهيمة *n* (*pl* **bahaayim**) domestic animal
bahja بهجة *n* delight; good spirits, gladness
bahlawaan بهلوان *n* (*pl* **-aat**) buffoon, clown
bahlawaaniyya بهلوانيّة *n* buffoonery
baḥar بحر *n* (*pl* **buḥuur**) **1** river; **al-baḥar** the Nile **2** sea; **al-baḥar al-maaliḥ** the sea; **al-baḥar al-aḥmar** the Red Sea; **al-baḥar al-abyaḍ al-mutawassiṭ** the Mediterranean Sea
baḥas بحس *vi* (**a, baḥis**) **ᶜan fi** to look sth. up; to do research

baḥḥaar بحّار *n* (*pl* **baḥḥaara**) sailor; **baḥḥaara** ship's crew

baḥri بحري *adj* pertaining to the river or the sea • *adv* northward; **al-kharṭuum baḥri** Khartoum North

baḥs بحس *n* (*pl* **buḥuus**) research

bajaʿ بجع *coll n* (*unit n* **bajʿa**) pelican(s)

baka بكى *vi* (**-i, bika**) (ʿ**ala**) to cry, weep, lament

bakaan بكان *n* (*pl* **-aat**) place

bakaara بكارة *n* virginity

bakkaash بكّاش *adj* flatterer (in order to win a favour)

bakkaay بكّاي *adj* crying a lot (a baby)

bakkash بكّش *vi* (**bikkeesh, bakash**) (ʿ**ala**) to ingratiate o.s. (with), flatter a lot in order to win a favour

bakra بكرة *n* pulley; reel

bakshiish بكشيش *n* tip (gratuity)

baktiriya بكتريا *n* (*pl* **-aat**) bacteria

bakhiil بخيل (*pl* **bukhala**) *adj* stingy, mean • *n* miser

bakhiit بخيت *adj* bringing good luck

bakhit بخت *n* luck; **ya bakht-ak** you're lucky, you lucky one!

bakhkha بخّ (**u, bakhkh**) *vi* to atomize, spray out • *vt* to spray

bakhkhaakh بخّاخ *n* (*pl* **-aat**) spray (can), atomizer

bakhkhaakha بخّاخة *n* spray (can), atomizer

bakhkhar بخّر *vt* **1** (**bikhkheer**) to cense, fumigate **2** (**bakhra**) to cense for healing (by burning a charm) **3** (**bakhra**) (*slang*) to cheat in exams (with a crib sheet)

bakhra بخرة *n* **1** charm (of paper) **2** crib sheet

bakhuur بخور *n* (homemade) incense

balʿuum بلعوم *n* oesophagus, gullet

bala بلا *n* (*pl* **balaawi**) disaster

balaʿ بلع *vt* (**a, bali**ʿ) to swallow

balaada بلادة *n* stupidity

balaagh بلاغ *n* (*pl* **-aat**) official complaint, report of a fault or problem; **fataḥ balaagh** he filed a complaint

balaali بلالي *n pl* (*unit n* **biliyya**) ball bearings

balaash بلاش *adj invar* free of charge, gratis; **be-balaash** free of charge, gratis

balad بلد *n* **1** (*pl* **bilaad, buldaan**) place of origin **2** (*pl* **bilaad, buldaan**) country **3** (*pl* **buluud, bilaad, buldaan**) town, village

baladi بلدي *adj, usually invar* **1** local **2** native **3** pertaining to the countryside; having simple manners; **baladi ashaw** uncivilized, having bad manners

baladiyya بلديّة *n* town hall; municipality

balaḥ بلح *coll n* date(s) (fruit)

balak بلك *n* (*pl* **balakkaat**) electric socket

balakoona بلكونة *n* balcony

balal بلل *n* moisture

balaṣ بلص *vt* (**u, balṣa**) to bribe

balbaaṣ بلباص *n* flatterer (in order to win a favour)

balbal بلبل *vt* **1** (**bilbeel**) to wet; to moisten, dampen **2** (**balbala**) to confuse; to make trouble

balbala بلبلة *n* confusion

balbaṣ بلبص *vi* (**balbaṣa**) (ʿ**ala**) to ingratiate o.s. (with), flatter in order to win a favour

balgham بلغم *n* phlegm

balif بلف *n* (*pl* **-aat**) valve

baliid بليد *adj* (*pl* **bulada**) stupid; foolish

baliigh بليغ *adj* eloquent

baliila بليلة *n* **1** adzuki beans **2** any kind of grain or beans, boiled and eaten at a **karaama** or to break a fast, particularly during Ramadan

baliyya بليّة *n* (*pl* **-aat, balaawi**) disaster

baljiika بلجيكا *prop n* Belgium

baljiiki بلجيكي (*pl* **-yyiin**) *adj* Belgian • *n* a Belgian

balla بلّ *vt* (**i, balla**) to wet

ballaal بلال *n* wetting solution or oil

ballaaṭ بلاط *n* **1** professional plasterer of interior walls with cement **2** tiler

ballagh بلّغ *vt* **1** (**billeegh**) to inform, notify; to pass on, convey **2** (**balaagh, tabliigh**) **ʿan** to inform on/against, report to the police

ballal بلّل *vt* (**balal**) to wet

ballash بلّش *vt* (**billeesh**) to stop, quit; **ballish al-kooraak** stop shouting

ballaṭ بلّط *vt* (**billeeṭ, tabliiṭ**) **1** to plaster (top layer) **2** to tile

balluur بلّور *n* (*pl* **-aat**) crystal

balluushi بلّوشي *adj invar* (*slang*) gratis, for free; **da ḥaaja balluushi** that's a real bargain

balṭa بلطة *n* (*pl* **-aat, balaaṭi**) pickaxe

balṭaji بلطجي *n* (*pl* **-yya**) outlaw

balṭo بالطو *n* (*pl* **-haat**) coat, overcoat

balwa بلوى *n* (*pl* **balaawi**) disaster

bambar بمبر *n* (*pl* **banaabir**) stool (chair); **wagaʿ min al-bambar sabaʿ marraat** (*lit* he fell from his stool seven times) he's hard to be cheated

bambi بمبي *adj* pink

bana بنى *vt* (**-i, buna**) to build

banaḍoora بنضورة *n* tomato(es)

banafsaji بنفسجي *adj* purple; violet (colour)

band بند *n* (*pl* **bunuud**) (*leg*) clause; article

bandar بندر *n* (*pl* **banaadir**) **1** a populated region (as opposed to wilderness) **2** provincial town

bango بنقو *n* marijuana

bani بني *n pl* (*sg* **ibin**) the children of; those associated with; **bani aadam** (*m*) human being; **bani aadma** (*f*) human being; **bani aadmiin** human beings

banij بنج *n* anaesthetic; **banij kaamil** general anaesthetic; **banij mawḍiʿi** local anaesthetic

banjar بنجر *coll n* (*unit n* **banjaraaya**) beetroot(s)

bank بنك *n* **1** (*fin*) (*pl* **bunuuk**) bank **2** (*pl* **bunukka**) counter

banna بنّا *n* (*pl* **bannaayiin**) builder, mason

banshar بنشر *n* (*pl* **banaashir**) tyre repair shop

banṭaloon بنطلون *n* (*pl* **banaaṭliin**) trousers

banṭoon بنطون *n* (*pl* **-aat, banaaṭiin**) ferry, pontoon

banyo بنيو *n* (*pl* **-haat**) bathtub

banziin بنزين *n* **1** benzine, petrol, gasoline **2** accelerator

baqqaal بقّال *n* grocer

baqqaala بقّالة *n* grocery

bara برى *vt* (**-i, bariya, bari**) to sharpen (pencil)

baraa- برا. *adv* alone, on one's own, of one's own accord; **ja baraa-ho** he came alone; **baraa-ho** of his own accord; **hi ʿamalat-o baraa-**

ha she did this herself, on her own

baraa'a براءة *n* innocence; **baraa'at ikhtiraa**ʿ patent

baraaḥ براح *n* **1** plenty of room (e.g. in a house); **fii baraaḥ** there is more than enough room **2** ease; **az-zool da bitḥiss ma'aa-ho be-baraaḥ** one feels at ease with this guy

barabandi بربااندي *n* (*pl* **-yyaat**) large nail used as a hook or peg (to fix things together); tent peg

barad برد *vt* (**i, biraada**) to file (metal)

barad برد *n* hail

barad برد *coll n* African electric fish

barafaan برافان *n* cosmetics

barag برق *vi* (**i, barig**) to flash, sparkle

barak برك *vi* (**u, barik**) to kneel

baraka بركة *n* **1** blessing, grace, benediction **al-baraka fii-k** blessing be on you: my condolences; (*reply*) **al-baraka fi j-jamii**ʿ blessing be on all **2** spiritual power of saints

baram برم *vt* (**u, barim**) **1** to twist (a rope) **2** to screw

baranda برندة *n* **1** veranda **2** arcade

baraṣ برص *n* vitiligo (skin disease)

barashoot برشوت *n* (*pl* **-aat**) parachute

baraziil برازيل *prop n* **al-baraziil** Brazil

baraziili برازيلي (*pl* **-yyiin**) *adj* Brazilian • *n* a Brazilian

barbaḥ بربح *vt* (**barbaḥa**) to strip a branch of its thorns

barbari بربري (*pl* **baraabra**) *adj* Berber (pertaining to a North-African Berber tribe) • *n* a Berber

bardaan بردان *adj* cold (of persons)

barḍ- برضـ *adv* (*used only with second person sg*) also, too; **inta barḍ-ak masheet maʿaa-hum** you too went with them

barḍo برضو *adv* also, too

bargiyya برقيّة *n* telegram

barhan برهن *vi* (**barhana, burhaan**) to prove

barid برد *n* cold weather

barig برق *n* (*pl* **buruug**) flash (of lightning)

barii' بريء *adj* (*pl* **-iin, abriyaa**) innocent

bariid بريد *n* mail, post; **bariid iliktrooni** e-mail; **bariid jawwi** airmail; **bariid sarii**ʿ express mail

bariyya بريّة *n* invocation to God for protection from any kind of evil (said when s.o. is ill)

barjal برجل *n* (*pl* **baraajil**) compasses

barjal برجل *vt* (**birjeel, barjala**) to muddle, make a mess of

barjala برجلة *n* mess, muddle, disorder

barlamaan برلمان *n* (*pl* **-aat**) parliament

barmaj برمج *vt* (**barmaja**) to plan or make a programme; to program

barmiil برميل *n* (*pl* **baraamiil**) barrel

barnaamij برنامج *n* (*pl* **baraamij**) programme; program

barniiṭa برنيطة *n* (**baraaniiṭ**) European type of hat

barr بر *n* land (as opposed to sea and air)

barra برا *prep* outside • *adv* outside; **saafar bilaad barra** he travelled abroad

barra' برّأ *vt* (**-i, tabri'a**) to acquit

barraad برّاد *n* (*pl* **-aat, baraariid**) teapot

barraad برّاد *n* filer, person who has the job of filing metal

barraag برّاق *n* lightning

barraay برّاي *adj* talkative

barraaya برّاية *n* pencil sharpener

barrad برّد *vt* (**birreed, tabriid**) **1** to cool, make cold **2** to bathe **3** to prepare a corpse before burial

barrar برّر *vt* (**tabriir**) to justify

barri برّي *adj* **1** wild (animals) **2** pertaining to land (as opposed to sea and air)

barriima برّيمة *n* (*pl* **-aat, baraariim, barraayim**) hand drill (boring tool)

barsiim برسيم *n* alfalfa

barsham برشم *vt* (**barshama**) to rivet, fix tightly

barṭaᶜ برطع *vi* (**barṭaᶜa, birṭeeᶜ**) **1** to gallop about, run and prance about **2** (*slang*) to gallivant, gad about

barṭuush برطوش *n* (*pl* **baraaṭiish**) a worn out slipper

baruud برود *n* **1** bathroom **2** preparation of a corpse before burial

barwa بروة *n* used piece of soap

barwaz برْوز *vt* (**barwaza, burwaaz**) to frame (e.g. a picture)

basam بسم *vi* (**u, basma**) to smile

basaṭ بسط *vt* (**i, inbisaaṭ**) to make s.o. happy, delight

basboor بسبور *n* (*pl* **-taat, basaabiir**) passport

basbuusa بسبوسة *n* a variety of pastry

basiiṭ بسيط *adj* **1** (*pl* **-iin**) few; little **2** (*pl* **busaṭa**) simple, plain

baskawiit بسكويت *n pl* (*sg* **baskoota**) biscuits

baskoota بسكوتة *n* (*pl* **baskawiit**) biscuit

basma بسمة *n* smile

bassبس *conj* **1** but **2** except • *adv* only, if only, just; **ana bass law ᶜarrasta al-bineyya di…** if only I had married this girl… • *interj* stop! enough!

bastilla بستلّة *n* tiffin tin

basṭoona بسطونة *n* (*pl* **-aat, basaaṭiin**) cane or reed for beating

baṣaara بصارة *n* wisdom

baṣal بصل *coll n* (*unit n* **baṣala, baṣalaaya**) onion(s); **baṣal makaada** garlic

baṣar بصر *n* eyesight

baṣiir بصير (*pl* **-iin, buṣara**) *n* **1** traditional healer who practises by applying heat to specific parts of the body **2** bone setter

baṣma بصمة *n* (*pl* **baṣamaat**) fingerprint

bashaasha بشاشة *n* joy showing on the face

bashar بشر *n* mankind

bashar بشر *vt* (**u, bashir**) to grate

bashari بشري *adj* human

bashka بشكة *n* tangle

bashsha بشّ *vt* (**i, bashsh, bashaasha**) to welcome (guests) generously and joyfully

bashshar بشّر *vi* **1** (**bishsheer**) **ᶜala/le-** to show appreciation to a bridegroom, special guest, or singer at a party by raising the hand and snapping the fingers **2** (**bushaara**) **be-** to give good news, bring good tidings **3** (**tabshiir**) (**be-**) to evangelise

bashtan بشتن *vt* (**bashtana**) to neglect (one's appearance, clothes, house), be dowdy
bashuush بشوش *adj* friendly, amiable
batar بتر *vt* (**u, batir**) to amputate
batir بتر *n* amputation
baṭaala بطالة *n* idleness; unemployment
baṭaaṭis بطاطس *n pl* (*sg* **baṭaaṭsa, baṭaaṭsaaya**) potatoes; **baṭaaṭis muḥammara** fried potatoes
baṭaḥ بطح *vi* (**a, baṭiḥ**) to knock down
baṭal بطل *n* (*pl* **abṭaal**) hero; champion
baṭari بطري *n* (*pl* **bayaaṭra**) veterinarian
baṭii بطي *adj* (*pl* **-'iin**) slow
baṭraan بطران *adj* arrogantly ungrateful for God's gifts
baṭṭ بط *coll n* duck(s)
baṭṭaal بطال *adj* bad
baṭṭaaniyya بطّانيّة *n* (*pl* **-aat, baṭaaṭiin**) blanket
baṭṭaariyya بطّاريّة *n* **1** battery **2** (electric) torch, flashlight
baṭṭal بطّل (**biṭṭeel**) *vi* **1** to quit, stop **2** to break down • *vt* to quit, stop doing sth.
baṭṭan بطّن *vt* (**tabṭiin**) to line or pad a garment
baṭṭiikh بطّيخ *coll n* watermelon(s)
baṭun بطن *n f* (*pl* **buṭuun**) **1** abdomen, belly; stomach **2** pregnancy (*in the sense of counting the number of births*); **di baṭun-a at-taalta** this is her third pregnancy; this is her third child **3** section of a tribe **4** interior, inside; **baṭn-o faarigha** it is hollow; **baṭn al-kuraa**ʿ the sole of the foot

bawaagi بواقي *n* (*sg* **baagi**) remains, remnants
bawaasiir بواسير *n pl* piles, haemorrhoids
bawaẓaan بوظان *n* decay, rottenness
bawṣala بوصلة *n* compass
bawwaab بواب *n* doorkeeper, doorman
bawwaaba بوابة *n* (large) gate
bawwakh بيّخ *vt* (**biwweekh**) to fumigate (clothes, a room) with incense
bawwal بوّل *vt* to help s.o. to urinate
bawwar بوّر *vt* (**tabwiir**) to leave fallow; to leave unsold
bawwaz بوّز (**biwweez**) *vi* to pout • *vt* to drink (from a bottle)
bawwaẓ بوّظ *vt* (**biwweeẓ, bawaẓaan**) to spoil sth./s.o., damage, corrupt; to cause to decay
bayaaḍ بياض *coll n* catfish
bayaaḍ بياض *n* **1** plaster **2** bleach **3** white of egg **4** film (over eyes) **5** small part of the fee of a **faki**, given in advance
bayaakha بياخة *n* tediousness; silliness
bayaan بيان *n* (*pl* **-aat**) statement, declaration notice, notification; **bayaan ṣaḥafi** press release
bayyaaʿ بيّاع *n* seller, vendor
bayyaaḍ بيّاض *n* plasterer
bayyaḍ بيّض *vt* **1** (**biyyeeḍ, tabyiiḍ**) to plaster (top layer); **bayyaḍ be-j-jiir** to whitewash **2** (**biyyeeḍ, tabyiiḍ**) to bleach **3** (**tabyiiḍ**) to correct a draft of a document
bayyaḍ بيّض *vi/vt* (**biyyeeḍ, beeḍa**) to lay (eggs)

bayyakh بيّخ *vt* (**biyyeekh**) to spoil, mess up

bayyan بيّن *vt* (**biyyeen**) to reveal; to make clear

bayyat بيّت *vi* (**bayataan, mabiit**) to spend the night

bayyina بيّنة *n* evidence, proof

bazag بزق *vi* (**u, bazig, buzaag**) to spit

bazzaaza بزّازة *n* baby's feeding bottle

bazzar بزّر *vt* (**bizzeer, tabziir**) to waste

be- بـ *prep* at; with (things); in by; through; **be-la** without

beeʿ بيع *n* (*pl* **-aat**) sale; **le-l-bee**ʿ for sale; **bee**ʿ **wa shira** commerce, trade

beeʿ**a** بيعة *n* sale

beeḍ بيض *coll n* egg(s); **beeḍ maslu-ug** boiled eggs; **beeḍ be-ṭ-ṭawwa/ beeḍ magli** fried eggs; **beeḍ** ʿ**iyuun** fried eggs (yolk not broken)

beeḍa بيضة *unit n* **1** egg **2** (*pl* **-aan**) testicle

beeḍaawi بيضاوي *adj* egg-shaped

beeji بيجي *adj* beige

been بين *prep* between, among; **been-i wa-been-ak** between the two of us

beenaat بينات *prep* between, among

beerag بيرق *n* (*pl* **bayaarig**) flag, banner

beet بيت *n* (*pl* **biyuut**) house; **fi l-beet** at home; **beet birish** tent of matting; **beet sha**ʿ**ar** tent of camel hair; **beet al-adab** lavatory, toilet; latrine; **beet abu/ umm shabatu** spider's web; **beet an-naḥal** beehive

berri برّي *interj* no (*used by women only*); **berri, berri** no, no!

biʿ**eew** بعيو *n* (*pl* **-aat**) dwarf

biʿ**id** بعد *vi* (**i, bu**ʿ**aad**) **1** to be(come) distant, be far away; to stay at a distance **2** (**min**) to keep a distance (to), stay away (from)

biʿ**sa** بعسة *n* mission (delegation)

bidʿ**a** بدعة *n* (*pl* **bida**ʿ) **1** innovation **2** heresy

bidaaya بداية *n* beginning, start

biga بقى *vt* (**-a, bagiya, bagayaan**) to become, get; **al-biga shinu** what (has) happened?; **al-bibga shinu** what will happen?; **ma bibga** (*m*), **ma bitabga** (*f*) it is impossible; **hu bibga lee-y** he is my relative

bihit بهت *vi* (**a, bahta, bahataan**) to fade

bii'a بيئة *n* environment

bii'i بيئي *adj* environmental

biim بيم *n* (*pl* **abyaam**) beam

biir بير *n f* (*pl* **abyaar, aabaar**) well; **biir as-sayfon** soakaway; **biir as-silim** stair well, stair opening

biira بيرة *n* beer

bijaama بجامة *n* pyjamas

bika *n* (*pl* **bikyaat**) abbreviation of; **beet al-bika** mourning place, a house where people go to condole with a bereaved family

bikir بكر *n* firstborn child; **bitt bikir** first girl; **walad bikir** first son

bikr بكر *n* (*pl* **-aat**) virgin

bikra بكرة *n* virgin

bikriyya بكريّة *adj f* pregnant for the first time

bilaad بلاد *n pl* (*sg* **balad**) country; countries

bildaat بلدات *n pl* agricultural fields

bilenti بلنتي *n* (*pl* **-iyyaat**) **1** penalty (*football*) **2** violation that leads to a penalty

bilhaarsiya بلهارسيا *n* bilharzia
billi بلي *coll n* (*unit n* **biliyya**) marble(s)
bilyaardo بلياردو *n* billiards
bilyoon بليون *n* (*pl* **balaayiin**) billion
binaaya بناية *n* building
bineyya بنيّة *n* girl
bint بنت *n* (*pl* **banaat, bannuut**) girl
bira برى *vi* (**-a, bariya, barayaan**) **1** to heal **2 min** to recover (from an injury)
bira برا *vt* (**-i, mabaaraa**) to follow; **bira d-darib** to track, follow a track
biraada برادة *n* filings (metal)
birid برد *vi* (**a, barid**) to become cold, cool
birish برش *n* (*pl* **buruush**) reed mat
biriṭaani بريطاني (*pl* **-yyiin**) *adj* British • *n* a Briton
biriṭaaniya بريطانيا *prop n* Britain
birka بركة *n* (*pl* **birak**) pool, pond, small lake
bisilla بسلّة *n* peas
bishkiir بشكير *n* (*pl* **bashaakiir**) towel
bitaaᶜ بتاع *adj m* (*f* **bitaaᶜat**) *in construction indicating* **1** *possession:* to belong to; **al-musaddas bitaaᶜ-i** the pistol is mine; my pistol; **al-mufḥaḍa bitaaᶜat-i** the purse is mine; my purse **2** *association:* **bitaaᶜ al-mooya** water carrier, water seller; **an-nuur bitaaᶜ al-ᶜarabiyya** the car lights; **mara bitaaᶜat rabb-a-na** a pious woman **bitaaᶜ an-niswaan** philanderer
biteen بتين *interrog* when
bitrool بترول *n* petroleum; refined oil; **bitrool khaam** crude oil, petroleum
bitt بت *n* (*pl* **banaat, bannuut**) **1** daughter; **bitt marat-i, bitt raajil-i** my stepdaughter; **bitt ᶜamm/ᶜamma** female cousin on father's side; **bitt khaal/khaala** female cousin on mother's side; **bitt akhu/ukhut** niece; **bitt ḥaraam/bott zina** bastard daughter, illegitimate daughter **2** girl; **bitt umm laᶜᶜaab** doll, puppet
bizir بزر *coll n* (*unit n* **bizra**, *pl* **buzuur**) seed(s); pip(s)
biznis بزنس *n* business
bizr بزر *n* clitoris
bizza بزّة *n* (*pl* **bizzaz**) baby's feeding bottle
blaastik بلاستيك *adj* plastic • *n* plastic
blok بلوك *n* (*pl* **-aat**) **1** block **2** one row of houses (in a street)
boksi بكسي *n* (*pl* **bakaasi**) pickup truck
boobaar بوبار *n* swank, braggart
boobiina بوبينة *n* (*mech*) ignition distributor
boofeeh بوفيه *n* (*pl* **-aat**) buffet
bool بول *n* urine
booliis بوليس *n* **1** police; **booliis al-ḥaraka** traffic police **2** (*pl* **bawaaliis**) policeman
booliiṣa بوليصة *n* bill; policy (insurance); **booliiṣat shaḥan** bill of lading
boorsiliin بورسلين *n* china, porcelain
boosa بوسة *n* kiss
boostar بوستر *n* (*pl* **-aat**) poster
boosh بوش *n* **1** meal consisting of bread crumbled in water in which fava beans have been cooked **2** crowd at a wedding

broofa بروفة *n* rehearsal
brustaata برستاتا *n* prostate
buʿud بعد *n* **1** remoteness; **al-buʿud biziid aj-jafa** out of sight, out of mind **2** (*pl* **abʿaad**) range; dimension
bu's بؤس *n* misery
budaa'i بدائي *adj* (*pl* **-yyiin**) primitive
budd بد *n* **la budda** it is inevitable
budra بودرة *n* powder
buḍaaʿa بضاعة *n* (*pl* **baḍaayiʿ**) goods, merchandise; **buḍaaʿa baayra** unsold goods; **buḍaaʿa muharraba** contraband
bufteek بفتيك *n* beefsteak
bugʿa بقعة *n* (*pl* **bugaʿ**) **1** spot, stain **2** spot, place; **al-bugʿa** old Omdurman, Omdurman of the Mahdi
bugbug بقبق *n* **umm bugbug** okra stew
bugga بقّة *n* sip
buggaag بقّاق *coll n* blister(s)
bugja بقجة *n* (*pl* **bugaj**) knapsack, pack
buhaag بهاق *n* skin disease that discolours parts of the skin, pityriasis alba; vitiligo
buhaaraat بهارات *n pl* spices
buḥeera بحيرة *n* lake
bukra بكرة *n* tomorrow
bukhaar بخار *n* steam, vapour
bukhsa بخسة *n* (*pl* **bukhas**) calabash
bukhul بخل *n* stinginess
bulaaṭ بلاط *coll n* tile(s)
bulbul بلبل *coll n* (*pl* **balaabil**) nightingale(s)
buldoozar بلدوزر *n* (*pl* **-aat**) bulldozer
bulootiin بولتين *n* (*pl* **-aat**) platinum point (for car)
bulṭi بلطي *coll n* tilapia (fish)
buluk بلك *n* (*mil*) (*pl* **-aat**) company
buluufar بلوفر *n* (*pl* **-aat**) pullover, jersey; sweater
buluuza بلوزة *n* blouse
buna بنا *n* construction (building)
bundugiyya بندقيّة *n* (*pl* **banaadig**) rifle, gun; **bundugiyyat kharṭuush** small-bore rifle; air-gun, air rifle
bungus بنقس *n* triple drum
bunn بن *coll n* **1** coffee beans **2** ground coffee
bunni بنّي *adj* brown
bunya بنية *n* (*pl* **-aat, bunaj**) a blow with the fist, a punch
burʿum برعم *n* (*pl* **baraaʿim**) bud
buraaz براز *n* faeces
burhaan برهان *n* (*pl* **baraahiin**) proof, evidence
burjum برجم *n* chickenpox
burma برمة *n* (*pl* **buraam, buram**) earthenware pot; cooking pot, pan; **siid al-buraam** (*m*) potter; **sitt al-buraam** (*f*) potter
burshaam برشام *n* (*pl* **-aat, baraashiim**) rivet
burtukaan برتكان *coll n* orange(s); **burtukaan abu ṣ-ṣurra** navel orange(s)
burtukaani برتكاني *adj* orange
burṭumaaniyya برطمانيّة *n* jar with lid
buruj برج *n* (*pl* **abraaj**) **1** tower **2** star sign
buruud برود *n* coldness, insensitivity
buruuda برودة *n* cold (of weather)
burwaaz برواز *n* (*pl* **baraawiiz**) picture frame
busaaṭ بساط *n* (**-aat, absiṭa**) carpet

busṭa بسطة *n* post (mail); **al-busṭa** the post office
busṭaji بسطجي *n* (*pl* **-yya**) postman
bushaara بشارة *n* (*pl* **-aat, bashaayir**) good news
bushra بشرى *n* (*pl* **bushaaraat**) good news; **bushra saara** good news
butajaaz بوتجاز *n* (*pl* **-aat**) gas cooker
buttaab بتاب *coll n* husk(s) of grain
buṭaan بطان *n* (*trad*) ritual before a wedding: friends and peers whip the groom while he is supposed not to utter a sound
buṭaan بطان *n* (*pl* **-aat, abṭina**) saddle girth
buṭaana بطانة *n* lining of a garment
buṭaaqa بطاقة *n* card; **buṭaaqa shakhṣiyya** identity card
buṭeyni بطيني *adj* gluttonous, having a voracious appetite
buṭuula بطولة *n* **1** championship **2** heroism
buuʿ بوع *n* (*pl* **buuʿeen**) wrist; **ma biʿraf kuuʿ-o min buuʿ-o** (*lit* he doesn't know the difference between his elbow and his wrist) he doesn't know anything
buug بوق *n* (*pl* **abwaag**) horn (musical instrument)
buuhya بوهية *n* paint
buuji بوجي *n* (*pl* **bawaaji**) spark plug
buulistar بولستر *n* polyester
buum بوم *coll n* owl(s)
buum بوم *adj invar* dull, thick, stupid
buur بور *adj invar* fallow; **ariḍ buur** fallow land
buuri بوري *n* (*pl* **bawaari**) horn (of car)
buurṣa بورصة *n* stock market
buuṣ بوص *coll n* reed(s), cane
buuṣa بوصة *n* inch
buut بوت *n* (*pl* **abwaat**) boot (footwear)
buuz بوز *n* (*pl* **-aat, abwaaz**) pouting mouth; **buuz aj-jazma** toe/toe cap of a shoe
buzaag بزاق *n* spittle

d – د

da دا *dem pron m* this
daʿa دعا *vt* **1** (**-u, duʿaa**) to pray to, invoke **daʿa (Allah) be-baraka le-** to invoke a blessing upon; **daʿa (Allah) be-laʿna ʿala** to invoke a curse upon **2** (**-u, daʿwa**) to invite
daʿaaya دعاية *n* publicity; propaganda
daʿak دعك *vt* (**a, daʿik**) to rub (the skin)
daʿam دعم *n* **1** support; **daʿam maʿnawi** moral support **2** subsidy; **daʿam maali** subsidy • *vt* (**a, daʿam**) **1** to support **2** to subsidize
daʿwa دعوى *n* (**daʿaawi**) lawsuit
daʿwa دعوة *n* invitation; **ma lee-k daʿwa** it's none of your business
daaʿi داعي *n* **ma fih daaʿi** there's no need (to do sth.)
daa'iri دائري *adj* round, circular; **ṭariig daa'iri** ring road; **baaṣṣ daa'iri** circular bus
daab داب *vi* (**u, dawabaan**) to melt, dissolve

daabba دابّة *n* (*pl* **dawaabb**) beasts of burden
daabi دابى *n* (*pl* **dawaabi**) snake
daada دادة *n* nurse (for children)
daaḍḍa داضّ *vt* (**-i, mudaaḍḍa**) to oppose; to be against
daafaᶜ دافع *vi* (**difaaᶜ**) to defend
daafag دافق *vi* (**dufaag**) to miscarry (humans); **hi daafagat** she had a miscarriage
daafi دافي *adj* warm
daafiᶜ دافع *n* (*pl* **dawaafiᶜ**) motive
daafuuri دافوري *n* informal football match (in the street)
daagash داقش *vi* (**mudaagasha**) **maᶜa** to bump, collide, crash into
daagis داقس *adj* inattentive
daak داك *dem pron m* that
daakh داخ *vi* (**u, dawakhaan**) to faint; to be(come) dizzy
daakhil داخل *prep* inside; **abga daakhil** please come in! • *n* interior
daakhili داخلي *adj* internal, inner
daakhiliyya داخليّة *n* boarding house, dormitory
daam دام *vi* (**u, dooma**) to last; **ma daam** as long as; since; **ma daam jiit, agᶜud** since you have come you may stay
daar دار *n* (*pl* **diyaar**) **1** home; homeland **2** house; **daar an-nashir** publishing house
daar دار *vi* (**u, doora, dawaraan**) **1** to turn (round), move in a circle **2** to revolve, rotate **3 al-mawduuᶜ biduur ḥawaleen** the subject is about
daar دار *vt* (**u, deera**) **1** to want, need; **bitduur/bidduur shinu** what do you want? **2** to be about to; **ash-shamis taduur taghiib** the sun is about to set
daariji دارجي *adj* **ad-daariji** the colloquial (language), spoken Arabic
daarijiyya دارجيّة *adj f* **ad-daarijiyya** the colloquial (language), spoken Arabic
daas داس (**u, doosa, dawasaan**) *vi* **ᶜala 1** to step on, tread on, trample on **2** to put pressure on, press; to click (on a button) • *vt* to hit; to kick; **dustaa-ho be-ᶜarabiyyat-i** I hit him with my car; **daas-o** he snubbed/humiliated him; **daas banziin** to accelerate; **daas fuul** (*slang*) to eat **fuul**
daash داش *vi* (**u, dawashaan**) to be(come) dizzy
daawa داوى *vt* (**-i, mudaawaa**) to treat medically, cure, heal
daawam داوم *vi* (**mudaawama**) to continue
daawas داوس *vt* (**duwaas, mudaawasa**) to fight with
daaya داية *n* midwife
daayikh دايخ *adj* dizzy, giddy
daayim دايم *adj* constant, lasting, permanent
daayin داين *n* creditor
daayir داير *adj* (*f* **daayra**, *pl* **daayriin**) (*used for*) *to want, need;* **hu ma daayir-o** he doesn't want it/him; **hi daayraa-ho** she wants it/him
daayish دايش *adj* dizzy, giddy
daayman دايما *adv* always
daayra دايرة *n* (*pl* **dawaayir**) circle, ring
dabaara دبارة *n* wisdom
dabagh دبغ *vt* (**u, dibaagha**) to tan leather

dabal دبل *vt* (**i, dabil**) to punch (with fist)
dabalaan دبلان *n* calico
dabar دبر *coll n* healing wound(s) or sore(s)
dabba دبّة *n* (*pl* **-aat, dibab**) sand dune
dabbaaba دبّابة *n* (*mil*) tank
dabbaagh دبّاغ *n* tanner
dabbaasa دبّاسة *n* stapler
dabbal دبّل (**dibbeel**) *vt* to double; **dabbalta al-gamiiṣ** I put on a second shirt (over the first one) • *vi* **dabbal ʿala marat-o** he married a second wife
dabbar دبّر *vt* (**dibbeer, tadbiir**) to manage (financial matters on a domestic level)
dabbuur دبّور *n* (*pl* **dabaabiir**) a type of large wasp
dabbuura دبّورة *n* (*pl* **dabaabiir**) (*mil*) star (badge of rank)
dabbuus دبّوس *n* (*pl* **dabaabiis**) **1** pin; safety pin; hairpin; **dabbuus mashbak** paperclip; **dabbuus ḍaghiṭ** drawing pin, thumbtack **2** staple
dabiib دبيب *n* (*pl* **dabaayib**) snake; **dabiib al-baḥar** eel
dabras دبرس *vi* (**dabrasa, dibrees**) to be(come) depressed; **be-** to depress, cause a depression
dabrasa دبرسة *n* depression, gloom
dabul دبل *adj* double
dafʿa دفعة *n* push
dafa دفا *n* warmth
dafaʿ دفع *vt* (**a, dafiʿ**) **1** to pay **2** to push
dafan دفن *vt* (**a, dafin**) to bury
dafar دفر *vt* (**i, dafir**) to push
daffa دفّة *n* rudder
daffa دفى *vt* (**-i, diffeey**) to warm
daffaʿ دفّع *vt* (**diffeeʿ**) to make s.o. pay
daffaara دفّارة *n* lorry, bus
daffag دفّق *vt* (**diffeeg**) **1** to spill (e.g. milk, salt) **2** to throw away (any liquid, e.g. dirty water) • *vi* to spill over, run over (of liquid or vessel); **al-beet bidaffig** the roof is leaking
dafiʿ دفع *n* (*pl* **dafʿiyyaat**) payment
dafiiʿa دفيعة *n* a child given to another family that does not have (enough) children
dafin دفن *n* burial
dafra دفرة *n* push
daftar دفتر *n* (*pl* **dafaatir**) notebook; register
dagas دقس *vi* (**u, dagis**) to be unaware of a profit; to be deceived, cheated
dagash دقش *vt* (**u, dagish, dagsha**) to bump into, collide, crash into
dagdaag دقداق *n* **1** (of an unpaved road) unevenness **2** (*slang*) trouble, problems • *adj invar* troublemaker
dagga دقّة *n* blow, stroke
dagga دقّ *vt* (**u, dagg**) **1** (**on**) to hit, beat, strike, hammer, knock (on); to pound; **daggoo-hu dagg** they thrashed him; **bidugg aj-jaras** he rings the bell; **dagga l-washam** to tattoo; **dagga sh-shalluufa** to tattoo the lips; **dagga j-jirsa** to call for mercy **2** to thresh • *vi* to ring, be knocked on; **aj-jaras bidugg** the bell is ringing; **al-baab bidugg** s.o. is knocking on the door
daggaag دقّاق *n* **daggaag al-buraam** potter

daggas دقّس *vt* (**dagsa**) to cheat, deceive
dagiig دقيق *n* flour; **abu d-dagiig** moth; butterfly
dagiiga دقيقة *n* (*pl* **dagaayig**) minute; **antaẓir dagiiga** wait a moment
dagsha دقشة *n* bump, collision, crash
daghash دغش *n* dawn, early morning
daghmas دغمس *vt* (**daghmasa**) to blur (e.g. facts)
dahab دهب *n* gold
dahabi دهبي *adj* golden
dahan دهن *vt* (**i, dihin**) to grease the skin
dahnas دهنس *vi* (**dahnasa, dihnees**) **le-** to ingratiate o.s. with, flatter in order to win a favour
dahsha دهشة *n* amazement, astonishment
daḥash دحش *n* (*pl* **duḥuush**) young donkey
daḥiin دحين *adv* just now
dajjaal دجّال *n* impostor, charlatan, quack
dakka دكّ *vt* (**u, dakk, dakakaan**) **1** to tamp down, pound firmly (e.g. ground) **2** (**min**) to play truant (from school or work)
dakwa دكوة *n* peanut butter, groundnut paste
dakhal دخل *vt* (**u, dukhuul**) to enter, come in; **dakhal al-khidma al-ʿaskariyya** to enlist (military service)
dakhkhal دخّل *vt* (**dikhkheel**) to make s.o. enter, permit to enter; to put inside
dakhkhan دخّن *vi/vt* (**tadkhiin**) to smoke
dakhl دخل *n* income
dalaja دلجة *n* any surface empty of loose sand and vegetation (desert, town or house); **dagga d-dalaja** he found himself in a difficult situation, he failed, he went bankrupt
dalak دلك *vt* (**i, dalik**) to massage
dalduum دلدوم *n* **umm dalduum** (*pl* **umm dalaadiim**) a punch with the back of the fist
daleeb دليب *coll n* doleib palm(s)
dalguun دلقون *n* (*pl* **dalaagiin**) rag, tatter; cloth (for cleaning)
daliil دليل *n* (*pl* **adilla**) **1** evidence, proof **2** guide
dalik دلك *n* massage
dalla دلّ *vt* (**i, dalla**) to guide
dalla دلّى *vt* (**-i, dilleey**) to lower (things)
dallaʿ دلّع *vt* (**dilleeʿ, dalaʿ**) to pet, pamper, spoil
dallaal دلال *n* **1** auctioneer **2** vendor of secondhand goods
dallaaliyya دلاليّة *n* female peddler, selling on credit
dallak دلّك *vt* (**dilleek, tadliik**) to massage
dallal دلّل *vt* (**dalaal, tadliil**) to pet, pamper, spoil
dalluuka دلّوكة *n* (*pl* **dalaaliik**) small drum, usually of clay with stretched hide
damʿa دمعة *n* **1** (*pl* **dumuuʿ**) teardrop **2** thin meat stew; thin sauce
damaar دمار *n* destruction
damawi دموي *adj* **1** bloody; **zool damawi** killer, murderer **2** pertaining to blood; **ad-dawra ad-damawiyya** circulation of the blood
damgha دمغة *n* duty stamp; **waraga damgha** stamped document

damm دم *n* blood; **beenaat-na laḥam wa damm** the same blood runs in our veins; **been-um/ beenaat-um damm** there's a blood feud between them; **damm at-taayir** allergy rash; **damm-o khafiif** he is light-hearted; he's funny; **damm-a tagiil** she is a bore

dammaam دمّام *n* **abu dammaam** spleen

dammar دمّر *vt* (**tadmiir**) to destroy

dammuuriyya دمّوريّة *n* unbleached cotton

dandurma دندرمة *n* homemade ice cream

dangar دنقر *vi* (**dingeer, dangara**) to bend down/over

dangas دنقس *vi* (**dingees, dangasa**) to bend down/over

dani دني *adj* (*pl* **-yyiin**) low, mean, ignoble

dankas دنكس *vt* (**dinkees, dankasa**) **1** to tilt **2** to lower (e.g. a flag)

dannaan دنّان *n* **abu dannaan** type of large wasp

dantilla دنتلة *n* **1** lace **2** tassel

daqiiq دقيق *adj* precise, accurate

darabukka دربكّة *n* triple drum

darabziin درابزين *n* (*pl* **-aat**) railing, fence (of reed or metal)

daraga درقة *n* (*pl* **-aat, dirag**) armour; shield

daraja درجة *n* **1** degree; school mark; class; grade; rank; **daraja uula** first class, first degree; **le-d-daraja** to the extent **2** step of stairs or ladder

daran درن *n* tuberculosis

daras درس *v* (**u, daris, diraasa**) to study

darash درش *vt* (**u, darish**) to grind (with stones)

darat درت *n* period of time before the harvest (between the end of the rains and the beginning of winter)

darbakiin دربكين *n* (*pl* **-aat**) electric drill

dardaag درداق *n* **abu d-dardaag** dung beetle

dardaaga درداقة *n* wheelbarrow

dardag دردق *vt* (**dardaga**) to roll sth.

dardash دردش *vi* (**dardasha**) to chat

darib درب *n* (*pl* **duruub**) unpaved road; track; **darb al-arbaʿiin** the Forty Days Road

daris درس *n* (*pl* **duruus**) lesson

darra درّ *vi/vt* (**u, darr, dararaan**) to lactate

darrab درّب *vt* (**dirreeb, tadriib**) to train s.o.

darras درّس *vt* (**tadriis**) to teach

darwash دروش *vi* (**darwasha**) to live in an enlightened state (of a mystic or dervish)

darwiish درويش *n* (*pl* **daraawish**) dervish, member of a Sufi brotherhood; holy man

dasiisa دسيسة *n* (*pl* **dasaayis**) intrigue, scheme

dassa دسّ *vt* **1** (**i, dassa, dasasaan**) to hide, conceal **2** (**i, dasiisa**) to intrigue

dasta دستة *n* (*pl* **disat**) dozen

dastar دستر *vi* (**dastuur**) to be possessed by spirits

dastuur دستور *n* (*pl* **dasaatiir**) **zaar** spirit

dastuur دستور *n* (*pl* **dasaatiir**) constitution

dasuusiyya دسوسيّة *n* hide and seek (game)
dashdash دشدش *vt* (**dishdeesh, dashdasha**) to smash, break into pieces
dawa دوا *n* **1** (*pl* **adwiya**) medicine, remedy, drug; **dawa sharaab** medical syrup; **dawa baladi** local or home remedy **2** (*pl* **diwyaat**) spices
dawaajin دواجن *n pl* poultry
dawaali دوالي *n pl* varicose veins
dawaam دوام *n* perpetuity, permanence, infinity; **ad-dawaam le-llaah** permanence is for God (*a reply when being offered condolences*)
dawash دوش *vi* (**yidwish, dawsha**) to make a din, hubbub, commotion
dawla دولة *n* (*pl* **duwal**) state (nation)
dawra دورة *n* cycle, cyclic stage; **ad-dawra** menstruation; **ad-dawra ad-damawiyya** the circulation of the blood; **dawra tadriibiyya** training cycle, course
dawri دوري *adj* periodical
dawriyya دوريّة *n* **1 a** patrol **b** roadblock **2** periodical
dawsha دوشة *n* din, hubbub; fuss; commotion
dawwaam دوّام *n* (*pl* **-aat**) shift (at work)
dawwaama دوامة *n* whirlpool
dawwab دوّب *vt* (**diwweeb, tadwiib**) to melt sth.; to dissolve sth.
dawwad دوّد *vi* (**diwweed**) to get worms
dawwan دوّن *vt* (**tadwiin**) **1** to write down, note, record **2** to blog
dawwar دوّر *vt* (**diwweer, tadwiir**) to start (a car), turn on (an engine)
dayyan ديّن *vt* (**deen**) to lend
deedabaan ديدبان *n* (*pl* **-aat**) sentry
deel ديل *dem pron pl* these
deelaak ديلاك *dem pron pl* those
deelak ديلك *dem pron pl* those
deen دين *n* (*pl* **diyuun**) debt
deer دير *n* (**adiira**) monastery
di دي *dem pron f* this
dibeebu ديبيبو *n* **umm dibeebu** eel
dibla دبلة *n* (*pl* **dibal**) wedding ring
diblomaasi دبلوماسي (*pl* **-yyiin**) *adj* diplomatic • *n* diplomat
difaaʿ دفاع *n* defence
difteeriya دفتيريا *n* diphtheria
diggeen دقّين *n* small beard
digin دقن *n* (*pl* **duguun**) **1** beard **2** chin
dihaan دهان *n* (*pl* **-aat**) **1** fat, grease, cream (for cosmetic use) **2** paint
dihin دهن *n* (*pl* **duhuun**) **1** fat, grease **2** perfumed fat used as skin cream
diḥeesh دحيش *n* (*m*) young donkey
diḥeesha دحيشة *n* (*f*) young donkey
diik ديك *dem pron f* that
diik ديك *n* (*pl* **diyuuk, dayaka**) rooster, cock; **diik ruumi** turkey
diimuqraaṭi ديمقراطي *adj* democratic • *n* democrat
diimuqraaṭiyya ديمقراطيّة *n* democracy
diin دين *n* (*pl* **adyaan**) religion
diini ديني *adj* religious
diiwaan ديوان *n* (*pl* **dawaawiin**) reception room, lounge
diizil ديزل *n* diesel (fuel)
diktaatoor دكتاتور *n* (*pl* **-iyyiin**) dictator

diktaatooriyya دكتاتوريّة *n* dictatorship
diktoor دكتور *n* (*pl* **dakaatra**) **1** medical doctor, physician; **diktoor ʿiyuun** optician **diktoor aʿṣaab** neurologist; **diktoor amraaḍ nisa** gynaecologist; **diktoor asnaan** dentist; **diktoor aṭfaal** paediatrician; **diktoor baaṭiniyya** internist; **diktoor baṭari** veterinary; **diktoor jildiyya** dermatologist; **diktoor nafsi** psychiatrist; psychologist **2** Ph.D. holder, doctor
dilaaha دلاهة *adj invar* foolish
dilaala دلالة *n* auction **suug ad-dilaala** secondhand goods market
dilka دلكة *n* skin scrub made from millet or sorghum flour, ground cloves, scented oil and perfumes, smoked with sandalwood or acacia wood
dimeeʿaat دميعات *n pl* **abu dimeeʿaat** cattle plague
dingil دنقل *n* (*pl* **danaagil**) axle
diqqa دقّة *n* accuracy; **be-diqqa** accurately
diraasa دراسة *n* study; **ad-diraasaat al-ʿulya** higher studies
diriʿ درع *n* (*pl* **duruuʿ**) armour
dirib درب *n* (*pl* **-aat**) intravenous drip
diriksoon دركسون *n* (*pl* **-aat**) steering wheel
disembar ديسمبر *n* December
dish دش *n* (*pl* **dashasha, dushuush**) **1** satellite dish **2** (*slang*) bottom, backside (of girls, women)
dishin دشن *adj* rough, tough
diyaana ديانة *n* religion
diyya ديّة *n* blood money
dooba دوبى *v* (**-i, doobaay, doobeey**) to sing (bedouin songs)
doobaay دوباي *n* nomad's poem or song
dookha دوخة *n* giddiness, dizziness; vertigo
doolaab دولاب *n* (*pl* **dawaaliib**) chest of drawers, cupboard, cabinet, wardrobe
doolaar دولار *n* (*pl* **-aat**) dollar
doom دوم *coll n* (*unit n* **dooma, doomaaya**) **1** doum palm(s) **2** fruit(s) of the doum palm
doonki دونكي *n* (*pl* **dawaanki**) small pump used to raise water from a water source, donkey engine
door دور *n* (*pl* **adwaar**) **1** turn (in succession); **da door-ak inta** it's your turn **2** round; **door kushteena** a round of cards; **door al-leela** this day next week **3** storey, floor; **ad-door al-arḍi** the ground floor **4** role; **bilʿab door** it plays a role
doosha دوشة *n* giddiness, dizziness
dooshka دوشكا *n* (*pl* **-aat**) automatic weapon
dosseeh دسّيه *n* (*pl* **-aat**) file, dossier
draama دراما *n* drama
duʿaa دعا *n* (*pl* **adʿiya**) invocation to God
duʿaash دعاش *n* cool breeze (after rain)
dubaara دبارة *n* thin rope (of jute)
dubb دب *n* (*pl* **dababa**) bear
dubbilyuusii دبليوسي *n* lavatory, toilet; latrine
dufʿa دفعة *n* (*pl* **-aat, dufaʿ**) draft (army); class (of one school year)
dufaag دفاق *n* (*pl* **-aat**) miscarriage
dugaag دقاق *adj* very fine (of flour, powder)

dugul دقل *n* (*pl* **duguul**) stump of a tree

dughri دغري *adj* **1** candid, forthright, straightforward **2** just, fair • *adv* straight, straight ahead

dughshiyya دغشيّة *n* **1** dawn **2** (*agr*) work in the early morning

dughush دغش *n* dawn, early morning

dukkaan دكّان *n* (*pl* **dakaakiin**) shop, store

dukhaan دخّان *n* **1** (*pl* **dakhaakh-iin**) smoke; **dukhaan al-ʿazaba** weaver bird **2** smoke bath, fumigation

dukhla دخلة *n* consummation of marriage on the wedding night; **leelat ad-dukhla** the wedding night

dukhun دخن *n* pearl millet, bulrush millet

dukhuul دخول *n* entrance, way in

dulgaan دلقان *n* (*pl* **dalaagiin**) rag, tatter; cloth (for cleaning)

dullung دلّنق *n* (*pl* **dalaaling**) small earthenware pot (for beer)

dumaagh دماغ *n* (*pl* **admigha**) **1** head **2** mind

dunya دنيا *n* earthly existence, world

dura درة *n* **1** sorghum **2** corn, maize; **dura shaami** corn, maize

duraash دراش *adj invar* coarse ground (e.g. of grain)

durdur دردر *n* (*pl* **daraadir**) round mud or stone building with a thatched roof

durraab درّاب *coll n* **1** clod (of dried sand or mud) **2** rude talk

duruj درج *n* (*pl* **adraaj**) **1** drawer **2** school desk

dusuntaarya دسنتاريا *n* dysentery

dush دش *n* (*pl* **dushuush**) shower; **akhad dush** to take a shower; shower

dut دت *adv* **ma...dut** never, at all

duud دود *coll n* (*unit n* **duuda, duudaaya**, *pl* **deedaan**) worm(s), maggot(s); **duud ghiiniyya** guinea worm(s); **duuda shariiṭiyya** tapeworm; **duudat faraasha** caterpillar

duud دود *n* (*no pl*) lion

duun دون *prep* without; **be-duun** without

duwaas دواس *n* fight

duwali دولي *adj* international

ḍ - ض

ḍaʿiif ضعيف *adj* (*pl* **ḍuʿaaf**) **1** thin, slim **2** feeble, weak, powerless, spineless

ḍaaʿ ضاع *vi* (**i, ḍeeʿa**) to get lost, be lost

ḍaaʿaf ضاعف *vt* (**muḍaaʿafa, ḍiʿʿeef**) double

ḍaabiṭ ضابط *n* (*pl* **ḍubbaaṭ**) officer

ḍaag ضاق *vt* (**u, ḍuwaaga, ḍooga**) to taste

ḍaag ضاق *vi* (**i, ḍiig**) to become tight

ḍaalli ضالّي *adj* (*pl* **ḍaalliin**) lost, astray

ḍaamin ضامن *n* guarantor; bailor

ḍaan ضان *coll n* sheep

ḍaanaaya ضاناية *unit n* **1** ewe, female sheep **2** dimwitted person

ḍaani ضاني *adj* mutton (meat)
ḍaara ضارى *vt* (**-i, muḍaaraa**) to hide sth./s.o.
ḍaarab ضارب *vt* (**ḍarib, muḍaaraba**) to fight
ḍaarr ضار *adj* harmful
ḍaayag ضايق *vt* (**muḍaayaga**) to bother, annoy; to harass, pester
ḍaayar ضاير *vt* (**muḍaayara**) to arrange, put in order
ḍabʿa ضبعة *n* (*pl* **ḍibaaʿ**) hyena
ḍabaab ضباب *n* mist, fog
ḍabaḥ ضبح *vt* (**a, ḍabiḥ**) to slaughter, butcher
ḍabaṭ ضبط *vt* (**u, ḍabit**) to discipline
ḍabb ضب *n* (*pl* **ḍababa, ḍububba**) gecko, house lizard
ḍabba ضبّ *vt* (**u, ḍabb**) to take a firm hold (of s.o.)
ḍabiṭ ضبط *n* discipline
ḍablaan ضبلان *adj* **1** withered **2** having poor health
ḍablan ضبلن *vi* (**ḍablana**) **1** to wither **2** to look unhealthy
ḍabṭ ضبط *n* discipline; **be-ḍ-ḍabt** exactly
ḍafar ضفر *v* (**u, ḍafir**) **1** to plait, braid (hair) **2** to kick a football with the toes
ḍafḍaʿa ضفضعة *n* (*pl* **ḍafaaḍiʿ**) frog
ḍaffaara ضفّارة *n* nail clipper
ḍaffar ضفّر *vt* (**ḍiffeer**) **1** to plait, braid (hair) **2** to cut nails
ḍafiira ضفيرة *n* (*pl* **ḍafaayir**) plait, braid
ḍaghaṭ ضغط *vi* (**a, ḍaghiṭ**) (**ʿala**) to put pressure on
ḍaghiṭ ضغط *n* pressure; **ḍaght ad-damm** blood pressure
ḍahar ضهر *n* (*pl* **ḍuhuur**) **1** back; **ḍahr al-murkab** deck of a boat; **ḍahr at-toor** a roof sloping on both sides; **ʿind-o ḍahar** he has s.o. in the family with power or wealth who can back him **2** small island in a river
ḍahbaan ضهبان *adj* astray, lost
ḍaḥawiyya ضحويّة *n* (*agr*) work in the late morning
ḍaḥḥa ضحّى *vt* (**-i, taḍḥiya**) to sacrifice
ḍaḥik ضحك *n* laughter
ḍaḥil ضحل *adj* shallow
ḍaḥiyya ضحيّة *n* (*pl* **ḍaḥaaya**) **1** sacrifice **2** victim
ḍaḥka ضحكة *n* laugh
ḍaḥwa ضحوة *n* late morning
ḍajiij ضجيج *n* loud noise, din, hubbub
ḍajja ضجّة *n* loud noise, din, hubbub
ḍajja ضجّ *v* (**i, ḍajj, ḍajja, ḍajiij**) to be noisy, make a din, hubbub
ḍakar ضكر *n* (*pl* **ḍukuur**) **1** male **2** penis
ḍakariyya ضكريّة *adj f* **1** woman behaving like a man **2** lesbian
ḍakraan ضكران *adj* courageous and trustworthy
ḍakham ضخم *adj* big, huge
ḍakhkha ضخّ *vt* (**u, ḍakhkh**) to pump
ḍalʿa ضلعة *n* (*pl* **ḍuluuʿ**) rib
ḍalaam ضلام *n* darkness
ḍalfa ضلفة *n* (*pl* **ḍilaf**) leaf (of a door, window)
ḍalla ضلّ *vi* (**i, ḍall, ḍalalaan**) to go astray, lose one's way
ḍallal ضلّل *vt* (**ḍilleel**) to deceive, cheat
ḍallam ضلّم *vi* (**ḍilleem, ḍalaam**) to become dark; **washsh-o ḍallam** his face fell

ḍalma ضلمة *n* darkness • *adj invar* dark

ḍamaan ضمان *n* **1** guarantee, warranty; **ḍamaan miyya fi l-miyya** guaranteed hundred percent **2** bail

ḍamaana ضمانة *n* **1** guarantee, warranty **2** bail

ḍaman ضمن *vt* (**a, ḍamaan, ḍamaana**) **1** to guarantee, vouch for **2** to bail

ḍamiir ضمير *n* (*pl* **ḍamaayiir**) conscience

ḍamma ضمّ *vt* (**u, ḍamm**) **1** to include **2** (**le-/ila**) to attach (to); to cause to join **ḍammoo-ho le-l-faṣil** they accommodated him in the class

ḍanab ضنب *n* (*pl* **ḍunuub, ḍunubba**) tail

ḍarab ضرب *vt* (**a, ḍarib**) **1** to hit, beat, knock, strike; **ḍarab buuhya** to paint; **ḍarab be-j-jiir** to whitewash; **ḍarab fuul** to eat **fuul**; **ḍarab ḥaaja baarda** to drink a soft drink; **ḍarab-o kaff** he smacked him; **ḍarab naar** to shoot; **ḍarab orneesh** to polish; **ḍarab be-r-raṣṣaaṣ** to shoot; **ḍarab raqam** to dial; **ḍarab ta-lafoon** to telephone **2** (*arith*) to multiply; **ḍarb khamsa fi sitta yisaawi talaatiin** five times six equals thirty *vi* **1** to ring; **aj-jaras biḍrab** the bell is ringing **2** to throb (heart) **3** **ʿala** to play a musical instrument

ḍarar ضرر *n* (*pl* **aḍraar**) damage; **fii-ho ḍarar** damaged

ḍarba ضربة *n* blow, stroke; kick, shot; **ḍarba be-n-naar** shot; **ḍarba ḥurra** a free kick; **ḍarba rukniyya** a corner (football); **ḍarbat shamis** sunstroke

ḍariiba ضريبة *n* (*pl* **ḍaraayib**) tax; **ḍariibat aj-jamaarik** customs duty

ḍariiḥ ضريح *n* (*pl* **ḍaraayiḥ, aḍriḥa**) saint's tomb

ḍariir ضرير *adj* blind

ḍarr ضر *coll n* a species of small ant(s)

ḍarra ضرّ *vt* (**u, ḍarra**) to harm, damage

ḍarra ضرّة *n* co-wife

ḍarra ضرّى *vt* (**-i, ḍirreey**) to winnow

ḍarraʿ ضرّع *vt* (**ḍirreeʿ, taḍriiʿ**) to measure (e.g. cloth)

ḍarraaya ضرّاية *n* winnowing fork

ḍarrab ضرّب *vt* (**ḍirreeb, taḍriib**) (*arith*) to multiply

ḍaruura ضرورة *n* necessity

ḍaruuri ضروري *adj* necessary

ḍaruuriyyaat ضروريّات *n pl* necessities

ḍaw ضو *n* (*pl* **aḍwaa**) light; **ʿala ḍaw** in the light of

ḍawaaḥi ضواحي *n pl* surroundings; **ḍawaaḥi l-madiina** suburbs

ḍawwa ضوّى (**-i, ḍiwweey**) *vi* to give light • *vt* illuminate, give light to

ḍawwag ضوّق *vt* (**ḍiwweeg**) to let s.o. taste sth.

ḍayaaʿ ضياع *n* loss, waste

ḍayyaʿ ضيّع *vt* (**ḍiyyeeʿ, ḍeeʿa**) to lose

ḍayyag ضيّق *vt* (**taḍyiig**) to nar-row (down)

ḍayyig ضيّق *adj* tight; narrow

ḍeef ضيف *n* (*pl* **ḍiyuuf**) guest, visitor

ḍiʿif ضعف *vi* (**a, ḍuʿuf**) **1** to become thin **2** to become feeble, weak
ḍidd ضد *prep* against
ḍiffa ضفّة *n* (*pl* **ḍifaaf**) riverbank
ḍihib ضهب *vi* (**a, ḍahab, ḍahabaan**) to go astray, lose one's way
ḍiḥik ضحك *vi* **1** (**a, ḍaḥik, ḍaḥka**) (**ʿala**) to laugh (at); to giggle **2** (**a, ḍaḥik**) **ʿala** to deceive, cheat
ḍiig ضيق *n* **1** narrowness; **ḍiig an-nafas** breathlessness **2** anxiety, distress
ḍiriʿ ضرع *n* (*pl* **ḍuruuʿ**) udder
ḍiris ضرس *n* (*pl* **ḍuruus, aḍraas**) molar tooth; **ḍirs al-ʿagul** wisdom tooth
ḍiyaafa ضيافة *n* hospitality
ḍuʿuf ضعف *n* weakness
ḍubbaan ضبّان *coll n* flies; **ḍubbaan al-ḥamiir** horseflies
ḍufra ضفرة *n* dried cartilaginous remains of shellfish (a basic ingredient for a kind of home-made perfume)
ḍufur ضفر *n* (*pl* **aḍaafir, aḍaafreen**) fingernail, toenail
ḍuhur ضهر *n* midday; noon **baʿd aḍ-ḍuhur** afternoon
ḍuḥa ضحا *n* late morning
ḍulaaf ضلاف *n* **abu ḍulaaf** anteater
ḍull ضل *n* (*pl* **ḍalala**) shadow, shade
ḍullaala ضلالة *n* makeshift sun shelter
ḍuluf ضلف *n* (*pl* **ḍalafeen, ḍuluuf**) hoof
ḍulumma ضلمّة *n* darkness • *adj invar* dark; **al-waaṭa ḍulumma** it's dark
ḍumana ضمنة *n* dominoes
ḍuraaʿ ضراع *n* (*pl* **-aat**) arm
ḍurus ضرس *n* (*pl* **ḍuruus, aḍraas**) molar tooth; **ḍurs al-ʿagul** wisdom tooth

e

eeh ايه *interrog* what
eeraqaan ايرقان *n* hepatitis, jaundice

f – ف

faad فاد *vt* (**i, faayda**) to be useful
faaḍ فاض *vi* (**i, fayaḍaan**) to flood, overflow (e.g. of a river); **faaḍ bee-y min-na-ha** I am fed up with her
faaḍi فاضي *adj* (*pl* **-yyiin**) empty; blank; free, vacant, unoccupied, available
faaḍil فاضل *adj* remaining; **faaḍil lee-y nuṣṣ as-saaʿa** I have half an hour left
faaḍil فاضل *adj* good-hearted, generous
faag فاق *vi* (**u, fooga**) to return to consciousness; to sober up
faaḥish فاحش *adj* using obscene language
faaja' فاجأ *vt* (**mufaaja'a**) to surprise; to take by surprise
faajir فاجر *adj* immoral

faakar فاكر *vi* (**mufaakara**) to hold a consultation
faaks فاكس *n* (*pl* **-aat**) fax
faakha فاكهة *n* (*pl* **fawaakih**) a fruit
faakhir فاخر *adj* luxurious
faal فال *n* **1** good omen **2** hope; **faal Allah wa-la faal-ak** rest your hope on God
faaliḥ فالح *adj* **1** (of children) good, honest, sensible, clever; **ya faaliḥ** you're a good boy, you're a clever boy! **2** (of adults) successful
faalso فالسو *adj invar* fake
faanuus فانوس *n* (*pl* **fawaaniis**) lantern, paraffin lamp, oil lamp
faar فار *vi* (**u, foora, fawaraan**) **1** to rise (of dough) **2** to boil
faar فار *n* (*pl* **fiiraan**) (male) rat; mouse; **faar tajaarib** guinea pig, an animal being used for an experiment
faara فارة *n* **1** (female) rat; mouse; **da faara daagis** (*slang*) that is a gullible person **2** calf (of leg)
faara فارة *n* plane (tool)
faaraaya فاراية *n* mouse
faarag فارق *vi* (**furaag, mufaaraga**) to part
faarigh فارغ *adj* empty; **baṭn-o faargha** it is hollow; **kalaam faarigh** nonsense
faaris فارس *n* (*pl* **fursaan**) horse rider, knight; **faaris aḥlaam-i** the prince of my dreams
faas فاس *n* (*pl* **fu'uus**) axe, hatchet
faasid فاسد *adj* corrupt (dishonest)
faaṣal فاصل *vi* (**mufaaṣala, fiṣaal**) to haggle, bargain
faaṣil فاصل *n* (*pl* **fawaaṣil**) **1** partition boundary **2** interval, interlude
faaṣuulya فاصوليا *n* beans; **faaṣuulya khaḍra** green beans, French beans; **faaṣuulya beeḍa** white beans
faat فات *vi* (**u, foota, fawataan**) **1** to go; to leave; **ash-shahar al-faat** last month **2 ʿala** to call in at, drop in on • *vt* to pass, overtake
faatḥa فاتحة *n* **al-faatḥa** the opening **suura** or chapter of the Koran; **gara l-faatḥa** to recite the opening chapter of the Koran (e.g. to thank God; to conclude a wedding contract); **shaal al-faatḥa** to recite the opening chapter of the Koran (when offering condolences)
faatiḥ فاتح *adj* **1** open **2** bright (of colour)
faatiyya فاتية *n* bully
faatna فاتنة *adj f* attractive, charming
faatuura فاتورة *n* (*pl* **fawaatiir**) bill, invoice; **faatuura mabda'iyya** pro forma invoice; quotation; **faatuura nihaa'iyya** final invoice
faaṭir فاطر *adj* not fasting; having had breakfast
faaṭṭi فاطي *adj* **faaṭṭi saṭur** silly, crazy
faawa فاوة *adj invar* light (of weight); **baṭn-o faawa** he's useless
faawil فاول *n* (*pl* **faawlaat**) (*sports*) foul, foul play
faayda فايدة *n* (*pl* **fawaayid**) **1** benefit; use, utility; **da faaydat-o shinu** what's the use of it?; **be-la/be-duun/min gheer faayda** in vain **2** profit, interest **3** royalty
faayiḍ فايض *n* surplus (in balance), reserves (accounts)

faayig فايق *adj* said about an irresponsible, lazy person
faayiz فايز *adj* winning • *n* winner
faayl فايل *n* (*pl* **-aat**) file (of papers)
faayruus فيروس *n* (*pl* **-aat**) virus
faayẓ فايظ *n* incorrect behaviour (in business, construction); **ishtaghal lee-na be-l-faayẓ** he cheated us with his work
faaz فاز *vi* (**u, fooz**) (**be-**) to win; **faaz be-jaayza** to win a prize
faaẓa فاظة *n* vase; flowerpot, plant pot
fabraayir فبراير *n* February
fabrak فبرك *vt* (**fabraka**) **1** to manufacture in a shoddy way **2** to fabricate a lie
fada فدى *vt* (**-i, fidiya**) to ransom
faḍaa فضا *n* cosmic space
faḍaa'i فضائي *adj* spatial, space; **qanaa faḍaa'iyya** satellite channel
faḍaaya فضاية *n* open space
faḍaḥ فضح *vt* (**a, faḍiḥ, faḍiiḥa**) to scandalize, bring shame on
faḍalaat فضلات *n pl* **1** leftovers **2** faeces
faḍḍa فضّة *n* silver
faḍḍa فضّى *vt* (**-i, fiḍḍeey, tafḍiya**) to empty; to unload
faḍḍa فضّ *vt* (**i, faḍḍ, faḍaḍaan**) to put an end to
faḍḍal فضّل *vt* **1** (**tafḍiil**) (**ʿala**) to favour, prefer s.o./sth. (to) **2** (**fiḍḍeel**) to leave (food for s.o. else)
faḍḍi فضّي *adj* silver
faḍfaḍ فضفض *vi* (**faḍfaḍa**) to relieve one's feelings, unburden one's mind
faḍiiḥa فضيحة *n* (*pl* **faḍaayiḥ**) public disgrace, scandal
faḍiil فضيل *adj* kind
faḍiila فضيلة *n* (*pl* **faḍaayil**) virtue
faḍla فضلة *n* (*pl* **faḍalaat**) rest, remnant, remainder
faḍul فضل *n* (*pl* **afḍaal**) grace, goodness, favour; **min faḍl-ak** please (requesting)
faḍwa فضوة *n* free time
fagaʿ فقع *vt* (**a, fagiʿ, fagʿa**) to break open, split (e.g. nuts, fruit, eggs); **fagaʿ maraart-i** (*lit* he split my gall) he gave me a very hard time
fagad فقد *vt* (**i, fagid, fugdaan**) to lose
fagash فقش *vt* (**i, fagish**) to break open
faggaʿ فقّع *vt* (**figgeeʿ, fagʿa, tafgiiʿ**) to break open, split (e.g. nuts, fruit, eggs)
faggaaʿa فقّاعة *n* (*pl* **-aat, fagaagiiʿ**) air bubble
faggash فقّش *vt* (**figgeesh**) to break into pieces
fagiir فقير (*pl* **fugara**) *adj* poor • *n* mystic
fagraan فقران *adj* poor
fagri فقري *adj* very good in doing a job, proficient
fagur فقر *n* poverty
faham فهم *n* understanding; **suu' al-faham** misunderstanding
fahham فهّم *vt* (**fihheem, faham**) to explain, make s.o. understand
fahras فهرس *vt* (**fahrasa**) to make a list of; to index, catalogue
fahrasa فهرسة *n* (*pl* **fahaaris**) index
faḥam فحم *n* coal, charcoal
faḥaṣ فحص *vt* (**a, faḥiṣ**) **1** to check (mechanics) **2** to do a laboratory test
faḥḥa فحّ *vi* (**i, faḥḥiiḥ**) to hiss (snake)

faḥḥaṭ فحّط *vi* (**fiḥḥeeṭ, tafhiiṭ**) to brake suddenly (in joyriding)
faḥiṣ فحص *n* (*pl* **fuḥuuṣaat**) **1** checkup (mechanics) **2** laboratory test
faj'a فجأة *adv* (*and* **faj'atan**) suddenly, unexpectedly, by surprise
fajaq فجق *vt* (**a, fajiq**) to crush with the foot
fajjar فجّر *vt* (**tafjiir**) to explode
fajriyya فجريّة *n* (*agr*) work at dawn
fajur فجر *n* dawn
fajwa فجوة *n* gap
fakak فكك *n* dislocation
fakii فكي *n* (*pl* **fukaya**) **1** traditional healer who uses verses of the Koran or charms as a form of magic **2** holy man **3** (*Isl*) religious teacher
fakk فك *n* (*pl* **fukuuk, afkaak**) jaw (animals)
fakka فكّة *n* coins; small change; **fakka ḥadiid** coins
fakka فكّ *vt* **1** (**i, fakk, fakakaan**) to undo, untie, unscrew; to loosen **2** (**i, fakk, fakakaan**) to take to pieces, take apart, dismantle **3** (**i, fakk, fakka**) to set free, release (e.g. from prison) **4** (**i, fakka**) to give change (money)
fakkar فكّر *vi* (**tafkiir**) (**fi**) to think (about)
fakhar فخر *vi* (**a, fakhr**) (**be-**) to be proud (of)
fakhda فخدة *n* (*pl* **fikhad**) leg (meat)
fakhfakha فخفخة *n* pomposity
fakhkh فخ *adj* brittle
fakhr فخر *n* pride
fakhuur فخور *adj* (**min, be-**) proud (of)
falaaḥa فلاحة *n* **1** (of children) honesty, probity, sensibility **2** (of adults) success
falaḥ فلح *vi* (**a, falaaḥa**) (**fi**) to succeed (in), prosper
falaja فلجة *n* space between the front teeth (sign of beauty)
falak فلك *n* **1** (*pl* **aflaak**) star; planet **2** **ʿilim al-falak** astronomy, universe
falas فلس *n* bankruptcy
falgasa فلقسة *n* exaggeration in one's way of talking, in content or style
falhama فلهمة *n* affectation, airs, showing off
falla فلّى *vt* (**-i, tafliya**) to pick out vermin (e.g. from head, clothes)
fallaati فلاتي *n* (*pl* **fallaata**) one of the Fellata (collective term applied to immigrants of West African origin)
fallal فلّل *vi* (**filleel**) to become dark
fallas فلّس *vi* (**tafliis**) to be(come) bankrupt, broke, penniless • *vt* (*slang*) to break open (e.g. a lock)
falluuka فلّوكة *n* (*pl* **fallaayik**) small sailing boat (river)
faniila فنيلة *n* (*pl* **fanillaat, fanaayil**) undershirt, vest; **faniila be-ḥammaalaat** undershirt, vest; **faniilat ṣuuf/faniilat ṣagaṭ** pullover, sweater, cardigan
fanjaṭ فنجط *vi* (**finjeeṭ, fanjaṭa**) to gallop about, run and prance about
fann فن *n* (*pl* **funuun**) art
fanna فنّ *vt* (**i, fann**) to throw (stones)
fannaan فنّان *n* (*m*) artist
fannaana فنّانة *n* (*f*) artist

fanni فنّي *adj* **1** technical **2** artistic
fantuut فنتوت *n* (*pl* **fanaatiit**) little blighter, plucky little devil
fanṭaaẓ فنطاظ *n* (*pl* **fanaaṭiiẓ**) **1** tank (for water) **2** tanker (lorry)
faqiih فقيه *n* (*pl* **fuqaha**) expert in Islamic law
faqra فقرة *n* **1** paragraph **2** short series of songs
faqri فقري *adj* spinal
far^coon فرعون *n* (*pl* **faraa^cna**) pharaoh
far^cooni فرعوني *adj* pharaonic
faraagh فراغ *n* (*pl* **-aat**) emptiness; vacuum
faraash فراش *coll n* butterflies
faraawla فراولة *n* strawberries
farad فرد *vt* (**i, farid**) to unfold
faraḍ فرض *vt* (**i, fariḍ**) (**^cala**) to impose (on)
farag فرق *vi* (**i, farig**) to differ, be different; **da ma bifrig** that doesn't make a difference
faraga فرقة *n* little space; little time; **addii-ni faraga ma^caa-k** make me some space; make some time for me
faraḥ فرح *n* (*pl* **afraaḥ**) **1** joy, happiness, delight **2** wedding
faraj فرج *n* **1** relief **2** (*pl* **furuuj**) vulva
farak فرك *vt* (**i, farik**) **1** to rub **2** to stir with a **mufraaka**
faram فرم *vt* (**u, farim**) to mince
farandiit فرنديت *n* guinea worm
farash فرش *vt* (**u, farish**) to cover (e.g. with a sheet, a carpet)
faraz فرز *vt* (**i, fariz**) to sort out
fard فرد *n* (*pl* **afraad**) individual
farda فردة *n* (*pl* **-aat, firad**) **1** one of a pair **2** (*slang*) friend, boyfriend/girlfriend **3** a bus route (one way)
fardi فردي *adj* **1** individual **2** odd (of numbers)
farfar فرفر (**farfara**) *vi* to move convulsively • *vt* (*slang*) to mess up (e.g. a room) while searching for sth.
farfara فرفرة *n* convulsion; **farfarat madbuuḥ** convulsion of a slaughtered animal
farfash فرفش *vi/vt* (**firfeesh, farfasha**) to cheer up
farga^c فرقع *vi* (**firgee^c, farga^ca**) to burst open; to explode • *vt* to cause to burst open; to explode
farga^ca فرقعة *n* bursting; explosion
farḥaan فرحان *adj* happy, glad, joyful
fari^c فرع *n* (*pl* **furuu^c**) **1** branch, twig **2** branch, section
fariḍ فرض *n* **1** (*pl* **furuuḍ**) duty, obligation **2** (*pl* **faraayiḍ**) (*Isl*) religious duty
farig فرق *n* (*pl* **furuugaat**) difference
fariid فريد *adj* unique
fariiḍa فريضة *n* (*pl* **faraayiḍ**) sacrament (protestant)
fariig فريق *n* (*pl* **firag**) **1** quarter of a town or village **2** section of a bedouin camp
fariiq فريق *n* (*pl* **furaqa**) general, lieutenant general, major general
fariiq فريق *n* (*pl* **firaq**) team, crew
fariisa فريسة *n* (*pl* **faraayis**) prey
farikh فرخ *n* (*pl* **furuukh**) sheet of paper
farikh فرخ *n* (*pl* **furuukh**) **1** **farikh al-ḥamaam** young pigeon, squab **2** male slave

farish فرش *n* **1** bedspread, bedding (mattress and sheet) **2** furnishing, fitting up

farkha فرخة *unit n* **1** (*pl* **firaakh**) chicken, hen **2** (*pl* **-aat**) female slave

farmal فرمل *vi* (**farmala**) to brake

farmala فرملة *n* (*pl* **faraamil**) brake

farra فرّ *vi* (**i, farr**) to flee, run away • *vt* (**i, farra**) to unfold

farraan فرّان *n* baker

farraar فرّار *n* (*pl* **-aat, faraariir**) hatchet, chopper, meat cleaver; **abu farraar** cerebrospinal fever; meningitis

farraash فرّاش *n* (*m*) sweeper, cleaner

farraasha فرّاشة *n* (*f*) sweeper, cleaner

farrag فرّق *vi* (**tafriig**) **been** to distinguish, differentiate • *vt* (**firreeg, tafriig**) to separate, set apart

farragh فرّغ *vt* (**firreegh, tafriigh**) to empty; to unload

farraḥ فرّح *vt* (**firreeḥ, tafriiḥ**) to make happy, delight

farrash فرّش *vt* (**firreesh, farish**) to spread a cover over, cover (e.g. with a sheet, a carpet)

farraz فرّز *vt* (**firreez**) to sort out

farruuja فرّوجة *n* (*pl* **faraariij**) young chicken

fartak فرتك (**fartaka, firteek**) *vt* **1** to disperse, scatter (a group) **2** to take to pieces, take apart, dismantle • *vi* (*slang*) to run off, clear off, escape

faru فرو *coll n* (*unit n* **farwa**, *pl* **faraaw**) fur; hide

farwa فروة *unit n* (*pl* **faraaw**) **1** hide **2** prayer mat **3** carpet (of hide)

farzaʿ فرزع *vt* (**farzaʿa**) to scatter (individuals)

fasa فسى *vi* (**-i, fasu**) to fart

fasaad فساد *n* corruption

fasaala فسالة *n* avarice, stinginess

fasad فسد *vi* (**i, fasaad**) to be(come) corrupted morally

fasaḥa فسحة *n* open space, open area

fasakh فسخ *vt* (**a, fasikh**) **1** to peel (of skin) **2** to annul, cancel (of a wedding engagement) **3** to declare (a contract) invalid

fasiikh فسيخ *n* **1** salt-cured fish **2** paste of salt-cured fish with peanut butter

fasil فسل *adj* (*pl* **fusala**) avaricious; **al-khala wa-la r-rafiig al-fasil** better to be in the desert than to have an avaricious companion

fassad فسّد *vt* (**fasaad**) to corrupt

fassaḥ فسّح *vt* (**fisseeḥ, fusḥa**) **1** to let s.o. have fun, take around, take out on a trip **2** (*slang*) to finish s.o. off, kill

fassar فسّر *vt* (**tafsiir**) to interpret, explain

faswa فسوة *n* fart

fasya فسية *n* fart

faṣal فصل (**i, faṣil**) *vt* **1** to separate; to disconnect **2** to dismiss, depose (from office, function) • *vi* **1** to be disconnected (e.g. of electricity, water, telephone) **2 been** to cause to separate

faṣiiḥ فصيح *adj* eloquent

faṣiila فصيلة *n* (*pl* **faṣaayil**) faction

faṣil فصل *n* (*pl* **fuṣuul**) **1** classroom **2** season **3** chapter **4** dismissal

faṣli فصلي *adj* seasonal

faṣṣ فص *n* (*pl* **fuṣuuṣ**) segment of fruit or vegetable; **faṣṣ tuum** a clove of garlic
faṣṣal فصّل *vt* **1** (**fiṣṣeel, tafṣiil**) to cut out a pattern (for garments) **2** (**tafṣiil**) to tell or explain in detail
fasha فشا (**-i, fashiya, fashayaan**) *vi* to be disclosed (of a secret) • *v* to betray (a secret)
fashal فشل *vi* (**a, fashal**) to fail • *n* failure; **fashal kilawi** kidney failure
fashfaash فشفاش *coll n* lung(s) (as meat)
fashshar فشّر *vi* (**fishsheer, fashar**) (**be-**) to boast, brag
fashshaar فشّار *n* boaster, braggart
fataa فتاة *n* (*pl* **fatawaat**) girl
fatag فتق *vt* (**i, fatig**) to rip open at the seams
fataḥ فتح *vt* (**a, fatiḥ**) **1** to open; **aftaḥ ash-shaariʿ** clear the way! **2** to switch on, turn on (light, gas, radio, etc.) **3** (*slang*) to ignore; **aftaḥ lee-ho** forget about him/it!
fatal فتل *vt* (**i, fatil**) to twist (a rope)
fatan فتن *vt* (**i, fitna**) **1** to cause discord between people **2** to charm, enchant; to tempt; to seduce
fatar فتر *vi* (**a, futuur, fatar**) to be(come) tired • *n* fatigue
fatariita فتريتة *n* a (reddish) variety of sorghum (*pej*) **ʿeesh ḥamaam** pigeon food
fatfuuta فتفوتة *n* (*pl* **fataafiit**) crumb
fatḥa فتحة *n* **1** the act of opening; **fatḥat al-khashum** the first payments towards a bride price **2** opening, aperture; **fatḥat ash-sharaj** anus
fatiḥ فتح *n* the act of opening; **fatḥ al-kitaab** fortune telling by a **faki**
fatiil فتيل *n* (*pl* **fataayil**) small bottle
fatiila فتيلة *n* (**fataayil**) wick
fatra فترة *n* (*pl* **-aat, fataraat**) period (of time), term
fatraan فتران *adj* tired, exhausted
fatta فتّة *n* dish of soup, sauce or stew poured over crumbled bread or **kisra**
fatta فتّ *vt* (**i, fatt**) to crumble (bread or **kisra** in soup or sauce)
fattaaḥa فتّاحة *n* bottle opener, can opener
fattaan فتّان *n* intriguer
fattaan فتّان *adj* attractive, charming
fattag فتّق *vt* (**fitteeg**) to rip open at the seams
fattar فتّر *vt* (**fitteer**) to tire
fattash فتّش *vi* (**fitteesh, taftiish**) **le-/ʿala** to search for; look for • *vt* (**taftiish**) to inspect; to search
fatwa فتوى *n* (*pl* **fataawi**) Islamic ruling, legal opinion
fatwana فتونة *n* toughness, bullying
faṭam فطم *vt* (**i, faṭim, fiṭaam**) to wean
faṭar فطر *vi* (**u, faṭuur**) to have breakfast; to break the fast
faṭiira فطيرة *n* (*pl* **faṭaayir**) type of fried pastry
faṭiis فطيس *adj invar* (*pl* **faṭaayis**) not slaughtered according to Islamic law and therefore considered inedible
faṭiisa فطيسة *n* (*pl* **faṭaayis**) carrion carcass
faṭṭa فطّ *vt* (**u, faṭṭ**) to skip; to pass over

faṭuur فطور *n* breakfast; breaking of the fast

fawaakih فواكه *n pl* (*sg* **faakha**) fruit(s)

fawaayid فوايد *n pl* (*sg* **faayda**) profits, interests; royalties

fawḍa فوضى *n* disorder, muddle, mess; chaos

fawwaḍ فوّض *vt* (**tafwiiḍ**) to authorize, commission s.o.; to delegate

fawwat فوّت (**fiwweet, tafwiit**) *vi* **1** to become crazy **2** to be(come) loose (e.g. of a screw) • *vt* **1** to let go; allow to pass **2** to skip, leave out; to pass over **3** to send away, chase away

fawwaṭ فوّط *vt* (**fiwweeṭ**) to dry or clean with a dishcloth

fawwaz فوّز *vt* (**fooz**) to make s.o. win

fayaaga فياقة *n* irresponsibility and laziness

fayaḍaan فيضان *n* (*pl* **-aat**) inundation, flood (from river)

fayrus فايروس *n* (*pl* **-aat**) virus

faza‘ فزع *vi* (**a, faz‘a**) to come together to help s.o. in need; **jibnaa-k faz‘a bigiit waj‘a** we brought you in to help but you've become a pain • *vt* **faza‘ ḥaṭab** to collect firewood

fazuura فزورة *n* (*pl* **fawaaziir**) riddle

fazza فزّ *vi* (**i, fazza, fazazaan**) to flee

fazza فزّة *n* flight (escape)

faẓii‘ فظيع *adj* awful, terrible

fi في *prep* **1** in at; about; among; **fi l-beet** in the house; at home; **fi sh-shughul** at work; **fi s-saa‘a khamsa** at five o'clock; **‘ind-i ma‘aa-k ḥadiis fi mas'ala** I want to talk to you about a matter; **fi-ma ba‘ad** afterwards **2** (*arith*) **khamsa fi sitta yasaawi talaatiin** five times six equals thirty

fi‘il فعل *n* **1** (*pl* **fi‘aal**) deed (act); action **2** (*pl* **af‘aal**) verb

fidiya فدية *n* ransom

fiḍa فضى *vi* (**-a, faḍayaan**) **1** to become empty **2** to make time

fiḍil فضل *vi* (**a, faḍla**) to remain, be left over

figsha فقشة *n* (*pl* **figash**) half a piece of fruit or vegetable

fihim فهم (**a, faham**) *vt* to understand, comprehend • *vi* (**fi**) to be knowledgeable (about)

fihrist فهرست *n* (*pl* **fahaaris**) index

fii في *part* there is/are; **hu ma fii** he/it isn't there; **hi ma fiisha** she isn't there; **hum ma fiishiin** they aren't there; **hu fii, gaa‘id** he is around

fiil فيل *n* (*pl* **afyaal**) elephant; **daa' al-fiil** elephantiasis

fiish فيش *coll n* counters, tokens (in games)

fiish فيش *n* (*pl* **afyaash**) certificate of good conduct

fiisha فيشة *unit n* (*pl* **-aat, fiish**) chip, counter, token (in games) • *n* electric socket

fiiziyya فيزيا *n* physics

fijil فجل *coll n* (*unit n* **fijla**) radish(es)

fijja فجّة *n* (*pl* **-aat, fijaj**) place

fikir فكر *n* (*pl* **afkaar**) opinion

fikra فكرة *n* (*pl* **afkaar**) **1** thought, idea **2** indication

filaan فلان *n* **filaan al-filaani** so-and-so

filfil فلفل *coll n* (*unit n* **filfiliyya**) pepper; **filfil aḥmar** (dried) red pepper(s); **filfil akhḍar** fresh green pepper(s); **filfil aswad** (**filfil ruumi**) black pepper; sweet pepper(s)

filim فيلم *n* (*pl* **aflaam**) **1** film, movie **2** photographic film

filtar فيلتر *n* (*pl* **-aat, falaatir**) filter

finjaan فنجان *n* (*pl* **fanaajiin**) small handleless coffee cup

fiqh فقه *n* Islamic jurisprudence

firaakh فراخ *coll n* (*unit n* **farkha**) chicken(s), hen(s), poultry

firansa فرنسا *prop n* France

firansaawi فرنساوي (*pl* **-yyiin**) *adj* French • *n* a Frenchman

firansi فرنسي (*pl* **-yyiin**) *adj* French • *n* a Frenchman

firdoos فردوس *n* paradise

firiḥ فرح *vi* (**a, faraḥ**) (**be-**) to be(come) happy, glad (about); to rejoice

firqa فرقة *n* (*pl* **firaq**) (music) band, company, troupe, ensemble

firra فرة *n/n pl* **al-firra** nightjar (bird)

fishaar فشار *n* popcorn

fitaag فتاق *n* rupture

fitga فتقة *n* (*pl* **fitag**) piece of cloth ripped from a garment at the seams

fitna فتنة *n* (*pl* **-aat, fitan**) **1** conflict, discord **2** (*Isl*) conflict, dissension between Muslims **3** sedition

fiṭis فطس *vi* (**a, faṭsa**) to die (animals)

fiyuus فيوس *n* (*pl* **-aat**) (*elec*) fuse

foog فوق *prep* **1** on, on top of, upon, in, along; over, above; **hi maasha foog ash-shaari**ᶜ she's walking on/along the street; **al-guruush foog ash-shanṭa** the money is in the bag; **waga**ᶜ **min foog aṭ-ṭarabeeza** it fell from the table **2** over, above • *adv* up, upstairs, above

foogaani فوقاني *adj* upper

foorm فورم *n* (*pl* **-aat**) form (document)

fooz فوز *n* victory (in a game)

freem فريم *n* (*pl* **-aat**) frame (of spectacles)

fuḍuul فضول *n* curiosity

fuḍuuli فضولي *adj* curious

fugdaan فقدان *n* loss, bereavement; **wafaat-o fugdaan** his death is a loss; **shihaadat fugdaan** police certificate for reported missing items

fuggaaᶜ فقّاع *n* (*pl* **fagaagii**ᶜ) bubble

fukaaha فكاهة *n* fun

fukaahi فكاهي *adj* comic

fukhkhaar فخّار *n* pottery, earthenware • *adj* clay

fulkluur فلكلور *n* folklore

full فل *coll n* Arabian jasmine

fulla فلّة *n* (*pl* **-aat, fulal**) cork; bottle cap

funduk فندك *n* (*pl* **fanaadik**) mortar (for pounding grain etc.)

funduq فندق *n* (*pl* **fanaadiq**) hotel

furaag فراق *n* parting, separation

furaash فراش *n* (*pl* **-aat**) bed with bedspread, bedding; **beet al-furaash** mourning place, a house where people go to condole with the bereaved family; **rafa**ᶜ **al-furaash** to end the official mourning ceremony

furṣa فرصة *n* (*pl* **furaṣ**) chance, opportunity, occasion

furṣa فرصة *n* cream (of milk)

fursha فرشة *n* (*pl* **furash**) brush; **furshat asnaan** toothbrush; **naḍḍaf be-fursha** to brush

furun فرن *n* (*pl* **afraan**) **1** oven, furnace **2** bakery

fusḥa فسحة *n* stool (faeces)

fusḥa فسحة *n* (*pl* **fusaḥ**) **1** trip, outing; picnic **2** little space

fustaan فستان *n* (*pl* **fasaatiin**) frock, gown

fuṣḥa فصحى *adj f* **al-fuṣḥa** *abbreviation of* **al-lugha al-ʿarabiyya al-fuṣḥa** the pure Arabic language, i.e. the literary or classical Arabic language

fuṭriyyaat فطريّات *n pl* parasitic fungi

fuul فول *coll n* (*unit n* **fuulaaya, fuula**) fava beans, broad beans, horse beans; **fuul suudaani** groundnuts, peanuts; **zeet fuul** groundnut oil

fuula فولة *n* (*pl* **-aat, fuwal**) pool of rain water

fuut فوت *imp* (*v* **faat**) go away!

fuuṭa فوطة *n* (*pl* **fuwaṭ**) **1** small cover for decoration on a table or chair **2** serviette, napkin **3** cloth (for cleaning); dishcloth

g – ق

gaʿʿad قعّد *vt* (**giʿʿeed, gaʿda**) **1** to make s.o. sit down, seat **2** to cause to stay

gaʿad قعد *vi* (**u, guʿaad**) **1** to sit (down); **itfaḍḍal agʿud** have a seat, sit down please!; **gaʿad mutgangin** to squat; **gaʿad mutrabbiʿ** to sit with legs crossed **2** to stay, to remain **3** (*followed by a verb in the present tense:*) to begin, start

gaʿar قعر *n* (*pl* **guʿuur**) bottom, backside

gaʿda قعدة *n* informal gathering, get-together

gaaʿid قاعد *adj* present; **ana gaaʿid** I am staying put; **hu fii, gaaʿid** he is around • *part* (*used with* **fi** *expresses past or present continuous tense*) **kaan gaaʿid yashrab fi l-laban** he was drinking milk

gaabal قابل *vt* (**mugaabala**) to encounter, meet

gaabil قابل *adj* susceptible to; **gaabil le-l-kasir** fragile; **gaabil le-l-ishtiʿaal** inflammable, combustible

gaabiliyya قابليّة *n* **1** faculty, power, ability **2** tendency, disposition, liability

gaadir قادر *adj* able; capable; powerful

gaaḍa قاضى *vt* (**-i, mugaaḍaa**) to sue, prosecute

gaaḍi قاضي *n* (*pl* **guḍaa**) judge, magistrate; **gaaḍi sharʿi** (*Isl*) religious judge

gaafila قافلة *n* (*pl* **gawaafil**) camel caravan; **gaafilat ʿarabaat** convoy

gaal قال *vt* (**u, gool**) to say; **gaal inn-/inno** to allege, claim

gaalib قالب *n* (*pl* **gawaalib**) mould; cake pan; shoemaker's last

gaam قام *vi* (**u, gooma, giyaam**) **1** to stand up, get up;

to be(come) erect **2** to sprout; to grow (of plants); **gaam buruus** to sprout spontaneously (of edible plants) **3** to take off, depart, leave; **gaam barraa-ho** he left alone, he left on his own; **gaam ṣuuf** he ran off very fast **4** (*with following verb*) *and then...*; **gaam gaal** and then he said

gaamar قامر *vi* (**mugaamara, gumaar**) to gamble

gaardiya قارديا *n* giardiasis

gaas قاس *vt* (**i, giyaas**) to measure

gaasa قاسى *vi* (**-i, mugaasaa**) to suffer

gaasam قاسم *vt* (**mugaasama**) to share with; **gaasamat ukhut-a al-huduum** she shared her clothes with her sister

gaasi قاسي *adj* stern, severe, hard, tough, brutal, cruel, merciless

gaaṣid قاصد *adj* purposely, on purpose

gaaṣir قاصر *n* (*pl* **guṣṣar**) minor, under age

gaashar قاشر *vt* (**mugaashara**) (*slang*) to hate

gaashir قاشر *adj* smart, elegant, chic

gaaṭaʿ قاطع *vt* (**mugaaṭaʿa**) **1** to interrupt **2** to cut in (of a car overtaking)

gaaṭiʿa قاطعة *adj f* having passed the menopause

gaaṭira قاطرة *n* locomotive (railway)

gaawal قاول *vi* (**mugaawala**) to undertake (e.g. an enterprise); to contract

gaawt قاوت *n* gout

gaayaḍ قايض *vt* (**mugaayaḍa**) to exchange

gaayil قايل *adj* thinking that, *as in* **kunta gaayil-ak shaaṭir** I thought that you were clever

gaayim قايم *adj* standing, erect; **gaayim be-nafs-o** he's independent

gaayim قايم *n* (*pl* **gawaayim**) any vertical support, prop, pole; **gaayim al-marma** goalpost

gabaaḥa قباحة *n* ugliness

gabaḍ قبض (**u, gabiḍ**) *vt* to seize, arrest • *vi* **ʿala** to seize, arrest

gabbal قبّل *vi* (**gibbeel**) to come back, return **gabbal raajiʿ** to come back, return

gabḍa قبضة *n* a handful; **gabḍat yadd/iid** a handful

gabiḍ قبض *n* capture, arrest; **amr gabiḍ** arrest warrant

gabiiḥ قبيح *adj* (*pl* **-iin, gubaaḥ**) ugly

gabiila قبيلة *n* (*pl* **gabaayil**) tribe, ethnic group

gabil قبل *prep - see* **gabli**

gabli قبلى *prep* before; ago; **jiina gabli shahreen** we came two months ago; **gabli kida** previously; already, before; **gabli ma** before

gabul قبل *prep - see* **gabli**

gabur قبر *n* (*pl* **gubuur**) grave; tomb

gadaḥ قدح *n* (*pl* **gudaaḥa, agdaaḥ**) **1** (wooden) bowl; **abu l-gadaḥ** tortoise; turtle **2** large plate

gadal قدل *vi* (**i, gadla**) to walk in a conceited way

gadam قدم *n* **1** (*pl* **gadameen**) foot **2** (*pl* **agdaam**) foot (12 inches)

gadd قد *n* (*pl* **guduud**) hole (in cloth)

gadda قدّ *vt* (**i, gadd, gadda**) to perforate, pierce, make or bore a (small) hole, pierce, perforate

gaddaf قدّف *vi* (**giddeef, gadaf**) to row (a boat)

gaddam قدّم *vt* **1** (**tagdiim**) to present, offer; to introduce; to submit **2** (**qiddeem**) to show out in leave-taking **3** (**qiddeem**) to bring forward (a date) • *vi* (**taqdiim**) **le-** to apply for

gadduum قدّوم *n* (*pl* **gadaadiim**) **1** mouth; muzzle **2** kiss **3** chisel (wood)

gadgad قدقد *vt* (**gadgada, gidgeed**) to pierce, perforate, bore small holes

gadḥa قدحة *n* fried garlic (added to a stew)

gadiim قديم *adj* (*pl* **gudaam**) old (of things); ancient, from ancient times

gadur قدر *n* amount; extent; **gadur shinu** how much? • *conj* as, as much as, like (amount, weight, height); the same; **gadur ma** however much, much as

gaḍa قضى (**-i, gaḍiya, gaḍayaan**) *vt* to finish • *vi* **ʿala** to finish with, terminate; to eliminate

gaḍaf قضف *vi/vt* (**i, gaḍif**) to vomit, throw up

gaḍḍa قضّى *vt* (**giḍḍeey**) to spend time

gaḍiyya قضيّة *n* (*pl* **gaḍaayaa**) **1** case, matter, question, affair **2** lawsuit, legal case; **rafaʿ gaḍiyya ʿala** to bring a lawsuit against, sue

gafa قفا *n* (*pl* **agfiya**) back of the neck; **be-gafa** behind

gafal قفل *vt* (**i, gafil**) to close, shut; to lock; to switch off, turn off/out (light, gas, radio, etc.)

gafaṣ قفص *n* (*pl* **agfaaṣ**) cage

gafash قفش *vt* (**i, gafish**) to see through; to catch red-handed; **gafashta malʿuub-o** I saw through his trick

gaffal قفّل *vt* (**giffeel**) to close, shut; to lock; to switch off

gafiis قفيس *n* (*pl* **gafaayis**) ring or sleeve for tightening or attaching sth. (e.g. water hose to tap, padlock to door)

gaham قهم *vt* (**a, gaham**) to treat s.o. in a bad or disappointing way, to disappoint

gahwa قهوة *n* (*pl* **gahaawi**) **1** coffee (beverage) **2** coffee shop

gaḥḥa قحّ *vi* (**u, guḥḥa**) to cough

galʿa قلعة *n* (*pl* **gilaaʿ**) citadel, castle

gala قلى *vt* (**-i, galayaan**) to fry

galaʿ قلع *vi* (**a, galiʿ**) to undress • *vt* **1** to take off (clothes or jewellery) **2** to take away by force

galab قلب *vt* (**i, galib, galba**) to turn upside down/inside out; **galab al-huuba** to somersault

galaba قلبة *n* reverse side of a piece of cloth; **laabis-o be-l-galaba** he's wearing it inside out

galad قلد *vt* (**i, galda, galadaan**) to embrace (while greeting)

galag قلق *n* worry, anxiety, uneasiness

galaga قلقة *n* testicle (of animals)

galalo قللو *n* **gaʿad umm galalo** to squat

galam قلم *vt* (**i, galim**) to break off

galam قلم *n* (*pl* **aglaam**) pen **galam raṣaaṣ** pencil

galawooẓ قلووظ *n* **1** thread of a screw; **musmaar galawooẓ** screw; **lambat galawooẓ** screw-in light bulb **2** screw

galgaan قلقان *adj* (**ʿala**) anxious, worried (about)

galib قلب *n* (*pl* **guluub**) heart; **ziyaada fi ḍarbaat al-galib** palpitation; **galb-o aswad** he's malicious
galiil قليل *adj* (*pl* **gulaal**) little, few
galiri قالري *n* (*pl* **-haat**) art gallery
galla قلّ *vt* (**i, gall**) to lift
galla قلّ *vi* (**i, gilla**) to become less, decrease
gallaʿ قلّع *vi* (**gillee**ʿ) to undress • *vt* **1** to take off (clothes or jewellery) **2** to pull out, uproot; to root out
gallaab قلاب *n* (*pl* **-aat**) tipper truck
gallab قلّب *vt* (**galba**) to turn over (once) (**gilleeb**) to turn over (more than once, e.g. cakes in oil)
gallad قلّد *vt* (**tagliid**) to imitate • *vi* **fi** to imitate
gallag قلّق *vt* (**gilleeg**) to worry, bother • *vi* ʿ**ala/be-** to worry about
gallal قلّل *vt* (**gilleel, tagliil**) to lessen, reduce • *vi* **min** to lessen, reduce; **gallal min gadr-o** to disrespect
galluubiyya قلوبيّة *n* bird trap
galwaẓ قلوظ *vt* (**galwaẓa**) to screw
gamar قمر *n* (*pl* **agmaar**) moon **gamar arba**ʿ**ṭaashar** full moon; **gamar ṣinaa**ʿ**i** satellite; **gamar ad-diin** paste of apricot concentrate, to be diluted with water and consumed at breakfast during Ramadan
gamara قمرة *n* cabin, compartment
gamaz قمز *vi* (**i, gamiz**) to flinch; (**min**) to recoil (from)
gambuur قمبور *n* (*pl* **ganaabiir**) traditional nomad hairstyle for boys; ʿ**ind-i gambuur** am I stupid?
gamḥi قمحي *adj* light brown (also of skin)
gamiḥ قمح *n* wheat
gamiiṣ قميص *n* (*pl* **gumṣaan**) shirt; **gamiiṣ noom** nightgown
gammal قمّل *vi* (**tagmiil**) to be covered with lice
gamul قمل *coll n* (*unit n* **gamla**) louse (lice)
ganʿ**aan** قنعان *adj* (**min**) **1** fed up (with) **2** desperate, in despair (about)
gana قنا *coll n* (*unit n* **ganaaya**) bamboo, bamboo cane(s)
ganaṣ قنص *vi* (**u, ganiiṣ**) (**le-**) to hunt; **ganaṣ le-l-arnab be-kalib** he hunted the rabbit with a dog
ganat قنت *vi* (**i, ganataan, ganit**) to moan; to groan
ganduul قندول *n* (*pl* **ganaadiil**) ear (head of grain)
ganiiṣ قنيص *n* game (animals)
ganjar قنجر *vt* (**ganjara**) to abduct, kidnap
gannaaṣ قناص *n* hunter
gannab قنب *vi* (**ginneeb**) to sit
ganṭara قنطرة *n* (*pl* **ganaaṭir**) aqueduct
gara قرا (**-a, giraaya**) *vt* **1** to read **2** to study (law, medicine, etc.) • *vi* **fi** to read
garaʿ قرع *coll n* (*unit n* **gar**ʿ**a**) pumpkin(s), gourd, squash
garaaba قرابة *n* **1** family relationship; kinship; consanguinity **2** closeness
garaaneet قرانيت *n* granite
garaḍ قرض *vt* (**u, gariḍ**) **1** to gnaw; to nibble **2** to cause a three cornered tear **3** to scrub (clothes) **4** (*slang*) to finish completely (e.g. a book); to

know by heart (e.g. a subject for an exam)

garam قرم *vi* (**u, garim**) to nibble

garaṣ قرص *vt* (**u, gariṣ**) **1** to bite (of insects) **2** to pinch

garash قرش *vt* (**u, garish, garashaan**) to chew

garḍaan قرضان *adj* (*slang*) exhausted

garfaan قرفان *adj* disgusted

gargariiba قرقريبة *n* piece of palm frond used for spreading **kisra** batter on the griddle

gargoosh قرقوش *n* (*pl* **garaagiish**) dry/dried bread

garguur قرقور *n/n pl* (*pl* **garaagiir**) **1** snail(s) **2** shield-head catfish

gariḍ قرض *coll n* pods of the acacia (sunt) tree (used medicinally and for incense)

gariib قريب *n* (*pl* **garaayib, agaarib**) relative

gariib قريب *adj* (*pl* **-iin, guraab**) (**min/le-**) near (to), close (to), nearby; **hu gariib** he is around • *adv* **1** nearby **2** soon, shortly **3** recently • *prep* by; towards; going, getting on for; just (close) on; just before; **khallaṣ gariib aḍ-ḍuhur** by noon he had finished; **gariib ʿashara jineeh** just (close) on ten pounds

garin قرن *n* (*pl* **guruun**) horn; **waḥiid al-garin** rhinoceros

garma قرمة *n* (*pl* **-aat, guram**) a bite (of food)

garmaan قرمان *adj* **le-** longing for

garmaṣiiṣ قرمصيص *n* silk headscarf (worn by a bride or by a girl to be circumcised)

garmuuṭ قرموط *n* (*pl* **garaamiiṭ**) eel catfish

garnabiiṭ قرنبيط *coll n* cauliflower

garra قرّا *vt* (**-i, giraaya**) to teach

garra قرّ *vi* (**i, igraar**) **be-** to acknowledge, admit, confess to

garraash قرّاش *n* (*pl* **-aat**) garage

garrab قرّب *vi* (**girreeb, tagriib**) **1** (**min/le-**) to approach, draw near, come near (to) **2** to be about to; **garrabta akhalliṣ** I am about to finish, I have nearly finished

garrad قرّد *vi* (**girreed**) to be infested with ticks

garraḍ قرّض *vt* (**girreeḍ**) **1** to gnaw; to nibble **2** to give a final turn to a screw • *vi* (*slang*) **ʿala** to close a subject at a particular moment; to leave it (at that)

garraf قرّف *vt* (**girreef**) to disgust

garraḥ قرّح *vt* (**tagriiḥ**) to vaccinate

garraṣ قرّص *vt* (**girreeṣ, tagriiṣ**) **1** to bite (of insects) **2** to pinch

garrash قرّش *vt* (**girreesh**) to park a car inside

garrash قرّش *vi* (**guruush**) to have become rich

garṣa قرصة *n* **1** sting; bite (by an insect) **2** pinch

garṭaʿ قرطع *vt* (**girṭeeʿ, garṭaʿa**) to gulp loudly

garuuḥa قروحة *n* vaccination

garya قرية *n* (*pl* **gura**) village

gasaawa قساوة *n* difficulty in life

gasam قسم *vt* (**i, gasim, gisma**) to divide

gasiima قسيمة *n* wedding certificate

gasiṭ قسط *n* (*pl* **agsaaṭ**) installment (of money due or paid)

gassam قسّم *vt* (**gisseem, tagsiim**) to divide; to share out, distribute

gassaṭ قسّط *vt* (**gisseeṭ, tagsiiṭ**) to sell on credit

gassiis قسّيس *n* (*pl* **gasaawsa, gusus**) priest, clergyman

gasṭara قسطرة *n* catheter
gaswa قسوة *n* cruelty
gaṣaʿ قصع *vt* (**a, gaṣiʿ**); **gaṣaʿ aj-jirra** to chew the cud
gaṣab قصب *coll n* (*unit n* **gaṣabaaya, gaṣaba**) **1** cane; **gaṣab sukkar** sugar cane; **al-qaṣaba al-hawa'iyya** trachea, windpipe **2** straw (dried stems)
gaṣad قصد *vt* (**u, gaṣid**) to aim, intend, to mean
gaṣgaṣ قصقص *vi* (**gaṣgaṣa**) to pare, trim (e.g. of nails), to prune (trees, shrubs)
gaṣid قصد *n* (*no pl*) purpose, aim, intention, goal, object, objective; **be-gaṣd-o** on purpose; **be-duun/min gheer gaṣid** unintentionally
gaṣiida قصيدة *n* (*pl* **gaṣaayid**) poem
gaṣiir قصير *adj* (*pl* **guṣaar**) short
gaṣriyya قصريّة *n* chamber pot, potty
gaṣṣa قصّ *vt* (**u, gaṣṣ**) **1** to cut (with scissors); to clip, shear **2** to tell, recount (a story) **3 gaṣṣa l-atar** to track
gaṣṣaaṣ قصّاص *n* **1** tracker **2** a good storyteller
gaṣṣar قصّر (**giṣṣeer, tagṣiir**) *vt* to shorten • *vi* to be insufficient; **ma gaṣṣartu maʿaa-na** you've been generous to us
gaṣur قصر *n* (*pl* **guṣuur**) palace, castle
gashar قشر *vi* (**i, gashra**) to dress well
gashaṭ قشط *vt* (**u, gashiṭ**) to flick with a whip
gashsh قش *coll n* **1** grass, weed **2** alfalfa or any freshly cut leaves (for fodder) **3** dry grass, hay **4** straw
gashsha قشّ *vt* (**u, gashsh**) to sweep
gashsha قشة *unit n* straw; **ma ʿind-o gashsha murra** he is not picky; **hu gashsha murra** he is a difficult person
gashshaara قشّارة *n* threshing machine
gashshar قشّر *vt* (**gishsheer, tag-shiir**) **1** to peel, husk **2** to thresh
gaṭaʿ قطع *vt* (**a, gaṭiʿ**) **1** to cut; to shred; to chop; to fell (trees); **gaṭaʿ miʿaad** to make an ap-pointment; **gaṭaʿ tazkara** to buy a ticket **2** to disconnect, block; **gaṭaʿ ad-darib** to lay an ambush; **gaṭaʿ banziin** to run out of petrol (vehicle) **3** to boycott **4** to pass, cross (street, bridge) • *vi* **1** (**a, gaṭiʿ**) to be cut, disconnected (e.g. of electricity, water, tele-phone line) **2** (**a, gaṭiiʿa**) **fi** to gossip about
gaṭaf قطف *vt* (**i, gaṭif**) to empty of water
gaṭar قطر *n* (*pl* **giṭaaraat, guṭaara**) railway train **gaṭar al-buḍaaʿa** freight train
gaṭar قطر *vt* (**u, gaṭir**) to tow
gaṭiʿ قطع *n* **gaṭiʿ ad-darib** ambush
gaṭiiʿ قطيع *n* (*pl* **guṭʿaan**) flock, herd
gaṭiiʿa قطيعة *n* **1** gossip(ing), backbiting **2 gaṭiiʿa fi ḍ-ḍahar** pain in the back
gaṭiifa قطيفة *n* (*pl* **gaṭaayif**) velvet
gaṭra قطرة *n* medicinal drop
gaṭṭa قطّ *vi* (**i, gaṭṭ**) to run out, be used up (e.g. of water in well, goods)
gaṭṭaʿ قطّع *vt* (**giṭṭeeʿ, tagṭiiʿ**) to tear (up, apart), rip apart

gaṭṭaaʿ قطّاع *n* (*pl* **-iin, guṭṭaa**ʿ); **gaṭṭaa**ʿ **aṭ-ṭurug** robber
gaṭṭaaʿ**a** قطّاعة *n* cutter; shredder
gaṭṭaaʿ**i** قطّاعي *adj* retail
gaṭṭaara قطّارة *n* dropper (e.g. for eye drops)
gaṭṭar قطّر *vt* (**giṭṭeer, tagṭiir**) to drip (e.g. eye drops)
gawaayim قوايم *n pl* (*sg* **gaayma**) supporting structure of a building
gawwa قوّى *vt* (**-i, tagwiya**) to strengthen
gawwaal قوّال *n* a gossip
gawwaam قوّام *adv* hurry up!
gawwal قوّل *vt* (**giwweel**); **gawwal al-kalaam** to twist words
gawwam قوّم *vt* (**giwweem**) to make s.o. stand up
gawwi قوّي *adj* (*pl* **-yyiin, agwiya**) strong
gayyad قيّد *vt* (**geed, giyyeed**) **1** to hobble, tether, tie up; to restrict **2** to register, record
gayyal قيّل *vi* (**giyyeel, magiil**) to spend the afternoon (in one place)
gazaaz قزاز *coll n* glass (material)
gazaaza قزازة *unit n* (*pl* **gazaayiz**) bottle
gazgaz قزقز *vi* (**gizgeez, gazgaza**) (**be-**) to eat (snacks, nuts, seeds)
geed قيد *n* (*pl* **giyuud**) **1** fetter; hobble, restriction **2** record (register)
geef قيف *coll n* shore(s), riverbank(s)
gelti قلتي *n* (*pl* **guluut**) natural reservoir of water in rock
gibeel قبيل *adv* before (of time), previously
gibil قبل (**a, gubuul**) *vi* (**be-**) to accept • *vt* to accept
gibla قبلة *n* **1** direction towards which Muslims face in prayer (the direction of Mecca) **2** niche in the wall of a mosque indicating the direction for praying
gibṭi قبطي (*pl* **agbaaṭ, gibaṭ**) *adj* Coptic • *n* Copt
gidda قدّة *adj invar* (*slang*) talkative
giddaam قدّام *prep* in front (of) • *adv* ahead; **be-giddaam** in front (of)
giddaami قدّامي *adj* front
gidim قدم *vi* (**a, gudum**) to become old (of things)
gidir قدر *n* (*pl* **guduur**) cooking pot
gidir قدر (**a, gudra**) *vi* ʿ**ala** **1** to bear; **ma bagdar** ʿ**alee-ho** I cannot bear it **2** to be strong enough for, to be a match for; **ma bagdar** ʿ**alee-ho** I am not a match for him •*vt* to be able (to), can; **ma bagdar a**ʿ**mil-o** I cannot do it
giḍa قضى *vi* (**-a, gaḍayaan, gaḍiya**) to end
gifil قفل *n* (*pl* **agfaal**) lock
giḥif قحف *n* (*pl* **guḥuuf**) **1** earthenware bowl **2** potsherd
giima قيمة *n* stew of minced meat and tomatoes
gilig قلق *vi* (**a, galag**) ʿ**ala/be-** to worry about
gilla قلّة *n* littleness, fewness; **gillat al-ḥaya** indecency, impertinency; **gillat al-adab** impoliteness, rudeness
giniʿ قنع *vi* (**a, gani**ʿ) (**min**) **1** to be fed up (with) **2** to despair
ginilla قنلّة *n* underskirt; petticoat, slip
ginneeṭa قنيطة *n* (*pl* **ganaaniiṭ**) (*slang*) anus
giraaṭ قراط *n* carat (gold)
giraaya قراية *n* reading, studying; study

girba قربة *n* (*pl* **girab**) skin for holding water
girdaan قردان *n* **abu girdaan** heron
gireen قرين *n* **gireen ḥashshaash** carmine bee-eater (bird)
gireeshaat قريشات *n pl* small amount of money
girfa قرفة *n* cinnamon
girid قرد *n* (*pl* **guruud**) monkey
girif قرف *coll n* (*unit n* **girfa**) bark (of a tree), bast, rind
girif قرف *vi* (**a, garaf**) to be disgusted
girim قرم *vi* (**a, garam**) **le-** to long for, miss
girinti قرنتي *coll n* (*unit n* **girinti-yya**) hippopotamus
girish قرش *n* (*pl* **guruush**) piastre
gisim قسم *n* (*pl* **agsaam**) department, section **gisim al-booliis** large police station
gisma قسمة *n* **1** (*pl* **agsaam**) division, share **2** (*pl* **-aat, gisam**) destiny, fate
giss قس *n* (*pl* **gasaawsa, gusus**) priest, clergyman
gissiis قسّيس *n* (*pl* **gasaawsa, gusus**) priest, clergyman
giṣayyir قصيّر *adj* **1** (*pl* **giṣayriin, guṣaar**) short **2** shallow (of well)
giṣdiir قصدير *n* (*pl* **gaṣaadiir**) **1** tin (material) **2** solder
giṣṣa قصّة *n* (*pl* **giṣaṣ**) tale, story
gishir قشر *coll n* (*unit n* **gishra**, *pl* **gushuur**) **1** (natural) outer skin or layer, husk(s), chaff, pod(s); **gishir as-samak** fish scale(s); **gishir al-beeḍ** eggshell(s) **2** dandruff
gishra قشرة *unit n* (*pl* **gushuur**) **1** peel, rind, skin (of fruit, nuts, beans); pod **2** scab; callus, callosity, horny skin
gishṭa قشطة *n* cream (milk)
giṭʿa قطعة *n* (*pl* **giṭaʿ**) piece, cut, fragment; **giṭʿat ariḍ** a piece of land, plot
giṭaaʿ قطاع *n* (*pl* **-aat**) sector; **al-giṭaaʿ al-ʿaamm** the public sector; **al-giṭaaʿ al-khaaṣṣ** the private sector
giyaafa قيافة *n* elegance
giyaam قيام *n* departure, takeoff
giyaama قيامة *n* resurrection **ʿiid al-giyaama** Easter; **yoom al-giyaama** the Day of Judgment
giyaas قياس *n* (*pl* **-aat**) measurement
giyyeed قيّيد *n* **1** tying up, hobbling (camel) **2** registration, recording
giyyeela قيّيلة *n* spending of the day (at one place); midday rest
goʿoonj قعونج *coll n* frog(s)
goḍḍeem قضّيم *coll n* **1** species of small tree (*Grewia bopulifolia*) **2** fruit of this tree
gongolees قنقليس *coll n* (*unit n* **gongoleesaaya**) fruit of the baobab tree
googa قوقى *vi* (**-i, googaay**) to coo
gool قول *n* **1** talk; **shin gool-ak** what is your opinion? **2** (*pl* **agwaal**) a saying
goomaak قومك *interj* let's get up
goon قون *n* (*pl* **agwaan**) (*sports*) goal (both score and net)
gooz قوز *n* (*pl* **geezaan**) **1** sand dune **2** large cooking pot
greeb قريب *coll n* grapefruit(s)
green قرين *coll n* grapefruit(s)
gubba قبّة *n* (*pl* **gubab**) dome
gubbaal قبّال *prep* before; ago; **jiina gubbaal yoomeen** we came two days ago; **gubbaal kida** previously; already, before; **gubbaal ma** before

gubuul قبول *n* acceptance; approval
guddaam قدّام *prep* in front (of) • *adv* ahead; **be-guddaam** in front (of)
gudra قدرة *n* power, strength, capacity; ability
gudum قدم *n* state of being old (things)
guffa قفّة *n* (*pl* **gufaf**) basket
guḥḥa قحّة *n* coughing, cough
gujja قجّة *n* (*pl* **gujaj**) forelock
gulla قلّة *n* (*pl* **gulal**) small earthenware jar
gumaar قمار *n* gambling, gamble
gumaash قماش *n* (*pl* **-aat, agmisha**) cloth, fabric, brake lining; material
gumbula قمبلة *n* (*pl* **ganaabil**) bomb; shell (projectile)
gumri قمري *coll n* (*unit n* **gumriyya**, *pl* **gamaari**) dove(s); laughing dove(s)
gumurti قمرتي *n* (*pl* **-yya**) gambler
gunduraani قندراني *n* (*pl* **-yyaat**) large truck
gunfud قنفد *n* (*pl* **ganaafid**) *and* **abu gunfud** hedgehog
gurʿa قرعة *n* drawing of lots (e.g. in assigning plots of land)
guraad قراد *coll n* tick(s)
gurgud قرقد *n* woolly (African) hair
gurḥa قرحة *n* (*pl* **guraḥ**) ulcer
gurr قر *n* cold weather
gurraaṣa قرّاصة *n* (*pl* **garaariiṣ**) pancake-like flat bread made from wheat flour and water, with yeast
gurṭaaṣ قرطاص *n* (*pl* **garaaṭiiṣ**) cornet, ice cream cone
gurumbuʿ قرمبع *coll n* cockroach(es); **abu gurumbuʿ** cockroach
gurunful قرنفل *n* (*unit n* **gurunfulaaya**) **1** clove(s) **2** carnation(s)
guruush قروش *n pl* (*sg* **girish**) money
guṣaad قصاد *prep* facing; opposite
guṣayyir قصيّر *adj* **1** (*pl* **guṣayriin, guṣaar**) short **2** shallow (of well)
guṣṣa قصّة *n* fringe (hair)
guṣur قصر *n* shortness
guṭb قطب *n* (*pl* **agṭaab**) (*geog*) pole
guṭraan قطران *n* tar
guṭṭiyya قطّيّة *n* (*pl* **gaṭaaṭi**) thatched hut, round (stone) hut
guṭun قطن *n* cotton
guub قوب *coll n* scurf
guwaala قوالة *n* hearsay
guwwa قوّة *n* strength; force, power; **guwwat ḥuṣaan** horse power; **guwwat raas** obstinacy

gh – غ

ghaab غاب *vi* (**i, ghiyaab**) **1** to be absent **2** to set (of sun)
ghaaba غابة *n* forest, woodland
ghaadi غادي; **be-ghaadi** *adv* over there, (on) that side
ghaafal غافل *vi* (**mughaafala**) **ʿan** to ignore
ghaagha غاغة *n* din
ghaalaṭ غالط *vt* (**mughaalaṭa**) to contradict
ghaali غالي *adj* expensive, valuable, precious, dear
ghaalib غالب *adj* winning • *n* **1** winner **2 fi l-ghaalib** probably
ghaaliban غالبا *adv* probably

ghaamiḍ غامض *adj* unclear, obscure, mysterious
ghaamig غامق *adj* dark (of colour)
ghaar غار *n* (*pl* **gheeraan**) cave, cavern
ghaar غار *vi* (**i, ghiira**) (**min/ʿala**) to be jealous (about)
ghaar غار *vt* (**i, ghaara**) to raid
ghaara غارة *n* raid, razzia
ghaaya غاية *n* purpose, goal; **le-ghaayat** until; **le-ghaayat daak** till then
ghaayib غايب *adj* absent, away
ghaayto غايتو *adv* **1** hence, consequently, thus, so **2** in fact; anyhow, anyway
ghaaz غاز *n* (*pl* **-aat**) gas
ghaaẓ غاظ *vt* (**i, ighaaẓa, gheeẓ**) to anger, irritate
ghabaa غبا *n* stupidity
ghabaawa غباوة *n* stupidity
ghabba غبّى *vi* (**-i, ghaybuuba**) to lose consciousness; to fall into a coma; to go into a trance
ghabbash غبّش *vt* (**ghabaash, ghabsha**) to cover or pollute with dust or mud; **al-walad da ghabbash nafs-o ghabsha** the boy got himself really dusty/ muddy
ghabi غبي *adj* (*pl* **aghbiya**) stupid, dumb, foolish
ghabiina غبينة *n* (*pl* **ghabaayin**) resentment, grudge
ghabsha غبشا *adj f* (*m* **aghbash**) (of water) polluted with dust or mud
ghabyaan غبيان *adj* stupid, dumb
ghada غدا *n* lunch
ghadda غدّى *vt* (**-i, ghada**) to give lunch to
ghaddaar غدّار *adj* treacherous, perfidious
ghaḍab غضب *n* anger
ghaḍbaan غضبان *adj* angry
ghaḍruuf غضروف *n* (*pl* **ghaḍaariif**) **1** gristle, cartilage **2** hernia
ghafa غفى *vi* (**-u, ghafwa**) to doze (off), drop off to sleep
ghafar غفر (**i, ghufraan**) *vt* to forgive; **rabba-na yaghfir zunuub-ak** may God forgive you your sins • *vi* **le-** to forgive; **ghafarta lee-ho** I have forgiven him
ghaffal غفل *vt* (**ghiffeel**) to take by surprise; **al-maṭara ghaffalat-ni** I was caught in the rain
ghafiir غفير *n* (*pl* **ghufara**) guard, watchman, doorkeeper, caretaker
ghafla غفلة *n* inattentiveness, carelessness; **ʿala ghafla** suddenly, unexpectedly
ghafwa غفوة *n* nap, snooze
ghala غلى *vt* (**-i, ghaliya**) to boil
ghala غلا *n* high cost, high price
ghalaawa غلاوة *n* preciousness
ghalab غلب (**i, ghulub**) *vi* to overcome, win • *vt* to overcome, defeat
ghalabaawi غلباوي *adj* (*pl* **-yyiin**) troublemaker, fussy
ghalafa غلفة *n* foreskin, prepuce
ghalaṭ غلط *adj* wrong • *n* (*pl* **-aat, ghalṭaat**) mistake, error, fault
ghalbaan غلبان *n* miserable
ghalbaana غلبانة *n f* **1** miserable **2** pregnant
ghalfa غلفا *adj f* (*m* **aghlaf**) uncircumcised female; **ya wadd al-ghalfa** you son of a bitch!
ghaliid غليد *adj* obese, fat
ghallab غلّب *vt* (**ghilleeb**) to make s.o. crazy

ghallaf غلّف *vt* (**ghilleef, taghliif**) to wrap; to encase
ghalṭa غلطة *n* error; fault; mistake
ghalṭaan غلطان *adj* wrong, mistaken
ghamaam غمام *coll n* cloud(s)
ghamaḍ غمض *vt* (**i, ghamiḍ, ghimeeḍa**); **ghamaḍ al-ʿiyuun** to close one's eyes
ghamaz غمز *vi* (**i, ghamiz**) to wink
ghamḍa غمضة *n* short nap, snooze
ghamm غم *n* deep grief, sorrow
ghammaaz غماز *n* (*pl* **-aat**) trigger
ghammas غمّس *vt* (**ghimmees**) to dip (e.g. bread in sauce, a biscuit in tea)
ghamra غمرة *n* unconsciousness
ghamraan غمران *adj* unconscious
ghamza غمزة *n* wink
ghanam غنم *coll n* (*unit n* **ghanamaaya**) goat(s)
ghanamaaya غنماية *n* she-goat
ghani غني *adj* (*pl* **aghniya**) rich, wealthy
ghanna غنّى *vi/vt* (**-i, ghuna**) to sing
ghannaay غنّاي *n* a good singer
ghanwa غنوة *n* (*pl* **ghunwaat**) song
ghanyaan غنيان *adj* rich, wealthy
gharaama غرامة *n* a fine
gharaḍ غرض *n* (*pl* **aghraaḍ**) objective, purpose, goal
gharaf غرف *vt* (**i, gharif**) to scoop
gharaz غرز *vt* (**i, ghariz**) **1** to stitch **2** to insert a stick firmly in the ground
gharbaawi غرباوي (*pl* **gharraaba**) *adj* pertaining to the west of Sudan, western Sudanese • *n* westerner (of Sudan)
gharbal غربل *vt* (**gharbala**) to sift
gharbi غربي (*pl* **-yyiin**) *adj* western, pertaining to the west • *n* westerner
ghargaan غرقان *adj* **1** drowning; drowned **2** in a state of ecstasy (of dervishes); in a trance
gharghariina غرغرينا *n* gangrene
gharib غرب *n* west; **be-l-gharib** westward
ghariib غريب *adj* (*pl* **-iin**) **1** strange, unknown **2** weird, odd • *n* (*pl* **ghuraba**) stranger
ghariig غريق *adj* deep (water); **baṭn-o ghariiga** said about a quiet person who might have sth. to hide • *n* (*pl* **gharga**) drowned person
ghariiza غريزة *n* (*pl* **gharaayiz**) instinct
gharraabi غرّابي *n* (*pl* **gharraaba**) westerner (of Sudan)
gharraafa غرّافة *n* ladle
gharrag غرّق *vt* (**ghirreeg**) to drown s.o.
gharram غرّم *vt* (**gharaama**) to fine s.o.
ghasal غسل *vt* (**i, ghasiil**) to wash, launder
ghasiil غسيل *n* washing, laundry
ghassaal غسّال *n* washerman, laundryman
ghassaala غسّالة *n* **1** washerwoman, laundress **2** washing machine
ghassal غسّل *vt* (**ghisseel, ghasiil**) to wash, launder
ghaṣab غصب *vt* (**i, ghaṣib**) to force, compel
ghaṣban غصبا *adv* **ghaṣban ʿan-o/ghaṣban ʿan ʿeen-o** against his will, by force
ghaṣib غصب *n* force, compulsion, coercion **be-l-ghaṣib** by force

ghashaawa غشاوة *n* film (over eyes)
ghashiim غشيم *adj* (*pl* **ghushama**) stubborn, obstinate
ghashsha غشّ *vt* (**u, ghishsh, ghashsh**) to cheat, deceive
ghashshaash غشّاش *adj* deceitful • *n* cheat, fraud, swindler
ghashwa غشوة *n* **inta maashi hinaak ṭawaali wa-la ʿind-ak ghashwa** are you going straight there or are you going to call in at s.o. on the way?
ghataata غتاتة *n* nastiness
ghatiit غتيت *n* (*pl* **ghutata**) nasty
ghaṭa غطا *n* (*pl* **aghṭiya**) blanket
ghaṭas غطس *vi* (**i, ghaṭis**) to plunge; to dive
ghaṭrasa غطرسة *n* arrogance, authoritarian behaviour, despotism
ghaṭṭa غطّى *vt* (**-i, taghṭiya**) to cover
ghawiiṭ غويط *adj* deep; **baṭn-o ghawiiṭa** said about a quiet person who might have sth. to hide
ghaybuuba غيبوبة *n* coma
ghayraan غيران *adj* jealous
ghayuur غيور *adj* jealous
ghayyab غيّب *vi* (**ghiyyeeb**) to go into a trance
ghayyam غيّم *vi* (**gheem**) to be clouded
ghayyar غيّر *vt* (**ghiyyeer, taghyiir**) to change; to shift; **ghayyar le-j-jariḥ** to change a dressing on a wound
ghazaal غزال *coll n* (*pl* **ghuzlaan**) gazelle(s); antelope(s) (generic); deer (generic)
ghazal غزل *n* love poetry
ghazal غزل *vt* (**i, ghazil**) to spin (yarn)
ghaziir غزير *adj* thick (e.g. hair, forest)
ghazza غزّ *vt* (**u, ghazz**) **1** to erect **2** to insert a stick in the ground
gheem غيم *coll n* (*pl* **ghiyuum**) clouds
gheer غير *prep* except, apart from; else; **ma ḥaḍar zool gheer al-awlaad deel** nobody came except for these boys; **min gheer** without • *neg part* non-, un-; **gheer ḥakuumi** non-governmental
gheer- غير *n* other(s); another; **wa gheer-um** and others; **waaḥid gheer-o/waaḥda gheer-a** another one
ghiḍib غضب *vi* (**a, ghaḍab**) to be(come) angry
ghifil غفل *vi* (**a, ghafil**) **ʿan** to be inattentive
ghiira غيرة *n* jealousy
ghila غلى *vi* (**-i, ghalayaan**) to boil
ghila غلى *vi* (**-a, ghala**) to be(come) expensive
ghilaaf غلاف *n* (*pl* **-aat, aghlifa**) cover (e.g. of a book)
ghilib غلب *vi* (**a, ghulub**) (**min**) to be fed up (with)
ghiliṭ غلط *vi* (**a, ghalaṭ**) **1** to be wrong, mistaken; to make a mistake, err **2** **fi/ʿala** to wrong s.o., offend (verbally or physically)
ghimir غمر *vi* (**a, ghamra**) to faint; to lose consciousness
ghina غنى *n* wealth, riches
ghina غنى *vi* (**-a, ghina**) to be(come) rich
ghira غرا *n* strong type of glue
ghirig غرق *vi* (**a, gharag**) **1** to sink **2** to drown
ghisha غشى *vt* (**-a, ghashwa, ghashayaan**) to drop in on, call in at

ghishaa' **غشاء** *n* (*pl* **aghshiya**) membrane; **ghishaa' al-bakaara** hymen, virginal membrane

ghishsh **غش** *n* cheating, deceit, swindle

ghiweesha **غويشة** *n* (*pl* **-aat, ghawaayish**) bracelet

ghiyaab **غياب** *n* absence

ghiyaar **غيار** *n* spare clothes (e.g. when travelling)

ghiza **غزا** *n* (*pl* **aghziya**) nutrition

ghizaa'i **غزائي** *adj* nutritious

ghubaar **غبار** *n* dust brought by the wind

ghubaasha **غباشة** *n* drink of curdled milk mixed with water

ghubun **غبن** *n* (*pl* **ghabaayin**) grievance; grudge

ghubush **غبش** *n pl* miserable people, very poor people

ghudda **غدّة** *n* (*pl* **ghudad**) gland

ghulub **غلب** *n* victory (in a game)

ghuluuṭiyya **غلوطيّة** *n* riddle, word game, tongue-twister, e.g.; **bitt banat beet been beeteen**

ghunya **غنية** *n* (*pl* **aghaani**) song

ghuraab **غراب** *n* (*pl* **ghirbaan**) crow

ghurba **غربة** *n* absence from the homeland, state of being a stranger

ghurbaal **غربال** *n* (*pl* **gharaabiil**) large sieve, strainer

ghurfa **غرفة** *n* (*pl* **ghuraf**) room

ghurṭaaṣiyya **غرطاصيّة** *n* stationery

ghurunjaal **غرنجال** *n* ginger-like, reddish root, used in e.g. a meat stew, *also called* **ʿirig aḥmar**

ghuruub **غروب** *n* **ghuruub ash-shamis** sunset

ghuruur **غرور** *n* arrogance, haughtiness, conceit

ghurza **غرزة** *n* (*pl* **ghuraz**) stitch

ghuṣṣa **غصة** *n* (*pl* **ghuṣaṣ**) (*also fig*) lump (in throat)

ghuṭa **غطا** *n* (*pl* **ghuṭaayaat**) lid, cover, top (e.g. of pot, bottle)

ghuṭaaya **غطاية** *n* lid, cover, top (e.g. of pot, bottle)

ghuul **غول** *n* (*pl* **ghiilaan**) ghoul, a desert demon appearing in ever varying shapes

ghuula **غولة** *n* a female desert demon

h – ه

haadi **هادي** *adj* (*f* **haadya, hadiyya**) calm, quiet; **hadiyya wa raḍiyya** said about an easy-going, calm woman

haaj **هاج** *vi* (**i, hayajaan**) **1** to be(come) very angry, go berserk **2** to be(come) sexually aroused

haajam **هاجم** *vt* (**hujuum, muhaajama**) to attack, assault

haajar **هاجر** *vi* (**hijra**) **1 le-/ila** to migrate (to) **2 min** to emigrate (from)

haak **هاك** *imp m* (*f* **haaki**, *pl* **haakum**) take!

haalik **هالك** *adj* perishing; **diyuun haalka** bad debts

haamish **هامش** *n* (*pl* **hawaamish**) **1** margin **2** (foot)note

haamm **هام** *adj* important

haammi **هامّي** *adj* (**be-**) concerned, anxious, worried (about)

haan **هان** *vt* (**i, ihaana**) to humiliate

haatif **هاتف** *n* (*pl* **hawaatif**) telephone

haawad هاود *vt* (**huwaada**) to add a free gift to an item being sold
haawi هاوي *n* (*pl* **huwaa**) amateur
haawya هاوية *n* chasm, abyss
haayij هايج *adj* sexually aroused
habaala هبالة *n* stupidity, silliness
habash هبش *vt* (**i, habish**) to touch
habba هبّ *vi* (**i, habba, habuub**) to blow (wind)
habbaaba هبّابة *n* hand fan
habbab هبّب *vt* (**hibbeeb**) to fan
habbash هبّش *vt* (**hibbeesh, tahbiish**) to touch
habbuud هبّود *n* ash
habhab هبهب *vi* (**habhaba, hibheeb**) to flutter (birds)
habiil هبيل *adj* stupid, silly
habuub هبوب *n* (*pl* **habaayib**) sandstorm, dust storm
hada هدى *vt* **1** (**-i, hadayaan**) to guide **2** (**-i, ihda**) to give s.o. a present
hadaf هدف *n* (*pl* **ahdaaf**) **1** target, aim, purpose, objective, goal **2** (*sports*) goal (score)
hadam هدم *vt* (**i, hadim**) to destroy, demolish
hadda هدّ *vi* (**i, hadd**) **fi/ʿala** to come off (colour)
hadda هدّى *vt* (**-i, hiddeey, tahdiya**) **1** to calm, pacify **2** to tranquillize, sedate; **hadda as-surʿa** to slow down
haddad هدّد *vt* (**hiddeed, tahdiid**) to threaten
haddam هدّم *vi* (**hiddeem, tahdiim**) to destroy, demolish
hadeek هديك *pron pl* those
hadeel هديل *pron pl* these
hadiyya هديّة *n* (*pl* **hadaayaa**) gift, present
hadiyya هديّة *adj f* calm, quiet - *see* **haadi**
haḍam هضم *vt* (**i, haḍm**) to digest (of the stomach)
haḍrab هضرب *vi* (**haḍraba**) to talk deliriously; to talk in one's sleep
hajam هجم *vi* (**i, hajma**) **ʿala** to attack, assault
hajiij هجيج *n* dancing at a party, excitement
hakar هكر *n* junk, rubbish
hamad همد *vi* (**a, hamadaan, humuud**) to die down (fire)
hamaji همجي *adj* (*pl* **-yyiin, hamaj**) uncouth, uncivilized, savage
hamajiyya همجيّة *n* uncivilized behaviour, savagery
hamal همل *vt* (**i, ihmaal, hamala**) to neglect, disregard
hamala هملة *n* negligence, neglect
hamas همس *vi* (**i, hams**) to whisper
hamaz همز *vt* (**i, hamiz**) to poke, spur on
hambaati همباتي *n* (*pl* **hambaata**) bandit
hambariib همبريب *n* cool breeze
hambuul همبول *n* (*pl* **hamaabiil**) scarecrow
hamham همهم *vi* (**himheem, hamhama**) **1** to hum **2** to talk gibberish (in anger)
hamiim هميم *adj* diligent, zealous, energetic; helpful
hamm هم *n* (*pl* **humuum**) worry
hamma همّ *vt* (**i, hamm**) to matter, be important to; **da ma yahimm-ak** that's none of your business • *vi* **be-** to be concerned about; **wa-la yahimm-ak** don't worry!

hammash همّش *vt* (**tahmiish**) to marginalize
hammaz همّز *vt* (**himmeez**) to poke more than once, spur on
hamsa همسة *n* whisper
hana هنا *n* well-being, happiness; **be-l-hana wa sh-shifa** I/we hope you are enjoying/have enjoyed the food
handasa هندسة *n* **1** engineering **2** geometry
handasi هندسي *adj* pertaining to engineering
hangar هنقر *n* (*pl* **hanaagir**) hangar
hanna هنّى *vt* (**-i, tahniya**) (**be-**) to congratulate (on)
hannag هنّق *vi* (**hinneeg**) to bray
haraakil هراكل *n/n pl* parakeet(s); budgerigar(s)
harab هرب *vi* (**a, huruub, harabaan**) (**min**) to run away; to escape (from)
haraj هرج *vi* (**i, harja**) **fi** to scold
haram هرم *n* (*pl* **ahraam, ahraamaat**) pyramid
haras هرس *vt* (**i, haris**) to squash, mash, crush
harash هرش *vt* (**i, harish**) to threaten
harjal هرجل (**hirjeel, harjala**) *vi* (of voices) buzz, to be noisy • *vt* to put in disarray, mess up
harrab هرّب *vt* (**hirreeb, tahriib**) to smuggle
hassa' هسّع *adv* now; **le-hassa'** until now, hitherto
hassi هسّي *adv* now
hashaab هشاب *coll n* species of gum-bearing acacia tree
hashsh هش *adj* delicate, fragile
hataf هتف *vi* (**u, hutaaf**) to cheer; **hataf be-shi'aaraat** to shout slogans
hatash هتش *n* junk, rubbish
hatrash هترش *vi* (**hatrasha**) to talk deliriously
hawa هوا *n* **1** air **2** wind
hawas هوس *n* craze, madness, frenzy; rapture
hawhaw هوهو *vi* (**hawhawa**) **fi/foog** to bark (at) (dogs)
hawwa هوّى *vt* (**-i, tahwiya**) to ventilate (e.g. a room)
hawwan هوّن *vi* (**tahwiin**) (of God) to ease, make (life) bearable
hay'a هيئة *n* corporation, organization board of corporation
hayajaan هيجان *n* excitement
hayyaj هيّج *vt* (**hiyyeej, tahyiij**) to stir, provoke, excite, arouse (desire)
hayyin هيّن *adj* **1** easy **2** easy-going; **hayyin u layyin** easy-going
hazam هزم *vt* (**i, haziima**) to defeat
haziima هزيمة *n* (*pl* **hazaayim**) defeat
hazza هزّا *vt* (**-i, tahziya**) to mock
hazza هزّ *vt* (**i, hazz**) to shake; to jolt; **hazza r-raas** to nod
hazza هزّة *n* **1** jolt **2** earthquake
haẓẓaar هظّار *n* joker, wag
haẓẓar هظّر *vi* (**hiẓaar**) to joke, jest; **ma'a** to tease
heeja هيجة *n* tumult
heem هيم *coll n* chicken lice
hi هى *pron sg f* she
hida هدى *vi* (**-a, huduu**) to be(come) calm
hidim هدم *n* (*pl* **huduum**) garment
hidma هدمة *n* (*pl* **huduum**) garment
hijliij هجليج *n* desert date (tree); **shajarat hijliij** a desert date tree
hijra هجرة *n* **1** migration **2** emigration

hilaal هلال *n* crescent moon; **al-hilaal al-aḥmar** the Red Crescent
hilib هلب *n* (*no pl*) anchor
hilik هلك *vi* (**a, halik, halakaan**) to die (of animals)
himma همة *n* zeal
hin هن *pron pl f* they
hina هنا *adv* here
hinaak هناك *adv* there
hinaay هناي *n* thingy, thingummy; 'what's-his-name'
hind هند *prop n* **al-hind** India
hindi هندي (*pl* **hunuud**) *adj* Indian • *n* an Indian
hini هني *adv* here
hittiifa هتّيفة *n* crowd recruited for shouting slogans
hiwaaya هواية *n* hobby
hiya هي *pron sg f* she
hiẓaar هظار *n* fun, joking
hooy هوي *interj* hey!
hu هو *pron sg m* he
hubuuṭ هبوط *n* fall, drop (in level, e.g. of temperature, blood pressure)
hudhud هدهد *n* (*pl* **hadaahid**) hoopoe
huduu هدو *n* quietness; **be-huduu** quietly
huduum هدوم *n* (*sg* **hidim, hidma**) garments, clothes
hujuum هجوم *n* (*pl* **-aat**) attack, assault
hum هم *pron pl m/f* they
huraar هرار *n* faeces
huruub هروب *n* flight; escape
huwaada هوادة *n* a free gift added to a purchase
huwiyya هويّة *n* identity
huwwa هوّ *pron sg m* he

ḥ - ح

ḥaadd حاد *adj* sharp; acute; fierce, vehement (also of talk)
ḥaadda حادّة *adj f* (woman) in mourning
ḥaadig حادق *adj* sharp, sour, tart (of taste)
ḥaadis حادس *n* (*pl* **ḥawaadis**) accident
ḥaadsa حادسة *n* (*pl* **ḥawaadis**) accident
ḥaaḍ حاض *vi* (**i, ḥeeḍ**) to menstruate
ḥaaḍir حاضر *interj* **1** present! **2** at your service! • *n* **al-ḥaaḍir** the present (time)
ḥaaffa حافّة *n* (*pl* **ḥawaaff**) edge, rim
ḥaafiz حافز *n* (*pl* **ḥawaafiz**) incentive
ḥaafiẓa حافظة *n* water flask
ḥaafla حافلة *n* city bus
ḥaagid حاقد *adj* spiteful, malicious
ḥaaḥa حاحا *vt* (**-i, ḥiḥeey, muḥaaḥaa**) to scare off (birds)
ḥaaja حاجة *n* thing, object; something; **wa-la ḥaaja** nothing
ḥaajib حاجب *n* (*pl* **ḥawaajib**) eyebrow
ḥaajiz حاجز *n* (*pl* **ḥawaajiz**) **1** barrier **2** (small) embankment, dyke
ḥaajj حاج *n* (*m*) **1** pilgrim (to Mecca) **2** title of respect for elderly man
ḥaajja حاجّة *n* (*f*) **1** pilgrim (to Mecca) **2** title of respect for elderly woman
ḥaaka حاكى *vt* (**-i, muḥaakaa**) to imitate
ḥaakam حاكم *vt* (**muḥaakama**) to try, put on trial

ḥaakim حاكم *n* (*pl* **ḥukkaam**) governor, ruler

ḥaal حال *n* (*pl* **aḥwaal**) situation, state, condition; **al-ḥaal maayil** the situation is bad; **ḥaal makshuuf** state of a husband who does not provide his wife with the necessities of life; **ḥaal mastuur** state of a husband who provides his wife with the necessities of life; **ʿala kulli ḥaal/fi kull al-aḥwaal** anyhow, anyway; **fi ayyi ḥaal** in any case; **fi l-ḥaal** immediately

ḥaala حالة *n* (*pl* **-aat, aḥwaal**) situation, state, condition; **fi ayyi ḥaala** in any case; **al-ḥaala sayyi'a** the situation is bad; **az-zool da ḥaala khaaṣṣa** this guy is a special case

ḥaalan حالا *adv* immediately

ḥaalib حالب *n* (*pl* **ḥawaalib**) ureter

ḥaam حام *vi* (**u, ḥuwaama**) to roam, wander; **ḥaam ḥawaleen** **1** to circle **2** to prowl

ḥaami حامي *adj* warm; **ṭabʿ-o ḥaami** he's touchy

ḥaamiḍ حامض *adj* sour

ḥaamil حامل *adj* (*pl* **ḥummal**) pregnant

ḥaamil حامل *n* (*pl* **ḥawaamil**) stand (e.g. for a blackboard, flip chart); support; brace

ḥaamuḍ حامض *n* sourdough, leaven

ḥaamya حامية *n* garrison

ḥaara حارة *n* part of a town district

ḥaarab حارب *vt* (**ḥarib, muḥaaraba**) to wage war; to fight

ḥaaris حارس *n* (*pl* **ḥurraas**) guard, doorman **ḥaaris al-marma** goalkeeper

ḥaarr حار *adj* **1** painful **2** hot

ḥaasab حاسب *vt* (**muḥaasaba**) to settle an account with

ḥaasib حاسب *imp* watch out!

ḥaasid حاسد *adj* (*pl* **ḥussaad**) envious; malicious; causing the evil eye

ḥaassa حاسّة *n* (*pl* **ḥawaass**) sense (one of the five senses)

ḥaasuub حاسوب *n* (*pl* **ḥawaasiib**) computer

ḥaaṣar حاصر *vt* (**ḥiṣaar, muḥaaṣara**) to besiege

ḥaash حاش *vt* (**u, ḥayashaan, ḥoosha**) to pen up (animals)

ḥaaṭ حاط *vt* (**i, ḥeeṭa**) to surround

ḥaawal حاول *vi* (**muḥaawala**) to try, attempt

ḥaawi حاوي *n* (*pl* **ḥuwaa**) conjurer, magician, juggler

ḥaawya حاوية *n* large container for transport

ḥaaza حازى *vt* (**-i, muḥaazaa, ḥiza**) to run parallel to

ḥaazim حازم *adj* earnest

ḥaba حبى *vi* (**-u, ḥabayaan**) to crawl (child)

ḥabaab حباب *n* (*sg* **ḥabiib**); **ḥabaab-ak** welcome!; **ḥabaab-ak ʿashara** you're most welcome!

ḥabas حبس *vt* (**i, ḥabis, ḥabsa**) to lock up, confine, detain, imprison; **ḥabas ad-darib/aṭ-ṭariig** to ambush

ḥabash حبش *coll n* Ethiopians

ḥabasha حبشة *prop n* **al-ḥabasha** Ethiopia

ḥabashi حبشي *adj* (*pl* **ḥabash**) Ethiopian, Ethiopic • *unit n* an Ethiopian

ḥabb حب *coll n* seed(s); grain(s); **ḥabb ash-shabaab** acne

ḥabba حبّ *vt* (**i, ḥubb**) to love; to like

ḥabba حبّة *unit n* **1** (*pl* **ḥubuub**) seed **2** (*pl* **-aat, ḥubuub**) tablet, pill **3** (*pl* **ḥubuub**) pimple **4** (*pl* **-aat**) piece (item); **ḥabbat leemuun** one piece of lemon **5** a little bit; **ḥabbat sukkar** a little bit of sugar; **ḥabba ḥabba** one by one, bit by bit, gradually, slowly

ḥabbaaya حبّاية *unit n* **1** (*pl* **-aat**) piece (item) **2** (*pl* **-aat, ḥubuub**) pill, tablet **3** a little bit; **ḥabbaayat sukkar** a little bit of sugar

ḥabbahaan حبّهان *n* cardamom

ḥabbooba حبّوبة *n* granny, grandmother (also used to refer to any old woman)

ḥabiib حبيب (*pl* **aḥibba, aḥbaab**) *adj* dear, beloved • *n* friend; lover

ḥabiib حبيب *n/n pl* heron

ḥabil حبل *n* (*pl* **ḥibaal**) rope; cord, string; **ḥabil tiil** thick rope; hemp rope; **ḥabl as-surra/al-mashiima** umbilical cord

ḥabis حبس *n* **1** confinement, custody, detention **2** obstruction; **ḥabs bool** obstruction or retention of urine; **ḥabs ad-darib/aṭ-ṭariig** ambush

ḥadaad حداد *n* mourning

ḥadaba حدبة *n* hunchback

ḥadar حدر *vt* (**i, ḥadra**) to stare

ḥadas حدس *vi* (**u, ḥadas**) to happen, occur

ḥadas حدس *n* (*pl* **aḥdaas**) event

ḥadd حد *n* (*pl* **ḥuduud**) **1** limit, boundary; **le-ḥaddi** till; **le-ḥaddi miteen** till when?; **le-ḥaddi ma** until **2** (*Isl*) punishment prescribed by Islamic law

ḥadda حدّ *vi* (**i, ḥidd, ḥidaad**) to mourn

ḥadda حدّ *vi* (**i, ḥadd**) to limit, restrict

ḥaddaad حدّاد *n* (*pl* **-iin, ḥadaadiid**) blacksmith, smith

ḥaddaadi حدّادي *adj* **ḥaddaadi maddaadi** spacious (e.g. house)

ḥaddaas حدّاس *adj* talkative (in positive or negative sense)

ḥaddad حدّد *vt* (**taḥdiid**) to determine, specify; to fix a boundary

ḥaddag حدّق *vi* (**ḥiddeeg, taḥdiig**) (**fi/le-**) to stare (at)

ḥaddar حدّر *vi* (**ḥiddeer**) to glare

ḥaddas حدّس *vi* (**ḥiddees, ḥadiis**) to tell; **galb-i ḥaddas lee-y** it occurred to me

ḥaddi حدّ *n* - *see* **ḥadd**

ḥadiid حديد *coll n* **1** iron; **ḥadiid ṣulb** steel; **ḥadiid al-lijaam** bit (mouthpiece of bridle) **2** (money) change in coins

ḥadiida حديدة *unit n* piece of iron

ḥadiiga حديقة *n* (*pl* **ḥadaayig**) garden **ḥadiigat al-ḥayawaanaat** zoo

ḥadiis حديس *n* (*pl* **aḥaadiis**) **1** the Tradition(s) of the Prophet Mohammed **2** (formal) talk, conversation

ḥadiis حديس *adj* **1** modern **2** new

ḥaḍaana حضانة *n* nursery, kindergarten (for toddlers)

ḥaḍaara حضارة *n* civilization

ḥaḍan حضن *vt* (**i, ḥuḍun**) **1** to embrace, hug **2** to hatch (sit on eggs)

ḥaḍar حضر *n* a settled population (as opposed to nomads)

ḥaḍar حضر (**a, ḥuḍuur**) *vi* to be present • *vt* to be present at, attend

ḥaḍḍaana حضّانة *n* incubator

ḥaḍḍar حضّر *vt* (**ḥiḍḍeer, taḥḍiir**) to prepare

ḥaḍra حضرة *n term of respect*: **ḥaḍrat-ak ism-ak minu** what is your name, Sir?; **ḥaḍrat aḍ-ḍaabiṭ** the honourable officer

ḥafaḍ حفض *vt - see* **ḥafaẓ**

ḥafar حفر (**i, ḥafir**) *vt* to dig, excavate; to drill (for oil, water) • *vi* **le-** to set up a trap, to trick (a person)

ḥafat حفت *vi* (**i, ḥafit**) to dig with the hands

ḥafaẓ حفظ *vt* (**a, ḥifiẓ**) **1** to keep, preserve **2** to learn by rote, know by heart; **ḥafaẓ ṣamm** to know by heart thoroughly

ḥaffaar حفّار *n* professional digger

ḥaffaara حفّارة *n* drilling rig

ḥaffaaẓa حفّاظة *n* cooler

ḥaffar حفّر *vt* (**ḥiffeer**) to dig

ḥafiid حفيد *n* (*pl* **aḥfaad**) grandson

ḥafiida حفيدة *n* granddaughter

ḥafiir حفير *n* (*pl* **ḥafaayir**) cistern, manmade pool

ḥafla حفلة *n* party (celebration)

ḥafyaan حفيان *adj* barefoot

ḥagaara حقارة *n* contempt, scorn

ḥagaayig حقايق *n pl* (*sg* **ḥagiiga**) facts

ḥagad حقد *vi* (**i, ḥagid**) to be spiteful

ḥagan حقن *vt* (**i, ḥagin**) **1** to retain (urine) **2** to cork up (one's emotions) • *vi* (**i, ḥagin, ḥaganaan**) to be blocked (of e.g. water); to be(come) congested (of blood)

ḥagar حقر *n* contempt • *vt* (**i, ḥagaara**) to despise, treat with contempt, look down on

ḥagg حق *n* (*pl* **ḥuguug**) right; **ḥagg-o baarid** his right is well established; **maʿaa-ho/ʿalee-ho/lee-ho/ʿind-o ḥagg** he's right; **ḥagg-ak ʿalee-y** you are right and I am wrong; **ḥuguug al-insaan** human rights • *adj m* (*f* **ḥaggat**) *in construction indicating possession* to belong to; **al-kursi da ḥagg minu** whose chair is this?; **as-saaʿa di ḥaggat-i** this watch is mine, this is my watch

ḥaggaar حقّار *adj* contemptuous, wretched

ḥaggag حقّق *vt* (**taḥgiig**) **1** to make sth. come true **2** to investigate, carry out an investigation or inquiry

ḥagiiga حقيقة *n* (*pl* **ḥagaayig**) truth; fact; **al-ḥagiiga/fi-l-ḥagiiga** in fact, actually

ḥagiigi حقيقي *adj* **1** real, genuine **2** actual • *adv* really, certainly, for sure; **ḥagiigi** is that true?; is that so?; really?

ḥagiir حقير *adj* contemptible

ḥaguud حقود *adj* spiteful, malicious

ḥajar حجر *n* **1** (*pl* **ḥujaara, aḥjaar**) stone; rock; **ḥajar masann** whetstone; **galb-o ḥajar** he's ruthless **2** (*pl* **ḥujaara, aḥjaar**) dry battery **3** (*pl* **ḥujaara**) bowl of a hookah (water pipe)

ḥajaz حجز *vt* (**i, ḥajiz**) **1** to reserve; to book **2** to detain

ḥajim حجم *n* (*pl* **aḥjaam**) size

ḥajir حجر *n* **ḥajir ṣiḥḥi** quarantine

ḥajiz حجز *n* **1** reservation booking; **maktab al-ḥajiz** booking office **2** detention

ḥajj حج *n* pilgrimage to Mecca

ḥajja حجّى *vt* (**-i, ḥuja**) to tell a story to

ḥajjaam حجّام *n* a person specialized in bloodletting

ḥajjab حجّب *vt* (**ḥijaab**) to make s.o. wear a veil

ḥajjam حجّم *vt* (**ḥijjeem, ḥijaama**) to bleed (bloodletting)

ḥajwa حجوة *n* (*pl* **-aat, aḥaaji, ḥuja**) folktale

ḥaka حكى *vt* **1** (**-i, ḥaki**) (**le-**) to tell, relate **2** (**-i, ḥikaaya**) to tell (a story)

ḥakam حكم *vt* (**i, ḥukum**) to rule over, govern, reign • *vi* to rule, pronounce a verdict; **le-** to judge in s.o.'s favour; **ʿala** to sentence

ḥakam حكم *n* (*pl* **ḥukkaam**) referee

ḥakiim حكيم *adj* (*pl* **-iim, ḥukama**) wise • *n* (*pl* **ḥukama**) doctor's assistant

ḥakka حكّ *vt* (**u, ḥakk**) **1** to scrub **2** to scrape **3** to scratch o.s.

ḥakka حكّة *n* itch(ing)

ḥakkaama حكّامة *n* female bard judging in her songs the achievements or failures of her tribesmen

ḥakkaay حكّاي *adj* good at storytelling

ḥakuuma حكومة *n* government

ḥalaal حلال *n* that which is permitted by Islamic law; **wad ḥalaal** a trustworthy, decent person

ḥalaawa حلاوة *n* **1** candies, sweets; **giṭʿat ḥalaawa** candy **2** depilatory paste made from sugar, water and lime juice **3** sweetness; beauty; pleasantness

ḥalab حلب *vt* (**i, ḥalib**) to milk

ḥalab حلب *coll n* (*unit n* **ḥalabi**, *pl* **ḥalaba**) gipsies

ḥalaf حلف *vi* (**i, ḥalafaan**) (**be-**) to take an oath; **ḥalaf be-l-yamiin** to take an oath; **ḥalaf be-l-kiḍib** to commit perjury

ḥalafaan حلفان *n* swearing an oath; **ḥalafaan be-l-kiḍib** perjury

ḥalag حلق *n* (*pl* **ḥulgaan**) pair of earrings

ḥalag حلق (**i, ḥalga, ḥilaaga**) *vi* to have a shave and/or a haircut • *vt* to shave; to cut hair

ḥalaga حلقة *n* episode of a poem or a series (radio, TV)

ḥalaj حلج *vi* (**i, ḥalij**) to gin (cotton)

ḥalama حلمة *n* teat of a baby's bottle; **ḥalamat shaṭur** nipple

ḥalawaani حلواني *n* **1** (*pl* **-yyiin**) pastry chef **2** pastry shop, bakery

ḥalawaaya حلواية *n* (*pl* **ḥalawiyyaat**) candy

ḥalawiyyaat حلويّات *n pl* sweets, candies

ḥalguum حلقوم *n* (*pl* **ḥalaagiim**) throat

ḥalig حلق *n* (*pl* **ḥuluug**) throat; **ḥalg-i biyuujaʿ-ni/biyuujiʿ-ni** I have a sore throat

ḥaliib حليب *n* fresh milk

ḥaliif حليف *n* (*pl* **ḥulafa**) ally

ḥaliifa حليفة *n* (*pl* **ḥalaayif**) oath

ḥall حل *n* (*pl* **ḥuluul**) solution (of a problem)

ḥalla حلّة *n* (*pl* **ḥilal**) cooking pot, pan

ḥalla حلّى *vt* (**-i, taḥliya**) **1** to sweeten **2** to decorate (e.g. a door, curtain, dress)

ḥalla حلّ *vt* **1** (**i, ḥall**) to solve, resolve **2** (**i, ḥalla**) to undo, untie **3** (**i, ḥill**) (**min**) to absolve (of/from)

ḥallaag حلاق *n* barber

ḥallaf حلّف *vt* (**ḥilleef**) to make s.o. swear an oath

ḥallal حلّل *vt* (**taḥliil**) **1** to analyse **2** to declare to be permitted under Islamic law

ḥalluuf حلّوف *n* (*pl* **ḥalaaliif**) pig; boar

ḥama حمى *vt* (**-i, ḥimaaya**) to protect
ḥama حما *n* (*pl* **ḥimyaan**) father-in-law
ḥamaa حماة *n* (*pl* **ḥamawaat**) mother-in-law
ḥamaam حمام *coll n* pigeon(s)
ḥamaaqa حماقة *n* readiness to take offence
ḥamaas حماس *n* enthusiasm, zeal
ḥamaasa حماسة *n* enthusiasm, zeal
ḥamad حمد *vt* (**i, ḥamid**) to praise (God)
ḥamal حمل *n* (*pl* **ḥimlaan**) lamb
ḥambak حمبك *vi* (**ḥambaka, ḥimbeek**) **fi** to contest the result of a game or debate on false grounds
ḥambuuka حمبوكة *n* (*pl* **ḥanaabiik**) balloon
ḥamḥam حمحم *vi* (**ḥamḥama**) to whinny
ḥamid حمد *n* praise; **al-ḥamdu le-llaah** **1** thanks be to God, all is well **2** fortunately; **ḥamdi-llah ʿala s-salaama** thank God for the safe arrival
ḥamla حملة *n* campaign, expedition
ḥamma حمّى *vt* (**-i, ḥimmeey**) to bathe s.o.
ḥammaal حمّال *n* porter, carrier
ḥammaala حمّالة *n* **1** braces, suspenders; **ḥammaalat al-ʿarabiyya** chassis **2** stand (e.g. for a jar)
ḥammaam حمام *n* (*pl* **-aat**) **1** bath, bathroom; **akhad ḥammaam** to take a bath, bathe; **ḥammaam as-sibaaḥa** swimming pool **2** lavatory, toilet, latrine
ḥammaḍ حمّض *vi* (**ḥimmeeḍ**) **1** to be(come) sour **2** to leaven • *vt* (**taḥmiiḍ**) to develop (a film)
ḥammal حمّل *vt* (**taḥmiil**) **1** to load (e.g. a donkey) **2** to make pregnant illegally
ḥammam حمّم *vt* (**ḥammaam**) to bathe s.o.
ḥammar حمّر *vt* (**taḥmiir**) to fry
ḥammar حمّر *vi* (**ḥimmeer**) to glare
ḥammaṣ حمّص *vt* (**ḥimmeeṣ, taḥmiiṣ**) to roast (e.g. coffee beans)
ḥamu حمو *n* **ḥamu n-niil** prickly heat (rash)
ḥamu حمو *n* (*pl* **ḥimyaan**) father-in-law
ḥana حنى *vt* (**-i, ḥaniya, ḥanayaan**) to bend
ḥanaan حنان *n* affection, kindness, sympathy
ḥanafiyya حنفيّة *n* tap
ḥanak حنك *n* (*pl* **aḥnaak**) jaw (humans)
ḥanḍal حنضل *coll n* bitter apple (plant)
ḥaniin حنين *adj* merciful, compassionate; kind
ḥaniya حنية *n* **1** curve, bend **2** bow **3** bent back, humpback
ḥanjara حنجرة *n* (*pl* **ḥanaajir**) throat
ḥankuush حنكوش *adj* (*pl* **ḥanaakiish**) showy, vain
ḥanna حنّ *vi* (**i, ḥinn**) **ʿala** to be kind to
ḥannan حنّن *vt* (**ḥinneen, taḥniin**) to arouse sympathy
ḥannan حنّن *vt* (**ḥinneen**) to apply henna
ḥannas حنّس *vt* (**ḥinnees, taḥniis**) to dissuade s.o. from a course of action
ḥaraam حرام *n* that which is forbidden by Islamic law; **wad ḥaraam**

illegitimate son; **bitt ḥaraam** illegitimate daughter; **ʿalee-y al-ḥaraam** I'll divorce my wife!; **ḥaraam ʿalee-k** shame on you!

ḥaraami حرامي *n* (*pl* **-yya**) thief

ḥaraara حرارة *n* **1** heat **2** temperature; **darajat al-ḥaraara** degree of temperature **3** dial tone (telephone)

ḥarad حرد *vi* (**i, ḥarid, ḥaradaan**) **1** to refuse to move (of a donkey) **2** to sulk; to suddenly decide not to do sth. (out of anger); **ḥarad al-akal** to refuse to eat (out of anger)

ḥarag حرق *vt* **1** (**i, ḥarig, ḥariig, ḥariiga**) to burn **2** (**i, ḥarig**) to hurt • *vi* (**i, ḥarig**) to hurt, ache

ḥaraj حرج *n* embarrassment

ḥaraka حركة *n* **1** motion, movement; **ḥarakt-o tagiila** he is slow **2** traffic **ḥarakat al-muruur** traffic; (**booliis**) **al-ḥaraka** the traffic police **3** political or religious movement

ḥaram حرم *vt* (**i, ḥirmaan**) **1** (**min**) to deprive of **2** to forbid, prohibit

ḥaran حرن *vi* (**i, ḥarin, ḥaranaan**) to refuse to move (of a donkey)

ḥaras حرس *vt* (**i, ḥiraasa**) (**min**) to watch, guard (against), shield • *n* (*pl* **ḥurraas**) guard, escort

ḥarat حرت *vt* (**i, ḥiraata**) to plough

ḥarba حربة *n* (*pl* **ḥuraab**) spear, lance

ḥarbi حربي *adj* **1** military; martial **2** content with a simple way of living, keeping one's spirits up

ḥardaan حردان *adj* sulking, angry and refusing to cooperate

ḥarfana حرفنة *n* skill, proficiency, craftsmanship

ḥarfi حرفي *adj* literal

ḥarfiyyan حرفيا *adv* literally

ḥarib حرب *n f* (*pl* **ḥuruub, ḥuruubaat**) war; **ḥarib ahliyya** civil war

ḥarif حرف *n* (*pl* **ḥuruuf**) letter (of alphabet)

ḥariif حريف *adj* (*pl* **-iin, ḥurafa**) skilful, proficient

ḥariig حريق *n* (*pl* **ḥaraayig**) fire; conflagration

ḥariiga حريقة *n* (*pl* **ḥaraayig**) fire, conflagration

ḥariim حريم *coll n* (*sg* **ḥurma**) **1** (married) women **2** close female relatives for whom a man is responsible

ḥariir حرير *n* (*pl* **ḥaraayir**) silk

ḥariiri حريري *adj* silk; silky

ḥariiṣ حريص *adj* **1** cautious, careful; **khallii-k ḥariiṣ** be careful! **2** **ʿala** eager for

ḥarr حر *n* heat

ḥarraan حرّان *adj* feeling hot

ḥarraḍ حرّض *vt* (**ḥirreeḍ, taḥriiḍ**) (**ʿala**) to provoke; to incite, instigate (against)

ḥarrag حرّق *vt* **1** (**ḥirreeg**) to burn **2** (**ḥirreeg, ḥaragaan**) to hurt

ḥarrak حرّك *vt* (**ḥirreek, taḥriik**) to move s.o./sth.; to stir s.o./sth.; to arouse

ḥarram حرّم *vt* (**taḥriim**) to declare to be forbidden by Islamic law

ḥarrash حرّش *vt* (**ḥirreesh, taḥriish**) (**ʿala**) to incite (against)

ḥarreena حرّينة *n* tag (game)

ḥasaada حسادة *n* spite

ḥasaasiyya حساسيّة *n* sensitivity; allergy

ḥasab حسب *vt* (**i, ḥisaab**) **1** to calculate **2** to consider, regard

ḥasab حسب *prep* (**le-**) according to; **ḥasab aẓ-ẓuruuf** depending on circumstances

ḥasad حسد *n* spite, malice

ḥasad حسد *vt* (**i, ḥasaada, ḥasad**) to envy (causing the evil eye), be spiteful

ḥasana حسنة *n* alms, charitable donation, good deed

ḥasiib حسيب *adj* of noble descent; **al-ḥasiib wa l-nasiib** form of address to a person of noble descent

ḥassa حسّا *adv* now

ḥassa حسّ *vi* (**i, iḥsaas**) **1** (**be-**) to feel; **ḥassa be-milal** to feel bored, be(come) bored **2 be-** to be(come) aware of

ḥassaas حسّاس *adj* sensitive

ḥassas حسّس *vt* (**taḥsiis**) (**be-**) to make s.o. feel sth.; **ḥassas-ni be-j-joo**ʿ he made me feel hungry

ḥassi حسّي *adv* now

ḥasuud حسود *adj* envious; malicious; causing the evil eye

ḥaṣaad حصاد *n* (*pl* **-aat**) harvest

ḥaṣaaya حصاية *unit n* - *see* **ḥaṣḥaaṣ**

ḥaṣad حصد *vt* (**i, ḥaṣaad**) to harvest; to reap

ḥaṣal حصل *vi* (**a, ḥuṣuul**) **1** to happen, occur **2 ʿala** to obtain

ḥaṣḥaaṣ حصحاص *coll n* (*unit n* **ḥaṣaaya, ḥaṣḥaaṣaaya**) pebble(s), gravel

ḥaṣiila حصيلة *n* (*pl* **ḥaṣaayil**) **1** output, produce **2** outcome, result

ḥaṣiir حصير *coll n* **1** reed (dry stems) **2** reed matting

ḥaṣiira حصيرة *unit n* (*pl* **ḥaṣaayir**) reed mat

ḥaṣṣaala حصّالة *n* money box

ḥaṣṣal حصّل *vt* (**ḥiṣṣeel**) to catch up with • *vi* (**ḥiṣṣeel, taḥṣiil**) **ʿala** to obtain

ḥaṣwa حصوة *n* stone (e.g. in kidney)

ḥasha حشا *n* waist

ḥasha حشى *vt* (**-i, ḥashi**) to stuff

ḥashad حشد *vt* (**i, ḥashid**) to muster, mobilize (e.g. troops)

ḥashar حشر *vt* (**i, ḥashir**) **fi** to put inside (a bag, pocket), tuck sth. into; **ḥashar nafs-o/ragabt-o/ruuḥ-o fi** to interfere in

ḥashara حشرة *n* insect

ḥasharaat حشرات *n pl* vermin

ḥashid حشد *n* (*pl* **ḥushuud**) gathering, assembly, crowd; mobilization (e.g. of troops); **ḥashid jamaahiiri** rally

ḥashiish حشيش *coll n* **1** (*pl* **ḥashaayish**) grass; weed **2** marijuana (cannabis)

ḥashiya حشية *n* stuffing (e.g. for mattresses)

ḥashsha حشّ (**i, ḥashsh**) *vi* **1** to cut grass **2** to weed • *vt* to weed

ḥashshaash حشّاش *adj* a person who has the job of cutting grass; **ḥashshaash be-dign-o** (*lit* he cuts the grass with his beard) he doesn't keep his promises

ḥashshaasha حشّاشة *n* **1** grass cutter, sickle **2** weeding hoe

ḥashshar حشّر *vt* (**ḥishsheer, taḥshiir**) **fi** to put inside (a bag, pocket), tuck sth. into; **ḥashshar nafs-o/ragabt-o/ruuḥ-o fi** to interfere

ḥashwa حشوة *n* **1** filling (for a tooth or a sandwich) **2** sandwich

ḥatta حتّى *conj* **1** until **2** so that, in order that • *adv* even **ḥatta**

law, **ḥatta wa law** even if, even though

ḥaṭab حطب *coll n* firewood

ḥaṭṭaabi حطّابي *n* (*pl* **ḥaṭṭaaba**) woodcutter; wood vendor

ḥaṭṭam حطّم *vt* (**ḥiṭṭeem, taḥṭiim**) to destroy, wreck

ḥawa حوى *vt* (**-i, ḥawiya**) to contain

ḥawaafiz حوافز *n pl* (*sg* **ḥaafiz**) incentives

ḥawaali حوالي *adv* approximately, about

ḥawaleen حَوَلين *prep* **1** round **2** about; **al-mawduuʿ biduur ḥawaleen** the subject is about

ḥawiyya حويّة *n* (*pl* **-aat, ḥawaayaa**) packsaddle (camel)

ḥawja حوجة *n* want, need

ḥawl حول *prep* about • *n* power, might; **la ḥawl illaah** there is no power save in God! (*exclamation of helplessness*); **ya ḥawl illaah/ ya ḥawla** oh might of God! (*upon hearing bad news*)

ḥawwaasha حوّاشة *n* small cultivated field

ḥawwaati حوّاتي *n* (*pl* **ḥawwaata, ḥawwaatiyya**) fisherman

ḥawwad حوّد *vi* (**ḥiwweed, taḥwiid**) **1** to change direction, deviate **2 min** to avoid, keep clear of

ḥawwal حوّل *vt* (**taḥwiil**) **1** to transfer, shift **2** to change (money) **3** (**le-**) to transform (into)

ḥawwam حوّم *vt* (**ḥuwaama**) to take s.o. around

ḥawwash حوّش *vt* **1** (**ḥiwweesh**) to fence in **2** (**taḥwiish**) to save up

ḥawwaṭ حوّط *vt* (**ḥiwweeṭ**) (**min**) to take precautions to avoid (evil) by means of charms; **ḥawwaṭ al-beet min ash-shayaaṭiin** he protected the house against devils by means of charms

ḥaya حيا *n* modesty; politeness; **galiil al-ḥaya** indecent, impudent, impolite

ḥayaa حياة *n* life; **wa ḥayaat...**by the life of

ḥayawaan حيوان *n* (*pl* **-aat**) animal; **ḥayawaan khala** wild animal

ḥayawi حيوي *adj* lively; vital

ḥayraan حيران *adj* confused, at a loss

ḥayy حي *n* (*pl* **aḥyaa**) town district; quarter; neighbourhood; **aḥyaa ʿashwaa'iyya** unplanned, illegal settlements

ḥayy حي *adj* (*pl* **aḥyaa**) alive; **ḥayy moot** half-alive, sickly

ḥayya حيّى *vt* (**-i, taḥiya**) to greet; to salute

ḥayyar حيّر *vt* (**ḥiira, ḥiyyeer**) to confuse, bewilder, puzzle

ḥazam حزم *vt* (**i, ḥazim**) to bundle, tie in a bundle

ḥazar حزر *n* warning; **akhad ḥazar-o** to take precautions

ḥaziin حزين *adj* sad

ḥazlag حزلق *vi* (**ḥizleeg, ḥazlaga**) to overdo (in behaviour, dress), to talk in an affected way; to talk as if knowing everything on any subject

ḥaznaan حزنان *adj* sad

ḥazzar حزّر *vt* (**taḥziir**) (**min**) to warn (against)

ḥaẓiira حظيرة *n* reserve (for wild animals), game park

ḥaẓir حظر *n* prohibition, ban, embargo; **ḥaẓr at-tajawwul** curfew

ḥazẓ حظ *n* luck; **le-ḥasan al-ḥazẓ** fortunately; **le-suu' al-ḥazẓ** unfortunately
ḥeeḍ حيض *n* menstruation
ḥeel حيل *n* strength; **shidd ḥeel-ak** be brave, be strong, do your best; **be-l-ḥeel** strongly, very
ḥeeragaan حيرقان *n* heartburn
ḥeeṭa حيطة *n* (*pl* **ḥeeṭaan, ḥiyaṭ**) wall
ḥibin حبن *n* (*pl* **aḥbaan**) boil
ḥibir حبر *n* (*pl* **aḥbaar**) ink
ḥidaashar حداشر *num* eleven
ḥidd حد *n* mourning
ḥiddeey حدّيي *coll n* black kite(s); eagle(s)
ḥidwa حدوة *n* (*pl* **ḥidaw**) horseshoe
ḥiḍir حضر *vi* (**a, ḥuḍuur**) to be present
ḥifaaḍ حفاض *n* (*pl* **-aat**) nappy, diaper
ḥigid حقد *n* spite, malice
ḥiila حيلة *n* (*pl* **ḥiyal**) trick, ruse
ḥiira حيرة *n* confusion, bewilderment
ḥijaab حجاب *n* **1** (*pl* **-aat**) (*Isl*) headscarf (covering head, hair and neck) **2** (*pl* **ḥijbaat, aḥjiba**) amulet; charm
ḥijaama حجامة *n* bloodletting
ḥijeeri حجيري *adj* looking young for one's age
ḥijil حجل *n* (*pl* **ḥijuul**) anklet
ḥijil حجل *coll n* partridge(s)
ḥijir حجر *n* (*pl* **ḥujuur**) lap
ḥijja حجّة *n* (*pl* **ḥijaj**) proof; argument
ḥijla حجلة *n* hopscotch
ḥikaaya حكاية *n* **1** tale, story **2** matter (thing)
ḥikir حكر *n* (*pl* **aḥkaar**) ownership of land
ḥikma حكمة *n* (*pl* **ḥikam**) wisdom
ḥilaaga حلاقة *n* shave; haircut; **makanat ḥilaaga 1** safety razor **2** electric shaver
ḥilba حلبة *n* fenugreek
ḥileel حليل *n* **ya ḥleel-ak** how nice for you!; how wonderful for you!; **ya ḥleel zamaan** how wonderful it used to be!
ḥileela حليلة *n* small village
ḥilf حلف *n* (*pl* **aḥlaaf**) alliance, pact
ḥilim حلم *vi* (**a, ḥilim**) to dream • *n* (*pl* **aḥlaam**) dream
ḥill حل *n* (*Chr*) absolution
ḥilla حلّة *n* (*pl* **ḥilal, ḥallaal**) village
ḥilu حلو *adj* (*f* **ḥilwa**) sweet; delicious; beautiful; nice; **ḥilu murr** homemade drink consumed at breakfast during Ramadan, *also called* **aabree**
ḥimaaya حماية *n* protection defence
ḥimil حمل *vi* (**a, ḥimil**) to conceive
ḥimil حمل *n* (*pl* **aḥmaal**) pregnancy; **ḥimil khaarij ar-riḥim** ectopic pregnancy
ḥinayyin حنيّن *adj* kind, tender
ḥinna حنة *n* henna; henna plant
ḥinniyya حنّية *n* compassion, kindness, sympathy, affection
ḥiraasa حراسة *n* **1** guarding **2** detention
ḥirafi حرفي *n* (*pl* **-yyiin**) artisan craftsman
ḥirbooya حربوية *n* chameleon
ḥirfa حرفة *n* (*pl* **ḥiraf**) skilled craft, workmanship
ḥirfiyya حرفيّة *n* craftsmanship
ḥirid حرد *vt* (**a, ḥarid, ḥaradaan**) **1** to refuse to move (of a donkey) **2** to sulk; to suddenly decide not to do sth. (out of anger); **ḥirid al-akal** to refuse to eat (out of anger)

ḥirig حرق *vi* (a, **ḥarig**) to be burnt
ḥirṣ حرص *n* caution
ḥisaab حساب *n* (*pl* **-aat**) **1** bill, account; **aʿmal ḥisaab-ak** take care! **2** computation **3** arithmetic
ḥiss حس *n* **1** voice; **ma ʿind-o ḥiss** he is silent **2** presence; **ma ʿind-o ḥiss** he is absent **3** (*pl* **aḥaasiis, iḥsaasaat**) feeling; intuition
ḥiṣaar حصار *n* (*pl* **-aat**) siege; blockade; embargo
ḥiṣba حصبة *n* measles
ḥiṣeen حصين *n* **abu l-ḥiṣeen** fox
ḥiṣṣa حصّة *n* (*pl* **ḥiṣaṣ**) lesson, class
ḥishma حشمة *adj invar* decent • *n* decency (dress)
ḥitaala حتالة *adj invar* the youngest of the family
ḥitta حتة *n* (*pl* **ḥitat**) **1** piece (portion, fragment), **ḥittat ariḍ** piece of land, plot **2** place
ḥiwaar حوار *n* (*pl* **-aat**) dialogue
ḥiyaaza حيازة *n* (*leg*) possession, holding, tenure; custody of land or property by right of ownership or tenancy
ḥizaam حزام *n* (*pl* **-aat, aḥzima**) belt; **ḥizaam al-amaan** safety belt; **ḥizaam naari** shingles, herpes zoster
ḥizib حزب *n* (*pl* **aḥzaab**) political party
ḥizma حزمة *n* (**ḥizam**) bundle
ḥooḍ حوض *n* (*pl* **ḥeeḍaan, aḥwaaḍ**) **1** basin; **ḥooḍ as-sibaaḥa** swimming pool **2** washbasin, washstand, sink; **ḥooḍ al-banyo** bathtub **3** trough **4** (*agr*) seedbed; field plot sectioned off for irrigation **5** riverbed **6** pelvis
ḥool حول *n* (*pl* **-aat**) year
ḥoosh حوش *n* (*pl* **ḥeeshaan**) **1** enclosure, fence **2** courtyard, yard
ḥubaar حبار *coll n* bustard(s)
ḥubb حب *n* love
ḥubuub حبوب *n pl* (*coll n* **ḥabb**, *unit n* **ḥabba**) **1** kernels, seeds **2** tablets, pills; **ḥubuub manʿ al-ḥimil** birth control pills **3** pimples, boils, cysts
ḥuduud حدود *n pl* **1** border, frontier **2** Islamic penal code
ḥuḍun حضن *n* embrace
ḥuḍuur حضور *n* attendance; (*also fig*) presence; **takliif be-l-ḥuḍuur** summons
ḥufra حفرة *n* (*pl* **ḥufar**) hole in ground, pothole, pit
ḥugg حق *n* (*pl* **ḥagaga**) round box for perfumes
ḥugna حقنة *n* **1** (*pl* **ḥugan**) injection **2** basin, depression (land)
ḥugra حقرة *n* contempt
ḥuguug حقوق *n pl* (*sg* **ḥagg**) law (study); **ḥuguug al-insaan** human rights
ḥujja حجّة *n* (*pl* **ḥujaj**) proof; argument
ḥujra حجرة *n* (*pl* **ḥujar**) room (part of the house)
ḥujwa حجوة *n* (*pl* **-aat, aḥaaji, ḥuja**) folktale
ḥukum حكم *n* **1** (*pl* **-aat**) reign, rule, governance; **al-ḥukum ar-rashiid/ al-ḥukum ar-raashid** good governance **2** (*pl* **aḥkaam**) judgment, sentence, verdict; **al-ḥukum be-l-iʿdaam** the death penalty
ḥumaar حمار *n* (*pl* **ḥamiir**) donkey; **ḥumaar al-waḥsh; ḥumaar al-waadi** zebra

ḥumbuk حمبك *coll n* fruit(s) of the wild jujube tree
ḥumma حمّى *n f* fever; **ḥumma n-nufaas** childbed fever; **ḥumma ṣafra** yellow fever; **ḥumma umm barid** cold fever; **al-ḥumma al-faḥmiyya** anthrax; **al-ḥumma an-nazfiyya** Rift Valley fever; **ḥummat al-gashsh/ḥumma ad-dariis** hay fever
ḥumuuḍa حموضة *n* acidity
ḥumuula حمولة *n* capacity (holding power)
ḥurga حرقة *n* severe emotional pain
ḥurguṣ حرقص *coll n* worm(s); **abu ḥurguṣ** worm; **al-fi baṭn-o ḥurguṣ, baraa-ho birguṣ** he who has sth. to hide, shows it by his behaviour
ḥurma حرمة *n* (*pl* **ḥariim**) married woman
ḥurr حر *adj* (*pl* **aḥraar**) free
ḥurriya حريّة *n* freedom; **be-ḥurriya** freely
ḥuṣaan حصان *n* (*pl* **ḥaṣiin**) horse
ḥushari حشري (*pl* **-yyiin**) *adj* curious • *n* busybody, meddler
ḥutaala حتالة *adj invar* the youngest of the family
ḥutrub حترب *n* leftovers (of food remaining in a cooking pot), scrapings
ḥuṭaam حطام *n pl* ruins, wrecks
ḥuuliyya حوليّة *n* anniversary celebration of a Sufi order at the tomb of its sheikh or at his home
ḥuur حور *coll n* (*unit n* **ḥuuriyya**) 1 (*Isl*) houri(s); **wadd al-ḥuur/ bitt al-ḥuur** albino person 2 nymph(s); mermaid(s)
ḥuut حوت *coll n* (*unit n* **ḥuutaaya**, *pl* **ḥeeṭaan**) fish
ḥuwaala حوالة *n* money order
ḥuwaar حوار *n* (*pl* **ḥiiraan**) disciple of a sheikh
ḥuzun حزن *n* (*pl* **aḥzaan**) sadness, grief

i

iʿaada إعادة *n* repetition; **iʿaadat al-ḥuguug** rehabilitation **iʿaadat an-naẓar (fi)** reconsideration (of); **iʿaadat as-sana** repeating a year at school; **iʿaadat tawṭiin** resettlement
iʿaaqa إعاقة *n* handicap
iʿdaam إعدام *n* (*pl* **-aat**) **1** death penalty, capital punishment, execution **2** annihilation
iʿfaa إعفاء *n* pardon
iʿjaab اعجاب *n* admiration
iʿlaan إعلان *n* (*pl* **-aat**) **1** notice, notification, announcement, proclamation **2** advertisement; **ʿamal iʿlaan** to advertise
iʿtabar إعتبر *vt* (**iʿtibaar**) to consider
iʿtada اعتدى *vi* (**-i, iʿtidaa**) **ʿala** to act brutally or unlawfully against; to assail, assault
iʿtamad إعتمد (**iʿtimaad**) *vt* to endorse, approve • *vi* **ʿala** to rely on, to depend on
iʿtana اعتنى *vi* (**-i, iʿtina**) **be-** to care for, look after
iʿtaqal اعتقل *vt* (**iʿtiqaal**) to detain
iʿtaraḍ إعترض *vi* (**iʿtiraaḍ**) (**ʿala**) to object (to)

iʿtaraf إعترف *vi* (**iʿtiraaf**) (**be-**) to confess, acknowledge, admit
iʿtazar إعتزر *vi* (**iʿtizaar**) to apologize
iʿtibaar اعتبار *n* (*pl* **-aat**) consideration **akhad fi iʿtibaar-** to take into consideration
iʿtidaa اعتدا *n* (*pl* **iʿtida'aat**) assault
iʿtimaad إعتماد *n* (*pl* **-aat**) **1** endorsement, approval **2** dependence
iʿtiqaal اعتقال *n* (*pl* **-aat**) detention
iʿtiraaḍ إعتراض *n* (*pl* **-aat**) objection
iʿtiraaf إعتراف *n* (*pl* **-aat**) confession, acknowledgment
iʿtizaar إعتزار *n* (*pl* **-aat**) apology
ibaada إبادة *n* annihilation
ibdaaʿ إبداع *n* (*pl* **-aat**) creation (by humans)
ibil إبل *coll n* (*no unit n*) camels
ibin ابن *n* (*pl* **abnaa**) son
ibliis إبليس *n* (*pl* **abaaliis, abaalisa**) Satan, devil
ibra إبرة *n* (*pl* **ibar**) **1** needle; **lambat ibra** light bulb of bayonet type **2** sting (e.g. of a bee)
ibriig إبريق *n* (*pl* **abaariig**) jug, pitcher (for ablutions and usage in toilet)
ibtaʿad ابتعد *vi* (**ibtiʿaad**) (**ʿan**) to stay away (from)
ibtada إبتدا *vi* (**-i, bidaaya, ibtida**) to begin, start
ibtahaj إبتهج *vi* (**ibtihaaj**) to be delighted
ibtakar إبتكر *vt* (**ibtikaar**) to invent
ibtasam إبتسم *vi* (**ibtisaam**) to smile
ibtazza ابتز *vt* (**ibtizaaz**) to blackmail
ibtidaa'i ابتدائي *adj* primary
ibtikaar إبتكار *n* (*pl* **-aat**) invention
ibtisaam إبتسام *n* (*pl* **-aat**) smile
ibtisaama إبتسامة *n* smile
ibtizaaz ابتزاز *n* blackmail
idaana إدانة *n* conviction, guilty verdict
idaara إدارة *n* administration, management
iddaʿa ادّعى *vt* (**-i, iddiʿa**) to allege, claim • *vi* (**-i, iddiʿa, daʿwa**) **ʿala** to bring a lawsuit against, sue
iddaafar ادّافر *vi* (**mudaafara**) to push one another
iddaagash ادّاقش *vi* (**mudaagasha, dagsha**) **maʿa** to bump, collide, crash into
iddaawa ادّاوى *vi* (**-a, mudaawaa**) to be treated medically; to be cured
iddaawas ادّاوس *vi* (**duwaas**) to fight with one another
iddabba ادّبّ *vi* (**dabba, dibbeey**) to slink; **iddabba wara** to stalk
iddabras ادّبرس *vi* (**dabrasa, dibrees**) to be(come) depressed
iddafaʿ ادّفع *vi* (**dafiʿ**) to be paid
iddaffa ادّفا *vi* (**-a, diffeey**) to be warmed
iddaffag ادّفّق *vi* (**diffeeg**) **1** to be spilled (e.g. milk, salt) **2** to be thrown away (of liquid, e.g. dirty water)
iddagash ادّقش *vi* (**dagsha**) **maʿa** to bump, collide, crash into
iddagdag ادّقدق *vi* (**dagdaag**) to be uneven, have potholes (of an unpaved road)
iddagga ادّقّ *vi* (**dagg**) **1** to be hit, beaten, hammered, knocked, thrashed, threshed **2** to be ground (e.g. spices)
iddaggas ادّقّس *vi* (**diggees**) to be cheated, deceived
iddakhar ادّخر *vt* (**iddikhaar**) to store (for future use)
iddakhkhal ادّخّل *vt* (**tadakhkhul**) to interfere, intervene, meddle

iddalla ادّلّى *vi* (**-a, dilleey**) to descend, to go down
iddallaʿ ادّلّع *vi* (**dalaʿ, tidilliʿ**) **1** to be pampered, spoiled **2** to behave frivolously
iddallal ادّلّل *vi* (**dalaal**) to behave frivolously
iddammar ادّمّر *vi* (**tadmiir**) to be destroyed
iddangar ادّنقر *vi* (**dingeer, dangara**) to bend down/over
iddangas ادّنقس *vi* (**dingees, dangasa**) to bend down/over
iddankas ادّنكس *vi* (**dinkees, dankasa**) to tilt
iddardag ادّردق *vi* (**dirdeeg**) to roll
iddarrab ادّرّب *vi* (**dirreeb, tadriib**) to be trained
iddassa ادّسّ *vi* (**dass, dassa**) to hide o.s., to be hidden
iddashdash ادّشدش *vi* (**dashdasha**) to be smashed
iddashshaʿ ادّشّع *vi* (**dishsheeʿ**) to belch
iddashsha' ادّشّأ *vi* (**-a', dishsheey**) to belch
iddawwar ادّوّر *vi* **1** (**dawaraan**) to be(come) round (e.g. of the moon) **2** (**diwweer**) to be turned on, switched on (e.g. of engine)
iddayyan ادّيّن *vi* (**deen**) to borrow (money)
iddayyan ادّيّن *vi* (**tadayyun**) to become religious, devout; to make a show of being religious
idmaan ادمان *n* addiction
iḍaafa إضافة *n* addition; **be-l-iḍaafa le-** in addition to
iḍḍaara اضّارّ *vi* (**-a, muḍaaraa**) to hide o.s.; to be hidden; to shelter
iḍḍaarab اضّارب *vt* (**muḍaaraba**) to fight with one another
iḍḍaayag اضّايق *vi* (**muḍaayaga**) (**min**) to be annoyed (by)
iḍḍaayar إضّاير *vi* (**muḍaayara**) to be arranged, put in order
iḍḍarab اضّرب *vi* (**ḍarib**) to be beaten
iḍḍawwa اضّوّى *vi* (**-a, ḍawayaan**) to be illuminated
iḍeena إضينة *adj invar* spineless, weak-willed; **al-iḍeena tadugg-o wa taʿtazir lee-ho** a spineless person won't stand up for himself
iḍraab إضراب *n* (*pl* **-aat**) strike, labour stoppage
ifaada إفادة *n* notice, notification
ifraaj إفراج *n* **min** release (e.g. from prison; of goods, from a store, a ship)
ifriiqiya إفريقيا *prop n* Africa; **ifriiqiya aj-januubiyya** South Africa
iftakar افتكر *vt* (**iftikaar**) to think, believe
iftakhar افتخر *vi* (**fakhr, iftikhaar**) (**be-**) to be proud (of)
iftaraḍ افترض *vi* (**iftiraaḍ**) to suppose
iftataḥ افتتح *vt* (**iftitaaḥ**) to open (a ceremony)
iftiraaḍ إفتراض *n* (*pl* **-aat**) assumption
iftitaaḥ افتتاح *n* (*pl* **-aat**) official opening (ceremony)
ifṭaar إفطار *n* (*pl* **-aat**) the breaking of the fast; breakfast
igraar إقرار *n* (*pl* **-aat**) **1** confession, acknowledgment **2** (*with an adjective*) declaration, statement; **igraar ṭibbi** medical certificate; **igraar jumruki** customs declaration
ighaasa إغاسة *n* aid, relief
ightarab اغترب *vi* (**ightiraab**) to go abroad to work

ightaṣab اغتصب *vt* (**ightiṣaab**) to rape

ightiṣaab إغتصاب *n* (*pl* **-aat**) rape

ihaana إهانة *n* humiliation

ihmaal إهمال *n* negligence, neglect; carelessness, heedlessness

ihtamma اهتمّ *vi* (**ihtimaam**) (**be-**) to be concerned (with), care (about)

ihtimaam إهتمام *n* (*pl* **-aat**) concern; **ʿadam ihtimaam** carelessness

iḥaala احالة *n* transfer

iḥbaaṭ إحباط *n* frustration

iḥraaj احراج *n* (*pl* **-aat**) embarrassment

iḥsaan إحسان *n* alms; charitable deed

iḥsaas إحساس *n* (*pl* **-aat, aḥaasiis**) feeling; intuition

iḥṣa'aat إحصاءات *n pl* statistics

iḥṣaa'i إحصائي *adj* statistical

iḥṣaa'iyyaat إحصائيّات *n pl* statistics

iḥtaaj إحتاج *vi* (**iḥtiyaaj**) **le-** to need

iḥtaaṭ احتاط *vi* (**iḥtiyaaṭ**) to take precautions

iḥtafal احتفل *vi* (**iḥtifaal**) **be-** to celebrate

iḥtafaẓ احتفظ *vi* (**iḥtifaaẓ**) **be-** to keep, preserve

iḥtagar احتقر *vt* (**ḥagaara, iḥtigaar**) to despise, treat with contempt, look down on

iḥtajja احتجّ *vi* (**iḥtijaaj**) (**ʿala**) to protest (against)

iḥtakar احتكر *vt* (**iḥtikaar**) to monopolise

iḥtalla احتلّ *vt* (**iḥtilaal**) to occupy

iḥtaram احترم *vt* (**iḥtiraam**) to respect

iḥtaras احترس *vi* (**iḥtiraas**) (**min**) to beware (of); **iḥtaras min al-kalib** beware of the dog!

iḥtawa احتوى *vi* (**iḥtiwa**) **ʿala** to contain, include

iḥtifaal إحتفال *n* (*pl* **-aat**) celebration, ceremony

iḥtigaan إحتقان *n* congestion

iḥtijaaj إحتجاج *n* (*pl* **-aat**) protest

iḥtikaar إحتكار *n* (*pl* **-aat**) monopoly

iḥtilaal إحتلال *n* occupation

iḥtimaal إحتمال *n* (*pl* **-aat**) probability

iḥtiraam إحترام *n* respect

iḥtiyaaj إحتياج *n* (*pl* **-aat**) need

iḥtiyaal إحتيال *n* deceit

iḥtiyaaṭ إحتياط *n* (*pl* **-aat**) **1** reserve, store; **2** precaution; **al-iḥtiyaaṭ waajib** precaution is a duty

iḥtiyaaṭi إحتياطي *adj* **1** spare, reserve **2** precautionary

iid إيد *n f* (*pl* **iideen, ayaadi**) **1** hand; **malyat iid/gabḍat iid** a handful **2** handle; **iid al-funduk** pestle; **iid al-ukra** doorknob, door handle

iigaaʿ إيقاع *n* (*pl* **-aat**) rhythm

iijaabi ايجابي *adj* positive

iijaar إيجار *n* (*pl* **-aat**) rent, lease

iimaan إيمان *n* faith, belief

iiraad إيراد *n* (*pl* **-aat**) income, revenue

iiṣaal إيصال *n* (*pl* **-aat**) receipt; voucher

iiṭaali إيطالي (*pl* **-yyiin**) *adj* Italian • *n* an Italian

iiṭaalya إيطاليا *prop n* Italy

ijaaba إجابة *n* reply, answer

ijaaza إجازة *n* holiday, vacation, leave

ijbaari اجباري *adj* compulsory

ijhaaḍ اجهاض *prop n* (*pl* **-aat**) abortion; miscarriage

ijjaaṭ اجّاط *vi* (**jooṭa**) to be(come) a mess, to be muddled

ijraa إجرا *n* (*pl* **-'aat**) procedure

ijtahad اجتهد *vi* (**ijtihaad**) to be industrious, diligent; to do one's best

ijtamaʿ اجتمع *vi* (**ijtimaa**ʿ) to meet together, assemble; to have a meeting

ijtihaad إجتهاد *n* diligence

ijtimaaʿ إجتماع *n* (*pl* **-aat**) meeting, assembly

ikkiil اكّيل *n* (*pl* **akkaaliin**) glutton

ikraah إكراه *n* coercion, force, compulsion; **la ikraaha fi d-diin** (*Isl*) there should be no coercion in matters of religion

ikraam إكرام *n* generosity, hospitality

ikta'ab إكتأب *vi* (**ikti'aab**) to be(come) depressed

iktafa إكتفى *vi* (**-i, iktifa**) (**be-**) to be satisfied, content (with)

iktasab اكتسب *vt* (**iktisaab**) to gain, acquire

iktashaf اكتشف *vt* (**iktishaaf**) to discover, find out

ikti'aab إكتئاب *n* depression, gloom

iktifa إكتفا *n* contentment, satisfaction

iktishaaf إكتشاف *n* (*pl* **-aat**) discovery

ikhbaar إخبار *n* (*pl* **-aat**) announcement, official information

ikhlaaṣ إخلاص *n* faithfulness, loyalty

ikhtaar اختار *vt* (**ikhtiyaar**) to choose

ikhtabar اختبر *vt* (**ikhtibaar**) to test

ikhtafa اختفى *vi* (**-i, ikhtifa**) to disappear

ikhtalaf اختلف *vi* (**ikhtilaaf**) to differ, be different, vary; (**ma**ʿ**a, fi**) to disagree, have a different opinion; **bakhtalif ma**ʿ**aa-k fi l-mawḍuu**ʿ **da** I disagree with you about that subject

ikhtalas اختلس *vt* (**ikhtilaas**) to embezzle, misappropriate

ikhtaraʿ اخترع *vt* (**ikhtiraa**ʿ) to invent

ikhtarag اخترق *vt* (**ikhtiraag**) to penetrate

ikhtaṣar اختصر (**ikhtiṣaar**) *vi* to be brief, be concise • *vt* to summarize, condense; **ikhtaṣar aṭ-ṭariig** to take a short cut

ikhtasha اختشى *vi* (**-i, ikhtisha**) to be(come) shy, bashful

ikhtibaar إختبار *n* (*pl* **-aat**) test; **tiḥt al-ikhtibaar** on trial (at work)

ikhtilaaf إختلاف *n* (*pl* **-aat**) difference

ikhtilaas اختلاس *n* (*pl* **-aat**) embezzlement, misappropriation

ikhtiraaʿ إختراع *n* (*pl* **-aat**) invention

ikhtiṣaar إختصار *n* (*pl* **-aat**) **1** abbreviation **2** brevity; **be-ikhtiṣaar** in short, in brief

ikhtiṣaaṣ إختصاص *n* (*pl* **-aat**) jurisdictional competence

ikhtiṣaaṣi إختصاصي *n* (*pl* **-yyiin**) specialist

ikhtiṭaaf إختطاف *n* (*pl* **-aat**) abduction

ikhtiyaar إختيار *n* (*pl* **-aat**) choice

ila إلى *prep* to

ilaah إله *n* (*pl* **aaliha**) god

ilḥaad الحاد *n* heresy

ilḥaaḥ الحاح *n* insistence, persistence

illa إلا *prep* except; only; **ma** ʿ**ind-o illa bagara waaḥda** he has only one cow; **illa iza/illa law** unless

iltafat التفت *vi* (**iltifaat**) **le-** to turn one's head towards

iltahab التهب *vi* (**iltihaab**) to be(come) inflamed

iltazam التزم *vi* (**iltizaam**) (**be-**) to be committed (to)

iltihaab إلتهاب *n* (*pl* **-aat**) infection, inflammation; **iltihaab aj-jiyuub al-anfiyya** sinusitis; **iltihaab al-kabid** hepatitis; **iltihaab miʿda** gastritis; **iltihaab ri'awi** pneumonia; **iltihaab sadi** mastitis

iltizaam إلتزام *n* (*pl* **-aat**) commitment, engagement

ilzaami الزامي *adj* obligatory, mandatory; **(al-khidma al-ʿaskariyya) al-ilzaamiyya** obligatory military service

imaam إمام *n* (*pl* **a'imma**) (*Isl*) imam, prayer leader

imbahaṭ امبهط *vi* (**bahṭa, bahaṭaan**) to be stupefied

imdaad إمداد *n* (*pl* **-aat**) (*mil*) supply

imdaadaat إمدادات *n pl* (*mil*) **1** supplies **2** logistics

imḍa إمضا *n* (*pl* **imḍaa'aat**) signature

imkaaniyya إمكانيّة *n* possibility

imla إملا *n* (*pl* **imla'aat**) dictation

imma إمّا *conj* **1** unless; **imma ja, ana bamshi** unless he comes, I leave **2** (*see also* **ya-**) either…or; **imma da, imma daak** either this or that

imsaak إمساك *n* constipation

imtadda امتدّ *vi* (**imtidaad**) to be extended

imtaḥan امتحن (**imtiḥaan**) *vi* to sit for exams • *vt* to examine, test

imtalak امتلك *vt* (**imtilaak**) to own, possess

imtaṣṣa امتصّ *vt* (**imtiṣaaṣ**) to absorb

imtidaad إمتداد *n* (*pl* **-aat**) extension

imtiḥaan إمتحان *n* (*pl* **-aat**) exam, test

imtiyaaz إمتياز *n* **1** distinction, excellence **2** medical internship, housemanship **3** (*pl* **-aat**) privilege; franchise

in إن *conj* if; **in shaa allah** God willing, Deo volente; **in kaan** **1** if **2** whether; **ma baʿraf in kaan ṣaḥiiḥ wa-la kiḍib** I don't know whether it is true or a lie; **in ma** unless (*see also* **imma**)

inʿaash إنعاش *n* intensive care

inʿakas انعكس *vi* (**ʿaksa**) to be reflected (light)

inʿaṭan انعطن *vi* (**ʿaṭin**) to be soaked

inbahaṭ انبهط *vi* (**bahṭa, bahaṭaan**) to be stupefied

inbasaṭ انبسط *vi* (**inbisaaṭ**) (**min**) to be glad (about), happy (about), pleased (with)

inbashak انبشك *vi* (**bashka**) to be(come) tangled

inbatta انبتّ *vi* (**inbitaat**) to be cut off (e.g. family ties); **ḥeel-o inbatta** his power to act deserted him

inbaṭaḥ انبطح *vi* (**inbiṭaaḥ**) to lie on one's stomach

inbisaaṭ إنبساط *n* delight, pleasure, joy, happiness

indagga اندقّ *vi* (**dagg**) to be hit, beaten, hammered, knocked, thrashed, threshed

indahash اندهش *vi* (**dahsha, indihaash**) (**min**) to be amazed, surprised, astonished (by)

indassa اندسّ *vi* (**dass, dassa**) to hide o.s.; to be hidden

inḍamma انضمّ *vi* (**inḍimaam**) **le-** to join, associate with

inḍarab انضرب *vi* (**ḍarib**) to be hit, beaten

infaʿal انفعل *vi* (**infiʿaal**) to be(come) emotional, be(come) excited

infajjar انفجّر *vi* (**infijaar**) to explode
infaṣal انفصل *vi* (**infiṣaal**) to separate
infataḥ انفتح *vi* (**infitaaḥ, fatiḥ**) to be opened
infiʿaal انفعال *n* excitement
infijaar إنفجار *n* (*pl* **-aat**) explosion
infiṣaal انفصال *n* (*pl* **-aat**) separation
influwanza إنفلونزا *n* influenza, flu
ingadda انقدّ *vi* (**gadd**) to be(come) porous; to have a hole
ingalab انقلب *vi* **1** (**galba**) to be turned upside down/inside out; to somersault **2** (**ingilaab**) to be overthrown
ingaraṣ انقرص *vi* (**garṣa**) **1** to be bitten (by insects) **2** to be pinched
ingaṭaʿ انقطع *vi* (**ingiṭaaʿ**) **1** to break off, snap; **al-ḥabil bingaṭiʿ min maḥall rigeyyig** the rope snaps at its weakest point **2** to be cut (off), to be disconnected
ingilaab إنقلاب *n* (*pl* **-aat**) coup d'etat, overthrow
ingiltarra إنقلترا *prop n* England
inghamas انغمس *vi* (**inghimaas**) **fi** **1** to be immersed in **2** to be taken up by, engrossed in, preoccupied by
inghashsha انغشّ *vi* (**ghashsh, ghashashaan**) to be cheated, deceived
ingliiz إنقليز *coll n* English, Englishmen
ingliizi انقليزي *adj* (*pl* **ingliiz**) English • *unit n* an Englishman
inhaar انهار *vi* (**inhiyaar**) to collapse
inhadda انهدّ *vi* (**hadd**) to fall down, collapse (e.g. a house)
inhamak انهمك *vi* (**inhimaak**) **fi** to be taken up by, engrossed in, preoccupied by
inhazam انهزم *vi* (**haziima, inhizaam**) to be defeated
inhiyaar انهيار *n* collapse, breakdown **inhiyaar ʿaṣabi** nervous breakdown
inḥabba انحبّ *vi* (**ḥubb**) to be loved
inḥadar انحدر *vi* (**inḥidaar**) to slope
inḥalla انحلّ *vi* (**a, inḥilaal, ḥall**) **1** to be solved **2** to be(come) loose, untied; **inḥallat akhlaag-o** he has abandoned his principles
inḥana انحنى *vi* (**-i, ḥaniya**) to bend, curve; to meander, wind; to bow; to grow crooked (a person's back)
inḥarag انحرق *vi* (**ḥarig**) to be burnt; **inḥarig min** to eat one's heart out with jealousy about or hatred to (a person)
inḥasab انحسب *vi* (**ḥisaab**) to be calculated
inḥidaar إنحدار *n* (*pl* **-aat**) slope
injaaz إنجاز *n* (*pl* **-aat**) achievement, accomplishment
injaraḥ انجرح *vi* (**jariḥ**) to be wounded
injiil إنجيل *n* (*pl* **anaajiil**) Gospel
inkaar إنكار *n* denial
inkamad انكمد *vi* (**kamid**) to be filled to the brim
inkamash انكمش *vi* (**inkimaash**) **1** to shrink, contract **2 min** to withdraw socially
inkammad انكمّد *vi* (**kimmeed**) **be-** to stop (with an action); **inkammid** stop! (with what you're doing)
inkasa انكسى *vi* (**-i, kiswa**) to buy clothes
inkasaf انكسف *vi* (**kasfa**) to be(come) embarrassed

inkasar انكسر *vi* (**kasra, inkisaar**) to break (also of a heart); **ʿeen-o inkasarat** he felt ashamed
inkhabaṭ انخبط *vi* (**khabṭa**) to be hit; to be knocked; to be nudged
inkhanag انخنق *vi* (**khanig, inkhinaag**) to choke
inn- إنّ.. *conj* that; **gaalu inn-a marḍaana** they said that she is ill
inno إنو *conj* that; **biguulu inno ḥa-yakuun fih maṭar katiir** they say that there will be a lot of rain
inqaaz إنقاز *n* (*pl* **-aat**) salvation
insaan إنسان *n* (*pl* **naas**) human being
insaani انساني *adj* human, humanitarian
insadda انسدّ *vi* (**sadd, insidaad**) to be closed; to be blocked
insaḥab انسحب *vi* (**insiḥaab**) to retreat, withdraw o.s.
insarag انسرق *vi* (**sarga**) (**min**) to be stolen (from); to be robbed; **insaragat minn-i guruush-i** my money has been stolen
insiḥaab انسحاب *n* (*pl* **-aat**) retreat
insha انشا *n* (*pl* **insha'aat**) composition (in school)
inshagga انشقّ *vi* (**shagg, shagagaan**) to crack, be split
inshaghal انشغل *vi* (**inshighaal**) to be busy
inshaḥaṭ انشحط *vi* (**shaḥṭa, inshiḥaaṭ**) **1** to run aground (of ships) **2 fi** to merge into a crowd
insharaṭ انشرط *vi* (**shariṭ**) to be torn (up, apart)
inta انت *pron sg m* you
intaaj إنتاج *n* (*pl* **-aat**) production
intaajiyya إنتاجيّة *n* production
intaaya إنتاية *n* female (animals)
intabah انتبه *vi* (**intibaah**) (**le-**) to be attentive, pay attention (to)
intaha انتهى *vi* (**-i, nihaaya**) **1** to end **2 min** to finish, be finished with, have finished sth.
intahaak انتهاك *n* (*pl* **-aat**) violation
intahak انتهك *vt* (**intihaak**) to violate
intahaz انتهز *vt* (**intihaaz**); **intahaz al-furṣa** to take the opportunity
intaḥar انتحر *vi* (**intiḥaar**) to commit suicide
intakas انتكس *vi* (**intikaas**) to suffer a relapse (into sickness)
intakhab انتخب *vt* (**intikhaab**) to elect (in elections)
intaqam انتقم *vi* (**intiqaam**) (**le-, min**) to take revenge, avenge (sth., on); **intaqam le-sharaf-o** he defended his honour; **intaqam le-akhuu-ho min al-kaatil** he avenged his brother's death on the murderer
intaṣab إنتصب *vi* (**intiṣaab**) to become erect, be erected
intaṣar انتصر *vi* (**intiṣaar**) (**ʿala**) to gain victory (over), overcome
intashar انتشر *vi* (**intishaar**) to spread
intaẓam انتظم *vi* (**intiẓaam**) to be(come) regular
intaẓar انتظر *vi/vt* (**intiẓaar**) to wait (for)
inti انتي *pron sg f* you
intibaah إنتباه *n* attention
intifaaḍa انتفاضة *n* revolt
intihaazi إنتهازي *adj* (*pl* **-yyiin**) opportunist
intiḥaar إنتحار *n* suicide
intikhaabaat إنتخابات *n pl* elections
intiqaam إنتقام *n* (*pl* **-aat**) revenge, vengeance

intirnet إنترنت *n* internet
intiṣaab إنتصاب *n* (*pl* **-aat**) erection
intiṣaar إنتصار *n* (*pl* **-aat**) victory (in battle)
intiẓaam إنتظام *n* regularity, order; **be-intiẓaam** on a regular basis, regularly
intiẓaar نتظار *n* waiting; **niḥna fi intiẓaar-kum** we're waiting for you
intu انتو *pron pl m/f* you
inṭamas انطمس *vi* (**ṭamsa**) **1** to fade, to be blotted out **2** to lose one's talents, lose one's skills
inṭibaaʿ انطباع *n* (*pl* **-aat**) impression
inzaʿaj انزعج *vi* (**inziʿaaj**) to be annoyed; to be disturbed
inzaar إنزار *n* (*pl* **-aat**) warning
inzagham انزغم *vi* (**inzighaam**) to gatecrash
inzalag انزلق *vi* (**inzilaag**) to slide, slip, glide
inzarra انزرّ *vi* (**zarra**) to be trapped; to have no way out
inẓalam انظلم *vi* (**ẓulum**) to be treated unjustly
iqaama إقامة *n* residence, stay; **taṣriiḥ iqaama** stay permit, residence permit
iqliim إقليم *n* (*pl* **aqaaliim**) region
iqliimi إقليمي (*pl* **-yyiin**) *adj* regional • *n* a person from the countryside
iqtanaʿ إقتنع *vi* (**iqtinaaʿ**) to be convinced; to be persuaded
iqtaraḥ إقترح *vt* (**iqtiraaḥ**) to propose, suggest
iqtaṣad إقتصد *vi* (**iqtiṣaad**) to economise
iqtiraaḥ إقتراح *n* (*pl* **-aat**) proposal, suggestion
iqtiṣaad إقتصاد *n* economy
iqtiṣaadi إقتصادي *adj* **1** economic **2** economical, thrifty
iraada إرادة *n* will (desire)
irhaab إرهاب *n* terrorism
irhaabi إرهابي (*pl* **-yyiin**) *adj* terrorist • *n* terrorist
irhaaq إرهاق *n* exhaustion
iriitri إريتري (*pl* **-yyiin**) *adj* Eritrean • *n* an Eritrean
iriitriya إريتريا *prop n* Eritrea
irsaal إرسال *n* transmission, broadcasting (radio, TV)
irsaaliyya إرساليّة *n* **1** batch, consignment or shipment of goods **2** long distance transportation of a patient to hospital **3** (*Chr*) mission
irṣaad إرصاد *n* observation; **irṣaad jawwiyya** meteorological observation
irshaad إرشاد *n* (*pl* **-aat**) guidance
irtaaḥ ارتاح *vi* (**raaḥa, irtiyaaḥ**) **1** to feel comfortable, at ease **2** to find relief
irtabak ارتبك *vi* (**irtibaak**) to be(come) confused, bewildered
irtabaṭ ارتبط *vi* (**irtibaaṭ**) **be- 1** to be linked, connected with **2** to commit o.s. to
irtafaʿ ارتفع *vi* (**irtifaaʿ**) to go up, rise, ascend (e.g. prices, temperature)
irtajaf ارتجف *vi* (**rajafaan**) to shiver, tremble
irtakab ارتكب *vt* (**irtikaab**) to commit (a crime), to make (a mistake); **irtakab zanib/zanb** to sin, do wrong
irtakaz ارتكز *vi* (**irtikaaz**) **ʿala** to lean (on)
irtibaaṭ إرتباط *n* (*pl* **-aat**) **1** link, connection, relation **2** commitment, obligation

irtifaaʿ إرتفاع *n* **1** rise (in prices, temperature) **2** elevation **3** altitude, height

isʿaaf إسعاف *n* (*pl* **-aat**) medical service; **ʿarabiyyat isʿaaf** ambulance; **al-isʿaaf** first aid; **isʿaafaat awwaliyya** first aid

isaa'a إساءة *n* affront, offence

isbaat إسبات *n* (*pl* **-aat**) confirmation proof

isbeer إسبير *n* (*pl* **-aat**) spare part; **ʿajala isbeer, lastik isbeer** spare tyre

isbirit إسبيرت *n* (*chem*) spirit

isbitaalya إسبتالية *n* hospital

isfinja اسفنجة *n* sponge

ishaal إسهال *n* diarrhoea

isim إسم *n* **1** (*pl* **asaami, asmaa**) name **2** (*gram*) noun

isiyuubi إسيوبي (*pl* **-yyiin**) *adj* Ethiopian, Ethiopic • *n* an Ethiopian

isiyuubiya إسيوبيا *prop n* Ethiopia

iskaafi اسكافي *n* (*pl* **-yyiin**) shoe mender, cobbler; shoemaker

iskaan إسكان *n* housing; **wazaarat al-iskaan** the Ministry of Housing

iskeert إسكيرت *n* (*pl* **-aat**) skirt

islaam إسلام *n* Islam

islaami إسلامي *n* islamist

islaami إسلامي *adj* **1** islamic **2** islamist

isni اسني *adj* ethnic

istaʿadda استعدّ *vi* (**istiʿdaad**) to prepare o.s.; to be(come) ready

istaʿfa استعفى *vi* (**-a, istiʿfa**) to dismiss (from military service)

istaʿjal استعجل *vi* (**istiʿjaal**) to hurry

istaʿmal استعمل *vt* (**istiʿmaal**) to use

ista'naf استأنف *vi* (**isti'naaf**) (*leg*) to appeal

ista'zan استأزن *vt* (**izin, isti'zaan**) to ask permission • *vi* **min** to ask permission

istaad استاد *n* (*pl* **-aat**) stadium

istaahal استاهل *vt* (*no vn*) to deserve; to be worth; **al-ʿarabiyya tastaahil khamsa alif** the car is worth five thousand

istaandar استاندر *adj* original (quality)

istaayl استايل *n* (*pl* **-aat**) style (e.g. of clothing) • *adj invar* (of girls) slim

istabadda استبدّ *vi* (**istibdaad**) **1** to be arbitrary **2** to be(come) despotic, tyrannical

istaḍaaf استضاف *vt* (**i, ḍiyaafa, istiḍaafa**) to receive guests

istafaad استفاد *vi* (**i, istifaada**) to benefit

istafragh استفرغ *vi/vt* (**istifraagh**) to vomit, throw up

istafsar استفسر *vi* (**istifsaar**) (**ʿan**) to inquire (about)

istaghalla استغلّ *vt* (**istighlaal**) to exploit

istaghfar استغفر *vt* (**istighfaar**) to ask God for forgiveness; **astaghfaru-llaah** may God forgive me!

istaghna استغنى *vi* (**istighna**) **min** to manage without

istaghrab استغرب *vi* (**istighraab**) (**min**) to be amazed, surprised, astonished (by)

istahbal استهبل *vi* (**istihbaal**) to play the fool

istahlak استهلك *vt* (**istihlaak**) to consume

istaḥa استحى *vi* (**-a, istiḥa**) to be(come) shy, bashful

istaḥagga استحقّ *vt* (**istiḥgaag**) to deserve; to have the right to; to be worth; **al-beet daak yastaḥigg aktar min miit alif** that house is worth more than a hundred thousand

istaḥamma استحمّ *vi* (**a, ḥammaam**) to take a bath

istaḥmal استحمل *vt* (**istiḥmaal**) to bear, endure

istaḥsan استحسن *vi* (**istiḥsaan**) to be better to

istajwab استجوب *vt* (**istijwaab**) to cross-examine, interrogate

istakshaf استكشف *vt* (**istikshaaf**) to explore

istakhaffa استخفّ *vt* (**istikhfaaf**) to take lightly, treat with contempt

istakhdam استخدم *vt* (**istikhdaam**) to use, make use of

istakhraj استخرج *vt* (**istikhraaj**) **1** to extract (e.g. oil, minerals) **2** to procure by application (official documents)

istalaf استلف *vt* (**sulfa, salaf, istilaaf**) to borrow

istalam استلم *vt* (**istilaam**) to receive

istamarra استمرّ *vi* (**istimraar**) to continue

istamtaʿ استمتع *vi* (**istimtaaʿ**) **be-** to enjoy

istanad استند *vi* (**istinaad**) **ʿala** to rely on

istankar استنكر *vt* (**istinkaar**) to disapprove

istanna استنّ *vi/vt* (*no vn*) to wait (for)

istaqaal استقال *vi* (**a, istiqaala**) to resign

istaqarra استقرّ *vi* (**istiqraar**) to settle down, become settled

istaqbal استقبل *vt* (**istiqbaal**) to receive people

istarḥam استرحم *vt* (**istirḥaam**) to plead for mercy

istarkha استرخ *vi* (**istirkhaa**) to relax

istaslam استسلم *vt* (**istislaam**) to surrender

istashaar استشار *vt* (**istishaara**) to consult, ask for advice

istashhad إستشهد *n* (**istishhaad**) to quote

istashhad إستشهد *n* (**istishhaad**) to be martyred; to be killed (in a holy war)

istawa استوى *vi* (**-i, istiwa**) **1** to be well cooked, done **2** to ripen

istawrad استورد *vt* (**istiiraad**) to import

istiʿdaad إستعداد *n* readiness, preparedness

istiʿmaal إستعمال *n* (*pl* **-aat**) use

istiʿraaḍ إستعراض *n* (*pl* **-aat**) parade; **istiʿraaḍ ʿaskari** military review

isti'naaf إستئناف *n* (*leg*) appeal

istibdaad استبداد *n* arbitrariness; tyranny, despotism

istibyaan إستبيان *n* (*pl* **-aat**) **1** questionnaire **2** (opinion) poll

istidʿaa استدعا *n* summons

istiḍaafa استضافة *n* reception (of guests)

istifaada إستفادة *n* benefit

istifraagh استفراغ *n* vomit

istifsaar استفسار *n* (*pl* **-aat**) inquiry

istiftaa استفتا *n* (*pl* **-'aat**) referendum

istighlaal إستغلال *n* utilization, exploitation

istihlaak إستهلاك *n* (*pl* **-aat**) consumption

istiika إستيكة *n* rubber, eraser; blackboard rubber

istiiraad إستيراد *n* import, importation

istijwaab إستجواب *n* (*pl* **-aat**) cross-examination, interrogation
istik استك *n* (*pl* **asaatik**) elastic band
istikshaaf إستكشاف *n* (*pl* **-aat**) exploration, scouting
istikhdaam إستخدام *n* (*pl* **-aat**) use
istikhfaaf استخفاف *n* contempt
istimaara إستمارة *n* form (document)
istimraar إستمرار *n* continuation; **b-istimraar** continuously
istimraariyya إستمراريّة *n* continuation
istimtaaʿ استمتاع *n* enjoyment
istiqaala إستقالة *n* resignation
istiqbaal إستقبال *n* (*pl* **-aat**) reception lobby, reception desk; **ḥaflat istiqbaal** reception (party)
istiqlaal إستقلال *n* independence
istiqraar استقرار *n* stabilization, stability
istiraaḥa إستراحة *n* **1** pause, break **2** rest house
istirḥaam إسترحام *n* (*pl* **-aat**) mercy
istirkhaa استرخا *n* relaxation
istishaara استشارة *n* consultation
istishhaad إستشهاد *n* martyrdom
istishhaad إستشهاد *n* (*pl* **-aat**) quotation
istiwa إستوا *n* **khaṭṭ al-istiwa** equator
istiwaa'i إستوائي *n* equatorial, tropical, tropic
istob استوب *n* (*pl* **-aat**) traffic lights
istok استوك *n* (*pl* **-aat**) stock, store
iṣṭabil إسطبل *n* (*pl* **iṣṭablaat**) stable (horses)
iṣlaaḥ إصلاح *n* (*pl* **-aat**) reform
iṣṭaad اصطاد *vt* (**ṣeed, iṣṭiyaad**) to hunt

ishaaʿa إشاعة *n* rumour
ishaara إشارة *n* signal; sign, omen; **al-ishaara/ishaarat al-ḥaraka/ ishaarat al-muruur** traffic sign; traffic lights; **be-l-ishaara le-** with respect to, regarding
ishaarb إشارب *n* (*pl* **-aat**) scarf
ishfa إشفة *n* (*pl* **ishaf**) **1** awl **2** large needle **3** knitting needle
ishgaddi اشقدي *n* swollen glands
ishkaal إشكال *n* (*pl* **-aat**) problem
ishkaaliyya إشكاليّة *n* problem
ishlaag إشلاق *n* (*pl* **-aat**) barrack
ishraaf اشراف *n* supervision
ishtaag اشتاق *vi* (**shoog, ishtiyaag**) **le-** to long for, miss
ishtabah اشتبه *vi* (**ishtibaah**) **fi** to suspect; **nashtabih fii-hum** we suspect them
ishtabak إشتبك *n* (**ishtibaak**) to clash
ishtaghal اشتغل *vi* (**shughul**) to work
ishtaha اشتهى *vt* (**-i, shahwa, ishtiha**) to crave
ishtahar اشتهر *vi* (**shuhra**) **be-** to be famous for, well known for
ishtaka اشتكى *vi* (**-i, shakwa, shakiyya**) (**min**) to complain (about)
ishtara اشترى *vt* (**-i, shira**) to buy, purchase
ishtarak اشترك *vi* (**ishtiraak**) **fi** **1** to participate **2** to subscribe; to become a member of
ishtibaah إشتباه *n* suspicion
ishtibaak إشتباك *n* (*pl* **-aat**) clash, scuffle
ishtiraak إشتراك *n* (*pl* **-aat**) subscription
ishtiraaki اشتراكي *adj* socialist • *n* Socialist
ishtiraakiyya اشتراكيّة *n* Socialism

itʿaabaṭ اتعابط *vi* (**ʿabaaṭa**) to act dumb

itʿaada اتعادى *vi* (**-i, ʿadaawa, muʿaadaa**) to be against one another, be hostile to one another

itʿaadal اتعادل *vi* (**taʿaadul**) to balance; to be balanced

itʿaafa اتعافى *vi* (**-a, muʿaafaa**) (**min**) to recover (from), get well

itʿaagad اتعاقد *vi* (**taʿaagud**) to make up a contract

itʿaahad اتعاهد *vi* (**muʿaahada, taʿaahud**) (**ʿala**) to come to agreement (on)

itʿaalaj اتعالج *vi* (**muʿaalaja, ʿilaaj**) to be treated medically; to be cured

itʿaamal اتعامل *vi* **1** (**muʿaamala, taʿaamul**) **maʿa** to treat, behave towards, deal with **2** (**muʿaamala**) **be-** to handle, deal with (things)

itʿaaṭaf اتعاطف *vi* (**taʿaaṭuf**) **maʿa** to show sympathy or concern towards

itʿaawan اتعاون *vi* (**muʿaawana, taʿaawun**) (**maʿa**) to cooperate, collaborate (with)

itʿaawar اتعاور *vi* (**ʿawaara**) to act dumb

itʿadal اتعدل *vi* (**taʿdiil**) to be adjusted

itʿadda اتعدّ *vi* (**ʿadd**) to be counted

itʿadda اتعدّى (**-a, taʿaddi**) *vi* **ʿala** to wrong; to offend (verbally or physically), violate (s.o.'s rights) • *vt* to pass, overtake; to exceed, go beyond; **itʿadda ḥuduud-o** he went beyond what is acceptable

itʿaddal اتعدّل *vi* (**taʿdiil**) to be adjusted

itʿaḍḍa اتعضّ *vi* (**ʿaḍḍa**) to be bitten; to be stung (by scorpion)

itʿaffan اتعفّن *vi* (**ʿiffeen, taʿaffun**) to stink; to rot

itʿahhad اتعهّد *vi* (**taʿahhud**) (**be-**) to pledge, vow

itʿajan اتعجن *vi* (**ʿajna**) **1** to be kneaded **2** to be done badly (e.g. a job)

itʿajjab اتعجّب *vi* (**ʿijjeeb, taʿajjub**) (**min**) to be amazed, surprised, astonished (by)

itʿajjal اتعجّل *vi* (**ʿajala**) to hurry

itʿajjan اتعجّن *vi* (**ʿijjeen, tiʿijjin**) to be kneaded thoroughly

itʿakka اتعكّ *vt* (**ʿakka**) to be(come) a mess

itʿakkar اتعكّر *vi* (**ʿikkeer**) **1** to get muddy **2** to be disturbed (of mood)

itʿakkaz اتعكّز *vi* (**ʿikkeez**) **ʿala** to walk with crutches

itʿallag اتعلّق *vi* (**ʿilleeg**) to hang, be hanged

itʿallam اتعلّم *vt* (**taʿallum**) to learn

itʿama اتعمى *vi* (**-i, ʿama**) to be(come) blind

itʿamal اتعمل *vi* (**ʿamla**) **1** to be done **2** to be made

itʿammar اتعمّر *vi* **1** (**taʿmiir**) to be built on **2** (**ʿamra**) to be serviced (e.g. an engine) **3** (**ʿamra**) to be loaded (of a gun)

itʿankash اتعنكش *vi* (**ʿankasha**) **fi** to hold on firmly to, keep very close to (child to mother, friends to each other)

itʿarraf اتعرّف *vi* (**taʿarruf**) **be-/ʿala** to become acquainted with

itʿarraj اتعرّج *vi* (**ʿirreej, taʿriij, taʿarruj**) to bend (of road)

itʿaṣar اتعصر *vt* (**ʿaṣir**) to be squeezed; to be pressed (e.g. for oil)

itʿaṣṣab اتعصّب *vi* (**taʿaṣṣub**) to be(come) fanatical

itʿashsha اتعشّى *vi* (**-a, ʿasha**) to dine; to have supper, evening meal

itʿattar اتعتّر *vi* (**ʿataraan**) (**fi**) to stumble, trip (over)

itʿaṭan اتعطن *vi* (**ʿaṭin**) to be soaked

itʿaṭṭal اتعطّل *vi* **1** (**ʿuṭul**) to break down **2** (**ʿiṭṭeel, ʿaṭala**) to be physically unable to work **3** (**ʿiṭṭeel, ʿaṭala**) to be late, delayed

itʿaṭṭar اتعطّر *vi* (**ʿiṭṭeer, taʿṭiir**) to perfume o.s.

itʿawaj عوج *vi* (**ʿawja**) to bend (of road); to be bent (of materials)

itʿawwad اتعوّد *vi* (**taʿwiid**) (**ʿala**) to be(come) used (to), accustomed (to)

itʿawwag اتعوّق *vi* (**ʿiwweeg, taʿwiig**) to be injured, wounded

itʿawwaj اتعوّج *vi* (**ʿiwweej, ʿawja**) to bend (of road); to be bent (of materials)

itʿawwar اتعوّر *vi* (**ʿiwweer**) to be injured, wounded

itʿayyan اتعيّن *vi* (**taʿyiin**) to be appointed

itʿazal اتعزل *vi* (**ʿuzla**) **1** to be chosen, selected **2** to be dismissed (from military service) **3** to be(come) isolated

itʿazzab اتعزّب *vi* **1** (**ʿazaab, ʿizzeeb**) to suffer **2** (**taʿziib**) to be tortured

it'aakal اتآكل *vi* (**ta'aakul**) to corrode; to rot (of wood)

it'aamar اتآمر *vi* (**mu'aamara, ta'aamur**) (**ʿala/ḍidd**) to conspire, plot (against)

it'ajjal اتأجّل *vi* (**ta'jiil**) to be postponed, adjourned, suspended

it'akal اتأكل *vi* (**akla**) to be eaten

it'akkad اتأكّد *vi* **1** (**ikkeed**) to be verified **2** (**ta'kiid**) (**min**) to verify

it'akhkhar اتأخّر *vi* (**ta'khiir**) to be late; to be delayed, adjourned

it'allam اتألّم *vi* (**alam**) to have pain, suffer from pain

it'arjaḥ اتأرجح *vi* (**ta'arjuḥ**) to swing

it'assaf اتأسّف *vi* (**asaf, ta'assuf**) (**ʿala**) to express regret, be sorry (for)

it'assar اتأسّر *vi* (**ta'assur**) (**be-**) to be affected (by); to be influenced (by)

itbaaʿ اتباع *vi* (**beeʿ**) to be sold

itbaadal اتبادل *vt* (**tabaadul**) to exchange, swap

itbaalad اتبالد *vi* (**balaada**) to act dumb

itbaḍḍaʿ اتبدّع *vi* (**biḍḍeeʿ**) to buy (goods)

itbaggag اتبقّق *vi* (**biggeeg**) to blister

itbahdal اتبهدل *vi* (**bahdala**) to be treated without respect

itbakhkha اتبخّ *vi* (**bakhkh**) to be sprayed

itbakhkhar اتبخّر *vi* **1** (**tabkhiir**) to evaporate **2** (**bikhkheer**) to be censed

itbakhtar اتبختر *vi* (**bakhtara, tabakhtur**) to strut, to walk in a conceited way

itbalbal اتبلبل *vi* (**bilbeel**) to be(come) wet, moist, damp

itballa اتبلّ *vi* (**balal, balla**) to be(come) wet, moist, damp; **al-fuula ma bititballa fi khashm-o** (*lit* a peanut doesn't get wet in his mouth) he is not able to keep a secret

itballal اتبلّل *vi* (**billeel, tibillil**) to be(come) wet, moist, damp

itballam اتبلّم *vi* (**balam**) **1** to be unable to express o.s. **2** to cover o.s. with a **toob** completely except for the eyes

itbana اتبنى *vi* (**-i, buna**) to be built

itbanna اتبنّى *vt* (**-a, tabanni**) to adopt

itbaram اتبرم *vi* (**barma, baramaan**) to be twisted (of a rope)

itbarjal اتبرجل *vi* (**birjeel, barjala**) to be(come) a mess, to be muddled

itbarmaj اتبرمج *vi* (**barmaja**) to be programmed

itbarraʿ اتبرّع *vi* (**tabarruʿ**) **be-** to donate, make a donation

itbarrad اتبرّد *vi* (**birreed**) to take a bath

itbarrak اتبرّك *vi* (**baraka, tabarruk**) to seek a blessing

itbassam اتبسّم *vi* (**tibissim**) to smile

itbashak اتبشك *vi* (**bashka**) to be(come) tangled

itbashtan اتبشتن *vi* (**bashtana**) to be(come) untidy, to be neglected (of one's appearance, clothes, house)

itbatar اتبتر *vi* (**batra**) to be amputated

itbaṭṭal اتبطّل *vi* (**biṭṭeel**) to break down

itbaṭṭar اتبطّر *vi* (**tabaṭṭur**) to show off

itbawwakh اتبوّخ *vi* (**bookha**) to have a smoke bath

itboobar اتبوبر *vi* (**boobaar**) to brag, swank

itfaa'al اتفاءل *vi* (**mufaa'ala**) **1 be-** to perceive sth. as a good omen **2** to be(come) optimistic

itfaaham اتفاهم *vi* (**tafaahum**) to reach an understanding

itfaakar اتفاكر *vi* (**mufaakara**) to discuss, exchange ideas; to hold a consultation

itfabrak اتفبرك *vt* (**fabraka**) **1** to be manufactured in a shoddy way **2** to be fabricated (a story, etc.)

itfaḍḍa اتفضّى *vi* (**-a, tifiḍḍi**) to be emptied, to be unloaded

itfaḍḍal اتفضّل *imp* please (offering); **itfaḍḍal** please (offering); **itfaḍḍal agʿud** be seated, have a seat

itfagad اتفقد *vi* (**fugdaan**) to get lost, become lost

itfajjar اتفجّر *vi* (**fajra**) to explode

itfakka اتفكّ *vi* **1** (**fakk, fakakaan**) to be(come) untied, unscrewed; to be(come) loose **2** (**fakk, fakakaan**) to be taken to pieces, taken apart, to be(come) dismantled **3** (**fakk, fakka**) to be set free, to be released (e.g. from prison) **4** (**fakk**) to be relieved (of pain, pressure, etc.) **5** (**fakka**) to be changed (of money)

itfalgas اتفلقس *vi* (**falgasa**) to overdo (in behaviour, dress, eloquence), to talk in an affected way, to talk as if knowing everything on a subject

itfalham اتفلهم *vi* (**falhama**) to put on airs, show off

itfaraḍ اتفرض *vi* (**fariḍ**) **ʿala** to be imposed on

itfaraz اتفرز *vi* (**fariz**) to be sorted out

itfargaʿ اتفرقع *vi* (**firgeeʿ, fargaʿa**) to burst, explode

itfarkash اتفركش *vi* (**farkasha**) to be concluded, finished

itfarraʿ اتفرّع *vi* (**tafarruʿ**) to branch, fork

itfarrag اتفرّق *vi* (**firreeg, furga, tifirrig**) to be(come) separated; to split up

itfarragh اتفرّغ *vi* (**tafriigh**) **1** to be emptied; to be unloaded **2** to make time

itfarraj اتفرّج *vi* (**tafarruj**) **ʿala** to watch, look at

itfarraz اتفرّز *vi* (**firreez, tifirriz**) to be sorted out

itfarshakh اتفرشخ *vi* (**farshakha**) to sit with legs stretched out in front (*considered impolite*)

itfartak اتفرتك *vi* (**firteek**) **1** to fall apart **2** to be dispersed, scattered **3** to be taken to pieces, taken apart, dismantled

itfarzaʿ اتفرزع *vi* (**firzeeʿ, farzaʿa**) to split up

itfasakh إتفسخ *vi* (**faskha, fasakhaan**) **1** to peel, flake off (of the skin) **2** to be cancelled (of a wedding engagement)

itfassaḥ اتفسّح *vi* (**fusḥa, fisseeḥ**) to go on a trip, have an outing

itfaṣal اتفصل *vi* (**faṣla**) to be(come) separated

itfaṣal اتفصل *vi* (**faṣil, faṣalaan**) **1** to be dismissed (from a job) **2** to be dislocated (socket, joint)

itfaṣṣal اتفصّل *vi* **1** (**fiṣṣeel, tafṣiil**) to be cut out (of a pattern for garments) **2** (**tafṣiil**) to be told or explained in detail

itfashshar اتفشّر *vi* (**fishsheer, fashar**) (**be-**) to boast, brag

itfatag اتفتق *vi* (**fatga**) to be ripped open at the seams

itfataḥ اتفتح *vi* (**fatiḥ**) to be opened

itfatal اتفتل *vi* (**fatla**) to be twisted (of a rope)

itfaṭam اتفطم *vi* (**faṭim, fiṭaam**) to be weaned

itfawwaq اتفوّق *vi* (**tafawwuq**) **1** to be excellent, excel **2 ʿala** to surpass

itfawwar اتفوّر *vi* (**foora**) to boil

itfoolaḥ اتفولح *vi* (*slang*) to try to do a clever thing; **ja yatfoolaḥ, jaab dagal-a yatloolaḥ** he came to fix it but he spoiled it instead

itgaaʿad اتقاعد *vi* (*no vn*) to retire

itgaabal اتقابل *vi* (**mugaabala**) **maʿa** to meet

itgaal اتقال *vi* (**gool**) to be said; **itgaal inno** the rumour goes that

itgaasam اتقاسم *vt* (**mugaasama**) to share; **itgaasamat guruush-a maʿaa-ho** she shared her money with him

itgaawal اتقاول *vi* (**mugaawala**) **maʿa** to undertake, contract

itgabaḍ اتقبض *vi* (**gabiḍ**) to be seized, arrested

itgaddam اتقدّم *vi* (**taqaddum**) **1** to advance, progress, make progress **2 ʿala** to precede; to get ahead of

itgafal اتقفل *vi* (**gafla, gafalaan**) **1** to be closed, shut **2** to be turned off, switched off (engine)

itgaffal اتقفّل *vi* (**giffeel**) to be closed

itgaham اتقهم *vi* (**gaham**) to be disappointed

itgala اتقلى *vi* (**-i, gali**) to be fried

itgalab اتقلب *vi* (**galba**) to be turned upside down/inside out

itgalgal اتقلقل *vi* (**gilgeel, galgala**) to be restless, wriggle, wobble

itgallab اتقلّب *vi* (**gilleeb**) to be turned over

itgannaᶜ اتقنع *vi* (**ginnee**ᶜ, **tagnii**ᶜ) to veil o.s. with a **toob**
itgannan اتقنّن *vt* (**ginneen**) to give milk a burnt taste
itgara اتقرى *vi* (**-i, giraaya**) **1** to be read **2** to be studied
itgaraṣ اتقرص *vi* (**garṣa**) **1** to be bitten (by insects) **2** to be pinched
itgarraḥ اتقرّح *vi* (**girreeḥ**) to be vaccinated
itgarraṣ اتقرّص *vt* (**garṣa**) **1** to be bitten (by insects) **2** to be pinched
itgasam اتقسم *vi* (**gasim, gisma**) to be divided
itgassam اتقسّم *vi* (**gisseem, tag-siim**) to be divided
itgashshar اتقشّر *vi* (**gishsheer**) to peel, flake off; to be peeled off
itgaṭaᶜ اتقطع *vi* (**gaṭi**ᶜ) **1** to break off, snap **2** to be cut (off), be disconnected
itgaṭṭaᶜ اتقطّع *vi* (**giṭṭee**ᶜ) to be torn (up, apart), ripped apart
itghaatat اتغاتت *vi* (**ghataata, mughaatata**) to be(come) nasty
itghaaẓ اتغاظ *vi* (**gheeẓ**) (**min**) to be vexed, angered (by)
itghaban اتغبن *vi* (**ghabiina**) **1** to be done an injustice **2** (**min**) to resent; to bear a grudge (against)
itghabbash اتغبّش *vi* (**ghabsha**) to be covered or polluted with dust or mud
itghadda اتغدّى *vi* (**-a, ghada**) to have lunch
itghala اتغلى *vi* (**-i, ghaliya, gha-layaan**) to boil
itghalab اتغلب *vi* (**ghulub**) to lose (e.g. a game)
itghallaf اتغلّف *vi* (**ghilleef, tagh-liif**) to be wrapped
itghasal اتغسل *vi* (**ghasiil**) to be washed, laundered
itghassal اتغسّل *vi* (**ghisseel, ghasiil**) to be washed, laundered
itghashsha اتغشّ *vi* (**ghashsh, ghashashaan**) to be cheated, deceived
itghaṭras اتغطرس *vi* (**ghaṭrasa**) **1** to be(come) arrogant, conceit-ed **2** to be(come) authoritarian, despotic
itghayyar اتغيّر *vi* (**ghiyyeer, ta-ghayyur**) to be changed
itghaza اتغزى *vi* (**-i, taghziya**) to be fed (with food); to be supplied (with money)
ithaabal اتهابل *vi* (**habaala**) to act dumb
ithabbab اتهبّب *vi* (**hibbeeb**) to fan o.s.
ithadam إتهدم *vi* (**hiddeem**) to be destroyed, demolished
ithadda اتهدّ *vi* (**hadd**) **1** to be-come old (of fabric), lose colour **2** to collapse (e.g. a house)
ithaddam إتهدّم *vi* (**hiddeem, tihiddim**) to be destroyed, demolished
ithajja اتهجّى *vi/vt* (**-a, tahjiya**) to spell
ithara اتهرى *vi* (**-i, hari**) to be fed up
ithawas اتهوس *vi* (**hawas**) to be(come) crazy, mad, insane
ithawwar اتهوّر *vi* (**tahawwur**) to act without thinking, behave recklessly
ithayyaj اتهيّج *vt* (**hiyyeej, haya-jaan**) to be(come) excited, to be provoked, be stirred up
ithazza اتهزّ *vi* (**hazz**) to be shaken

itḥaakak اتحاكك *vt* (**muḥaakaka**) to touch each other, brush against each other

itḥaarab اتحارب *vi* (**muḥaaraba**) to fight with one another

itḥaawam اتحاوم *vi* (**ḥuwaama**) to hover (around)

itḥaayal اتحايل *vi* (**taḥaayul**) **ʿala** to cheat, play a trick on

itḥabas اتحبس *vi* (**ḥabsa, ḥabis**) to be detained, to be imprisoned

itḥabba اتحبّ *vi* (**ḥubb**) to be loved

itḥadda اتحدّى *vt* (**-a, taḥaddi**) to defy, challenge

itḥaḍḍar اتحضّر *vi* **1** (**ḥiḍḍeer, tiḥiddir**) to be prepared, ready **2** (**taḥaḍḍur**) to be(come) civilized

itḥaggag اتحقّق *vi* (**taḥgiig**) **1 fi** to investigate **2 min** to verify

itḥajaz اتحجز *vi* (**ḥajiz**) to be detained

itḥajjab اتحجّب *vi* (**ḥijaab**) to veil o.s.

itḥakam اتحكم *vi* (**ḥukum**) **be-** to be sentenced to

itḥakkam اتحكّم *vi* (**taḥakkum**) **fi** to control

itḥakkar اتحكّر *vi* (**ḥikkeer, tiḥikkir**) to sit cross-legged

itḥalaj اتحلج *vi* (**ḥalij**) to be ginned (of cotton)

itḥalla اتحلّ *vi* (**ḥall**) **1** to be(come) loose, untied **2** to be solved, resolved **3** to dissolve

itḥammaḍ اتحمّض *vi* **1** (**ḥimmeeḍ**) to be(come) sour; to be leavened **2** (**taḥmiiḍ**) to be developed (of a film)

itḥammal اتحمّل *vt* (**taḥammul**) to bear, endure; **itḥammal mas'uuliyya** to bear responsibility

itḥammar اتحمّر *vi* (**taḥmiir**) to be fried

itḥammas اتحمّس *vi* (**ḥamaas**) to be(come) enthusiastic, zealous

itḥankash اتحنكش *vi* (**ḥankasha**) to be showy

itḥannan اتحنّن *vi* (**ḥinneen**) to be decorated with henna

itḥarag اتحرق *vi* (**ḥarig**) to be burnt; **ma bitḥarig** fireproof; **itḥarig min** to eat one's heart out with jealousy about or hatred to (a person)

itḥaraj اتحرج *vi* (**ḥaraj**) to be(come) embarrassed

itḥargaṣ اتحرقص *vi* (**ḥirgeeṣ, ḥargaṣa**) to wriggle, squirm

itḥarrak اتحرّك *vi* (**ḥaraka**) to move, stir

itḥarrash اتحرّش *vi* (**taḥriish**) **be-** **1** to provoke, needle; to excite sexually **2** to be(come) sexually excited by

itḥassan اتحسّن *vi* (**taḥassun**) to be(come) better, improve

itḥassas اتحسّس *vt* (**taḥsiis**) to grope, feel one's way • *vi* (**ḥasaasiyya**) (**min**) to be(come) sensitive (about)

itḥaṣṣal اتحصّل *vi* (**ḥiṣṣeel**) **ʿala** **1** to acquire **2** to collect (money)

itḥasha اتحشى *vt* (**-i, ḥashi**) to be stuffed

itḥashshar اتحشّر *vi* (**ḥishsheer, taḥashshur**) to meddle, interfere

itḥaṭṭam اتحطّم *vi* (**ḥiṭṭeem, taḥaṭṭum**) to crash, be destroyed, wrecked

itḥawwal اتحوّل *vi* (**le-**) **1** (**taḥwiil**) to be transferred, shifted **2** (**taḥawwul**) (**le-**) to be transformed; to be changed (into)

itḥayyal اتحيّل *vi* (**ḥiyyeel, taḥayyul**) **ʿala/be-** to pretend to be sick or dead

itḥayyar اتحيّر *vi* (**ḥiira**) to be(come) puzzled, confused, perplexed

itḥazam اتحزم *vi* (**ḥazim**) to be bundled, tied in a bundle

itḥazzam اتحزّم *vi* (**ḥizzeem**) **1** to put on a (safety) belt **2** to be fully armed for a battle

itjaadal اتجادل *vi* (**jadal, mujaadala**) (**maʿa**) to argue, dispute (with)

itjaahal اتجاهل *vt* (**tajaahul**) to pretend not to see s.o. or sth., pass, ignore

itjaawaz اتجاوز *vt* (**tajaawuz**) to exceed, go beyond; to pass, overtake

itjadaʿ اتجدع *vt* (**jadʿa**) to be thrown, thrown away; **jadaʿ-o be-ḥajar** he threw a stone at him

itjaffaf اتجفّف *vi* (**jafaaf**) to dry

itjamaʿ اتجمع *vi* (**jamʿa**) **1** to be collected, gathered, assembled **2** (*arith*) to be added (up) **3** (*slang*) to be typed

itjammaʿ اتجمّع *vi* **1** (**jimmeeʿ, tajmiiʿ**) to be assembled, gathered, collected **2** (**tajmiiʿ**) to be assembled, put together

itjammad اتجمّد *vi* (**jimmeed**) to be frozen

itjannab اتجنّب *vt* (**tajannub**) to avoid

itjannan اتجنّن *vi* (**jinn**) **fi** to be(come) insane, crazy, go mad; to be crazy about

itjaraḥ اتجرح *vi* (**jariḥ**) to be wounded, injured

itjarra' اتجرّأ *vi* (**-a', jur'a**) **ʿala** to dare, to have the courage to

itjarraḥ اتجرّح *vi* (**jirreeḥ**) to be wounded, injured

itjarras اتجرّس *vt* (**jirrees, tijirris, jirsa**) (**min**) to be unable to bear sth. anymore

itjassas اتجسّس *vi* (**tajassus**) (**ʿala**) to spy (on)

itjawwal اتجوّل *vi* (**tajawwul**) to move from place to place, roam, wander

itjazab اتجزب *vi* (**jazba**) **1** to be attracted **2** to be in a state of religious ecstasy

itkaabas اتكابس *vi* (**mukaabasa**) to be squeezed into

itkaatal اتكاتل *vt* (**mukaatala**) to fight with one another

itkabas اتكبس *vi* (**kabsa**) to be filled to the brim

itkabba اتكبّ *vi* (**kabb**) to be poured (out)

itkabbar اتكبّر *vi* (**takabbur**) to be(come) conceited, arrogant, haughty

itkafa اتكفى *vi* (**-i, kafiya**) to have fallen/lie in an abnormal position (of things); to lie on one's stomach

itkaffa اتكفّى *vi* (**-a, kifaaya**) (**be-**) to be satisfied, content (with)

itkaffa اتكفّ *vi* (**kaff**) **1** to be hemmed **2** to be turned up (of sleeves or trouser legs)

itkahrab اتكهرب *vi* (**takahrub**) to be electrified

itkallaf اتكلّف (**taklifa, kulfa**) *vt* to cost

itkallaf اتكلّف *vt* (**takalluf**) **fi** to exaggerate; **itkallaf fi l-maskana** he exaggerated his misery

itkallam اتكلّم *vi* (**kalaam**) (**fi/ʿan**) to speak, talk (about)

itkammal اتكمّل *vi* (**kamaal, kamla**) to be made complete
itkarfas اتكرفس *vi* (**kirfees, karfasa**) **1** to shrink, contract (from cold); to huddle up for warmth **2** to be(come) crumpled, creased
itkarmash اتكرمش *vi* (**kirmeesh, karmasha**) to be(come) crumpled, creased; to be(come) wrinkled (clothes or face)
itkarraᶜ اتكرّع *vi* (**tikirriᶜ**) to belch
itkasaf اتكسف *vi* (**kasif, kasfa**) to be(come) embarrassed
itkasar اتكسر *vi* (**kasir, kisseer**) to break, be broken
itkassar اتكسّر *vi* (**kisseer, takassur**) to break, be broken (in pieces), to be smashed
itkashaḥ اتكشح *vt* (**kashḥa**) to be thrown away (any liquid, e.g. dirty water)
itkatal اتكتل *vi* (**katil**) to be killed
itkatam اتكتم (**katma**) *vi* **1** to be stifled; to be suppressed (of emotions) **2** to be lowered, muffled (of voice); to be dampened (of sound)
itkawa اتكوى *vi* (**kawi, kay, kawayaan**) to be ironed
itkawwam اتكوّم *vi* (**kiwweem**) to be piled up
itkawwan اتكوّن *vi* (**takawwun**) to be formed; to be set up
itkayyaf اتكيّف *vi* **1** (**kiyyeef**) **a le-** to like doing sth., to be glad to be with s.o. **b be-** to indulge o.s. (by smoking or drinking coffee, tea, or alcohol) **2** (**takayyuf**) **ᶜala** to become familiar with, accustomed to, adapted to
itkhabaṭ اتخبط *vi* (**khabṭa**) to be hit; to be knocked; to be nudged
itkhabbaṭ اتخبّط *vi* (**khibbeeṭ, takhbiiṭ**) **1** to knock on (e.g. of door) **2** to mess about, do a bad job; **itkhabbaṭ fi t-tafkiir** to think haphazardly and illogically; **maashi itkhabbaṭ** to reel
itkhadash اتخدش *vi* (**khadish**) to be scratched
itkhaddar اتخدّر *vi* (**khiddeer**) **1** to be drugged, anaesthetized **2** to be doped with cannabis
itkhaffaf اتخفّف *vi* (**khiffeef, takhfiif**) **1** to be(come) lighter (of weight) **2** to be relieved (of pain, pressure, etc.)
itkhalaᶜ اتخلع *vi* (**khulᶜa**) (**min**) to be frightened (by), be startled (by), to shy (at); **itkhalaᶜta khulᶜa** I jumped out of my skin, I had such a fright
itkhalkhal اتخلخل *vi* (**khilkheel, khalkhala**) to work loose (e.g. a tooth, a pole)
itkhallal اتخلّل *vi* (**khilleel, takhallul**) to be pickled
itkhallaṣ اتخلّص *vi* **min 1** (**khilleeṣ**) to be finished with **2** (**khalaas, takhalluṣ**) to get rid of
itkhammar اتخمّر *vi* (**khimmeer**) to ferment; to be leavened
itkhammas اتخمّس *vi* (**khimmees**) to be shared (e.g. a piece of bread, a cigarette, a chair)
itkhanag اتخنق *vi* (**khanig**) to choke, suffocate; to be stifled, strangled
itkharab اتخرب *vi* (**kharaab, kharba**) to be ruined, destroyed
itkharam اتخرم *vi* (**kharig**) to be porous; to have a hole
itkharra اتخرّ *vi* (**kharra**) to be leaked

itkharrab اتخرّب *vi* (**khirreeb, kharaab**) to be destroyed, ruined, wrecked

itkharraf اتخرّف *vi* (**kharfa, khirreef**) **1** to be(come) senile, feeble-minded **2** to talk nonsense

itkharraj اتخرّج *vi* (**takharruj**) to graduate

itkhaṭab اتخطب *vi* (**khuṭuuba**) to be(come) engaged to marry (of girls, women)

itkhaṭṭa اتخطّى *vt* (**-a, tikhiṭṭi**) to overtake, pass; to surpass, go beyond, exceed; **itkhaṭṭa ḥuduud-o** he went too far

itkhawwaf اتخوّف *vi* (**khoof**) (**min**) to fear

itkhayyal اتخيّل *vt* (**takhayyul**) to imagine

itkhazal اتخزل *vi* (**khazil**) to be disappointed

itkhazzan اتخزّن *vi* (**takhziin**) to be stored

itlaʿab اتلعب *vi* (**liʿib**) to be played (e.g. a match)

itlaaga اتلاقى *vi* (**-a, mulaagaa**) **maʿa** to meet

itlabbad اتلبّد *vi* (**libbeed, tilibbid**) to hide o.s.; to be hidden

itladagh اتلدغ *vi* (**ladgha**) to be stung; be bitten (by snakes)

itlaffa اتلفّ *vi* **1** (**laff, lafafaan**) to be turned **2** (**laffa, lafafaan**) to be twisted **3** (**laff, lafafaan**) to twist o.s. **4** (**laffa, lafafaan**) to be wrapped

itlaffat اتلفّت *vi* (**liffeet, lafta**) to turn one's head

itlaffaẓ اتلفّظ *vt* (**liffeeẓ, tiliffiẓ**) **maʿa** to swear at, use bad language

itlaflaf اتلفلف *vi* (**lifleef, laflafa**) **1** to be wound **2** to be wrapped **3** to be(come) tangled

itlaga اتلقى *vi* (**-i, lagayaan**) to be found

itlagha اتلغى *vi* (**-i, laghiya**) to be cancelled, abolished

itlaḥas اتلحس *vi* (**laḥis, laḥasaan**) **1** to be licked **2** (*slang*) to die, perish

itlajjam اتلجّم *vi* (**lijjeem**) **1** to have a bridle put on **2** to be dumbfounded

itlakham اتلخم *vi* (**lakhma**) to be(come) confused

itlakhbaṭ اتلخبط *vi* (**lakhbaṭa, likhbeeṭ**) **1** to be muddled; to be(come) a mess **2** to be(come) confused

itlakhlakh اتلخلخ *vi* (**likhleekh, lakhlakha**) to work loose (e.g. a tooth, a pole)

itlamlam اتلملم *vi* (**lamlama, tilimlim**) to be gathered, collected (of things)

itlamma اتلمّ *vi* (**lamma, lamamaan**) to be gathered, collected

itlaṣag اتلصق *vi* (**laṣga, laṣagaan**) to stick, be stuck

itlaṣṣag اتلصّق *vi* (**liṣṣeeg, tiliṣṣig**) to be glued, stuck

itlaṭaʿ اتلطع *vi* (**laṭʿa**) to have to wait for s.o. for a long time

itlaṭṭakh اتلطّخ *vi* (**liṭṭeekh**) to be(come) stained, blotted

itlawa اتلوى *vi* (**-i, lawiya**) **1** to be bent (of metal) **2** to warp

itlawlaw اتلولو *vi* (**liwleew, lawlawa**) **1** to curl **2** to coil **3** to wriggle **4** to prevaricate, twist and turn

itlawwa اتلوّى *vi* (**-a, liwweey**) to squirm

itlawwaʿ اتلوّع *vi* (**liwwee**ʿ) to be frightened
itlawwam اتلوّم *vi* (**loom, liwweem**) to be blamed; to be reproached
itlayyan اتليّن *vi* (**liyyeen**) **1** to be(come) moist; to be moistened **2** to be(come) supple
itlazag اتلزق *vi* (**lazga, lazagaan**) to stick, to be glued, stuck
itlazzag اتلزّق *vi* (**lizzeeg, tilizzig**) to stick, to be glued, stuck
itloolaḥ اتلولح *vi* (**loolaaḥ**) to swing
itmaaraḍ اتمارض *vi* (**tamaaruḍ**) to malinger
itmaasak اتماسك *vi* (**tamaasuk**) to hold hands
itmaaṭal اتماطل *vi* (**tamaaṭul, mumaaṭala**) to procrastinate; to buy time
itmaayaḥ اتمايح *vi* (**mayaḥaan**) to sway
itmaayal اتمايل *vi* (**mayalaan, tamaayul**) **1** to sway **2** to wobble (in walking)
itmadda اتمدّ *vi* **1** (**middeed**) to be extended **2** (**madda**) to lie (down)
itmaddad اتمدّد *vi* **1** (**middeed, tamdiid**) to be prolonged, extended **2** (**middeed**) to lie (down)
itmaddan اتمدّن *vi* (**tamaddun**) to be(come) civilized
itmaḍmaḍ اتمضمض *vi* (**maḍmaḍa**) to rinse the mouth
itmaghaṣ اتمغص *vi* (**maghaṣa**) (**min**) **1** to be vexed (by); to be treated unjustly (by) **2** to resent; to bear a grudge (against)
itmaghghaṣ اتمغّص *vi* (**mighgheeṣ, maghaṣa**) (**min**) **1** to be vexed (by); to be treated unjustly (by) **2** to resent; to bear a grudge (against)
itmaḥa اتمحى *vi* (**-i, maḥi**) to be obliterated
itmaḥḥan اتمحّن *vi* (**miḥḥeen**) to be(come) bewildered, perplexed, be at a loss
itmakan اتمكن *vi* (**makna**) (**min**) to be in a tight corner, be hard pressed (by)
itmakkan اتمكّن *vi* (**tamkiin**) **min** **1** to be very good at sth. **2** to be strong enough for, be a match for
itmakhkhaṭ اتمخّط *vi* (**mikhkheeṭ**) to blow one's nose
itmala اتملى *vi* (**-i, mali, malayaan**) to be filled
itmalakh اتملخ *vi* (**malakhaan**) **1** to be dislocated **2** to be sprained
itmalaṣ اتملص *vi* (**malṣa**) **min** **1** to slip out (of one's grip) **2** to slip/slide down, sag
itmallaq اتملّق *vt* (**tamalluq**) to ingratiate o.s. with, flatter in order to win a favour
itmallaṣ اتملّص *vi* (**milleeṣ**) **min** to break (a promise), to fail to keep (an appointment)
itmalmal اماLمل *vi* (**milmeel, malmala**) to wriggle (fidget)
itmanna اتمنّى *vi* (**-a, muna, tamanni**) to hope, wish
itmarmar اتمرمر *vi* (**marmara**) to play or roll in the sand
itmarrad اتمرّد *vi* (**tamarrud**) to rebel
itmarragh اتمرّغ *vi* (**mirreegh, margha**) **be-/fi** to cover o.s. (with dust or ashes, as an expression of grief)

itmarran اتمرّن *vi* (**tamriin**) to practise, exercise

itmarṣaᶜ اتمرصع *vi* (**mirṣeeᶜ, marṣaᶜa**) to swing one's hips

itmasaḥ اتمسح *vi* (**masiḥ, masaḥaan**) to be wiped out, erased, rubbed out

itmasak اتمسك *vi* (**maska**) **1** to be seized, arrested **2** to be taken hold of

itmassaḥ اتمسّح *vt* (**misseeḥ**) to oil (one's skin)

itmassak اتمسّك *vi* (**tamassuk**) (**be-**) to be firmly connected or attached (to)

itmasha اتمشى *vi* (**-a, mashi, mashiya**) to walk, stroll

itmattaᶜ اتمتّع *vi* (**tamattuᶜ**) to enjoy

itmaṭṭa اتمطّ *vi* **1** (**maṭṭ**) to stretch o.s. **2** (**miṭṭeeṭ**) to be stretched

itmaṭṭag اتمطّق *vi* (**miṭṭeeg**) to smack one's lips

itmaṭṭar اتمطّر *vi* (**maṭara**) **1** to rain **2** to shelter from the rain

itmayyaz اتميّز *vi* (**tamayyuz**) **be-** to be distinguished by, be characterized by

itnaᶜnash اتنعنش (**naᶜnasha**) *vi* to refresh o.s.

itnaasab اتناسب *vi* (**nasab**) **maᶜa** to be appropriate, suit; to match

itnaawal اتناول *vt* (**munaawala**) to take

itnaazal اتنازل *vi* (**tanaazul**) (**min/ ᶜan**) to step down, renounce (one's rights), yield

itnabba اتنبّا *vt* (**-a, tanabbu**) to predict, forecast

itnafakh اتنفخ *vi* (**nafikh**) to be inflated, filled with air (e.g. a tyre)

itnaffas اتنفّس *vi* (**tanaffus**) to breathe

itnagal اتنقل *vi* (**nagil**) to be transferred

itnaggaṭ اتنقّط (**niggeeṭ**) *vi* to trickle, drip • *vt* to add dots (to letters)

itnahab اتنهب *vi* (**nahib, nahba**) to be robbed, plundered

itnahhad اتنهّد *vi* (**nihheed, tanhiid**) to sigh

itnaḥas اتنحس *vi* (**naḥsa**) to be brought bad luck

itnajad اتنجد *vi* (**najda**) to be rescued, saved

itnajjad اتنجّد *vi* (**tanjiid, tinijjid**) **1** to be upholstered **2** to be stuffed (e.g. mattresses)

itnakab اتنكب *vi* (**nakba**) to be overcome by a disaster

itnakkar اتنكّر *vi* **1** (**nikkeer**) **le-** to ignore a person **2** (**tanakkur**) to disguise o.s., to be incognito

itnaqqab اتنقّب *vi* (**niqaab**) to put on a veil covering the face except the eyes

itnarfaz اتنرفز *vi* (**narfaza**) to be(come) bad-tempered, angry; **min** to be angered, annoyed, irritated by

itnashar اتنشر *vi* (**nashir**) **1** to be spread; to be hung or spread out (of clothes to dry) **2** to be published

itnashar اتنشر *vi* (**nashir**) to be sawn

itnashshag اتنشّق *vi* (**nishsheeg**) to inhale

itnawwaᶜ اتنوّع *vi* (**tanawwuᶜ**) to vary

itnawwar اتنوّر *vi* (**tanwiir**) **1** to be illuminated **2** to be knowledgeable, enlightened

itnazza اتنزّ (**naziiz**) *vt* to cause to ooze, seep, trickle

itnazzal اتنزّل *vi* (**nizzeel**) to be brought down; to be unloaded

itnaẓẓam إتنظّم *vi* (**niẓẓeem, tanẓiim**) to be(come) organized, systematized, to be arranged, put in order

itneen اتنين *num* two; **al-itneen** both

itraahan اتراهن *vi* (**muraahana, rihaan**) to bet

itraajaʿ اتراجع *vi* (**taraajuʿ**) (**min**) to go back (e.g. on a decision)

itraakam اتراكم *vi* (**taraakum**) to accumulate

itrabak اتربك *vi* (**rabka**) **1** to be(come) a mess, to be muddled **2** to be(come) confused

itrabba اتربّى *vi* (**-a, tarbiya**) to be brought up

itrabbaʿ اتربّع *vi* (**ribbeeʿ**) to sit cross-legged

itrabbash اتربّش *vi* (**rabsha**) to be(come) uneasy, troubled, confused

itraddad اتردّد *vi* (**taraddud**) to hesitate, to be reluctant

itraḍraḍ اترضرض *vi* (**riḍreeḍ, raḍraḍa**) to be bruised

itrafad اترفد *vi* (**rafid**) to be fired, dismissed (from office)

itragga اترقّى *vi* (**-a, targiya**) to be promoted (in rank, grade)

itrajja اترجّا *vt* (**-a, raja, tarjiya**) to implore, beseech, beg

itrajja اترجّ *vi* (**rajj**) to be shaken (liquid)

itrakab اتركب *vi* (**rukuub**) to be mounted

itrakkab اتركّب *vi* (**tarkiib**) to be assembled, put together

itrakkaz اتركّز *vi* **1** (**rikkeez, tarkiiz**) to be firmly fixed in the ground (e.g. a pole) **2** (**rikkeez, tarkiiz, tirikkiz**) **ʿala** to lean (on) **3** (**tarkiiz**) to be concentrated (e.g. juice, alcohol, perfume)

itrakha اترخى *vi* (**-i, rakhiya**) to be(come) loose

itrama اترمى *vi* (**-i, ramiya**) to be thrown (away)

itrassal اترسّل *vi* (**risseel**) to be sent

itraṣṣa اترصّ *vt* (**raṣṣ, raṣṣa**) to be stacked; put in order, arranged (of items)

itrashshaḥ اترشّح *vi* (**tarashshuḥ**) to be nominated

itrattab اترتّب *vt* (**tartiib**) to be arranged, to be put in order

itraṭṭab اترطّب *vt* (**tarṭiib**) to be(come) damp; to be dampened

itrawwa اتروّى *vi* (**-a, riwweey**) to be(come) calm

itrayyaḍ اتريّض *vi* (**riyaaḍa**) to practise sports

itrayyaḥ اتريّح *vi* (**riiḥa**) to perfume o.s.

itsaaʿad اتساعد *vi* (**musaaʿada**) to help one another

itsaabag إتسابق *vi* (**sabag, musaabaga**) to race

itsaafah اتسافه *vi* (**safaaha**) to behave immorally, be insolent

itsaalam اتسالم *vi* (**musaalama**) to greet each other

itsaawa اتساوى *vi* (**-a, musaawaa**) to be(come) equal

itsa'al اتسأل *vi* (**su'aal**) to be asked (question)

itsadda اتسدّ *vi* **1** (**sadd, insidaad**) to be closed; to be blocked; **niyyat-i itsaddat** I lost my appetite **2** (**sadda, siddeey**) **le-,** (**min**) to take revenge (on), avenge; **itsadda le-akhuu-ho min al-kaatil** he avenged his brother's death on the murderer; **itsadda le-sharaf-o** he defended his honour

itsaddad اتسدّد *vi* (**sadaad**) to be paid (of debt)

itsajan اتسجن *vi* (**sajna, sijin**) to be imprisoned

itsajjal اتسجّل *vi* (**tasjiil**) **1** to be noted down to be registered, recorded (also of music, etc.) **2** to be enrolled

itsakkat اتسكّت *vt* (**sikkeet**) to be silenced, pacified

itsakhkhan اتسخّن *vi* (**sikhkheen, taskhiin**) to be warmed, heated

itsalab اتسلب *vi* (**salba**) to be stolen (e.g. of livestock)

itsalla اتسلّى *vi* (**-a, tasliya**) to have a good time, amuse o.s.

itsallaf اتسلّف *vt* (**tasliif**) to borrow

itsallal اتسلّل *vi* (**tasallul**) **1** to trespass secretly, infiltrate **2** to make an offside move (in football)

itsama^c اتسمع *vi* (**sama^c**) to be heard

itsammam اتسمّم *vi* (**tasammum**) to be poisoned

itsarag اتسرق *vi* (**sarga**) (**min**) to be stolen (from); to be robbed; **itsarag minn-i kitaab-i** my book has been stolen

itsarra^c اتسرّع *vi* (**sur^ca**) to hurry; to do sth. in haste, dash off, rush into

itsarrab اتسرّب *vi* (**tasarrub**) **1** to leak, seep **2** to be smuggled **3** to sneak away; **itsarrab min-um** he gave them the slip

itsattar اتستّر *vi* (**tasattur**) **^cala** to shield s.o. (e.g. from scandal)

itsaṭal اتسطل *vi* (**saṭla, saṭalaan**) to be(come) high on cannabis

itsawwa اتسوّى *vi* (**-a, siwweey, suwaa**) to be made (e.g. of tea, food)

itsawwag اتسوّق *vi* (**siwweeg**) to shop, go shopping

itsawwak اتسوّك *vi* (**siwweek, taswiik**) to brush one's teeth

itsayṭar اتسيطر *vi* (**sayṭara**) **^cala** to dominate, control

itṣa^clak اتصعلك *vi* (**ṣa^claka**) to behave immorally

itṣaadam اتصادم *vi* (**ma^ca**) **1** (**muṣaadama**) to bump, collide, crash into **2** (**ṣidaam, muṣaadama**) to clash

itṣaalaḥ اتصالح *vi* (**muṣaalaḥa**) to be(come) reconciled

itṣabba اتصبّ *vi* (**ṣabb**) to be poured (out)

itṣadam اتصدم *vi* (**ṣadma**) (**fi**) to be shocked (by)

itṣadda اتصدّى *vi* (**-a, ṣiddeey, ṣadiya**) to rust, oxidize

itṣaddag اتصدّق *vi* **1** (**ṣiddeeg**) to be believed **2** (**taṣdiig**) to be approved, endorsed **3** (**taṣaddug**) (**^cala**) to give alms (to)

itṣaga^c اتصقع *vi* (**ṣag^ca**) **1** to be struck on the head **2** to be(come) high on cannabis

itṣaḥḥaḥ اتصحّح *vi* (**taṣḥiiḥ**) to be corrected

itṣallaḥ إتصلّح *vi* (**ṣilleeḥ, taṣliiḥ**) to be repaired; to be improved

itṣammagh اتصمّغ *vi* (**ṣimmeegh, ṣamugh**) to be glued

itṣana^c اتصنع *vi* (**ṣinaa^ca**) to be made, manufactured

itṣanna^c اتصنّع *vt* (**taṣannu^c**) to simulate

itṣannat اتصنّت *vi* (**taṣannut**) to eavesdrop; to bug

itṣarraf اتصرّف *vi* (**taṣarruf**) **1** to act, behave **2 fi** (things), **maʿa** (persons) to cope, manage

itṣawwar اتصوّر *vi* **1** (**taṣwiir**) to be photographed **2** (**taṣawwur**) to imagine

itshaʿbaṭ إتشعبط *vi* (**shiʿbeeṭ, shaʿbaṭa**) **fi** to climb (e.g. a tree)

itshaa'am اتشاءم *vi* (**mushaa'ama**) **1 be-** to perceive sth. as a bad omen **2** to be(come) pessimistic

itshaakal اتشاكل *vt* (**shakal**) to quarrel with one another

itshaal اتشال *vi* (**sheel, sheela**) to be taken away, removed

itshaarak اتشارك (**mushaaraka**) *vi* **1 fi** to share **2 maʿa** to collaborate, enter into partnership with one another • *vt* to share

itshaayal اتشايل *vt* (**sheela, shayalaan**) to carry together

itshabak اتشبك *vi* (**shabik**) to quarrel

itshabbaʿ اتشبّع *vi* (**tashabbuʿ**) to be(come) saturated

itshabbak اتشبّك *vi* (**shibbeek**) to be(come) complicated

itshabbar اتشبّر *vi* (**shibbeer, tishibbir**) to produce shoddy work, work on sth. without being skilled

itshadda اتشدّ *vi* (**shadda**) to be tightened; to be pulled; to be twisted (of a muscle)

itshagga اتشقّ *vi* (**shagg, shagga**) to crack, be split

itshaglab اتشقلب *vi* (**shigleeb, shaglaba, shaglabaan**) **1** to be overturned **2** to be turned upside down **ḥaal-o itshaglab** he became upset

itshaghal اتشغل *vi* (**shaghala**) (**be-**) to be busy (with), occupied (by)

itshaghghal اتشغّل *vi* (**shaghla**) to be(come) occupied (of a house)

itshahhag اتشهّق *vi* (**shihheeg**) to yawn

itshaḥan شحن *vi* (**shaḥin, shaḥna**) to be loaded; to be charged (with electricity)

itshaḥaṭ اتشحط *vi* (**shaḥṭa**) **1** to run aground (of ships) **2 fi** to get stuck (in traffic)

itshajjaʿ اتشجّع *vi* (**tashajjuʿ**) to be encouraged

itshakkal اتشكّل *vi* (**shikkeel**) to be formed

itshakkar اتشكّر *vi* (**shikkeer**) **le-** to express thanks to

itshalla اتشلّ *vi* (**shalal**) to be(come) paralysed

itshalwaṭ اتشلوط *vt* (**shalwaṭa**) to be(come) singed

itshangal إتشنقل *vi* (**shingeel, shangala**) to fall flat on one's back

itshankal اتشنكل *vi* (**shinkeel, shankala**) (**fi**) to trip (over)

itshannaj اتشنّج *vi* (**tashannuj**) to have convulsions

itsharag اتشرق *vi* (**sharagaan**) to swallow the wrong way, choke

itsharra اتشرّ *vi* (**sharr**) (*slang*) to have to wait a long time for a friend or a lover to appear

itsharraf اتشرّف *vi* (**sharaf**) to be honoured

itsharakh اتشرخ *vi* (**sharkha**) to crack, be cracked

itsharraṭ إتشرّط *vi* (**sharṭ**) to be stipulated; to be imposed as a condition

itsharraṭ إتشرّط *vi* (**shirreeṭ, tasharruṭ**) to be torn (up, apart)

itshattat اتشتّت *vi* (**shitteet, tashattut**) to be scattered

itshaṭab اتشطب *vi* (**shaṭib**) to be crossed out, erased, deleted; **raas-i itshaṭab** my mind went blank

itshaṭaf اتشطف *vi* (**shaṭfa**) **1** to wash one's face, hands and feet (without soap) **2** to be rinsed (of laundry) **3** to be scooped up (of water)

itshaṭṭab اتشطّب *vi* (**tashṭiib**) to be finished (of plastering, painting, etc. of a building)

itshaṭṭaf اتشطّف *vi* (**shiṭṭeef**) **1** to wash one's own face, hands and feet (without soap) **2** to be rinsed (of laundry)

itshawwash اتشوّش (**shiwweesh**) *vi* to suffer from interference, to be blurred

itshayṭan اتشيطن *vi* (**shayṭana**) to be(come) naughty, mischievous

itta'ta' اتّعتع *vi* (**ta'ta'a**) to speak unclearly

ittaakal اتّآكل *vi* (**ikkeel**) to be eaten

ittafag اتّفق *vi* (**ittifaag**) (**'ala**) to agree, come to an agreement (on)

ittaham اتّهم *vt* (**ittihaam, tuhma**) (**be-**) to accuse (of)

ittaḥad اتّحد *vi* (**ittiḥaad**) to unite

ittaka اتّكى *vi* (**-i, ittika, takiya**) **'ala** to lean on

ittakal اتّكل *vi* (**ittikaal**) **'ala** **1** to lean on/against **2; ittakal 'ala llaah** to seek support from God, depend on God; **nattakil 'ala llaah** let's go

ittallaj اتّلّج *vi* (**tilleej**) to be frozen

ittaltal اتّلتل *vi* (**taltala**) to be delayed unnecessarily

ittamma اتّمّ *vi* (**tamm, tamamaan**) to be finished, completed

ittana اتّنى *vi* (**-i, taniya**) to be bent (of metal)

ittarbas اتّربس *vi* (**tirbees**) to be bolted

ittarga' اتّرقع *vi* (**tirgee', targa'a**) to burst open

ittarra' اتّرّع *vi* (**titirri', tirree'**) to belch

ittartaḥ اتّرتح *vi* (**tirteeḥ, tartaḥa**) to stagger

ittaṣal اتّصل *vi* (**ittiṣaal**) **be-** to contact; to telephone

ittifaag إتّفاق *n* (*pl* **-aat**) agreement, accord; arrangement

ittifaagiyya إتّفاقيّة *n* agreement, accord

ittihaam إتّهام *n* (*pl* **-aat**) accusation

ittiḥaad إتّحاد *n* (*pl* **-aat**) union, association

ittijaah إتّجاه *n* (*pl* **-aat**) direction **ittijaah waaḥid** one way (traffic)

ittiṣaal إتّصال *n* (*pl* **-aat**) connection, link, contact; **'ala ittiṣaal be-** in contact with

itwaa'ad اتواعد *vi* (**muwaa'ada**) to promise to meet

itwaaḍa' اتواضع *vi* (**tawaaḍu'**) to be humble

itwaasa اتواسى *vi* (**-i, muwaasaa**) to be(come) equal, even

itwaaṣal اتواصل *vi* (**muwaaṣala, tawaaṣul**) **ma'a** to meet, communicate

itwaazan اتوازن *vi* (**tawaazun**) to balance

itwaḍḍa اتوضّى *vi* (**-a, wiḍḍeey, waḍu**) (*Isl*) to perform the ritual ablution

itwaḍḍab اتوضّب *vt* (**wiḍḍeeb, tawḍiib**) to be arranged; to be put in order
itwaḍḍaḥ وضّح *vi* (**wiḍḍeeḥ, waḍḥa**) to be(come) clear, to be explained
itwaffa اتوفّى *vi* (**-a, wafa, wafaat**) to pass away, die
itwaffar اتوفّر *vi* (**wafra**) to be abundant
itwaggaʿ اتوقّع *vt* (**tawaggu**ʿ) to expect
itwahhaṭ اتوهّط *vi* (**wihheeṭ**) to prosper
itwaḥam اتوحم *vi* (**waḥam**) to crave for certain food (during pregnancy)
itwajjah اتوجّه *vi* (**wijjeeh**) to go in a direction
itwalad اتولد *vi* (**miilaad, wilaada**) to be born
itwallaʿ اتولّع *vi* (**wal**ʿ**a, willee**ʿ) to be ignited; to be switched on, turned on (light)
itwallaf اتولّف *vi* (**willeef, wilfa**) **1** to be(come) tame, domesticated **2** ʿ**ala/be-** to be(come) familiar with, accustomed to, adapted to
itwannas اتونّس *vi* (**wanasa**) to chat
itwarram اتورّم *vi* (**tawarrum**) to swell up
itwarraṭ اتورّط *vi* (**warṭa, wirreeṭ**) to be(come) entangled, embroiled
itwassaʿ اتوسّع *vi* (**wissee**ʿ, **tawsii**ʿ) to be widened, broadened; to be extended, expanded
itwassakh اتوسّخ *vi* (**wisseekh**) to be(come) dirty, filthy
itwassaṭ اتوسّط *vi* (**tawassuṭ**) to mediate
itwaṣṣal اتوصّل *vi* **le- 1** (**waṣla**) to reach (e.g. of water, electricity); **al-mooya itwaṣṣalat lee-na** we gave been connected to the water system **2** (**tawaṣṣul**) to reach (the truth); **itwaṣṣalna le-l-ḥagiiga** we reached the truth
itwattar اتوتّر *vi* (**tawattur**) to be(come) tense, be(come) nervous
itwazzaʿ اتوزّع *vi* (**tawzii**ʿ) to be distributed
itwaẓẓaf اتوظّف *vi* (**tawẓiif**) to be employed
ityaggan اتيقّن *vi* (**tayaggun**) **be-** to verify
ityassar اتيسّر *vi* (**tayassur**) to be made easy, facilitated
itzaal اتزال *vi* (**zeela, izaala**) to be removed
itzagal اتزقل *vt* (**zagla**) to be thrown (away)
itzaḥḥa اتزحّ *vi* (**zaḥḥa**) to be moved, shoved, pushed aside
itzaḥzaḥ إتزحزح *vi* (**zaḥzaḥa, ziḥzeeḥ**) to be unsteady, unstable; to shift (e.g. of cargo)
itzakkar اتزكّر *vt* (**tazakkur**) to remember
itzalag اتزلق *vi* (**zalig, zalga**) to slide, slip, glide
itzammar اتزمّر *vi* (**tazammur**) **fi** to lose one's temper with
itzanag اتزنق *vi* (**zanig**) to be caught short; to get into a tight spot
itzaraʿ اتزرع *vi* (**zari**ʿ, **ziraa**ʿ**a**) to be sown, be cultivated
itzarra اتزرّ *vi* (**zarra**) to be trapped; to have no way out
itzarraʿ اتزرّع *vt* (**zirrii**ʿ**a**) to sprout
itzawwaj اتزوّج *vi* (**zawaaj**) to marry
itzawwar اتزوّر *vt* (**tazwiir**) to be forged, counterfeit

itzayyaf اتزيّف *vt* (**tazyiif**) to be forged, counterfeit

itzayyan اتزيّن *vi* **1** (**ziyaana**) to be shaved and have a haircut (men) **2** (**ziina, tazayyun**) to have one's hair done and makeup applied (women)

itẓaahar اتظاهر *vi* (**taẓaahur**) **be-** to pretend, simulate

itẓalam اتظلم *vi* (**ẓulum**) to be treated unjustly

itẓallam اتظلّم *vi* (**taẓallum**) **min** to raise a complaint against

iṭaar إطار *n* (*pl* **-aat**) frame (e.g. of picture, text etc. but not of spectacles)

iṭlaaq إطلاق *n* release (e.g. from prison), dispatch; **iṭlaaq an-naar** shooting; **ʿala l-iṭlaaq** (*with neg part*) absolutely not, not at all

iṭlaaqan إطلاقا *adv* absolutely (not), (not) at all

iṭnaashar اطناشر *num* twelve

iṭṭaʿʿam اطّعّم *vi* (**taṭʿiim**) to be vaccinated

iṭṭaʿan اطّعن *vi* (**ṭaʿin**) to be stabbed

iṭṭabakh اطّبخ *vi* (**ṭabikh**) to be cooked

iṭṭafa اطّفى *vi* (**-i, ṭafiya**) to be extinguished; to be switched off, turned off/out (light, gas)

iṭṭaffal اطّفّل *vi* (**taṭafful**) (**ʿala**) to intrude

iṭṭamman اطّمّن *vi* (**iṭmi'naan**) (**ʿala**) to be reassured (about), have one's mind set at rest (about); **kunta daayir aṭṭammin ʿalee-k** I wanted to make sure you are doing well

iṭṭarad اطّرد *vi* (**ṭarid**) to be sent away; to be sacked, fired, dismissed

iṭṭarshag اطّرشق *vi* (**ṭirsheeg, ṭarshaga**) to burst open

iṭṭawwaʿ اطّوّع *vi* (**taṭawwuʿ**) to volunteer

iṭṭawwal اطّوّل *vi* (**ṭiwweel**) to be lengthened

iṭṭawwar اطّوّر *vi* (**taṭawwur**) to develop

iṭṭooṭaḥ اطّوطح *vi* (**ṭooṭeeḥ**) to swing, dangle

izʿaaj إزعاج *n* disturbance, annoyance

iza إزا *conj* if; **iza amkan** if possible

izaaʿa إزاعة *n* **1** broadcast **2** broadcasting station; **maḥaṭṭat izaaʿa** broadcasting station

izdaḥam ازدحم *vi* (**izdihaam**) to be(come) crowded

izin إزن *n* (*pl* **uzuunaat**) permission, licence; **b-izni Allah** with God's permission; **ʿan izn-ak** excuse me!; **izin istiiraad** import licence

izmiil إزميل *n* (*pl* **azaamiil**) chisel (stone)

izzakkar ازّكّر *vt* (**tazakkur**) to remember

izzawwaj ازّوّج *vi* (**zawaaj**) to marry

izzay إزي *interrog* how; **izzayy-ak** how are you?

j – ج

ja جا *vi* (**-i, jayya**) **1** to come; **jeytan jiit** welcome, it's good that you came; **yaji s-saaʿa** about an hour **2** to arrive

jaʿʿar جعّر *vi* (**jiʿʿeer**) to wail (of men)

jaʿar جعر *vi* (**u, jaʿir**) **1** to low (of cattle) **2** to wail (of men)

jaʿba جعبة *n* buttock
jaʿiiṣ جعيص *adj* (*pl* **-iin, juʿaṣa**) expert
jaʿjaʿ جعجع *vi* (**jiʿjeeʿ, jaʿjaʿa**) to be all talk and no action
jaaʿ جاع *vi* (**u, juuʿ**) to be(come) hungry
jaab جاب *vt* **1** (**i, jeeba, jayabaan**) (**maʿa**) to bring, get, fetch **2** (**i, jeeba**) to yield, produce **3** (**i, jeeba**) to score (a goal)
jaabra جابرة *n* ground; **masak aj-jaabra** to sit on the ground
jaadal جادل (**jidaal**) *vi* (**maʿa**) to argue (with), dispute (with); **ma tajaadil maʿaa-y** don't argue with me • *vt* to argue with, dispute with; **ma tajaadil-ni** don't argue with me
jaadd جاد *adj* serious (no fun)
jaafa جافى *vt* (**-i, mujaafa, jafa**) to refrain from visiting family or friends
jaaff جاف *adj* **1** dry; arid **2** rude
jaafi جافي *adj* (*pl* **jaafiin**) neglecting family ties or friendships
jaahil جاهل *adj* (*pl* **-iin, juhala**) ignorant • *n* (*pl* **juhhaal**) young child, infant
jaahiliyya جاهليّة *adj* state of ignorance in pre-Islamic times
jaahiz جاهز *adj* ready
jaahiziyya جاهزيّة *n* readiness
jaaḥid جاحد *adj* ungrateful
jaalid جالد *adj* (*slang*) playing truant; **jaalid ramaḍaan** avoiding fasting during Ramadan
jaaluun جالون *n* (*pl* **jawaaliin**) gallon
jaamʿa جامعة *n* university
jaamal جامل *vt* (**mujaamala**) to treat with courtesy; **bijaamil-ak saay** he's only flattering you (with an empty courtesy)
jaamiʿ جامع *n* (*pl* **jawaamiʿ**) mosque
jaamid جامد *adj* **1** solid, strong **2** stiff, hard, inflexible • *adv* solidly, strongly
jaamuus جاموس *n* (*pl* **jawaamiis**) buffalo
jaani جاني *adj* (*pl* **junaat**) guilty of a crime
jaanib جانب *n* (*pl* **jawaanib, aj-naab**) side
jaann جان *n/n pl* helpful or harmful spirit(s), demon(s)
jaar جار *n* (*pl* **jeeraan**) neighbour
jaari جاري *adj* current
jaasir جاسر *adj* brave
jaasuus جاسوس *n* (*pl* **jawaasiis**) spy
jaaṭ جاط *vt* (**u, jooṭa**) **1** to muddle, make a mess of **2** to make a din; to make a fuss
jaawab جاوب *vi* (**ijaaba, jawaab**) (**ʿala**) to answer, reply (to)
jaay جاي *adj* coming, next; **be-jaay** over here, this side
jaayiz جايز *adv* maybe, perhaps
jaayza جايزة *n* (*pl* **jawaayiz**) prize, award
jaaz جاز *n* jazz
jaaz جاز *n* refined petrol; **jaaz abyaḍ** paraffin, kerosene; **jaaz aswad** diesel (fuel)
jaaza جازى *vt* (**-i, mujaazaa**) **1** to reward, recompense; **jaazaa-k Allah kheer** may God reward you, thank you **2** to punish
jaazaf جازف *vi* (**mujaazafa**) **1** to be adventurous; to be heedless, reckless **2** (*slang*) to search for or do an irregular job

jaazib جاذب *adj* attractive
jaazibiyya جاذبيّة *n* attraction, gravity
jabaan جبان *n* (*pl* **-iin, jubana**) coward
jabad جبد *vt* (**i, jabid**) to pull
jabakhaana جبخانة *n* ammunition
jabal جبل *n* (*pl* **jibaal**) mountain, hill
jabana جبنة *n* **1** coffee pot (for serving coffee) **2** coffee (drink)
jabar جبر *vt* (**i, jabur**) **1** (**ᶜala**) to force (to), compel (to) **2** to set bones; to splint
jabbaada جبّادة *n* fishing rod
jabbaar جبّار *adj* **1** strong **2** ruthless **3** stingy, mean • *n* (*Isl*) Omnipotent One (epithet of God)
jabbad جبّد *vt* (**jibbeed**) to pull
jabbar جبّر *vt* (**jibbeer**) to set bones; to splint
jabbas جبّس *vt* (**jibbees**) to plaster with gypsum
jabda جبدة *n* long distance
jabha جبهة *n* **1** forehead **2** (*mil/pol*) front
jabiira جبيرة *n* (*pl* **jabaayir**) splint
jabr جبر *n* **aj-jabr** algebra
jabur جبر *n* force, compulsion; **be-j-jabur** by force
jadaᶜ جدع *n* (*pl* **jidᶜaan**) a brave, upright and noble person
jadaᶜ جدع *vt* (**a, jadiᶜ**) to throw (at), throw away; **jadaᶜ-o** he threw it away; **jadaᶜ-o be-ḥajar** he threw a stone at him
jadaara جدارة *n* skill, proficiency, craftsmanship
jadal جدل *n* dispute, controversy
jadari جدري *n* smallpox; **jadari kaazib** chickenpox
jadd جد *n* seriousness (no fun); **jadd jadd** seriously; **be-j-jadd** seriously; really; **be-j-jadd** really?; is that so? • *adv* really
jaddaaᶜa جدّاعة *n* cushion
jaddad جدّد *vt* (**tajdiid**) to renew
jaddi جدّي *n* **aj-jaddi** pole star
jadiid جديد *adj* (*pl* **judaad**) new; **jadiid lanj** brand new
jadiir جدير *adj* (*pl* **judara**) skilful, proficient
jadla جدلة *n* (**jadaayil**) lock of hair
jadwal جدول *n* (*pl* **jadaawil**) **1** schedule, timetable **2** chart, list, table **3** small irrigation channel; drain
jaḍḍa جضّ *vi* (**i, jaḍḍ, jaḍḍa**) to be noisy, make a din, hubbub, commotion
jaḍḍa جضّة *n* loud noise, din
jaḍḍam جضّم *n* (**jiḍḍeem**) to pinch s.o.'s cheek (as punishment)
jafa جفا *n* social negligence, coldness
jafaaf جفاف *n* drought
jafal جفل *vi* (**i, jafla, jafalaan**) **1 min** to shy at **2** to bolt, run away
jaffa جفّ *vi* (**i, jaffa**) to become dry
jaffaf جفّف *vt* (**jiffeef**) to dry sth.
jaggam جقّم *vt* (**jiggeem**) to take small bites (from bread)
jagjag جقجق *vi* (**jigjeeg, jagjaga**) to bubble (of stew or porridge in pot, referred to as an indication that it has thickened enough and is done); **al-ḥalla bitjagjag** the pot is bubbling
jaglab جقلب *vi* (**jigleeb, jaglaba**) to gallop about, run and prance about
jagham جغم *vi* (**u, jaghim**) to gulp
jaghmas جغمس *vt* (**jighmees, jaghmasa**) to make a mess of • *vi* **jaghmas fi l-kalaam** to talk off the point

jahaama جهامة *adj invar* huge
jahal جهل *vi* (**a, jahl**) **be-** to be ignorant of
jahannam جهنّم *n* hell
jahannamiyya جهنّميّة *n* bougainvillea
jahar جهر *vt* (**a, jahra**) to dazzle
jahawi جهوي *adj* provincial or parochial in outlook
jahd جهد *n* (*pl* **juhuud**) effort
jahhal جهّل *vt* (**tajhiil**) to keep ignorant
jahhaz جهّز *vt* (**jihheez, tajhiiz**) to prepare
jahjah جهجه *vt* (**jahjaha**) to mislead
jahl جهل *n* ignorance
jaḥad جحد *vi* (**a, juḥuud**) to be ungrateful
jaḥam جحم *n* rabies
jaḥiim جحيم *n* hell
jaḥmaan جحمان *adj* **1** rabid, suffering from rabies **2** having a craving for sth., greedy
jakitta جكتّة *n* jacket (of suit)
jakk جك *n* (*pl* **jukukka, jukuuk**) jug
jakka جكّ *vi* (**u, jakk**) to run slowly; to trot; to jog
jakka جكّة *n* trot; **jara fi j-jakka** to trot
jalaafa جلافة *n* rudeness
jalab جلب *vt* (**i, jalib**) to bring for sale, hawk
jalad جلد *vt* (**i, jalid**) to flog, lash, whip
jalas جلس *vi* (**i, juluus**) to sit
jalda جلدة *n* lash (with whip)
jali جلي *n* jelly; jello
jaliid جليد *n* ice; snow
jalla جلّى *vi/vt* (**-i, jilleey**) to miss (in throwing, shooting)
jallaabi جلابي *n* (**jallaaba**) (*trad*) northern Sudanese itinerant trader (*now pej for northern Sudanese of Arab origin*)
jallaabiyya جلابيّة *n* (*pl* **-aat, jalaaliib**) jellabia (traditional men's dress; women's home dress)
jallad جلّد *vt* (**tajliid**) **1** to put a cover on (a book) **2** to bind (a book)
jalsa جلسة *n* meeting
jalṭa جلطة *n* **1** blood clot **2** thrombosis; stroke
jamʿiyya جمعيّة *n* society, association, organization; **jamʿiyya qaaʿidiyya** community-based organization; **aj-jamʿiyya al-ʿumuumiyya** the annual general meeting (of an organisation)
jamaʿ جمع (**a, jamiʿ**) *vt* **1** to bring together, assemble, collect, gather **2** (*arith*) to add (up) **3** (*slang*) to type
jamaaʿa جماعة *n* folks; a group or bunch (of people); **ya jamaaʿa** you folks
jamaaʿi جماعي *adj* collective
jamaahiir جماهير *n pl* **aj-jamaahiir** (*sg* **jamhuur**) the masses
jamaahiiri جماهيري *adj* pertaining to the masses; **liqaa jamaahiiri** rally
jamaal جمال *n* beauty
jamaarik جمارك *n pl* (*sg* **jumruk**) customs; **maʿfi min aj-jamaarik** duty-free
jamal جمل *n* (*pl* **jumaal, jimaal**) **1** camel **2** (*slang*) vulva
jamaloon جملون *n* (*pl* **-aat**) **1** hangar **2** shed (for machines, tractors, etc.)
jamb جمب *prep* next to, next by (*see also* **jaanib**); **ʿala jamb** aside; **zanb-o ʿala jamb-o** it's his own fault

jamba جمبة *n* side of the body
jambari جمبري *n* shrimps
jamhuur جمهور *n* (*pl* **jamaahiir**) public, audience
jamhuuri جمهوري (*pl* **-yyiin**) *adj* republican • *n* Republican
jamhuuriyya جمهوريّة *n* republic; **jamhuuriyyat ifriiqiya al-wusṭa** the Central African Republic
jamiᶜ جمع *n* **1** (*gram*) plural **2** (*arith*) addition
jamiiᶜ جميع *n* all
jamiil جميل *adj* beautiful, pretty, handsome • *n* (*pl* **jamaayil**) favour; **naakir aj-jamiil** ungrateful
jammaᶜ جمّع *vt* **1** (**jimmeeᶜ, tajmiiᶜ**) to assemble, bring together, collect **2** (**tajmiiᶜ**) to assemble, put together
jammaali جمّالي *n* (*pl* **jammaala**) camel driver
jammad جمّد *vt* (**jimmeed, tajmiid**) to freeze
jamra جمرة *unit n* hot coal, ember; **aj-jamra al-khabiisa** **1** anthrax **2** said about the system of an electric meter per household
jamur جمر *coll n* (*unit n* **jamra**) hot coals, embers
jana جنى *vi* (**-i, janiyya, jinaaya, tajanni**) **ᶜala** to offend (verbally or physically)
jana جنى *vt* (**-i, jani**) to reap, harvest
jana جنا *n* **1** (*pl* **jinyaat, jannuun**) baby, infant, (young) child; **janaa-y** my child **2** seed, germ of a seed **3** clitoris
janaab جناب *n* **janaab-ak** Your Honour (to army or police officers)
janaaḥ جناح *n* (*pl* **ajniḥa**) wing (of a bird; a building)
janaayni جنايني *n* (*pl* **-yya**) gardener
janareetar جنريتر *n* (*pl* **-aat**) generator
janb جنب *prep* next to, next by
janba جنبة *n* side of the body
jand جند *n* (*pl* **ajinda**) topic of an agenda
jandar جندر *n* gender
janguur جنقور *n* (*pl* **janaagiir**) rag (for cleaning)
janiin جنين *n* foetus; **aj-janiin sagaṭ** the foetus miscarried, aborted
janiyya جنيّة *n* crime, offence
janjabiira جنجبيرة *n* ginger
janna جنّة *n* paradise; **aj-janna** Paradise
janna جنّ *vi* (**i, jinn**) to be(come) insane, crazy, go mad
jannab جنّب *vt* (**jinneeb**) **min** to set/put aside
jannad جنّد *vt* (**jinneed, tajniid**) (*mil*) to recruit
jannan جنّن *vt* (**jinneen**) to drive s.o. mad, madden
januub جنوب *n* south
januubi جنوبي (*pl* **-yyiin**) *adj* southern; pertaining to the south (of Sudan) • *n* southerner
janzabiil جنزبيل *n* ginger
jara جرى *vi* (**-i, jari, jarayaan**) **1** to run **2** to flow
jaraad جراد *coll n* locust(s), grasshopper(s)
jaraaya جراية *n* ration (military, prison)
jarab جرب *n* scabies; scab; mange
jarabandi جربندي *adj* (*pl* **-yya**) bungler
jarabandiyya جربنديّة *n* shoddy way of working (without being skilled)

jaraboks جربكس *n* (*pl* **-aat**) gearbox
jarad جرد *vt* (**u, jarid**) to take an inventory
jaraf جرف *vt* (**i, jarif**) to wash away; **al-amṭaar jarafat al-khaṭṭ** the rains washed away the track
jaraḥ جرح *vt* (**a, jariḥ**) to wound, injure
jaras جرس *n* (*pl* **ajraas**) bell
jarasoon جرسون *n* (*pl* **-aat**) waiter
jarasoona جرسونة *n* waitress
jarayaan جريان *n* streaming
jarda جردة *n* military expedition
jardal جردل *n* (*pl* **jaraadil**) bucket, pail
jari جري *n* **aj-jari** running around, being busy with one's daily duties
jarid جرد *n* inventory; **qaaymat aj-jarid** inventory list
jarif جرف *n* (*pl* **juruuf**) (cultivated) river shore
jariḥ جرح *n* (*pl* **juruuḥ**) injury, wound
jarii' جريء *adj* daring, courageous, brave
jariid جريد *coll n* palm branch(es)
jariida جريدة *unit n* (*pl* **jaraayid**) **1** palm branch **2** newspaper
jariima جريمة *n* (*pl* **jaraayim**) crime, offence
jarikaana جركانة *n* jerrycan
jarjar جرجر *vt* (**jirjeer, jarjara**) **1** to drag; **jarjar kurᶜeen-o** he shuffled **2** to interrogate thoroughly for a long time
jarra جرّ *vt* (**u, jarr**) to pull; to drag
jarra جرّى *vt* (**-i, jirreey**) to make s.o. run
jarraaḥ جرّاح *n* surgeon
jarraay جرّاي *adj* quick, fast (runner)
jarrab جرّب *vt* (**jirreeb, tajriib**) to try out, test
jarrad جرّد *vt* (**tajriid**) to demote; to strip s.o. of his rank or weapons
jarraḥ جرّح *vt* (**jirreeḥ, tajriiḥ**) to wound, injure
jarras جرّس *vt* (**jirrees, jirsa**) to make s.o. plead for mercy
jarsuuma جرسومة *n* (*pl* **jarasiim**) microbe, germ
jasad جسد *n* (*pl* **ajsaad**) body
jassa جسّ *vt* (**i, jass**) to explore sth. by feeling round it; to try the weight by lifting (livestock); to test (e.g. eggs)
jashiᶜ جشع *adj* very greedy
jaw جو *n* (*pl* **ajwaa**) **1** weather **2** (*also fig*) atmosphere, climate
jawaahir جواهر *n pl* jewellery
jawaahirji جواهرجي *n* (**-iyya**) jeweller
jawaaz جواز *n* (*pl* **-aat**) passport; **jawaaz as-safar** passport
jawda جودة *n* good quality
jawhara جوهرة *n* (*pl* **jawaahir**) jewel
jawjawa جوجوة *n* instability (person)
jawla جولة *n* tour, trip
jawwaᶜ جوّع *vt* (**jiwweeᶜ, tajwiiᶜ**) to make s.o. hungry; to deprive of food; **jawwiᶜ kalb-ak, bitbaᶜ-ak** keep your dog hungry and he'll follow you
jawwaab جوّاب *n* (*pl* **-aat**) **1** answer **2** letter (message)
jawwaad جوّاد *n* (*pl* **jiyaad**) horse
jawwaafa جوّافة *n* guava
jawwaal جوّال *n* (*pl* **-aat**) mobile telephone
jawwi جوّي *adj* pertaining to air; **bariid jawwi** airmail; **khuṭuuṭ jawwiyya** airlines; **al-quwwaat aj-jawwiyya** the air force
jayyaashi جيّاشي *n* (*pl* **jayyaasha**) soldier

jayyar جيّر *vt* (**jiyyeer**) to limewash
jayyid جيّد *adj* good
jaza جزى *vt* (**-i, jiza**) **1** to recompense, reward **2** to punish
jazab جزب *vt* (**i, jazib**) to attract
jazar جزر *coll n* (*unit n* **jazara, jazaraaya**) carrot(s)
jaziira جزيرة *n* (*pl* **juzur, jazaayir**) island; **aj-jaziira** Gezira state
jazma جزمة *n* (*pl* **-aat, jizam**) shoe (also used as an insult)
jazmaji جزمجي *n* (*pl* **-iyya**) shoemaker; shoe mender, cobbler
jazoliin جازولين *n* diesel (fuel)
jazr جزر *n* low tide
jazr جزر *n* (*pl* **juzuur**) root
jazza جزّ *vt* (**i, jazz**) **1** to clip; to shear **2** to cut (e.g. grass)
jazzaab جزّاب *adj* attractive
jazzaar جزّار *n* butcher
jeeb جيب *n* (*pl* **jiyuub**) pocket; **iltihaab aj-jiyuub al-anfiyya** sinusitis
jeesh جيش *n* (*pl* **jiyuush**) army
jiʿaan جعان *adj* hungry
jibaaya جباية *n* taxation, levying of taxes
jibba جبّة *n* (*pl* **jibab**) jellabia (traditional men's dress)
jibis جبس *n* gypsum
jibna جبنة *n* (*pl* **ajbaan**) cheese; **jibna beeḍa** white cheese; **jibna muḍaffara** rope cheese; **jibna ruumiyya** type of yellow cheese (European)
jidaad جداد *coll n* chicken(s), hen(s), poultry; **jidaad al-waadi** guinea fowl(s); **jidaad ar-ruum** turkey(s)
jidd جدّ *n* (*pl* **juduud, ajdaad**) grandfather
jiddan جداً *adv* very, extremely
jifin جفن *n* (*pl* **jufuun**) eyelid
jigir جقر *n* (*pl* **juguur**) rat
jiha جهة *n* direction, side
jihaad جهاد *n* (*Isl*) holy war
jihaaz جهاز *n* (*pl* **ajhiza**) **1** appliance; apparatus, set; instrument, equipment(s) **2** system, apparatus **3** body, institution corps; staff
jihiz جهز *vi* (**a, jahiz**) to be ready; to get ready
jiḥim جحم *vi* (**a, jaḥam**) **1** to be rabid, suffer from rabies **2** to have a craving for sth.; to be greedy
jiiba جيبة *n* skirt
jiifa جيفة *n* (*pl* **jiyaf**) carcass, carrion
jiil جيل *n* (*pl* **ajyaal**) generation
jiilaati جيلاتي *n* ice cream
jiir جير *n* lime; **ḥajar jiir** limestone
jiira جيرة *n* neighbourliness
jilaad جلاد *n* (*pl* **-aat**) paper cover, book wrapper, book jacket
jilba جلبة *n* washer (for taps)
jilda جلدة *adj invar* stingy, mean
jilda جلدة *n* **1** foreskin, prepuce **2** washer (for taps)
jilid جلد *n* **1** skin; **jild-o takhiin** he is thick-skinned **2** (*pl* **juluud**) hide; leather
jilif جلف *n* (*and* **jilf**, *pl* **ajlaaf**) rude, uncivilized
jinaa'i جنائي *adj* criminal
jinaaḥ جناح *n* (*pl* **ajniḥa**) wing (of a bird; a building)
jinaaya جناية *n* crime, felony, capital offence
jinaaza جنازة *n* (*pl* **janaayiz**) **1** funeral, burial **2** corpse; **ʿangareeb aj-jinaaza** bier
jindi جندي *n* **abu j-jindi** house cricket

jindib جندب *n* **abu j-jindib** house cricket

jineeh جنيه *n* (*pl* **-aat**) pound (money)

jineena جنينة *n* (*pl* **janaayin**) orchard, garden

jiniraal جنرال *n* (*pl* **-aat**) (*mil*) general

jinis جنس *n* (*pl* **ajnaas**) **1** sort, kind, species **2** origin, ethnicity, race, tribe; **jins-ak shinu** to which tribe do you belong? **3** sex (male, female) **4** (*gram*) gender

jinjawiid جنجويد *n pl* janjaweed, armed horsemen

jinn جنّ *coll n* (*unit n m* **jinni**, *unit n f* **jinniyya**) helpful or harmful spirits, demons • *n* madness, mania, insanity; rapture; obsession, craze; **jinn-a fi shokolaata** she's crazy about chocolate

jins جنس *n* sex (intercourse)

jinsi جنسي *adj* sexual

jinsiyya جنسيّة *n* nationality

jinziir جنزير *n* (*pl* **janaaziir**) fetter, iron chain

jiraaḥa جراحة *n* surgery

jireef جريف *n* (*pl* **jiruuf**) (cultivated) river shore

jireew جريو *n* (*pl* **jireewaat**) cub, puppy

jirjiir جرجير *n* cress, rocket

jirra جرّة *n* cud

jirtig جرتق *n* a charms ritual for protection and prosperity (part of a wedding celebration)

jiru جرو *n* (*pl* **jireewaat**) cub, puppy

jisim جسم *n* (*pl* **ajsaam**) body

jisir جسر *n* (*pl* **jusuur**) bridge

jitta جتّة *n* (*pl* **jitat**) **1** body **2** corpse

jiwanti جونتي *n* (*pl* **-yyaat**) (pair of) gloves

jiza جزا *n* (*pl* **jiza'aat**) punishment (in military or civil service)

jizaara جزارة *n* butcher's shop

jizza جزّة *n* fleece

jookar جوكر (*pl* **jawaakir**) **1** joker (cards) **2** said of a person who takes any kind of job

jooṭa جوطة *n* **1** din, hubbub; fuss, commotion **2** mess, muddle, disorder

jooz جوز *n* **1** (*pl* **ajwaaz**) pair **2** (*pl* **jeezaan**) yoke

jooz جوز *n* **jooz aṭ-ṭiib** nutmeg

juʿraan جعران *n* (*pl* **jaʿaariin**) *and* **abu j-juʿraan** black house beetle

jubun جبن *n* cowardice

juḍum جضم *n* (*pl* **juḍuum**) cheek

jughma جغمة *n* gulp

jughraafi جغرافي *adj* geographic

jughraafiya جغرافية *n* geography

juhd جهد *n* (*pl* **juhuud**) effort

juḥur جحر *n* (*pl* **juḥuur, jaḥḥaar**) burrow

juḥuud جحود *n* ingratitude

jumʿa جمعة *n* **yoom aj-jumʿa** Friday; **aj-jumʿa al-ḥaziina** (*Chr*) Good Friday; **aj-jumʿa al-yatiima** (*Isl*) the last Friday of Ramadan

jumbaaz جمباز *n* gymnastics

jumjumma جمجمّة *n* (*pl* **jamaajim**) skull

jumla جملة *n* (*no pl*) **1** total, sum; **jumlat an-naas** all the people **2** bulk; wholesale; **al-intaaj be-j-jumla** mass production **3** (*pl* **jumal**) (*gram*) sentence

jummaada جمّادة *n* cream (milk)

jummeez جمّيز *coll n* various species of wild fig tree

jumruk جمرك *n* (*pl* **jamaarik**) customs

jumruki جمركي *adj* pertaining to customs

jundi جندي *n* (*pl* **junuud**) soldier; **jundi nafar** private soldier

junḥa جنحة *n* (*pl* **junaḥ**) misdemeanour

junuun جنون *n* madness, mania, insanity; rapture

jurʿa جرعة *n* draught, dose of liquid

jur'a جرءة *n* bravery, courage

juraab جراب *n* (*pl* **-aat**) leather pouch

jurun جرن *n* (*pl* **ajraan**) store for grain, granary

jussa جسّة *n* (*pl* **jusas**) corpse

juuʿ جوع *n* hunger

juud جود *n* generosity; **aj-juud be-l-mawjuud** (*lit* generosity is done with what is available) one can be generous with even a little

juudiyya جوديّة *n* (*trad*) mediation and arbitration process

juwaar جوار *n* neighbourhood; **fi j-juwaar** in the neighbourhood

juwwa جوّا *prep* inside, within • *adv* inside; **be-juwwa** inside

juwwaani جواني *adj* inner

juzaam جزام *n* leprosy

juz'i جزئي *adj* partially

juzlaan جزلان *n* (*pl* **-aat, jazaaliin**) wallet, purse (for men)

juzu جزو *n* (*pl* **azjaa**) part, portion segment, piece

k – ك

kaʿʿa كعّة *n* fighting, war

kaʿab كعب *adj* bad

kaʿab كعب *n* (*pl* **kuʿuub**) heel

kaʿak كعك *n* shortbread biscuits

kaʿba كعبة *n* **al-kaʿba** the Kaaba, the holy shrine in Mecca

ka'ann- كأن *conj* as if

ka'anno كأنو *conj* as if

kaab كاب *n* (*pl* **-aat**) cap

kaabuus كابوس *n* (*pl* **kawaabiis**) nightmare

kaad كاد *vi* (**i, keed, keeda**) to intrigue

kaaḍib كاضب *adj* false

kaafa كافى *vt* (**-i, mukaafaa**) to reward

kaaffa كافّة *n* all; **kaaffat an-naas** all the people

kaafi كافي *adj* sufficient, enough; **ma kaafi** insufficient

kaafir كافر *n* (**kuffaar, kafara**) unbeliever, infidel; blasphemer

kaafuur كافور *n* camphor

kaajar كاجر *vi* (**mukaajara**) to be obstinate

kaakaaw كاكاو *n* cocoa

kaal كال *vt* (**i, keela**) to measure (grain)

kaaluut كالوت *n* (*pl* **kawaaliit**) club (weapon)

kaamil كامل *adj* entire, whole; complete; **be-l-kaamil** completely

kaan كان *vi* (**u, koon**) to be (in past and future); **yakuun mawjuud bukra** he/it will be there tomorrow; **kaan mawjuud** it existed (in the past)

kaan كان *conj* **1** if; **kaan ma ḥabbeet, ma taʿmal-o** if you don't like it, don't do it; **kaan ma** unless **2** whether

kaanuun كانون *n* (*pl* **kawaaniin**) brazier, charcoal stove

kaarib كارب *adj* **1** excellent, well-made **2** said of a decent and reliable person

kaarro كارو *n* (*pl* **kaarroohaat, karroowaat, kawaarro**) donkey cart, horse cart

kaarsa كارسة *n* (*pl* **kawaaris**) catastrophe

kaaruusha كاروشة *n* itch

kaas كاس *n* (*pl* **-aat**) **1** drinking glass **2** vase; flowerpot, plant pot

kaas كاس *vt* (**u, kuwaasa**) to search, look for • *vi* **le-** to search for, look for

kaashif كاشف *adj* uncovered; bareheaded

kaatal كاتل *vi* (**kitaal, mukaatala**) to fight; to fight in a war

kaatib كاتب *n* **1** (*pl* **kataba**) clerk **2** (*pl* **kuttaab**) writer

kaatil كاتل *n* murderer, killer

kaatim كاتم *adj* suffocating, oppressive (of atmosphere); **kaatim ṣoot** silencer (of a gun)

kaawa كاوى *vt* (**-i, mukaawaa**) to tease

kaazib كازب *adj* false

kabaab كباب *n* cooked, fried or grilled meat; **kabaab ḥalla** stewed meat; **kabaab ṭawwa** meat fried in a saucepan

kabak كبك *n* (*pl* **kubaaka**) sports shoes

kabar كبر *vt* (**u, kabir**) to clear the ground for cultivation

kabareet كبريت *n* (*trad*) all the cosmetics required by a married woman (**dilka**, **khumra**, **bukhuur**, etc.)

kabas كبس *vi* (**i, kabis**) **ʿala** to take s.o. by surprise; to catch a person red-handed; **an-noom kabas ʿalee-y** I dropped off to sleep

kabba كبّ *vt* (**u, kabb**) to pour (out)

kabbaas كبّاس *n* (*pl* **kabaabiis**) nightmare; **abu kabbaas** nightmare

kabbar كبّر *vi* (**takbiir**) to say **al-lahu akbar** while raising one's hand or stick into the air • *vt* (**kibbeer**) to enlarge

kabbas كبّس *vt* (**kibbees**) to push, press down

kabbuut كبّوت *n* (*pl* **kabaabiit**) **1** bonnet (of car) **2** raincoat

kabda كبدة *n* (*pl* **kibad**) liver (as meat)

kabdi كبدي *adj* dark red, liver-coloured

kabid كبد *n* (*anat*) liver

kabiina كبينة *n* (**kabaayin**) **1** cabin, small room (on ship) **2** phone booth, phone box

kabiir كبير *adj* (*pl* **kubaar**) **1** big, large **2** elderly; **kabiir fi s-sinn** elderly; **al-kabiir** senior

kabish كبش *n* (*pl* **kibaash**) ram, male sheep; **majarr al-kabish** the Milky Way

kabkabee كبكبي *n* chickpeas

kabsuula كبسولة *n* capsule

kabsha كبشة *n* **1** a handful **2** ladle

kabtin كبتن *n* (**kabaatin**) captain

kadanka كدنكة *n* (*agr*) type of small hoe for clearing the soil

kaddaara كدّارة *n* sports shoes; football boots

kaddaari كدّاري *adv* on foot

kaddab كدّب *vi/vt* (**kiddeeb**) to weed

kade كدي *interj* **1** let me see…; so then… **2** let me see it, give it (to me)

kadi كدي *adv* like this, in this way
kadiis كديس *n* (*m*) (*pl* **kadaayis**) tomcat
kadiisa كديسة *n* (*f*) (*pl* **-aat, kadaayis**) cat
kadoos كدوس *n* (*pl* **-aat**) pipe (for tobacco)
kadruuk كدروك *n* (*pl* **kadaariik**) pig
kaḍab كضب *vi* (**i, kaḍba**) (**ʻala, fi**) to lie (to, about)
kaḍam كضم *vi* (**u, kaḍim**) to be unable to speak, be silent (as a result of shock)
kaḍba كضبة *n* (*pl* **-aat, kiḍib**) lie
kaḍḍaab كضّاب *n* liar
kaḍḍab كضّب *vi* (**kiḍib**) (**ʻala, fi**) to lie (to, about)
kafa كفى *vt* (**-i, kafiya**) to protect from (of God); **Allah yakfii-ni sharr-ak** God will protect me from your evil deeds
kafa كفى *interj* enough, that will do
kafaala كفالة *n* **1** guarantee **2** bail
kafan كفن *n* (*pl* **akfaan**) shroud
kafar كفر *vi* (**u, kufur**) to deny God's existence; to blaspheme
kafash كفش *vt* (**i, kafish**) to catch, seize (a person)
kafateera كفتيرة *n* (*pl* **-aat, kafaatiir**) kettle
kaff كفّ *n* (*pl* **kufuuf**) **1** palm of the hand **2** a slap; **addaa-ho kaff/ ḍarab-o kaff** he slapped him
kaffa كفّى *vt* (**-i, kifaaya**) to suffice, be enough for; to satisfy
kaffa كفّة *n* hem
kaffa كفّة *n* **kaffat al-miizaan** scale of a balance
kaffa كفّ *vt* (**i, kaff**) **1** to hem **2** to turn up (sleeves or trouser legs)
kaffaara كفّارة *n* **1** expression of sympathy to s.o. who is ill **2** penance, atonement
kaffan كفّن *vt* (**takfiin**) to shroud
kaffar كفّر *vt* **1** (**kaffaara**) to express sympathy when a person is ill **2** (**kaffaara**) (*of God*) to forgive; **Allah yakaffir sayyi'aat-ak** may God forgive your sins **3** (**kaffaara, takfiir**) to do penance, atone **4** (**kiffeer, takfiir**) to declare s.o. to be an infidel or blasphemer
kaffat كفّت *vt* (**kiffeet**) to smack, slap (on the face)
kafiif كفيف *adj* blind
kahaf كهف *n* (*pl* **kuhuuf**) cave
kahraba كهربا *n* electricity
kahrabaa'i كهربائي *adj* electrical
kahrabji كهربجي *n* (*pl* **-yya**) electrician
kahramaan كهرمان *n* amber
kajam كجم *vt* (**u, kajim**) to bite
kajjaama كجّامة *n* steel trap
kak كك *adj invar* (*slang*) mad, crazy
kakas ككس *n* (*slang*) money
kakko ككّو *n* (*pl* **-yaat**) type of small monkey
kalaam كلام *n* **1** talk, conversation **kalaam faarigh/saakit/ saay/faaḍi/khaarim baarim; ayyi kalaam** nonsense **2** speech (language) **3** matter, affair
kalaawi كلاوي *n pl* (*sg* **kilwa**) kidneys (as meat)
kalabsh كلبش *n* **1** (*pl* **-aat**) handcuffs **2** eclampsia
kalashinkoof كلشنكوف *n* (*pl* **-aat**) Kalashnikov (gun)
kalatsh كلتش *n* (*pl* **-aat**) clutch (of vehicle)
kalawi كلوي *adj* renal

kalazaar كلزار *n* kala azar
kalba كلبة *n* bitch
kalbash كلبش *vt* (**kalbasha**) to handcuff
kalib كلب *n* (*pl* **kilaab**) dog; **kalib ṣeed/kalib ganiiṣ** hound (for hunting)
kalkal كلكل *vt* (**kalkala, kilkeel**) to tickle, titillate
kallaaba كلابة *n* steel trap
kallaam كلام *adj* talkative (in positive or negative sense) • *n* a good talker
kallab كلّب *vi* (**killeeb**); **jild-o kallab** he had goose pimples; **shaʿrat jild-o kallabat** his hair stood on end
kallaf كلّف *vt* (**takliif**) **1** to cost; **bikallif kam** what does it cost? **2** (**be-**) to put in charge (of); **kallaf nafs-o** (**be-**) he made a great effort (to); **ma takallif nafs-ak** you don't have to go to so much trouble; **kallaf be-l-ḥuḍuur** to summon
kallam كلّم *vt* (**kalaam**) to talk to, speak to
kalma كلمة *n* (*pl* **kalimaat**) word
kaloonya كلونية *n* eau de cologne
kam كم *interrog* how much, how many; **be-kam** how much (price)
kamaan كمان *adv* also; too; **kamaan marra** once more
kamad كمد *vt* (**i/u, kamid**) to fill completely, fill to the brim
kamad كمد *n* deep grief
kamanja كمنجا *n* (*pl* **-aat**) violin
kamar كمر *n* waistband; money belt
kamara كمرة *n* (*pl* **kamiraat**) iron girder
kambiyaala كمبيالة *n* bill of exchange
kamiin كمين *n* (*pl* **kamaayin**) ambush, trap
kamiina كمينة *n* (*pl* **kamaayin**) kiln
kamira كمرا *n* (*pl* **kamiraat**) camera
kammaada كمّادة *n* compress
kammaama كمّامة *n* (*pl* **-aat, kamaayim**) face mask (e.g. against dust, pollution)
kammaasha كمّاشة *n* **1** pincers **2** large weeding hoe with two prongs **3** (*mil*) pincer movement
kammad كمّد *vt* (**takmiid**) to foment
kammal كمّل *vt* (**kamaal, kamla**) **1** to finish, end, complete **2** to spend all (e.g. money)
kammuniyya كمّونيّة *n* dish of tripe and liver
kammuun كمّون *n* black cumin
kamsha كمشة *n* ladle
kanaar كانار *n/n pl* canary/canaries
kanaba كنبة *n* (*pl* **-aat, kanab**) bench, couch, sofa
kanas كنس *vt* (**u, kanis**) to sweep
kandaaka كنداكة *n* sandstorm
kaniisa كنيسة *n* (*pl* **kanaayis**) church; **kaniisa katidraa'iyya** cathedral
kankash كنكش *vi* (**kankasha**) **fi** **1** to hold on firmly to, keep very close to (child to mother, friends to each other) **2** to be engrossed in (e.g. a job, a game)
kannaas كنّاس *n* street sweeper, street cleaner
kannaasa كنّاسة *n* rake
kantiin كنتين *n* (*pl* **kanaatiin**) grocery
kantuush كنتوش *n* (*pl* **kanaatiish**) earthenware cooking pot
kanz كنز *n* (*pl* **kunuuz**) treasure
karʿa كرعة *n* belch
karaahiyya كراهيّة *n* hatred

karaakiib كراكيب *n pl* rubbish, junk
karaama كرامة *n* dignity, self-respect
karaama كرامة *n* **1** sacrifice to get a blessing (slaughtering of a sheep) **2** alms giving **3** miracle done by a holy man or saint
karab كرب *vt* (**u, karib**) to tie
karad كرد *vt* (**u, karid**) to scrape
karaf كرف *vt* (**u, karif**) to sniff (perfume, incense)
karafitta كرفتّة *n* tie, necktie
karak كرنق *n* (*pl* **-aat**) **1** rake **2** hoe
karam كرم *n* generosity
karang كرنق *n* (*pl* **-aat**) rake
karanki كرنكي *n* crank (car); **ʿamuud al-karanki** crankshaft; **ʿilbat al-karanki** crankcase
karash كرش *vi* (**u, karish**) to scratch o.s.
karateeh كرتيه *n* karate
karawi كروي *adj* **1** round (like a ball) **2** pertaining to football or other ball games
karbareetar كربريتر *n* (*pl* **-aat**) carburettor
kardan كردن *vt* (**kardana**) to cordon off
kardoon كردون *n* (*pl* **-aat**) (*mil*) cordon
karfas كرفس *vt* (**kirfees, karfasa**) to crumple, crease, wrinkle
karfas كرفس *n* celery
kariih كريه *adj* unpleasant, nasty
kariim كريم *adj* **1** (*pl* **-iin, kurama**) generous **2** respectful form of address, *as in* **ism al-kariim(a) minu** what is your name?
karikateer كاركتير *n* (*pl* **-aat**) caricature; cartoon
karish كرش *n* (*pl* **kuruush**) paunch, potbelly
karit كرت *n* (*pl* **kuruut**) card, postcard

karkaar كركار *n* mixture of fat, sesame oil, cloves, orange peel and perfume (for hair)
karkab كركب *vi* (**karkaba**) to produce a loud noise,
karkaba كركبة *n* din bother, to-do
karkadee كركدي *n* **1** hibiscus **2** hibiscus tea
karkuur كركور *n* (*pl* **karaakiir**) cave
karmash كرمش *vt* (**kirmeesh, karmasha**) to crumple, crease, wrinkle
karmasha كرمشة *n sg/pl* wrinkle(s)
karnab كرنب *n* (*pl* **karaanib**) cabbage
karnafaal كرنافال *n* (*pl* **-aat**) festival
karoohaat كروهات *n pl*; **gumaash karoohaat** chequered cloth
karoor كرور *n* junk, rubbish
karooriyya كروريّة *n* small reel (for thread)
karoosa كروسة *n* pack of ten boxes of matches
karraaka كرّاكة *n* dredger, bulldozer
karraas كرّاس *n* (*pl* **-aat, karaariis**) copybook, exercise book
karrab كرّب *vt* (**kirreeb**) **1** to tie well **2** to do sth. well; to be(come) good at; **karrabta al-ʿuluum** I've become good at sciences
karrah كرّه *vt* (**kirreeh**) (**fi**) to cause to hate; **karrah-ni al-balad da** he made me hate this place; **karrah-ni fii-ho** he made me hate him/it
karram كرّم *vt* (**takriim**) to honour
karrar كرّر *vt* **1** (**tikraar**) to repeat **2** (**takriir**) to refine (e.g. petrol, sugar)
karsha كرشة *n* tripe
kartoon كرتون *n* (*pl* **-aat**) animated cartoon

kartoon كرتون *coll n* cardboard
kartoona كرتونة *unit n* (*pl* **-aat, karaatiin**) **1** piece of cardboard **2** cardboard box, carton
karwat كروت (**kirweet, karwata**) *vi* to be sloppy, produce slovenly work • *vt* to botch, bungle
karwata كروتة *n* shoddy work, (piece of) bungled job
kasa كسا *vt* (**i, kiswa**) to clothe
kasaafa كسافة *n* intensity
kasaf كسف *vt* (**i, kasif, kasafaan**) to embarrass
kasaḥ كسح *vi* (**a, kasiḥ**) to walk quickly (in a hurry)
kasal كسل *n* laziness
kasar كسر *vt* (**i, kasir**) to break; to break off
kasbaan كسبان *adj* gaining; winning
kasbara كسبرة *n* dried coriander; **kasbara khaḍra** fresh coriander
kasiiḥ كسيح *adj* (*pl* **kusaḥa**) suffering from rickets
kasir كسر *n* (*pl* **kusuur**) **1** fracture **2** fraction **alf jineeh u kasir** one thousand pounds plus a little more
kaslaan كسلان *adj* lazy
kasra كسرة *n* **1** (*pl* **kussaar**) splinter, sliver **2** (*pl* **-aat**) chip (in china, glass, etc.)
kassab كسّب *vt* (**kisseeb**) to make s.o. earn or gain sth.
kassaḥ كسّح (**kisseeḥ, taksiiḥ**) to work in iron
kassar كسّر *vt* (**kisseer, taksiir**) to smash, break into pieces
kastar كستر *n* custard; custard pudding
kashaf كشف *vt* (**i, kashif**) **1** to uncover, unveil; to reveal, disclose; to betray (a secret) **2** to examine, check medically
kashaḥ كشح *vt* (**a, kashiḥ, kashaḥaan**) to throw away (any liquid, e.g. dirty water)
kashaṭ كشط *vt* (**u, kashiṭ**) to scrape
kashbara كشبرة *n* dried coriander; **kashbara khaḍra** fresh coriander
kashif كشف *n* (*pl* **kushuufaat**) **1** medical checkup, medical examination **2 a** list; **kashf al-ujuur** payroll **b** list of persons and the amount of money they donated at a special occasion
kashkash كشكش *vi* **1** (**kishkeesh**) to jingle, rattle **2** (**kashkasha**) to be(come) crazy • *vt* **1** (**kashkasha**) to round up and lead away (a herd) **2** (**kishkeesh**) to pleat, smock
kashkasha كشكشة *n* **1** jingling; rattling **2** decoration of dresses, sheets, curtains with embroidery and/or tassels
kashkoosh كشكوش *n* (*pl* **kashaakiish**) rattle, bells and rattle
kashsha كشّة *n* police swoop, round-up, police raid; **al-kashsha** group of policemen doing a swoop; **tajii-k al-kashsha** go to hell!
kashsha كشّ *vi* (**i, kashsh**) **1** to shrink **2** (**min**) to recoil, shrink (from)
kashsha كشّ *vt* (**u, kashsha**) to drive (herd) together, to round up (livestock, school children, street vendors, criminals)
kashshaaf كشّاف *n* (*pl* **kashshaafa**) scout
kashshaafa كشّافة *n* **1** (electric) torch; searchlight; floodlight **2** scouting (children)
kashshaasha كشّاشة *n* sun shelter

kashshaf كشّف *vt* (**kishsheef**) to investigate
kashshan كشّن *vt* (**kushna**) to brown (onions)
kashshar كشّر *vt* (**kishsheer, takshiir**) to frown, scowl
katab كتب (**i, kitaaba**) *vi* to write • *vt* to write, note down; **katab kitaab-o** he signed the marriage contract; **katabat raajil-a** she had a charm put on her husband
kataḥ كتح *vt* (**a, katiḥ**) **1** (**be-**) to throw (dust) at (e.g. in a fight, of a passing car) **2** to drink at one go (a glass of alcohol)
katal كتل *vt* (**u, katil**) **1** to kill, murder **2** to switch off (e.g. the light)
katam كتم *vi* (**u, katma, katamaan**) to be oppressive (of weather) • *vt* (**u, katim, katamaan**) **1** to suppress, restrain, curb, stifle; **katam nafas-o** he held his breath; **katam as-sirr** to keep secret **2** to lower, muffle (voice); to muffle, dampen (sound)
katara كترة *n* large number, multitude; abundance; **be-l-katara** plentifully
katidraa'iyya كتدرائيّة *n* cathedral
katif كتف *n* (*pl* **katfeen, kutuuf, aktaaf**) shoulder; **looḥat al-katif** shoulder blade
katiiba كتيبة *n* (*pl* **kataayib**) battalion
katiina كتينة *n* (*pl* **kataayin**) timing chain (car)
katiir كتير *adj* (*pl* **kutaar**) many; much, plentiful • *adv* often, frequently
katil كتل *n* murder; **katil ʿamd/ katil maʿa sabaq al-iṣraar** premeditated murder
katjtjan كتجّن *vt* (**kitjtjeen**) to hate
katkat كتكت *vi* (**kitkeet, katkata**) to chatter (of teeth)
katkoota كتكوتة *n* whooping cough
katkuut كتكوت *n* (*pl* **kataakiit**) chick
katla كتلة *n* battle, fight
katma كتمة *n* suffocating atmosphere (because of absence of wind); **katmat nafas** apnoea
kattaaḥa كتّاحة *n* heavy sandstorm
kattaal كتّال *adj* a good killer
kattaf كتّف *vt* (**kitteef, taktiif**) to tie up by hands and feet
kattaḥ كتّح *vt* (**kitteeḥ**) (**be-**) to throw (dust) at s.o. (e.g. in a fight, of a passing car)
kattar كتّر *vt* (**kitteer**) to increase; **kattar kheer-ak** may your goodness increase, thank you
kawa كوى *vt* (**-i, kawi, kay, kawayaan**) **1** to iron **2** to brand, mark **3** to cauterize
kawaafeer كوافير *n* coiffeur, hairdresser
kawaariʿ كوارع *n pl* soup made from sheep or cow's foot
kawkab كوكب *n* (*pl* **kawaakib**) **1** planet **2** star **3** (*slang*) uninvited guest, sponger
kawn كون *part*; **maʿa kawn** though, although
kawn- كون. *conj* as long as; since, as; **kawn-ak jiit, ma ḥa-amrug** since you've come, I won't go out
kawntar كونتر *n* (**-aat**) counter (e.g. in a shop, bank)
kawwaʿ كوّع *vi* (**kiwweeʿ, takwiiʿ**) to recline on one elbow
kawwaaya كوّاية *n* soldering iron

kawwam كوّم *vt* (**kiwweem, takwiim**) to pile up, make a heap of sth.
kawwan كوّن *vt* (**takwiin**) **1** to form; to set up **2** to establish o.s.
kayfiyya كيفيّة *n* quality
kayluun كيلون *n* (*pl* **kawaaliin**) lock
kayyaad كيّاد *adj* spiteful • *n* intriguer
kayyaal كيّال *n* professional measurer (of grain, liquids)
kayyaf كيّف *vt* (**kiyyeef, takyiif**) **1** to make s.o. feel good **2** to offer s.o. a drink or a smoke **3** to furnish with an air cooler or air conditioner
kayyal كيّل *vt* (**kiyyeel**) to measure (grain)
kayyas كيّس *vt* (**kiyyees**) to put in a plastic bag
kazab كزب *vi* (**i, kazba, kizba**) (**ʿala, fi**) to lie (to, about)
kazba كزبة *n* (*pl* **-aat, akaaziib**) lie
kazzab كزّب *vi* (**kizib**) (**ʿala, fi**) to lie (to, about)
keef كيف *n* pleasure, enjoyment; **ʿala keef-ak** as you like, as you please
keef كيف *interrog* how; **keef al-ḥaal/keef ḥaal-ak/keef-ak** how are you?
keefin كيفن *interrog* how; **keefinn-ak** how are you?
keek كيك *n* cake
keela كيلة *n* measure, unit of weight equal to 12.58 kg
kibad كبد *n pl* (*sg* **kabda/kibda**) liver (as meat)
kibir كبر *vi* (**a, kubur**) **1** to grow (increase in size) **2** to grow old
kibriit كبريت *coll n* **1** sulphur **2** (*pl* **kabaariit**) matches; box of matches; **ʿuud kibriit** matchstick
kibriita كبريتة *n* (*pl* **kabaariit**) matches; box of matches
kida كدا *adv* so, like this, in this way; **gaal kida** he said so
kifaaya كفاية *n* sufficiency • *adj invar* enough, sufficient • *interj* enough
kiilo كيلو *n* **1** (*pl* **kiilohaat**) kilo, kilogram **2** (*pl* **kiilomitraat**) kilometre
kiilomitir كيلومتر *n* (*pl* **kiilomitraat**) kilometre
kiimaawi كيماوي (*pl* **-yyiin**) *adj* chemical • *n* chemist
kiimaawiyyaat كيماويّات *n pl* chemicals
kiimiya كيميا *n* chemistry
kiina كينا *n* quinine
kiini كيني (*pl* **-yyiin**) *adj* Kenyan • *n* a Kenyan
kiiniya كينيا *prop n* Kenya
kiir كير *n* (*pl* **kiiraan**) bellows
kiirii كيري *adj invar* illegal (of goods; of meat not slaughtered according to health regulations)
kiis كيس *n* (*pl* **akyaas**) bag (of plastic, paper, cloth); **kiis makhadda** pillowcase; **kiis duhni** lipoma
kiisha كيشة *n* duffer; a poor hand (at games)
kila كلى *n pl* (*sg* **kilwa**) (*anat*) kidneys
kilaash كلاش *n* (*pl* **-aat**) Kalashnikov (gun)
kilaw كلو *n pl* (*sg* **kilwa**) kidneys (both *anat* and as meat)
killding كلّدنق *n* **killding abu ṣalʿa** vulture
kilma كلمة *n* (*pl* **kalimaat**) word
kilwa كلوة *n* (*pl* **kila, kilaw**) (*anat*) kidney

kimil كمل *vi* (**a, kamla**) to finish; to be finished, completed; to be used up (food, goods)
kimmiyya كمّيّة *n* quantity
kinaasa كناسة *n* sweepings
kirdaan كردان *n* (*pl* **-aat**) breast piece (ornament)
kirih كره *vt* (**a, karih**) to dislike, hate, loathe
kirintiina كرينتينا *n* quarantine; **khaṭṭa fi kirintiina** to put in quarantine
kisaaḥ كساح *n* (*and* **kusaaḥ**) rickets
kisib كسب *vt* (**a, kasib**) to gain, earn, to win
kiskitta كسكتّة *n* cap
kisra كسرة *n* **1** very thin flat bread made from sorghum or millet flour and water, with sourdough **2** ʿ**aṣiida** (stiff porridge made from the same ingredients)
kissiib كسّيب *adj* successful in gaining wealth
kiswa كسوة *n* (*pl* **kasaawi**) **1** garment (especially when new) **2** the cover of the Kaaba
kitaab كتاب *n* (*pl* **kutub**) book; **al-kitaab** the Koran; **al-kitaab al-muqaddas** the Bible
kitaaba كتابة *n* **1** writing **2** amulet
kitaal كتال *n* battle, fight; fighting
kitir كتر *vi* (**a, katara**) to multiply, be(come) many, numerous; to increase
kiyyiif كيّيف *adj* said about s.o. who enjoys the luxuries of life, such as drinking tea, coffee, alcohol or using tobacco
kizba كزبة *n* (*pl* **-aat, akaaziib**) lie
kobs كبس *n* (*pl* **-aat**) **1** electric power point; electric socket; **kobs intaaya** electric socket **2** electric plug; **kobs ḍakar** electric plug
kobsi كبسي *n* (*pl* **-yyaat**) **1** electric power point; electric socket **2** electric plug
kolet كلت *n* wood of a species of acacia, used for incense and fumigation
kolira كلرا *n* cholera
kombyuutar كمبيوتر *n* (*pl* **-aat**) computer
komidiino كمدينو *n* (*pl* **komidiinaat**) bedside table
kondoom كندوم *n* (*pl* **-aat**) condom
konfooy كنفوي *n* (*pl* **-aat**) convoy
konk كنك *adj* concentrated (alcoholic drink)
kontraato كنتراتو *n* (*no pl*) contract
koodeeb كوديب *n* clearing and preparation of the soil for sowing
koofaara كوفارة *n* dyspepsia
koojan كوجن *vt* (**koojaan, koojeen**) (*also fig*) to concoct
kookaab كوكاب *n* (*pl* **-aat**) spear
koom كوم *n* (*pl* **keemaan, akwaam**) heap; pile
kooma كوما *n* **1** coma **2** comma
koomar كومر *n* (*pl* **kawaamir**) lorry, van (to transport detainees)
koon كون *n* universe
koora كورة *n* (*pl* **kuwar**) bowl
kooraak كوراك *n* (*pl* **kawaariik**) shouting, screaming
koorak كورك *vi* (**kooraak**) **1** to shout, yell, scream, call out **2** (ʿ**ala**) to cry; to wail; to lament **3** to crow (of bird)
kooreek كوريك *n* (*pl* **kawaariik**) spade, shovel
kooriyya كوريّة *n* (*pl* **kawaari**) bowl
koors كورس *n* (*pl* **-aat**) course

koosa كوسا *coll n* (*unit n* **koosa, koosaaya**) courgette, zucchini
koosha كوشة *n* throne for the bride and the bridegroom at a wedding
kooz كوز *n* (*pl* **keezaan**) **1** mug (of tin, steel) **2** (*slang*) islamist
koras كورس *n* choir
kreem كريم *n* (*pl* **-aat**) body cream
kuʿuubiyya كعوبيّة *n* badness
kubbaaniyya كبّانيّة *n* switchboard (electricity or telephone utility)
kubbaaya كبّاية *n* (*pl* **-aat, kabaabi**) drinking glass; cup, teacup; tumbler; **kubbaayat shubb** a tall drinking glass
kubri كبري *n* (*pl* **kabaari**) bridge
kubur كبر *n* old age
kudur كدر *n* (*pl* **kadaareen**) hoof; **ja kudur** he came on foot
kufta كفتة *coll n* (*unit n* **kuftaaya**) patties made of minced meat, fish or chicken and fried or grilled on a skewer; **kuftat samak** fried or grilled fishcakes
kufur كفر *n* **1** atheism **2** blasphemy
kuhna كهنة *n* (*pl* **kuhan**) rag (for cleaning shoes, boots or griddle)
kuḥli كحلي *adj* dark blue
kuḥul كحل *n* antimony, kohl
kuḥuul كحول *n* alcohol (drink); **al-kuḥuul** medicinal alcohol, methylated alcohol
kuj كج *n* **1** bad luck, misfortune **2** s.o. who brings bad luck or misfortune
kujuur كجور *n* (**kajara**) medicine man, diviner
kull كل *n* **1** whole; totality; entirety; all; **an-naas kull-um** all the people; everybody; **al-madiina kull-a** the whole town **2** each, every
kulli كلّي *adj* total
kulliyya كلّيّة *n* faculty (university); college
kullo كلّو *n* **1** all; **kullo n-naas** all the people, everybody **2** each, every; **kullo yoom** daily, every day; **kullo waaḥid** everyone; **kullo ma** every time, whenever; **kullo kullo** (not) at all; **ma saafarta kullo kullo** I never travelled
kumm كم *n* (*pl* **akmaam**) sleeve
kumsaari كمساري *n* (*pl* **kamaasra**) bus or train conductor; ticket collector
kumsha كمشة *n* ladle
kunaafa كنافة *n* a variety of pastry (usually stuffed with peanuts)
kunush كنش *n* (*pl* **aknaash**) implement for stirring porridge
kura كرة *n* **1** sphere; **al-kura al-arḍiyya** the globe **2** (*pl* **kuwar**) ball; football; **al-kura; kurat al-gadam** football (soccer); **kurat as-salla** basketball; **kura ṭaayra** volleyball
kuraaʿ كراع *n* (*pl* **kurʿeen**) leg; foot; **ja be-kurʿeen-o** he came on foot; **kuraaʿ-o fi ragabt-o** against his will; **kuraaaʿ-o ma ḥaarra** (*lit* his leg is indeed hot) *expression used to apologize for s.o. who wants to leave when s.o. else has just arrived*
kuraat كرات *n pl* **kuraat ad-damm** blood cells, blood corpuscles
kurbaaj كرباج *n* (*pl* **karaabiij**) whip (of rhinoceros hide)
kurdumma كردمّة *n* (*pl* **karaadiim**) **1** lump **2** bump (swelling)
kurkum كركم *n* turmeric
kurnuk كرنك *n* (*pl* **karaanik**) rectangular mud building with thatched, sloping roof

kurr-kurr كر كر *interj* expression used to ward off misfortune (by women only)

kursi كرسي *n* (*pl* **karaasi**) chair; **kursi juluus** armchair

kurusheeh كروشيه *n* **1** embroidery **2** crochet(ing)

kuruuki كروكي *n* rough sketch

kuss كسّ *n* (*pl* **kasasa**) (*slang*) vagina

kusuuf كسوف *n* **kusuuf ash-shamis** eclipse of the sun

kushteena كشتينة *n* (a pack of) playing cards

kushuk كشك *n* (*pl* **akshaak**) kiosk, small shop standing on its own

kutla كتلة *n* (*pl* **-aat, kutal**) **1** log, block (of wood) **2** bloc **3** (*phys*) mass

kutur كتر *adj invar* a lot (of)

kuuᶜ كوع *n* (*pl* **keeᶜaan, kuuᶜeen, akwaaᶜ**) elbow; **ma biᶜraf kuuᶜ-o min buuᶜ-o** (*lit* he doesn't know the difference between his elbow and his wrist) he doesn't know anything

kuur كور *n* (*pl* **kiiraan**) bellows

kuura كورة *n* (*pl* **kuwar**) ball; **al-kuura; kuurat al-gadam** football (soccer); **kuurat as-salla** basketball; **kuura ṭaayra** volleyball

kuusha كوشة *n* (*pl* **kuwash**) garbage heap

kuwwaara كوّارة *n* pebbly fish (species of *Alestes*)

kwayyis كويّس *adj* good, well • *adv* well

kh - خ

khaabuur خابور *n* (*pl* **khawaabiir**) **1** wedge **2** large meatbone

khaadim خادم *n* **1** (*pl* **khaddaamiin**) male servant **2** (*pl* **khadam**) female slave **3** (*pl* **khuddaam**) spirit (of the kind that possesses a person)

khaaḍ خاض *vt* (**u, khuwaaḍa**) to wade (in water); to slither (in mud)

khaaf خاف *vi* (**a, khoof**) (**min**) to be afraid (of), be scared (of)

khaal خال *n* (*pl* **akhwaal, kheelaan**) maternal uncle

khaala خالة *n* maternal aunt

khaalaf خالف *vt* **1** (**khilaaf**) to go against, contradict **2** (**mukhaalafa**) to violate, break (rules)

khaali خالي *adj* **1** empty, vacant **2 min** devoid of

khaaliṣ خالص *adv* **1** very, extremely **2** at all, ever

khaaliṭ خالط *adj* (*slang*) **khaaliṭ bitt** dating a girl; **khaalṭa walad** dating a boy

khaam خام *adj invar* raw, unprocessed; **maadda khaam** raw material

khaamis خامس *adj* fifth

khaan خان *vt* (**u, khiyaana**) to betray

khaaraj خارج *vt* (**mukhaaraja**) to help out

khaarij خارج *prep* outside; (**fi**) **al-khaarij** abroad

khaariji خارجي *adj* external

khaaṣam خاصم *vt* (**mukhaaṣama, khiṣaam**) **1** to cease to be on speaking terms with **2** to sue

khaaṣṣ خاصّ *adj* **1** special **2** private

khaaṣṣatan خاصّة *adv* especially, particularly

khaati خاتي *adj* mistaken, wrong, at fault

khaatim خاتم *n* (*pl* **khatam, khawaatim**) (finger) ring

khaaṭi خاطي *adj* mistaken, wrong, at fault • *n* (*Chr*) sinner

khaaṭib خاطب *adj* (*pl* **-iin, khuṭṭaab**) engaged to be married (of men)

khaaṭir خاطر *n* **ʿashaan khaaṭir** for the sake of; because of

khaawa خاوى *vt* (**-i, mukhaawaa**) to befriend

khaayib خايب *adj* good-for-nothing, a failure (of a person)

khaayif خايف *adj* (**min**) afraid (of)

khaayin خاين *adj* (*pl* **-iin, khawana**) unfaithful; traitor

khabar خبر *n* (*pl* **akhbaar**) message; news; **al-akhbaar** the news (in the media)

khabaṭ خبط *vt* (**i, khabiṭ, khabaṭaan**) to strike, hit; to nudge; (**ʿala**) to knock, tap

khabaz خبز *vt* (**i, khabiiz**) to bake

khabba خبّى *vt* (**-i, khibbeey**) to hide, conceal

khabbaaz خبّاز *n* baker

khabbar خبّر *vt* (**khibbeer**) to tell, inform

khabbaṭ خبّط *vt* (**khibbeeṭ, takhbiiṭ**) (**ʿala**) to knock, tap

khabiir خبير *n* (**khubara**) **1** expert **2** guide

khabiis خبيس *adj* (*pl* **-iin, khubasa**) **1** cunning, wily, shrewd **2** malignant (disease)

khabiiz خبيز *coll n* cookies

khabṭa خبطة *n* a bump, a knock, a blow

khadaʿ خدع *vt* (**a, khidaʿ**) to cheat, deceive, trick

khadam خدم *vt* (**i, khidma**) to serve

khadar خدر *n* numbness

khadash خدش *vt* (**i, khadish**) to scratch

khadd خد *n* (*pl* **khuduud**) cheek

khaddaʿ خدّع *vt* (**khiddeeʿ**) to fry (onions) lightly

khaddaam خدّام *n* (*m*) servant

khaddaama خدّامة *n* (*f*) servant, maid

khaddar خدّر *vt* (**khiddeer, takhdiir**) to anaesthetize, drug

khadraan خدران *adj* numb

khadsha خدشة *n* (*pl* **khuduush**) scratch

khaduum خدوم *adj* helpful

khaffa خفّ *vi* (**i, khiffa**) to be(come) light (of weight)

khaffaḍ خفّض *vt* (**khiffeeḍ, takhfiiḍ**) to reduce (e.g. price)

khaffaf خفّف *vt* (**khiffeef, takhfiif**) **1** to make lighter, lighten (of weight) **2** to relieve, ease (of pain, pressure, etc.)

khafiif خفيف *adj* (*pl* **-iin, khufaaf**) light (of weight); **damm-o khafiif** he is light-hearted, a humorous person

khajal خجل *n* shyness

khajla خجلة *n* (sense of) shame

khajlaan خجلان *adj* ashamed

khajuul خجول *adj* **1** shy, bashful **2** modest, polite

khala خلا *n* open country; wilderness; desert • *adj invar* empty; **al-beet khala** the house is empty

khalaʿ خلع *vt* (**a, khaliʿ**) to startle, frighten

khalaaṣ خلاص *adv* very, extremely • *interj* that's it, so much for that; enough

khalaaṣ خلاص *n* salvation, deliverance

khalaf خلف *vt* (**i, khilaafa**) **1** to succeed (come after) **2** to fail to keep to; **khalaf waʿid** to break a promise; **khalaf kalaam-o** he went back on his word
khalal خلل *n* defect; **al-beet da fii-ho khalal** the people of this house have bad morals
khalaq خلق *vt* (**i, khaliq**) to create (God)
khalaṭ خلط *vt* (**i, khaliṭ**) to mix
khalawi خلوي *adj* pertaining to the desert, wilderness
khalbaṭ خلبط (**khilbeeṭ, khalbaṭa**) *vt* to mess up, do a job badly
khalf خلف *prep* behind; **be-l-khalf** backwards
khaliiga خليقة *n* (*pl* **khalaayig**) deformed person (*also used as an insult*)
khaliij خليج *n* (*pl* **khiljaan**) gulf
khaliiṭ خليط *n* mixture
khaliyya خليّة *n* (*pl* **khalaaya**) **1** beehive, bees' nest **2** cell
khalkhal خلخل *vt* (**khilkheel, khalkhala**) to work loose (e.g. a tooth, a pole)
khall خل *n* vinegar
khalla خلّى *vt* (**-i, khilleey**) **1** to leave, abandon **2** to allow, let; **khallii-ho** leave him/it; don't do it; **khallii-ho yaʿmil-o** let him do it; **khalli baal-ak** take care!; **Allah yakhallii-k** may God preserve you, thank you
khallaaṭ خلاط *n* mixer, blender
khallaaṭa خلاطة *n* mixer, blender
khallal خلّل (**khilleel**) *vt* to pickle • *vi* **be-** to rub (oil, salve, shampoo)
khallaṣ خلّص *vt* **1** (**khalaaṣ**) (**min**) to finish (with), complete **2** (**takhliiṣ**) to obtain clearance for • *vi* (**khalaaṣ, khilleeṣ**) **min** to get rid of
khalq خلق *n* divine creation
khalṭa خلطة *n* mixture (e.g. sauce)
khaluug خلوق *adj* well-mannered, polite
khalwa خلوة *n* **1** spiritual retreat (Islamic) **2** (*pl* **khalaawi**) Koranic school
khamad خمد *vi* (**i, khamid**) to be extinguished
khamaj خمج *vt* (**i, khamij**) to be overgenerous
khamasṭaashar خمسطاشر *num* fifteen
khamash خمش (**i, khamish**) *vt* to take a handful of
khamiir خمير *adj* leavened or fermented more than necessary
khamiira خميرة *n* yeast, leaven; **khamiira biira** brewer's yeast
khamjaan خمجان *adj* not knowing proper etiquette, overdoing (e.g. in gesture, spending, dressing, hospitality)
khamma خمّ *vt* (**u, khamm**) **1** to scoop or gather with the hands **2** to mislead maliciously
khammaar خمّار *n* sourdough, leaven
khamman خمّن *vt* (**takhmiin**) to estimate, guess
khammar خمّر *vt* (**khimmeer, takhmiir**) to ferment, leaven
khammas خمّس *vt* (**takhmiis**) to share a single item (e.g. one loaf of bread, one cigarette, one chair)
khamra خمرة *n* (*pl* **khumuur**) any alcoholic drink, intoxicant; liquor
khamsa خمسة *num* five
khamsiin خمسين *num* fifty

khamsha خمشة *n* a handful
khanag خنق *vt* (**i, khanig**) to choke, suffocate, stifle, strangle
khandag خندق *n* (*pl* **khanaadig**) (*mil*) ditch, trench
khanjar خنجر *n* (*pl* **khanaajir**) dagger
khannag خنّق *vi* (**khinneeg**) to be in eclipse; **al-gamar khannag** the moon is in eclipse; **al-shamis khannagat** the sun is in eclipse
khanziir خنزير *n* (*pl* **khanaaziir**) pig (*also used as an insult*); **laḥam khanziir** pork
khara خرا *n* faeces, shit
kharaab خراب *n* destruction
kharaaba خرابة *n* a ruined house; **kharaabaat** ruins
kharab خرب *vt* (**i, kharib**) to ruin, destroy
kharag خرق *vt* (**i, kharig**) to violate
kharam خرم *vt* (**u, kharim**) to make or bore a hole, pierce, perforate
kharaṣaana خرصانة *n* **1** building gravel **2** concrete
kharash خرش *vt* (**i, kharish**) to scratch
kharat خرت *vt* (**i, kharit**) to win from s.o. in gambling
kharaṭ خرط *vt* (**i, khiraaṭa**) to carve
kharaṭ خرط *vt* (**i, khariṭ**) **1** to strip a branch of its leaves **2** to wipe off (e.g. remains of food from a plate)
kharbaan خربان *adj* broken, out of order
kharbash خربش *vt* (**khirbeesh, kharbasha**) to scratch
khardal خردل *n* mustard (seeds)
kharfaan خرفان *adj* senile, feeble-minded
kharig خرق *n* (**khuruugaat**) violation
khariif خريف *n* **al-khariif** the rainy season (autumn)
khariifi خريفي *adj* pertaining to the rainy season
khariita خريتة *n* (*pl* **khartooyaat, khurtaayaat**) small bag, pouch
khariiṭa خريطة *n* (*pl* **kharaayiṭ**) map, chart
kharmaan خرمان *adj* suffering withdrawal symptoms (from alcohol, tobacco, coffee, tea)
kharmaj خرمج *vt* (**khirmeej, kharmaja**) **1** to knead **2** to botch, bungle; to mess up
kharmaja خرمجة *n* **1** bungled job, shoddy work **2** jobbery, corrupt practices, rigging
kharra خرّ *vt* **1** (**u, kharr, kharra**) to leak **2** (**u, khariir**) to gush (water)
kharraaji خرّاجي *n* (*pl* **-yya**) water seller
kharraama خرّامة *n* hole punch
kharraaṭ خراط *n* carver, lathe turner
kharrab خرّب *vt* (**khirreeb, takhriib**) to destroy, ruin, wreck
kharraf خرّف *vi* (**khirreef, kharfa**) **1** to be(come) senile, feeble-minded **2** to talk nonsense
kharraf خرّف *vi* (**khirreef, khariif**) **1** to receive rain **al-waaṭa kharrafat** the land has been rained on **2** to spend the rainy season
kharraj خرّج *vt* (**khirreej**) to discharge (cause to leave)
kharraj خرّج *vt* (**takhriij**) **1** to take out, let out; to discharge **2** to cause to graduate
kharram خرّم *vt* (**khirreem, takhriim**) to perforate, punch, pierce; to bore (a hole)
kharsha خرشة *n* scratch

khartooya خرتوية *n* **1** pouch **2** nosebag
kharṭa خرطة *n* (*pl* **khuraṭ**) map, chart
kharṭuum خرطوم *n* (*pl* **kharaaṭiim**) trunk of an elephant
kharṭuum خرطوم *prop n* **al-kharṭuum** Khartoum
kharṭuush خرطوش *n* (*pl* **kharaaṭiish**) **1** hosepipe **2** cartridge (of a gun)
kharuuf خروف *n* (*pl* **khurfaan, khirfaan**) ram, male sheep
khasaara خسارة *n* loss; **baa**ᶜ **be-khasaara** to sell at a loss; **ya khasaara** what a loss! what a pity!
khasaasa خساسة *n* wickedness
khasiis خسيس *adj* mean, ignoble, false, wily
khasraan خسران *adj* **1** broken down, out of order, defective **2** loss-making
khass خس *coll n* lettuce
khassa خسّ *vi* (**i, khassa, khasasaan**) to lose weight
khassar خسّر *vt* (**khisseer, takhsiir**) to damage, spoil; to cause a loss
khastak خستك (**khisteek, khastaka**) *vt* to botch, bungle, work on sth. pretending to know all about it • *vi* **be-** to fool s.o. in an unpleasant way; **khastak be-na khastaka** he fooled us badly
khastaka خستكة *n* shoddy work, bungled job
khaṣa خصى *vt* (**-i, khaṣayaan**) to castrate, geld
khaṣaa'iṣ خصائص *n pl* (*sg* **khaaṣṣiyya**) attributes, properties
khaṣam خصم *vt* (**i, khaṣim**) to deduct, subtract
khaṣiib خصيب *adj* fertile
khaṣiim خصيم *n* (*pl* **khuṣama**) adversary, opponent
khaṣim خصم *n* (*pl* **khuṣuum**) adversary, opponent, party (in a lawsuit)
khaṣkhaṣ خصخص *vt* (**khaṣkhaṣa**) to privatize
khaṣkhaṣa خصخصة *n* privatization
khaṣṣa خصّ *vt* **1** (**u, khuṣuuṣ**) to concern, pertain to; **da ma yakhuṣṣa-ni** it doesn't concern me, that's none of my business **2** (**u, khaṣṣa**) to allot
khaṣṣaṣ خصّص *vi* (**takhṣiiṣ**) **1** to specialize **2** to allot, assign
khashab خشب *coll n* wood
khashaba خشبة *unit n* (*pl* **-aat, akhshaab**) **1** piece of wood **2** podium, stage
khashsha خشّ *vt* (**u, khashsh**) to enter, come in
khashum خشم *n* (*pl* **khushuum**) **1** mouth; muzzle; **khashm al-banaat** elephant-snout (fish) **2** opening; **khashm al-beet a** front door, gate **b** clan
khata ختا *n* (*pl* **akhtaa**) mistake, error, fault
khatam ختم *vt* (**i, khatim**) **1** to conclude, finish **2** to seal; to stamp
khatiya ختية *n* (*pl* **khataaya**) mistake, wrong, sin
khatta ختّ *vt* (**u, khatt**) to put, lay (deposit); **khatta baal-o** he paid attention
khaṭab خطب *vi* (**u, khuṭba**) to preach; to give a speech • *vt* (**u, khuṭuuba**) to get engaged to (of men)
khaṭaf خطف *vt* (**i, khaṭif**) to snatch; to kidnap, abduct

khaṭar خطر *vi* (**i, khaṭra**) to travel unexpectedly; **khaṭar fi baal-o** it occurred to him
khaṭar خطر *n* danger • *adj invar* (*slang*) great
khaṭii'a خطيئة *n* (*pl* **khaṭaaya**) (*Chr*) sin
khaṭiib خطيب *n* **1** (*pl* **khuṭaba**) (*Isl*) preacher **2** (*pl* **khuṭṭaab**) fiancé
khaṭiiba خطيبة *n* fiancée
khaṭiir خطير *adj* **1** dangerous **2** grave, serious, critical **3** (*slang*) great
khaṭiya خطية *n* (*pl* **khaṭaaya**) mistake, wrong, sin
khaṭṭ خط *n* (*pl* **khuṭuuṭ**) **1** line; stripe; **khaṭṭ anaabiib** pipeline; **khaṭṭ at-talafoon** the telephone line **2** track; route (e.g. of a bus) **3** (*agr*) furrow **4** handwriting; calligraphic style; font (printing, computer)
khaṭṭaaṭ خطّاط *n* calligrapher
khaṭṭaṭ خطّط *vt* (**takhṭiiṭ**) **1** to mark with lines or stripes **2** to plan, scheme
khaṭwa خطوة *n* (**khaṭawaat**) footstep, (*also fig*) step
khawaaja خواجة *n* (*f* **khawaajiyya**, *pl* **-aat**) white foreigner
khawwaaf خوّاف *adj* afraid • *n* coward
khawwaf خوّف *vt* (**takhwiif**) to frighten, scare
khawwal خوّل *n* (*pl* **-aat**) homosexual (dominant partner)
khayaal خيال *n* imagination fantasy
khaybaan خيبان *adj* good-for-nothing, a failure (of a person)
khayri خيري *adj* charitable; **ʿamal khayri** charity
khayyaala خيّالة *n* (*mil*) cavalry
khayyaaṭ خيّاط *n* tailor
khayyab خيّب *vt* (**kheeba**); **khayyab amal-i** he disappointed me
khayyaṭ خيّط *vt* (**khiyaaṭa**) to sew; to stitch
khaziina خزينة *n* (*pl* **khazaayin, khizan**) **1** safe; treasury **2** chamber of a gun
khazna خزنة *n* (*pl* **khizan**) **1** safe; treasury **2** chamber of a gun
khazzaan خزّان *n* (*pl* **-aat**) **1** water reservoir, cistern **2** dam
khazzan خزّن *vt* (**khizzeen, takhziin**) to store
kheeba خيبة *n* failure, flop; **kheebat amal** disappointment
kheel خيل *n* (*pl* **khiyuul**) horses
kheema خيمة *n* (*pl* **khiyaam, khiyam**) tent
kheer خير *n* **1** bounty, blessing, well-being, goodness; **be-kheer** in good health; **ḥasal kheer** no harm has been done; **taṣbaḥ ʿala kheer** sleep well; (*reply*) **w-inta min ahl al-kheer** (*lit* you belong to the good people) you too **2** (*pl* **-aat**) good deed; **ʿamal kheer** charity • *adj invar* good
kheesh خيش *coll n* canvas, jute
kheeṭ خيط *n* (*pl* **khiyuuṭ**) thread, string
kheezaraan خيزران *coll n* bamboo, bamboo cane(s)
khibra خبرة *n* experience
khidʿa خدعة *n* (*pl* **khidaʿ**) deception
khidir خدر *vi* (**a, khadar, khadaraan**) to be(come) numb
khidma خدمة *n* (*pl* **khadamaat**) **1** service; **al-khidma**

(al-ʿaskariyya) al-ilzaamiyya obligatory military service 2 favour (kindness)
khifaaḍ خفاض *n* female circumcision; **khifaaḍ firʿooni** pharaonic circumcision
khiffa خفّة *n* lightness (of weight); **khiffat ar-ruuḥ** light-heartedness
khijil خجل *vi* **1** (**a, khajal**) to be(come) shy, bashful **2** (**a, khajal, khajla**) to be(come) ashamed
khilaaf خلاف *n* (*pl* **-aat**) disagreement, dispute, quarrel • *prep* except, apart from; other than; **waaḥid khilaaf-o** another one
khilaal خلال *prep* during; within (time); **min khilaal** via, through
khilga خلقة *n* (*pl* **khilag**) shape or outward appearance (of a person); **ghayyar khilgat-o** he disguised himself
khiliṣ خلص *vi* **1** (**a, khalaaṣ**) to finish; to be finished; to be completed; to be used up (food, goods) **2** (**a, khalaaṣ**) to be(come) exhausted **3** (**a, khalaaṣ, khalṣa, khalaṣaan**) **min a** to finish sth. **b** to get rid of
khimir خمر *vi* (**a, khamaraan**) to ferment; to be leavened
khirib خرب *vi* (**a, kharaab**) to break down, to be out of order
khirim خرم *vi* (**a, kharam**) to suffer from withdrawal symptoms (alcohol, tobacco, coffee, tea)
khirriij خرّيج *n* graduate
khirtiit خرتيت *n* (*pl* **kharaatiit**) rhinoceros
khirwiʿ خروع *n* castor oil plant(s); **zeet khirwiʿ** castor oil
khisir خسر *vi* (**a, khasaara, khusraan**) **1** to be(come) spoiled, damaged; to break down **2** to lose (e.g. in a match)
khiṣb خصب *adj* fertile; **ariḍ khiṣba** fertile soil
khiṣla خصلة *n* (*pl* **khuṣal**) lock of hair
khiṣm خصم *n* (*pl* **khuṣuum**) adversary, opponent, party (in a lawsuit)
khiṣr خصر *n* (*pl* **khuṣuur**) waist
khiṣya خصية *n* testicle
khishin خشن *adj* coarse, rough, tough
khita ختى *vi* (**-i, khata, khatiya**) **1** to err, make a mistake, to be wrong, mistaken **2 ʿala** to wrong s.o.; to offend (verbally or physically)
khitaam ختام *n* end, conclusion
khitaami ختامي *adj* final
khitaan ختان *n* circumcision; **khitaan firʿooni** pharaonic circumcision
khitim ختم *n* (*pl* **akhtaam**) seal; stamp
khiṭa خطى *vi* (**-i, khaṭa, khaṭiya**) **1** to err, make a mistake, to be wrong, mistaken **2 ʿala** to wrong s.o.; to offend (verbally or physically)
khiṭaab خطاب *n* (*pl* **-aat**) **1** letter (message) **2** public address **3** discourse
khiyaana خيانة *n* betrayal
khiyaar خيار *coll n* cucumber(s) (of smooth variety)
khiyaar خيار *n* (*pl* **-aat**) choice
khiyaaṭa خياطة *n* sewing, stitching
khoof خوف *n* **1** fear **2** cowardice

khoor خور *n* (*pl* **kheeraan**) **1** seasonal streambed; seasonal stream **2** ditch dug for rain water, gutter (street)

khooza خوزة *n* (*pl* **-aat, khuwaz**) helmet

khubs خبس *n* cunning, shrewdness, slyness

khuḍaar خضار *n* vegetable(s)

khuḍra خضرة *n* **1** Jew's mallow, melukhia **2** greenness; vegetation

khuḍrawaat خضروات *n pl* vegetables

khuḍurji خضرجي *n* (*pl* **-yya**) greengrocer

khuff خفّ *n* (*pl* **akhfaaf**) **1** foot of a camel **2** a type of slippers

khulaaṣa خلاصة *n* **1** most important part, essence; conclusion **2** afterbirth

khumra خمرة *n* homemade perfume

khumsumiyya خمسميّة *num* five hundred

khunfus خنفس *coll n* (*unit n* **khunfusaana**, *pl* **khanaafis**) beetle(s)

khunn خنّ *n* **khunn al-murkab** hold of a ship

khuraafa خرافة *n* fable

khuraafi خرافي *adj* legendary

khurad خرد *coll n* (*unit n* **khurda**) scrap metal

khurda خردة *adj invar* (*slang*) useless, worthless

khurraaj خرّاج *coll n* abscess(es)

khurtaaya خرتوية *n* (*pl* **-aat, khartooyaat**) pouch; nosebag

khuruj خرج *n* (*pl* **akhraaj**) water skin

khurum خرم *n* (*pl* **akhraam**) hole (in wall, wood, cloth)

khuruuj خروج *n* exit, way out

khusuuf خسوف *n* eclipse of the moon

khuṣuuba خصوبة *n* fertility

khuṣuuma خصومة *n* situation of not being on speaking terms with each other

khuṣuuṣ خصوص *n* **be-khuṣuuṣ** concerning, regarding

khuṣuuṣan خصوصاً *adv* especially, specially, particularly, in particular

khuṣuuṣi خصوصي *adj* private

khuṣuuṣiyya خصوصيّة *adj* privacy

khuṭba خطبة *n* (*pl* **khuṭab**) **1** speech, public address **2** sermon

khuṭṭa خطّة *n* (*pl* **khuṭaṭ**) plan, scheme

khuṭuuba خطوبة *n* engagement to marry

khuṭuura خطورة *n* danger; seriousness

khuṭuuṭ خطوط *n pl* (*sg* **khaṭṭ**) lines; stripes; **khuṭuuṭ jawwiyya** airlines

khuwwa خوّة *n* brotherhood, friendship

l - ل

la لا *neg part* no; **la da…la daak/ la da…wa-la daak** neither this… nor that; **be-la** without

laʿan لعن *vt* (**a, laʿin**) to curse (of God)

laʿba لعبة *n* **1** (*pl* **luʿab**) toy **2** (*pl* **-aat, alʿaab**) game (play); **alʿaab naariyya** fireworks; **beet al-laʿba** (*trad*) the house where the wedding is celebrated

laᶜbanji لعبنجي *n* (*pl* **-yya**) funny-face, joker, wag
laᶜna لعنة *n* curse (of God)
laᶜuut لعوت *n* a species of acacia
la'ann- لأن *conj* because
la'anno لأنو *conj* because
la'iim لئيم *adj* (*pl* **lu'ama**) cunning, shrewd, sly, wily
laaᶜib لاعب *n* player
laafit لافت *adj* **laafit le-n-naẓar** attracting attention
laafta لافتة *n* signboard; nameplate
laaga لاقى *vt* (**-i, mulaagaa**) to meet
laaghi لاغي *adj* void, invalid
laaḥaẓ لاحظ *vt* (**mulaaḥaẓa**) to notice, take note of
laaji لاجي *n* (*pl* **-'iin**) refugee
laak لاك *vt* (**u, looka, lawakaan**) to chew
laakam لاكم *vi* (**mulaakama**) (*sports*) to box
laakin لاكن *conj* but, however, yet
laaloob لالوب *coll n* fruit(s) of the desert date tree
laalooba لالوبة *unit n* **1** a piece of fruit of the desert date tree **2** (*slang*) clitoris
laam لام *vt* (**u, loom**) to blame; to reproach
laamiᶜ لامع *adj* **1** shining, bright **2** famous
laarinja لارنجة *n* mandarin orange
laaṣig لاصق *adj* sticking; clingy; **hu laaṣig lee-kum** he doesn't know when he's not welcome, he's hard to get rid of
laawaz لاوز *vi* (**mulaawaza**) **le-** to confuse or scare s.o. by appearing suddenly or in a different shape than expected
laayḥa لايحة *n* (*pl* **lawaayiḥ**) set of regulations
laayig لايق *adj* proper, suitable; **gheer laayig** improper
laayuug لايوق *adj* (*also fig*) slimy
laazig لازق *adj* sticking; clingy
laazim لازم *part* to have to, must; it is necessary; **laazim tamshi** you must go, you have to go
labad لبد *vi* (**i, labda, labadaan**) to hide o.s.; **ḥamad labad** hide-and-seek
labakh لبخ *vt* (**a, labikh**) to apply bit by bit (e.g. cream, paint, mud)
labakh لبخ *coll n* a species of acacia
laban لبن *n* (*pl* **albaan**) milk; **laban ash-shajara** sap
labani لبني *adj* light blue, sky blue
labaṭ لبط *vt* (**u, labiṭ**) to hit, beat
labbad لبّد *vt* (**libbeed**) to hide, conceal
labbakh لبّخ *vi* (**libbeekh**); **labbakh fi l-kalaam** to be unable to express o.s. clearly
labbakh لبّخ *vt* (**talbiikh**) to apply plaster to a wall
labbas لبّس *vt* (**libbees**) to dress s.o.; to clothe
labsa لبسة *n* (*pl* **-aat, libis**) garment
labsa لبسة *n* dress, attire, clothing; **labsa rasmiyya** official dress, uniform
labṭa لبطة *n* blow, stroke
labwa لبوة *n* lioness
ladaaya لداية *n* hearthstone
ladagh لدغ *vt* (**a, ladigh, ladaghaan**) to sting; to bite (of snakes)
ladeetar لديتر *n* (*pl* **-aat**) radiator
ladgha لدغة *n* sting (wound); bite (of a snake)
laḍam لضم *vt* (**u, laḍim**) **1** to thread a needle **2** to string (beads)

lafakh لفخ *vt* (**a, lafikh**) to kick
lafat لفت *vt* (**i, lafit, lafataan**); **lafat an-naẓar** to attract attention; **lafat an-naẓar le-** to turn one's attention towards
laff لف *n* **laff wa dawaraan** prevaricating, twisting and turning
laffa لفّة *n* **1** turn, turning; **laffat raas** fit of giddiness/dizziness **2** side turning **3** tour **4** four pieces of **kisra** together
laffa لفّ *vi* **1** (**i, laffa**) to turn **2** (**i, laff**) to wind, coil up **3** (**i, laff, lafafaan**) **fi** to tour, go around, go about; **laffa dawaraan** to move in circles; **laffa wa dawwar** to go round a topic •*vt* **1** (**i, laff**) to turn, twist **2** (**i, laffa**) **be-** to wrap; **laffa be-shaash, laffa be-gumaash** to bandage **3** (**i, laff**) to wind **4** (**i, laffa**) to tour, go around, go about
lafkha لفخة *n* kick
laflaf لفلف *vt* (**lifleef, laflafa**) to scour, go from shop to shop; **laflafeena as-suug kullo wa ma ligeena al-gumaash al-daayriin-o** we scoured the whole market but didn't find the cloth we wanted
lagaṭ لقط *vt* (**u, lagiṭ**) to pick (e.g. cotton, flowers)
laggaḥ لقّح *vt* (**talgiiḥ**) to fertilize (plants)
laggaṭ لقّط *vt* (**liggeeṭ, talgiiṭ**) **1** to pick (cotton, flowers) **2** to clean (e.g. rice)
lagiya لقية *n* find (item found); **ligeet-o lagiya** I bought it as a bargain
lagha لغى *vt* (**-i, laghi, laghayaan**) to abolish, cancel
lagham لغم *n* (*pl* **alghaam**) landmine
lahab لهب *coll n* flame(s)
lahas لهس *vi* (**a, lahis, lahasaan**) to pant
lahja لهجة *n* **1** dialect, tongue, speech **2** accent **3** manner of speaking
laḥam لحم *n* (*pl* **luḥuum**) **1** flesh; **beenaat-na laḥam wa damm** we are blood relatives **2** meat; **laḥam ʿajjaali** veal; **laḥam bagar** beef; **laḥam ḍaani** mutton; **laḥam fakhda** leg of mutton, beef, etc.; **laḥam ṣaafi** meat without bones or fat
laḥam لحم *vt* (**a, laḥim**) to solder
laḥas لحس *vt* (**a, laḥasaan, laḥis**) to lick
laḥḥag لحّق *vt* (**liḥḥeeg**) to help to catch up; **laḥḥagtaa-ho ṭ-ṭayaara** I helped him to catch the plane
laḥḥas لحّس *vt* (**liḥḥees**) to bribe
laḥma لحمة *n* (*pl* **luḥuum**) meat; **laḥma mafruuma** minced/ground meat
laḥmiyya لحميّة *n* fibroids
laḥn لحن *n* (*pl* **alḥaan**) tune, melody
laḥsa لحسة *n* **1** lick **2** (*slang*) bribe
laḥẓa لحظة *n* moment
laja لجا *vi* (**-a, lujuu**) to take refuge, to seek asylum
lajam لجم *vt* (**i, lajim**) to reign in, restrain
lajjam لجّم *vt* (**lijjeem, taljiim**) to put a bridle on
lajjan لجّن *vt* (**lajna**) to consider as useless, write off
lajna لجنة *n* (*pl* **lijaan**) committee, board, commission

lakaᶜ لكع *vt* (**a, laki**ᶜ) **1** to use spurs (on a horse) **2** to accelerate

lakam لكم *vt* (**u, lakamaan, lakim**) to punch, box

lakaz لكز *vt* (**i, lakazaan**) to kick (a person, an animal)

lakonda لكوندة *n* basic hotel, pension, guesthouse

lakham لخم *vt* (**a, lakhma**) to confuse

lakhbaaṭ لخباط *n* troublemaker; dishonest person

lakhbaṭ لخبط *vt* (**likhbeeṭ, lakhbaṭa**) **1** to muddle, make a mess of **2** to confuse; to mix up

lakhbaṭa لخبطة *n* **1** mess, muddle, disorder **2** confusion

lakhkha لخّ (**u, lakhkh**) *vt* to mix (dough with other ingredients such as onions, etc.) • *vi* to work on sth. without being skilled; **as-sabbaak da bilukhkh saay** this plumber is useless

lakhkhaṣ لخّص *vt* (**talkhiiṣ**) to summarize

lakhlakh لخلخ *vt* (**likhleekh, lakhlakha**) to work loose (e.g. a tooth, a pole)

lakhma لخمة *n* confusion

lamaᶜ لمع *vi* (**a, lam**ᶜ**aan**) to gleam, shine

lamaḥ لمح *vt* (**a, lamaḥaan**) to glance (at)

lamas لمس *vt* (**a, lamis**) to touch, feel

lamba لمبة *n* (*pl* **-aat, limaḍ**) **1** lamp **2** light bulb; **lambat galawooẓ** screw-in light bulb; **lambat ibra** light bulb of bayonet type; **lambat naaylon** strip light, neon tube

lamḥa لمحة *n* glance, glimpse

lamlam لملم *vt* (**limleem, lamlama**) to gather, collect (things)

lamma لمّة *n* crowd

lamma لمّ (**i, lamm**) *vt* to gather, collect • *vi* **fi** to get hold of

lamma لما *conj* **1** when, as **2** while

lammaᶜ لمّع *vt* (**limmee**ᶜ**, talmii**ᶜ) to polish

lammaaᶜ لمّاع *n* the means to make sth. shine (e.g. polish, a brush, steel wool, lip gloss)

lamman لمّن *conj* **1** when **2** while

laqab لقب *n* (*pl* **alqaab**) **1** nickname **2** title of address

lastik لستك *n* (*pl* **lasaatik**) tyre; **lastik isbeer** spare tyre; **lastik juwwaani** inner tube of a tyre; **al-lastik naazil/munaffis** puncture

laṣag لصق *vt* (**i, laṣig, laṣga**) to glue, stick

laṣga لصقة *n* sticking plaster

laṣṣag لصّق *vt* (**liṣṣeeg, talṣiig**) to glue, stick

laṭaᶜ لطع *vt* (**a, laṭi**ᶜ) to keep s.o. waiting

laṭakh لطخ *vt* (**a, laṭikh, liṭṭeekh**) to stain, blot

laṭam لطم *vt* (**u, laṭim**) to slap

laṭiif لطيف *adj* (*pl* **-iin, luṭaaf**) amiable, friendly, gentle, nice

laṭkha لطخة *n* (*pl* **luṭakh**) stain, blot, spot

laṭma لطمة *n* slap

laṭṭaᶜ لطّع *vt* (**liṭṭee**ᶜ) to keep s.o. waiting

law لو *conj* if; **law kaan** if; **law ma** unless; **ḥatta law; ḥatta wa law** even though, even if; **law samaḥta** excuse me

lawᶜ**a** لوعة *n* passion

lawa لوى *vt* (**-i, lawi, lawiya, lawayaan**) **1** to make crooked, bend (materials) **2** to warp

lawaaya لوايا *n* spasms, cramps in the bowels

lawaayiḥ لوايح *n pl* (*sg* **laayḥa**) regulations; statutes

lawaazim لوازم *n pl* necessities

lawḥa لوحة *n* a painting (art)

lawiya لوية *n* bend (in materials)

lawlab لولب *n* (*pl* **lawaalib**) coil (intrauterine device)

lawlaw لولو *vi* (**liwleew, lawlawa**) to prevaricate, twist and turn

lawwam لوّم *vt* (**liwweem**) to blame; to reproach

lawwan لوّن *vt* (**talwiin**) to colour

lawwas لوّس *vt* (**talwiis, talawwus**) to pollute, contaminate

layli ليلي *adj* pertaining to the night; **ʿasha layli** night blindness

layyan ليّن *vt* (**liyyeen**) **1** to moisten, dampen **2** to make supple

layyas ليّس *vt* (**liyyees, talyiis**) to plaster

layyin ليّن *adj* **1** moist, wet **2** supple, flexible (material); **yadd-o layna** he is generous

lazag لزق *vi* (**i, lazig**) to stick

lazag لزق *vt* (**i, lazig, lazga**) to glue, stick

lazam لزم (**a, luzuum**) *vi* to have to, must; to be necessary, to be imperative; **yalzam tamshi l-mustashfa** you have to go to the hospital • *vt* to have to, must; to be necessary; **yalzam-ak tamshi l-mustashfa** you have to go to the hospital

lazam لزم *adj invar* (referring to first cousin, niece or nephew:); **da wad khaal-i lazam** this is my male cousin from mother's side; **deel banaat ʿamm-i lazam** these are my nieces from father's side; **da wad akhuu-y lazam** this is my nephew from my brother's side

lazga لزقة *n* sticking plaster

laziiz لزيز *adj* delicious

lazij لزج *adj* sticky, viscous

lazza لزّ *vt* (**i, lazz**) to push

lazza لزّة *n* push

lazzaag لزّاق *n* glue

lazzag لزّق *vt* (**lizzeeg, talziig**) to glue, stick

le- لـ *prep* **1** to, for; **lee-y shahreen hina** I have been here for two months **2** until **3** (*indicating possession*) **lee-k akhawaat kutaar** you have a lot of sisters; **lee-ho ʿind-i miit jineeh** I owe him a hundred pounds

leeh ليه *interrog* why

leel ليل *coll n* nighttime; **be-l-leel** at night; in the evening; **nuṣṣ al-leel** midnight

leela ليلة *unit n* (*pl* **-aat, layaali**) night; **al-leela** today; **le-l-leela** until now

leemuun ليمون *coll n* lime(s), lemon(s)

liʿib لعب (**a, liʿib**) *vi* to play • *vt* to play (e.g. a game, football); **liʿib door** to play a role

libaas لباس *n* (*pl* **-aat**) underpants

libda لبدة *n* (*pl* **libad**) **1** saddle pad **2** large breastpiece (women)

libis لبس (**a, libis**) *vi* to get dressed, put on clothes • *vt* to wear, put on (clothes) • *n pl* attire, clothes

lidigh لدغ *vi* (**a, ladigh**) to be stung

liga لقى *vt* (**-a, lagayaan**) to find

ligeemaat لقيمات *n pl* fritters
liḥa لحا *n* bark (of a tree)
liḥaaf لحاف *n* (*pl* **-aat**) light mattress
liḥaam لحام *n* solder
liḥig لحق *vt* (**a, laḥagaan, laḥig**) **1** to catch up with; to reach sth. or s.o. on time **2** to rescue, protect (of a saint)
liḥis لحس *vt* (**a, laḥasaan, laḥis**) to lick
liibi ليبي (*pl* **-yyiin**) *adj* Libyan • *n* a Libyan
liibiya ليبيا *prop n* Libya
liif ليف *coll n* fibre
liifa ليفة *unit n* loofah
liin لين *n* moisture
lijaam لجام *n* (*pl* **-aat**) reins, bridle
likka لكّة *n* sticky mud (when walking) • *adj invar* stupid, dimwitted
limis لمس *vt* (**a, lamis**) to touch, feel
liqaaḥ لقاح *n* pollen
lisaan لسان *n* (*pl* **alsina**) tongue; **abu lisaan** foot and mouth disease
lissa لسّة *n* gums
lissaᶜ لسّع *adv* **1** still; **lissaᶜ badri** it's still early **2** not yet; **lissaᶜ ma khallaṣta** I haven't finished yet **3** (*with an active participle*) just, just now, only recently; **ana lissaᶜ shaarib ḥaaja** I've just had a drink
lista لستة *n* (*pl* **lisat**) list; menu
listik لستك *n* (*pl* **lasaatik**) tyre; **listik isbeer** spare tyre; **listik juwwaani** inner tube of a tyre; **al-listik naazil/munaffis** puncture
listika لستكة *n* (*pl* **lasaatik**) (piece of) elastic
liṣig لصق *vi* (**a, laṣga**) to be(come) stuck (e.g. of key in lock)
liwa لوا *n* (*mil*) **1** (*pl* **-'aat**) brigadier **2** (*pl* **alwiya**) brigade
liwweeᶜ لوّيع *adj* frightening, alarming (person)
liyaaga لياقة *n* collar
liyuuna ليونة *n* flexibility, suppleness
lizig لزق *vi* (**a, lazga**) to be(come) stuck (e.g. of key in lock)
lizza لزّة *n* sensual pleasure
lojisti لوجستي *adj* logistical
looḥ لوح *n* (*pl* **alwaaḥ, leeḥaan**) plank; wooden board
looḥa لوحة *n* **1** board; **looḥat al-katif** shoulder blade; **looḥat iᶜlaan** noticeboard; **looḥa iᶜlaaniyya** billboard **2** licence plate **3** a painting (art)
loola لولى *vt* (**-i, loolaay**) to rock a child; to sing to sleep
loolaḥ لولح *vt* (**looleeḥ**) to swing
loom لوم *n* blame
loon لون *n* (*pl* **alwaan**) colour
loori لوري *n* (*pl* **lawaari**) lorry
looza لوزة *n* (*pl* **-aat, luwaz**) tonsil
luᶜaab لعاب *n* dribble, slobber
luᶜabi لعبي *n* (*pl* **luᶜabanjiyya**) funny-face, joker, wag
lubaan لبان *coll n* **1** chewing gum **2** incense made of gum
lubb لب *n* essence; inner part; **fi lubb** inside
lubnaan لبنان *prop n* Lebanon
lubnaani لبناني (*pl* **-yyiin**) *adj* Lebanese • *n* a Lebanese
lugma لقمة *n* (*pl* **lugam**) **1** morsel, mouthful **2** **ᶜaṣiida**, stiff porridge made with sorghum or millet flour
lugha لغة *n* language; **al-lugha ad-daarija/al-lugha ad-daarijiyya/ al-ᶜaammiyya** the colloquial language; spoken Arabic; **al-lugha al-ᶜarabiyya al-fuṣḥa** the

(eloquent) literary or classical Arabic language
lughz لغز *n* (*pl* **alghaaz**) riddle, puzzle
lujuu لجو *n* refuge, asylum
luṭf لطف *n* gentleness
luuba لوبا *coll n* black-eyed bean(s)
luubya لوبيا *coll n* black-eyed bean(s)
luuli لولي *coll n* (*unit n* **luuliyya**) pearl(s)
luuṭi لوطي (*pl* **lawaayṭa**) *adj* homosexual (submissive partner)
luwaaṭa لواطة *n* homosexuality
luwaz لوز *n pl* tonsils; **iltihaab al-luwaz** tonsilitis
luzuum لزوم *n* need, necessity

m – م

ma ما *part* **1** (*neg*) **a** not **b** neither; **ma daayir yagʿud wa-la yamrug** he will neither stay nor go out **2** (*affirm*) indeed; **ma tatwannasi maʿaa-na shwayya** why don't you chat a bit with us; **ṭabʿan ma shaghghaal, inta ma ʿayyaan** of course you're not working, you are ill **3** (*excl*) what; **ma shaa Allah a** whatever God may intend! (*exclamation to ward off the evil eye*) **b** well I never! (*exclamation of wonder or admiration*) **4** *occurring in phrasal conjunctions, for example* **gabli ma** before; **miteen ma** whenever
ma ما *interrog* (*also* **maa**) what; **maa l-ak** what's the matter with you?; **inta maa l-ak** (*lit* what is it to you) it's not your business!
maʿa مع *prep* **1** with (persons); **maʿa baʿaḍ** together; **maʿa inno/maʿa inn-** although; **maʿa zaalik** nevertheless; **maʿa kawn** though, although **2** (*used for*) to have with; **maʿaa-k karraas-ak** do you have your copybook with you?
maʿaash معاش *n* (*pl* **-aat**) **1** retirement; **nazal al-maʿaash** to retire **2** pension
maʿadiyya معديّة *n* ferry boat
maʿalaga معلقة *n* (*pl* **maʿaalig**) spoon
maʿarraṣ معرّص *n* pimp
maʿaṭ معط *vt* (**a, maʿiṭ**) to pull out (e.g. hair); to pluck (e.g. a chicken)
maʿbad معبد *n* (*pl* **maʿaabid**) temple (of worship)
maʿdan معدن *n* (*pl* **maʿaadin**) mineral; **maʿdan-o kwayyis/ṭayyib** he is from a decent family; his morals are good
maʿdani معدني *adj* mineral; **mooya maʿdaniyya** mineral water
maʿduum معدوم *adj* nonexistent, absent (of things); **as-sukkar maʿduum** there's no sugar at all
maʿfi معفي *adj* exempted
maʿguul معقول *adj* reasonable; **ma maʿguul** unreasonable; unbelievable!
maʿhad معهد *n* (*pl* **maʿaahid**) institute
maʿida معدة *n* stomach
maʿiisha معيشة *n* (*pl* **maʿaayish**) means of existence; livelihood
maʿjuun معجون *n* putty; **maʿjuun asnaan** toothpaste; **maʿjuun ḥilaaga** shaving cream
maʿleesh معليش *interj* **1** never mind, don't worry about it, it doesn't matter **2** sorry

maʿluumaat معلومات *n pl* data, information
maʿmal معمل *n* (*pl* **maʿaamil**) laboratory
maʿmuudiyya معموديّة *n* baptism
maʿmuul معمول *adj* made; **maʿmuul min shinu** what is it made of?
maʿna معنى *n* (*pl* **maʿaani**) meaning, sense; **maʿnaa-ho/-ha shinu** what does it mean?; **maʿnaat-o/-a shinu** what does it mean?
maʿnawi معنوي *adj* mental; **daʿam maʿnawi** moral support
maʿnawiyyaat معنويّات *n pl* morale, spirits
maʿraḍ معرض *n* (*pl* **maʿaariḍ**) exhibition **maʿraḍ al-kitaab** book fair
maʿraka معركة *n* (*pl* **maʿaarik**) battle
maʿrifa معرفة *n* **1** knowledge **2** (*pl* **maʿaarif**) acquaintance
maʿruuf معروف *adj* well-known
maʿruuf معروف *n* favour (kindness); **ʿamal lee-y/fi-yya maʿruuf** he did me a favour
maʿṣuur معصور *adj* **1** squeezed; being in a tight spot, under pressure **2** **ʿala** feeling responsible for
maʿyuun معيون *adj* stricken by the evil eye
ma'kuulaat مأكولات *n pl* food(s)
ma'luuf مألوف *adj* familiar
ma'suur مأسور *n* prisoner of war
ma'zuun مأزون *n* a person authorized to perform Muslim marriages and divorces
maaʿuun ماعون *n* (*pl* **mawaaʿiin**) kitchen utensil
maadda مادّة *n* (*pl* **mawaadd**) **1** substance, matter; material; **maadda khaam** raw material **2** school or university subject
maaddi مادّي *adj* material; materialistic
maaḍi ماضي *adj* sharp (e.g. a knife)
maaḍi ماضي *n* **al-maaḍi** **1** the past **2** (*gram*) perfect (past) tense
maahir ماهر *adj* (*pl* **mahara**) skilful, proficient
maahiyya ماهيّة *n* (*pl* **mawaahi**) monthly salary
maakil ماكل *adj* (*v* **akal**) **ana lissaʿ maakil ḥaaja** I have just eaten sth.
maakin ماكن *adj* big, huge
maal مال *n* (*pl* **amwaal**) property, money
maal مال *vi* (**i, mayalaan, meel**) (**le-, ila**) **1** to slant, slope, lean (to/toward) **2** to be inclined to, favourably disposed toward
maali مالي *adj* financial
maaliḥ مالح *adj* salty
maalik مالك *n* (*pl* **mullaak**) owner
maama ماما *n* title of and respectful form of address or reference to an older woman, applied in particular by children to a schoolteacher
maaniʿ مانع *n* (*pl* **mawaaniʿ**) obstacle, impediment, obstruction, objection; **ma fii maaniʿ** there's no objection
maaniʿ مانع *adj* very strong (person)
maaniḥ مانح *n* donor
maaras مارس *vt* (**mumaarasa**) to practise
maareeg ماريق *n* a variety of sorghum
maarig مارق *adj* leaving, going out; **abga maarig** let's go!
maaris مارس *n* March
maarka ماركة *n* **1** chip, counter, token (in a restaurant) **2** brand,

trade name; **maarka tijaariyya** trademark

maaroog ماروق *n* manure; **ya ḥumaar al-maaroog, ya ʿadiim az-zoog** (*lit* you donkey of the manure, having no manners) said to s.o. who is impolite

maas ماس *coll n* diamond(s); **fii-ho maas** it could give an electric shock, it's live

maasuura ماسورة *n* (*pl* **-aat, mawaasiir**) **1** pipe, tube; **maasuurat al-bundugiyya** gun barrel **2** tap **3** (*slang*) said about sth./s.o. that/who raised false expectations

maaṣ ماص *vi* (**u, mooṣa**) to dissolve

maasha ماشة *n* tongs for picking up hot coals

maashiyya ماشيّة *n* (*pl* **mawaashi**) cattle; livestock

maat مات *vi* (**u, moot**) to die; **maat be-j-juuʿ** to starve; **ash-shaah maat** checkmate

maayiʿ مايع *adj* **1** liquid **2** pliable; **mawgif maayiʿ** unclear, undecided position **3** womanish (of a man)

maayo مايو *n* May

mabaaḥis مباحس *n pl* state investigation department; **raajil mabaaḥis** secret agent

mabda مبدا *n* (*pl* **mabaadi**) principle

mabda'i مبدئي *adj* initial; fundamental; **faatuura mabda'iyya** pro forma invoice

mabḥuuḥ مبحوح *adj* hoarse

mabiit مبيت *n* any place where one spends the night

mablagh مبلغ *n* (*pl* **mabaaligh**) amount of money, sum; **al-mablagh al-kulli** the total amount

mabluul مبلول *adj* wet

mabna مبنى *n* (*pl* **mabaani**) building

mabruuk مبروك *interj* congratulations; **alf mabruuk** hearty congratulations

mabsuuṭ مبسوط *adj* **1** (**be-, min**) happy, glad (about), pleased (with) **2** slightly drunk **3** well-off

mabṣam مبصم *n* thumb

mabshara مبشرة *n* grater

mabwala مبولة *n* urinal

mabyaḍ مبيض *n* (*pl* **mabaayiḍ**) ovary

mada مدى *n* range, extent

madaam مدام *n* madam, lady

madagg مدق *n* (*pl* **-aat**) pestle

madaḥ مدح *vt* (**a, madiḥ**) to praise

madani مدني *adj* civil, civic; **al-mujtamaʿ al-madani** civil society; **at-tasqiif al-madani** civic education

madaniyya مدنيّة *n* civilized world

madassa مدسّة *n* **1** hiding place **2** untruthful speech

madbagha مدبغة *n* (*pl* **madaabigh**) tannery

madd مد *n* high tide (at the seaside)

madda مدّة *n* rest (lying down)

madda مدّ *vt* (**i, madd**) **le-** to extend (e.g. a hand); to hand over • *vi* (**i, madda**) (**fi**) to prolong, lengthen; **Allah yamidd fi ayaam-ak** may God give you a long life

maddaad مدّاد *n* (*pl* **-aat**) rafter; beam or strut (laid lengthways)

maddad مدّد *vt* (**middeed, tamdiid**) **1** to extend, expand **2** to prolong

madfuuʿ مدفوع *adj* paid; prepaid

madiida مديدة *n* (thin) porridge

madiiḥ مديح *n* (*pl* **madaayiḥ**) **1** praise **2** poem or song in praise of the prophet Mohammed

madiina مدينة *n* (*pl* **mudun**) **1** city, town **2** district of a town

madkhal مدخل *n* (*pl* **madaakhil**) **1** entrance **2** access

madkhana مدخنة *n* (*pl* **madaakh-in**) chimney

madrasa مدرسة *n* (*pl* **madaaris**) school; **madrasat al-asaas** primary (basic) school; **al-madrasa al-ibtidaa'iyya** primary school; **al-madrasa as-saanawiyya** secondary school; **al-madrasa as-saanawiyya al-ʿulya** higher secondary school

madrasi مدرسي *adj* pertaining to school

madyuun مديون *adj* indebted, in debt; **ana madyuun lee-ho** I owe him

maḍa مضا *vi* (**-i, imḍa**) to sign

maḍaagha مضاغة *n* temple (head)

maḍabb مضبّ *n* (*pl* **-aat**) alley, narrow passage, bottleneck

maḍakhkha مضخّة *n* hand pump

maḍarra مضرّة *n* harm; **ʿawaja ma fii, illa l-maḍarra ḥaaṣla** there's no problem, but harm there is

maḍghuuṭ مضغوط *adj* being in a tight spot, under pressure

maḍmaḍ مضمض *vt* (**maḍmaḍa**) to rinse out the mouth

maḍmuun مضمون *adj* guaranteed, sure; reliable, trustworthy

maḍmuun مضمون *n* (*pl* **maḍaamiin**) content(s) (of e.g. a book)

maḍrab مضرب *n* (*pl* **maḍaarib**) **1** racquet, bat **2** egg whisk

maḍyuuf مضيوف *adj* having guests

mafakk مفك *n* (*pl* **-aat**) screwdriver

mafarr مفر *n* escape; **ma fii mafarr** there is no way out, it's inevitable

mafhuum مفهوم *n* (*pl* **mafaahiim**) concept, notion, idea

maframa مفرمة *n* mincer, meat grinder

mafrash مفرش *n* (*pl* **mafaarish**) **1** bedspread **2** tablecloth

mafruuḍ مفروض *adj invar* considered proper; **mafruuḍ/ al-mafruuḍ** it is assumed; it is supposed

mafruuma مفرومة *n* minced meat, ground meat

mafṣal مفصل *n* (*pl* **mafaaṣil**) joint (of the body)

mag مق *n* (*pl* **-aat**) mug

magʿad مقعد *n* (*pl* **magaaʿid**) seat

magaas مقاس *n* (*pl* **-aat**) size (of clothes, shoes)

magannan مقنّن *adj* having a burnt taste (of milk)

magaṣṣ مقص *n* (*pl* **-aat**) scissors

magbuul مقبول *adj* acceptable

magdara مقدرة *n* (*and* **magdira**) ability, capacity, power; **ṣaaḥib magdara** powerful, influential

magiil مقيل *n* any place where one spends a midday rest

maglab مقلب *n* (*pl* **magaalib**) pitfall

magluub مقلوب *adj* inside out, upside down

magṣuuṣa مقصوصة *n* (*pl* **magaaṣiiṣ**) slotted ladle, skimmer

magṭuuʿiyya مقطوعيّة *n* piecework

maghaṣ مغص *n* abdominal pain; stomach ache; menstruation cramps

maghaṣ مغص *vt* (**i, maghaṣ**) to treat unjustly; to vex

maghaṣa مغصة *n* resentment, grudge

maghfira مغفرة *n* forgiveness

maghghaṣ مغّص *vt* (**mighgheeṣ**) to treat unjustly; to vex
maghlag مغلق *n* (*pl* **maghaalig**) builder's merchant, store for building materials
maghnaṭiis مغنطيس *n* magnet
maghnaṭiisi مغنطيسي *adj* magnetic
maghrab مغرب *vi* (**mighrab**) to be dusk
maghruur مغرور *adj* conceited, haughty, arrogant
maghshuush مغشوش *adj* counterfeit
maghyuuẓ مغيوظ *adj* furious
mahaana مهانة *n* humiliation
mahaara مهارة *n* skill, proficiency, craftsmanship
mahal مهل *n* **ʿala mahl-ak** take your time!
mahar مهر *n* (*pl* **muhuur**) dowry
mahdi مهدي *adj* (*Isl*) rightly guided; **al-mahdi** the Mahdi
mahhal مهّل *vt* (**mihheel, tamhiil**) respite
mahla مهلة *n* respite
mahma مهما *conj* whatever, no matter what
mahmuum مهموم *adj* (**be-**) concerned, anxious, worried (about)
mahoogani مهوقني *n* mahogany
mahrajaan مهرجان *n* (*pl* **-aat**) festival
mahzala مهزلة *n* (*pl* **mahaazil**) laughing stock, farce; **da/hu mahzala** this/he is ridiculous
maḥabba محبّة *n* love, affection
maḥalabiyya محلبيّة *n* essence of mahaleb (used in cosmetics and henna)
maḥall محل *n* (*pl* **-aat**) **1** place **2** shop
maḥalli محلّي *adj* local, indigenous
maḥalliyya محلّيّة *n* administrative district of a town municipality; governorate
maḥammad محمّد *n* **maḥammad aḥmad** Mr Average, the man in the street; **maḥammad walad** said about a boyish girl
maḥanna محنّة *n* affection, kindness, sympathy, compassion
maḥaṭṭa محطّة *n* **1** station; **maḥaṭṭat al-banziin** petrol station, gas station; **maḥaṭṭat as-sikka ḥadiid** railway station; **maḥaṭṭat izaaʿa** broadcasting station **2** bus stop
maḥbuub محبوب *adj* beloved; favourite
maḥbuus محبوس (*pl* **maḥaabiis**) *adj* imprisoned • *n* prisoner
maḥduud محدود *adj* limited
maḥḍar محضر *n* (*pl* **maḥaaḍir**) **1** formal record of a police case **2** minutes, record (e.g. of a meeting)
maḥfaẓa محفظة *n* (*pl* **maḥaafiẓ**) wallet, purse (for women)
maḥguur محقور *adj* contemptible
maḥḥan محّن *vt* (**miḥḥeen**) to bewilder
maḥkama محكمة *n* (*pl* **maḥaakim**) tribunal, court; **maḥkamat al-mashaayikh** traditional tribal court; **al-maḥkama ad-dastuuriyya** constitutional court; **maḥkama ʿulya** high court; **maḥkama jinaa'iyya** criminal court; **maḥkama juz'iyya** summary court; **maḥkama sharʿiyya** islamic court; **maḥkamat al-isti'naaf** court of appeal
maḥkuum محكوم *adj invar* **ʿala** sentenced, convicted; **hi maḥkuum ʿalee-ha be-l-iʿdaam** she is sentenced to death
maḥkuumiyya محكوميّة *n* court sentence

maḥlab محلب *n* mahaleb seeds (used as a basic ingredient for perfume and **dilka**)

maḥluul محلول *n* (*pl* **maḥaaliil**) (*chem*) solution

maḥmuul محمول *adj* burdened (e.g. with responsibilities)

maḥmuum محموم *adj* feverish

maḥnaan محنان *adj* bewildered, perplexed, at a loss

maḥni محني *adj* curved

maḥsuubiyya محسوبيّة *adv* on the basis of a personal or family relationship; **ʿayyan-a maḥsuubiyya saakit** he appointed her only because she is family/a friend of the family

maḥṣuul محصول *n* (*pl* **maḥaaṣiil**) crop, produce, yield

maḥshi محشي *n* stuffed vegetables

maḥẓuuẓ محظوظ *adj* lucky

majaaʿa مجاعة *n* famine

majaal مجال *n* (*pl* **-aat**) field, domain, scope

majaari مجاري *n pl* (*sg* **majra**) sewer, drains

majalla مجلّة *n* magazine, periodical

majar مجر *prop n* **al-majar** Hungary

majaraawi مجراي (*pl* **-yyiin**) *adj* Hungarian • *n* a Hungarian

majari مجري (*pl* **-yyiin**) *adj* Hungarian • *n* an Hungarian

majduuʿ مجدوع *adj* thrown (away); **ligeet-o majduuʿ** I bought it as a bargain

majhuud مجهود *n* (*pl* **-aat**) effort, exertion **ʿamal majhuud** to make an effort

majjaan مجّان *adj* free of charge, gratis

majjaanan مجّانا *adv* free of charge, gratis

majjaani مجّاني *adj* free of charge, gratis

majlis مجلس *n* (*pl* **majaalis**) council, assembly, board; **majlis ʿaskari** military court; **majlis al-idaara** board of directors, management board; **majlis al-umana** board of trustees; **al-majlis al-waṭani** the national assembly; **majlis ash-shaʿb** parliament; **majlis ash-shiyuukh** council of elders; senate

majmaʿ مجمع *n* (*pl* **-aat**) cooperative, collective; **majmaʿ ṭibbi** medical practice

majmuuʿ مجموع *n* (*pl* **-aat**) total

majmuuʿa مجموعة *n* group, collection, complex; **majmuuʿa mustahdafa** target group

majnuun مجنون (*pl* **majaaniin**) *adj* crazy, mad, insane, lunatic

majra مجرى *n* (*pl* **majaari**) channel, irrigation channel, streambed; drain; **majra al-bool** urethra

majzara مجزرة *n* (*pl* **majaazir**) slaughter, massacre

majzuub مجزوب *adj* (*pl* **majaaziib**) in a state of ecstasy (of dervishes)

majzuum مجزوم (*pl* **majaaziim**) *adj* leprous • *n* leper

makaan مكان *n* (*pl* **amaakin**) **1** place; **makaan muʿayyan** somewhere **2** room, space

makaana مكانة *n* standing, esteem; respectable position

makaaniiki مكانيكي *n* (*pl* **-iyya**) mechanic, fitter

makaasib مكاسب *n pl* (*sg* **maksab**) earnings

makana مكنة *n* machine; engine; **makanat khiyaaṭa** sewing

machine; **makanat ḥilaaga** **1** safety razor **2** electric shaver
makaroona مكرونة *n* macaroni; pasta
makashshan مكشّن *adj* browned (of onions); **makashshan be-la baṣal** (*lit* browned without onions) no need to sing his praises, he's his own best advertisement
makḥala مكحلة *n* (*pl* **makaaḥil**) kohl container
makiida مكيدة *n* (*pl* **makaayid**) intrigue, scheme
makk مك *n* (*pl* **mukuuk**) chief of a tribe
makkaar مكّار *adj* cunning, shrewd
maknasa مكنسة *n* (*pl* **makaanis**) broom; **maknasa kahraba'iyya** vacuum cleaner
makrafoon مكرفون *n* (*pl* **-aat**) microphone
maksab مكسب *n* (*pl* **makaasib**) profit, gain, earning
maksuuf مكسوف *adj* shy, bashful
makshaṭa مكشطة *n* scraper (workshop)
maktab مكتب *n* (*pl* **makaatib**) desk; office; **maktab al-istiʿlaamaat** inquiry office
maktaba مكتبة *n* **1** bookcase **2** library **3** bookshop **4** stationery shop
maktuub مكتوب *adj* **1** written **2** decreed by God
makwa مكوة *n* (*pl* **makaawi**) iron (for pressing clothes)
makwaji مكوجي *n* (*pl* **-iyya**) laundryman
makhaaḍa مخاضة *n* (**makhaayiḍ**) ford
makhadda مخدّة *n* pillow
makhaḍ مخض *vt* (**a, makhiḍ**) to churn (milk)
makhbaz مخبز *n* (*pl* **makhaabiz**) bakery
makhlab مخلب *n* (*pl* **makhaalib**) claw
makhluug مخلوق *n* (*pl* **makhaaliig**) creature
makhraṭa مخرطة *n* (*pl* **makhaariṭ**) lathe
makhruuga مخروقة *n* (*pl* **makhaarig**) hip
makhṣi مخصي *adj* (*pl* **-yyiin**) castrated
makhṣuuṣ مخصوص *adj* specific, particular • *adv* **le-** specially for, especially for
makhtuuf مختوف *adj* **makhtuuf al-loon** pale (of skin)
makhṭuuba مخطوبة *adj f* engaged to be married
makhzan مخزن *n* (*pl* **makhaazin**) store, storeroom, warehouse
makhzanji مخزنجي *n* (*pl* **-yya**) storekeeper
malʿab ملعب *n* (*pl* **malaaʿib**) playground
malʿaga ملعقة *n* (*pl* **malaaʿig**) spoon
malʿuub ملعوب *n* (*pl* **malaaʿiib**) trick
malʿuun ملعون *adj* (*pl* **malaaʿiin**) **1** cursed **2** naughty
mala ملى *vt* (**-a, mali**) **1** to fill **2** to wind up (e.g. a clock)
malaabis ملابس *n pl* clothes; **malaabis daakhiliyya** underwear
malaahi ملاهي *n pl* funfair, amusement park
malaak ملاك *n* (*pl* **malaayka**) angel
malaama ملامة *n* blame; reproach
malaamiḥ ملامح *n pl* (*sg* **malmaḥ**) features

malaff ملف *n* (*pl* **-aat**) file (of papers); folder (computer); portfolio
malak ملك *vt* (**i, malik**) to own, possess; **malak nafs-o** to restrain o.s.
malaki ملكي *adj* **1** royal **2** civil (as opposed to military)
malakh ملخ *vt* (**a, malikh, malakhaan**) **1** to dislocate **2** to sprain
malal ملل *n* boredom, tediousness; **ḥassa be-malal** to feel bored
malaṣ ملص *vi* (**u, maliṣ**) to undress • *vt* to take off (clothes or jewellry)
malfaḥa ملفحة *n* (*pl* **malaafiḥ**) large shawl (worn by men)
malghi ملغي *adj* **1** cancelled **2** void, invalid
malḥuuẓa ملحوظة *n* remark, observation
malik ملك *n* (*pl* **muluuk**) king
malika ملكة *n* queen
malja ملجا *n* (*pl* **malaaji**) place of refuge, shelter; **malja yutama** orphanage
malka ملكة *n* queen
malkhuum ملخوم *adj* **1** confused **2** very busy
malla ملّى *vt* (**-i, tamliya**) to dictate
mallaaki ملاكي *adj invar* privately owned; **ʿarabiyya mallaaki** a private car
mallaala ملالة *n* hot sand
mallaḥ ملّح (**milleeḥ**) *vi* to bring more food; **ya walad, malliḥ lee-na** hey boy, bring us some more food
mallas ملّس (**millees, tamliis**) *vt* **1** to smoothe (the surface) **2** to caress • *vi* **le-** to flatter in order to win a favour
mallaṣ ملّص *vi* (**milleeṣ, tamliiṣ**) to undress • *vt* to take off (clothes or jewellry)
malooda ملودة *n* large weeding hoe
malwa ملوة *n* (*pl* **malaawi**) unit of weight equal to 3.145 kg
malwi ملوي *adj* bent, crooked, curved
malyaan مليان *adj* **1** full **2** plump
mamaḥḥan ممحن *adj* perplexed, bewildered, at a loss
mamarr ممر *n* (*pl* **-aat**) passage; corridor, aisle
mamkuun ممكون *adj* **min** being cornered, hard pressed by
mamlaka مملكة *n* (*pl* **mamaalik**) kingdom
mamsuukh ممسوخ *adj* having bad manners
mamsuus ممسوس *adj* insane
manaʿ منع *vt* (**a, maniʿ**) to forbid, prohibit; to prevent
manaakh مناخ *n* (*pl* **-aat**) climate
manaakhreen مناخرين *n pl* nose
manaama منامة *n* sleeping car (on train)
manaara منارة *n* lighthouse; beacon
manaḥ منح *vt* (**a, minḥa**) to grant, award
manaṣṣa منصّة *n* dais, podium
manbaʿ منبع *n* (*pl* **manaabiʿ**) source of a river
mandoola مندولة *n* food basket
manduub مندوب *n* (*pl* **-iin, manaadiib**) delegate, representative; **manduub sharika** company representative
manfa منفى *n* (*pl* **manaafi**) exile
manfaʿa منفعة *n* (*pl* **manaafiʿ**) benefit
manfuukh منفوخ *adj* **1** inflated **2** conceited; pompous

manga منقة *n* (*pl* **manga**) mango(es)
mangad منقد *n* (*pl* **manaagid**) brazier, charcoal stove
mangala منقلة *n* (*pl* **manaagil**) protractor (geometry)
manghooli منغولي *adj* (*pl* **-yyiin**) having Downs syndrome
manhaj منهج *n* (*pl* **manaahij**) method; **manhaj ad-diraasa** curriculum
manḥuus منحوس *adj* unlucky, unfortunate
manihool منهول *n* (*pl* **-aat**) manhole
manjam منجم *n* (*pl* **manaajim**) mine (e.g. coal, iron)
mansaj منسج *n* (*pl* **manaasij**) loom (for weaving cloth)
manshaṭ منشط *n* (*pl* **manaashiṭ**) activity (such as a workshop, seminar)
manshuur منشور *n* (*pl* **-aat, manaashiir**) circular, brochure, pamphlet, leaflet, flyer
mantuuj منتوج *n* produce, yield
manṭig منطق *n* logic
manṭiga منطقة *n* (*pl* **manaaṭig**) area, zone
manṭigi منطقي *adj* logical
manzil منزل *n* (*pl* **manaazil**) house; residence; dwelling
manẓar منظر *n* (*pl* **manaaẓir**) view, sight, lookout
maqaabir *n pl* مقابر (*sg* **maqbara**) cemetery, graveyard
maqaala مقالة *n* article (in journal or magazine)
maqaaṣṣa مقاصّة *n* exchange of debts
maqbara مقبرة *n* (*pl* **maqaabir**) grave, tomb
marʿa مرعى *n* (*pl* **maraaʿi**) pasture, grazing land
marʿuub مرعوب *adj* frightened, terrified
mara مرة *n* (*pl* **niswaan, nasaawiin**) **1** woman **2** wife; **marat abuu-y** my stepmother
maraakbi مراكبي *n* (*pl* **-yya**) boatman; **ʿazuumat maraakbiyya** an insincere invitation
maraara مرارة *n* **1** gall **2** a dish of raw liver and tripe served with lemon and hot pepper
marabba مربّى *n* jam
maraḍ مرض *n* (*pl* **amraaḍ**) disease; sickness; **maraḍ as-sukkari** diabetes
maraḍraḍ مرضرض *adj* feeling pain all over the body
marag مرق *vi* (**u, muruug**) to go out, leave • *vt* to discharge (e.g. from hospital)
maraga مرقة *n* broth
maragoot مرقوت *coll n* bedbug(s)
maraṣ مرص *v* (**u, mariṣ, maraṣaan**) to knead **kisra** with water
marashsha مرشّة *n* sprinkler
marazabba مرزبّة *n* sledgehammer
marbuuʿ مربوع *adj* **1** stocky **2** medium (of height) • *n* **1** (*pl* **-aat**) block, group of houses **2** (*pl* **maraabiiʿ**) square
marbuuk مربوك *adj* **1** muddled **2** confused, bewildered
marḍaan مرضان *adj* ill, sick
marfaʿiin مرفعين *n* (*pl* **maraafiʿiin**) hyena
marga مرقة *n* (*trad*) outing (women leaving the house for a visit to family, friends, or market)
margoot مرقوت *coll n* bedbug(s)
marham مرهم *n* (*pl* **maraahim**) ointment, salve, cream

marḥab مرحب *interj* welcome; **marḥab bee-k** welcome!; **marḥabteen/maraaḥib** you're most welcome!
marḥaban مرحبا *interj* welcome
marḥala مرحلة *n* (*pl* **maraaḥil**) stage (period)
marḥuum مرحوم *n* (*pl* **maraaḥiim**); **al-marḥuum** the late (said of a deceased person)
marii' مريء *n* **al-marii'** oesophagus, gullet
mariiḍ مريض (*pl* **marḍa**) *adj* ill, sick • *n* patient
mariina مرينة *n* (*pl* **maraayin**) supporting beam (roof)
mariisa مريسة *n* (*pl* **maraayis**) millet beer
marin مرن *adj* flexible (person, position)
markaz مركز *n* (*pl* **maraakiz**) **1** central place, centre; **markaz ṣiḥḥi** health centre; **markaz ar-ri'aasa** headquarters **2** station (government post)
markazi مركزي *adj* central
markuub مركوب *n* (*pl* **maraakiib**) (*trad*) shoe; **abu markuub** shoe bill stork
markhi مرخي *adj* **1** loose, slack **2** tasteless, insipid (of food)
marma مرمى *n* **1** range (e.g. of a gun) **2** goal (net); **ḥaaris al-marma** goalkeeper; **gaayim al-marma** goalpost
marra مرّة *n* instant of time; **marra waaḥda** once; **marrateen** twice; **marra marra** sometimes, occasionally; **be-l-marra** in one go; **kull marra** every time; **marra min al-marraat** once upon a time; **marra taanya/marra taani/kamaan marra** once more, again • *adv* once
marra مرّ (**u, muruur**) *vi* **1** to pass **2 fi** to pass (an exam) **3 be-/ʿala** to go past, pass by **4 ʿala** to call in at, drop in on • *vt* to pass (an exam)
marraat مرّات *adv* sometimes, occasionally; **marraat katiira** often, frequently
marrag مرّق *vt* (**marga, mirreeg**) to take out, bring out; to discharge (e.g. from a hospital, prison)
marran مرّن *vt* (**tamriin**) to cause, practise
marrar مرّر *vt* (**tamriir**) to hand, pass (e.g. the salt, football)
marsa مرسى *n* (*pl* **maraasi**) anchorage, small harbour
martaba مرتبة *n* (*pl* **maraatib**) **1** mattress **2** position, function, rank
marwaḥa مروحة *n* (*pl* **maraawiḥ**) electric fan, ventilator
marwaḥiyya مروحيّة *n* helicopter
marwuush مرووش *adj* scatterbrained
maryala مريلة *n* (*pl* **-aat, maraayil**) **1** bib **2** apron
mas'ala مسألة *n* (*pl* **masaa'il**) issue, question, affair, matter
mas'uul مسؤول *adj* responsible, liable; **mas'uul min** responsible for, in charge of
mas'uuliyya مسؤوليّة *n* responsibility, liability
masa مسا *n* afternoon evening; **fi l-masa, be-l-masa;** in the evening; **masaa l-kheer/masaa n-nuur** good afternoon; good evening
masaa'an مساء *adv* in the evening
masaafa مسافة *n* **1** distance **2** period of time

masaaj مساج *n* (*pl* **-aat**) massage
masaam مسام *n* (*pl* **-aat**) pore
masaana مسانة *n* bladder
masaḥ مسح *vt* (**a, masiḥ**) to survey (land; inhabitants)
masaḥ مسح *vt* (**a, masiḥ, masaḥaan**) to wipe, erase, rub out, raze; **masaḥ be-l-faara** to plane; **masaḥ shanab-o/masaḥ lee-ho shanab-o** he bribed him •*vi* **ʿala** to stroke; **masaḥ ʿala shanab-o** he bribed him
masak مسك *vt* (**i, masik, masakaan**) **1** to hold, take hold of; to cling to; **masak nafs-o** to restrain o.s. **2** to catch; to seize, arrest
masal مسل *n* (*pl* **amsaal**) **1** proverb, saying **2** example (illustration), instance
masalan مسلا *adv* for example
masalla مسلّة *n* large needle
masḥa مسحة *n* ointment
masḥana مسحنة *n* (*pl* **masaaḥin**) mill
masḥuug مسحوق *n* powder
masiḥ مسح *n* (*pl* **musuuḥaat**) survey
masiid مسيد *n* (*pl* **masaayid**) Koranic school
masiiḥ مسيح *n* **al-masiiḥ** the Messiah, Christ
masiiḥi مسيحي *adj* (*pl* **-yyiin**) Christian
masiikh مسيخ *adj* tasteless, insipid
masiil مسيل *n* **ma lee-ho masiil** there's no one like him
masiira مسيرة *n* (*pl* **masaayir**) hair plait
masiira مسيرة *n* peaceful demonstration, march
masjid مسجد *n* (*pl* **masaajid**) mosque
masjuun مسجون *n* (*pl* **masaajiin**) prisoner
maskan مسكن *n* (*pl* **masaakin**) dwelling, residence
maskuun مسكون *adj* haunted by spirits
maskhara مسخرة *n* (*pl* **masaakhir**) laughing stock, farce; **da/hu maskhara** this/he is ridiculous
masookar مسوكر *adj* firmly locked, securely locked
masraḥ مسرح *n* (*pl* **masaariḥ**) **1** theatre; stage; **masraḥ al-ʿaraayis** puppet theatre **2** scene (e.g. of a crime)
masraḥi مسرحي *adj* theatrical
masraḥiyya مسرحيّة *n* theatre play, theatrical performance
massaaḥ مسّاح *n* land surveyor; **massaaḥ jookh** flatterer
massaaḥa مسّاحة *n* wiper; erasing rubber
massaḥ مسّح *vt* (**misseeḥ**) to oil (s.o.'s skin)
massal مسّل (**tamsiil**) *vt* **1** to represent **2** to act (a role) • *vi* to act
masṭara مسطرة *n* (*pl* **masaaṭir**) ruler (for lines)
masṭariina مسطرينة *n* trowel (for cement)
masṭuul مسطول *adj* (*pl* **masaaṭiil**) **1** stoned, i.e. under the influence of cannabis **2** dullard, duffer
maṣaariif مصاريف *n pl* (*sg* **maṣruuf**) costs, expenses; expenditure
maṣaariin مصارين *n pl* (*sg* **muṣraan**) bowels, entrails, intestines
maṣaḥḥa مصحّة *n* specialized clinic
maṣar مصر *vt* (**u, maṣir**) to wring (out)

maṣdar مصدر *n* **1** (*pl* **maṣaadir**) source, origin (e.g. of information) **2** (*gram*) verbal noun
maṣduum مصدوم *adj* shocked; **nafs-i maṣduuma** I have no desire at all
maṣfa مصفى *n* (*pl* **maṣaafi**) sieve, strainer; **maṣfat shaay** tea strainer
maṣfaa مصفاة *n* (*pl* **maṣaafi**) **1** filter **2** refinery
maṣil مصل *n* (*pl* **amṣaal**) vaccine
maṣir مصر *prop n* Egypt
maṣri مصري (*pl* **-yyiin**) *adj* Egyptian • *n* an Egyptian
maṣlaḥa مصلحة *n* (*pl* **maṣaaliḥ**) **1** interest, stake **2** department, government agency
maṣmaṣ مصمص *vt* (**maṣmaṣa**) **1** to rinse (e.g. dishes) **2** to suck the marrow out of a bone **3** (*slang*) to kiss
maṣnaᶜ مصنع *n* (*pl* **maṣaaniᶜ**) factory
maṣnaᶜiyya مصنعيّة *n* cost of labour
maṣnuuᶜ مصنوع *adj* (**min**) made (of), manufactured
maṣraf مصرف *n* (*pl* **maṣaarif**) **1** drain water outlet **2** (*fin*) bank
maṣruuf مصروف *n* (*pl* **-aat, maṣaariif**) household expenses (for one day); **maṣruuf aj-jeeb** pocket money
maṣṣa مصّ *vt* (**u, maṣṣ**) **1** to suck **2** to absorb **3** to cup (wounds)
maṣṣaaṣ مصّاص *adj* sucking; **maṣṣaaṣ damm** vampire •*n* (*pl* **-aat**) soakaway for sewage system
maṣṭaba مصطبة *n* (*pl* **maṣaaṭib**) raised platform (next to a house)
masha مشى *vi* **1** (**-i, mashi**) to go; to leave; **ana masheet** I'm off; **an-namshi** let's go; **masha be-washsh-o** he left for good; **al-buluuza di ma tamshi maᶜa al-iskeert da** this blouse doesn't go with that skirt **2** (**-i, mashi, mashiya**) to walk
mashaakil مشاكل *n pl* (*sg* **mushkila**) problems, trouble; **ᶜamal mashaakil** to make trouble
mashaayikh مشايخ *n pl* (*sg* **sheekh**) tribal elders
mashammaᶜ مشمّع *n* (*pl* **-aat**) oilcloth; linoleum; tarpaulin
mashbak مشبك *n* (*pl* **mashaabik**) clasp; clothes peg
mashbuuh مشبوه *adj* suspect, suspicious; **da mashbuuh** this is suspect/suspicious; **hi mashbuuha** she is a suspect
mashghuul مشغول *adj* occupied, busy; **al-khaṭṭ mashghuul** the (telephone) line is busy
mashghuuliyya مشغوليّة *n* responsibility (in work)
mashhad مشهد *n* (*pl* **mashaahid**) scene (e.g. of a theatre play)
mashhuur مشهور *adj* (**be-**) famous (for)
mashiima مشيمة *n* placenta; afterbirth; **ḥabl al-mashiima** umbilical cord
mashiya مشية *n* **1** walk, stroll **2** errand
mashluul مشلول *adj* paralysed
mashnaga مشنقة *n* (*pl* **mashaanig**) gallows, scaffold
mashookash مشوكش *adj* jilted (as a lover or a friend)
mashraḥa مشرحة *n* (*pl* **mashaariḥ**) mortuary, morgue

mashruuᶜ مشروع *n* (*pl* **-aat, mashaariiᶜ**) project, scheme, enterprise
mashruuṭ مشروط *adj* torn
mashsha مشّى *vt* (**-i, mishsheey**) **1** to send away, dismiss **2** to teach or cause to walk
mashshaaṭa مشّاطة *n* hairdresser (traditional)
mashshaay مشّاي *adj* quick, fast walker
mashshaṭ مشّط *vt* (**mushaaṭ**) **1** to comb **2** to plait hair; to dress hair
mashtal مشتل *n* (*pl* **mashaatil**) plant nursery
mashwi مشوي *adj* grilled; roasted
mata متى **mata ma** *conj* when, whenever
mataaha متاهة *n* labyrinth
matḥaf متحف *n* (*pl* **mataaḥif**) museum
matiin متين *adj* solid, strong
matni متنى *adj* curved (of materials)
matsh ماتش *n* (*pl* **-aat**) match (sport)
mattaᶜ متّع *vt* (**mitteeᶜ**) to make s.o. enjoy sth.
mattar متّر *vt* (**mitteer**) to measure (length)
maṭᶜam مطعم *n* (*pl* **maṭaaᶜim**) restaurant
maṭaafi مطافي *n pl* **al-maṭaafi** the fire brigade; **ᶜarabiyyat al-maṭaafi** fire engine
maṭaar مطار *n* (*pl* **-aat**) airport
maṭabb مطبّ *n* (*pl* **-aat**) **1** pothole **2** airpocket
maṭar مطر *coll n* rain(s)
maṭara مطرة *unit n* (*pl* **amṭaar**) rain; shower of rain
maṭbaᶜa مطبعة *n* (*pl* **maṭaabiᶜ**) printing press
maṭbaga مطبقة *n* (*pl* **maṭaabig**) purse, wallet (women)
maṭbakh مطبخ *n* (*pl* **maṭaabikh**) kitchen
maṭbuuᶜa مطبوعة *n* printed matter
maṭluug مطلوق *n* (*pl* **maṭaaliig**) of questionable morals
maṭmuura مطمورة *n* (*pl* **maṭaamiir**) granary
maṭmuus مطموس *n* (*pl* **maṭaamiis**) stupid, silly
maṭṭa مطّ *vt* (**i, miṭṭeeṭ**) to stretch
maṭṭaaṭ مطّاط *n* rubber (material)
maṭṭaaṭi مطّاطي *adj* made of rubber; elastic, stretchable
maṭṭar مطّر *vi* (**miṭṭeer, maṭara**) **1** to rain **2** to shelter from the rain
maṭwa مطوى *n* (*pl* **maṭaawi**) pocket knife, penknife
mawᶜid موعد *n* (*pl* **mawaaᶜiid**) appointment
mawaaᶜiid مواعيد *n pl* (*sg* **miiᶜaad**) appointments; **fi mawaaᶜiid-o** he is punctual
mawaaᶜiin مواعين *n pl* kitchen utensils
mawaarid موارد *n pl* (*sg* **mawrid**) resources; **al-mawaarid al-bashariyya** human resources
mawḍuuᶜ موضوع *n* (*pl* **-aat, mawaaḍiiᶜ**) matter, issue; subject, topic
mawgif موقف *n* (*pl* **mawaagif**) **1** car park; place where vehicles stop or park; **mawgif al-ᶜarabaat/al-baaṣṣaat/al-ḥaaflaat** bus station **mawgif at-taksi** taxi rank **2** position (opinion), standpoint
mawhiba موهبة *n* (*pl* **mawaahib**) talent

mawhuub موهوب *adj* talented
mawjuud موجود *adj* present; **yakuun mawjuud bukra** he/it will be there tomorrow; **kaan mawjuud** it existed (in the past)
mawlaana مولانا *n* term of address to a judge or a Muslim leader
mawluud مولود *adj* born; **al-mawluud(a)** the newborn child
mawrid مورد *n* (*pl* **mawaarid**) **1** source, resource **2** small harbour
mawruud موورود *adj* feverish
mawsuuq موسوق *adj* **mawsuuq fii-ho** reliable, trustworthy
mawwal موّل *vt* (**tamwiil**) to finance, fund, sponsor
mawwan موّن *vt* (**tamwiin**) (**be-**) to supply, provide (with)
mawwaṣ موّص *vt* (**miwweeṣ**) to cause to dissolve (e.g. of mud bricks in rainy season; of **kisra** in water)
mawwat موّت *vt* (**miwweet**) **1** to kill, to murder **2** to sit at a deathbed
maysara ميسرة *n* prosperity
maysuur ميسور *adj* prosperous
mayyal ميّل *vi* (**meel, mayalaan**) **1** **ʿala** to lean on **2** **le-** to tend to, be inclined to
mayyaz ميّز *vi* (**tamyiiz**) **been** to distinguish • *vt* (**meez**) to share (costs of food)
mayyit ميّت *adj* **1** dead **2** blunt (e.g. a knife)
mazaad مزاد *n* (*pl* **-aat**) auction
mazaaj مزاج *adj* (*pl* **-aat**) mood; **mazaaj ʿakraan** a bad mood
mazbaḥa مزبحة *n* (*pl* **mazaabiḥ**) slaughter, massacre
mazḥuum مزحوم *adj* busy; crowded; **mazḥuum zaḥma** very busy; very crowded
mazlagaan مزلقان *n* (*pl* **-aat**) **1** a treacherous (slippery) part of a road or path **2** level crossing on the railway
maznuug مزنوق *adj* (**fi**) caught short, in a tight spot (for); **kunta maznuug wa ma ligeet ḥammaam** I was caught short and didn't find a toilet
mazraʿa مزرعة *n* (*pl* **mazaariʿ**) (*agr*) **1** plantation; field **2** farm
mazza مزّة *n* (*pl* **mizzaz**) appetizer, snack
mazzag مزّق *vt* (**mizzeeg**) to tear to pieces (e.g. paper)
maẓalla مظلّة *n* **1** sunshade, parasol, umbrella **2** parachute
maẓalli مظلّي *adj* (*pl* **-yyiin**) uninvited guest, sponger, parasite (appearing uninvited at meals)
maẓbuuṭ مظبوط *adj* right, correct; **ma maẓbuuṭ** incorrect
maẓluum مظلوم (*pl* **maẓaaliim**) *adj* treated unjustly; oppressed • *n* victim of injustice, victim of oppression
meedaan ميدان *n* (*pl* **mayaadiin**) **1** open space in a town, public square; field **2** sports track; **meedaan as-sibaaq, meedaan as-sabag** race track
meel ميل *n* inclination, slope
meez ميز *n* (*pl* **-aat**) lounge at the work place
meez ميز *n* (*sports*) finish
meydaani ميداني *adj* relating to a field (of work, research); **baḥis meydaani** field research

meyḍana ميضنة *n* (*pl* **mayaaḍin**) minaret
miʿda معدة *n* stomach; **wajaʿ miʿda** gastritis
miʿyaar معيار *n* (*pl* **maʿaayiir**) criterion, gauge, standard measure
miʿza معزة *n* (*pl* **maaʿiz, maʿiiz**) goat
mi'zana مئزنة *n* (*pl* **ma'aazin**) minaret
midda مدّة *n* pus
miḍyaaf مضياف *adj* hospitable
migdaar مقدار *n* (*pl* **magaadiir**) quantity
mihani مهني *adj* professional, vocational
mihaniyya مهنيّة *n* craftsmanship
mihbal مهبل *n* (*pl* **mahaabil**) vagina
mihna مهنة *n* (*pl* **mihan**) profession, occupation
miḥin محن *vi* (**a, miḥna**) to be(come) bewildered, perplexed, be at a loss
miḥna محنة *n* (*pl* **miḥan**) bewilderment
miḥraat محرات *n* (*pl* **maḥaariit**) plough
miḥwar محور *n* (*pl* **maḥaawir**) axis
miiʿaad ميعاد *n* (*pl* **mawaaʿiid**) appointment; **fi mawaaʿiid-o** punctual
miidaaliya ميدالية *n* medal
miidaaliyya ميداليّة *n* medal
miidaan ميدان *n* (*pl* **mayaadiin**) **1** open space in a town, public square; field **2** sports track; **miidaan sabaag** race track
miikaaniiki ميكانيكي *n* (*pl* **-iyya**) mechanic, fitter
miil ميل *n* (*pl* **amyaal**) mile
miilaad ميلاد *n* birth; **ʿiid miilaad** birthday
miina مينا *n* (*pl* **mawaani**) harbour, port
miiraas ميراس *n* (*pl* **mawaariis**) inheritance, legacy
miiri ميري *adj invar* civilian (clothes, as opposed to military uniform)
miita ميتة *n* death; **miita faj'a** an accidental death, a sudden death
miiteen ميتين *num* two hundred
miiza ميزة *n* **1** feature, characteristic **2** advantage
miizaan ميزان *n* (*pl* **mawaaziin**) scales, balance
miizaaniyya ميزانيّة *n* budget
mijdaaf مجداف *n* (*pl* **majaadiif**) oar
mikyaaj مكياج *n* makeup
milaarya ملاريا *n* malaria
milaaya ملاية *n* sheet, bed linen
miliḥ ملح *n* (*pl* **amlaaḥ**) salt • *adv* (*slang*) for free, gratis
milik ملك *n* (*pl* **amlaak**) property
milkiyya ملكيّة *n* ownership; possession
milla ملّة *n* (*pl* **milal**) **1** religious community **2** group of people or tribe, referred to in a negative sense; **di milla ghariiba** they are a strange sort of people
milli ملّي *n* millimetre
milyoon مليون *n* (*pl* **malaayiin**) million
min من *prep* **1** from; of **2** about **3** since; ago; **min zamaan** a long time ago, from long ago; **min wakit/min yoom** since **4** than
minbar منبر *n* (*pl* **manaabir**) **1** minbar; pulpit (in a mosque) **2** (*also fig*) platform

mindiil منديل *n* (*pl* **manaadiil**) handkerchief; **mindiil warag** paper handkerchief

minḥa منحة *n* (*pl* **minaḥ**) grant; **minḥa diraasiyya** scholarship

minu منو *interrog* who; **ism-ak minu** what is your name?

minẓaar منظار *n* (*pl* **manaaẓiir**) binoculars; telescope; any medical '-scope' (e.g. laryngoscope)

miqyaas مقياس *n* (*pl* **maqaayiis**) criterion, gauge, standard measure; **miqyaas al-baḥar** Nilometer

miraaya مراية *n* mirror

miriḍ مرض *vi* (**a, maraḍ**) to be(come) sick, ill

mirigمرق *n* (*pl* **muruug**) roof beam; rafter

mirr مر *n* bile

mirriikh مرّيخ *n* **al-mirriikh** Mars

misa مسا *n* afternoon; evening; **fi l-misa/ be-l-misa** in the evening; **misaa l-kheer/ misaa n-nuur** good afternoon; good evening

misaal مسال *n* (*pl* **amsila**) example (illustration)

misaali مسالي *adj* ideal, exemplary

misik مسك *n* musk; (synthetic) white musk

miskiin مسكين *adj* (*pl* **masaakiin**) **1** miserable; **shakl-o miskiin** he looks poor, miserable **2** kind, good-hearted, naive, modest, humble; quiet (person)

misl مسل *prep* **1** like; resembling; **walad misl da...**such a boy... **2** such as • *conj* as

mistika مستكا *n* **1** mastic gum (used in incense); chewing gum **2** species of grass of which the dried form is put in drinking water to improve its taste

mishmish مشمش *coll n* apricot(s)

miteen متين *interrog* when; **miteen ma** whenever

mitil متل *prep* **1** like; resembling; **bitt mitil di...**such a girl... **2** such as

mitir متر *n* **1** (*pl* **amtaar**) metre **2** tape measure

mitl متل *prep* as, like, such as

miyya ميّة *num* hundred; **khamsiin fi l-miyya** fifty percent; **miyya miyya** excellent, perfect

mizziiga مزّيقا *n* (*pl* **mazaaziig**) music

modeel موديل *n* (*pl* **-aat**) model

moobaayl موبايل *n* (*pl* **-aat**) mobile telephone

mooj موج *coll n* (*pl* **-aat, amwaaj**) wave(s)

mooja موجة *unit n* wave; **moojat ḥarr** heat wave

moorada موردة *n* (*pl* **mawaarid**) **1** slope leading down to the water's edge (of a river or a canal) **2** landing stage (boats), anchorage, dock

mooṣ موص *n* **kisra** mixed with water (consumed by women to gain weight)

moot موت *n* death

mootar موتر *n* (*pl* **mawaatir**) motorcycle

mooya موية *n* water; **mooya ḥilwa** fresh water; **mooya murra** brackish water; **mooya maʿdaniyya** mineral water; **mooya magaṭṭara** distilled water; **mooya sharaab** drinking water; **mooya samiina** very cold drinking water; **mooya**

zarga pure water, without additions; **al-mooya/al-mooyaat** breaking of the fast (during Ramadan); **mooya fi l-ʿeen/al-mooya al-beeḍa** cataract (in eye); **al-mooya as-sooda** glaucoma

mooz موز *coll n* banana(s)

motoor موتور *n* (*pl* **-aat**) engine

muʿaag معاق *adj* handicapped, disabled

muʿaahada معاهدة *n* treaty, convention

muʿaakis معاكس *adj* contrary, opposite

muʿaalaja معالجة *n* (*med*) treatment

muʿaamala معاملة *n* treatment; handling

muʿaaraḍa معارضة *n* opposition

muʿaaṣir معاصر *adj* contemporary

muʿaayana معاينة *n* **1** job interview **2** on-the-spot inspection

muʿaffar معفّر *adj* dusty

muʿaffin معفّن *adj* stinking; decayed, rotten, putrid

muʿaggad معقّد *adj* complex, complicated

muʿajjiz معجّز *adj* **1** old (of humans) **2** in deficit (account)

muʿakkar معكّر *adj* turbid, muddy; **washsh muʿakkar** looking disturbed, a grumpy face

muʿallim معلّم *n* (*m*) **1** teacher, master **2** boss (term of address to boss of craftsmen)

muʿallima معلّمة *n* (*f*) teacher

muʿammir معمّر *adj* durable, lasting

muʿammish معمّش *adj* shortsighted

muʿaskar معسكر *n* (*pl* **-aat**) camp

muʿattit معتّت *adj* weevil-ridden

muʿaṭṭal معطّل *adj* out of order, defective

muʿaṭṭar معطّر *adj* **1** perfumed **2** flavoured

muʿawwag معوّق *adj* handicapped, disabled

muʿayyan معيّن *adj* particular; **shakhiṣ muʿayyan** a certain person; **mawḍuuʿ muʿayyan** a certain issue

muʿdi معدي *adj* contagious, infectious

muʿjab معجب *adj* **be-** delighted by, admiring; **ana muʿjab be-fustaan-ik** I like your dress

muʿjiza معجزة *n* miracle, wonder

muʿtamad معتمد *n* commissioner, authorized agent

muʿẓam معظم *n* most of, the majority of

mu'aamara مؤامرة *n* conspiracy, plot

mu'addab مؤدّب *adj* polite, well-mannered; decent; **ma mu'addab** impolite, impertinent, impudent

mu'ahhal مؤهّل *adj* qualified

mu'ahhil مؤهّل *n* (*pl* **-aat**) qualification

mu'ajjir مؤجّر *n* tenant

mu'akkad مؤكّد *adj* certain, sure; **al-kalaam da mu'akkad** this is certain

mu'akhkharan مؤخّرا *adv* recently

mu'akhkhira مؤخّرة *n* **1** rear end; **mu'akhkhirat al-murkab** stern of a boat **2** bottom, backside

mu'allif مؤلّف *n* (*m*) author, novelist, writer, composer

mu'allifa مؤلّفة *n* (*f*) author, novelist, writer, composer

mu'ammil مؤمّل *adj* hopeful

mu'annas مؤنّس *adj* (*gram*) feminine

mu'assasa مؤسّسة *n* foundation, institution

mu'ashshir مؤشّر *n* (*pl* **-aat**) pointer, indicator

mu'azzin مأزّن *n* muezzin
mu'lim مؤلم *adj* painful
mu'min مؤمن *n* believer
mu'tamar مؤتمر *n* (**-aat**) conference, congress; **mu'tamar ṣaḥafi** press conference
mu'zi مؤزي *adj* harmful
mubaʿzig مبعزق *adj* squandering
mubaadala مبادلة *n* exchange
mubaara مباراة *n* (*pl* **-yaat**) (*sports*) match
mubaashir مباشر *adj* direct; live (of broadcast)
muballiṭ مبلّط *n* **1** professional plasterer of interior walls with cement **2** tiler
mubargaʿ مبرقع *adj* (jellabia) covered with patches
mubarrir مبرّر *n* (*pl* **-aat**) justification, excuse
mubashshir مبشّر *n* (*Chr*) catechist, evangelist, (*Chr/Isl*) missionary
mubashtan مبشتن *adj* untidy, slovenly, unkempt
mubayyiḍ مبيّض *n* plasterer
mubkhar مبخر *n* (*pl* **mabaakhir**) incense burner
mubrad مبرد *n* (*pl* **mabaarid**) file (tool)
mudaawasa مداوسة *n* fighting
mudabbir مدبّر *adj* managing (financially); thrifty
mudabris مدبرس *adj* depressed
mudardam مدردم *adj* circular, round
mudarraj مدرّج *n* (*pl* **-aat**) **1** section, block (e.g in theatre, stadium) **2** tiered lecture room; **mudarraj ṭayyaaraat** runway
mudarrajaat مدرّجات *n pl* gallery (in stadium)
mudarrib مدرّب *n* (*m*) trainer
mudarriba مدرّبة *n* (*f*) trainer
mudarris مدرّس *n* (*m*) teacher
mudarrisa مدرّسة *n* (*f*) teacher
mudawwana مدوّنة *n* blog
mudawwar مدوّر *adj* round, circular
mudayyin مديّن *n* creditor; **hu mudayyin-ni** I owe him
mudda مدّة *n* (*pl* **-aat, mudad**) period, length of time; **le-mudda** for a while; **min mudda** some time ago; for a while
muddaʿa مدّعى *n* **muddaʿa ʿaleeho** defendant
muddaʿi مدّعي *n* (*pl* **-yyiin**) plaintiff, prosecutor; **al-muddaʿi al-ʿaamm** the public prosecutor
muddanni مدّني *adj* low
muddarrib مدّرّب *n* (*m*) trainee
muddarriba مدّرّبة *n* (*f*) trainee
muddayyin مدّيّن *adj* devout, religious
mudfaʿ مدفع *n* (*pl* **madaafiʿ**) cannon; **mudfaʿ haawun** mortar
mudgaag مدقاق *n* (*pl* **-aat**) flail, threshing tool
mudiir مدير *n* (*m*) (*pl* **-iin, mudara**) director, manager, boss; **mudiir madrasa** principal, headmaster
mudiira مديرة *n* (*f*) director, manager, boss; **mudiirat madrasa** headmistress
mudmaak مدماك *n* (*pl* **madaamiik**) bricklayer
mudmin مدمن *adj* addicted • *n* addict
muḍaaʿafaat مضاعفات *n pl* side effects
muḍaadd مضاد *adj* anti-, counter-; **muḍaadd ḥayawi** antibiotic; **hujuum muḍaadd** counterattack
muḍaariʿ مضارع *n* **al-muḍaariʿ** (*gram*) imperfect (present) tense

muḍaayaga مضايقة *n* annoyance; harassment
muḍablin مضبلن *adj* looking ill
muḍallim مضلّم *adj* dark (of light)
muḍayyig مضيّق *adj* (**min**) quickly irritated (by)
muḍḥik مضحك *adj* funny, comic
muḍiif مضيف *n* host, steward
muḍiifa مضيفة *n* hostess, stewardess
mufaaja'a مفاجأة *n* surprise
mufaaji مفاجي *adj* sudden
mufaḍḍal مفضّل *adj* preferred, favourite
mufakkira مفكّرة *n* **1** pocket diary, day-planner **2** note
mufallis مفلّس *adj* bankrupt, penniless
mufargaʿaat مفرقعات *n pl* explosives
mufaṣṣala مفصّلة *n* hinge
mufattiḥ مفتّح *n* streetwise
mufattish مفتّش *n* inspector
mufawwaḍ مفوّض *n* commissioner
mufiid مفيد *adj* useful, advantageous; **ma mufiid** useless
muflis مفلس *adj* **1** bankrupt, penniless **2** using bad language
mufraaka مفراكة *n* (*pl* **mafaariik**) stirring stick
mufrad مفرد *n* (*gram*) singular
muftaaḥ مفتاح *n* (*pl* **mafaatiiḥ**) **1** key **2** bottle opener, can opener **3** switch **4** spanner, wrench; **muftaaḥ ingiliizi** monkey wrench; **muftaaḥ ṣaamuula** spanner
mufti مفتي *n* (*pl* **-yyiin**) mufti, official exponent of Islamic law, deliverer of formal legal opinions
mugaabala مقابلة *n* **1** encounter **2** interview
mugaabil مقابل *n* **fi mugaabil** in return for; **be-duun mugaabil** without compensation, for free
mugaaḍaa مقاضاة *n* prosecution
mugaaṭaʿa مقاطعة *n* interruption
mugaawil مقاول *n* contractor
mugaayaḍa مقايضة *n* exchange
mugaddam مقدّم *n* **1** lieutenant colonel **2** rank in a Sufi order
mugaddam مقدّم *adv* in advance • *n* advance payment, down payment, deposit
mugaddar مقدّر *adj* decreed by God
mugallig مقلّق *adj* (**ʿala**) anxious, worried (about)
mugargar مقرقر *adj* hollow
mugarram مقرّم *adj* (*slang*) clever, experienced
mugrif مقرف *adj* disgusting
mugshaasha مقشاشة *n* (*pl* **magaashiish**) broom
mughaadara مغادرة *n* departure
mughabbar مغبّر *adj* dusty
mughaffal مغفّل *adj* stupid, dimwitted
mughanni مغنّي *n* (*m*) (*pl* **-yyiin**) singer
mughanniyya مغنّيّة *n* (*f*) singer
mughayyib مغيّب *adj* **1** in a coma **2** in a trance
mughayyim مغيّم *adj* cloudy; hazy
mughram مغرم *adj* **be-** in love with
mughri مغري *adv* attractive; tempting
mughrib مغرب *n* sunset
mughtarib مغترب *n* living abroad
muhaajir مهاجر *n* immigrant
muhaddi مهدّي *n* (*pl* **-'aat**) tranquilizer, sedative
muhandis مهندس *n* engineer; **muhandis mabaani/muhandis miʿmaari** architect
muharrib مهرّب *n* smuggler
muharrij مهرّج *n* buffoon, clown
muhazzab مهزّب *adj* polite, well-mannered, decent

muhimm مهم *adj* important
muhimma مهمّة *n* mission, assignment
muhla مهلة *n* respite
muhmil مهمل *adj* careless, negligent, slack
muhr مهر *n* (*pl* **muhuur**) foal, colt
muḥaadasa محادسة *n* (formal) talk, conversation
muḥaaḍara محاضرة *n* lecture
muḥaafaẓa محافظة *n* province, district
muḥaafiẓ محافظ *n* governor (of a district)
muḥaakama محاكمة *n* trial (in court)
muḥaal محال *adj* impossible
muḥaami محامي *n* (*pl* **-yyiin**) lawyer, advocate
muḥaara محارة *n* trowel (plaster)
muḥaaraba محاربة *n* fighting
muḥaarib محارب *n* fighter
muḥaasaba محاسبة *n* **1** bookkeeping, accountancy **2** settling of an account with s.o. **3** accountability
muḥaasib محاسب *n* (*m*) accountant
muḥaasiba محاسبة *n* (*f*) accountant
muḥaayid محايد *adj* neutral
muḥaazi محازي *adj* parallel
muḥallil محلّل *n* **1** analyst **2** (*Isl*) intermediate husband employed to enable a man to remarry his wife again after he has divorced her
muḥarram محرّم *adj* taboo
muḥiiṭ محيط *n* (*pl* **-aat**) ocean; **al-muḥiiṭ al-aṭlanṭi** the Atlantic Ocean; **al-muḥiiṭ al-haadi** the Pacific Ocean
muḥtaaj محتاج *adj* **le-** in need of
muḥtaajiin محتاجين *n pl* **al-muḥtaajiin** the needy
muḥtaal محتال *adj* deceitful, cheat
muḥtaar محتار *adj* at a loss
muḥtamal محتمل *adj* probable; **min al-muḥtamal** it's probable that
muḥtarif محترف *adj* professional; proficient
muḥtashim محتشم *adj* decent (females)
mujaahid مجاهد *n* (*Isl*) fighter in a holy war
mujaamala مجاملة *n* courtesy; **mujaamala saay** empty courtesy, false compliment
mujaazafa مجازفة *n* recklessness
mujammaᶜ مجمّع *n* (*pl* **-aat**) cooperative, collective, association (e.g. of schools, businessmen, medical doctors); **mujammaᶜ ṭibbi** group medical practice; **mujammaᶜ tijaari** trade association
mujarrad مجرّد *adv* only
mujarrib مجرّب *adj* experienced
mujawwaf مجوّف *adj* hollow
mujazzim مجزّم *adj* leprous • *n* leper
mujrim مجرم *n* criminal
mujtahid مجتهد *adj* diligent, industrious, zealous
mujtamaᶜ مجتمع *n* (*pl* **-aat**) community; society
mukaᶜᶜab مكعّب *adj* cubic • *n* (*pl* **-aat**) cube
mukaafaa مكافاة *n* (*pl* **mukaafa'aat**) gratification, reward, bonus
mukaajara مكاجرة *n* obstinacy
mukaajir مكاجر *adj* obstinate, going against the grain
mukaalama مكالمة *n* telephone call
mukaataba مكاتبة *n* correspondence
mukaatala مكاتلة *n* fighting

mukammada مكمّدة *n* compress
mukarfas مكرفس *adj* crumpled, creased
mukarmash مكرمش *adj* crumpled, creased; wrinkled (of clothes or face)
mukarmish مكرمش *adj* crumpled, creased; wrinkled (of clothes or face)
mukassaf مكسّف *adj* intensive; **ʿinaaya mukassafa** intensive care
mukassaḥ مكسّح *adj* crippled
mukassar مكسّر *adj* **1** broken **2 fi** having a crush on, crazy about
mukassaraat مكسّرات *n pl* snacks such as nuts, salted beans, popcorn, etc.
mukashkish مكشكش *adj* scatter-brained; crazy
mukawwin مكوّن *n* (*pl* **-aat**) ingredient, component
mukayyif مكيّف *n* (*pl* **-aat**) air cooler; air conditioner
mukta'ib مكتئب *adj* depressed, gloomy
muktafi مكتفي *adj* satisfied
mukur مكر *n* cunning, shrewdness, slyness
mukhaabaraat مخابرات *n pl* intelligence services
mukhaalafa مخالفة *n* **1** infraction, traffic violation **2** a fine (for a traffic violation)
mukhaddir مخدّر *n* (*pl* **-aat**) anaesthetic, sedative, narcotic, drug; **mukhaddiraat** anaesthesia, narcotics; (illegal) drugs
mukhallal مخلّل *n* (*pl* **-aat**) pickle
mukhalliṣ مخلّص *n* **al-mukhalliṣ** saviour (of Jesus Christ)
mukhalliṣ مخلّص *n* customs clearance agent
mukhammar مخمّر *adj* fermented; leavened
mukharrif مخرّف *adj* senile, feeble-minded
mukhiif مخيف *adj* frightening
mukhkh مخ *n* (*pl* **amkhaakh**) brain **mukhkh al-ʿaḍum** bone marrow
mukhkhaata مخّاتة *n* (*pl* **makhaakhiit**) mucus
mukhlaaya مخلاية *n* nosebag
mukhliṣ مخلص *adj* faithful, devoted, loyal; sincere
mukhraz مخرز *n* (*pl* **makhaariz**) **1** awl **2** a comb with one tooth
mukhtal مختل *adj* **mukhtal al-ʿagul** crazy, mad, lunatic
mukhtalaṭ مختلط *adj* mixed (e.g. boys and girls)
mukhtalif مختلف *adj* different, various; odd
mukhtaṣar مختصر *adj* concise • *n* (*pl* **-aat**) synopsis, outline, summary
mukhtaṣṣaat مختصّات *n pl* competencies
mukhtashi مختشي *adj* shy, bashful
mulaaḥ ملاح *n* stew; sauce; **mulaaḥ luuba** stew made of black-eyed bean(s); **mulaaḥ roob** sauce of curdled milk with onions; **mulaaḥ warag** stew with leaves of the black-eyed beans plant; **mulaaḥ weeka** stew with dried okra powder
mulaaḥaẓa ملاحظة *n* remark, note, observation, comment
mulaaḥiẓ ملاحظ *n* superintendent, overseer
mulaazim ملازم *n* (*mil*) lieutenant
mulakhkhaṣ ملخّص *n* (*pl* **-aat**) summary
mulawlaw ملولو *adj* curly

mulayyin ملـيّن *n* (*pl* -aat) laxative

mulfit ملفت *adj*; **mulfit le-n-naẓar** attracting attention

mulgaaṭ ملقاط *n* (*pl* **malaagiiṭ**) tweezers (used for medical or cosmetic purposes)

mulḥag ملحق *n* (*pl* **malaaḥig**) 1 supplement, appendix, attachment 2 annexe, (local) branch

mulḥid ملحد *n* heretic

muliḥḥ ملح *adj* 1 (ʿala) insisting (on) 2 persistent

multazim ملتزم *adj* engaged, committed

mulukhiyya ملخيّة *coll n* melukhia, Jew's mallow

mulzim ملزم *part* obligated, under obligation

mumaarasa ممارسة *n* practice

mumarriḍ ممرّض *n* (*m*) nurse

mumarriḍa ممرّضة *n* (*f*) nurse

mumassil ممسّل *n* (*m*) 1 representative, delegate 2 actor (as in theatre)

mumassila ممسّلة *n* (*f*) 1 representative, delegate 2 actress (as in theatre)

mumawwil مموّل *n* sponsor

mumayyaz ممـيّز *adj* distinctive; unique

mumayyiz ممـيّز *adj* distinctive

mumill ممل *adj* 1 dull, boring, tedious 2 annoying

mumkin ممكن *adj* possible · *adv* possibly

mumtaaz ممتاز *adj* excellent

mumtalakaat ممتلكات *n pl* possessions

mumtiʿ ممتع *adj* enjoyable

mumṭir ممطر *adj* rainy

munaafaqa منافقة *n* hypocrisy

munaafasa منافسة *n* competition

munaafiq منافق *adj* hypocrite

munaasaba مناسبة *n* (special) occasion **be-munaasabat** on the occasion of; **be-l-munaasaba** by the way

munaasib مناسب *adj* appropriate, proper, suitable, convenient; **ma munaasib** inappropriate, unsuitable, inconvenient; **fi wakit munaasib** in due course

munaaṣara مناصرة *n* advocacy

munaawala مناولة *n* (*Chr*) communion

munaawara مناورة *n* manoeuvre

munabbih منبّه *n* (*pl* -aat) 1 alarm clock 2 any hot drink that wakes s.o. up

munaghnigh منغنغ *adj* rich, wealthy

munassiq منسّق *n* coordinator

munawwaʿ منوّع *adj* various, diverse

munawwim منوّم *n* (*pl* -aat) sleep-inducing drug, sleeping pill

munaẓẓam منظّم *adj* tidy, orderly, well-organized, systematic; **be-shakil munaẓẓam** systematically

munaẓẓama منظّمة *n* organization, institution; **munaẓẓama gheer ḥakuumiyya** non-governmental organization; **munaẓẓama gheer ribḥiyya** non-profit organization

munaẓẓim منظّم *n* 1 organizer 2 (*pl* -aat) regulating device, regulator

munḍabiṭ منضبط *adj* punctual

munfaakh منفاخ *n* (*pl* **ma-naafiikh**) air pump

munfaṣil منفصل *adj* apart, separated

mungaar منقار *n* (*pl* **manaagiir**) 1 beak 2 (*slang*) a kiss

mungaash منقاش *n* (*pl* **manaagi-ish**) tool consisting of a needle and tweezers (used by rural men)

munḥaaz منحاز *adj* partial; prejudiced, biased
munḥall منحل *adj* immoral, base
munḥaṭṭ منحط *adj* low, base, mean, ignoble
muniya منية *n* (*pl* **amaani**) wish
munjal منجل *n* (*pl* **manaajil**) sickle; reaping hook; billhook
munkhaas منخاس *n* (*pl* **manaakhiis**) tool consisting of a needle and tweezers (used by rural men)
munkhafiḍ منخفض *adj* low; **jawda munkhafiḍa** inferior quality
munshaar منشار *n* (*pl* **manaashiir**) saw
muntaj منتج *n* (*pl* **-aat**) product
muntaẓim منتظم *adj* regular, steady
muntij منتج *n* producer
muqaarana مقارنة *n* comparison; **be-muqaaranat** in comparison with
muqaatil مقاتل *n* fighter
muqaaṭaʿa مقاطعة *n* rift in a relationship
muqaawama مقاومة *n* resistance
muqaddas مقدّس *adj* sacred, holy; **al-kitaab al-muqaddas** the Holy Scripture, the Bible; **al-qurbaan al-muqaddas** the Blessed Sacrament
muqaddima مقدّمة *n* introduction
muqandil مقندل *adj* (*slang*) well-off
muqtaraḥ مقترح *n* (*pl* **-aat**) suggestion, proposal
murʿib مرعب *adj* frightening, terrifying
muraad مراد *n* (*pl* **-aat**) **1** desire **2** goal
muraahig مراهق *n* (*m*) adolescent
muraahiga مراهقة *n* (*f*) adolescent
muraaḥ مراح *n* (**-aat, murḥaat**) herd, flock
muraajaʿa مراجعة *n* revision, audit
muraaqaba مراقبة *n* observation, monitoring
muraaqib مراقب *n* observer, monitor, overseer
muraasala مراسلة *n* correspondence
muraasil مراسل *n* (*m*) correspondent, reporter
muraasila مراسلة *n* (*f*) correspondent, reporter
muraasla مراسلة *n m* (*pl* **-aat**) orderly, messenger, courier (in an office)
murabbaʿ مربّع *adj* square; **mitir murabbaʿ** square metre • *n* (*pl* **-aat**) **1** square; **gumaash murabbaʿaat** checkered cloth **2** part of a town district
muraggaṭ مرقّط *adj* piebald
murakkaz مركّز *adj* concentrated (e.g. juice, alcoholic drink, perfume); **ʿinaaya murakkaza** intensive care
murakkiz مركّز *adj* concentrated, focussed
murashshaḥ مرشّح *n* (*m*) nominee, candidate
murashshaḥa مرشّحة *n* (*f*) nominee, candidate
murattab مرتّب *adj* tidy, orderly
murattab مرتّب *n* (*pl* **-aat**) pay, wage, salary
muraṭṭabaat مرطّبات *n pl* refreshments (cold drinks; fruits)
muraṭṭib مرطّب *adj* **1** damp **2** cool **3** (*slang*) well-off
murawwig مروّق *adj* (*slang*) well-off
murayyish مريّش *adj* (*slang*) well-off
murbargaʿ مبرقع *adj* piebald
murḍi مرضي *adj* acceptable
murhaq مرهق *adj* exhausted, worn out

murhiq مرهق *adj* exhausting
murḥaaka مرحاكة *n* (*pl* **maraaḥiik**) grindstone, millstone
muriiḥ مريح *adj* comfortable
murjaan مرجان *n* coral
murjeeḥa مرجيحة *n* (*pl* **maraajiiḥ**) swing
murkab مركب *n* (*pl* **maraakib**) boat; shuttle (loom)
murr مر *adj* bitter
mursaal مرسال *n* (*pl* **maraasiil**) messenger, courier
mursil مرسل *n* sender
murshid مرشد *n* guide (person)
murtaaḥ مرتاح *adj* at ease, comfortable
murtabik مرتبك *adj* confused, bewildered
murtafiʿ مرتفع *adj* high
muruuna مرونة *n* flexibility
muruur مرور *n* traffic
muruwwa مروّة *n* helpfulness; **ʿind-o muruwwa** he helps a lot of people
musaaʿada مساعدة *n* help, aid, assistance
musaaʿid مساعد *n* assistant
musaabaqa مسابقة *n* contest
musaafir مسافر *n* traveller; passenger
musaalim مسالم *adj* mild-tempered, peaceful
musaamaḥa مسامحة *n* forgiveness; tolerance
musaawaa مساواة *n* equality
musaddas مسدّس *n* (*pl* **-aat**) revolver, pistol
musahhil مسهّل *n* (*pl* **-aat**) laxative
musajjil مسجّل *n* **1** registrar **2** (*pl* **-aat**) tape recorder
musakkin مسكّن *n* (*pl* **-aat**) pain-killer, sedative, tranquilizer
musakhkhin مسخّن *adj* feeling hot
musallas مسلّس *n* triangle
musalli مسلّي *adj* amusing, entertaining
musalsal مسلسل *n* (*pl* **-aat**) series
musannin مسنّن *adj* developing teeth
musaqqaf مسقّف *adj* intellectual
musaṭṭaḥ مسطّح *adj* flat
musaṭṭiḥ مسطح *adj* having no knowledge (about a certain subject)
musawwis مسوّس *adj* **1** worm-eaten, weevil-ridden **2** having a cavity (tooth)
musiiqa موسيقا *n* music
musiiqaar موسيقار *n* musician
musiiqi موسيقي *n* (*pl* **-yyiin**) musician
musiir مسير *adj* interesting
musimm مسم *adj* poisonous, toxic
muslim مسلم *n* Muslim
musmaar مسمار *n* (*pl* **masaamiir**) metal nail; bolt, metal pin; **musmaar galawooẓ/musmaar burma** screw; **musmaar miḥwari** pivot bolt
mustaʿjil مستعجل *adj* urgent; in a hurry
mustaʿmal مستعمل *adj* used, secondhand
mustabidd مستبد *adj* arbitrary; tyrannical, despotic
mustadaam مستدام *adj* sustainable
mustahlik مستهلك *n* consumer
mustaḥi مستحي *adj* shy, bashful
mustaḥiil مستحيل *adj* impossible
mustajidd مستجد *n* fresh recruit; new employee
mustamirr مستمر *adj* constant, continuous
mustanad مستند *n* (*pl* **-aat**) document; title deed; file, computer file

mustangaʿ مستنقع *n* (*pl* **-aat**) marsh, swamp
mustaqbal مستقبل *n* future
mustaqill مستقل *adj* independent
mustaqirr مستقر *adj* settled; stable; steady
mustaraaḥ مستراح *n* latrine, lavatory, toilet
mustarda مستردة *n* mustard (ready)
mustashaar مستشار *n* consultant
mustashfa مستشفى *n* (*pl* **-yaat**) hospital
mustawa مستوى *n* (*pl* **-yaat**) level
mustawi مستوي *adj* **1** even (ground); flat (level) **2** ripe **3** well-cooked
mustawradaat مستوردات *n pl* imported goods, imports
muswaak مسواك *n* (*pl* **masaawiik**) stick from the **araak** tree, used as a toothbrush
muswaaṭ مسواط *n* (*pl* **masaawiiṭ**) stirring utensil (porridge, stew)
muswadda مسودّة *n* draft, rough copy
muṣaadara مصادرة *n* confiscation
muṣaalaḥa مصالحة *n* reconciliation
muṣaariʿ مصارع *n* wrestler
muṣaddi مصدّي *adj* rusty
muṣaggir مصقّر *adj* rusty
muṣalla مصلّى *n* place of prayer
muṣalliʿ مصلّع *adj* bald-headed
muṣammim مصمّم *n* designer
muṣawwir مصوّر *n* photographer
muṣawwiraati مصوّراتي *n* (*pl* **-yya**) photographer
muṣbaʿ مصبع *n* (*no pl*) finger; **al-muṣbaʿ al-kabiir** thumb; **muṣbaʿ ar-rijil** toe
muṣḥaf مصحف *n* (*pl* **maṣaaḥif**) a copy of the Koran
muṣiiba مصيبة *n* (*pl* **maṣaayib**) disaster, calamity, catastrophe
muṣirr مصر *adj* determined
muṣlaaya مصلاية *n* (*pl* **maṣaali**) prayer mat
muṣliḥ مصلح *adj* peacemaker
muṣraan مصران *n* (*pl* **maṣaariin**) intestine, gut
muṣṭalaḥ مصطلح *n* (*pl* **-aat**) technical term
muṣṭanaʿ مصطنع *adj* artificial
mush مش *interrog* isn't it?; **mush kida** isn't it?
mushaa مشاة *n* **1** pedestrians **2** infantry
mushaaghaba مشاغبة *n* **1** row, quarrel **2** riot, uproar
mushaahara مشاهرة *n* system of a monthly contract (e.g. when hiring s.o. after his retirement or to avoid a permanent contract)
mushaajara مشاجرة *n* quarrel
mushaaraka مشاركة *n* participation
mushaarik مشارك *n* participant
mushaaṭ مشاط *n* hair plaiting, braids
mushakkal مشكّل *adj* mixed (fruits, sweets)
mushawwash مشوّش *adj* vague, unclear (of speech; of radio or television signal)
mushiir مشير *n* field marshal
mushkaar مشكار *n* nickname
mushkila مشكلة *n* (*pl* **mashaakil**) problem; **fi mushkila** in trouble; **ma ʿinda-k mushkila** don't worry
mushooṭin مشوطن *adj* insane, mad, crazy, lunatic
mushraʿ مشرع *n* (*pl* **mashaariʿ**) landing stage (boats, ferry, pontoon), anchorage, dock

mushrif مشرف *n* supervisor
mushrig مشرق *adj* bright (of light)
mushtabah مشتبه *adj* **fi** suspect, suspicious; **di ḥaaja mushtabih fii-ha** this is suspect/suspicious; **hi mushtabih fii-ha** she is a suspect
mushtarak مشترك *adj* common, shared • *n* (*pl* **-aat**) (electric) multi-outlet socket
mushuṭ مشط *n* (*pl* **amshaaṭ**) comb
mushwaar مشوار *n* (*pl* **mashaawiir**) errand
mutʿa متعة *n* enjoyment
mutʿaawin متعاون *n* cooperator, helper, aide, assistant
mutʿaddid متعدّد *n* various, diverse, multiple; **mutʿaddid al-alwaan** multicoloured; **mutʿaddid as-saqaafaat** multicultural; **mutʿaddid az-zoojaat** polygamous
mutʿahhid متعهّد *n* contractor, regular supplier
mutʿallim متعلّم *n* educated person
mutʿaṣṣab متعصّب *adj* fanatical • *n* fanatic
mutʿib متعب *adj* tiring, exhausting
mut'akkid متأكّد *adj* (**min**) being certain, sure (about/of)
mut'akhkhiraat متأخّرات *n pl* overdue payments, arrears
mutadanni متدنّي *adj* (*pl* **-yyiin**) low, mean, ignoble
mutadarrib متدرّب *n* (*m*) trainee
mutadarriba متدرّبة *n* (*f*) trainee
mutarjim مترجم *n* (*m*) translator; **mutarjim fawri** interpreter, simultaneous translator
mutarjima مترجمة *n* (*f*) translator; **mutarjima fawriyya** interpreter, simultaneous translator
mutaṭaffil متطفّل *n* uninvited guest, sponger
mutbaṭṭil متبطّل *adj* idle, unemployed
mutfaa'il متفائل *adj* optimistic • *n* optimist
mutfajjiraat متفجّرات *n pl* explosives
mutfarriʿ متفرّع *adj* branching out; **shaariʿ mutfarriʿ min** a side street of
mutfarrij متفرّج *n* spectator
mutfarrijiin متفرّجين *n pl* audience
mutfattiḥ متفتّح *adj* open-minded
mutgalgil متقلقل *adj* restless
mutgangin متقنقن *adj* **gaʿad mutgangin** to squat
mutghaṭris متغطرس *adj* **1** arrogant, conceited **2** authoritarian, despotic
muthaawid متهاود *adj* selling cheap
mutḥaamil متحامل *n* **ʿala** partial; prejudiced, biased
mutḥaḍḍir متحضّر *adj* civilized
mutḥammis متحمّس *adj* enthusiastic, zealous
mutḥankish متحنكش *adj* showy
mutḥarrik متحرّك *adj* moving; mobile
mutḥashshir متحشّر *adj* curious • *n* busybody, meddler
mutḥayyir محتار *adj* confused, perplexed
mutḥayyiz متحيّز *adj* partial, prejudiced, biased
mutkabbir متكبّر *adj* conceited, haughty
mutkallif متكلّف *adj* artificial
mutkhallif متخلّف *adj* mentally retarded
mutkham متخم *adj* suffering from indigestion
mutlabbis متلبّس *adj* red-handed

mutlaflif متلفلف *adj* tangled
mutlakhbaṭ متلخبط *adj* **1** muddled, in disorder **2** confused
mutlakhbiṭ متلخبط *adj* confused
mutlakhim متلخم *adj* confused
mutlawliw متلولو *adj* curly
mutmakkin متمكّن *adj* skilful, proficient
mutmarrid متمرّد *n* rebel, mutineer
mutnaaqiḍ متناقض *adj* contradicting
mutnakkir متنكّر *adj* in disguise, incognito
mutnawwiᶜ متنوّع *adj* various, diverse
mutraar مترار *n* (*pl* **-aat, mataari-ir**) spindle
mutrabbiᶜ متربع *adj* **gaᶜad mutrabbiᶜ** to sit with legs crossed
mutraddid متردّد *adj* hesitating, reluctant
mutsaamiḥ متسامح *adj* tolerant
mutsaawi متساوي *adj* equal, even
mutshaa'im متشائم *adj* pessimistic • *n* pessimist
mutsharrid متشرد *n* homeless person
muttaaka متّاكى *adj* ajar
muttaḥid متّحد *adj* united; **al-umam al-muttaḥida** the United Nations; **al-wilaayaat al-muttaḥida** the United States; **al-mamlaka al-muttaḥida** the United Kingdom
muttarkash متّركش *adj* ajar
muttazin متّزن *adj* sensible, sober
mutwaaḍiᶜ متواضع *adj* humble
mutwaazin متوازن *adj* balanced
mutwaffir متوفّر *adj* abundant
mutwaḥḥish متوحّش *adj* savage, wild
mutwassiṭ متوسّط *adj* average; medium
mutwattir متوتّر *adj* (**tawattur**) tense
muṭaalaᶜa مطالعة *n* reader (book)
muṭaalaba مطالبة *n* request
muṭabbag مطبّق *n* (*pl* **-aat**) leaflet
muṭallaga مطلّقة *adj f* divorced (of a woman)
muṭallig مطلّق *adj* divorced (of a man)
muṭiiᶜ مطيع *adj* obedient
muṭraan مطران *n* (*pl* **maṭaarina**) bishop
muṭraaniyya مطرانيّة *n* diocese
muṭrag مطرق *n* (*pl* **maṭaarig**) **1** twig; rod (for beating) **2** bow for teasing cotton
muṭrib مطرب *n* (*m*) accomplished singer
muṭriba مطربة *n* (*f*) accomplished singer
muṭṭaffil متطفّل *n* uninvited guest, sponger
muṭṭarrif مطرّف *adj* extreme • *n* extremist
muṭṭawwiᶜ مطوّع *n* volunteer
muulaaṣ مولاص *n* molasses
muulid مولد *n* celebration of the birthday of a prophet or a saint; **muulid an-nabi** celebration of the birthday of the prophet Mohammed
muuna مونة *n* mortar (for building)
muus موس *n* (*pl* **amwaas**) razor blade
muusiliin موسلين *n* muslin
muusim موسم *n* (*pl* **mawaasim**) season
muusimi موسمي *n* seasonal
muwaafaga موافقة *n* approval, agreement
muwaajaha مواجهة *n* confrontation
muwaajih مواجه *adj/prep* opposite
muwaasa مواسى *adj* equal; even
muwaaṣafaat مواصفات *n pl* specifications, standards

muwaaṣala مواصلة *n* communication
muwaaṣalaat مواصلات *n pl* public transport
muwaaṭana مواطنة *n* citizenship
muwaaṭin مواطن *n* citizen
muwaazi موازي *adj* parallel
muwaffaq موفق *adj* **muwaffaq, in shaa Allah** success!
muwaqqat موقّت *adj* temporary
muwaẓẓaf موظّف *n* (*m*) civil servant, employee in an office; official; **muwaẓẓaf al-istiqbaal** receptionist; **al-muwaẓẓafiin** the staff
muwaẓẓafa موظّفة *n* (*f*) civil servant, employee in an office; official
muyassir ميسّر *n* facilitator
muzʿij مزعج *adj* annoying, irritating
muzaariʿ مزارع *n* farmer
muzakkar مزكّر *adj* (*gram*) masculine
muzakkira مزكّرة *n* **1** note (reminder), notice **2** memorandum; **muzakkirat at-tafaahum** memorandum of understanding;
muzakkiraat مزكّرات *n pl* memoirs
muzawwar مزوّر *adj* counterfeit
muzayyaf مزيّف *adj* counterfeit, false
muziiʿ مزيع *n* (*m*) announcer, broadcaster (radio, television)
muziiʿa مزيعة *n* (*f*) announcer, broadcaster
muziil مزيل *n* remover; **muziil ʿarag** deodorant; **muziil shaʿar** hair removal cream
muzmin مزمن *adj* chronic
muznib مزنب *adj* guilty
muẓaahara مظاهرة *n* demonstration, rally

n - ن

naʿʿam نعّم *vt* (**niʿʿeem**) to soften
naʿaal نعال *n* (*pl* **niʿlaat, niʿleen**) pair of shoes or slippers
naʿaam نعام *coll n* ostrich(es)
naʿaas نعاس *n* drowsiness
naʿal نعل *n* (*pl* **niʿlaat, niʿleen**) sole (of shoe)
naʿam نعم *interj* (*as conversation response*) **1** yes? **2** I beg your pardon?
naʿiiman نعيما *interj* (*said to a person after a bath or haircut*) may you feel comfortable; (*reply*) **anʿam Allah ʿalee-k** may God make you feel comfortable too
naʿja نعجة *n* (*pl* **niʿaaj**) **1** ewe, female sheep **2** dimwitted person
naʿnaaʿ نعناع *n* mint (plant)
naʿnash نعنش *vt* (**naʿnasha**) to refresh
naʿsaan نعسان *adj* sleepy, drowsy
naaʿim ناعم *adj* smooth; soft
naa'ib نائب *n* (*pl* **nuwwaab**) deputy, attorney; member of parliament; **naa'ib ar-ra'iis** vice-president; **an-naa'ib al-ʿaamm** the attorney general
naab ناب *n* (*pl* **nawaayib**) front tooth
naada نادى *vt* (**-i, munaada**) to call
naadi نادي *n* (*pl* **andiya, nawaadi**) club, social centre
naadir نادر *adj* rare • *adv* seldom
naafaq نافق *vi* (**nifaaq, munaafaqa**) to be hypocritical
naafas نافس *vt* (**munaafasa**) to compete
naafiʿ نافع *adj* useful, advantageous; **ma naafiʿ** useless

naafuura نافورة *n* fountain (for ornamental purpose)
naaga ناقة *n* (*pl* **niyaag**) she-camel
naagiṣ ناقص *adj* lacking, deficient; being short of; **naagiṣ-ni beeḍ** I am short of eggs • *prep* minus; **khamsa naagiṣ talaata yasaawi itneen** five minus three equals two
naagham ناغم *vt* (**munaaghama**) to call
naahiik ناهيك *part* **naahiik anno** not to mention, let alone
naaḥya ناحية *n* (*pl* **nawaaḥi**) side; direction **min an-naaḥya ad-dawliyya** from the international point of view; **min naaḥya…min naaḥya ukhra** on one hand…on the other hand… • *prep* **naaḥyat…**in the direction of, towards
naajiḥ ناجح *adj* successful
naak ناك *vt* (**i, neek**) (*vulgar*) to have sexual intercourse
naam نام *vi* (**u, noom**) to sleep
naamuus ناموس *coll n* mosquitoes
naamuusiyya ناموسيّة *n* mosquito net
naaqash ناقش *vt* (**niqaash, munaaqasha**) to discuss
naar نار *n f* (*pl* **niiraan**) fire; **an-naar gaamat/walaʿat** fire broke out; **an-naar** hell
naas ناس *n pl* (*sg* **insaan**) **1** people; **naas al-balad/naas al-ḥallaal** country people; peasantry; **naas ḥalaal** trustworthy, decent people **2** (*followed by a personal name*) the people of so-and-so's household or so-and-so themselves; **zurta naas Faaṭma** I visited Fatma; I visited Fatma's family
naasab ناسب *vt* (**nasab**) **1** to be appropriate, suit; to match **2** to marry into (a family)
naasuur ناسور *n* (*pl* **nawaasiir**) fistula
naaṣya ناصية *n* (*pl* **nawaaṣi**) street corner
naash ناش *vt* (**i, neesha**) to hit (of a weapon)
naashif ناشف *adj* **1** dry **2** stiff; **iid-o naashfa** he is stingy
naaṭig ناطق *n* spokesperson, spokesman
naawal ناول *vt* (**munaawala**) to give
naayib نايب *n* (*pl* **nuwwaab**) deputy, attorney; member of parliament; **naayib ar-ra'iis** vice-president; **an-naayib al-ʿaamm** the attorney general
naayim نايم *adj* sleeping, asleep
naaylon نايلون *n* **1** nylon **2** neon; **lambat naaylon** neon light; strip light
naaziḥ نازح *adj* displaced (person) • *n* internally displaced person
naaẓir ناظر *n* (*pl* **nuẓẓaar**) **1** master, headmaster, principal; station master **2** state-appointed administrative chief of a tribe
nabaʿ نبع *vi* (**u, nabʿ**) to well up (of water)
nabaaha نباهة *n* smartness, intelligence
nabaat نبات *coll n* (*pl* **-aat**) plants
nabaati نباتي *adj* vegetarian
nabag نبق *coll n* fruit(s) of the jujube tree; **shajar an-nabag** jujube tree
nabaḥ نبح *vi* (**a, nabiiḥ, nabaḥaan**) (**fi/foog**) to bark (at)
nabash نبش *vt* (**u, nabish**) **1** to scrabble in the dirt; **nabashu siirt-o** they gossiped about him **2** to reopen a grave

nabat نبت *vi* (**i, nabataan**) to sprout
nabatshi نبتشي *n* (*pl* **-yya**) orderly
nabawi نبوي *adj* pertaining to the prophet Mohammed
nabbah نبّه *vt* (**tanbiih**) to alert, warn
nabbaz نبّز *vt* (**nibbeez, nabaz**) to insult, abuse verbally, call names; to swear at
nabi نبي *n* (*pl* **anbiya**) prophet
nabiḍ نبض *n* (*pl* **nabaḍaat**) pulse
nabiih نبيه *adj* (*pl* **nubaha**) smart, clever
nabza نبزة *n* insult
nada ندى *n* dew
nadaama ندامة *n* remorse; repentance
nadah نده *vt* (**a, nadih, nadiiha**) **1** to call **2** to invoke (God, a saint)
nadar ندر *vt* (**u, nadir**) to invoke (God, a saint)
nadd ندّ *n* incense stick(s)
nadiid نديد *n* (*pl* **andaad, nadada**) peer (same age)
nadwa ندوة *n* (*pl* **nadawaat**) forum, seminar
naḍaafa نضافة *n* **1** cleaning; **ʿaamil naḍaafa** garbage collector **2** cleanliness; hygiene
naḍam نضم *vi* (**u, naḍim**) (**fi/ʿan**) to talk, speak (about)
naḍḍaam نضّام *adj* talkative (in positive or negative sense) • *n* a good talker
naḍḍaara نضّارة *n* spectacles, glasses
naḍḍaf نضّف *vt* (**niḍḍeef, naḍaafa, tanḍiif**) to clean; **naḍḍaf be-fursha** to brush
naḍiif نضيف *adj* clean; neat • *adv* (*slang*) very
nafa نفى *vt* (**-i, nafi**) **1** to deny **2** to banish, exile
nafaʿ نفع *vt* (**a, nafiʿ**) to be useful; **ma binfaʿ** it's no use
nafaḍ نفض *vt* (**u, nafiḍ**) to wipe off dust
nafaga نفقة *n* maintenance paid by a man to a divorced wife and their children
nafakh نفخ *vt* (**u, nafikh, nafakhaan**) **1** to inflate, pump up (e.g. a tyre); to puff, blow **2** (*slang*) to threaten
nafar نفر *n* (*pl* **anfaar**) **1** one person (when counting) **2 ʿaskari nafar** private (soldier)
nafas نفس *n* (*pl* **anfaas**) breath; **nafas gaayim** out of breath; breathlessness
nafasa نفسا *n* (*pl* **nafasawaat**) a woman who has just given birth (until 40 days afterwards)
nafash نفش *vt* (**u, nafashaan, nafish**) **1** to tease (wool, cotton), card (wool) **2** to undo hair plaits
nafayaat نفايات *n pl* garbage
naffaaj نفّاج *n* small door between backyards of neighbours
naffaakh نفّاخ *n* boaster, braggart
naffaasa نفّاسة *n* midwife
naffas نفّس *vt* (**niffees, tanfiis**) **1** to perforate; to deflate sth. **2** to assist at a birth **3** to make breathe again • *vi* **ʿala** (*slang*) to cause s.o. to fail
naffaz نفّز *vt* (**tanfiiz**) to carry out, execute
nafi نفي *n* negative
nafiir نفير *n* (*pl* **nafaayir**) voluntary working party
nafis نفس *n f* **1** (*pl* **nufuus**) soul **2** (*pl* **anfus**) self; **min nafs-o** of his own accord; **akhdim nafs-ak be-nafs-ak** serve yourself!; **shaayif nafs-o** he's vain, conceited **3** same; **di al-bitt be-nafis-a/**

di nafs al-bitt this is the same girl; **fi nafs al-wakit** at one and the same time, simultaneously **4** (**fi**) desire, appetite; **nafis-a fi s-safar** she would very much like to travel; **nafs-i masduuda** I have no appetite; **nafs-o maṣduuma** he has no desire at all; **ma ʿind-i nafis** I'm not in the mood

nafsi نفسي *adj* psychological

nafṭ نفط *n* crude oil, petroleum

nafṭi نفطي *n* crude oil, petroleum

nagʿa نقعة *n* (*pl* **-aat, nagaayiʿ**) any surface empty of loose sand and vegetation (desert, town or house)

nagaada نقادة *n pl* Egyptians living in Sudan

nagad نقد *vt* (**u, nagid**) to peck (of a bird)

nagaḍ نقض *vt* (**u, nagiḍ**) to break (e.g. a promise)

nagal نقل *vt* (**u, nagil**) **1** to transfer; to transport **2** to copy

nagar نقر *vt* (**u, nagir**) **1** to tap, knock **2** (*slang*) to guess

nagaṣ نقص (**u, nagṣ, nugṣaan**) *vi* **1** to be deficient; **as-sukkar nagaṣ** there was not enough sugar **2 min** to reduce, lessen; **nagaṣta min as-sukkar** I took (off) a bit of sugar • *vt* to reduce, lessen; **nagaṣta as-sukkar** I took less sugar

nagash نقش *vt* **1** (**u, nigaasha**) to paint (e.g. a house; skin with henna) **2** (**u, nigaasha**) to engrave **3** (**u, nagish, nagashaan**) (*slang*) to grasp, understand

nagdiyya نقديّة *n* cash

nagga نقّى *vt* **1** (**-i, niggeey**) to select **2** (**-i, niggeey**) to sort out, clean (e.g. rice) **3** (**-i, tanqiya**) to purify; to refine (e.g. sugar, petrol)

nagga نقّ *vi* (**i, nigga**) to nag; to grumble

naggaag نقّاق *n* grumbler

naggaala نقّالة *n* stretcher (for carrying the sick)

naggaar نقّار *n* **naggaar al-khashab** woodpecker

naggaash نقّاش *n* house painter

naggar نقّر *vt* (**niggeer, nagir**) to beat a drum

naggaṣ نقّص *vt* (**niggeeṣ, tangiiṣ**) **min** to reduce, lessen

naggaṭ نقّط (**niggeeṭ**) *vi* to leak, to cause to trickle, drip • *vt* to add dots (to letters)

nagiiṣa نقيصة *n* (*pl* **nagaayiṣ**) shortcoming

nagil نقل *n* **1** transportation; **ʿarabiyyat nagil** truck **2** transmission

nagnaaga نقناقة *n* light rain, drizzle

nagnag نقنق *vi* (**nagnaga**) to nag; to grumble

nagra نقرة *n* (*pl* **nugar**) scar

nagṣ نقص *n* deficiency, deficit, shortage

nagham نغم *n* (*pl* **anghaam**) melody, tune

naghama نغمة *n* (*pl* **anghaam**) melody, tune

naha نهى *vt* (**-i, nihaaya, inhaa**) to end, terminate; **naheet-o minʿ/an al-kiḍib** I told him to stop lying

nahaar نهار *n* daytime, day; **an-nahaar da** today; **nuṣṣ an-nahaar** noon

nahab نهب *vt* (**a, nahib**) to loot, rob, plunder

nahad نهد *vi* (**a, nahid**) to pant
nahar نهر *n* (*pl* **anhaar**) river
nahar نهر *vt* (**a, nahir, naharaan**) to scold
nahash نهش *vt* (**a, nahsha**) to tear to pieces (of an animal)
nahaz نهز *vt* (**a, nahiz**) to raise (a heavy item) from the floor
nahd نهد *n* (*pl* **nuhuud**) woman's breast
nahhaab نهّاب *n* robber, thief
nahhar نهّر *vt* (**nihheer**) to scold
nahim نهم *adj* gluttonous, greedy
naḥal نحل *coll n* (*unit n* **naḥla**) bee(s)
naḥas نحس *vt* (**a, naḥis, naḥasaan**) to bring bad luck upon
naḥs نحس *n* bad luck
naḥu نحو *n* grammar
naja نجا *vi* (**-u, najaa, najaat**) (**min**) to survive, escape (e.g. from an accident)
najaʿ نجع *vi* (**a, naji**ʿ) (of head of the family) to flee from one's responsibilities, run off, disappear
najaaḍa نجاضة *n* smartness
najaaḥ نجاح *n* success
najaala نجالة *n* a lot of talk but no action; **hum gaa'diin kutur najaala saay** they are doing nothing but talk
najaasa نجاسة *n* (*Isl*) impurity
najad نجد *vt* (**i, najda**) to rescue, save
najaḥ نجح *vi* (**a, najaaḥ**) (**fi**) to succeed, be successful; to pass (an exam)
najar نجر *vi* (**u, najir**) **1** to do carpentry work; to work wood **2** (*slang*) to make up (a story)
najda نجدة *n* rescue; **an-najda/ booliis an-najda** accident and emergency department (of police)
najḍaan نجضان *adj* exhausted
najiiḍ نجيض *adj* (*pl* **nujaaḍ**) **1** ripe **2** mature **3** done, well-done (food) **4** smart, clever, proficient, skilful, handy
najiila نجيلة *n* lawn (grass)
najim نجم *coll n* (*unit n* **najma**) **1** star(s) **2** planet(s)
najis نجس *adj* (*Isl*) impure
najja نجّى *vt* (**-i, nijjeey**) to rescue, save
najjaama نجّامة *n* (*agr*) small weeding hoe with two prongs
najjaar نجّار *n* **1** carpenter **2** (*pl* **najaajiir**) chisel (carpentry)
najjad نجّد *vt* (**nijjeed, tanjiid**) **1** to upholster **2** to stuff (e.g. mattresses)
najjaḍ نجّض *vt* **1** (**nijjeeḍ, tanjiiḍ**) to cook food till done **2** (**najaaḍ**) **najjaḍ-ni najaaḍ** he gave me a very hard time
najma نجمة *unit n* **1** (*pl* **-aat, nujuum**) star; **najma umm ḍanab** comet **2** planet
nakar نكر *vt* (**u, nakaraan**) to deny
nakash نكش *vt* (**u, nakish**) to undo (hair plaits)
nakhal نخل *coll n* (*unit n* **nakhla**) date palm(s)
nakhara نخرة *n* (*pl* **-aat, nikhreen**) **1** nose **2** nostril
nakhas نخس *vt* (**a, nakhis**) to poke
nakhiil نخيل *coll n* (*unit n* **nakhla**) date palm(s)
nakhla نخلة *n sg/pl* wart
namaṭ نمط *n* (*pl* **anmaaṭ**) **1** pattern (style) **2** type, stereotype
namaṭi نمطي *adj* **1** stereotypical **2** formal, stiff

namiim نميم *n* bedouin poetry
namiima نميمة *n* gossip
namil نمل *coll n* (*unit n* **namla**) ant(s); **namil abu r-riish** ant(s) in winged stage; **namil al-ʿeesh** a species of very large ant(s); **namil as-sukkar** a species of large red ant(s)
namli نملي *n* (*and* **silik namli**) fine wire netting; mosquito screening
namliyya نمليّة *n* cupboard with wire netting; dish rack of wire netting
namm نم *n* bedouin poetry
namma نمّ *vi* (**i, namm**) to sing (bedouin songs)
nammaam نمّام *n* a gossip
nammal نمّل *vi* (**nimmeel, tanmiil**) to tingle
namuuzaj نموزج *n* (*pl* **namaazij**) example, model
namuuzaji نموزجي *adj* exemplary, model; **madrasa namuuzajiyya** model school
naqaaba نقابة *n* trade union, syndicate
naqad نقد *vt* (**u, naqd**) to criticize
naqi نقي *adj* pure
naqiib نقيب *n* (*mil*) captain
naqiiq نقيق *n* croaking
naqqab نقّب *vt* (**tanqiib**) to make a woman veil herself
naqqab نقّب *vt* (**tanqiib**) to prospect (minerals, oil)
narfaz نرفز *vt* (**narfaza**) to anger, irritate
nasab نسب *vi* (**i, nasab**) **le-** to trace one's pedigree back to
nasab نسب *n* (*pl* **ansaab**) pedigree; genealogy; **shajarat an-nasab** genealogical tree, pedigree; **beet ḥasab wa nasab** a distinguished family; **ʿind-o ḥasab wa nasab** he is of noble descent
nasaj نسج *vt* (**u, nasiij, nisaaja**) to weave
nasakh نسخ *vt* (**a, nasikh**) to copy, to photocopy
nasal نسل *vt* (**i, nasil**) to pull loose threads out of cloth; to remove fluff from cloth
nasiib نسيب *n* (*pl* **nasaaba, nasaayib**) **1** father-in-law **2** brother-in-law
nasiiba نسيبة *n* **1** mother-in-law **2** sister-in-law
nasiij نسيج *n* (*pl* **ansija**) **1** textile, fabric **2** (*anat*) tissue
nasiim نسيم *n* breeze; **shamm an-nasiim** secular spring feast (Monday following Coptic Easter)
nasl نسل *n pl* offspring, descendants
nasma نسمة *n* breeze
nasnaas نسناس *n* (*pl* **nasaaniis**) type of small monkey
nasnaas نسناس *n* gossip
nasnas نسنس *vi* (**nisnees, nasnasa**) **fi** to gossip
nassaaj نسّاج *n* **1** weaver **2** weaver bird
nassaq نسّق *n* (**tansiiq**) to coordinate
naṣab نصب (**u, naṣb**) *vt* to erect; to pitch (a tent) • *vi* **ʿala** to swindle, deceive, cheat
naṣb نصب *n* deceit, fraud, scam, swindle
naṣiib نصيب *n* (*pl* **anṣiba**) **1** share **2** fate, lot, destiny; **ya-naṣiib** lottery
naṣiiḥ نصيح *adj* intact
naṣiiḥa نصيحة *n* (*pl* **naṣaayiḥ**) advice
naṣr نصر *n* victory (in battle)

naṣraani نصراني *n* (*pl* **naṣaara**) Christian
naṣṣ نص *n* (*pl* **nuṣuuṣ**) text, wording
naṣṣaab نصّاب *n* cheat, fraud, swindler, impostor
nasha نشا *n* starchy drink of boiled dura flour, gruel
nashaadir نشادر *n pl* ammonia
nashaaṭ نشاط *n* (*pl* **-aat, anshiṭa**) activity
nashal نشل *vt* (**i, nashil**) **1** to pull up (a water vessel) from a well **2** to pickpocket
nashar نشر *vt* (**u, nashir**) **1** to spread **2** to spread or hang clothes to dry **3** to publish
nashar نشر *vt* (**u, nashir**) to saw
nashiid نشيد *n* (*pl* **anaashiid**) official song, anthem; **an-nashiid al-waṭani** the national anthem
nashiiṭ نشيط *adj* (*pl* **-iin, nushaaṭ**) active, energetic
nashra نشرة *n* a wound that does not heal quickly
nashra نشرة *n* (*pl* **-aat, nasharaat**) news broadcast
nashshaab نشّاب *n* (*pl* **-aat**) bow and arrow
nashshaal نشّال *n* pickpocket
nashshaf نشّف *vt* (**nishsheef**) to dry s.o./sth.
nashshan نشّن *vi* (**nishsheen, tanshiin**) (**ʿala**) to aim (at) (e.g. in shooting)
nashshaṭ نشّط *vt* (**tanshiiṭ**) to activate
nataḥ نتح *vi* (**a, natiḥ**) to throb (pulse)
nataj نتج *vi* (**i, natiija**) **min/ʿan** to result from • *vt* (**i, intaaj**) to produce, yield
natal نتل *vt* (**i, natil**) to drag away by force
natar نتر *vi* (**u, natir**) to roar (e.g. of a lion)
natiija نتيجة *n* (*pl* **nataayij**) **1** result, outcome, consequence; conclusion **2** calendar
naṭag نطق *vi* (**u, nuṭug**) to utter; to pronounce
naṭaḥ نطح *vt* (**a, naṭiḥ**) to gore (with the horns)
naṭṭa نطّ *vi* (**u, naṭṭ, naṭaṭaan**) (**be-**) to jump (over) • *vt* to jump over
naṭṭa نطّة *n* jump
naṭṭaṭ نطّط *vt* (**niṭṭeeṭ**) to jump, hop, skip, bounce
nawa نوى *v* (**-i, niyya**) to intend
nawaaya نواية *n* kernel (fruit)
nawwa نوّة *n* storm with rains
nawwaʿ نوّع *vt* (**tanwiiʿ**) to diversify
nawwaati نوّاتي *n* (*pl* **nawwaatiyya**) sailor
nawwam نوّم *vt* (**niwweem**) to make s.o. sleep
nawwar نوّر *vt* (**tanwiir**) to illuminate, light up • *vi* (**nuwaar**) to blossom
nayy ني *adj* **1** raw, uncooked **2** unripe
nazaf نزف *vi* (**i, naziif**) to bleed
nazaḥ نزح *vi* (**a, nuzuuḥ**) to be forced to migrate, be displaced by war or natural disaster
nazal نزل *vi* (**i, nuzuul**) **1** (**min**) to descend, come down to land; to dismount; to get off (e.g. a bus); **nazal al-maʿaash** to retire **2** to go into a trance
naziif نزيف *n* bleeding, haemorrhage
naziih نزيه *adj* just, fair, impartial
nazla نزلة *n* **1** influenza **2** catarrh, common cold; **nazla shuʿabiyya** bronchitis

nazza نزّ (**i, nazz, nazza**) *vi* to ooze, seep, trickle • *vt* to cause to ooze, seep, trickle
nazzal نزّل *vt* (**nizzeel**) **1** to lower, bring down, take down **2** to unload
naẓar نظر *vi* (**u, naẓir**) **1 le-** to look at **2 fi** to take into consideration
naẓar نظر *n* **1** eyesight, sight; **naẓar-o ḍaʿiif** he is shortsighted **2** consideration **iʿaadat naẓar** reconsideration; **be-ṣarf an-naẓar min** regardless of
naẓara نظرة *n* look
naẓari نظري *adj* theoretical
naẓariyya نظريّة *n* theory
naẓariyyan نظريّا *adv* theoretically
naẓẓam نظّم *vt* (**niẓẓeem, tanẓiim**) to put in order, arrange, systematize, organize, regulate
naẓẓar نظّر *vi* (**tanẓiir**) (*pej*) to theorize
nejef نجف *coll n* party lights
niʿaal نعال *n* (*pl* **niʿlaat, niʿleen**) pair of shoes or slippers
niʿis نعس *vi* (**a, naʿaas**) to be(come) sleepy, drowsy
niʿma نعمة *n* (*pl* **niʿam**) **1** grace (of God) **2** comfort, ease of life
nibla نبلة *n* (*pl* **nibal**) catapult, sling
nidim ندم *vi* (**a, nadam**) **ʿala** to repent
nifaaq نفاق *n* hypocrisy
nifeesa نفيسة *n* a piece of rich food given to a poorer person (as protection against the evil eye)
nigaasha نقاشة *n* house painting
nihaa'i نهائي *adj* final; **gabli n-nihaa'i** semifinal •*adv* absolutely, completely, totally
nihaaya نهاية *n* end
nihheeda نهّيدة *n* sigh
niḥaas نحاس *n* **1** copper; **niḥaas aṣfar** brass **2** copper drum (emblem of chieftainship)
niḥna نحنا *pron pl* we
niil نيل *n* **an-niil** the Nile; **an-niil al-abyaḍ** the White Nile; **an-niil al-azrag** the Blue Nile
niim نيم *coll n* neem tree(s)
niishaan نيشان *n* (*pl* **-aat, nayaashiin**) medal
nija نجا *vi* (**-u, najaa, najaat**) (**min**) to survive, escape (e.g. from an accident)
nijaada نجادة *n* **1** upholstery **2** stuffing (e.g. of mattresses)
nijaara نجارة *n* carpentry
nijiḍ نجض *vi* (**a, najaaḍ**) **1** to ripen **2** to be cooked, done; **al-baṭaaṭis nijiḍ/nijḍat** the potatoes are done, ready
nikis نكس *n* (*pl* **ankisa**) underpants, knickers
niksi نكسي *n* (*pl* **ankisa**) underpants, knickers
nikhaala نخالة *n* bran
nikhreen نخرين *n* nose
nimir نمر *n* (*pl* **numuur**) leopard
nimra نمرة *n* (*pl* **nimar**) **1** number **2** school mark **3** number plate
nimsa نمسا *prop n* **an-nimsa** Austria
nimsaawi نمساوي (*pl* **-yyiin**) *adj* Austrian • *n* an Austrian
niqaab نقاب *n* (*pl* **-aat**) veil (covering the face except the eyes)
nirweej نرويج *prop n* **an-nirweej** Norway
nirweeji نرويجي (*pl* **-yyiin**) *adj* Norwegian • *n* a Norwegian
nisa نسى *vt* (**-a, nasayaan**) to forget
nisaaja نساجة *n* weaving

nisaala نسالة *n* fluff; loose thread
nisba نسبة *n* proportion, rate; percentage; **be-n-nisba le-** concerning, with respect to
nisbi نسبي *adj* relative; percentual; proportional
nisbiyyan نسبيّاً *adv* relatively
nisl نسل *n* offspring, descendants
nisha نشا *n* starchy drink of boiled dura flour, gruel
nishaara نشارة *n* sawdust
nishif نشف *vi* (**a, nashaaf**) to dry
niyaaba نيابة *n* representation, proxy, deputyship; **an-niyaaba** office of a public prosecutor, office of a public attorney; **wakiil(at) niyaaba** public prosecutor, public attorney; **mudiir(a) be-n-niyaaba** acting director
niyoon نيون *n* neon **lambat niyoon** neon light; strip light
niyya نيّة *n* intention; **niyya sooda/suu' niyya** bad intention; **salaamat niyya/khalaaṣ niyya** good faith
niẓaam نظام *n* **1** (*pl* **nuẓum**) system, proper order, orderliness; **be-n-niẓaam** systematically; in order **2** (*pl* **nuẓum, anẓima**) **a** system, institution **b** regime, political system
njimitti نجميتّي *coll n* (*unit n* **njimittaaya**) species of flies that are found in swarms in wet places (e.g. near river, in cultivated fields)
nofembar وفمبر *n* November
noo' نوع *n* (*pl* **anwaa'**) **1** kind, sort, type **2** gender
noo'iyya نوعيّة *n* quality
nooba نوبة *n* **1** bout, fit (of illness) **2** traditional Sufi drumming
noom نوم *n* sleep; **maraḍ an-noom** sleeping sickness
noona نونى *vi* (**-i, noonaay**) to lull to sleep
noota نوتة *n* (*pl* **nuwat**) **1** notebook **2 noota musiiqiyya** musical note
nubuwwa نبوّة *n* prophecy
nudra ندرة *n* scarcity
nufaakh نفاخ *n* abdominal distension
nufaas نفاس *n* state of having recently given birth; **beet an-nufaas** any house where a woman is cared for during the 40 days following childbirth
nufuuz نفوز *n* influence; (political) power; **'ind-o nufuuz** he is influential
nuggaara نقّارة (*pl* **nagaagiir**) *n* **1** type of drum **2** (tribal) dancing party with drums
nugla نقلة *n* (*pl* **nugal**) patch (on shoe)
nugṣaan نقصان *n* lack, shortage
nugṭa نقطة *n* **1** (*pl* **nugaṭ**) drop **2** (*pl* **nugaṭ**) dot; spot; (*also fig*) point **3** (*pl* **nigaaṭ**) police post; **nugṭat al-booliis/an-nugṭa** police post
nugulti نقلتي *n* (*pl* **-yya**) shoemender, cobbler; shoemaker
nukta نكتة *n* (*pl* **nukat, nikaat**) joke
numuu نمو *n* development, growth
nuquud نقود *n pl* money
nuskha نسخة *n* (*pl* **nusakh**) copy, photocopy; **nuskha aṣliyya** original
nuṣṣ نص *n* **1** half **2** middle, centre; **nuṣṣ al-balad** the town centre, down-town **3** waist
nuṭu' نطع *n* (*pl* **nuṭa'**) circular reed mat with a hole in the middle, used for a smoke bath
nuṭug نطق *n* pronunciation
nuuna نونة *n* dimple (in cheek)

Library!

LYNX! CONSORTIUM
BOISE MAIN LIBRARY

Items that you checked out

Title:
Sudanese Arabic-English English-Suda
ID: 31150013877184
Due: Wednesday, April 06, 2016

Total items: 1
Account balance: 0
Wednesday, March 09, 2016 5:58 PM
Ready for pickup: 0

For library hours call 384-4114
To Renew any items
Phone 384-4450 or visit
http://www.boisepubliclibrary.org

nuur نور *n* (*pl* **anwaar**) light; **nuur guddaami** headlight(s); **nuur warraani** rear light(s)
nuwwaar نوّار *coll n* blossom(s)
nuzuuḥ نزوح *n* displacement
nuzuul نزول *n* descent

O

ooḍa أوضة *n* (*pl* **owaḍ**) room; **ooṭṭ an-noom** bedroom
oogad أوقد *vt* (**yoogid, wuguud**) to light a fire, ignite
oorṭa اورطة *n* (*pl* **uraṭ**) battalion, regiment
orneek ارنيك *n* (*pl* **araaniik**) form (document)
orneesh ارنيش *n* polish

q – ق

qaaᶜa قاعة *n* hall; **qaaᶜat aṣ-ṣadaaga** the Friendship Hall
qaaᶜida قاعدة *n* (*pl* **qawaaᶜid**) **1** rule; principle **2** base, stand, pedestal **3** military base
qaa'id قائد *n* **1** (*pl* **quwwaad**) commander **2** (*pl* **qiyaadaat**) leader
qaad قاد *vt* (**u, qiyaada**) to lead; to guide
qaafya قافية *n* (*pl* **qawaafi**) rhyme
qaama قامة *n* stature, build (of a person)
qaamuus قاموس *n* (*pl* **qawaamiis**) dictionary
qaanuun قانون *n* (*pl* **qawaaniin**) law, act, bill; **qaanuun al-ᶜuguubaat** penal code; **qaanuun aj-jinaa'iyyaat** criminal code
qaanuuni قانوني *adj* legal; **gheer qaanuuni** unlawful, illegal
qaaran قارن *vi* (**muqaarana**) **been** to compare; **bitqaarin been-o wa been ar-raajil at-taani** she compares him with the other guy
qaari قاري *n* (*pl* **qurraa**) reader (person)
qaarra قارّة *n* continent
qaawam قاوم *vt* (**muqaawama**) to resist
qaayid قايد *n* **1** (*pl* **quwwaad**) commander **2** (*pl* **qiyaadaat**) leader
qaayma قايمة *n* (*pl* **qawaayim**) list
qabali قبلي *adj* tribal
qadar قدر *n* (*pl* **aqdaar**) fate, destiny; **leelat al-qadar** night of the revelation of the Koran
qaddar قدّر *vt* (**taqdiir**) **1** to value, assess; to estimate **2** to appreciate
qaḍaa قضاء *n* **1** settlement, winding up **2** destiny, fate; **qaḍaa wa qadar** by fate and divine decree **3** judgment **4** jurisprudence **5** **ᶜala** elimination
qanaa قناة *n* (*pl* **qanawaat**) canal, channel; **qanaa faḍaa'iyya** satellite channel
qanaaᶜa قناعة *n* contentment, satisfaction
qannan قنّن *vt* (**taqniin**) to legislate
qanuuᶜ قنوع *adj* contented, content

qaraar قرار *n* (*pl* **-aat**) decision
qarn قرن *n* (*pl* **quruun**) century
qarrar قرّر *vt* (**qaraar**) to decide
qasam قسم *n* oath
qasam قسم *vi* (**i, qasam**) **1** to swear an oath **2** (**be-**) to swear (on/by)
qawaaʿid قواعد *n pl* (*sg* **qaaʿida**) **1** rules **2** grammatic rules, grammar
qawmi قومي *adj* national
qayyam قيّم *vt* (**taqyiim**) to assess, value; to evaluate
qayyim قيّم *adj* valuable
qazaf قزف *vt* (**i, qazif**) to slander
qibla قبلة *n* **1** direction of Mecca **2** niche in mosque indicating the direction of Mecca
qiddiis قدّيس *n* (*Chr*) saint
qiima قيمة *n* (*pl* **qiyam**) value; **bela qiima** worthless
qimma قمّة *n* (*pl* **qimam**) **1** mountain top, summit **2** conference, summit
qinaaʿ قناع *n* (*pl* **-aat, aqniʿa**) mask
qiyaada قيادة *n* leadership
qiyaama قيامة *n* resurrection **ʿiid al-qiyaama** Easter; **yoom al-qiyaama** the Day of Judgment; **al-qiyaama** the Day of Judgment has come!
qoos قوس *n* (*pl* **aqwaas**) **1** bow (weapon); **qoos quzaḥ** rainbow **2** arch, vault **3** parenthesis, bracket (punctuation); **been qooseen** in parentheses, between brackets
quddaas قدّاس *n* (*pl* **-aat**) mass (in church)
qudwa قدوة *n* example (to be followed)
qur'aan *n* **al-qur'aan** القرآن the Koran
qur'aani قرآني *adj* Koranic
qurbaan قربان *n* **al-qurbaan al-aqdas** the Blessed Sacrament
quwwaat قوّات *n* (armed) forces; **al-quwwaat al-musallaḥa** the armed forces; **al-quwwaat an-niẓaamiyya** the armed forces (army, police and security forces); **al-quwwaataj-jawwiyya** the air force; **al-quwwaat al-baḥriyya** the navy; **quwwaat al-mushaa** infantry; **quwwaat ad-difaaʿ ash-shaʿbi** the Popular Defence Forces

r – ر

raʿa رعى *vt* **1** (**-a, raʿi**) to herd, shepherd, graze **2** (**-a, riʿaaya**) to protect
raʿad رعد *n* (*pl* **ruʿuud**) thunder
raʿiyya رعيّة *n* (*pl* **raʿaaya**) subject (of a country or ruler)
ra'a رأى *vt* (**yara, ruu'ya**) to see in a dream or vision
ra'as رأس *vt* (**a, riyaasa, ri'aasa**) to head, to lead; to preside over, chair
ra'iis رئيس *n* (*pl* **ruwasa, ru'asa**) head, leader, chief; president; superior; **ra'iis wuzara** prime minister; **ra'iis aj-jalsa/ ra'iis al-ijtimaaʿ/ra'iis al-majlis** chairperson; **ra'iis ʿummaal** foreman
ra'iisi رئيسي *adj* main, leading
ra'si رأسي *adj* vertical
ra'y رأي *n* (*pl* **araa'**) opinion, view

raaᶜa راعى *vt* (**-i, muraaᶜaa**) to look after • *vi* **le-** to stand by, to help out

raaᶜi راعي *n* (*pl* **rawaaᶜiyya, ruᶜᶜaa**) **1** shepherd, herdsman **2** (*pl* **ruᶜᶜaa**) parish priest, pastor

raa'iᶜ رائع *adj* splendid, marvellous

raa'id رائد *n* (*pl* **ruwwaad**) (*mil*) major

raab راب *vi* (**u, roob**) to be(come) curdled

raabiᶜ رابع *adj* fourth

raabiṭa رابطة *n* (*pl* **rawaabiṭ**) association (club)

raad راد *vt* (**i, reeda**) to like, love

raadi رادي *n* (*pl* **raadiyohaat, rawaadi**) radio

raafᶜa رافعة *n* (*pl* **rawaafiᶜ**) lever

raafag رافق *vt* (**muraafaga**) to accompany, escort

raag راق *vi* (**u, rooga, rawaag, ruwaaga, rawagaan**) to be(come) calm, quiet, to calm down

raagid راقد *adj* abundant, plentiful (e.g. goods)

raahan راهن *vt* (**muraahana, rihaan**) to bet with

raahba راهبة *n* (*pl* **raahibaat**) nun

raaḥ راح *vi* **1** (**u, rooḥa, rawaḥaan**) **a** to lose one's way, be lost **b** to get lost, become lost **2** (**-u,** *no vn*) to go; to leave; to go for good

raaḥa راحة *n* **1** rest, relaxation, ease; comfort; break, pause; **akhad raaḥa** to take a rest; to take a break; **be-raaḥa** slowly; carefully; quietly; **raaḥt al-baal** peace of mind; **2 raaḥat al-yadd/al-iid** palm of the hand; **raaḥat al-kuraaᶜ** sole of the foot

raajaᶜ راجع *vt* (**muraajaᶜa**) to revise; to check

raajil راجل *n* (*pl* **rujaal, rijaal**) **1** man **2** husband; **raajil umm-i** my stepfather

raakib راكب *n* (*pl* **rukkaab**) passenger

raakuuba راكوبة *n* (*pl* **rawaakiib**) sun shelter

raaqab راقب *vt* (**muraaqaba**) to observe, watch; to monitor

raaqi راقي *adj* refined (manners), gentle; elegant

raas راس *n* (*pl* **ruus, ru'uus, ruuseen, reeseen**) **1** head; **raas-o gawwi/naashif** he is stubborn, obstinate, disobedient; **raakib raas-o** he is stubborn **2** tip; **foog raas al-aṣaabiᶜ** on tiptoe; **raas al-beet** roof; **raas as-sana** New Year; **raas kheeṭ/raas mawḍuuᶜ** **a** the origin (e.g. of a story; lineage) **b** indication

raasal راسل *vt* (**muraasala**) to correspond with

raasi راسي *adj* (*pl* **raasiin**) calm, self-controlled

raasib راسب *n* (*pl* **rawaasib**) residue; sediment

raasmaal راسمال *n* (*fin*) **1** capital **2** the basic cost of sth.

raasmaali راسمالي (*pl* **-yyiin**) *adj* capitalist • *n* capitalist

raasmaaliyya راسماليّة *n* capitalism

raashid راشد *adj* mature; **al-ḥukum ar-raashid** good governance

raatib راتب *n* (*pl* **rawaatib**) pay, wage, salary

raay راي *n* (*pl* **aaraa**) opinion, view; **ar-raay al-ᶜaamm** the public opinion

raaya راية *n* flag, banner

raayiᶜ رايع *adj* wonderful

raayig رايق *adj* calm, quiet
rabaaba ربابة *n* (*mus*) instrument with one to five strings, played with a bow
rabak ربك *vt* (**i, rabka**) **1** to muddle, make a mess of **2** to confuse
rabaṭ ربط *vt* (**u, rabiṭ**) to tie (up), bind, fasten; to attach
rabb رب *n* **ar-rabb** the Lord, God; **rabb-a-na** our Lord, God
rabba ربّى *vt* (**-i, tarbiya**) **1** to bring up, raise children **2** to breed, raise cattle
rabbaaba ربّابة *n* (*mus*) instrument with one to five strings, played with a bow
rabbaaṭa ربّاطة *n* gang
rabbaaṭi ربّاطي *n* (*pl* **rabaaṭiyya, rabaabiiṭ**) bandit, robber
rabbash ربّش *vt* (**rabsha**) to be(come) uneasy, troubled, confused
rabbat ربّط *vt* (**ribbeet**) (**ʿala**) to tap (on shoulder)
rabbaṭ ربّط *vt* (**rubaaṭ, ribbeeṭ**) to tie (up), bind, fasten
rabiiʿ ربيع *n* spring (season)
rabiit ربيت *n* crackling (from fat of a sheep tail)
rabiṭ ربط *n* tying, binding, fastening; **rabṭ ad-darib** ambush
rabka ربكة *n* **1** mess, muddle, disorder **2** confusion
rabrab ربرب (**rabraba**) to be talkative
rabraab ربراب *adj* talkative
radam ردم *vt* (**u, radim**) to fill in with sand or earth (e.g. a pit, uneven ground)
radd رد *n* (*pl* **ruduud**) answer, reply; **radd fiʿil** reaction
radda ردّة *n* coarsely ground grain
radda ردّ *vi* (**u, radd**) (**ʿala**) to answer (to), reply (to)
raddad ردّد *vt* (**riddeed, tardiid**) to repeat
radi ردي *adj* vile, base
radmiyya ردميّة *n* **1** layer of sand or earth **2** filling in with sand or earth **3** dyke, embankment
raḍakh رضخ *vt* (**a, raḍikh**) to crush
raḍḍ رض *n* (*pl* **ruḍuuḍ**) bruise
raḍḍa رضّى *vt* (**-i, riḍḍeey, tarḍiya**) to appease, seek to please
raḍḍaʿ رضّع *vt* (**a, riḍḍeeʿ, riḍaaʿa**) to suckle, breastfeed, nurse
raḍi رضي *adj* easygoing, peaceful (person)
raḍiiʿ رضيع *adj* unweaned • *n* (*pl* **ruḍḍaʿ**) foster child
raḍraḍ رضرض *vi* (**riḍreeḍ, raḍraḍa**) to bruise
raḍyaan رضيان *adj* consenting, agreeing
rafaʿ رفع *vt* (**a, rafiʿ**) to raise, lift; to hold up high; **rafaʿ daʿwa ʿala** to bring a case against, sue; **raafiʿ nakhart-o** he's haughty, arrogant
rafaahiyya رفاهية *n* luxury
rafad رفد *vt* (**i, rafid**) to dismiss, sack, depose (from office)
rafaḍ رفض (**u, rafiḍ, rafḍ**) *vi* to refuse, decline • *vt* to refuse, reject
rafas رفس *vt* (**i, rafis**) to kick
rafdiyya رفديّة *n* dismissal (from office)
raff رف *n* (*pl* **rufuuf**) shelf
raffaas رفّاس *n* **abu raffaas** motorboat
rafid رفد *n* dismissal (from office, function)
rafiḍ رفض *n* refusal, rejection

rafiiᶜ رفيع *adj* **1** thin, slim **2** fine, delicate

rafiig رفيق *n* (*pl* **rafaaga**) companion, comrade; **ar-rafiig gabli ṭ-ṭariig** choose your companion before you choose the route

rafraf رفرف *n* (*pl* **rafaarif**) mudguard, fender, bumper (car)

rafraf رفرف *vi* (**rafrafa**) **1** to flutter, flap **2** to waggle the eyebrows

rafsa رفسة *n* a kick

ragaᶜ رقع *vi* (**a, ragiᶜ**) to patch (e.g. a garment)

ragaba رقبة *n* (*pl* **rugaab**) **1** neck; **ᶜamal/ᶜind-o ragaba** he killed s.o. **2** self; **katal ragabt-o** he killed himself; **ja be-ragabt-o** he himself came; he came by himself; **zanb-o ᶜala ragabt-o** it's his own fault

ragad رقد *vi* (**u, rugaad, ragda**) **1** to lie (down); **ragad maᶜa** to have sex with **2** to be hospitalized **3 ragad foog al-beeḍ** to hatch, sit on eggs • *vt* to hospitalize

ragaṣ رقص *v* (**u, ragiiṣ**) to dance

ragash رقش *vi* (**i, ragish**) to sparkle, glitter, shine

ragda رقدة *n* rest (lying down)

ragga رقّى *vt* (**-i, targiya**) to promote (in rank, grade)

raggaᶜ رقّع *vt* (**riggeeᶜ**) to patch

raggaaṣ رقّاص *n* professional dancer; a good dancer

raggad رقّد *vt* (**riggeed, rugaad, ragda**) **1** to make s.o. lie down **2** to hospitalize

ragiig رقيق *n pl* slaves

ragiiṣ رقيص *n* dancing

ragiṣ رقص *n* dance; dancing; **ragṣ al-ḥamaama** traditional bride's pigeon dance

ragraag رقراق *adj* giving broken shade

ragrag رقرق *vi* (**ragraga, rigreeg**) (of eyes) to be(come) filled with tears

ragṣa رقصة *n* dance

ragha رغى *vi* (**-i, raghayaan**) to foam (of soap)

raghba رغبة *n* (*pl* **raghabaat**) desire

raghgha رغّى *vt* (**-i, righgheey**) to foam (of soap)

raghiif رغيف *coll n* (*pl* **arghifa**) loaves of bread

raghm رغم *prep* **raghmi inn-/anno** although, despite the fact that; **maragat raghmi inn-a ᶜind-a ḥumma** she went out although she has a fever; **be-raghmi min** despite, in spite of

rahad رهد *n* (*pl* **ruhuud**) large watercourse

rahan رهن *vt* (**a, rahin**) to pawn; to mortgage

rahaw رهو *coll n* crane(s) (bird)

rahiif رهيف *adj* thin, transparent; delicate

rahiifa رهيفة *n* one piece of **kisra**

rahiina رهينة *n* (*pl* **rahaayin**) hostage

rahn رهن *n* (*pl* **ruhuunaat**) mortgage

raḥal رحل *vi* (**a, ruḥuul, raḥiil**) to move away; to leave, depart

raḥam رحم *vt* (**a, raḥma**) **1** to have mercy on (of God, on the dead); **Allah yarḥam-o** may God have mercy on his soul; he is dead **2** to be merciful to, have compassion for

raḥaṭ رحط *n* waist fringe (of a bride)

raḥḥab رحّب *vt* (**tarḥiib**) to welcome

raḥḥal رحّل *vi* (**tarḥiil**) **1** to transport (persons); to transfer **2** to dispatch; to deport

raḥiil رحيل *n* departure
raḥiim رحيم *adj* (*pl* **ruḥama**) merciful, compassionate • *n* (*Isl*) Merciful One, Compassionate One (epithet of God)
raḥma رحمة *n* mercy
raḥmaan رحمن *n* (*Isl*) Merciful One (epithet of God)
raja رجا *n* hope
raja رجا *vt* (**-u, raja**) to beg, implore, beseech
rajaʿ رجع *vi* (**a, rujuu**ʿ) to return to come back; **raja**ʿ **khalif** to reverse (e.g. a car)
rajaa' رجاء *n* (*pl* **-aat**) request for a favour
rajaf رجف *vi* (**i, rajif, rajafaan**) to shiver, tremble, wince
rajfa رجفة *n* **1** shiver **2** tremor
rajja رجّة *n* hubbub, din
rajja رجّ (**u, rajja**) *vt* to shake (liquid) • *vi* to chatter
rajjaʿ رجّع *vt* (**rijjee**ʿ) **1** to return sth.; to give back; to send back **2** to restore (e.g. electricity)
rakʿ**a** ركعة *n* bow (also in prayer)
rakaʿ ركع *vi* (**a, raki**ʿ**, rak**ʿ**a**) to bow (also in prayer)
rakan ركن *vt* (**i, rakin**) **1** to put aside **2** to park a car
rakaz ركز *vt* (**i, rakiz, rakazaan**) to take a firm stand, to withstand (an attack)
rakiiza ركيزة *n* (*pl* **rakaayiz**) pole (in support of a leaning wall or an old roof)
rakkab ركّب *vt* (**rikkeeb, tarkiib**) **1** to cause to mount/to board **2** to assemble, put together; to combine, compound
rakkaz ركّز *vi* (**tarkiiz**) (**fi**) to concentrate, focus (on) • *vt* **1** (**rikkeez, tarkiiz**) to fix firmly into the ground (e.g. a pole) **2** (**tarkiiz**) to concentrate (e.g. juice, alcohol, perfume)
rakwa ركوة *n* pitcher, jug (for religious purposes)
rakha رخا *n* **abu rakha** said appraisingly about a cheap purchase
rakha رخى *vt* (**-i, rakhiya, rakhayaan**) to ease off, slacken (e.g. a rope), loosen
rakhaa رخا *n* easy life
rakham رخم *coll n* Egyptian vulture(s)
rakhama رخمة *unit n* Egyptian vulture; **hu zool rakhama** he's a foolish and lazy person
rakhi رخي *adj* **1** easy (of life) **2** cheap (of price)
rakhiiṣ رخيص *adj* cheap
rakhkham رخّم *vi* (**rikhkheem**) to be(come) sleepy
rakhkhaṣ رخّص *vt* **1** (**rikhkheeṣ, tarkhiiṣ**) to reduce the price of **2** (**tarkhiiṣ**) to issue a permit
rama رمى *vt* (**-i, ramiya, ramayaan**) to throw (at), throw away
ramaad رماد *n* (*pl* **armida**) ash; **khamm ar-ramaad** Eve of Ramadan
ramaadi رمادي *adj* grey
ramad رمد *n* inflammation of the eye
ramaḍaan رمضان *n* (*Isl*) Ramadan, name of the month of fasting; **ramaḍaan kariim** (*wish*) a good/generous Ramadan
ramash رمش *vi* (**i, ramashaan**) to blink
ramla رملة *n* (*pl* **rimaal**) sand
ramli رملي *adj* sandy
rammal رمّل *vt* (**tarmiil**) to make a widow(er)

rammal رمّل *vt* (**tarmiil**) **1** to cover the floor with sand **2** to cover the interior walls with plaster

rammam رمّم *vt* (**tarmiim**) to renovate

ramz رمز *n* (*pl* **rumuuz**) symbol, token

randook رندوك *n* secret language (of street kids)

ranna رنّ *vi* (**i, raniin**) to tinkle; to ring

rannag رنّق *vi* (**rinneeg**) (**le-**) to stare (at)

raqaaba رقابة *n* censorship

raqam رقم *n* (*pl* **arqaam**) number; figure

raqiib رقيب *n* (*pl* **ruqaba**) (*mil*) sergeant

raqiiq رقيق *adj* gentle

raqraq رقرق *vi* (**raqraqa, riqreeq**) (of eyes) to be(come) filled with tears

rasam رسم *vt* (**u, rasim**) **1** to sketch, draw, paint **2** to scheme, to plan (illegal actions)

rasim رسم *n* (*pl* **rusuumaat**) drawing, picture; **rasim handasi** technical drawing; **rasim galib** electrocardiogram

rasm رسم *n* (*pl* **rusuum**) duty (customs); tax

rasmi رسمي *adj* official, formal; **ma rasmi; gheer rasmi** unofficial

rassaam رسّام *n* (*art*) painter; draftsman

rassal رسّل *vt* (**risseel**) to send

rasuul رسول *n* (*pl* **rusul**) **1** (*Isl*) prophet, messenger of God; **ar-rasuul** the Prophet Mohammed **2** (*Chr*) apostle

raṣaᶜ رصع *vt* (**a, raṣiᶜ**) to beat, hit, slap

raṣiid رصيد *n* credit

raṣiif رصيف *n* (*pl* **arṣifa**) platform, pavement, quay

raṣṣa رصّ *vt* (**u, raṣṣ**) to stack, put in order

raṣṣa رصّة *n* stack

raṣṣaaṣ رصّاص *coll n* lead (metal); **galam raṣṣaaṣ** pencil

raṣṣaaṣ رصّاص *coll n* crossbeams, transverse beams or struts (roof)

raṣṣaaṣa رصّاصة *unit n* bullet

raṣṣaaṣi رصّاصي *adj* grey

rasha رشى *vt* (**-i, rashwa**) to bribe

rashaaga رشاقة *adj* elegance

rashaaḥa رشاحة *n* ignition (in car)

rashaḥ رشح *vi* (**a, rashiḥ, rashaḥaan**) **fi** to seep through

rashiid رشيد *adj* reasonable, wise; mature; **al-ḥukum ar-rashiid** good governance

rashiig رشيق *adj* elegant

rashsha رشّ *vt* (**u, rashsh**) to sprinkle

rashshaash رشّاش *n* (*pl* **-aat**) **1** machine gun **2** sprinkler

rashshaḥ رشّح *vt* (**tarshiiḥ, tarashshuḥ**) to nominate

rashwa رشوة *n* (*pl* **-aat, rashaawi**) bribe

ratiina رتينة *n* (*pl* **rataayin**) oil lamp, paraffin lamp, lantern

rattab رتّب *vt* (**ritteeb, tartiib**) to arrange, to put in order, tidy

rattal رتّل *vt* (**tartiil**) **1** to recite/chant the Koran (according to fixed rules) **2** to chant hymns, sing church songs

raṭan رطن *vi* (**u, ruṭaana**) **1** to speak a local non-Arabic language **2** to speak broken Arabic

raṭib رطب *adj* damp, humid

raṭṭab رطّب *vt* (**tarṭiib**) to dampen, moisten • *vi* (**riṭṭeeb, tarṭiib**)

1 to relax in a cool place, chill out 2 to be(come) rich

raṭul رطل *n* (*pl* **arṭaal**) unit of weight equal to 449.28 grammes, a pound

rawa روى *vt* (**-i, rayy**) to irrigate

rawaasib رواسب *n pl* (*sg* **raasib**) residues, sediments

rawḍa روضة *n* kindergarten, nursery school

rawwaab روّاب *n* kind of clay (used to purify water)

rawwab روّب *vt* (**roob**) to curdle

rawwab روّب *vt* (**riwweeb**) to purify water with a kind of clay

rawwag روّق *vt* (**riwweeg**) to purify (water) by letting the mud settle • *vi* (*slang*) (**rooga**) to be(come) rich, be well-off

rawwaḥ روّح *vi* (*no vn*) to go, leave; to go for good • *vt* (**rooḥa, rawaḥaan, riwweeḥ**) to lose sth.

rayy ري *n* irrigation

rayyaḥ ريّح *vt* **1** (**riyyeeḥ, taryiiḥ**) to give relief to, ease (pain, pressure) **2** (**riiḥa**) to perfume

rayyal ريّل *vi* (**riyaala**) to dribble, slobber

rayyash ريّش *vi* (**riyyeesh, taryiish**) to be(come) rich

rayyis ريّس *n* (*pl* **ruwasa**) foreman; boss; president

razaala رزالة *n* vice, immorality

razag رزق *vt* (**i, rizig**) to provide (of God)

raziil رزيل *adj* (*pl* **ruzala**) immoral

raziila رزيلة *n* (*pl* **razaayil**) immoral act

reeda ريدة *n* love

reeka ريكة *n* tray of basketwork

reet ريت *part* **ya reet...**I wish...; if only...

riᶜaaf رعاف *n* nosebleed

riᶜaaya رعاية *n* care, protection, providence

ri'a رئة *n* lung

ri'aasa رئاسة *n* chairmanship, presidency; **ar-ri'aasa** headquarters

riba ربى *vi* (**-a, ribaaya**) to grow up

riba ربا *n* interest, usury

ribiḥ ربح *n* (*pl* **arbaaḥ**) profit, interest

ribiḥ ربح (**a, ribiḥ**) *vi* to make a profit • *vt* to gain, win; **ribiḥ salaamt-o** he escaped unharmed; **ribiḥ jaayza** to win a prize

rida ردا *n* (*pl* **ardiya**) shorts

riḍa رضا *n* consent

riḍa رضى (**-a, riḍa**) *vi* **1** (**be-**) to accept, to consent (to) **2** (**ᶜan**) to forgive

riḍaaᶜa رضاعة *n* breastfeeding; **akhu fi/be- r-riḍaaᶜa** foster brother

riḍiᶜ رضع *vi* (**a, riḍaaᶜa**) to be breastfed

rifga رفقة *n* companionship, company

rigeeṭa رقيطة *n* kind of clay (used in a mixture for plastering the outer walls and the roof)

rigeyyig رقيق *adj* (*f* **rigeyga**) fine, thin, slim; **umm rigeyga** thin broth with dried okra

rigg رق *n sg/pl* tambourine

riggeeᶜ رقّيع *n* **abu riggeeᶜ** (*zool*) bat

righib رغب *vt* (**a, raghba**) **fi** to desire

righwa رغوة *n* foam, suds

rihaab رهاب *n* (*pl* **-aat**) mirage

rihaan رهان *n* (*pl* **-aat**) bet

riḥim رحم *n* (*pl* **arḥaam**) womb, uterus; **ḥimil khaarij ar-riḥim** ectopic pregnancy
riḥla رحلة *n* **1** (*pl* **-aat, riḥal**) journey, trip, tour, outing **2** (*pl* **-aat**) flight (on plane)
riif ريف *n* (*pl* **aryaaf**) countryside
riifi ريفي *adj* rural, from the countryside
riig ريق *n* saliva; **ʿala r-riig** on an empty stomach
riiḥ ريح *n* (*pl* **riyaaḥ**) spirit (of the kind that possesses a person)
riiḥa ريحة *n* (*pl* **aryaaḥ, rawaayiḥ**) **1** smell **2** scent, perfume
riiḥaan ريحان *n* (*pl* **rayaaḥiin**) basil (plant)
riish ريش *coll n* (*pl* **-aat, riyash**) feather(s)
rija رجا *vt* (**-a, rajayaan**) to wait for
rijiim رجيم *n* diet
rijil رجل *n* **1** (*pl* **rijleen**) leg **2** (*pl* **rijleen**) foot **3** (*pl* **arjila**) leg (e.g. of a table)
rijla رجلة *n* purslane
rikaab ركاب *n* (*pl* **-aat**) stirrup
rikib ركب *vt* (**a, rukuub**) **1** to mount; to board, get into **2** to ride
riksha ركشة *n* rickshaw
rikha رخى *vi* (**-a, rakhaa**) to be(come) easy (of life); **as-suug rikha** the market is full of cheap goods
rikhaam رخام *n* marble
rimish رمش *n* (*pl* **rumuush**) eyelash
rimma رمّة *n* (*pl* **rimam**) carcass, carrion
riqq رق *n* slavery
risaala رسالة *n* (*pl* **rasaayil**) **1** message **2** letter (missive) **3** mission (objective)
riwaaya رواية *n* novel
riyaaḍa رياضة *n* sports, gymnastics, physical exercise
riyaala ريالة *n* dribble, slobber
riyaasa رياسة *n* presidency
rizma رزمة *n* (*pl* **rizam**) bundle
roob روب *n* (thick) curdled milk, curds, buttermilk
roog روق *n* (*pl* **reegaan**) queue, line, row
rooga روقة *n* serenity; calm, quietness
rooj روج *n* lipstick
rooshetta روشتّة *n* medical prescription
ruʿb رعب *n* terror, horror
rubaaṭ رباط *n* (*pl* **-aat, arbiṭa**) **1** drawstring; shoelace **2** bandage **3** (*Chr*) **rubaaṭ muqaddas** a holy union (e.g. marriage)
rubṭa ربطة *n* (*pl* **rubaṭ**) bundle
rubuʿ ربع *n* (*pl* **arbaaʿ**) one fourth; quarter
rugʿa رقعة *n* (*pl* **rugaʿ**) patch
rugaag رقاق *n* flakes made of sorghum flour, consumed at breakfast during Ramadan
ruḥḥal رحّل *n pl* (*sg* **raḥḥaal**) nomads
rujuula رجولة *n* **1** manliness **2** heroism, bravery and nobility
rukab ركب *n pl* (*sg* **rukba**) knees; **abu rukab** foot and mouth disease
rukba ركبة *n* (*pl* **rukab, rakaabeen**) knee
rukun ركن *n* (*pl* **arkaan**) corner
rukhṣa رخصة *n* (*pl* **rukhaṣ**) licence; permit; **rukhṣat qiyaada** driving licence
rumatizim روماتيزم *n* rheumatism; rheumatoid arthritis
rummaana رمّانة *unit n* pomegranate; **rummaana yaddawiyya** hand grenade

rusuum رسوم *n pl* (*sg* **rasm**) duty (customs); taxes; fees
rushaash رشاش *n* light rains (at the beginning of the rainy season)
rushrush رشرش *n* (*pl* **rashaarish**) eyelash
rutba رتبة *n* (*pl* **rutab**) (*mil*) rank
ruṭaana رطانة *n* any local non-Arabic language
ruṭuuba رطوبة *n* **1** moisture, humidity **2** coolness **3** rheumatism; arthritis
ruu'ya رؤيا *n* vision, dream
ruu'ya رؤية *n* **1** eyesight **2** view, opinion
ruuḥ روح *n f/m* (*pl* **arwaaḥ**) **1** soul, spirit; **ar-ruuḥ al-amiin** the Archangel Gabriel; **ar-ruuḥ al-qudus** the Holy Spirit **2** life, self; **katal ruuḥ-o** he killed himself **3** ghost **4** essence (e.g. of perfume), spirit; **ruuḥ an-nashaadir** ammonia **5** barrel (of a gun); **umm ruuḥeen** double-barrelled gun
ruuḥi روحي *adj* spiritual (as opposed to material)
ruus روس *coll n* Russians
ruusi روسي *adj* (*pl* **ruus**) Russian • *unit n* a Russian
ruusiya روسيا *prop n* Russia
ruwaaba روابة *n* leavening agent made of curdled milk
ruzz رز *n* rice

S – س

saʿa سعى *vi* (**-a, saʿi**) **le-** to strive for, make an effort to
saʿaada سعادة *n* happiness, joy; gladness
saʿaf سعف *coll n* (*unit n* **saʿfa**) palm fibre
saʿar سعر *n* rabies
saʿiid سعيد *adj* (*pl* **-iin, suʿada**) glad, happy
saʿiyya سعيّة *n* livestock
saʿlab سعلب *n* (*pl* **saʿaalib**) fox
saʿlaba سعلبة *n* loss of hair
saʿraan سعران *adj* **1** rabid, suffering from rabies **2** greedy, voracious
sa'al سأل *vt* (**a, su'aal**) to ask • *vi* **min/ʿan** to ask about
saaʿa ساعة *n* **1** hour; **as-saaʿa kam** what's the time? **2** clock; watch • *conj* **saaʿt-a/saaʿat ma** when, whenever; **saaʿt-a/ saaʿit-ha** then, at that time; by then
saaʿaat ساعات *adv* sometimes, occasionally; **saaʿaat-a/saaʿaat-ha** then, at that time; by then
saaʿaati ساعاتي *n* (*pl* **-iyya**) seller or repairer of watches
saaʿad ساعد *vt* (**musaaʿada**) (**fi**) to help s.o. (with), to assist s.o. (in)
saa'iḥ سائح *n* (*pl* **suyyaaḥ, suwwaaḥ**) tourist
saab ساب *vt* (**i, sayabaan**) to leave; to abandon, desert
saabag سابق *vt* (**sabag, musaabaga**) to race
saabiʿ سابع *adj* seventh
saabiqa سابقة *n* (*pl* **sawaabiq**) **1** precedent **2** previous criminal conviction
saabit سابت *adj* firm, solid; constant, fast (of colour)
saada سادة *adj invar* plain, simple, *as in*: **shaay saada** tea without

sugar or milk; **gahwa saada** coffee without sugar (or milk); **gumaash saada** unpatterned cloth (of one colour)
saadis سادس *adj* sixth
saafar سافر *vi* (**safar**) to travel, depart
saafil سافل *adj* (*pl* **safala**) base, low, vile • *n* bastard; **as-saafil** downriver (Nile), north, northerly
saafuuta سافوتة *n* **ʿind-o saafuuta** said about a person who wants to eat continuously
saag ساق *vt* (**u, suwaaga**) **1** to drive (cattle); to lead (away) **2** to drive (a car), to steer
saag ساق *n* (*pl* **seegaan**) **1** trunk of a tree; stem, stalk **2** leg (of humans)
saagiṭ ساقط *adj* cold
saagiya ساقية *n* (*pl* **sawaagi**) water-wheel
saaham ساهم *vi* (**musaahama**) **1 be-** (**fi**) to contribute (to) **2 fi** to be(come) a shareholder
saahil ساهل *adj* easy
saaḥ ساح *vi* (**i, sayaḥaan, sooḥa**) to melt
saaḥ ساح *vi* (**u, siyaaḥa, seeḥa**) to roam
saaḥa ساحة *n* large open space, open area
saaḥil ساحل *n* (*pl* **sawaaḥil**) coast
saaḥir ساحر *n* (*pl* **saḥara**) conjurer, magician
saakin ساكن *n* (*pl* **sukkaan**) inhabitant; **as-sukkaan** population
saakit ساكت *adj* silent • *adj invar* baseless, without a (specific) reason; **kalaam saakit** nonsense • *adv* **1** without a (specific) reason; **gaaʿid saakit** idle **2** only, just (because); **al-fariig itghalab min al-ḥakam saakit** the team only lost because of the referee **3** for free, gratis
saal سال *vi* (**i, seel, sayalaan**) to flood
saalam سالم *vi* (**musaalama**) to greet
saalim سالم *adj* (*pl* **saalmiin**) safe; sound, intact
saaluus سالوس *n* trinity; **as-saaluus al-aqdas** the Blessed Trinity
saam سام *vt* (**u, soom**) to sell
saamaḥ سامح *vt* (**musaamaḥa**) to forgive
saanawi سانوي *adj* secondary
saanya سانية *n* (*pl* **sawaani**) second
saar سار *vi* (**i, seera**) to go in procession to the bride's house
saaraṭ سارط *n* (**mushaaraṭa, shuraaṭ**) to bet
saari ساري *n* (*pl* **saariya**) mast
saari ساري *adj* operational, in force, valid; **saari l-leel** young locust(s), hopper(s)
saariḥ سارح *adj* inattentive, absent-minded
saas ساس *n* foundation (e.g. of a building)
saaṭ ساط *vt* (**u, suwaaṭa**) to stir (tea, soup)
saaṭuur ساطور *n* (*pl* **sawaaṭiir**) **1** butcher's knife **2** machete
saawa ساوى *vi* (**-i, musaawaa**) **been** to treat equally • *vt* **1** (**-i, musaawaa**) to make equal, level or even **2** (**-i, musaawaa**) to equal; **sitta zaayid talaata yasaawi tisʿa** six plus three equals nine **3** (**-i, taswiya**) to settle, reach an agreement on; **saawa al-mas'ala** he settled the matter

saay ساي *adj invar* baseless, without a (specific) reason; **kalaam saay** nonsense • *adv* **1** without a (specific) reason; **gaaʿid saay** idle **2** only, just (because); **di daʿaaya saay** this is only propaganda **3** for free, gratis

saayfun سايفون *n* (*pl* **-aat**) **1** cistern (of lavatory) **2** flush toilet

saayiḥ سايح *n* (*pl* **suyyaaḥ, suwwaaḥ**) tourist

saayil سايل *n* (*pl* **sawaayil**) liquid

saazij سازج *adj* naive, silly

sabʿa سبعة *num* seven

sabʿiin سبعين *num* seventy

sabʿṭaashar سبعطاشر *num* seventeen

sabaanikh سبانخ *n* spinach

sabaata سباتة *n* reed mat

sabab سبب *n* (*pl* **asbaab**) cause, reason, ground; **be-sabab** owing to, because of

sabag سبق *vt* (**u, sabag**) to precede

sabag سبق *n* contest, race; **meedaan as-sabag** race track

sabahlal سبهلل *adj* slovenly, disorganized, chaotic; careless

sabahlaliyya سبهلليّة *n* disorder, chaos as a result of carelessness

sabaḥ سبح *vi* (**a, sibaaḥa**) to swim

sabalooga سبلوقة *n* (*pl* **sabaaliig**) gutter (of roof); rainspout

sabat سبت *n* (*pl* **subaata**) basket

sabba سبّ *vt* (**i, sabb**) to insult (a religion), to swear

sabbaaba سبّابة *n* index finger

sabbaabi سبّابي *n* (*pl* **sabbaaba**) hawker

sabbaak سبّاك *n* plumber

sabbab سبّب *vt* (**sabab, tasbiib**) to cause

sabbaḥ سبّح *vi* (**sibbeeḥ, tasbiiḥ**) to pray with prayer beads

sabbak سبّك *vt* (**sibbeek**) to cook (a stew or sauce) perfectly (have the perfect formula to cook a good stew or sauce)

sabbat سبّت *vt* (**sibbeet, tasbiit**) to fix firmly

sabbuura سبّورة *n* (*pl* **-aat, sabaabiir**) blackboard

sabiib سبيب *coll n* straight hair

sabiibi سبيبي *adj* straight, soft (of hair)

sabiil سبيل *n* (*pl* **sabaayil**) public supply of drinking water such as a water jar or drinking fountain

sabiiṭa سبيطة *n* (*pl* **sabaayiṭ**) cluster (of fruit)

sadd سد *n* (*pl* **suduud**) closure; barrier; blockage; dam; **sadd al-maal** payment made by a bridegroom to the family of the bride

sadda سدّ *vt* (**i, sadd**) to close, shut; to bar, block, plug; **sadda n-niyya/n-nafis** to take away the appetite or one's enthusiasm

saddaada سدّادة *n* (*pl* **-aat, sadaadiid**) stopper, plug, cork

saddad سدّد *vt* (**siddeed**) to settle (a debt); **as-saddad deen-o naamat ʿeen-o** whoever has paid his debts sleeps well

safaaha سفاهة *n* insolence

safaara سفارة *n* embassy

safah سفه *vt* (**a, safahaan**) to be disrespectful towards s.o. by ignoring them

safak سفك *vt* (**i, safik**) to shed (blood)

safanna سافنّا *n* savannah

safar سفر *n* (*pl* **asfaar**) journey, travel

safari سفري *adj* takeaway (food)
safariyya سفريّة *n* journey
safaroog سفروق *n* (*pl* **safaariig**) boomerang
saffa سفّ *vt* (**i, saff**) **1** to chew tobacco **2** to eat or chew (powdered food like flour or sugar) in small quantities **3** (*slang*) to embezzle
saffa سفّة *n* quid of chewing tobacco
saffaaḥ سفّاح *n* killer, murderer
saffaaya سفّاية *n* wind bringing fine dust
saffah سفّه *vt* (**siffeeh**) to be disrespectful towards s.o. by ignoring them
safiih سفيه (**sufaha**) *adj* insolent • *n* immoral person
safiina سفينة *n* (*pl* **sufun**) ship
safiir سفير *n* (*pl* **sufara**) ambassador
safik سفك *n* **safk ad-damm** bloodshed
safinja سفنجة *n* plastic or rubber slipper(s), flipflop(s)
saflat سفلت *vt* (**saflata**) to cover with asphalt or tarmac
safra سفرة *n* (*pl* **safariyyaat**) journey, travel
safuufa سفوفة *n* stomach powder (of dried green herbs)
saga سقى *vt* (**-i, sagi**) **1** to water; to irrigate **2** to give s.o. water to drink
sagaf سقف *vt* (**i, sagif**) to roof (house); to thatch
sagaṭ سقط *vi* (**u, suguuṭ**) **1** to fail (e.g. in exams); **sagaṭ fi naẓar-i** he has lost my respect **2 aj-janiin sagaṭ** the foetus miscarried, aborted
sagaṭ سقط *n* cold (of weather)
saggaṭ سقّط (**siggeeṭ**) *vt* **1** to cause to fail (e.g. in an examination) **2** to abort (a pregnancy), cause an abortion; **saggaṭat aj-janiin** she had an abortion • *vi* to miscarry, abort; **hi saggaṭat** she had a miscarriage
sagif سقف *n* (*pl* **suguuf**) roof; ceiling
sahala سهلة *n* (*pl* **sahlaat**) plain
saham سهم *n* (*pl* **sihaam**) arrow
saham سهم *n* (*pl* **ashum**) share (of company stock)
sahhal سهّل *vt* (**tashiil**) to make easy, facilitate
sahwan سهوا *adv* unintentionally
saḥaab سحاب *coll n* cloud(s)
saḥab سحب *vt* (**a, saḥib**) to withdraw sth.
saḥan سحن *vt* (**a, saḥin**) to grind (mill)
saḥar سحر *vt* (**a, siḥir**) **1** to bewitch **2** to cast the evil eye on
saḥḥaar سحّار *n* (*pl* **saḥaaḥiir**) **1** sorcerer **2** person with an evil eye
saḥsuuḥ سحسوح *adj* (*pl* **saḥaasiiḥ**) womanish (of a man)
sajad سجد *vi* (**u, sajda, sujuud**) (*Isl*) to prostrate o.s. (in prayer)
sajam سجم *n* soot; **sajam-i** (*lit* soot is mine) expression used by women on receiving bad news
sajan سجن *vt* (**i, sajna, sijin**) to imprison, take prisoner
sajda سجدة *n* (*Isl*) prostration (in prayer)
sajiin سجين *n* (*pl* **sujana**) prisoner
sajjaada سجّادة *n* (*pl* **-aat, sajaajiid**) carpet; rug
sajjaan سجّان *n* (*m*) jailer

sajjaana سجّانة *n (f)* jailer
sajjal سجّل *vt* (**tasjiil**) **1** to note down, register, record (also music, etc.) **2** to enroll; to subscribe **3** to score (football)
sajjar سجّر *vi* (*no vn*) to smoke a cigarette
sajmaan سجمان *adj* slack (person), good-for-nothing
sakan سكن *n* soot
sakan سكن *vi* (**u, sakan**) to live (in a place), dwell • *n* lodging, accommodation
sakar سكر *n* drunkenness
sakat سكت *vi* (**u, sukuut**) to be(come) silent
sakka سكّ *vt* (**u, sakk, sakakaan**) to run after; to chase
sakkan سكّن *vt* (**sakan, iskaan**) to house, provide accommodation for
sakkan سكّن *vt* (**sikkeen, taskiin**) to ease, relieve (pain); to sedate, tranquilize
sakkar سكّر *vt* **1** (**sukkar**) to sweeten with sugar **2** (**sikkeer, taskiir**) to intoxicate
sakkat سكّت *vt* (**sikkeet**) to silence, pacify; **ya noom taʿaal wa sakkit aj-juhhaal** come, sleep, and make the children be quiet
saklab سكلب *vi* (**saklaba**) to wail (of women)
saklaba سكلبة *n* (*pl* **sakaaliib**) wail (of women)
sakraan سكران *adj* (*pl* **-iin, sakaara**) drunk, intoxicated
saksak سكسك *vi* (**saksaka**) to dance
sakta سكتة *n* silence; **sakta galbiyya** heart failure
sakhaafa سخافة *n* ridiculous or disagreeable behaviour; folly; silly or nasty thing to do
sakhaana سخانة *n* heat
sakhaf سخف *n* ridiculous or disagreeable behaviour; folly; silly or nasty thing to do
sakhal سخل *coll n* (*pl* **sukhlaan**) kid(s) (of goat)
sakhala سخلة *unit n* young she-goat
sakhiif سخيف *adj* (*pl* **-iin, sukhafa**) absurd, silly, ridiculous; nasty, disagreeable
sakhiina سخينة *n* thin vegetable stew
sakhkhaan سخّان *n* (*pl* **-aat**) heater
sakhkhan سخّن *vt* (**sikhkheen, taskhiin**) **1** to heat, warm **2** to warm up (e.g. for sports)
salaam سلام *n* **1** peace; **as-salaam(u) ʿalee-kum** may peace be upon you; (*reply*) **wa ʿalee-kum as-salaam** may peace be upon you too; **ya salaam** my goodness! good heavens! **2** (*pl* **-aat**) greeting
salaama سلامة *n* safety, well-being; **ḥamdi-llah ʿala s-salaama** thank God for the safe arrival; **salaamat niyya** good faith; **maʿa s-salaama** goodbye; **salaamt-ak** expression of sympathy to s.o. who is ill
salaat سلات *n* meat grilled on hot stones
salab سلب *coll n* hawser(s), thick rope(s)
salab سلب *vt* (**i, salib**) **1** to steal (e.g. livestock) **2** to cut meat from the bone
salaf سلف *n* (*pl* **-iyyaat**) loan
salafiyya سلفيّة *n* loan
salag سلق *vt* (**i/u, salig, salga**) to boil (food)
salak سلك *v* (**u, suluuk**) to behave

salakh سلخ *vt* (**a, salikh**) to skin
salakhaana سلخانة *n* slaughter-house, abattoir
salaṭa سلطة *n* salad; **salaṭa ḥamra** mixed salad
salbi سلبي *adj* negative
saliiga سليقة *n* broth
saliim سليم *adj* **1** correct; **ma saliim** incorrect **2** intact
salij سلج *coll n* (Swiss) chard, leaf beet
salla سلّة *n* (*pl* **-aat, silaal**) basket
salla سلّ *vt* (**i, sall**) **1** to extract, pull out (e.g. a knife, a thorn, one of many) **2** to take off (clothes or jewellery)
salla سلّى *vt* (**-i, tasliya**) to amuse s.o.
sallaf سلّف *vt* (**tasliif**) to lend
sallaḥ سلّح *vt* (**tasliiḥ**) to arm
sallak سلّك *vt* (**silleek**) **1** to clear, unblock (pipes) **2** to pick clean (teeth) **3** to run in (a car)
sallam سلّم *vt* (**tasliim**) **1** to deliver, hand over, submit; **sallam nafs-o le-l-booliis** he gave himself up to the police **2** to keep safe, protect (of God); **Allah yasallim-ak** may God protect you • *vi* (**salaam**) **ʿala** to greet, give a greeting; **sallim lee-y ʿalee-hum** greetings to them, say hello to them
salluuka سلّوكة *n* (*pl* **-aat, salaaliik**) dibble stick
salṭana سلطنة *n* chieftaincy; kingdom, sultanate
sama سما *n* (*pl* **samawaat**) **1** heaven **2** sky
samaʿ سمع *n* (sense of) hearing
samaad سماد *n* dung, manure
samaaḥ سماح *n* **1** tolerance; pardon, forgiveness **2** beauty
samaaḥa سماحة *n* beauty
samaḥ سمح *vi* (**a, samaaḥ**) **le-** to allow, to permit; **law samaḥta** excuse me
samak سمك *coll n* (*pl* **asmaak**) fish
samara سمرة *n* beneficial to one's health (said of certain food)
samiḥ سمح *adj* good, fine, nice; beautiful, pretty, handsome; **di samḥa samaaḥa** she is very beautiful • *adv* okay, fine, all right!
samiin سمين *adj* (*pl* **sumaan**) fat, thick, obese
samin سمن *n* clarified butter, ghee
samkar سمكر *vi* (**samkara**) to do metalwork
samkari سمكري *n* (*pl* **-yya**) tinsmith, tinplater; metalworker, panel beater
samma سمّى *vt* (**-i, simaaya**) to name, give a name to
sammaʿ سمّع *vt* (**simmeeʿ, tasmiiʿ**) to let s.o. hear (sth.), cause to hear
sammaaʿa سمّاعة *n* **1** loudspeaker **2** telephone receiver **3** earphone **4** stethoscope
sammaaki سمّاكي *n* (*pl* **sammaaka**) fisherman, fishmonger
sammad سمّد *vt* (**simmeed, tasmiid**) to fertilize (soil)
sammam سمّم *vt* (**simmeem, tasmiim**) to poison
samman سمّن *vt* (**tasmiin**) to fatten
sammar سمّر *vt* (**simmeer, tasmiir**) to nail
samni سمني *adj* beige
samsaar سمسار *n* (*pl* **samaasra**) estate agent, broker, middleman
samsara سمسرة *n* brokerage
sana سنة *n* (*pl* **sanawaat, siniin**) year; **sana kabiisa** leap year; **raas as-sana** New Year

sanad سند *vt* (**i, sanad**) to support (hold up)
sanad سند *n* (*pl* **-aat**) document, title deed
sanawi سنوي *adj* annual
sanawiyyan سنويّا *adv* annually
sandewiitsh سندويتش *n* (*pl* **-aat**) sandwich
saniin سنين *adj* sharp
sanna سنّ *vt* (**i, sann**) to sharpen, grind (knives)
sannan سنّن (**tasniin**) *vi* to develop teeth • *vt* to examine a person's teeth to determine their age
sansara سنسرة *n* censorship (act of censoring)
santar سنتر *vt* (**santara**) to centralize • *n* (*pl* **-aat**) centre (of attention, position)
santi سنت *n* (*pl* **santimitraat**) centimetre
santimitir سنتمتر *n* (*pl* **santimitraat**) centimetre
saqaafa سقافة *n* culture
saqaafi سقافي *adj* cultural
saqiil سقيل *adj* (*pl* **suqala**) a bore (person)
saqqaf سقّف *vt* (**tasqiif**) to educate (impart knowledge or culture to)
saraab سراب *n* mirage
saraaya سرايا *n* (*pl* **-aat**) palace
sarag سرق *vt* (**i, sarig, sarga**) to steal, rob
saraḥ سرح *vi* **1** (**a, sarḥa**) **be-** to herd, graze (feed); **bisraḥ be-ghanam ibliis** (*lit* he is herding Satan's sheep) he is an unrealistic person **2** (**a, saraḥaan**) to be(come) absent-minded, to daydream
sarat سرت *vi* (**u, sarit**) to extract, to pull out one of many
saraṭaan سرطان *n* (*med*) cancer; **saraṭaan ad-damm** leukemia
sarga سرقة *n* (*pl* **sarigaat**) theft
sarḥaan سرحان *adj* inattentive, absent-minded, daydreaming
sariiᶜ سريع *adj* quick, fast; prompt
sariiḥa سريحة *n* (*pl* **saraayiḥ**) **1** splinter, sliver (in skin) **2** strip (of land)
sariir سرير *n* (*pl* **saraayir**) bed
sarij سرج *n* (*pl* **suruuj**) saddle
sariyya سريّة *n* (*mil*) squad, part of a platoon
sarraᶜ سرّع *vt* (**sirreeᶜ**) to hasten
sarrab سرّب *vt* (**sirreeb, tasriib**) to cause to leak (out)
sarraḥ سرّح *vt* **1** (**sirreeḥ, tasriiḥ**) to comb **2** (**tasriiḥ**) to release from prison to dismiss from the army
sarsaar سرسار *adj* chatterer
sarwa سروة *n* wealth
satar ستر (**u, sitir**) *vt* **1** to cover (at an attack), shield (from scandal) **2** (**u, sutra**) (*Isl*) to bury (a person) • *vi* (**u, sutra**) to protect (of God); **rabb-a-na yastur** may the Lord preserve us!
sattaf ستّف *vi* (**sitteef, tastiif**) to pack (luggage)
saṭal سطل *vi* (**u, saṭil**) to be(come) high on cannabis
saṭḥi سطحي *adj* superficial
saṭiḥ سطح *n* (*pl* **suṭuuḥ**) **1** surface **2** (flat) roof
saṭṭaḥ سطّح *vi* (**siṭṭeeḥ**) **1** to ride on the top of a train **2** **be-** to fool s.o.
saṭṭal سطّل *vi* (**siṭṭeel**) to be(come) high on cannabis
saṭṭar سطّر *vt* (**tasṭiir**) to rule a line

saṭur سطر *n* (*pl* **suṭuur**) line (of writing)
saṭwa سطوة *n* (**ʿala**) power, authority (over)
sawa سوى *adv* together
sawaabiq سوابق *n pl* (*sg* **saabiqa**) **1** precedents **2** previous criminal convictions
sawaari سواري *n* cavalry
sawra سورة *n* revolution; **sawrat al-inqaaz** the Salvation Revolution (1989)
sawri سوري *adj* revolutionary
sawwa سوّى *vt* (**-i, siwweey, suwaa**) to make (e.g. tea, food); **sawwa (lee-ho) ʿarabiyya** he (worked and) got himself a car • *vi* (**-i, siwweey, suwaa**) **fi** to do, to be up to; **bitsawwi fi shinu** what are you doing?; what are you up to?
sawwaag سوّاق *n* driver
sawwaaṭ سوّاط *adj* intriguer
sawwaay سوّاي *n* doer, person who gets things done; **as-sawwaay ma ḥaddaas** a doer doesn't talk much
sawwag سوّق *vi* (**taswiig**) to market
sawwar سوّر *vt* (**siwweer, taswiir**) to fence in, put a fence round
sawwas سوّس *vi* (**siwwees, taswiis**) to be(come) infested with weevils or woodworm
sawwaṭ سوّط *vi* (**suwaaṭa, siwweeṭ**) (**fi**) to gossip (about), intrigue
sawwiyyan سوّيّاً *adv* together
sayalaan سيلان *n* gonorrhea
sayfon سيفون *n* (*pl* **-aat**) **1** lavatory cistern **2** flush toilet
sayṭar سيطر *vi* (**sayṭara**) **ʿala** to dominate, control
sayyaara سيّارة *n* car
sayyaḥ سيّح *vt* (**siyyeeḥ, tasyiiḥ**) to melt sth.
sayyaj سيّج *vt* (**siyyeej, siyaaj, tasyiij**) to fence in, put a fence round
sayyas سيّس *vi* (**siyaasa**) to be diplomatic
sayyi' سيّئ *adj* bad
sayyi'a سيّئة *n* sin (Islamic)
sayyid سيّد *n* (*pl* **saada**) **1** mister, sir **2** master
sayyida سيّدة *n* lady, madam
sazaaja سزاجة *n* naivety
sebtembar سبتمبر *n* September
seef سيف *n* (*pl* **siyuuf**) sword
seel سيل *n* (*pl* **siyuul**) flood (from rain), torrent
seer سير *n* (*pl* **siyuur**) strap; belt, transmission belt
seera سيرة *n* visit in procession of a bridegroom, his family and other guests to the house of the bride
seeraamiik سيراميك *n* tiles; **as-seeraamiik sa-yarmii-k** (*lit* the tiles throw you down) you'll slip on these tiles
seesabaan سيسبان *coll n* sesbania, River Bean, Danchi plant
seetaan سيتان *n* satin
siʿa سعة *n* capacity (volume)
siʿid سعد *coll n* (*unit n* **siʿda**) (bed of) rushes, sedge; **al-biʿid wa-la l-ariḍ umm siʿid** (*lit* a distance or a place full of rushes) it's advisable to keep one's distance from problems
siʿin سعن *n* **abu siʿin** marabou stork(s)
siʿir سعر *n* (*pl* **asʿaar**) price
siʿir سعر *vi* (**a, saʿar**) to be rabid, suffer from rabies

sibaaḥa سباحة *n* swimming; **ḥooḍ as-sibaaḥa** swimming pool

sibba سبّة *n* (*pl* **asbaab**) cause, reason, ground (of a quarrel)

sibḥa سبحة *n* (*pl* **sibaḥ**) prayer beads, rosary

sibir سبر *n* (*pl* **asbaar, subuur**) amulet

sidaada سدادة *n* (*pl* **-aat, sadaa-diid**) stopper, plug, cork

sidir سدر *coll n* (*unit n* **sidra**) jujube tree(s)

sigaala سقالة *n* (*pl* **-aat, sagaayil**) gangway; scaffolding

sigaaya سقاية *n* irrigation

siha سها *vi* (**-u, sahwa**) (**min**) to be inattentive (to), pay no attention (to)

siḥir سحر *n* witchcraft; magic, sorcery

siḥliyya سحليّة *n* (*pl* **saḥaali**) lizard

siid سيد *n* (*pl* **asyaad**) owner; **siid al-beet** landlord; **siid ad-dukkaan** shopkeeper

siija سيجة *n* draughts (game)

siikh سيخ *coll n* (*pl* **siyakh**) **1** rod(s), bar(s) **2** skewer(s)

siira سيرة *n* conduct (of life); **jaabu siirt-o** they spoke about him; **siira zaatiyya** curriculum vitae

siirinj سيرنج *n* (*pl* **-aat**) syringe

siisi سيسي *n* **umm siisi** mouse

siiwsiiw سيوسيو *n* (*pl* **sawaasiiw**) small chick

sijaara سجارة *n* (*pl* **sajaayir**) cigarette

sijill سجل *n* (*pl* **-aat**) register; list, index; **as-sijill al-madani** the population register

sijillaat سجلات *n pl* records, archives

sijin سجن *n* (*pl* **sujuun**) prison, jail

sikir سكر *vi* (**a, sakar**) to become drunk

sikirteer سكرتير *n* (*m*) secretary

sikirteera سكرتيرة *n* (*f*) secretary

sikka سكّة *n* (*pl* **sikak**) road; way; **as-sikka ḥadiid** railway; **maḥaṭṭat as-sikka ḥadiid** railway station

sikkiin سكّين *n* (*pl* **sakaakiin**) knife; blade

sikkiina سكّينة *n* (*pl* **sakaakiin**) **1** knife; blade **2** ledge, ridge on top of the roof

sikhin سخن *vi* (**a, sakhaana**) to be(come) hot

sikhir سخر *vi* (**a, sukhriyya**) **min** to mock, ridicule, scorn

silaaḥ سلاح *n/n pl* (*pl* **asliḥa**) weapon(s), firearms; **silaaḥ aṭ-ṭayaraan** the Air Force; **as-silaaḥ aṭ-ṭibbi** the Medical Corps

silik سلك *n* (*pl* **aslaak**) **1** wire; **silik araanib** chicken wire; **silik namli** fine wire netting; mosquito screening **2** steel wool **3** spoke (e.g. of a bike)

silim سلم *vi* (**a, salaama**) (**min**) to survive, stay safe, be cured

sillim سلّم *n* (*pl* **salaalim**) stairs; ladder

silmi سلمي *adj* peaceful

silsila سلسلة *n* (*pl* **salaasil**) necklace; chain

simaaya سماية *n* naming ceremony of a child

simbatiik سمبتيك *adj invar* **1** sympathetic **2** nice, beautiful (of things)

simbir سمبر *coll n* (*unit n* **simbiriyya**) Abdim's stork(s)

simiʿ سمع *vt* (**a, samaʿ**) to hear; to listen **simiʿ al-kalaam** to obey

simin سمن *vi* (**a, sumun**) to gain weight, grow fat
siminaar سمينار *n* (*pl* **-aat**) seminar
simm سم *n* (*pl* **sumuum**) poison, venom
simsim سمسم *coll n* sesame; **zeet simsim** sesame oil
sinama سينما *n* cinema
sindaala سندالة *n* anvil
sinkiit سنكيت *n* meat from the hump on the back of a bull
sinn سن *n* **1** (*pl* **asnaan, sunuun**) tooth; **sinn al-fiil** elephant's tusk; ivory **2** age
sinna سنّة *n* **1** cog **2** sharp point, tip (e.g. of pen, knife) • *adv* a little (bit); **ʿaamil sinna** tipsy
sinnaara سنّارة *n* (*pl* **-aat, sanaaniir**) **1** fishhook **2** knitting needle
sinner سنّر *n* turpentine, thinner
siqa سقة *n* confidence, trust
sirig سرق *vi* (**a, sarga**) to be stolen to be robbed; **guruush-i sirgat** my money has been stolen; **kitaab-i sirig** my book has been stolen
sirk سرك *n* circus
sirmus سيرمس *n* (*pl* **saraamis**) thermos, vacuum flask
sirr سر *n* (*pl* **asraar**) **1** secret; **ana gutta fi sirr-i** I said to myself; **be-sirr** secretly **2** sacrament (Catholic)
sirri سرّي *adj* secret, confidential • *adv* secretly, confidentially
sirriyya سرّيّة *n* **1** secrecy **2** concubine (slave)
sirwaal سروال *n* (*pl* **saraawiil**) loose cotton trousers, worn under a jellabia
sirwiis سرويس *n* (*pl* **saraawiis**) large plate
sistar سيستر *n* nun, sister
sitaara ستارة *n* (*pl* **-aat, sataayir**) curtain screen
sitt ست *n* (*pl* **-aat**) **1** lady, madam **2** female owner; **sitt al-beet** landlady; **sitt al-wadiʿ** fortune-teller, seer; **sitt ash-shaay** tea vendor
sitta ستّة *num* six
sittiin ستّين *num* sixty
sityaan ستيان *n* (*pl* **-aat**) bra(ssiere)
siṭṭaashar سطّاشر *num* sixteen
siweed سويد *prop n* **as-siweed** Sweden
siweedi سويدي (*pl* **-yyiin**) *adj* Swedish • *n* a Swede
siwiitar سويتر *n* (*pl* **-aat**) **1** sweater **2** jacket (with zipper)
siwisra سويسرا *prop n* Switzerland
siwisri سويسري (*pl* **-yyiin**) *adj* Swiss • *n* a Swiss
siyaada سيادة *n* sovereignty; **siyaatt-ak** Your Honour (to army or police officers)
siyaaḥa سياحة *n* tourism
siyaaḥi سياحي *adj* tourist
siyaaj سياج *n* (*pl* **-aat, asyija**) fence, enclosure
siyaaq سياق *n* context
siyaasa سياسة *n* **1** politics **2** policy
siyaasi سياسي (*pl* **-yyiin**) *adj* political • *n* politician
siyuubar سيوبر *adj* super; **siyuubar maarkit** supermarket
siyuula سيولة *n* liquidity; fluidity
siyuutar سيوتر *n* (*pl* **-aat**) **1** sweater **2** jacket (with zipper)
sokit سكت *n* (*pl* **-aat**) electric socket
soomiit سوميت *n* agate
soonki سونكي *n* (*pl* **sawaanki**) bayonet
sooṭ سوط *n* (*pl* **seeṭaan**) whip

suʿaal سعال *n* **suʿaal diiki** whooping cough
suʿbaan سعبان *n* (*pl* **saʿaabiin**) snake
su'aal سؤال *n* (*pl* **as'ila**) question
subʿumiyya سبعميّة *num* seven hundred
subḥaan سبحان *n* (*Isl*); **subḥaan-o wa-taʿaala** may He be praised (*formula used after the mentioning of God's name*); **subḥaan Allaah** God be praised! (*exclamation of wonder*)
sufli سفلي *adj* lower • *n/n pl* evil spirit(s) (that can possess s.o.); **ʿind-o sufli** he is homosexual
sufraji سفرجي *n* (*pl* **-yya**) waiter
sugud سقد *adj invar* sleepless; **ṭeerat as-sugud** a species of small nocturnal bird
suhuula سهولة *n* easiness; **be-suhuula** easily
suḥaa'i سحائي *n* meningitis
sujuud سجود *n* (*Isl*) prostration (in prayer)
sujuuk سجوك *n pl* sausages; **giṭʿat sujuuk** sausage
sukkar سكّر *n* sugar
sukkari سكّري *n* diabetes; **maraḍ as-sukkari** diabetes
suksuk سكسك *coll n* (*unit n* **suksuka, suksukaaya**) bead(s)
sukurji سكرجي *n* (*pl* **-yya**) drunkard
sukuut سكوت *n* silence
sukhra سخرة *n* **hu shaghghaal sukhra** he's working with only food as payment
sukhriyya سخريّة *n* scorn, mockery
sukhun سخن *adj* hot
sulfa سلفة *n* (*pl* **sulaf**) loan
sull سل *n* tuberculosis
sulṭa سلطة *n* authority, (political) power
sulṭaan سلطان *n* (*pl* **salaaṭiin**) tribal leader, clan leader, chief; sultan
sulṭaaniyya سلطانيّة *n* large dish or plate
sulṭawi سلطوي *n* (*pl* **-yyiin**) authoritarian
suluuk سلوك *n* (*pl* **-iyaat**) behaviour, conduct, manners
sumʿa سمعة *n* reputation
sumun سمن *n* obesity
sumuu سمو *n* highness; **as-sumuu wa rifʿa** Her/His Highness
sumuum سموم *n* hot wind
sunna سنّة *n* **as-sunna** the Sunna, i.e. the customs and usages of the Prophet Mohammed; **anṣaar as-sunna** those who live according to the Sunna
sunni سنّي (*pl* **-yyiin**) *adj* Sunni, pertaining to the Sunna • *n* Sunni, a follower of the Sunna of the Prophet Mohammed
sunuṭ سنط *coll n* sunt tree, scented-pod acacia
surʿa سرعة *n* speed, pace, tempo; haste; **be-surʿa** quickly, fast, promptly
surayya سريّا *n* satellite telephone
susta سستة *n* (*pl* **susat**) zip, zipper
sutra سترة *n* decency
suttumiyya ستّميّة *num* six hundred
suṭuuḥ سطوح *n pl* (*sg* **saṭiḥ**) roof (top layer)
suu' سوء *n* badness, bad state; **suu' ḥaẓẓ** bad luck, misfortune; **suu' idaara** mismanagement; **suu' muʿaamala** mistreatment; **suu' niyya** bad intention; **suu' faham** misunderstanding; **suu' tafaahum** mutual

misunderstanding; **suu' taghziya** malnutrition
suudaan سودان *prop n* **as-suudaan** Sudan, the Sudan
suudaani سوداني (*pl* **-yyiin**) *adj* Sudanese • *n* a Sudanese
suug سوق *n m/f* (*pl* **aswaag**) market, shopping area; **as-suug ḥaarr** the market is lively; **as-suug baarid** the market is sluggish; **as-suug al-ḥurr(a)** duty-free shops
suur سور *n* (*pl* **aswaar**) enclosure, fence, wall
suura سورة *n* (*pl* **suwar**) sura, chapter of the Koran
suus سوس *coll n* weevil(s); woodworm(s); **fii-ho suus** it has a cavity (tooth); **ʿarga suus** liquorice root; liquorice
suwaa سواة *n* action, doing
suwaama سوامة *n* selling (of hawkers)
suwaar سوار *n* (*pl* **aswira, asaawir**) bracelet
suwaaṭa سواطة *n* **1** stirring **2** gossiping
suweeba سويبة *n* granary

Ṣ – ص

ṣaʿab صعب *adj* hard, difficult; **ʿumla ṣaʿba** hard currency
ṣaʿiid صعيد *n* **aṣ-ṣaʿiid** southward, southerly, upriver (Nile)
ṣaʿluuk صعلوك *n* (*pl* **ṣaʿaaliik**) immoral person, vagabond, pauper, down-and-out
ṣaʿuudi صعودي (*pl* **-yyiin**) *adj* Saudi • *n* a Saudi
ṣaʿuudiyya صعودية *prop n* **aṣ-ṣaʿuudiyya** (*abbreviation of*) **al-mamlaka al-ʿarabiyya aṣ-ṣaʿuudiyya** the Kingdom of Saudi Arabia
ṣaʿuuṭ صعوط *n* chewing tobacco; snuff
ṣaabir صابر *adj* patient
ṣaabuun صابون *coll n* soap; **ṣaabuun ghasiil** laundry soap; **ṣaabuun ḥammaam** toilet soap
ṣaabuuna صابونة *unit n* a piece of soap
ṣaad صاد *vt* (**i, ṣeed**) to hunt; **ṣaad samak** to fish
ṣaadaf صادف *vt* (**muṣaadafa**) to come across or meet by chance
ṣaadag صادق *vi* (**muṣaadaga**) **ʿala** to approve, endorse, pass • *vt* (**ṣadaaga**) to befriend
ṣaadam صادم *vt* (**ṣadma, muṣaadama**) **maʿa** to bump into, collide, crash into
ṣaadar صادر *vt* (**muṣaadara**) to confiscate
ṣaadig صادق *adj* truthful, sincere; **ma ṣaadig** dishonest
ṣaadiraat صادرات *n pl* exports, exported goods
ṣaafi صافي *adj* pure
ṣaagʿa صاقعة *n* (*pl* **ṣawaagiʿ**) lightning strike
ṣaaḥab صاحب *vt* (**muṣaaḥaba**) to befriend
ṣaaḥba صاحبة *n* (*f*) **1** friend **2** owner; **ṣaaḥbat al-beet** landlady
ṣaaḥḥ صاح *adj invar* correct, right, true; **ma ṣaaḥḥ** incorrect

ṣaaḥi صاح *adj* (*pl* **ṣaaḥiin**) **1** awake **2** sober, not drunk
ṣaaḥib صاحب *n* (*m*) (*pl* **aṣḥaab**) **1** friend **2** owner; **ṣaaḥib al-beet** landlord
ṣaaj صاج *n* (*pl* **ṣiijaan**) griddle
ṣaala صالة *n* hall
ṣaalaḥ صالح *vt* (**muṣaalaḥa**) to make peace between, pacify, conciliate, reconcile
ṣaaliḥ صالح *adj* **1** fit (for use); valid; **ma ṣaaliḥ** useless **2** righteous, close to God • *n* (*Isl*) a righteous person
ṣaaloon صالون *n* (*pl* **ṣawaaliin**) reception room, lounge; **ʿarabiyya ṣaaloon** estate car, station wagon
ṣaam صام *vi* (**u, ṣiyaam, ṣoom**) to fast
ṣaamit صامت *adj* silent
ṣaamuula صامولة *n* (*pl* **ṣawaamiil**) nut (of a bolt), screw-nut; **ṣaamuult-o faakka/maḥluuja** (*lit* he has a screw loose) he's crazy
ṣaan صان *vt* (**i, ṣiyaana**) to repair, maintain
ṣaan صان *vt* (**u, ṣoon**) to preserve (e.g. one's honour)
ṣaanni صانّي *adj* (*pl* **ṣaanniin**) silent
ṣaaraʿ صارع *vi* (**muṣaaraʿa**) to wrestle
ṣaaraḥ صارح *vi* (**ṣaraaḥa**) to be honest, speak out frankly
ṣaargeel صارقيل *coll n* earthworm(s), lobworm(s) (used as bait in fishing)
ṣaarim صارم *adj* stern
ṣaaruukh صاروخ *n* (*pl* **ṣawaariikh**) **1** rocket **2** kite (toy)
ṣaayiʿ صايع *n* (*pl* **-iin, ṣuyyaʿ**) vagabond
ṣaayigh صايغ *n* (*pl* **ṣuyyaagh**) jeweller; goldsmith; silversmith
ṣabaaḥ صباح *n* morning; **fi ṣ-ṣabaaḥ** in the morning; **ṣabaaḥ al-kheer/ṣabaaḥ an-nuur** good morning
ṣabaaḥan صباحا *adv* in the morning
ṣabagh صبغ *vt* (**i, ṣabigh**) to dye, colour (hair or clothes)
ṣabar صبر *coll n* squirrel(s)
ṣabar صبر *vi* (**u, ṣabur**) to be patient
ṣabba صبّ (**u, ṣabb**) *vt* to pour out • *vi* to pour heavily (of rain)
ṣabbaaba صبّابة *n* funnel
ṣabbaar صبّار *coll n* succulent plant(s); cacti
ṣabbagh صبّغ *vt* (**ṣibbeegh, taṣbiigh**) to dye, colour (hair or clothes)
ṣabbaḥ صبّح *vi* (**ṣibbeeḥ**) **ʿala** to wish s.o. a good morning
ṣabi صبي *n* (*pl* **ṣubyaan**) a brave young man
ṣabiib صبيب *n* diarrhoea
ṣabna صبنة *n* absence of rain during the rainy season
ṣabur صبر *n* patience
ṣabuur صبور *adj* patient
ṣada صدى *n* echo
ṣada صدا *n* rust, oxidation
ṣadaaga صداقة *n* friendship
ṣadaf صدف *vi* (**u, ṣudfa**) to happen by chance, by coincidence; **ṣadaf anno laagaa-o** he met him by coincidence
ṣadaf صدف *coll n* **1** seashell(s) **2** mother-of-pearl
ṣadafiyya صدفيّة *n* psoriasis
ṣadag صدق *vi* (**i, ṣidig**) to tell the truth

ṣadaga صدقة *n* alms, charitable donation

ṣadam صدم *vt* (**u, ṣadma**) **1** to bump, crash into, collide with **2** to shock

ṣadar صدر *vi* (**u, ṣuduur**) to be issued; to be published

ṣadda صدّ *vt* **1** (**u, ṣadd**); **ṣadda raajiᶜ** to come back, return **2** (**u, ṣadd, ṣuduud**) (*slang*) (of girls) to refuse to meet (a lover)

ṣadda صدّى *vi* (**-i, ṣiddeey, ṣadiya**) to rust, oxidize

ṣaddag صدّق *vt* (**taṣdiig**) **1** to believe s.o. or sth. **2** to approve, endorse

ṣaddar صدّر *vt* (**taṣdiir**) to export

ṣadiid صديد *n* (*pl* **ṣadaayid**) pus

ṣadiig صديق *n* (*m*) (*pl* **aṣdigaa**) friend, confidant

ṣadiiga صديقة *n* (*f*) friend, confidant

ṣadma صدمة *n* **1** bump, collision, crash **2** emotional shock, disappointment; **ṣadma nafsiyya** psychological shock

ṣadur صدر *n* (*pl* **ṣuduur**) chest; breast

ṣafaᶜ صفع *vt* (**a, ṣafᶜaan**) to slap (on the face)

ṣafaar صفار *n* **ṣafaar al-beeḍ** yolk

ṣafag صفق *coll n* leaves

ṣafaga صفقة *n* bargain, deal, conclusion of transaction

ṣaff صف *n* (*pl* **ṣufuuf**) **1** queue, line of people **2** row (e.g in theatre, stadium) **3** year, grade of schooling

ṣaffa صفّى *vt* **1** (**-i, ṣiffeey**) to sift, filter, clarify; to strain **2** (**-i, taṣfiya**) to refine (e.g. petrol, sugar) **3** (**-i, taṣfiya**) to kill in revenge

ṣaffaaya صفّاية *n* cloth for straining (foods)

ṣaffag صفّق *vi* (**ṣiffeeg, ṣafga, taṣfiig**) to clap hands, applaud

ṣaffar صفّر (**taṣfiir**) *vi* to whistle

ṣaffar صفّر (**ṣiffeer**) *vi* to be(come) yellow; to wither (of plants) • *vt* to colour yellow

ṣafga صفقة *n* clapping of hands, applause

ṣafḥa صفحة *n* (*pl* **ṣafaḥaat**) page (of book)

ṣafiiḥ صفيح *coll n* tin plate, sheet iron

ṣafiiḥa صفيحة *unit n* (*pl* **ṣafaayiḥ**) **1** piece of tin plate **2** large can

ṣafra صفرة *n* a variety of sorghum

ṣafra صفرا *n* **aṣ-ṣafra** hepatitis, jaundice

ṣafṣaaf صفصاف *coll n* willow(s)

ṣagaᶜ صقع (**a, ṣagiᶜ**) *vt* to strike on the head • *vi* (of cannabis) to cause to be high

ṣagar صقر *n* rust

ṣaggar صقّر *vi* (**ṣiggeer**) to rust, oxidize

ṣagiiᶜa صقيعة *n* (*pl* **ṣagaayiᶜ**) plain

ṣagur صقر *n* (*pl* **ṣuguur**) **1** eagle (generic), hawk, falcon bird of prey **2** (*slang*) homosexual (dominant partner)

ṣaghghar صغّر *vt* (**taṣghiir, ṣighgheer**) to make sth. small(er)

ṣaghiir صغير *adj* (*pl* **ṣughaar**) **1** small **2** young, minor; **aṣ-ṣaghiir** junior

ṣahal صهل *vi* (**a, ṣahiil**) to neigh

ṣaḥaafa صحافة *n* journalism, press

ṣaḥafi صحفي *adj* (*pl* **-yyiin**) journalistic, pertaining to journalism; **bayaan ṣaḥafi, tasriiḥ ṣaḥafi** press release • *n* journalist

ṣaḥan صحن *n* (*pl* **ṣuḥuun**) **1** plate; dish **2** saucer
ṣaḥḥ صح *adj invar* true; right
ṣaḥḥa صحّة *n* **1** health **2** rightness, correctness
ṣaḥḥa صحّى *vt* (**-i, ṣiḥḥeey, taṣḥiya**) to wake s.o. up, rouse
ṣaḥḥa صحّ *vi* (**i, ṣaḥḥa**) to be true
ṣaḥḥaḥ صحّح *vt* (**taṣḥiiḥ**) to correct
ṣaḥii صحي *adj* true; correct; right
ṣaḥiifa صحيفة *n* (*pl* **ṣuḥuf**) newspaper
ṣaḥiiḥ صحيح *adj* true; correct; right; **ma ṣaḥiiḥ** incorrect
ṣaḥraa صحرا *n* (*pl* **ṣaḥaari**) desert
ṣaḥraawi صحراوي *adj* pertaining to the desert
ṣaḥṣaḥ صحصح *vi* (**ṣiḥṣeeḥ, ṣaḥṣaḥa**) to wake up; **ya awlaad, ṣaḥṣaḥu maᶜaa-y** hey kids, pay attention!
ṣakhr صخر *coll n* (*pl* **ṣukhuur**) rock(s)
ṣalᶜa صلعة *n* (*pl* **ṣilaᶜ**) baldness; **ᶜind-o ṣalᶜa** he is bald; **abu ṣalᶜa** the bald guy
ṣalaa صلاة *n* (*pl* **ṣalawaat**) prayer; (*Isl*) **ṣalaat aṣ-ṣubuḥ** morning prayer; **ṣalaat al-ḍuhur** prayer at noon; **ṣalaat al-ᶜaṣur** afternoon prayer; **ṣalaat al-mughrib** prayer at sunset; **ṣalaat al-ᶜisha** evening prayer; **ṣalaat at-taraawiiḥ** prayers performed during Ramadan, after the breaking of the fast
ṣalaaḥ صلاح *n* righteousness, goodness, piety; **ᶜind-o/fii-ho ṣalaaḥ** he is a righteous and pious person
ṣalaaḥiyya صلاحيّة *n* validity
ṣalb صلب *adj invar* solid, hard
ṣaliib صليب *n* **1** (*pl* **ṣulbaan**) cross (e.g. of Christ); **aṣ-ṣaliib al-aḥmar** the Red Cross **2** (*pl* **ṣalaayib**) unit of measurement of sugar in blood
ṣalla صلّى *v* (**-i, ṣalaa**) to pray
ṣallaᶜ صلّع *vi* (**ṣilleeᶜ**) to become bald
ṣallab صلّب *vi* (**taṣliib**) **1** (*Chr*) to make the sign of the cross **2** to put a cross (for marking or deleting)
ṣallaḥ صلّح *vt* (**ṣilleeḥ, taṣliiḥ**) to repair, mend; to correct; to improve sth.
ṣalṣa صلصة *n* tomato sauce, tomato paste
ṣamat صمت *vi* (**u, ṣamt**) to be silent
ṣamm صم *adv* **ḥafaẓ ṣamm** to know by heart thoroughly
ṣamma صمّ *vt* (**u, ṣamm**) to close up; **ṣamma khashm-o** he was silent
ṣammaagha صمّاغة *n* glue pot or bottle
ṣammagh صمّغ *vt* (**taṣmiigh**) to glue
ṣammam صمّم (**taṣmiim**) *vi* (**ᶜala**) to be determined • *vt* to design
ṣamt صمت *n* silence
ṣamugh صمغ *n* **1** gum, resin gum arabic **2** glue; **lazzaag ṣamugh** glue
ṣanaᶜ صنع *vt* (**a, ṣinaaᶜa**) to make, manufacture
ṣandal صندل *coll n* sandalwood
ṣandal صندل *n* (*pl* **ṣanaadil**) **1** sandal(s) **2** barge
ṣandaliyya صندليّة *n* essence of sandalwood
ṣanduug صندوق *n* (*pl* **ṣanaadiig**) **1** (large) box, trunk, case, chest;

ṣanduug al-busṭa, ṣanduug al-bariid, ṣanduug bariidi post office box; **ṣanduug al-intikhaabaat** ballot box **2** informal credit association, savings club **3** fund
ṣanf صنف *n* (*pl* **aṣnaaf**) kind, species; category
ṣanfara صنفرة *n* sandpaper
ṣangaᶜ صنقع *vi* (**ṣingeeᶜ**, **ṣangaᶜa**) to look upwards
ṣangar صنقر *vi* (**ṣingeer**) to sit
ṣanguur صنقور *n* (*pl* **ṣanaagiir**) top of the head
ṣanna صنّ *vi* (**i, ṣann**) to pause, be silent for a short while
ṣanna صنّة *n* short silence; **akhad lee-ho ṣanna** he was silent for a while; **addii-ha ṣanna** wait a little!
ṣannaf صنّف *vt* (**taṣniif**) to categorize, classify
ṣarᶜa صرعة *n* epilepsy
ṣaraaḥa صراحة *n* frankness, honesty, sincerity; **be-ṣaraaḥa** frankly, honestly
ṣaraf صرف *v* (**u, ṣarif**) **1** to spend **2** to receive one's salary **3** to cash (a cheque)
ṣarakh صرخ *vi* (**a, ṣariikh, ṣuraakh**) (**fi**) to shout, yell, scream (at)
ṣarfa صرفة *n* payment of one's share by an informal credit association or savings club
ṣarfiyya صرفيّة *n* amount of money to be received (from work, friends, etc.)
ṣariif صريف *n* (*pl* **ṣurfaan**) fence, enclosure (of reed or straw)
ṣariiḥ صريح *adj* frank, honest; **ma ṣariiḥ** dishonest
ṣarkha صرخة *n* a cry, a shout, a yell
ṣarmaan صرمان *adj* needy
ṣarmaati صرماتي *n* (*pl* **-yya**) shoemaker; shoe mender, cobbler
ṣarra صرّ *vi* (**u, ṣariir**) to squeak • *vt* **1** (**u, ṣarra, ṣararaan**) to tie up (as in a cloth) **2** (**u, ṣarra**) **ṣarra washsh-o** to frown, to screw up one's eyes
ṣarraaf صرّاف *n* cashier, moneychanger
ṣarraf صرّف *vt* (**ṣirreef, taṣriif**) **1** to drain **2** to give s.o. money, distribute money
ṣarraḥ صرّح (**taṣriiḥ**) *vi* **1 be-** to declare **2 le-** to permit, give permission
ṣarrakh صرّخ *vi* (**ṣuraakh, ṣirreekh**) to shout, yell, scream
ṣarṣaar صرصار *n* (*pl* **ṣaraaṣiir**) **1** (field) cricket **2** cockroach
ṣarṣar صرصر (**ṣarṣara**) *vi* to squeak • *vt* **ṣarṣar washsh-o** to frown, to screw up one's eyes
ṣarṣuur صرصور *n* (*pl* **ṣaraaṣiir**) **1** (field) cricket **2** cockroach
ṣawaab صواب *coll n* nit(s)
ṣawwaan صوّان *n* granite
ṣawwam صوّم *vt* (**ṣiyaam**) to enable s.o. to fast
ṣawwar صوّر *vt* (**taṣwiir**) to photograph, take a picture; to film
ṣawwat صوّت *vi* (**taṣwiit**) to vote
ṣaydali صيدلي *n* (*pl* **ṣayaadla**) pharmacist
ṣaydaliyya صيدليّة *n* pharmacy
ṣayyaad صيّاد *n* hunter; **ṣayyaad samak** fisherman
ṣayyaf صيّف *vi* (**ṣeef, ṣeefa**) to be summer
ṣeed صيد *n* hunting, hunt, game; **ṣeed as-samak** fishing

ṣeeda صيدة *n* prey
ṣeef صيف *n* hot weather; summer
ṣeefi صيفي *adj* pertaining to the summer
ṣeewaan صيوان *n* (*pl* **-aat**) marquee, pavilion awning
ṣibgha صبغة *n* dye, tincture
ṣidaam صدام *n* (*pl* **-aat**) clash
ṣideeri صديري *n* (*pl* **-yyaat**) **1** sleeveless jacket **2** waistcoat
ṣidig صدق *n* truthfulness, sincerity
ṣifa صفة *n* **1** characteristic, quality, attribute **2** position, capacity; **be-ṣifat-o** as, in his capacity of **3** way, manner; **be-ṣifa khaaṣṣa** in particular, especially; **be-ṣifa ma/gheer rasmiyya** unofficially **4** (*gram*) adjective
ṣifir صفر *n* bronze; brass
ṣifir صفر *num* zero
ṣighayyir صغير *adj* (*pl* **-iin, ṣughaar**) **1** small **2** young
ṣihriij صهريج *n* (*pl* **ṣahaariij**) water tank; water tower
ṣiḥa صحا *vi* (**-a, ṣaḥayaan**) to wake up
ṣiḥḥi صحّي *adj* healthy; relating to health, sanitary; hygienic
ṣiin صين *prop n* **aṣ-ṣiin** China
ṣiini صيني *adj* (*pl* **-yyiin**) Chinese • *n* **1** (*pl* **-yyiin**) a Chinese **2** china, porcelain
ṣiiniyya صينيّة *n* **1** (*pl* **ṣawaani**) tray; baking tray **2** roundabout (at road junction)
ṣiit صيت *n* fame
ṣila صلة *n* link, connection
ṣinʿa صنعة *n* profession; **sinʿa fi l-yadd amaan min al-fagur** to have a profession is a guarantee against poverty
ṣinaaʿa صناعة *n* industry, manufacture
ṣinaaʿi صناعي *n* (*pl* **ṣanaayʿiyya**) artisan, craftsman
ṣinaaʿi صناعي *adj* industrial
ṣiraaʿ صراع *n* (*pl* **-aat**) conflict
ṣiraafa صرافة *n* bureau de change
ṣirfa صرفة *n* **ma ʿirifna lee-ho ṣirfa** we didn't know how to deal with him/it
ṣiyaam صيام *n* (*rel*) fast; fasting
ṣiyaana صيانة *n* repair; maintenance
ṣool صول *n* sergeant major
ṣoom صوم *n* (*rel*) fast; fasting
ṣoon صون *n* protection
ṣoot صوت *n* (*pl* **aṣwaat**) **1** sound, noise **2** voice **3** vote
ṣuʿuuba صعوبة *n* difficulty
ṣubaaʿ صباع *n* (*pl* **-aat**) **1** tube (e.g. toothpaste); **ṣubaaʿ amiir** small tube containing a type of strong glue **2** (*mus*) peg (of a stringed musical instrument) **3 ḥajar ṣubaaʿ** small battery (e.g. for remote control)
ṣubḥiyya صبحيّة *n* any part of a wedding celebrated by daylight
ṣubuḥ صبح *n* morning
ṣudaaʿ صداع *n* headache; **ṣudaaʿ niṣfi** migraine
ṣudaag صداق *n* (*pl* **-aat**) dowry
ṣudfa صدفة *n* (*pl* **ṣudaf**) coincidence; **ṣudfa/be-ṣudfa** accidentally, by chance, by coincidence
ṣuffaara صفّارة *n* (*pl* **-aat, ṣafaafiir**) whistle
ṣuffeer صفّير *n* **abu ṣuffeer** hepatitis, jaundice
ṣufra صفرة *n* (*pl* **ṣufar**) dining room; dining table
ṣufuufi صفوفي *adj* (*mil*) promoted from the ranks (of an officer)

ṣughayyir صغير *adj* (*pl* **-iin, ṣughaar**) **1** small **2** young
ṣughur صغر *n* smallness
ṣuḥba صحبة *n* friendship
ṣulb صلب *n* solid, hard; **ḥadiid ṣulb** steel
ṣulub صلب *n* (*pl* **-aat, ṣulubba, aṣlaab, ṣalabeen**) bottom, backside
ṣuluḥ صلح *n* reconciliation
ṣunaaḥ صناح *n* bad smell (of body); **al-wad shamma ṣunaaḥ-o** the boy has reached the age of discretion
ṣunaan صنان *n* bad smell (of body)
ṣurra صرة *n* **1** navel; **ḥabl aṣ-ṣurra** umbilical cord; **burtukaan abu ṣ-ṣurra** navel orange(s) **2** bundle; knapsack
ṣurṣaar صرصار *n* (*pl* **ṣaraaṣiir**) **1** cockroach **2** house cricket
ṣuuf صوف *n* (*pl* **aṣwaaf**) fleece; wool
ṣuufi صوفي *adj* pertaining to Sufism • *n* Sufi, adherent of mystical Islam, mystic
ṣuufiyya صوفيّة *n* **aṣ-ṣuufiyya** Sufism
ṣuura صورة *n* (*pl* **ṣuwar**) image, picture; photo

sh - ش

shaʿar شعر *coll n* (*unit n* **shaʿaraaya, shaʿara**, *pl* **shuʿuur**) hair
shaʿar شعر *vi* (**u, shuʿuur**) **be-** to feel sth.
shaʿb شعب *n* (*pl* **shuʿuub**) **1** people; nation **2** Christian congregation
shaʿbi شعبي *adj* popular; folk; **funuun shaʿbiyya** folk art, folklore
shaʿbiyya شعبيّة *n* popularity
shaʿiir شعير *n* barley
shaʿlal شعلل *vt* (**shaʿlala**) to cause to flare up (also of a quarrel, fight)
sha'an شأن *n* (*pl* **shu'uun**) affair, matter, question
shaaʿir شاعر *n* (*pl* **shuʿara**) poet
shaa' شاء *vt* to want, wish, intend; **in shaa' Allah/in shaa Allah/ in sha-llah** God willing, Deo volente; **ma shaa' Allah/ma shaa Allah** **1** whatever God may intend! (*exclamation to ward off the evil eye*) **2** well I never! (*exclamation of wonder or admiration said in response to information given*)
shaabb شاب *n* (*pl* **shabaab**) young man, adolescent
shaabba شابّة *n* young woman, adolescent
shaabik شابك *adj* dense (e.g. hair, forest)
shaaduuf شادوف *n* (*pl* **shawaadiif**) irrigation device of a scoop or bucket on the end of a pole and operated by a rope
shaaf شاف *v* (**u, shoof**) to see; **shaayif nafs-o** he is self-centered; he is vain
shaaff شاف *n* species of tree of which the wood is used for fumigation
shaafiʿ شافع *n* (*pl* **shuffaʿ**) child
shaaghal شاغل (**mushaaghala**) *vt* **1** to tease; to pester **2** to flirt with • *vi* **fi 1** to tease; to pester **2** to flirt with

shaahad شاهد *vt* (**mushaahada**) to watch; to witness
shaahi شاهي *n* tea
shaahid شاهد *n* (*pl* **shuhuud**) witness; **shaahid isbaat** witness for the prosecution **shaahid nafi** witness for the defence; **shaahid zuur** false witness
shaaḥib شاحب *adj* pale (of skin)
shaaḥin شاحن *adj* loading; charging; **ʿarabiiya shaaḥna** lorry, truck • *n* (*pl* **-aat**) battery charger
shaaḥna شاحنة *adj* pregnant
shaakal شاكل *vt* (**shakal**) to quarrel (with), fight
shaakir شاكر *adj* grateful
shaakki شاكّي *adj m* (*f* **shaakka**) **fi** suspicious of
shaakuush شاكوش *n* (*pl* **shawaakiish**) hammer; **addaa-ha shaakuush** he jilted her
shaal شال *n* (*pl* **-aat**) scarf, shawl
shaal شال *vt* (**i, sheel, sheela**) **1** to take; to take away, remove; to pick up; **shaal al-faatḥa** to recite the opening chapter of the Koran (when offering condolences) **2** (**i, sheela, shayalaan**) to carry • *vi* (**i, sheela**) (of rain) to be imminent; **al-maṭara shaalat** it is going to rain
shaama شامة *n* mole (spot on skin)
shaamil شامل *adj* complete, thorough
shaan شان *part* **fi shaan/ʿala shaan** for the sake of; because of; **fi shaan kida/kadi** therefore
shaaqq شاق *adj* hard, tough; **ashghaal shaaqqa** hard labour (punishment)
shaarak شارك (**mushaaraka**) *vi* **1 fi** to participate **2 be-** to contribute; **shaarak be-khamsa jineeh** he contributed five pounds **3 fi** to share (expenses), contribute to; **shaarak fi l-akil** he contributed to the meal • *vt* to join **shaarak-ni fi akl-i** he joined me for a meal
shaariʿ شارع *n* (*pl* **shawaariʿ**) street, road, way; **shaariʿ masdud** a blind alley; **shaariʿ turaab** unpaved road; **shaariʿ ẓalaṭ** paved road
shaarib شارب *adj* **ana lissaʿ shaarib ḥaaja** I have just drunk sth.
shaarid شارد *n* runaway, deserter
shaaseeh شاسيه *n* (*pl* **-aat**) chassis
shaash شاش *coll n* gauze
shaasha شاشة *n* screen
shaat شات *vt* (**u, shoot**) **1** to shoot a goal **2** to kick **3** to kick s.o. out
shaaṭi شاطي *n* (*pl* **shawaaṭi**) riverbank, shore, coast, beach
shaaṭir شاطر *adj* (*pl* **shaaṭriin, shuṭṭaar**) clever, smart, intelligent
shaawar شاور *vt* (**mushaawara**) to ask for advice; to consult
shaawiish شاويش *n* (*pl* **-iyya**) staff sergeant
shaay شاي *n* tea
shaayib شايب *n* (*pl* **shiyaab**) elderly, old person
shaazz شاذ *adj* deviating, perverse
shabʿaan شبعان *adj* **1** satisfied (with food) **2** drunk on local beer **3** (*slang*) well-off
shabaab شباب *n* youth • *n pl* (*sg* **shaabb**) youngsters, young people
shabah شبه *vt* (**a, shabah**) (*only used in imperfect tense*) to resemble; **kaan bishbah ar-raʾiis** he looked like the president

shabaḥ شبح *n* (*pl* **ashbaaḥ**) ghost, spectre

shabaḥ شبح *vi* (**a, shabiḥ**) to walk quickly (by taking big steps)

shabak شبك *coll n* **1** netting; net(s) **2** trelliswork

shabak شبك *vi* (**u, shabik, shabka**) to get stuck (e.g. of paper in photocopier) • *vt* (**u, shabka**) to get engaged to (of men)

shabaka شبكة *unit n* **1** (*pl* **-aat, shibak, shibaak**) net **2** (*pl* **-aat**) grid; grille (of car) **3** (*pl* **-aat**) network (e.g. group of people, computer); **shabakat al-intirnet** the internet

shabatu شبتو *n* **abu shabatu/umm shabatu** spider; **beet abu shabatu/umm shabatu** spider's web

shabaṭ شبط *n* (*pl* **shubaaṭa**) sandal

shabb شب *n* alum

shabba شبّ *vi* (**i, shababaan**) to be brought up (with morals, behaviour)

shabbaʿ شبّع *vt* (**shibbeeʿ, tashbiiʿ**) **1** to satiate, satisfy (of food) **2** to saturate

shabbaal شبّال *n* (*trad*) woman's gesture in a dance of flicking the hair at a person as a form of greeting

shabbah شبّه *vt* (**shibbeeh, tashbiih**) **ʿala** to mistake one person for another person

shabbak شبّك *vt* **1** (**shibbeek**) to net **2** (**tashbiik**) to connect people; to network; **waliid shabbak amiir wa aḥmad** Waleed brought Amir and Ahmed in contact with each other **a fi** to be(come) involved in; **ash-shabbak-ni fii-k shinu** how did I get involved in your problems? **b maʿa** to cause a problem between two people; **waliid shabbak amiir maʿa aḥmad** Waleed caused a problem between Amir and Ahmed

shabbuura شبّورة *n* mist

shabḥa شبحة *n* pace, step

shabiih شبيه *adj* **le-** like; resembling; similar to

shabka شبكة *n* wedding present of jewellery (the main part of the dowry)

shadar شدر *coll n* tree(s); bush(es); plant(s)

shadda شدّة *n* erection

shadda شدّ *vt* (**i, shadd**) **1** to pull; to tighten; **shadda as-sarij** to saddle; **shadda al-lijaam** to rein in; **shadda ʿaḍala** to twist a muscle; **shidd ḥeel-ak** be brave, be strong, do your best **2** to become erect, be erected • *vi* (**i, shadda**); **shadda ʿala iid-** to shake s.o.'s hand

shadiid شديد *adj* (*pl* **shudaad**) strong; severe • *adv* very, extremely

shafa شفى *vt* (**-i, shifa**) to heal, cure (of God)

shafaayif شفايف *n pl* (*sg* **shiffa**) lips

shafaga شفقة *n* pity

shafaq شفق *n* twilight

shafareen شفرين *n pl* labia

shafaṭ شفط *vt* (**u, shafiṭ**) **1** to slurp **2** to suck in **3** to drain away, siphon off

shaff شف *n* (*pl* **shufuuf**) necklace

shaffa شفّ *vi* (**i, shaff**) to cheat in exams (with a crib sheet)

shaffaaf شفّاف *adj* transparent

shaffaafiyya شفّافيّة *n* transparency
shaffaaṭ شفّاط *n* suction pump
shaffaaṭa شفّاطة *n* **1** drinking straw **2** pipette
shafgaan شفقان *adj* **1** impatient **2** (**ʿala**) anxious (about)
shafra شفرة *n* code
shafuug شفوق *adj* (**ʿala**) feeling pity (for)
shagaag شقاق *n* dyspepsia
shagaawa شقاوة *n* **1** naughtiness **2** hardship; misery
shagg شق *n* (*pl* **shuguug**) crack, split
shagga شقّة *n* (*pl* **shugag**) flat, apartment
shagga شقّ *vt* **1** (**i, shagg, shagagaan**) to crack; to cause to burst **2** (**i, shagg, shagga**) to slit, split, cut into two pieces; **shagga al-ḥilla** he passed through the village
shaggag شقّق *vt* (**shiggeeg**) to crack; to slit, split
shagi شقي *adj* **1** naughty **2** miserable
shagiig شقيق *n* (*pl* **ashigga**) full brother
shagiiga شقيقة *n* full sister
shaglab شقلب *vt* (**shigleeb, shaglaba**) **1** to overturn **2** to turn upside down
shagshag شقشق *vi* (**shagshaga**) to chirp, twitter
shagyaan شقيان *adj* miserable
shagyaana شقيانة *n* pair of rubber shoes
shaghab شغب *n* riot, uproar
shaghal شغل *vt* **1** (**a, shaghala**) to occupy (of work, mind); **da shaghalat baal-i** it occupied my mind **2** (**a, shaghil**) to occupy (space); **al-kutub tashghal al-ooḍa** the books fill the room
shaghala شغلة *n* sth. that keeps one busy; **ma ʿind-o shaghala** he has nothing (else) to do; **ʿamal al-mawduuʿ shaghala** he made quite a fuss about it
shaghalaaniyya شغلانيّة *n* **1** work that takes a long time to finish **2** worry; **da ʿamal lee-y shaghalaaniyya** it caused me worry
shaghalaat شغلات *n pl* things, stuff; **shaghalaat-i ween-a** where are my things?; where is my stuff?
shaghghaal شغّال *n* tin coffee pot (for boiling coffee)
shaghghaal شغّال *adj* working; **ma shaghghaal** out of order • *n* (*m*) servant
shaghghaala شغّالة *n* (*f*) servant, maid
shaghghal شغّل *vt* (**shighgheel, tashghiil**) **1** to employ; to make/give s.o. work; **shaghghal nafs-o** he busied himself **2** to start (car), switch on, turn on (engine)
shahad شهد *vi* (**a, shihaada**) (*Isl*) to utter the profession of faith, to bear witness to God and the Prophet Mohammed
shahag شهق *vi* **1** (**a, shahiig**) to inhale **2** (**a, shahig, shahagaan**) to hiccup
shahar شهر *n* (*pl* **shuhuur**) month; (*in construction:* **shahri**) **shahri waaḥid** January; **shahri itneen** February; **shahri talaata** March; **shahri arbaʿa** April; **shahri khamsa** May; **shahri sitta** June; **shahri sabʿa** July; **shahri tamaanya** August; **shahri tisʿa**

September; **shahri ʿashara** October; **shahri ḥidaashar** November; **shahri iṭnaashar** December

shahiid شهيد *n* (*pl* **shuhada**) martyr; killed in a holy war

shahiir شهير *adj* famous

shahiyya شهيّة *n* appetite

shahri شهري *adj* monthly

shahriyyan شهريّاً *adv* monthly

shahwa شهوة *n* lust

shaḥad شحد *vi* (**a, shaḥda, shiḥda**) to beg (for alms)

shaḥam شحم *n* (*pl* **shuḥuum**) grease, fat

shaḥan شحن *vt* (**a, shaḥin**) to load; to charge (with electricity)

shaḥḥaad شحّاد *n* beggar

shaḥḥam شحّم *vt* (**shiḥḥeem, tashḥiim**) (*mech*) to grease

shaḥmaan شحمان *adj* fat, obese

shaḥmuuṭa شحموطة *coll n* a species of small ant(s) that bite

shajaaʿa شجاعة *n* courage, bravery, boldness; **be-shajaaʿa** courageously, bravely, boldly

shajar شجر *coll n* **1** (*pl* **ashjaar**) tree(s) **2** bush(es), plant(s)

shajjaʿ شجّع *vt* (**shijjeeʿ, tashjiiʿ**) to encourage

shaka شكى (**-i, shakwa, shakiyya**) *vi* (**min**) to complain (about) • *vt* **shakaa-ho le-l-gaaḍi** he filed a complaint against him (in court)

shakal شكل *n* (*pl* **shaklaat**) quarrel, row

shakali شكلي *n* wailing (of women)

shakar شكر (**u, shukur**) *vi* **fi/le-** to be grateful to • *vt* (**ʿala**) to thank (for)

shakil شكل *n* (*pl* **ashkaal**) shape, form, outward appearance

shakiyya شكيّة *n* complaint

shakk شك *n* (*pl* **shukuuk**) doubt

shakka شكّ *vi* (**u, shakk**) (**fi**) to doubt (about); to be suspicious of

shakkaal شكّال *adj* quarrelsome; troublemaker

shakkaay شكّاي *n* grumbler

shakkak شكّك *vi* (**shikkeek, tashkiik**) (**fi**) to doubt (about); to be suspicious of

shakkal شكّل *vt* (**shikkeel**) to make up, constitute, form

shakkar شكّر *vt* (**shikkeer**) to praise (gratefully)

shakla شكلة *n* quarrel, row

shakshaaka شكشاكة *n* drizzle, light rain

shakshak شكشك *vi* (**shakshaka**) to behave immorally (of women)

shakshuuka شكشوكة *n* a dish of fried eggs with tomatoes

shakshuuka شكشوكة *n* (*pl* **shakaashiik**) prostitute

shakwa شكوى *n* (*pl* **shakaawi**) complaint

shakhar شخر *vi* (**u, shakhiir**) to snore

shakhbaṭ شخبط *vi* (**shakhbaṭa**) to scribble, scrawl

shakhkhar شخّر *vi* (**shikhkheer**) to snore

shakhkhaṣ شخّص *vt* (**tashkhiiṣ**) to diagnose

shakhṣ شخص *n* (*pl* **ashkhaaṣ**) person

shakhṣi شخصي *adj* personal

shakhṣiyya شخصيّة *n* personality; character

shakhṣiyyan شخصيّاً *adv* personally

shakhshakh شخشخ *vi* (**shakhshakha**) to rustle, swish

shalaʿ شلع *vi* (**a, shaliʿ**) **1** to flash (of light) **2** to be(come) very drunk

shalaᶜ شلعة *coll n* (*unit n* **shalᶜa**) flashes (of light)

shalal شلل *n* paralysis; **shalal kaamil** quadriplegia; **shalal niṣfi** hemiplegia; **shalal al-aṭfaal** polio

shalikh شلخ *n* (*pl* **shuluukh**) tribal scar (on face)

shalla شلّ *vt* (**i, shalal**) to paralyze

shallaal شلال *n* (*pl* **-aat**) cataract; waterfall

shallakh شلّخ *vt* (**shilleekh**) to scarify, cut the skin (tribal marks)

shallat شلّت *vt* (**shilleet**) to kick

shalluufa شلّوفة *n* (*pl* **shalaaliif**) lip

shalluut شلّوت *n* (*pl* **shalaaliit**) a kick

shalwaṭ شلوط *vt* (**shalwaṭa**) (of fire) to singe, scorch

shamᶜa شمعة *unit n* **1** (*pl* **-aat, shumuuᶜ**) candle **2** neon tube **3** water filter candle

shamᶜadaan شمعدان *n* (*pl* **-aat**) **1** candlestick **2** table lamp

shamaar شمار *n* **1** green cumin **shamaar akhḍar** dill **2** (*pl* **-aat**) a juicy piece of news

shamaata شماتة *n* malicious joy, schadenfreude

shamat شمت *vi* (**a, shamaata**) **fi** to take malicious pleasure in (another's misfortune)

shambar شمبر *n* (*pl* **shanaabir**) sleeve (to shut off air/oil, in motor of car)

shamboo شامبو *n* (*pl* **-haat**) shampoo

shamboora شمبورة *n* (*pl* **shanaabiir**) (*slang*) **1** penis **2** clitoris

shamiᶜ شمع *coll n* wax; **shamiᶜ aḥmar** sealing wax

shamis شمس *n f* (*pl* **shumuus**) sun; **ḍarbat shamis** sunstroke; **ᶜabbaad ash-shamis** sunflower(s)

shamish شمش *n f* (*pl* **shumuus**) sun

shamla شملة *n* (*pl* **shimal**) rug of wool or goatshair

shamma شمّ *vt* (**i, shamm**) **1** to smell **2** to sniff (e.g. glue, cocaine) **3** (*slang*) to hate, dislike; **shammeet-o shamm** I hate(d) him/it bitterly

shammaᶜ شمّع *v* (**tashmiiᶜ**) **1** to pack (goods) in plastic, cover (a load) with plastic sheets **2** to seal with wax **3** (*slang*) to (have to) travel by bus standing

shammaaᶜa شمّاعة *n* coat hanger, clothes hanger; **al-buluuza di ḥilwa, bass ash-shammaaᶜa aḥla** this blouse is nice, but the one who's wearing it is nicer

shammaam شمّام *coll n* sweet melon(s)

shammaasi شمّاسي *n* (*pl* **shammaasa**) (*slang*) streetkid, homeless person

shammaashi شمّاشي *n* (*pl* **shammaasha**) (*slang*) streetkid, homeless person

shamsi شمسي *adj* pertaining to the sun **naḍḍaara shamsiyya** sunglasses

shamsiyya شمسيّة *n* (*pl* **-aat, shamaasi**) parasol, umbrella

shamshar شمشر *vi* (**shamshara**) to gossip, spread rumours

shana شنا *n* ugliness

shanab شنب *n* (*pl* **ashnaab, shunubba**) moustache

shanag شنق *vt* (**i, shanig**) to hang (as capital punishment)

shangal شنقل *vt* (**shingeel, shangala**) **1** to overturn **2** to turn (a person) upside down

shankal شنكل *n* (*pl* **shanaakil**) **1** hook (for lifting, pulling) **2** anchor

shankal شنكل *vt* (**shinkeel, shankala**) **1** to hook; to anchor **2** to trip (up) • *vi* **le-** to trip (up)

shanna شنّ *vt* (**i, shann**) (**ʿala**) to launch (e.g. a campaign, an attack) (against)

shanna شنّة *n* **lee-ho shanna wa ranna** he is very famous

shannaaf شنّاف *n* very negative person for whom nothing is ever good enough

shanṭa شنطة *n* (*pl* **shinaṭ**) **1** bag, handbag; suitcase, briefcase **2** boot (of car)

sharʿi شرعي *adj* (*Isl*) legal, legitimate; **gheer sharʿi** illegitimate

shara شرا *coll n* (*unit n* **sharaaya**) husk(s), chaff (of grain)

sharaab شراب *n* (*pl* **-aat, ashriba**) drink; **dawa sharaab** medical syrup

sharaaka شراكة *n* partnership

sharaara شرارة *n* (*pl* **-aat, sharar**) spark

sharad شرد *vi* (**u, sharid, sharadaan**) to run away, desert; to make an escape

sharaf شرف *n* honour

sharaḥ شرح *vt* (**a, shariḥ**) to explain

sharak شرك *n* (*pl* **ashraak**) trap, snare, pitfall

sharakh شرخ *vt* (**a, sharikh, sharkha**) to crack, make a crack in

sharaṭ شرط *vt* (**u, shariṭ**) to tear, tear up, tear apart

sharbuut شربوت *n* slightly fermented homemade drink of dates and spices, drunk at the Feast of the Sacrifice (Eid al Adha)

sharda شردة *n* flight, escape

sharga شرقة *n* swallowing the wrong way, fit of choking

shargaawi شرقاوي *adj* (*no pl*) pertaining to the east of Sudan, eastern Sudanese • *n* easterner (of Sudan)

shargi شرقي (*pl* **-yyiin**) *adj* eastern, pertaining to the east • *n* easterner

sharig شرق *n* east; **be-sh-sharig** eastwards; **naas ash-sharig** easterners (of Sudan)

shariḥ شرح *n* (*pl* **shuruuḥaat**) explanation

sharikh شرخ *n* (*pl* **shuruukh**) crack, fissure

shariiʿa شريعة *n* **ash-shariiʿa** the Islamic law

shariif شريف *adj* (*pl* **ashraaf, shurafa**) noble, honourable

shariiḥa شريحة *n* (*pl* **sharaayiḥ**) **1** slice; layer **2** SIM card (of a mobile telephone)

shariik شريك *n* (*pl* **shuraka**) partner; **shariik fi j-jariima** accomplice (in crime)

shariiṭ شريط *n* (*pl* **sharaayiṭ, ashriṭa**) **1** ribbon **2** tape **3** strip **4** wick (of kerosene lamp or stove)

sharika شركة *n* **1** company; firm **2** (*Chr*) communion

sharis شرس *adj* ferocious, vicious

shariṭ شرط *adj invar* pretty; **shariṭ le-l-ariḍ** very pretty

sharkha شرخة *n* (*pl* **shuruukh**) crack, fissure

sharmuuṭ شرموط *n* dried meat

sharmuuṭa شرموطة *n* (*pl* **sharaamiiṭ, sharammaṭ**) prostitute

sharr شر *n* **1** (*pl* **shuruur**) evil **2** wickedness

sharra شرّ *vt* (**u, sharr**) **1** to spread or hang clothes to dry **2** (*slang*) to let (a friend or a lover) wait for a long time

sharra' شرّع *vt* (**tashrii'**) to legislate

sharraani شرّاني *adj* (*pl* **-yyiin**) **1** vicious, wicked **2** quarrelsome, aggressive • *n* troublemaker

sharrab شرّب *vt* (**shirreeb**) to give to drink

sharrad شرّد *vt* (**tashriid**) to displace, render homeless

sharrak شرّك *vi* (**shirreek, tashriik**) **le-** to snare, set a trap for (animals); **yasharrik wa yaḥaaḥi** (*lit* he sets a trap and chases the birds away) to do sth. the wrong way

sharraṭ شرّط *vt* (**sharṭ**) to stipulate; put a condition

sharraṭ شرّط *vt* (**shirreeṭ, tashriiṭ**) to tear, tear up, tear apart

sharṭ شرط *n* (*pl* **shuruuṭ**) condition (requirement); stipulation, term; **'ala sharṭ, be-sharṭ** on the condition that, provided that

sharṭa شرطة *n* **1** tear, rip **2** diagonal stroke, slash; hyphen

shatal شتل *vt* (**i, shatil**) to take cuttings of (plants)

shatam شتم *vt* (**u, shatiima**) to abuse verbally, swear at, insult

shatiima شتيمة *n* (*pl* **shataayim**) verbal abuse, insult

shatla شتلة *n* (*pl* **-aat, shutuul**) cutting of a plant; seedling, young plant

shattat شتّت *vt* (**shitteet, tashtiit**) to scatter, disperse (individuals) • *vi* (*slang*) (**shitteet**) to leave

shaṭaara شطارة *n* cleverness, smartness, intelligence

shaṭab شطب (**u, shaṭib**) *vt* to cross out, strike out, erase, delete; **da shaṭab raas-i** my mind went blank • *vi* **'ala** to cross out, strike out, erase, delete

shaṭaf شطف *vt* (**u, shaṭif**) **1** to wash s.o.'s face, hands and feet (without soap) **2** to rinse (laundry) **3** to scoop up (water)

shaṭaranj شطرنج *n* chess

shaṭṭa شطّة *n* hot peppers; **shaṭṭa ḥamra/shaṭṭa naashfa** dried red peppers; **shaṭṭa khaḍra** fresh (green) peppers

shaṭṭab شطّب *vi* (**shiṭṭeeb**) to be finished (of goods, food) • *vt* (**tashṭiib**) to finish work on a building (plastering, painting, etc.)

shaṭṭaf شطّف *vt* (**shiṭṭeef, tashṭiif**) **1** to wash s.o.'s face, hands and feet (without soap) **2** to rinse (laundry)

shaṭur شطر *n* (*pl* **shuṭuur**) **1** udder **2** breast (of both men and women)

shawa شوى *vt* (**-i, shawi**) to grill; to roast

shawla شولة *n* comma

shawwaal شوّال *n* (*pl* **-aat**) large sack

shawwah شوّه *vt* (**tashwiih**) to harm (a reputation)

shawwash شوّش (**tashwiish**) *vi* **'ala** to blur, cause to be vague; to cause interference in signal (radio, television) • *vt* to disturb by interfering

shayaaka شياكة *n* chic, elegance

shayyaal شيّال *n* porter

shayyab شيّب *vi* (**shiyyeeb, sheeba**) to get/have white hair

shayyal شيّل *vt* (**shiyyeel, shayalaan**) to make s.o. carry sth.

sheek شيك *n* (*pl* **-aat**) cheque

sheekh شيخ *n* (*pl* **shiyuukh**) **1** sheikh, title of respect and form of address to a man with religious status **2** title of respect and form of address to an elder **3** leader of a Sufi order **4** (*pl* **shiyuukh, mashaayikh**) tribal elder; tribal leader, clan leader; chief; headman of a village

sheekha شيخة *n* (*f*) leader of a **zaar**

sheel شيل *n* load

sheela شيلة *n* **1** wedding gifts, including the dowry and foods, from the bridegroom to the bride and her family **2** visit of the female relatives of the bridegroom to the house of the bride, bringing with them the wedding gifts

sheen شين *adj* **1** ugly; **shakl-o sheen** he/it is ugly; **di bitt sheena shiita bass** this girl is as ugly as Tarzan's ape **2** bad (of manners or behaviour)

sheeṭaan شيطان *n* (*pl* **shayaaṭiin**) **1** devil; **ash-sheeṭaan** the devil, Satan **2** a naughty child; a clever child

sheykhuukha شيخوخة *n* old age (humans)

sheyya شيّة *n* grilled or roast meat

shiʿaar شعار *n* (*pl* **-aat**) slogan, motto; logo

shiʿba شعبة *n* (*pl* **shiʿaab**) forked stick or pole

shiʿeeriyya شعيرية *n* vermicelli

shiʿir شعر *n* poetry

shibak شبك *n pl* (*sg* **shibka**) problems; quarrels; **bitaaʿ shibak** troublemaker

shibiʿ شبع *vi* (**a, shabiʿ**) **1** to be(come) satisfied (with food) **2** to be(come) saturated

shibir شبر *n* (*pl* **ashbaar**) handspan (measurement of length); **az-zool shibir wa koom turaab** (*lit* man is nothing but a handspan and a pile of dust) everyone is equal in the grave

shibka شبكة *n* (*pl* **shibak**) problem; quarrel • *adj invar* quarrelsome, troublesome

shibsi شبسي *n* chips, French fries

shibshib شبشب *n* (*pl* **shabaashib**) pair of slippers; pair of sandals

shidda شدّة *n* (*pl* **shadaayid**) strength, intensity; **be-shidda** vehemently; **shiddat al-ḥaraami** the cleverness of the thief

shidda شدّة *n* pair of plastic sandals

shideera شديرة *n* small tree; bush

shidig شدق *n* (*pl* **shuduug**) cheek

shifa شفى *vi* (**-a, shifaa**) (**min**) to recover (from illness); to get well

shifaa شفا *n* healing, recovery; **be-l-hana wa sh-shifa** (said after a meal) I/we hope you enjoyed it

shiffa شفّة *n* (*pl* **shafaayif**) **1** lip **2** edge

shifig شفق *vi* (**a, shafaga**) **1** **ʿala** to have compassion on, to pity **2** to be impatient

shihaada شهادة *n* (*pl* **-aat, shahaayid**) **1** evidence; testimony; **shihaadat zuur** false testimony, perjury; **gaddam shihaada** to give evidence, testify **2** (*pl* **-aat, shahaayid**) certificate; **shihaadat**

fugdaan police certificate for reported missing items
shihaada شهادة *n* (*Isl*) profession of faith, the Muslim creed
shihheeg شهيق *n* **abu sh-shih-heeg** hiccup
shihid شهد *vi* (**a, shihaada**) to bear witness, testify, give evidence
shiḥim شحم *vi* (**a, shaḥam**) to grow fat
shii شي *n* (*pl* **ashyaa**) object, thing
shiiʿa شيعة *n* **ash-shiiʿa** the Shiah; Shiites
shiiʿi شيعي *adj* (*pl* **shiiʿa**) Shiite
shiik شيك *adj invar* chic, stylish, elegant
shiikolaata شيكولاتة *n* chocolate
shiish شيش *coll n* shutter(s)
shiisha شيشة *n* (*pl* **-aat, shiyash**) hookah, water pipe
shilbaaya شلباية *n* species of catfish
shimaal شمال *n* **1** north **2** left; **be-/ʿala sh-shimaal** to the left
shimaali شمالي (*pl* **-yyiin**) *adj* northern, pertaining to the north (of Sudan) • *n* northerner (of Sudan)
shimbanzi شمبانزي *n* chimpanzee
shin شن *interrog* what
shinu شنو *interrog* what; **le-shinu** what for? why?
shirib شرب *vt* (**a, sharaab**) **1** to drink **2** to absorb **3** to smoke
shirriir شرّير *adj* (*pl* **ashraar**) evil, vicious, wicked
shiryaan شريان *n* (*pl* **sharaayiin**) jugular vein
shita شتا *n* winter
shitwi شتوي *adj* pertaining to the winter
shiwayya شويّة *n* - *see* **shwayya**
shokolaata شوكولاتة *n* chocolate
shoof شوف *n* eyesight, sight; **shoof-o galiil** he is shortsighted
shoofaan شوفان *n* oats
shook شوك *coll n* **1** (*pl* **-aat, ashwaak**) thorn(s), prickle(s); **abu shook** porcupine; hedgehog **2** thistle(s) **3** fish bone(s)
shooka شوكة *unit n* **1** (*pl* **shu-wak**) (table) fork **2** hand of a clock **3** exactly, *as in*: **as-saaʿa tamaanya shooka** it's eight o'clock exactly
shoorba شوربة *n* soup
shooṭ شوط *n* (*pl* **ashwaaṭ**) half (in football match, etc.); **gataʿna shooṭ** we have done quite a good part of the job
shooṭan شوطن *vi* (**shawṭana**) to be(come) insane, crazy, go mad
short شورت *n* (*pl* **-aat**) shorts
shuʿaaʿ شعاع *n* (*pl* **ashiʿʿa**) ray
shuʿabi شعبي *adj* bronchial; **ilti-haab shuʿabi** bronchitis
shuʿba شعبة *n* (*pl* **shuʿab**) **1** sec-tion, department (e.g. of a school) **2** bronchus
shuʿla شعلة *n* torch (of fire)
shuʿuur شعور *n* feeling
shubbaak شبّاك *n* (*pl* **shabaabiik**) **1** window **2** counter (e.g. of a post office); **shubbaak at-ta-zaakir** ticket office, box office
shubha شبهة *n* (*pl* **shubuuhaat**) suspicion • *adj invar* suspicious (person)
shuffaʿ شفّع *n pl* (*sg* **shaafiʿ**) children
shughul شغل *n* (*pl* **ashghaal**) **1** work, labour **2** occupation, job; **shughul ma saabit** odd job **3** business
shuhra شهرة *n* fame

shuḥna شحنة *n* (*pl* **-aat, shuḥan**) load, cargo; **takaaliif ash-shuḥna** freight
shuḥuub شحوب *n* pallor
shujaaʿ شجاع *adj* (*pl* **shijʿaan, shujʿaan**) brave, courageous
shukran شكرا *interj* thanks; **shukran jaziilan** thank you very much
shukur شكر *n* **1** thankfulness, gratefulness, gratitude **2** praise
shuluukh شلوخ *n pl* (*sg* **shalikh**) tribal scars (on face)
shuraaʿ شراع *n* (*pl* **-aat, ashriʿa**) sail
shuraaṭ شراط *n* (*pl* **shuraaṭ-shuraaṭ**) bet
shurraab شرّاب *n* (*pl* **-aat**) sock; stocking
shurṭa شرطة *n* police; **ash-shurṭa al-amniyya** riot police
shurṭi شرطي *n* (*pl* **shurṭa**) policeman
shuruud شرود *n* flight, escape
shuruug شروق *n* **shuruug ash-shamis** sunrise
shuum شوم *n* bad omen
shuuna شونة *n* **1** granary, store (e.g. for grain) **2** grain market
shuura شورة *n* consultation, deliberation **majlis ash-shuura** state council
shuyuuʿi شيوعي (*pl* **-yyiin**) *adj* communist • *n* communist
shuyuuʿiyya شيوعيّة *n* communism
shuzuuz شزوز *n* deviation, perversion
shwayya شويّة *n* a little, a bit; few • *adv* a bit, a little, somewhat; **shwayya shwayya** bit by bit, gradually; slowly
shweesh شويش *n* **be-shweesh** slowly

t – ت

taʿʿab تعّب *vt* (**tiʿʿeeb**) to make suffer; to tire; to trouble
taʿaal تعال *imp m* (*f* **taʿaali**, *pl* **taʿaalu**) come!
taʿaamul تعامل *n* treatment (behaviour towards)
taʿaawun تعاون *n* cooperation
taʿab تعب *n* fatigue; discomfort
taʿaddi تعدّي *n* (*pl* **-yyaat**) offence (verbally or physically); violation
taʿaddud تعدّد *n* variety, diversity, plurality; **taʿaddud az-zoojaat** polygamy
taʿahhud تعهّد *n* (*pl* **-aat**) pledge, vow
taʿaṣṣub تعصّب *n* fanaticism
taʿbaan تعبان *adj* feeling unwell; tired
taʿbiya تعبية *n* mobilization
taʿbiir تعبير *n* (**-aat**) **1** expression **2** composition (in school)
taʿdiil تعديل *n* (*pl* **-aat**) adjustment
taʿiis تعيس *adj* wretched, miserable; unhappy
taʿlamji تعلمجي *n* (*pl* **-yya**) drill sergeant
taʿliim تعليم *n* education
taʿliimaat تعليمات *n pl* instructions, directives
taʿliiq تعليق *n* **1** suspension **2** (*pl* **-aat**) comment
taʿmiish تعميش *n* shortsightedness
taʿqiim تعقيم *n* (*pl* **-aat**) disinfection, sterilization
taʿriifa تعريفة *n* (*pl* **taʿaariif**) tariff
taʿriisha تعريشة *n* (*pl* **taʿaariish**) trellis

ta'shiiga تعشيقة *n* (*pl* **-aat, ta'aashiig**) gear lever
ta'ta' تعتع *vi* (**ta'ta'a**) to speak unclearly
ta'ṭiil تعطيل *n* (*pl* **-aat**) holding up, delay
ta'wiiḍ تعويض *n* (*pl* **-aat**) compensation, replacement
ta'yiin تعيين *n* (*pl* **-aat**) **1** appointment (to a job) **2** ration (military, prison)
ta'ziib تعزيب *n* (*pl* **-aat**) torture
ta'ziiz تعزيز *n* (*pl* **-aat**) promotion, strengthening (e.g. of ideas)
ta'ziya تعزية *n* condolences
ta'biin تابين *n* memorial ceremony for a deceased person 40 days after their death
ta'jiil تأجيل *n* (*pl* **-aat**) postponement, adjournment, suspension
ta'khiir تأخير *n* (*pl* **-aat**) delay
ta'kiid تأكيد *n* (*pl* **-aat**) confirmation; **be-t-ta'kiid** certainly, surely
ta'miin تأمين *n* (*pl* **-aat**) insurance
ta'siir تأسير *n* (*pl* **-aat**) effect, influence
ta'siis تأسيس *n* establishment, founding
ta'shiira تأشيرة *n* visa, travel permit
taab تاب *vi* (**u, tooba**) to repent
taaba' تابع *vt* (**mutaaba'a**) to follow (e.g. a person, a series, a subject)
taabuut تابوت *n* (*pl* **tawaabiit**) coffin
taafih تافه *adj* trivial, insignificant
taah تاه *vi* (**u, tawahaan**) **1** to get lost **2** to lose the thread of a story or discussion
taaj تاج *n* (*pl* **tiijaan**) crown; **taaj ad-diik; abu taaj** cock, rooster
taajar تاجر *vi* (**tijaara**) to trade
taajir تاجر *n* (*pl* **tujjaar**) merchant, trader
taaka تاكى *vt* (**-i, mutaakaa**) to leave ajar
taalit تالت *num* third
taamin تامن *adj* eighth
taamm تام *adj* complete, perfect
taani تاني *num* second • *adj* other, another; **waaḥid taani** another one; **marra taanya** once more, again **ḥaaja taani, ḥaaja taanya** sth. else; anything else; **at-taani** the next (one) • *adv* **1** secondly **2** again **marra taani, taani marra** again
taaniyyan تانيّاً *adv* secondly
taar تار *n* (*pl* **-aat**) blood feud; **akhad/shaal taar** to take revenge (feud); **akhad be-taar akhuu-ho/shaal taar akhuu-ho** he avenged his brother's death
taariikh تاريخ *n* **1** (*pl* **tawaariikh**) date **2** history
taasi' تاسع *adj* ninth
taawag تاوق *vi* (**mutaawaga**) to look round, have a second look (out of curiouity)
taayfooyd تايفويد *n* typhoid
taayih تايه *adj* astray, lost; lost, not knowing what to do
tabaldi تبلدي *coll n* (*unit n* **tabaldiyya**) baobab tree(s)
tabarooga تبروقة *n* prayer mat
tabarru' تبرّع *n* (*pl* **-aat**) donation
tabb تب *adv* completely, absolutely, totally; **hu abkam tabb** he's completely deaf
tabii'a تبيعة *n* afterbirth, placenta; **dafan aj-jana wa khalla t-tabii'a** (*lit* he buried the child

and kept the afterbirth) he is stupid

tabtab تبتب (**tibteeb, tabtaba**) to tap (on shoulder)

tadakhkhul تدخّل *n* (*pl* **-aat**) interference

tadbiir تدبير *n* (*pl* **tadaabiir**) management (of e.g. a household)

tadliik تدليك *n* massage

tadriib تدريب *n* (*pl* **-aat**) training

taḍaamun تضامن *n* solidarity

taḍriiᶜ تضريع *n* (*pl* **-aat**) measurement (of e.g. cloth)

tafaahum تفاهم *n* mutual understanding; **suu' at-tafaahum** mutual misunderstanding

tafaaṣiil تفاصيل *n pl* (*sg* **tafṣiil**) particulars, details

tafaḍḍal تفضّل *imp* please (offering); **tafaḍḍal ag**ᶜ**ud** be seated, have a seat

tafarruᶜ تفرّع *n* (*pl* **-aat**) branching, ramification

taffa تفّ *vi* (**u, taff**) to spit

tafkiir تفكير *n* thinking, consideration

tafliis تفليس *n* bankruptcy

tafliisa تفليسة *n* bankruptcy

tafriqa تفرقة *n* discrimination **tafriqa** ᶜ**unṣuriyya** racial discrimination

tafsiir تفسير *n* (*pl* **-aat**) interpretation (explanation)

tafṣiil تفصيل *n* (*pl* **tafaaṣiil**) **1** cut (of a garment) **2** detail; **be-t-tafṣiil** in detail

taftiiḥa تفتيحة *adj invar* streetwise

taftiish تفتيش *n* (*pl* **-aat**) search, inspection

tafwiiḍ تفويض *n* authorization, delegation mandate

taga تقة *n* threshing floor

tagaaṭuᶜ تقاطع *n* road junction, intersection, crossroads

tagaawi تقاوي *n* seeds (for sowing)

tagaliyya تقليّة *n* **mulaaḥ tagaliyya** stew of minced meat, fried onions, tomatoes and dried okra powder

taggal تقّل *vi* (**tiggeel, tagal**) **1** ᶜ**ala** to behave unpleasantly towards; to be(come) a burden on **2** to be(come) very drunk

tagiilتقيل *adj* **1** (*pl* **tugaal**) heavy **2** strong (of beverages)

tagiila تقيلة *adj f* pregnant

tagliid تقليد *n* imitation (of a product)

tagliidi تقليدي *adj* traditional

tagnad تقند *n* (*pl* **tagaanid**) (*agr*) raised strip separating arable field plots or seedbeds

tagriir تقرير *n* (*pl* **tagaariir**) report

tagsiim تقسيم *n* (*pl* **-aat**) division, distribution

taghayyur تغيّر *n* (*pl* **-aat**) change

taghliif تغليف *n* (*pl* **-aat, taghaaliif**) wrapping; packaging

taghyaan تغيان *adj* tyrannical, despotic

taghyiir تغيير *n* (*pl* **-aat**) change

taghziya تغزية *n* nutrition; **suu' taghziya** malnutrition

tahdiid تهديد *n* (*pl* **-aat**) threat

tahmiish تهميش *n* marginalization

tahriib تهريب *n* (*pl* **-aat**) smuggling

tahwiya تهوية *n* ventilation

tahziib تهزيب *n* good manners, decency

taḥaaluf تحالف *n* alliance

taḥaddi تحدّي *n* (*pl* **-yaat**) challenge

taḥakkum تحكّم *n* control

taḥakkumi تحكّمي *adj* arbitrary

taḥakkumiyya تحكّميّة *n* arbitrariness

taḥassun تحسّن *n* (*pl* **-aat**) improvement
taḥashshur تحشّر *n* (*pl* **-aat**) interference
taḥawwul تحوّل *n* (*pl* **-aat**) change, transformation
taḥḍiir تحضير *n* (*pl* **-aat**) preparation
taḥgiig تحقيق *n* (*pl* **-aat**) investigation **taḥgiig ṣaḥafi** reportage
taḥiyya تحيّة *n* (*pl* **-aat, taḥaaya**) greeting; **taḥiyyaat** greetings, regards
taḥliil تحليل *n* (*pl* **taḥaaliil**) analysis
taḥliya تحلية *n* **1** sweetening **2** dessert, sweet course of a meal
taḥriir تحرير *n* **1** liberation **2** editing
taḥtiim تحطيم *n* destruction
taḥwiil تحويل *n* (*pl* **-aat, taḥaawiil**) transfer; money transfer
taḥziir تحزير *n* (*pl* **-aat**) warning; alarm
tajammuʿ تجمّع *n* gathering
tajannub تجنّب *n* avoidance
tajassud تجسّد *n* (*Chr*) incarnation
tajhiiz تجهيز *n* (*pl* **-aat**) preparation
tajliid تجليد *n* (*pl* **-aat**) binding (of book)
tajmiil تجميل *n* beautification; **adawaat tajmiil** cosmetics
tajniid تجنيد *n* (*pl* **-aat**) recruitment
tajriid تجريد *n* **1** degradation **2** abstraction
tajriida تجريدة *n* military expedition
tajruba تجربة *n* (*pl* **tajaarib**) **1** experience; **akhad tajruba** to gain/have experience **2** experiment, test, trial
takaaliif تكاليف *n pl* (*sg* **takliif**) costs, expenses, charges, overhead
takabbur تكبّر *n* haughtiness, conceit, arrogance
takal تكل (**i, takil, takalaan**) *vt* to put against (for support); **takalta al-ʿaṣaaya ʿala l-ḥeeṭa** I put my stick against the wall • *vi* **ʿala** to lean on/against • *n* **ma ʿalee-ho takal** you cannot depend on him
takfiir تكفير *n* **1** atonement, penance **2** charge of infidelity or blasphemy
taklifa تكلفة *n* basic cost; expense
takniik تكنيك *n* (*pl* **-aat**) technique
taknolojiya تكنولوجيا *n* technology
takriim تكريم *n* honouring; **ḥaflat takriim** party given in s.o.'s honour
takriir تكرير *n* refinement (e.g. of petrol, sugar)
takriis تكريس *n* **1** dedication, devotion **2** (*Chr*) consecration
taksi تاكسي *n* (*pl* **takaasi**) taxi; **mawgif at-taksi** taxi rank
taktak تكتك *vi* (**taktaka**) to tick (e.g. a clock)
takyiif تكييف *n* (*pl* **-aat**) air conditioner
takhaṣṣuṣ تخصّص *n* (*pl* **-aat**) specialization
takhfiiḍ تخفيض *n* (*pl* **-aat**) reduction, discount
takhiin تخين *adj* (*pl* **tukhaan**) **1** thick **2** obese
takhliiṣ تخليص *n* (*pl* **takhaaliiṣ**) clearance from customs
takhmaan تخمان *adj* suffering from indigestion
takhmiin تخمين *n* (*pl* **-aat**) estimate, guess
takhriij تخريج *n* graduation
takhta تختة *n* (*pl* **tikhat**) blackboard
takhṭiiṭ تخطيط *n* (*pl* **-aat**) planning

takhwiif تخويف *n* scaring, intimidation
talaata تلاتة *num* three
talaatiin تلاتين *num* thirty
talafoon تلفون *n* (*pl* **-aat**) telephone; **addii-ni talafoon** give me a call
talaṭṭaashar تلطّاشر *num* thirteen
talawwus تلوّس *n* pollution, contamination
talayyuf تليّف *n* cirrhosis; **talayyuf kabid** cirrhosis of the liver
talfaan تلفان *adj* decayed, rotten, putrid
talij تلج *n* ice; snow; **bikassir at-talij lee-ho** he's flattering him in order to win a favour
talkhiiṣ تلخيص *n* summary
tallaaja تلاجة *n* refrigerator, fridge
tallab تلب *vi* (**tilleeb**) to jump from
tallaj تلّج *vt* (**tilleej**) to freeze
tallat تلّت *vi* (**tilleet**) to do sth. for a third time (e.g. to have a third child, to drink a third cup of coffee)
taltal تلتل *vt* (**taltala**) to frustrate plans by causing unnecessary delays, cause trouble by wasting s.o. else's time
tamaam تمام *n* completeness; **be-t-tamaam wa l-kamaal** in an excellent way • *adj invar* perfect; excellent; splendid; **kullo tamaam** everything is okay; **tamaam at-tamaam** excellent, perfect, splendid • *adv* perfectly, exactly; **zayyi da tamaam** exactly like this one
tamaaman تماماً *adv* exactly
taman تمن *n* (*pl* **atmaan**) price; charge; cost; value; **be-ayyi taman** by all means; **kullo shii be-taman-o** everything has its price
tamaniin تمنين *num* eighty
tamanni تمني *n* (*pl* **-yaat**) wish
tamanṭaashar تمنطاشر *num* eighteen
tamanya تمنية *num* eight
tamarji تمرجي *n* (*m*) (*pl* **-yya**) nursing assistant
tamarjiyya تمرجيّة *n* (*f*) nursing assistant
tamarrud تمرّد *n* rebellion, mutiny
tambalbaay تمبلباي *n* cooking pot
tamkiin تمكين *n* empowerment
tamma تمّ *vt* (**i, tamm**) to finish, complete • *vi* (**i, tamma**) to be finished, completed
tammam تمّم *vi* (**tamaam**) **1** (*mil*) to stand at attention **2** (**'ala**) to check attendance at school
tamman تمّن *vt* (**timmeen**) to determine the value of sth.
tamriin تمرين *n* (*pl* **-aat, tamaariin**) exercise, drill
tamsiil تمسيل *n* **1** acting (as in theatre) **2** representation
tamsiiliyya تمسيليّة *n* theatrical performance; radio play
tamtam تمتم *vi* (**tamtama, timteem**) to stammer, stutter
tamur تمر *coll n* (*unit n* **tamra**) date(s) (fruit)
tamwiil تمويل *n* funding; sponsorship
tamyiiz تمييز *n* discrimination **tamyiiz 'unṣuri** racial discrimination **tamyiiz ḍidd al-mar'a** discrimination against women
tana تنى *vt* (**-i, tani, taniya**) to bend (materials)
tanaaquḍ تناقض *n* (*pl* **-aat**) contradiction
tanaazul تنازل *n* (*pl* **-aat**) condescension, yielding; concession

tanabbu تنبّو *n* (*pl* **-'aat**) prediction, forecast; prophecy
tanawwuʿ تنوّع *n* variety, diversity
tanfiiz تنفيز *n* (*pl* **-aat**) execution of orders, implementation
tangiya تنقية *n* refinement (e.g. of petrol, sugar)
tanjiid تنجيد *n* **1** upholstery **2** stuffing (e.g. of mattresses)
tank تنك *n* (*pl* **-aat, tunukka**) tank (for petrol, gas, water)
tankar تنكر *n* (*pl* **tanaakir**) tanker (lorry, for water)
tanmiya تنمية *n* development, growth
tanna تنّى *vt* (**-i, tanna, tinneey**) to do sth. again, do sth. for a second time
tanqiya تنقية *n* purification
tansiiq تنسيق *n* coordination
tanwiir تنوير *n* (*pl* **-aat**) enlightenment; briefing; **gaddam tanwiir** to brief
tanẓiim تنظيم *n* (*pl* **-aat**) arrangement, organization
taqaaliid تقاليد *n pl* traditions
taqaddum تقدّم *n* progress
taqdiir تقدير *n* (*pl* **-aat**) estimate; assessment
taqi تقي *adj* pious
taqni تقني *adj* technical
taqriib تقريب *n* **be-t-taqriib** approximately, about
taqriiban تقريبا *adv* approximately, about
taqwa تقوة *n* piety
taqyiim تقييم *n* (*pl* **-aat**) evaluation, assessment
tarʿa ترعة *n* belch
tara ترى *part* **ya tara** I wonder
taraakum تراكم *n* accumulation
taraawiiḥ تراويح *n pl* Ramadan prayers, prayed in the mosque after breakfast
tarabeeza تربيزة *n* (*pl* **-aat, taraabiiz**) table
taraddud تردّد *n* hesitation
taraktar تركتر *n* (*pl* **-aat**) tractor
tarallelli ترلّلي *adj* mad, crazy
taras ترس *n* (*pl* **turuus**) embankment, dyke
tarbaal تربال *n* (*pl* **taraabla**) farm labourer
tarbaas ترباس *n* (**taraabiis**) bolt
tarbas تربس *vt* (**tirbees, tarbasa**) to bolt
tarbiya تربية *n* upbringing, education
targaʿ ترقع (**tirgeeʿ, targaʿa**) *vi* to burst open • *vt* to cause to burst open
targiya ترقية *n* promotion (by grade)
tarḥiil ترحيل *n* transportation (persons)
tarjam ترجم *vi* (**tarjama**) to translate
tarjama ترجمة *n* translation **tarjama fawriyya** simultaneous translation
tarkash تركش *vt* (**tirkeesh, tarkasha**) to leave ajar
tarkiib تركيب *n* (*pl* **-aat**) compound, combination
tarkiiba تركيبة *n* (*pl* **-aat, taraakiib**) compound, mixture
tarkiiz تركيز *n* concentration
tarmiim ترميم *n* (*pl* **-aat**) renovation
tarniima ترنيمة *n* (*pl* **taraaniim**) church song
tarra ترّ *vt* (**u, tarr**) to spin (yarn)
tarraʿ ترّع *vi* (**tirreeʿ, tatriiʿ**) to belch
tartiib ترتيب *n* (*pl* **-aat**) arrangement, order; combination

tarṭiiba ترطيبة *adj invar* (*slang*) relaxed; well-off
taryaan تريان *adj* well-off
tarzi ترزي *n* (*pl* **-yya**) tailor
tasaali تسالي *n pl* roasted water-melon or pumpkin seeds
tasaamuḥ تسامح *n* tolerance
tasammum تسمّم *n* poisoning
tasarruᶜ تسرّع *n* haste
tasawwus تسوّس *n* dry rot; **tasaw-wus al-asnaan** caries (dents)
tasjiil تسجيل *n* (*pl* **-aat**) registra-tion, recording
tasliim تسليم *n* (*pl* **-aat**) delivery
tasliya تسلية *n* amusement, entertainment
tasniin تسنين *n* determination of one's age on the basis of the teeth
tasqiif تسقيف *n* education, *as in* **at-tasqiif al-madani** civic education
tasriib تسريب *n* (*pl* **-aat**) leak(age)
tasriiḥ تسريح *n* release (e.g. from prison); **tasriiḥ ṣaḥafi** press release
tasriiḥa تسريحة *n* hairdo, hairstyle
taswiig تسويق *n* marketing
taswiya تسوية *n* settlement (e.g. of a business matter, a loan, accounts)
tasyiil تسييل *n* (*pl* **-aat**) clearing; liquidation (financial)
taṣaadum تصادم *n* **1** bumper (e.g. of a car) **2** (*pl* **-aat**) collision, crash
taṣarruf تصرّف *n* (*pl* **-aat**) behaviour
taṣawwur تصوّر *n* (*pl* **-aat**) con-cept, plan
taṣbiira تصبيرة *n* any snack or small dish to take the edge off hunger before a meal
taṣdiig تصديق *n* (*pl* **-aat**) approv-al; permit; licence
taṣdiir تصدير *n* (*pl* **-aat**) export; **izin/taṣriiḥ taṣdiir** export licence
taṣfiya تصفية *n* **1** sifting; filtering; refinement (e.g. of petrol, sugar) **2** clearing; liquidation (financial) **3** murder, revenge killing
taṣliiḥ تصليح *n* (*pl* **-aat**) repair
taṣmiim تصميم *n* (*pl* **-aat**) design layout
taṣniif تصنيف *n* (*pl* **-aat**) classifi-cation, categorisation
taṣriif تصريف *n* (*pl* **-aat**) drainage
taṣriifa تصريفة *n* drainage
taṣriiḥ تصريح *n* (*pl* **taṣaariiḥ**) permit, licence; **taṣriiḥ istiiraad** import licence; **taṣriiḥ iqaama** stay/residence permit
taṣwiir تصوير *n* photography; **aalat taṣwiir** photocopier
tashaabuh تشابه *n* (*pl* **-aat**) resemblance
tashaad تشاد *prop n* Chad
tashaadi تشادي (*pl* **-yyiin**) *adj* Chadian • *n* a Chadian
tashannuj تشنّج *n* (*pl* **-aat**) convul-sion seizure
tashbiik تشبيك *n* (*pl* **-aat**) networking
tashiil تسهيل *n* (*pl* **-aat**) facilita-tion facility
tashkhiiṣ تشخيص *n* diagnosis
tashriiḥ تشريح *n* **1** dissection **2** study of anatomy
tashsha تشّ *vt* (**i, tashsh, ta-shashaan**) to singe
tashshaashi تشّاشي *n* (**tash-shaasha**) hawker, pedlar
tashwiish تشويش *n* disturbance (by sound), interference (in radio signal)
tatanus تتانوس *n* tetanus

taṭᶜiim تطعيم *n* vaccination
taṭarruf تطرّف *n* extremism
taṭawwuᶜ تطوّع *n* volunteering
taṭawwur تطوّر *n* (*pl* **-aat**) development; **taṭawwuraat siyaasiyya** political developments
taṭbiig تطبيق *n* (*pl* **-aat**) implementation
taṭhiir تطهير *n* cleansing, purification disinfection; **taṭhiir ᶜirgi** ethnic cleansing
taṭriiz تطريز *n* embroidery
taṭwiir تطوير *n* development
tawᶜiya توعية *n* awareness raising
taw'am توءم *n* (*pl* **teemaan**) a twin
tawaaḍuᶜ تواضع *n* humility
tawaaṣul تواصل *n* (*pl* **-aat**) communication
tawaazun توازن *n* (*pl* **-aat**) equilibrium, balance
tawagguᶜ توقّع *n* (*pl* **-aat**) expectation
tawaleet توليت *n* **1** toiletries (comb, cream, perfume, etc. for women) **2** toilet table, dressing table
tawaqquᶜ توقّع *n* (*pl* **-aat**) expectation
tawattur توتّر *n* (*pl* **-aat**) tension
tawḍiiḥ توضيح *n* (*pl* **-aat**) clarification, explanation
tawfiiq توفيق *n* **tawfiiq, in shaa Allah** success!
tawfiir توفير *n* saving (money)
tawḥiid توحيد *n* **at-tawḥiid** (*Isl*) the doctrine of the oneness of God
tawqiiᶜ توقيع *n* (*pl* **-aat**) signature
tawriid توريد *n* (*pl* **-aat**) supply
tawṣiila توصيلة *n* extension lead
tawṣiya توصية *n* recommendation
tawwar توّر *vt* (**tiwweer**) to wake s.o. up, rouse • *vi* (**tatwiir**) to develop teeth
tawziiᶜ توزيع *n* (*pl* **-aat**) distribution
tayyaar تيّار *n* (*pl* **-aat**) current, stream; **ᶜaks/ḍidd at-tayyaar** upstream, (*also fig*) against the stream
tazkira تزكرة *n* (*pl* **tazaakir**) ticket
tazkiya تزكية *n* recommendation
tazwiir تزوير *n* forgery, falsification
teebaar تيبار *n* (*pl* **-aat**) large earthenware vessel (for water)
teemaan تيمان *n pl* (*sg* **toom**) twins
teerab تيرب *vt* (**teeraab**) to sow
tees تيس *n* (*pl* **tiyuus**) he-goat
teetal تيتل *n* (*pl* **tayaatil**) hartebeest
teras ترس *n* (*pl* **turuus**) (*agr*) terrace
termomitir ترمومتر *n* (*pl* **-aat**) thermometer
testa تستة *n* roadworthiness test (of a car)
tiᶜdaad تعداد *n* census
tiᶜib تعب *vi* (**a, taᶜab**) to be(come) tired; to suffer; **ma tatᶜab nafsak** don't bother
tibiᶜ تبع *vt* (**a, tabaᶜaan**) to follow, go along behind (e.g. a car)
tibin تبن *n* hay (used for roofing)
tibish تبش *coll n* a round variety of cucumber(s); **ᶜaḍalaat tibish** strong biceps
tifil تفل *n* dregs (e.g. of coffee, tea)
tigil تقل *n* (*pl* **tuguul**) baboon
tiḥishshir تحشّر *n* curiosity
tiḥit تحت *prep* under • *adv* down
tiḥtaani تحتاني *adj* lower
tiibii تيبي *n* tuberculosis
tiik تيك *n* **khashab tiik** teak
tiil تيل *n* **1** hemp **2** linen
tiim تيم *n* (*pl* **atyaam**) team
tiin تين *coll n* fig(s)
tiishirt تيشرت *n* (*pl* **-aat**) t-shirt

tijaara تجارة *n* trade, commerce
tijaari تجاري *adj* commercial
tikraar تكرار *n* repetition **be-t-tikraar** repeatedly
tilfaan تلفان *adj* rotten (person)
tilif تلف *vi* (**a, talaf**) to be(come) spoiled; to rot, decay
tilifizyoon تلفزيون *n* (*pl* **-aat**) television
tilifoon تلفون *n* (*pl* **-aat**) telephone; **addii-ni tilifoon** give me a call
tilighraaf تلغراف *n* (*pl* **-aat**) telegraph; telegram
tilit تلت *n* one third
tilmiiz تلميز *n* (*m*) (*pl* **talaamiiz**) pupil, cadet
tilmiiza تلميزة *n* (*f*) pupil
tiltaawi تلتاوي *adj* third
timsaal تمسال *n* (*pl* **tamaasiil**) statue
tinis تنس *n* tennis; **tinis aṭ-tawla** table tennis
tiris ترس *n* (*pl* **turuus**) cogwheel; gearwheel; **ʿilbat at-turuus** gearbox
tirmus تيرمس *n* (*pl* **taraamis**) thermos, vacuum flask
tiryaaq ترياق *n* (*pl* **-aat**) antidote
tisʿa تسعة *num* nine
tisʿaṭaashar تسعطاشر *num* nineteen
tisʿiin تسعين *num* ninety
tishaasha تشاشة *n* peddling (wares)
titik تتك *n* (*pl* **-aat**) trigger
tjakkas تجكّس *vt* (**jikkees, tijikkis**) (*slang*) to have a relationship, to see s.o.
tjatt تجت *adv* (with an adjective) totally, completely
tjiks تجكس *n/n pl* (*slang*) **1** girl(s) **2** boyfriend(s); girlfriend(s)
tjiksooya تجكسوية *n* (*slang*) girlfriend
toob توب *n* (*pl* **tiyaab**) traditional women's outer garment
tooba توبة *n* repentance
toom توم *n* (*pl* **teemaan**) a twin
toor تور *n* (*pl* **teeraan**) bull, ox; **toor makhṣi** bullock; **ḍahr at-toor** a roof sloping on both sides
torta تورتة *n* cake, tart
triiko تريكو *n* knitting; **bitashtaghil triiko** she is knitting
trotwaar تروتوار *n* (*pl* **-aat**) **1** platform **2** small dyke, embankment
tufaaf تفاف *n* spittle
tuffaaḥ تفّاح *coll n* apple(s)
tugul تقل *n* (*fig*) weight
tuhma تهمة *n* (*pl* **tuham**) accusation
tukul تكل *n* (*pl* **takkaal**) kitchen (made of mud or grass)
tukhma تخمة *n* indigestion
tullub تلّب *n* **naas tullub** thieves
tultumiyya تلتميّة *num* three hundred
tumbaak تمباك *n* tobacco; snuff
tumnumiyya تمنميّة *num* eight hundred
tumsaaḥ تمساح *n* (*pl* **tamaasiiḥ**) crocodile
turʿa ترعة *n* (*pl* **turaʿ**) irrigation channel
turaab تراب *n* **1** earth, soil; **shaariʿ turaab** unpaved road **2** dust
turaabi ترابي *adj* **1** pertaining to earth, soil or dust **2** sand-coloured, dust-coloured
turabi تربي *n* (*pl* **-yya**) gravedigger; cemetery attendant
turba تربة *n* (*pl* **turab**) **1** grave **2** earth, soil; land

turki تركي (*pl* **atraak**) *adj* Turkish • *n* a Turk
turkiya تركيا *prop n* Turkey
turmus ترمس *coll n* **1** Egyptian lupin **2** seeds of Egyptian lupin, eaten as a snack
turmusa ترمسة *n* (*pl* **taraamis**) thermos, vacuum flask
turumbeeta ترمبيتة *n* trumpet
tusʿumiyya تسعميّة *num* nine hundred
tuum توم *coll n* garlic
tuuna تونة *n* tuna fish
tuutya توتيا *n* galvanised iron (roofing, fencing)

ṭ – ط

ṭaʿʿam طعم *vt* **1** (**ṭiʿʿeem**) to season, add flavourings (spices), to sweeten (with sugar) **2** (**taṭʿiim**) to vaccinate
ṭaʿam طعم *n* flavour, taste
ṭaʿan طعن *vt* (**a, ṭaʿin**) **1** to stab; **ṭaʿan fi l-ḥukum** to appeal against a sentence **2** to inject
ṭaʿmiyya طعميّة *n* small cakes of ground chickpeas with flavourings
ṭaaʿ طاع *vt* (**i, ṭaaʿa**) to obey
ṭaaʿa طاعة *n* obedience; **beet aṭ-ṭaaʿa** (*Isl*) a husband's house to which a deserting wife is legally obliged to return
ṭaaʿim طاعم *adj* **1** tasty **2** nice (person)
ṭaaʿuun طاعون *n* plague, pestilence; **ṭaaʿuun bagari** cattle plague, rinderpest
ṭaab طاب *vi* (**i, ṭayabaan**) (**min**) to get well, recover
ṭaabʿa طابعة *n* **1** (*pl* **ṭawaabiʿ**) postage stamp **2** (*pl* **ṭaabiʿaat**) printing machine, printer
ṭaabig طابق *n* (*pl* **ṭawaabig**) storey, floor (of a building); **taman-o ṭaabig** its price is double
ṭaabuuna طابونة *n* (*pl* **ṭawaabiin**) bread bakery
ṭaabuur طابور *n* (*pl* **ṭawaabiir**) **1** queue, line, roll call (in school or army); **ṭaabuur ʿarabaat** convoy **2** (military) parade **3 aṭ-ṭaabuur al-khaamis** the fifth column
ṭaaga طاقة *n* vent, small window
ṭaagiyya طاقيّة *n* (*pl* **-aat, ṭawaagi**) skullcap, hat
ṭaahir طاهر *adj* ritually clean
ṭaaḥ طاح *vi* (**i, ṭeeḥ, ṭeeḥa**) to slip, slide, lose one's footing
ṭaaḥuuna طاحونة *n* (*pl* **ṭawaaḥiin**) mill
ṭaal طال *vi* (**u, ṭuul**) to become tall, long
ṭaalab طالب *vt* (**muṭaalaba**) request
ṭaaliʿ طالع *n* star of destiny; **ʿind-o ḥusn aṭ-ṭaaliʿ** he is lucky, fortunate; **ʿind-o suuʾ aṭ-ṭaaliʿ** he is unfortunate, ill-fated
ṭaalib طالب *n* (*m*) (*pl* **ṭalaba, ṭullaab**) student
ṭaaliba طالبة *n* (*f*) student
ṭaalig طالق *adj* (*Isl*) (*formula used by a man to divorce his wife*) **inti ṭaalig/ṭaalga** you are divorced!
ṭaaqa طاقة *n* energy
ṭaar طار *n* (*pl* **-aat**) large tambourine without jingles

ṭaar طار *vi* (**i, ṭayaraan**) to fly
ṭaara طارة *n* any round frame
ṭaarad طارد *vt* (**muṭaarada**) to run after, chase, pursue, stalk; to persecute
ṭaari طاري *n* (*pl* **ṭawaari**) emergency; **ḥaalat ṭawaari** state of emergency
ṭaari طاري *adj* emergent
ṭaasa طاسة *n* bowl
ṭaash طاش *vi* (**i, ṭeesha**) to miss its target (e.g. of spear, bullet)
ṭaashim طاشم *adj* (*pl* **ṭaashmiin**) drunk
ṭaawaʿ طاوع *vt* (**muṭaawa**ʿ**a**) to obey
ṭaayiʿ طايع *adj* **1** pliable **2** obedient
ṭaayish طايش *adj* reckless
ṭaaza طازة *adj invar* fresh
ṭaazij طازج *adj* fresh
ṭabʿ *n* **be-ṭ-ṭab**ʿ بالطبع of course, naturally
ṭabʿ**an** طبعاً *adv* of course, naturally
ṭabaʿ طبع *vt* (**a, ṭibaa**ʿ**a**) **1** to print **2** to type
ṭabaashiir طباشير *n* blackboard chalk
ṭabaashiira طباشيرة *n* piece or stick of blackboard chalk
ṭabag طبق *n* (*pl* **ṭubaaga**) traditional food cover
ṭabag طبق (**u, ṭabig, ṭabagaan**) *vt* **1** to double; to repeat once **2** to fold (up); to double up
ṭabakh طبخ *vt* (**u, ṭabiikh**) to cook (food)
ṭabal طبل *vt* (**u, ṭabil**) to lock
ṭabanja طبنجة *n* pistol; revolver
ṭabaqa طبقة *n* **1** layer; storey **2** social class; **aṭ-tabaqa al-wusṭa** the middle class; **aṭ-tabaqa al-**ʿ**aamila** the working class
ṭabaz طبز *vt* (**u, ṭabiz, ṭabza**) to do sth. the wrong way; **ṭabaz al-**ʿ**een** to hurt one's eye by accidentally putting one's finger into it
ṭabbaakh طبّاخ *n* cook
ṭabbaal طبّال *n* drummer
ṭabbag طبّق *vt* (**taṭbiig**) to apply, implement
ṭabbag طبّق *vt* (**ṭibbeeg, taṭbiig**) to fold (up); to double up • *vi* (**ṭibbeeg**) to marry for a second time
ṭabbal طبّل (**ṭibbeel**) *vi* **1** to drum **2 le-** to flatter in order to win a favour
ṭabiʿ طبع *n* character, nature; **ṭab**ʿ**-o sheen** he's bad-mannered; **ṭab**ʿ**-o ḥaami** he's touchy
ṭabiiʿ**a** طبيعة *n* **1** nature (natural world) **2** character; **aṭ-ṭabii**ʿ**a jabal** (*lit* nature is a mountain) one's character cannot be changed
ṭabiiʿ**i** طبيعي *adj* natural
ṭabiib طبيب *n* (*pl* **aṭibba**) medical doctor, physician
ṭabiikh طبيخ *n* (*pl* **ṭabaayikh**) cooked food; cuisine
ṭabla طبلة *n* **1** (*pl* **ṭubuul**) a clay or wooden drum **2** eardrum
ṭabla طبلة *n* (*pl* **ṭibal**) padlock
ṭabliyya طبليّة *n* (*pl* **ṭabaali**) tray hung around the neck, used for displaying small items for sale
ṭabṭab طبطب *vi* (**ṭabṭaba, ṭibṭeeb**) ʿ**ala** to pat
ṭafa طفى *vt* (**-i, ṭafi, ṭafayaan**) **1** to put out (e.g. a fire, a cigarette), extinguish **2** to switch off, turn off (light, gas)
ṭafag طفق *vt* (**i, ṭafig, ṭafga**) to dent

ṭafaḥ طفح *vi* (**a, tafiḥ**) to overflow (drain, sewage)
ṭafash طفش *vi* (**u, ṭafsha, ṭafashaan**) (of head of the family) to flee from one's responsibilities; to run off, disappear
ṭaffaaya طفّاية *n* **1** fire extinguisher **2** ashtray
ṭaffag طفّق *vt* (**ṭiffeeg**) to dent
ṭaffaḥ طفّح *vi* (**ṭiffeeḥ**) to float
ṭaffar طفّر *vi* (**ṭiffeer**) to leap; to jump over (e.g. a hole), jump down
ṭaffash طفّش *vt* (**ṭiffeesh, ṭafsha**) to cause s.o. to run off, get rid of (a person)
ṭafga طفقة *n* dent
ṭafra طفرة *n* leap
ṭagash طقش *vt* (**u, ṭagish**) to bump, collide, crash into
ṭagga طقّ *vt* (**u, ṭagg**) **1** to hit, beat, strike, hammer, knock (on) **2** to tap a gum tree **3** to sew (with a sewing machine)
ṭagim طقم *n* (*pl* **ṭuguum**) set (of jewels, clothes, etc.)
ṭahhar طهّر *vt* **1** (**ṭihheer, taṭhiir**) to purify, cleanse; to disinfect **2** (**ṭahaara, ṭahuur**) to circumcise
ṭahuur طهور *n* (*pl* **-aat**) circumcision
ṭaḥan طحن *vt* (**a, ṭaḥin**) to grind (mill)
ṭaḥiina طحينة *n* paste of crushed sesame seeds
ṭaḥniyya طحنيّة *n* halva, hard paste of crushed sesame seeds, with caramel
ṭalaᶜ طلع *vi* (**a, ṭuluuᶜ**) **1** to come out, get out, go out; **ṭalaᶜ be-gadd al-guffa** (*lit* he came out through a hole in the basket) he failed, he's a loser **2** to emerge, appear **3** to ascend, go up **4 fi** to climb into
ṭalaag طلاق *n* divorce; (*Isl*) **ᶜalee-y aṭ-ṭalaag** (**be-talaata**) (*swearing*) I'll divorce my wife (with the threefold formula, i.e. irrevocable)
ṭalab طلب *vt* (**u, ṭalab**) to ask for, request, claim, demand, order (e.g. in a restaurant); **hu ṭaalib-ni** I owe him
ṭalab طلب *n* (*pl* **-aat**) **1** request, demand, claim, order (e.g. in a restaurant) **2** application
ṭalabiyya طلبيّة *n* request (list of things), order (e.g. in a restaurant)
ṭalga طلقة *n* (*pl* **-aat, ṭilag**) **1** shot **2** bullet
ṭalgaana طلقانة *adj f* **inti ṭalgaana** (*formula used by a man to divorce his wife*) you are divorced!
ṭalig طلق *n* labour pains
ṭaliḥ طلح *n* species of acacia, of which the wood is used for fumigation
ṭalis طلس *adj* enamel
ṭallaᶜ طلّع *vt* (**tilleeᶜ**) to bring out, bring forward, take out; **ṭallaᶜ riiḥa** to smell; **ṭallaᶜ zeet-i** he gave me a very hard time
ṭallag طلّق *vt* **1** (**ṭalaag**) to divorce **2** (**ṭilleeg, taṭliig**) **ṭallag al-rijleen** to stretch one's legs, go for a walk
ṭamaᶜ طمع *n* greed
ṭamaaṭim طماطم *n pl* (*sg* **ṭamaṭmaaya**) tomatoes
ṭamas طمس *vt* (**u, ṭamis**) to efface, blot out
ṭamaṭmaaya طمطماية *n* (*pl* **ṭamaaṭim**) tomato
ṭambuur طمبور *n* (*pl* **ṭanaabiir**) (*mus*) instrument with one to five strings, played with a bow
ṭami طمي *n* **1** silt **2** river clay

ṭamma طمّ *vi* (**u, ṭumaam**); **baṭun-...ṭammat/ṭaamma (min)** **1** to feel sick (from), to be(come) nauseated (by); **baṭn-o ṭaamma** he is feeling sick; **as-sama baṭun-a ṭaamma** it is going to rain **2** to be(come) fed up (with); **baṭn-i ṭammat/ṭaamma min ash-shughul da** I am fed up with this work

ṭammaaʿ طمّاع *adj* greedy

ṭammam طمّم *vt* (**ṭimmeem**) (**min**) to make s.o. feel sick, to cause to be(come) nauseated (by)

ṭamman طمّن *vt* (**ṭimmeen**) to reassure, set s.o.'s mind at rest

ṭanaash طناش *n* (*slang*) indifference; **iddeet-o ṭanaash** I gave him the cold shoulder, I gave him the go-by

ṭaniin طنين *n* **1** indistinct sound heard at a distance **2** buzzing of insects

ṭann طن *n* (*pl* **aṭnaan**) ton (weight)

ṭannash طنّش *vt* (**ṭanaash, ṭinneesh**) (*slang*) to be indifferent towards, ignore

ṭanṭan طنطن *vi* (**ṭanṭana**) to mutter (in anger)

ṭaqs طقس *n* (*pl* **ṭuquus**) rite

ṭaraawa طراوة *n* coolness, cool weather

ṭarab طرب *n* singing

ṭarabeeza طربيزة *n* (*pl* **-aat, ṭaraabiiz**) table

ṭarad طرد *vt* (**u, ṭarid**) to drive away, expel, banish; to dismiss, sack

ṭaraf طرف *n* (*pl* **aṭraaf**) **1** edge **2** a party (e.g. in dispute, contract); **min ṭaraf** without knowing anything about the subject; **sallam ʿala n-naas min ṭaraf** he greeted the people without knowing them

ṭaraga طرقة *n* two pieces of **kisra** together

ṭaraḥ طرح *vi* (**a, ṭaraḥaan**) to miscarry (of animals)

ṭaraḥ طرح *vt* (**a, ṭariḥ**) **1** (*arith*) to subtract **2** to pose (e.g. a question)

ṭaraḥaan طرحان *n* miscarriage (of animals)

ṭarash طرش *vi/vt* (**u, ṭuraash**) to vomit, throw up

ṭarash طرش *n* deafness

ṭargaʿ طرقع (**ṭargaʿa, ṭirgeeʿ**) *vi* to snap or click one's fingers • *vt* **ṭargaʿ al-aṣaabʿeen** to crack one's knuckles

ṭarḥa طرحة *n* (*pl* **-aat, ṭiraḥ**) scarf, headscarf • *adj invar* said about a minibus, taxi or rickshaw that is used for public transport; **riksha ṭarḥa** public rickshaw, having a fixed route

ṭari طري *adj* **1** supple, flexible (material) **2** fresh (vegetables, bread) **3** tender (meat)

ṭarid طرد *n* (*pl* **ṭuruud**) parcel, package

ṭariid طريد *n* (*m*) (*pl* **ṭarada**) the boy following (in line of births); **ḥaydar ṭariid aḥmad** Haydar was born after Ahmed

ṭariida طريدة *n* (*f*) (*pl* **-aat, ṭarada**) the girl following (in line of births); **iḥsaan ṭariidat ʿaadil** Ihsan was born after Adil

ṭariig طريق *n* (*pl* **ṭurug**) way, road, route; **fi ṭ-ṭariig** under way, on one's way; **ʿan ṭariig** through

ṭariiga طريقة *n* (*pl* **ṭurug**) **1** way; method; approach, style, behaviour; **ma fii ṭariiga** (there's) no way; **be-ayyi ṭariiga** by any means **2** religious brotherhood, Sufi order

ṭariin طرين *adj* sharp

ṭarram طرّم *vi* (**ṭirreem**); **washsh-o ṭarram** he pouted

ṭarran طرّن *vt* (**ṭirreen**) **1** to sharpen (e.g. a knife) **2** to trim (a piece of wood)

ṭarraz طرّز *vt* (**ṭirreez, taṭriiz**) to embroider

ṭarruuma طرّومة *n* **abu ṭarruuma** said about a child that is always pouting

ṭarshag طرشق (**ṭirsheeg, ṭarshaga**) *vi* to burst open • *vt* to cause to burst open

ṭarṭuur طرطور *n* (**ṭaraaṭiir**) (*trad*) conical cap, such as is worn by: **1** followers of the Mahdi **2** a clown

ṭashaash طشاش *adj* having poor eyesight; **shoof-u ṭashaash** he has poor eyesight, he is half blind • *adv* **bishuuf ṭashaash ṭashaash** he has poor eyesight, he is half blind

ṭasham طشم *vi* (**u, ṭashma**) to be(come) drunk

ṭashashaan طشّشان *n* poor eyesight • *adj* having poor eyesight, half blind; **shoof-u ṭashashaan** he has poor eyesight, he is half blind

ṭashit طشت *n* (*pl* **ṭushaata**) washbowl, wash tub

ṭashsha طشّ *vi* (**i, ṭashsh, ṭashsha**) **1** to lose one's way, get lost **2** to get lost (of radio, television signal) **3 min** to lose, get lost; **walad-i ṭashsha min-ni fi s-suuq** my son got lost in the market

ṭawʿi طوعي *adj* voluntary

ṭawa طوى *vt* (**-i, ṭawi**) to coil, roll up

ṭawaari طواري *n pl* (*sg* **ṭaari**) state of emergency

ṭawiil طويل *adj* (*pl* **ṭuwaal**) long; tall

ṭawwa طوّة *n* frying pan, casserole, saucepan **beeḍ be-ṭ-ṭawwa** fried eggs

ṭawwaʿ طوّع *vi* (**ṭiwweeʿ, taṭwiiʿ**) to retch

ṭawwaali طوّالى *adv* **1** straight ahead, direct **2** immediately, at once **3** always; continuously, all the time

ṭawwaḥ طوّح *vi* (**ṭiwweeḥ, ṭooḥa**) to sway to and fro, to reel; to drift about; **ṭawwaḥ be-l-ʿarabiyya** his car came off the road

ṭawwal طوّل (**ṭiwweel, taṭwiil**) *vt* to lengthen; **Allah yiṭawwil ʿumr-ak** may God give you a long life • *vi* **1** to take a long time; **inta ṭawwalta min-na-na** we didn't see you for a long time **2** to be old

ṭawwar طوّر *vt* (**taṭwiir**) to develop sth.

ṭayaraan طيران *n* aviation airline(s); **aṭ-ṭayaraan al-ḥarbi** military aviation

ṭayyaani طيّاني *n* (*pl* **-yya**) maker or layer of mud bricks

ṭayyaar طيّار *n* pilot

ṭayyaara طيّارة *n* airplane, aircraft; **ṭayyaara naffaasa** jet aircraft; **ṭayyaarat warag** kite (toy)

ṭayyiʿ طيّع *adj* supple, flexible (material)

ṭayyib طيّب *adj* **1** kind, goodhearted **2** well, good; **kullo sana wa intu ṭaybiin** (*greeting on annually celebrated occasions*) may

you be well every year; (*reply*) **wa inta ṭayyib** may you also be well • *interj* okay, fine, all right
ṭeer طير *coll n* (*pl* **ṭiyuur**) bird(s)
ṭeera طيرة *unit n* bird; **ṭeerat aj-janna** firefinch; **ṭeerat al-bagar** cattle egret
ṭeesh طيش *n* recklessness
ṭibaaʿa طباعة *n* **1** printing **2** typing; **makanat ṭibaaʿa** printing machine, printer
ṭibb طب *n* medical science; study of medicine
ṭibbi طبّي *adj* medical
ṭifil طفل *n* (*pl* **aṭfaal**) child
ṭiib طيب *n* complete set of perfumes
ṭiiba طيبة *n* kindness, goodness
ṭiin طين *n* (*pl* **aṭyaan**) **1** clay **2** mud **3** soil, agricultural land
ṭiish طيش *adj* the last one in a race, game or class; **aṭ-ṭiish** the dunce
ṭiiẓ طيظ *n* (*pl* **aṭyaaẓ**) (*slang*) anus
ṭilyaani طلياني (*pl* **ṭilyaan, ṭalaayna**) *adj* Italian • *n* an Italian
ṭimiʿ طمع *vi* (**a, ṭamaʿ**) **fi** to covet; to be greedy for
ṭira طرى *vi* (**-a, ṭariya**) to become soft or pliant • *vt* (**-a, ṭariya, ṭarayaan**) to recollect
ṭirish طرش *vi* (**a, ṭarash**) to become deaf
ṭoof طوف *n* (*pl* **ṭoofeen, aṭwaaf**) **1** patrol **2** raft
ṭoog طوق *n* (*pl* **aṭwaag**) neckband
ṭooṭaḥaaniyya طوطحانيّة *n* swing
ṭuʿum طعم *n* bait
ṭufayli طفيلي *n* (*pl* **-yyaat**) parasite
ṭulba طلبة *n* (*pl* **ṭulab**) day labourer (construction work)
ṭuluuʿ طلوع *n* **ṭuluuʿ ash-shamis** sunrise
ṭumaam طمام *n* nausea
ṭumuuḥ طموح *n* (*pl* **-aat**) ambition
ṭundub طندب *n* capers
ṭuquus طقوس *n pl* (*sg* **ṭaqs**) rites
ṭuraash طراش *n* vomit
ṭurumba طرمبة *n* **1** water pump **2** petrol station, gas station **ṭurumbat al-banziin** petrol station, gas station **3** trumpet
ṭuub طوب *coll n* brick(s); **ṭuub aḥmar** fired bricks; **ṭuub akhḍar, ṭuub nayy** mud bricks, unfired, sun-dried bricks
ṭuul طول *n* (**aṭwaal**) **1** length; height; **ʿala ṭuul** straight ahead/on **2** (*geog*) longitude • *prep* throughout; **ṭuul al-leel** all night long • *conj* **ṭuul ma** as long as
ṭuuriyya طوريّة *n* (*pl* **-aat, ṭawaari**) hoe (for digging)
ṭuẓẓ طظ *interj* (*slang*) I don't give a damn **ṭuzz fii-ho** he can go to hell

u

u و *conj* and
ufuq أفق *n* (*pl* **aafaaq**) horizon
ufuqi أفقي *adj* horizontal
ughniya أغنية *n* (*pl* **-aat, aghaani**) song
ujra أجرة *n* (*pl* **ujuur**) fare; wage for piecework
ukra اكرة *n* (*pl* **ukar**) doorknob, door handle; **iid/yadd al-ukra** doorknob, door handle

uksijiin أكسجين *n* oxygen
uktoobar أكتوبر *n* October
ukhra أخرى *adj f* (*m* **aakhar**) other, another
ukhut أخت *n* (*pl* **akhawaat**) sister
umbaariḥ أمبارح *n* yesterday; **awwal umbaariḥ** the day before yesterday
umbaaz أمباز *n* pulp
umm أم *n* (*pl* **-aat, ummahaat**) **1** mother; **umm-i** my mother; mummy; **yumma** mummy; **umm awlaad-i** my wife **2** (*denotes a distinguishing feature, for instance*); **umm ash-shuluukh** the woman with tribal marks on her face; **umm rigeyga** thin broth (with dried okra)
umma أمة *n* (*pl* **umam**) nation; **al-umam al-muttaḥida** the United Nations
ummi أمي *adj* illiterate
ummiyya أمّيّة *n* illiteracy
ummiyya أمّيّة *n* electric transformer
umniya أمنية *n* (*pl* **-aat, amaani**) wish
umuur امور (*sg* **amr/amur**) *n* issues, matters, affairs
urbuʿmiyya أربعميّة *num* four hundred
urdun أردن *prop n* **al-urdun** Jordan; the Jordan River
urduni أردني (*pl* **-yyiin**) *adj* Jordanian • *n* a Jordanian
urubba أوروبّا *prop n* Europe
urubbaawi اوروبّاي (*pl* **-yyiin**) *adj* European • *n* a European
urubbi اوروبّي (*pl* **-yyiin**) *adj* European • *n* a European
usbuuʿ أسبوع *n* (*pl* **asaabiiʿ**) week
usbuuʿi أسبوعي *adj* weekly
usbuuʿiyyan أسبوعيّاً *adv* weekly
usluub أسلوب *n* (*pl* **asaaliib**) style
usquf أسقف *n* (*pl* **asaaqifa**) bishop; **ra'iis al-asaaqifa** archbishop
usqufi أسقفي *adj* Episcopal
usra أسرة *n* (*pl* **usar**) family
ustaaz أستاذ *n* (*m*) (*pl* **asaatza, asaatiza**) teacher, master
ustaaza أستاذة *n* (*f*) teacher
usturaali أسترالي (*pl* **-yyiin**) *adj* Australian • *n* an Australian
usturaaliyya أستراليا *prop n* Australia
usṭa اسطى *n* (*pl* **usṭawaat**) **1** foreman, boss **2** title of address to a craftsman
usṭuul أسطول *n* (*pl* **asaaṭiil**) (*mil*) fleet
usṭuura اسطورة *n* legend
usṭuwaana أسطوانة *n* CD, diskette, gramophone record
uṣuuli اصولي *n* (*pl* **-iyyiin**) fundamentalist
uula أولى *num f* (*m* **awwal**) first

V

vidiyuu فديو *n* (*pl* **-haat**) video
viiza فيزا *n* (*pl* **-aat**) visa
villa فيلا *n* (*pl* **vilal**) villa
vooli فولي *n* volleyball

W – و

wa و *conj* **1** and **2** by (in swearing an oath); **w Allaahi** (I swear) by God

wa-la ولا *conj* **1** or **2** (*preceded by a negation*) nor; **ma daayir yaakul wa-la yashrab** he will neither eat nor drink **3** not even; **ma ᶜind-i wa-la girish** I don't have even a penny; **wa-la ḥata** not even

waᶜᶜa وعّى *vt* (**-i, tawᶜiya**) (**be-**) to make conscious or aware (of)

waᶜad وعد *vt* (**yuuᶜid/yawᶜid, waᶜad**) (**be-**) to promise; **waᶜattaa-ho be-l-ᶜamal da** I promised him I would do this work • *n* (*pl* **wuᶜuud**) promise

waᶜaẓ وعظ *vt* (**yooᶜiẓ, waᶜiẓ**) to preach, lecture

waᶜiẓ وعظ *n* (*pl* **mawaaᶜiiẓ**) sermon, lecture

waaᶜi واعي *adj* conscious, aware

waaᶜiẓ واعظ *n* (*pl* **wuᶜᶜaaẓ**) preacher

waabuur وابور *n* (*pl* **-aat**) **1** pump; **waabuur mooya** irrigation pump **2** engine; **waabuur baḥar** steamboat, steamer; **waabuur al-gaṭar** railway engine **3** generator

waadi وادي *n* (*pl* **widyaan**) **1** wadi, valley, dry riverbed, seasonal streambed; **hi fi waadi w inta fi waadi** she and you are not on the same wavelength **2** seasonal stream

waaḍiḥ واضح *adj* clear, plain

waafag وافق *vi* (**muwaafaga**) (**ᶜala**) to agree (about), approve (of)

waafir وافر *adj* plentiful

waagid واقد *adj* burning, alight

waaḥa واحة *n* oasis

waaḥda واحدة *adj f* one • *n* (*f*) some woman

waaḥdaat واحدات *n pl* (*f*) some women

waaḥdiin واحدين *n pl* some people

waaḥid واحد *num* one • *adj m* one • *n* (*pl* **waaḥdiin**) someone, somebody; **wa-la waaḥid** nobody

waajah واجه *vt* (**muwaajaha**) to face, confront

waajib واجب *n* (*pl* **-aat**) duty, obligation task, homework (studies); **waajib ᶜalee-k al-mushwaar da** you must do this errand

waajiha واجهة *n* front (of building)

waakhid واخد *adj* (*v* **akhad**) taking; having taken

waalaf والف *vi* (**wilif, muwaalafa**) **ᶜala, be-** to be(come) familiar with, accustomed to, adapted to

waalda والدة *n* mother

waali والي *n* (*pl* **wulaa**) governor of a state

waalid والد *n* father

waalideen والدين *n dual* parents; **waalidee-k** your parents

waaqiᶜ واقع *n* (*pl* **waqaaᶜi**) fact; **al-waaqiᶜ** reality

waaqiᶜi واقعي *adj* realistic

waarid وارد *adv* probably

waaridaat واردات *n pl* imports, imported goods

waaris وارس *n* (*pl* **wurraas, warasa**) heir

waasa واسى *vt* (**-i, muwaasaa**) **1** to console, comfort **2** to make equal, even

waasiᶜ واسع *adj* wide; spacious

waasiq واسق *adj* (**min**) trusting, confident; being certain, sure (about/of)
waasṭa واسطة *n* intermediary, influential backing; **be-waasṭat** through (by means of)
waasuug واسوق *n* (*pl* **-aat**) board with ropes for levelling the soil
waaṣal واصل *vt* (**muwaaṣala**) **1** to continue, pursue **2** to visit regularly
waaṭa واطا *n* **1** ground, floor **2** earth, land; **al-waaṭa khala** open country, empty of people **3** world; earthly existence; **al-waaṭa aṣbaḥat** morning has come; **al-waaṭa ḍulumma** it is dark; **al-waaṭa sukhna** it is hot, the weather is hot
waaṭi واطي *adj* (*also fig*) low
waaza وازى *vt* (**-i, muwaazaa**) to run parallel to
waazan وازن (**muwaazana**) *vt* to counterbalance • *vi* **been** to weigh one against another
waba وبا *n* (*pl* **awbiya**) epidemic
wabbakh وبّخ *vt* (**wibbeekh, tawbiikh**) to rebuke
wad ود *n* (*in construction with an article:* **wadd**) (*pl* **awlaad**) boy; son; **wad ʿamm/ʿamma** male cousin on father's side; **wad khaal/khaala** male cousin on mother's side; **wad akhu/ukhut** nephew; **wad ibn Aadam** male human being; **wad ḥalaal** a trustworthy person **wad ḥaraam/wad zina** illegitimate son; **wadd allaziina** (*mild insult*) son of those; **wadd al-ʿeen** pupil (of the eye)
wadaaʿ وداع *n* farewell
wadak ودك *n* fat used as a cosmetic
wadda ودّى *vt* (**-i, widdeey**) (**le-**) **1** to convey; to bring or take to (a place) **2** to send
waddaʿ ودّع *vt* (**wadaaʿ, widdeeʿ**) to see off; to bid farewell
waddar ودّر *vi* (**widdeer, wadaar**) to lose one's way, go astray • *vt* (**widdeer**) **1** to lose **2** to waste; **biwaddir ʿumr-o** he is wasting his life
wadiʿ ودع *coll n* (*unit n* **wadʿa**) seashell(s); **ḍarb al-wadiʿ** way of fortune-telling by throwing down shells and examining the positions in which they fall
wadiiʿ وديع *adj* quiet (person)
wadiiʿa وديعة *n* (*pl* **wadaayiʿ**) deposit (sth. held in safekeeping)
waḍʿ وضع *n* (*pl* **awḍaaʿ**) position situation
waḍaʿ وضع *vt* (**yaḍaʿ, wuḍuuʿ**) **1** to give birth to **2** to put • *vi* to give birth
waḍaḥ وضح *vi* (**yooḍaḥ, waḍḥa, wuḍuuḥ**) to be(come) clear (of things)
waḍḍab وضّب *vt* (**wiḍḍeeb, tawḍiib**) to put in order, arrange, tidy
waḍḍaḥ وضّح *vi* (**wiḍḍeeḥ, tawḍiiḥ**) to make clear, explain
waḍu وضو *n* (*Isl*) ritual ablution before prayer
wafa وفاة *n* (*pl* **wafiyaat**) death (of s.o.)
wafa وفى *vi* (**yuufi, wafaa**) to be faithful; **wafa be-l-waʿad** to keep a promise
wafaat وفاة *n* (*pl* **wafiyaat**) death (of s.o.)
wafd وفد *n* (*pl* **wufuud**) delegation

waffa وفّى *vi* (**-i, wafayaan**) **be-** to fulfil; **waffa be-l-ʿalee-ho** he fulfilled his obligations • *vi* to fulfil; **waffa l-ʿalee-ho** he fulfilled his obligations
waffar وفّر *vt* (**tawfiir**) to save up
wafi وفي *adj* (*pl* **awfiya**) loyal
wagʿa وقعة *n* fall; **wagʿa sheena/ sooda** big trouble
wagaʿ وقع *vi* (**yoogaʿ, wuguuʿ**) **1** to fall (down) **2 le-** to grasp, understand **3 fi** to lash out at; **wagaʿ fii-ho nabaz** he lashed out at him with insults; **wagaʿ fii-ho dagg** he gave him a beating
wagaf وقف *vi* (**yagiif, wuguuf**) **1** to halt, stop; to pause **2** to stand; to stand up **3 maʿa** to stand up for, stand by, support
wagfa وقفة *n* **1** pause **2** eve (of a religious feast)
waggaʿ وقّع *vt* (**wiggeeʿ**) to make s.o. fall
waggaf وقّف *vt* (**wiggeef, tawgiif**) **1** to halt, stop; to quit **2** to turn off, switch off
wagiyya وقيّة *n* unit of weight equal to 37.44 grammes; ounce
waham وهم *n* (*pl* **awhaam**) illusion
waḥda وحدة *n* loneliness
waḥiid وحيد *adj* **1** alone **2** lonely **3** sole, only; single
waḥish وحش *adj* (*pl* **waḥshiin**) brutal, savage
waḥsh وحش *n* (*pl* **wuḥuush**) wild animal
waḥsha وحشة *n* loneliness; **lee-k waḥsha** I miss you very much
wajʿa وجعة *n* (*pl* **-aat, awjaaʿ**) pain, ache
wajaʿ وجع *vi* (**yuujiʿ/yuujaʿ, wajiʿ, wajʿa**) to hurt, ache • *vt* to hurt; **ḥalg-i biyuujiʿ-ni/biyuujaʿni** I have a sore throat • *n* pain, ache; **wajaʿ baṭun** abdominal pain; **wajaʿ raas** headache
wajba وجبة *n* meal
wajh وجه *n* (*pl* **wujuuh**) **1** face **2** surface (e.g. of coffee, soup, pudding)
wajiih وجيه *adj* (*pl* **wujaha**) **1** good-looking **2** eminent **3** sensible (e.g. of a question)
wajjaʿ وجّع *vt* (**wijjeeʿ, wajʿa**) to hurt
wajjah وجّه *vt* (**wijjeeh, tawjiih**) to give directions to, direct; to offer guidance to
wakiil وكيل *n* (*pl* **wukala**) agent; **wakiil niyaaba** public prosecutor, public attorney
wakit وكت *n* (*pl* **awkaat**) time; point in time; **min wakit** since; **wakit ma** when, whenever; **baʿḍ al-awkaat** sometimes; **fi l-wakit daak** then, at that time; **fi wakt-o** punctual; **fi nafs al-wakit** at one and the same time, simultaneously
wala ولا *conj* - *see* **wa-la**
walad ولد *n* (*pl* **awlaad**) boy; son; **walad marat-o** stepson of a man; **walad raajil-a** stepson of a woman; **awlaad joon** (*lit* the sons of John) the British; white foreigners
wali ولي *n* (*pl* **awliya**) (*Isl*) holy man, saint; **wali l-amr** legal guardian; curator
waliima وليمة *n* (*pl* **walaayim**) banquet, meal for a large number of people
wallaʿ ولّع *vt* (**willeeʿ**) to light, ignite; to switch on, turn on (light, gas)

wallaaʿa ولاعة *n* cigarette lighter
wallad ولّد *vt* (**willeed, tawliid**) to give birth to
wallaf ولّف *vt* **1** (**tawliif**) to cobble together, to replace by a non-original spare part **2** (**tawliif**) to graft (plants) **3** (**willeef, wilfa**) to tame, domesticate
waluuf ولوف *adj* affectionately familiar with
walwal ولول *vi* (**wilweel, walwala**) to ululate, wail
wanasa ونسة *n* chat
wannaas ونّاس *adj* an entertaining talker
wannas ونّس *vi* (**wanasa**) to chat
waqf وقف *n* (*pl* **awqaaf**) (*Isl*) religious endowment; endowment fund; inalienable property
waqf وقف *n* **waqf iṭlaaq an-naar** ceasefire
waqqaʿ وقّع *vi* (**tawqiiʿ**) to sign
waquur وقور *adj* decent (**person**)
wara ورا *prep* behind • *adv* behind, in or at the back; **be-wara** behind
warad ورد *vi* (**i, warid**) to be mentioned, occur (in a written text)
warad ورد *vi* (**yoorid, wuruud**) **min/le-** to fetch water (from); **bitoorid le-l-biir** she fetches water from the well
warag ورق *coll n* **1** paper; **warag muqawwa** cardboard **2** leaves **3** leaves of the black-eyed bean plant
waraga ورقة *unit n* (*pl* **-aat, awraag**) **1** leaf **2** a piece or sheet of paper; a paper **3** a (written) paper **4** amulet; **waraga min al-ʿeen** amulet against the evil eye
waral ورل *n* (*pl* **-aat, wurulla**) monitor lizard
waram ورم *n* (*pl* **awraam**) swelling, bump; tumor
waras ورس *vt* (**i, wiraasa**) to inherit
ward ورد *coll n* (*pl* **wuruud**) **1** rose(s) **2** flower(s)
wardi وردي *adj* pink, rose-pink
wardiyya ورديّة *n* shift (at work)
wariis وريس *n* (*pl* **wurraas, warasa**) heir
warisa ورسة *n* inheritance
warnash ورنش *vt* (**wirneesh**) to polish
warra ورّى *vt* (**-i, wirreey**) to show
warraani ورّاني *adj* rear; back
warrad ورّد *vt* (**wirreed, tawriid**) to supply; **warrad lee-hum al-buḍaaʿa** he supplied them with the goods
warram ورّم *vt* (**wirreem**) **1** to cause to swell **2** (*slang*) to bore (of a person)
warraṭ ورّط *vt* (**warṭa, tawarruṭ**) to embroil in difficulties, to put on the spot
warsha ورشة *n* (*pl* **wirash**) repair shop; **warshat ʿamal** workshop
warṭa ورطة *n* dilemma, awkward position, predicament; **fi warṭa** in trouble
wasaakha وساخة *n* dirt; garbage, litter
wasaayil وسايل *n pl* (*sg* **wasiila**) means
wasakh وسخ *n* (*pl* **awsaakh**) dirt
wasaq وسق *vi* (**yasiq, siqa**) **fi** to trust
wasaṭ وسط *n* (*pl* **awsaaṭ**) **1** centre, middle; **fi wasaṭ** among **2** waist
wasiiʿ وسيع *adj* wide; spacious
wasiila وسيلة *n* (*pl* **wasaayil**) means

wasiim وسيم *adj* handsome
wasiiqa وسيقة *n* (*pl* **wasaayiq**) document, title deed
wasiiṭ وسيط *n* (*pl* **wusaṭa**) mediator
wasim وسم *n* (*pl* **awsaam**) mark, brand (e.g. cattle)
waskhaan وسخان *adj* dirty, filthy
wassaᶜ وسّع *vt* (**wisseeᶜ**, **tawsiiᶜ**) **1** to widen, broaden, extend, expand **2** to make room (for a person)
wassakh وسّخ *vt* (**wisseekh**, **wasaakha**) to dirty, soil
wassam وسّم *vt* (**wisseem**) to brand (mark); to mark (belongings, goods)
wassaq وسّق *vt* (**tawsiiq**) to document, authenticate, draw up a notarial deed
wasṭaani وسطاني *adj* middle
waswaas وسواس *n* **1** (*pl* **wasaawiis**) devil **2** chaotic thoughts (e.g. caused by anxiety); bad ideas
waswas وسوس *vi* (**waswasa**, **wiswees**) **1** to whisper **2 le-** to tempt (of devil), put bad ideas into s.o.'s head
waṣaf وصف *vt* (**yooṣif**, **waṣif**) **1** to describe, depict **2** to prescribe medicine
waṣal وصل *vi* (**yaṣal/yuuṣal**, **wuṣuul**) (**le-**) to arrive (at), reach
waṣfa وصفة *n* **1** prescription **waṣfa ṭibbiyya** medical prescription **2** recipe
waṣi وصي *n* (*pl* **awṣiya**) legal guardian
waṣif وصف *n* (*pl* **awṣaaf**) description
waṣil وصل *n* (*pl* **wuṣuulaat**) receipt; voucher
waṣiyya وصيّة *n* (*pl* **waṣaaya**) **1** message **2** testament, will; **al-waṣaaya al-ᶜashara** the Ten Commandments
waṣla وصلة *n* extension lead
waṣṣa وصّى *vt* (**-i**, **tawṣiya**) **ᶜala** to recommend sth.
waṣṣaf وصّف *vt* (**wiṣṣeef**) to describe
waṣṣal وصّل *vt* (**wiṣṣeel**) **1** (**le-**) to convey; to bring or take to (a place) **2** (**be-**) to connect, bring into contact (with)
washam وشم *vt* (**i**, **washim**) to tattoo
washim وشم *n* (*pl* **washmaat**, **awshaam**) tattoo
washsh وش *n* (*pl* **wushuush**) **1** face **2** surface (e.g. of coffee, soup, pudding)
washwash وشوش *vi* (**wishweesh**, **washwasha**) **1** to rustle **2** to whisper
watar وتر *coll n* (*pl* **awtaar**) **1** (*mus*) string **2** (*geom*) chord
waṭan وطن *n* (*pl* **awṭaan**) homeland
waṭani وطني *adj* **1** national **2** nationalistic
waṭaniyya وطنيّة *n* nationalism
waṭṭa وطّى *vt* (**-i**, **wiṭṭeey**) to lower (voice, sound)
waṭṭaaya وطّاية *n* sole of foot; sole of shoe
waṭwaaṭ وطواط *n* (*pl* **waṭaawiiṭ**) (*zool*) bat
wazaara وزارة *n* ministry; **wazaarat al-ᶜadl** the Ministry of Justice; **wazaarat al-iskaan** the Ministry of Housing; **wazaarat (ash-shu'uun) ad-daakhiliyya** the Ministry of the Interior; **wazaarat ash-shu'uun al-insaaniyya** the Ministry of Humanitarian Affairs; **wazaarat (ash-shu'uun) al-khaarijiyya** the Ministry

of Foreign Affairs; **wazaarat (ash-shu'uun) al-maaliyya** the Ministry of Finance; **wazaarat at-tarbiyya wa t-taʿliim** the Ministry of Education

wazan وزن *vt* (**yoozin, wazin, wazna**) to weigh

waziir وزير *n* (*m*) (*pl* **wuzara**) **1** minister; **waziir ad-dawla** state minister; **ra'iis wuzara** prime minister **2** best man (of bridegroom)

waziira وزيرة *n* (*f*) **1** minister **2** bridesmaid, maid of honour at a wedding

wazin وزن *n* weight

wazna وزنة *n* (*pl* **awzaan**) weight of a balance

wazzaʿ وزّع *vt* (**tawziiʿ**) to hand out; to distribute, disseminate

wazzaan وزّان *n* professional weigher (e.g. of grain, cotton)

waẓiifa وظيفة *n* (*pl* **waẓaayif**) **1** function, post; **da waẓiift-o shinu** what is it used for? what is its function? **2** job, occupation **waẓiifa khaalya** job vacancy

waẓẓaf وظّف *vt* (**tawẓiif**) to employ

weeka ويكة *n* dried okra powder

weekaab ويكاب *n* ash of a type of leaves, used to flavour a sauce of curdled milk

ween وين *interrog* where; **ʿala/le-ween** where to?; **min ween** from where? • *conj* where; **ana ma ʿaarif hu masha ween** I don't know where he has gone

wiʿa وعى *vi* (**yawʿa, waʿi**) **be-** to be(come) aware, conscious of

widir ودر *vi* (**a, wadaar**) to get lost, lose one's way, go astray

wiḍiḥ وضح *vi* (**yooḍaḥ, waḍḥa, wuḍuuḥ**) to be(come) clear

wigaaya وقاية *n* stand for a coffee pot

wiḥda وحدة *n* **1** unit **2** unity

wiḥil وحل *vi* (**yooḥal, waḥla**) to get stuck (e.g. of a car in sand or mud)

wijha وجهة *n* **wijhat naẓar** point of view

wikaala وكالة *n* agency

wilaada ولادة *n* delivery, childbirth

wilaaya ولاية *n* (*pl* **wilaayaat**) state (political entity); governorate

wileed وليد *n* (*pl* **-aat**) boy; **wileedaat** children

wilid ولد (**i, wilaada**) *vi* to give birth • *vt* to give birth to

wilif ولف *n* **ʿala** affectionate familiarity; **al-wilif kattaal** (*lit* affectionate familiarity is killing) familiarity breeds contempt

winish ونش *n* (*pl* **awnaash**) crane (machine)

winka ونكة *n* busy lizzie (flowers)

wiqaaya وقاية *n* prevention, precaution

wiraasa وراسة *n* inheritance

wirda وردة *n* fever

wirid ورد *vi* (**a, wirda**) to have a fever

wirid ورد *n* (*pl* **awraad**) a period of private prayer or reading from the Koran

wirik ورك *n* (*pl* **awraak**) thigh

wirim ورم *vi* (**a, waram**) to swell

wiris ورس *vt* (**a, waris, wiraasa**) to inherit

wisaakha وساخة *n* dirt; garbage, litter

wisaam وسام *n* (*pl* **awsima**) sash

wisiʿ وسع *vi* (**a, wasaaʿ**) to be(come) wide, broad

wisikh وسخ *adj* (*also fig*) dirty
wiṣaaya وصاية *n* guardianship; tutelage
wishaaḥ وشاح *n* (*pl* **awshiḥa**) sash
witid وتد *n* (*pl* **awtaad**) peg, tent peg
wiṭa وطى *vt* (**yowṭa, waṭi**) to step on
wizziin وزين *coll n* geese (goose)
woob ووب *n* **woob ʿalee-y** wail with me! cry with me! (*expression used by women upon news of a disaster or a death*)
wujuud وجود *n* being; existence; presence
wuquud وقود *n* fuel
wusṭa وسطى *adj f* (*m* **awsaṭ**) middle; **aṭ-ṭabaga al-wusṭa** the middle class
wusuʿ وسع *n* width
wuṣuul وصول *n* (*no pl*) arrival

y – ي

ya يا *conj* **ya da, ya daak** either this or that; **ya-imma** either… or; **ya-imma da, ya-imma daak** either this or that
ya يا *part* **1** (*voc*) **ya Faṭma** Fatma!; **ya siid-i** sir!; **ya sitt-i** madam!; **ya-akh-i** my brother!; **ya-ho** here he/it is!; **ya-ha** here she/it is! **2** (*excl*) **ya salaam** good heavens!; **ya bakht-ak** you're lucky, you lucky one!; **ya reet** I wish…, if only…
yaʿni يعني *part* **1** (*often used to express hesitation*) it means, that's to say, that is **2** so-so, sort of
ya's يأس *n* despair; **sinn al-ya's** menopause
yaa'is يائس *adj* desperate
yaabis يابس *adj* **1** dry; **yadd-o yaabsa** he is stingy **2** hard, tough (material) **3** stingy
yaabuusa يابوسة *n* constipation
yaadoob يادوب *adv* **1** just; just now; **da yaadoob kifaaya** it's just enough; **yaadoob khiliṣ** it/he has just finished; **yaadoob ma** as soon as **2** at last, finally; **yaadoob khallaṣ-o** he has finally finished it
yaadoob- يادوب- *adv* just now; **yaadoob-na rajaʿna** we came back just now
yaadoobak يادوبك *adv* just now; **yadoobak rajaʿna** we came back just now
yaafṭa يافطة *n* (*pl* **-aat, yifaṭ**) signboard; nameplate
yaarda ياردة *n* yard (measure)
yaat- ياتـ *interrog* which; **al-beet yaat-o**?which house; **al-bitt yaat-a** which girl?
yaato ياتو *interrog* which; **yaato girid** which monkey?; **yaato madrasa** which school?
yaawur ياور *n* (*pl* **yaawraat**) (*mil*) aide-de-camp
yaay يايي *n* (*pl* **-aat**) (metal) spring
yabaan يابان *prop n* **al-yabaan** Japan
yabaani ياباني (*pl* **-yyiin**) *adj* Japanese • *n* a Japanese
yadd يد *n f* (*pl* **yaddeen, ayaadi**) **1** hand; **malyat yadd/gabḍat yadd** a handful **2** handle; **yadd al-funduk** pestle; **yadd al-ukra** doorknob, door handle

yaddawi يدّوي *adj* manual
yagiin يقين *n* certainty; ʿ**ind-i yagiin fi** I am certain of
yahuud يهود *coll n* Jews
yahuudi يهودي *adj* (*pl* **yahuud**) Jewish • *unit n* a Jew
yajuuz يجوز *part* maybe, perhaps
ya-khi ياخي *excl part* **1** *informal term of address to any person, male or female*; **ya-khi, khallii-ni** hey you, leave me alone! **2** (*used when expressing surprise*) what are you telling me? is it true?
ya-khṣi يخصي *excl part* **ya-khṣi** ʿ**alee-k** shame on you!
yalla يلا *interj* come on, get on, let's…; **yalla namshi** let's go; **yallaa-k** let's go
yansuun ينسون *n* aniseed
yamiin يمين *n* (*pl* **-aat**) oath; ʿ**alee-y al-yamiin** I swear; **yamiin zuur** perjury
yamiin يمين *n* right (right-hand side); **be-l-yamiin,** ʿ**ala l-yamiin** on the right; ʿ**ala yamiin-ak** on your right; **al-yamiin** (*pol*) the Right • *adj invar* right (right-hand side) • *adv* **khushsh yamiin** enter at the right-hand side
yanaayir يناير *n* January
ya-naṣiib يا نصيب *n* lottery
yaraqa يرقة *n* caterpillar
yaraqaan يرقان *n* hepatitis, jaundice
yasaar يسار *n* **al-yasaar** (*pol*) the Left
yassar يسّر *vt* (**taysiir**) to facilitate, make easy
yatiim يتيم *n* (*pl* **yutama**) orphan
yi'is يئس *vi* (**a, ya's**) to despair
yibis يبس *vi* (**a, yabaas, yaba-saan**) to dry, be(come) dry
yikhṣ يخص *n* **yikhṣ** ʿ**alee-k** shame on you!
yimkin يمكن *part* maybe, perhaps; possibly
yoom يوم *n* (*pl* **ayyaam**) day (24 hours); **yoom al-aḥad** Sunday; **yoom al-itneen** Monday; **yoom at-talaata** Tuesday; **yoom al-arbi**ʿ**a** Wednesday; **yoom al-khamiis** Thursday; **yoom aj-jum**ʿ**a** Friday; **yoom as-sabat** Saturday; **al-yoom, al-yoom da** today; **yoom min al-ayyaam** once upon a time; **yoom ma** when
yoomaati يوماتي *adj* daily
yoomi يومي *adj* daily
yoomiyya يوميّة *n* **1** work per day **2** daily wages
yoomiyyaat يوميات *n pl* diary
yoomiyyan يوميّا *adv* daily
yughanda اوغندا *prop n* Uganda
yughandi اوغندي (*pl* **-yyiin**) *adj* Ugandan • *n* a Ugandan
yunaan يونان *prop n* **al-yunaan** Greece
yunaani يوناني (*pl* **-yyiin**) *adj* Greek • *n* a Greek
yuniforim يونيفورم *n* (*pl* **-aat**) uniform
yustaḥsan يستحسن *part* it would be better to
yuulyo يوليو *n* July
yuunyo يونيو *n* June
yuuro يورو *n* (*pl* **-haat**) euro
yuusif يوسف **yuusif effendi** *coll n* tangerine(s)

z – ز

za‘‘aafa زعّافة *n* long-handled broom for sweeping the ceiling
za‘‘al زعّل *vt* (**zi‘‘eel, za‘al**) to anger, upset; (to anger)
za‘al زعل *n* anger
za‘faraan زعفران *n* saffron
za‘iim زعيم *n* (*pl* **zu‘ama**) leader
za‘laan زعلان *adj* angry; upset
za‘nafa زعنفة *n* (*pl* **za‘aanif**) fin
zaa‘ زاع *vt* (**i, izaa‘a**) to broadcast
zaa'id زائد *prep* plus, in addition to; (*arith*) plus; **sitta zaa'id talaata yasaawi tis‘a** six plus three equals nine
zaad زاد *n* provisions (when travelling)
zaad زاد (**i, zeeda, ziyaada**) *vi* **1** to increase (e.g. of price, number); to rise (e.g. of water in river) **2** **‘an** to exceed, go beyond • *vt* to add, increase
zaakar زاكر *vi/vt* (**muzaakara**) to study (lessons)
zaakira زاكرة *n* memory
zaani زاني *n* (*pl* **zunaa**) adulterer
zaaq زاق *vi* (**u, zooqa, zawaqaan**) **1** (**min**) to sneak away, slip away (from) **2** **min** to dodge, evade
zaar زار *n* (*no pl*) **1** ritual of sacrifices, incantations, drumming and dancing performed for the purpose of appeasing a spirit by which a person is possessed **2** spirit(s), *as in* **‘ind-o zaar** he is possessed by spirits
zaar زار *vt* (**u, ziyaara**) to visit
zaat زات *n* **be-z-zaat** specially, especially, particularly; in particular
zaat- زات- *n* **1** self; **hu zaat-o ja, ja be-zaat-o** he himself came; **hi ‘amalat-o be-zaat-a** she did it herself; **di saa‘at-i zaat-a** this is my watch **2** too; **ana zaat-i daayir shaay** I (myself) also want tea **3** same; **di saa‘at-i be-zaat-a** this watch looks exactly the same as my watch
zaato زاتو *n* **1** self; **ana zaato amshi** I (myself) am leaving (too) **2** same; **da l-walad zaato** this is the very boy
zaawad زاود *vi* (**muzaawada**) (**‘ala**) to bid (for), **be-** to raise a bid by; **zaawad ‘alee-ho be-‘ashara** he raised the bid by ten
zaawal زاول *vi* (**muzaawala**) **le-** **1** to appear (in a dream) **2** to appear frequently with demands
zaawiya زاوية *n* (*pl* **zawaaya**) **1** corner; angle **2** prayer corner **3** dwelling of a sheikh where he prays and teaches the Koran **4** (*instr*) set square
zaayad زايد *vt* (**muzaayada**) to outbid s.o.
zaayda زايدة *n* (*anat*) appendix; **iltihaab zaayda/az-zaayda** appendicitis
zaayid زايد *prep* plus, in addition to; (*arith*) plus; **khamsa zaayid itneen yasaawi sab‘a** five plus two equals seven
zaayir زاير *n* (*pl* **zuwwaar**) visitor
zabaadi زبادي *n* yoghurt
zabad زبد *n* foam (river, sea)

zabbaal زبّال *n* plasterer (of walls and roofs with a mixture of dung, clay and water)
zabbad زبّد *vi* (**zibbeed**) to foam at the mouth (as a result of illness; out of anger)
zabbal زبّل *vt* (**zibbeel**) to plaster (walls and roofs) with a mixture of dung, clay and water
zabḥa زبحة *n* abbreviation of **zabḥa ṣadriyya** heart attack
zabiib زبيب *coll n* raisin(s)
zabuun زبون *n* (*pl* **zabaayin**) customer
zafar زفر *vi* (**u, zafiir**) to exhale
zaffa زفّة *n* wedding procession
zagal زقل *vt* (**u, zagil**) to throw (away)
zaghlal زغلل *vt* (**zaghlala, zighleel**) to blind, dazzle
zaghrad زغرد *vi* (**zaghrada**) to produce a trilling cry (by women, for joy)
zaghruuda زغرودة *n* (*pl* **zaghaari-id**) a trilling cry, produced by women for joy
zaghzagh زغزغ *vi* (**zaghzagha**) to chirp
zahaj زهج *n* boredom
zahar زهر *coll n* (*unit n* **zahra**, *pl* **zuhuur**) flower(s)
zahar زهر *coll n* (*unit n* **zahra**) dice
zahhaj زهّج *vt* (**zihheej**) **1** to annoy, irritate, disturb **2** to bore
zahjaan زهجان *adj* bored, fed up, weary
zaḥaf زحف *vi* (**a, zaḥif, zaḥafaan**) to creep; to crawl
zaḥḥa زحّ (**i, zaḥḥa, zaḥaḥaan**) *vi* to move aside, to give way • *vt* to move, shove, push aside
zaḥma زحمة *n* crowded; **fii zahma** it is crowded
zakaa زكا *n* cleverness, intelligence
zakaat زكاة *n* (*pl* **zakawaat**) (*Isl*) alms (one of the five pillars of Islam)
zakar زكر *vt* (**u, zikir**) to mention
zaki زكي *adj* (*pl* **azkiya**) clever, intelligent
zakka زكّى *vt* (**-i, zakaat**) **1** to give as alms **2** (**-i, tazkiya**) to recommend
zakkar زكّر *vt* (**zikkeer, tazkiir**) to remind
zakhiira زخيرة *n* (*pl* **zakhaayir**) ammunition
zakhraf زخرف *vt* (**zakhrafa, zikhreef**) to decorate
zalag زلق *vt* (**i, zalig**) to cause to slip; **bi-yazlig** it is slippery
zalageeba زلقيبة *n* a slippery spot or place
zallag زلّق *vt* (**zilleeg**) to cause to slip
zalluuma زلّومة *n* (*pl* **zalaaliim**) elephant's trunk
zalzaal زلزال *n* (*pl* **zalaazil**) earthquake
zamaala زمالة *n* fellowship, comradeship
zamaan زمان *adv* in times past, in the old days; **min zamaan** a long time ago, ages ago; for a long time; **gadiim az-zamaan** once upon a time
zaman زمن *n* (*pl* **azmina, azmaan**) time; (*pl* **azmina**) period of time; age, era; **zaman iḍaafi** overtime; **min zaman baʿiid** a long time ago, ages ago; **zaman ṭawiil** (for) a long time; (*Chr*) **az-zaman al-arbaʿiini** Lent; **zaman al-majii'** Advent

zambalak زمبلك *n* (*pl* **-aat**) (metal) spring

zambar زمبر *vi* (**zambara**) to play a flute

zamiil زميل *n* (*pl* **zumlaan, zumala**) colleague, teammate, schoolmate; comrade

zammar زمّر *vi* (**zimmeer**) to play the flute

zamzamiyya زمزميّة *n* water flask (for travelling)

zana زنى *vi* (**-i, zina**) to commit adultery

zanag زنق *vi* (**i, zanig**) to wedge in, corner

zanb زنب *n* (*and* **zanib**, *pl* **zunuub**) **1** guilt **2** sin, fault; **zanb-o ʿala ragabt-o/zanb-o ʿala jamb-o** it's his own fault

zanga زنقة *adj invar* **1** narrow; **fii zanga** it is crowded **2** suffocating (of hot weather, caused by absence of wind)

zanna زنّ *vi* (**i, zann**) **1** to buzz **2** to whine, go on and on

zannaan زنّان *n* **abu zannaan** wasp

zannaana زنّانة *n* whizzer (toy)

zannag زنّق *vt* (**zinneeg, zanga**) to corner, wedge in

zarʿa زرعة *n* greenery; crop(s)

zaraʿ زرع *vt* **1** (**a, zariʿ, ziraaʿa**) to plant; to sow; to grow **2** (**a, ziraaʿa**) to transplant

zaraaf زراف *coll n* giraffe(s)

zariiba زريبة *n* (*pl* **zaraayib**) **1** any enclosure **2** corral, cattle pen, sheepfold, stable **3** market for charcoal, wood and earthenware; **zariibat al-ʿeesh** grain market

zarra زرّ *vt* (**-a, zarr, zararaan**) to trap

zarraʿ زرّع *vt* (**tazriiʿ**) to cause to sprout

zarradiyya زرّديّة *n* (pair of) pliers

zarrar زرّر *vt* (**zirreer**) to button up

zarwa زروة *n* **saaʿat az-zarwa** rush hour

zarzuur زرزور *n/n pl* (*pl* **zaraaziir**) **1** starling(s) **2** various species of small birds (that are pests to grain farmers)

zawaaj زواج *n* (*pl* **ziijaat**) marriage

zawji زوجي *adj* even (of numbers)

zawwad زوّد *vi* (**ziyaada**) **ʿala** to add to; **zawwid lee-ho** give him some more

zawwaj زوّج *vt* (**ziwweej, tazwiij**) to give (a girl) in marriage

zawwaq زوّق *vi* (**ziwweeq, zawaqaan**) **1** (**min**) to sneak away, slip away (from) **2 min** to dodge, evade

zawwar زوّر *vt* (**tazwiir**) to counterfeit (e.g. documents, paper money), forge

zayy زي *prep* **1** like; resembling; **naas zayy deel...** such people... **2** such as • *conj* as; **zayy ma (inta) ʿaarif** as you know; **zayy ma (inti) ʿaayza** as you like

zayyaf زيّف *vt* (**tazyiif**) to counterfeit, forge (e.g. money)

zayyan زيّن *vt* **1** (**ziyyeen, tazyiin**) to decorate; to put on makeup **2** (**ziyyeen**) to cut hair; to shave s.o.'s head (men)

zayyat زيّت *vt* (**ziyyeet, tazyiit**) (*mech*) to oil, to lubricate

zeebag زيبق *n* mercury, quicksilver

zeen زين *interj* good, all right, okay

zeet زيت *n* (*pl* **ziyuut**) oil; **zeet bizra, zeet fahad** cotton seed oil;

zeet fuul groundnut oil; **zeet dura** corn oil, maize oil; **zeet simsim** sesame oil; **zeet zeetuun** olive oil
zeeti زيتي *adj* olive-green
zeetuun زيتون *coll n* olive(s)
ziʿil زعل *vi* (**a, zaʿla**) to be(come) angry
zibaala زبالة *n* **1** dung, manure **2** fermented mixture of dung, clay and water, used for plastering walls and roofs as a protection from rain
zibb زب *n* (*pl* **zubuub, zababa**) (*vulgar*) penis
zibda زبدة *n* butter
zifit زفت *n* pitch, tar
zihij زهج *vi* (**a, zahaj**) (**min**) to be fed up, to get bored
ziifa زيفة *n* cold wind
ziina زينة *n* decoration, ornament
ziir زير *n* (*pl* **azyaar**) large earthenware jar for storing water
ziiro زيرو *num* zero
zikir زكر *n* (*pl* **azkaar**) Sufi ritual based on the repeated mention of the name and epithets of God
zikra زكرى *n* (*pl* **zikrayaat**) reminiscence, remembrance; memorial ceremony
zikrayaat زكريات *n pl* memoirs
zilzaal زلزال *n* (*pl* **zalaazil**) earthquake
zimma زمّة *n* (*pl* **zimam**) conscience, integrity, sense of decency; **be-zimmat-ak** honestly?; is that really so?; **as-sakraan fi zimmat al-waaʿi** the sober person has to take responsibility for the drunkard
zina زنا *n* adultery; **wad zina** illegitimate son; **bitt zina** illegitimate daughter
zinaad زناد *n* (*pl* **-aat**) **1** trigger **2** cigarette lighter
zindiyya زندية *adv* by force; **be-z-zindiyya** by force
zink زنك *n* zinc, galvanized iron
zinzaana زنزانة *n* prison cell
ziraaʿa زراعة *n* **1** agriculture; cultivation **2** transplantation (of body organs)
ziraaʿi زراعي *adj* agricultural
ziraara زرارة *n* (*pl* **zaraayir**) button (clothes)
zirr زر *n* (*pl* **azraar**) (*mech*) button
zirriiʿa زرّيعة *n* sprouted seeds, shoots
ziyaada زيادة *n* extra, more; **ziyaada ʿala zaalik** moreover
ziyaara زيارة *n* visit
zoog زوق *n* taste
zooj زوج *n* (*pl* **azwaaj**) husband
zooja زوجة *n* wife
zool زول *n* (*no pl*) person, fellow, guy; **ma fii zool** there's nobody
zoola زولة *n* (*no pl*) woman
zubaab زباب *coll n* flies; **az-zubaaba ar-ramliyya** sandfly; **zubaabat at-tisii tisii** tsetse fly
zugaag زقاق *n* (*pl* **-aat**) alley
zuhri زهري *n* syphilis
zuhriyya زهريّة *n* vase; flowerpot, plant pot
zukaam زكام *n* catarrh, common cold
zukma زكمة *n* catarrh, common cold
zulaali زلالي *n* oedema
zumaam زمام *n* (*pl* **-aat, zamaayim**) (*trad*) nose ring (women)
zumbaara زمبارة *n* (*pl* **zanaabiir**) flute, reed pipe
zumurrud زمرّد *n* emerald
zura زرة *n* sorghum; **zura shaami** corn, maize

zuraar زرار *n* **1** (*pl* **zaraayir**) button (clothes) **2** (*pl* **azraar**) (*mech*) button
zurrii'a زرّيعة *n* sprouts, shoots
zurriyya زرّيّة *n* descendants, offspring
zuwaada زوادة *n* provisions (when travelling)

ẓ – ظ

ẓaabiṭ ظابط *n* (*pl* **ẓubbaaṭ**) officer
ẓaahir ظاهر *adj* evident, clear, visible • *conj* apparently
ẓaalim ظالم (*pl* **-iin, ẓalama**) *adj* unjust • *n* wrongdoer, oppressor
ẓabaṭ ظبط *vt* (**u, ẓabiṭ**) **1** to fix, put sth. right **2** to catch (e.g. thieves)
ẓabbaṭ ظبّط *vt* (**taẓbiiṭ**) to put sth. right; to fix (firmly)
ẓabṭ ظبط *n* **be-ẓ-ẓabṭ** exactly
ẓabṭiyya ظبطيّة *n* police station
ẓagg ظق *n* droppings (of birds)
ẓahar ظهر *vi* (**a, ẓuhuur**) to appear, emerge, become visible; **yaẓhar** it seems
ẓahara ظهرة *n* laundry blue
ẓahhar ظهّر *vt* **1** (**ẓihheer, taẓhiir**) to make visible **2** (**ẓihheer**) to add laundry blue (to a white wash)
ẓahri ظهري *adj* blue
ẓalam ظلم *vt* (**u, ẓulum**) to wrong, deny justice to, oppress
ẓalaṭ ظلط *coll n* large pebbles • *n* asphalt; **shaari' ẓalaṭ** paved road • *vt* (**u, ẓaliṭ**) to graze, chafe the skin
ẓalṭa ظلطة *n* graze
ẓann ظن *n* (*pl* **ẓunuun**) thought; assumption **ẓann-um fii-ho jamiil** they have a good opinion about him
ẓanna ظنّ *vt* (**i, ẓann**) to think, assume; to suppose, believe; **aẓunn-o kida** it appears to be so
ẓaraafa ظرافة *n* pleasantness
ẓaraṭ ظرط *vi* (**u, ẓariṭ, ẓuraaṭ, ẓirreeṭ**) to fart
ẓarf ظرف *n* (*pl* **ẓuruuf**) circumstance
ẓarif ظرف *n* (*pl* **ẓuruuf**) **1** envelope **2** magazine of a gun
ẓariif ظريف *adj* (*pl* **-iin, ẓuraaf, ẓurafa**) nice, pleasant
ẓarṭa ظرطة *n* (*pl* **-aat, ẓuraaṭ**) a fart
ẓuhuur ظهور *n* appearance; **'iid aẓ-ẓuhuur** Epiphany
ẓulum ظلم *n* (*pl* **maẓaalim**) injustice
ẓuruuf ظروف *n pl* (*sg* **ẓarf**) circumstances

English—Sudanese Arabic

A - a

abandon khalla خلّى (-i, khilleey); saab ساب (i, sayabaan)
abattoir salakhaana سلخانة
abbreviation ikhtiṣaar إختصار (*pl* -aat)
abdomen baṭun بطن (*pl* buṭuun)
abduct khaṭaf خطف (i, khaṭif)
ability gudra قدرة ; magdara/magdira مقدرة ; gaabiliyya قابليّة
able gaadir قادر ; **to be able** gidir قدر (a, gudra)
ablution waḍu وضو ; **to perform the ritual ablution** itwaḍḍa اتوضّى (-a, wiḍḍeey, waḍu)
abolish lagha لغى (-i, laghi, laghayaan); **to be abolished** itlagha اتلغى (-i, laghiya)
abort (**a pregnancy**) *vi* daafag دافق (dufaag); asgaṭ أسقط (yusgiṭ, isgaaṭ); ajhaḍ اجهض (i, ijhaaḍ); **the foetus aborted** aj-janiin sagaṭ • *vt* saggaṭ سقّط (siggeeṭ); ajhaḍ اجهض (i, ijhaaḍ)
abortion ijhaaḍ اجهاض (*pl* -aat); **to cause an abortion** saggaṭ سقّط (siggeeṭ); ajhaḍ اجهض (i, ijhaaḍ)
about fi في ; ʿan عن ; (**approximately**) ḥawaali حوالي ; be-t-taqriib; taqriiban تقريبا ; **about an hour** yaji s-saaʿa; **to be about to** garrab قرّب (girreeb, tagriib)
above foog فوق
abroad (fi) al-khaarij; **living abroad** mughtarib مغترب ; **to go abroad to work** ightarab اغترب (ightiraab)
abscess(es) khurraaj خرّاج
absence ghiyaab غياب
absent ghaayib غايب ; **to be absent** ghaab غاب (i, ghiyaab)
absent-minded sarḥaan سرحان ; saariḥ سارح ; **to be absent-minded** sarah سرح (a, sarahaan)
absolutely nihaaʾi نهائي ; tabb تب ; **absolutely not** iṭlaaqan إطلاقا ; ʿala l-iṭlaaq
absolution ḥill حل
absolve (**from/of**) ḥalla (min) حلّ (i, ḥall); **he is absolved from** hu fi ḥill min
absorb maṣṣa مصّ (u, maṣṣ); shirib شرب (a, sharaab)
abundance katara كترة
abundant mutwaffir متوفّر ; raagid راقد ; **to be abundant** itwaffar اتوفّر (wafra)
abuse asaa le- اسا (yusii, isaa'a); (**verbally**) nabbaz نبّز (nibbeez, nabaz); shatam شتم (u, shatiima)
abyss haawya هاوية
acacia **scented-pod acacia** sunuṭ سنط ; (**a gum-bearing species**) hashaab هشاب ; (**species of which the wood is used for fumigation**) ṭaliḥ طلح ; (**other species**) laʿuut لعوت ; labakh لبخ
accelerate lakaʿ لكع (a, lakiʿ); daas banziin
accent lahja لهجة
accept gibil (be-) قبل (a, gubuul); riḍa (be-) رضى (-a, riḍa)
acceptable magbuul مقبول ; murḍi مرضي

acceptance gubuul قبول
access madkhal مدخل (*pl* madaakhil)
accident ḥaadis حادس (*pl* ḥawaadis); ḥaadsa حادسة (*pl* ḥawaadis)
accidentally ṣudfa صدفة; be-ṣudfa
accommodation sakan سكّن; **to provide accommodation for** sakkan سكّن (sakan, iskaan)
accompany raafag رافق (mu-raafaga); **to accompany s.o. to a place** waṣṣal وصّل (wiṣṣeel)
accomplice shariik fi j-jariima
accomplish anjaz أنجز (i, injaaz)
accomplishment injaaz إنجاز (*pl* -aat)
according (**to**) ḥasab (le-) حسب
account ḥisaab حساب (*pl* -aat); **to settle an account with** ḥaasab حاسب (muḥaasaba)
accountability muḥaasaba محاسبة
accountancy muḥaasaba محاسبة
accountant (*m*) muḥaasib محاسب; (*f*) muḥaasiba محاسبة
accumulate itraakam اتراكم (taraakum)
accuracy diqqa دقّة
accurate daqiiq دقيق
accurately be-diqqa
accusation ittihaam إتّهام (*pl* -aat); tuhma تهمة (*pl* tuham)
accuse ittaham (be-) اتّهم (itti-haam, tuhma)
accustom s.o. to ʿawwad ʿala عوّد (taʿwiid); wallaf ʿala/be- اتولّف (willeef); **to be**(**come**) **accus-tomed** (**to**) itʿawwad (ʿala) اتعوّد (taʿwiid); itwallaf (ʿala/be-) اتولّف (willeef)
ache *n* wajʿa وجعة (*pl* -aat, awjaaʿ) • *v* ḥarag حرق (i, ḥarig); wajaʿ وجع (yuujiʿ/yuujaʿ, wajiʿ, wajʿa)
achieve anjaz أنجز (i, injaaz)
achievement injaaz إنجاز (*pl* -aat)
acidity ḥumuuḍa حموضة
acknowledge iʿtaraf be- إعترف (iʿtiraaf); garra be- قرّ (i, igraar)
acknowledgment iʿtiraaf إعتراف (*pl* -aat); igraar إقرار (*pl* -aat)
acne ḥabb ash-shabaab
acquainted **to become acquainted with** itʿarraf be-/ʿala اتعرف (taʿarruf)
acquaintance maʿrifa معرفة (*pl* maʿaarif)
acquire itḥaṣṣal ʿala اتحصّل (ḥiṣṣeel); iktasab اكتسب (iktisaab)
acquit barra' برّأ (-i, tabri'a)
act (**behave**) itṣarraf اتصرّف (taṣarruf); (**a role**) massal مسّل (tamsiil)
acting (**as in theatre**) tamsiil تمسيل; **acting director** mudiir(a) be-n-niyaaba
action fiʿil فعل (*pl* fiʿaal); suwaa سواة
activate nashshaṭ نشّط (tanshiiṭ)
active nashiiṭ نشيط (*pl* -iin, nushaaṭ)
activity nashaaṭ نشاط (*pl* -aat, anshiṭa); (**such as a workshop, seminar**) manshaṭ منشط (*pl* manaashiṭ)
actor mumassil ممسّل
actress mumassila ممسّلة
actual ḥagiigi حقيقي
actually al-ḥagiiga; fi-l-ḥagiiga
adaptor adabtar أدبتر (*pl* -aat)
add zaad زاد (i, ziyaada); aḍaaf اضاف (yuḍiif, iḍaafaa); **to add up** jamaʿ جمع (a, jamiʿ)
addict *n* mudmin مدمن
addicted mudmin مدمن; **to be**(**come**) **addicted** (**to**) adman (ʿala) أدمن (i, idmaan)

addiction idmaan ادمان
addition iḍaafa إضافة ; **(in arithmetic)** jamiᶜ جمع ; **in addition to** be-l-iḍaafa le-; **in addition to this** ᶜala l-ᶜalee-h
address ᶜunwaan عنوان (*pl* ᶜanaawiin); **public address** khiṭaab خطاب (*pl* -aat)
adjective ṣifa صفة
adjourn ajjal أجل (ta'jiil); akhkhar أخّر (ya'akhkhir, ta'khiir); **to be adjourned** it'ajjal اتأجّل (ta'jiil); it'akhkhar اتأخّر (ta'khiir)
adjournment ta'jiil تأجيل (*pl* -aat)
adjust ᶜadal عدل (i, ᶜadil); ᶜaddal عدّل (taᶜdiil); **to be adjusted** itᶜaddal اتعدّل (taᶜdiil)
adjustment taᶜdiil تعديل (*pl* -aat)
administer adaar أدار (yudiir, idaara)
administration idaara إدارة
admiration iᶜjaab اعجاب
admit iᶜtaraf (be-) إعترف (iᶜtiraaf); garra (be-) قرّ (i, igraar)
adolescent (*m*) muraahig مراهقة ; (*f*) muraahiga مراهقة
adopt itbanna اتبنّى (-a, tabanni)
adult baaligh بالغ
adulterer zaani زاني (*pl* zunaa)
adultery zina زنا ; **to commit adultery** zana زنى (-i, zina)
advance *v* **(go ahead)** itgaddam اتقدّم (tagaddum); **(bring forward, e.g. a date)** gaddam قدّم (giddeem); **in advance** mugaddam مقدّم
advantage miiza ميزة
advantageous mufiid مفيد ; naafiᶜ نافع
Advent zaman al-majii'
advertise ᶜamal iᶜlaan
advertisement iᶜlaan إعلان (*pl* -aat)
advice naṣiiḥa نصيحة (*pl* naṣaayiḥ); **to ask for advice** shaawar شاور (mushaawara); istashaar استشار (istishaara)
advocacy munaaṣara مناصرة
advocate *n* muḥaami محامي (*pl* -yyiin)
aerial ariyal أريل (*pl* araayil)
affair amr أمر (*pl* umuur); sha'an شان (*pl* shu'uun); mas'ala مسألة (*pl* masaa'il)
affect assar ᶜala/fi أسّر (ya'assir, ta'siir); **to be affected (by)** it'assar (be-) اتأسّر (ta'assur)
affectation falhama فلهمة
affection ḥanaan حنان ; maḥabba محبّة
afraid khawwaaf خوّاف ; khaayif خايف ; **to be afraid (of)** khaaf (min) خاف (a, khoof); itkhawwaf (min) اتخوّف (khoof)
Africa ifriiqiya إفريقيا ; **South Africa** ifriiqiya aj-januubiyya
African *adj/n* afriiqi افريقي (*pl* -yyiin)
after *conj* baᶜad ma • *prep* baᶜad بعد ; ᶜugub عقب
afterbirth tabiiᶜa تبيعة ; khulaaṣa خلاصة ; mashiima مشيمة
afternoon baᶜd aḍ-ḍuhur; masa/misa مسا ; **late afternoon** ᶜaṣur عصر ; ᶜaṣriyya عصريّة ; **good afternoon** masaa al-kheer, masaa an-nuur; **to spend the afternoon** gayyal قيّل (giyyeel, magiil)
afterwards baᶜdeen بعدين ; fi-ma baᶜad
again taani تاني ; marra taani, marra taanya; taani marra
against ḍidd ضد ; **against his will** ghaṣban ᶜan-o/ᶜan ᶜeen-o; kuraaᶜ-o

fi ragabt-o; **to be against s.o.** daaḍḍa داضّ (-i, mudaaḍḍa)

agate soomiit سوميت

age ʿumur عمر (*pl* aʿmaar); **what's your age?** ʿumr-ak kam?; **old age** kubur كبر ; **to reach old age** ʿammar عمّر (taʿmiir)

agency wikaala وكالة ; government agency maṣlaḥa مصلحة (*pl* maṣaaliḥ)

agenda (**of a meeting**) ajinda أجندة

agent wakiil وكيل (*pl* wukala)

aggregate (**in building**) kharasaana خرسانة

aggression ʿadaawa عداة و

aggressive ʿudwaani عدواني (*pl* -yyiin); sharraani شرّاني (*pl* -yyiin)

ago gabli قبلى ; gubbaal قبّال ; **we came two months ago** jiina gabli shahreen; **ages ago** min zamaan; min zaman baʿiid; **some time ago** min mudda

agree (**about**) waafag (ʿala) وافق (muwaafaga); (**on**) ittafag (ʿala) اتّفق (ittifaag)

agreement ittifaag إتّفاق (*pl* -aat); ittifaagiyya إتّفاقيّة ; **to reach an agreement** (**on**) ittafag (ʿala) اتّفق (ittifaag); itʿaahad (ʿala) اتعاهد (muʿaahada, taʿaahud)

agricultural ziraaʿi زراعي

agriculture ziraaʿa زراعة

aground **to run aground** (**of ships**) inshaḥaṭ انشحط (shaḥṭa, inshiḥaaṭ); itshaḥaṭ اتشحط (shaḥṭa)

ahead giddaam قدّام ; guddaam قدّام ; **to get ahead of** itgaddam ʿala اتقدّم (tagaddum)

aid *n* musaaʿada مساعدة ; ʿoon عون ; (**relief**) ighaasa إغاسة ; **first aid** al-isʿaaf; isʿaafaat awwaliyya

aide mutʿaawin متعاون

aide-de-camp yaawur ياور (*pl* yaawraat)

aim *n* gaṣid قصد (*pl* agṣaad); hadaf هدف (*pl* ahdaaf) • *v* gaṣad قصد (u, gaṣid); **to aim** (**at**) (**e.g. in shooting**) nashshan (ʿala) نشّن (nishsheen, tanshiin)

air hawa هوا ; **air pump** munfaakh منفاخ (*pl* manaafiikh)

air conditioner mukayyif مكيّف (*pl* -aat); takyiif تكييف (*pl* -aat)

air cooler mukayyif مكيّف (*pl* -aat)

aircraft ṭayyaara طيّارة

airline ṭayaraan طيران ; **airlines** khuṭuuṭ jawwiyya

airmail bariid jawwi

airplane ṭayyaara طيّارة

airport maṭaar مطار (*pl* -aat)

aisle (**in plane**) mamarr ممر (*pl* -aat)

ajar muttarkash متّركش ; muttaaka متاكى ; **to leave ajar** tarkash تركش (tirkeesh, tarkasha); taaka تاكى (-i, mutaakaa)

alarm *n* taḥziir تحزير ; **alarm clock** munabbih منبّه (*pl* -aat)

albino person (*m*) wadd al-ḥuur; (*f*) bitt al-ḥuur

alcohol (**drink**) kuḥuul كحول ; (**chemical**) al-kuḥuul

alert *v* nabbah نبّه (tanbiih)

alfalfa barsiim برسيم

algebra aj-jabr

alive ḥayy حي (*pl* aḥyaa); ʿaayish عايش ; **to be alive** ʿaash عاش (i, ʿeesh, ʿeesha); **to keep alive** ʿayyash عيّش (iʿaasha)

all kull كل ; kullo كلّو ; jamiiʿ جميع ; **all the people** kullo

n-naas; jumlat an-naas; kaaffat an-naas; **all the time** ṭawwaali طوّالى; **all right** ṭayyib طيّب; samiḥ سمح
allege gaal inn-/inno; iddaʿa ادّعى (-i, iddiʿa)
allergy ḥasaasiyya حساسيّة
alley maḍabb مضبّ (*pl* -aat); zugaag زقاق (*pl* -aat); **a blind alley** shaariʿ masduud
alliance ḥilf حلف (*pl* aḥlaaf); taḥaaluf تحالف
allot khaṣṣaṣ خصّص (takhṣiiṣ); khaṣṣa خصّ (u, khaṣṣa)
allow samaḥ le- سمح (a, samaaḥ); azanle- أزن (ya'zin, izin)
allowance badal بدل (*pl* badalaat); **travel allowance** badal safariyya
ally ḥaliif حليف (*pl* ḥulafa)
alms ṣadaga صدقة; ḥasana حسنة; zakaat زكاة (*pl* zakawaat); iḥsaan إحسان; **to give alms (to)** adda zakaat (le-); itṣaddag (ʿala) اتصدّق (taṣaddug); **to give as alms** zakka زكّى (-i, zakaat)
almsgiving karaama كرامة
alone baraa- برا.; waḥiid وحيد; **he came alone** ja baraa-ho
already gibeel قبيل; gabli kida; gabul da; gabil da
also barḍo برضو; kamaan كمان
alternative *adj* badiil بديل • *n* badiil بديل (*pl* badaayil)
although maʿa inn-/inno; raghmi inn-/inno; maʿa kawn
altitude irtifaaʿ إرتفاع
alum shabb شب
always daayman دايما; ṭawwaali طوّالى
amateur haawi هاوي (*pl* huwaa)
amazed to be amazed itʿajjab اتعجّب (ʿijjeeb, ʿajab); istaghrab استغرب (istighraab); indahash اندهش (dahsha, indihaash)
amazement dahsha دهشة; ʿajab عجب
ambassador safiir سفير (*pl* sufara)
amber kahramaan كهرمان
ambergris ʿambar عمبر
ambition ṭumuuḥ طموح (*pl* -aat)
ambulance ʿarabiyyat isʿaaf
ambush kamiin كمين (*pl* kamaay-in); gaṭiʿ ad-darib; ḥabs ad-darib; rabṭ ad-darib
America amriika أمريكا
American *adj/n* amriiki امريكي (*pl* amriikaan); amrikaani امريكاني (*pl* amriikaan)
amiable bashuush بشوش; ẓariif ظريف (*pl* -iin, ẓuraaf, ẓurafa); laṭiif لطيف (*pl* -iin, luṭaaf)
ammonia nashaadir نشادر
ammunition zakhiira زخيرة (zakhaayir); jabakhaana جبخانة
amnesty ʿafu عفو
among fi في; been بين; beenaat بينات
amount gadur قدر; ʿadad عدد (*pl* aʿdaad); **amount of money** mablagh مبلغ (*pl* mabaaligh)
amputate batar بتر (u, batir); **to be amputated** itbatar اتبتر (batra)
amputation batir بتر
amulet ḥijaab حجاب (*pl* ḥijbaat, aḥjiba); sibir سبر (*pl* asbaar, subuur)
amuse salla سلّى (-i, tasliya); **(o.s.)** itsalla اتسلّى (-a, tasliya)
amusing musalli مسلّي
amusement tasliya تسلية; **amusement park** malaahi ملاهي
anaesthetic banij بنج; mukhaddir مخدّر (*pl* -aat); **general anaesthetic**

banij kaamil; **local anaesthetic** banij mawḍiʿi
anaesthetist akhiṣṣaa'i takhdiir
anaesthetize khaddar خدّر (takhdiir); **to be anaesthetized** itkhaddar اتخدّر (khiddeer)
analyse ḥallal حلّل (taḥliil)
analysis taḥliil تحليل (*pl* taḥaaliil)
analyst muḥallil محلّل
anatomy (**study**) tashriiḥ تشريح
ancestors ajdaad أجداد
anchor *n* hilib هلب (*no pl*); shankal شنكل (*pl* shanaakil) • *v* shankal شنكل (shinkeel, shankala)
anchorage marsa مرساة (*pl* maraasi); moorada موردة (*pl* mawaarid); mushraʿ مشرع (*pl* -aat, mashaariʿ)
ancient gadiim قديم (*pl* gudaam)
and wa و ; u و
angel malaak ملاك (*pl* malaayka)
anger *n* zaʿal زعل ; ghaḍab غضب • *v* zaʿʿal زعّل (ziʿʿeel, zaʿal); ghaaẓ غاظ (i, ighaaẓa, gheeẓ); narfaz نرفز (narfaza); **to be angered** (**by**) itghaaẓ (min) اتغاظ (gheeẓ); itnarfaz (min) اتنرفز (narfaza)
angle zaawya زاوية (*pl* zawaaya)
angry zaʿlaan زعلان ; ghaḍbaan غضبان ; **to become angry** ziʿil زعل (a, zaʿla); ghiḍib غضب (a, ghaḍab); **to be**(**come**) **very angry** haaj هاج (i, hayajaan)
animal ḥayawaan حيوان (*pl* -aat); **wild animal** ḥayawaan barri; ḥayawaan khala; **domestic animal** bahiima بهيمة (*pl* bahaayim)
aniseed yansuun ينسون
ankle ʿarguub عرقوب (*pl* ʿaraagiib); ʿaḍum ash-sheeṭaan
anklet ḥijil حجل (*pl* ḥijuul)
annexe *n* mulḥag ملحق (*pl* malaaḥig)
annihilation ibaada إبادة ; iʿdaam إعدام (*pl* -aat)
announce aʿlan ʿan أعلن (yuʿlin, iʿlaan)
announcement iʿlaan إعلان (*pl* -aat); ikhbaar إخبار (*pl* -aat)
announcer (**radio, television**) (*m*) muziiʿ مزيع ; (*f*) muziiʿa مزيعة
annoy zahhaj زهّج (zihheej, tazhiij); azʿaj أزعج (i, izʿaaj); ḍaayag ضايق (muḍaayaga); **to be annoyed** inzaʿaj انزعج (inziʿaaj); iḍḍaayag (min) اضّايق (muḍaayaga)
annoyance izʿaaj إزعاج ; muḍaayaga مضايقة
annoying muzʿij مزعج ; mumill ممل
annual sanawi سنوي
annually sanawiyyan سنويّا
another (*m*) aakhar آخر (*f*) ukhra; taani تاني ; gheer غير ; khilaaf خلاف ; **another one** waaḥid taani; waaḥid gheer-o/khilaaf-o
answer *n* ijaaba إجابة ; jawwaab جوّاب (*pl* -aat); radd رد (*pl* ruduud) • *v* jaawab ʿala جاوب (ijaaba); radda (ʿala) ردّ (u, radd)
ant(**s**) namil نمل (*unit n* namla); **large red species** namil as-sukkar; **very large species** namil al-ʿeesh; **small species** ḍarr ضر ; **small biting species** shaḥmuuṭa شحموطة ; **in winged stage** namil abu r-riish; **white ants** arḍa أرضة
anthem nashiid نشيد (*pl* anaashiid); **the national anthem** an-nashiid al-waṭani

anthrax aj-jamra al-khabiisa; al-ḥumma al-faḥmiyya
antibiotic muḍaadd ḥayawi
antidote tiryaaq ترياق (*pl* -aat)
antimony kuḥul كحل
antique *n* antiika انتيكة (*pl* anaatiik)
antiquities aasaar آسار
anus fatḥat ash-sharaj
anvil sindaala سندالة
anxiety ḍiig ضيق; galag قلق
anxious (**about**) galgaan (ʿala) قلقان; shafgaan (ʿala) شفقان; mahmuum (be-) مهموم
any ayyi أي; **in any case** fi ayyi ḥaal; fi ayyi ḥaala
anybody ayyi waaḥid
anyhow ʿala kulli ḥaal; fi kull al-aḥwaal; ghaayto غايتو
anything ayyi ḥaaja; ayyi shi; **anything else** ḥaaja taani; ḥaaja taanya
anyway ʿala kulli ḥaal; fi kull al-aḥwaal; ghaayto غايتو
apart munfaṣil منفصل; **apart from** (**except**) gheer غير
apartment shagga شقّة (*pl* shugag)
apnoea katmat nafas
apologize iʿtazar إعتزر (iʿtizaar)
apology iʿtizaar إعتزار (*pl* -aat)
apostle rasuul رسول (*pl* rusul)
apparently baayin باين; ẓaahir ظاهر
appeal *n* isti'naaf إستئناف • *v* ista'naf استأنف (isti'naaf); (**against a sentence**) ṭaʿanfi l-ḥukum
appear ṭalaʿ طلع (a, ṭuluuʿ); ẓahar ظهر (a, ẓuhuur); **it appears to be so** aẓunn-o kida
appearance ẓuhuur ظهور; **outward appearance** shakil شكل (*pl* ashkaal); khilga خلقة
appendicitis iltihaab zaayda/az-zaayda
appendix (*anat*) zaayda زايدة
appetite shahiyya شهيّة; nafis (fi) نفس; **having a voracious appetite** buṭeyni بطيني; **I have no appetite** nafs-i masduuda
appetizer mazza مزّة (*pl* mizzaz); (**nuts, popcorn, etc.**) mukassaraat مكسّرات
applaud ṣaffag صفّق (ṣiffeeg, ṣafga, taṣfiig)
applause ṣafga صفقة
apple(s) tuffaaḥ تفّاح; **bitter apple** ḥanḍal حنضل; **Sodom apple** ʿushar عشر
apply (**e.g. cream, paint**) labakh لبخ (a, labikh); (**implement**) ṭabbag طبّق (taṭbiig); **to apply for** gaddam le- قدّم (tagdiim)
appoint ʿayyan عيّن (taʿyiin); **to be appointed** itʿayyan اتعيّن (taʿyiin)
appointment mawʿid موعد (*pl* mawaaʿiid); miiʿaad ميعاد (*pl* mawaaʿiid); (**to a job**) taʿyiin تعيين
appreciate qaddar قدّر (taqdiir)
approach *v* garrab (min/le-) قرّب (girreeb, tagriib) • *n* ṭariiga طريقة (*pl* ṭurug)
appropriate *adj* munaasib مناسب
approval gubuul قبول; muwaafaga موافقة; (**endorsement**) iʿtimaad إعتماد (*pl* -aat)
approve waafag (ʿala) وافق (muwaafaga); ṣaadag (ʿala) صادق (muṣaadaga); (**endorse**) iʿtamad إعتمد (iʿtimaad); ṣaddag صدّق (taṣdiig); **to be approved** itṣaddag اتصدّق (taṣdiig)
approximately ḥawaali حوالي; taqriiban تقريبا; be-t-taqriib

apricot(s) mishmish مشمش
April shahri arbaʿa; abriil أبريل
apron maryala مريلة (*pl* -aat, maraayil)
aqueduct gantara قنطرة (*pl* ganaaṭir)
Arabic ʿarabi عربي ; **spoken Arabic** ad-daariji; (al-lugha) ad-daarijiyya; (al-lugha) al-ʿaammiyya; **literary Arabic** al-lugha al-ʿarabiyya al-fuṣḥa
Arab *adj/n* ʿarabi عربي (*pl* ʿarab)
arak ʿaragi عرقي
arbitrariness taḥakkumiyya تحكّميّة ; istibdaad استبداد
arbitrary taḥakkumi تحكّمي ; mustabidd مستبد
arbitration juudiyya جوديّة
arcade baranda برندة
arch goos قوس (*pl* agwaas)
archbishop ra'iis al-asaaqifa
architect muhandis mabaani/miʿmaari
area manṭiga منطقة (*pl* manaaṭig); **open area** saaḥa ساحة ; fasaḥa فسحة ; meedaan/miidaan ميدان (*pl* mayaadiin)
argue jaadal (maʿa) جادل (jidaal); itjaadal (maʿa) اتجادل (jadal, mujaadala)
arid jaaff جاف
arithmetic ḥisaab حساب (*pl* -aat)
arm *n* ḍuraaʿ ضراع (*pl* -aat)
arm *v* sallaḥ سلّح (tasliiḥ)
armchair kursi juluus
armour daraga درقة (*pl* -aat, dirag); diriʿ درع
armpit abaaṭ أباط (*pl* -aat)
army jeesh جيش (*pl* jiyuush)
around **he is around** hu gariib; hu ma baʿiid; hu fii, gaaʿid
arouse ḥarrak حرّك (ḥirreek, taḥriik); (**desire**) hayyaj هيّج (hiyyeej, tahyiij); **to be(come) sexually aroused** haaj هاج (i, hayajaan)
arrange naẓẓam نظّم (niẓẓeem, tanẓiim); (**to put in order**) rattab رتّب (ritteeb, tartiib); ḍaayar ضاير (muḍaayara); waḍḍab وضّب (wiḍḍeeb, tawḍiib); (**objects**) raṣṣa رصّ (u, raṣṣ); **to be arranged** itnaẓẓam اننظم (niẓẓeem, tanẓiim); itrattab اترتّب (ritteeb, tartiib); iḍḍaayar إضّاير (muḍaayara); itwaḍḍab اتوضّب (wiḍḍeeb, tawḍiib); itraṣṣa اترصّ (raṣṣa)
arrangement tanẓiim تنظيم (*pl* -aat); (**order**) tartiib ترتيب (*pl* -aat); tawḍiib توضيب ; (**agreement**) ittifaag إتّفاق (*pl* -aat)
arrears mut'akhkhiraat متأخّرات
arrest *n* gabiḍ قبض ; arrest warrant amr gabiḍ • v masak مسك (i, masik, maska, masakaan); gabaḍ (ʿala) قبض (u, gabiḍ); **to be arrested** itmasak اتمسك (maska); itgabaḍ اتقبض (gabiḍ)
arrival wuṣuul وصول (*no pl*)
arrive waṣal (le-) وصل (yaṣal/yuuṣal, wuṣuul)
arrogance takabbur تكبّر ; ghuruur غرور ; ghaṭrasa غطرسة
arrogant mutkabbir متكبّر ; maghruur مغرور ; mutghaṭris متغطرس ; to be(come) arrogant itkabbar اتكبّر (takabbur); itghaṭras إتغطرس (ghaṭrasa)
arrow saham سهم (*pl* sihaam)
art fann فن (*pl* funuun); **faculty of arts** kulliyyat al-aadaab
arthritis ruṭuuba رطوبة ; **rheumatoid arthritis** uumaatizim روماتزم

article (**in journal**) maqaala مقالة ; (**legal**) band بند (*pl* bunuud)
artificial muṣṭanaᶜ مصطنع
artisan ṣinaaᶜi صناعي (*pl* ṣanaayᶜiyya); ḥirafi حرفي (*pl* -yyiin)
artist fannaan فنّان
artistic fanni فنّي
as *prep* (**like**) zayy زي ; mitil متل ; misl مسل ; (**in his capacity of**) be-ṣifat-o • *conj* (**because**) ᶜashaan عشان ; la'ann- لأن ; la'anno لأنو ; (**while**) lamman لمّن ; lamma لما ; wakit ma
ascend ṭalaᶜ طلع (a, ṭuluuᶜ)
Ascension ᶜiid aṣ-ṣuᶜuud
ash ramaad رماد (*pl* armida); habbuud هبّود
ashamed khajlaan خجلان ; **to be(come) ashamed** khijil خجل (a, khajal, khajla)
ashtray ṭaffaaya طفّاية
Asia aasiya آسيا
Asian *adj/n* aasiyawi آسيوي (*pl* -yyiin)
aside ᶜala jamb; **to set/put aside** jannab جنّب (jinneeb); **to move aside** zaḥḥa زحّ (i, zaḥḥ, zaḥaḥaan)
ask sa'al (min/ᶜan) سأل (a, su'aal); **to ask for** ṭalab طلب (u, ṭalab); **to ask for an explanation** istawḍaḥ استوضح (istiiḍaaḥ); **to be asked** (**question**) itsa'al اتسأل (su'aal)
asphalt ẓalaṭ ظلط ; **to cover with asphalt** saflat سفلت (saflata)
assault *n* hujuum هجوم (*pl* -aat); iᶜtidaa اعتدا (*pl* iᶜtida'aat) • *v* hajam ᶜala هجم (i, hajma); haajam هاجم (hujuum, muhaajama); iᶜtada ᶜala اعتدى (-i, iᶜtidaa)
assemble *vi* ijtamaᶜ اجتمع (ijtimaaᶜ) • *vt* (**gather**) jamaᶜ جمع (a, jamiᶜ); jammaᶜ جمّع (jimmeeᶜ, tajmiiᶜ); (**put together**) rakkab ركّب (rikkeeb, tarkiib); jammaᶜ جمّع (tajmiiᶜ); **to be assembled** itjamaᶜ اتجمع (jamᶜa); itjammaᶜ اتجمّع (jimmeeᶜ, jamᶜa); itrakkab اتكّب (tarkiib); itjammaᶜ اتجمّع (tajmiiᶜ)
assembly (**council**) majlis مجلس (*pl* majaalis); **the national assembly** al-majlis al-waṭani; (**meeting**) ijtimaaᶜ إجتماع (*pl* -aat)
assess qaddar قدّر (taqdiir); qayyam قيّم (taqyiim)
assessment taqyiim تقييم (*pl* -aat); taqdiir تقدير (*pl* -aat)
assign (**allot**) khaṣṣaṣ خصّص (takhṣiiṣ); khaṣṣa خصّ (u, khaṣṣa); (**appoint**) ᶜayyan عيّن (taᶜyiin)
assignment muhimma مهمة
assist saaᶜad (fi) ساعد (musaaᶜada); ᶜaawan عاون (muᶜaawana)
assistance musaaᶜada مساعدة
assistant musaaᶜid مساعد ; mutᶜaawin متعاون
association ittiḥaad إتّحاد (*pl* -aat); raabiṭa رابطة (*pl* rawaabiṭ); jamᶜiyya جمعيّة ; (**cooperative**) mujammaᶜ مجمّع (*pl* -aat); **trade association** mujammaᶜ tujaari
assume ẓanna ظنّ (u, ẓann, ẓunuun); iftaraḍ اتفرض (iftiraaḍ)
assumption ẓann ظن (*pl* ẓunuun); iftiraaḍ افتراض (*pl* -aat)
assure akkad le- اكّد (ya'akkid, ta'kiid)
asthma azma أزمة
astonished **to be astonished** itᶜajjab اتعجّب (ᶜijjeeb, ᶜajab);

istaghrab استغرب (istighraab); indahash اندهش (dahsha, indihaash)
astonishment taᶜajjub تعجّب
astray ḍahbaan ضهبان ; taayih تايه ; **to go astray** raaḥ راح (u, rooḥa, rawaḥaan); widir ودر (yawaddir, wadaar); waddar ودّر (widdeer, wadaar); ḍaaᶜ ضاع (i, ḍeeᶜa); ḍihib ضهب (a, ḍahab, ḍahabaan); ṭashsha طشّ (i, ṭashsh, ṭashsha)
astronomy ᶜilim al-falak
asylum lujuu لجو ; **to seek asylum** laja لجا (-a, lujuu)
at (**place**) fi في ; ᶜind عند ; (**time**) fi في
atmosphere (*also fig*) jaw جو (*pl* ajwaa)
atomizer bakhkhaakh بخّاخ (*pl* -aat); bakhkhaakha بخّاخة
atone kaffar كفّر (takfiir, kaffaara)
atonement takfiir تكفير ; kaffaara كفّارة
attach (**tie**) rabaṭ ربط (u, rabiṭ); (**include**) ḍamma (le-/ila) ضمّ (u, ḍamm); **to be firmly attached** (**to**) itmassak (be-) اتمسّك (tamassuk)
attachment (**supplement**) mulḥag ملحق (*pl* malaaḥig)
attack *n* hujuum هجوم (*pl* -aat) • *v* hajam ᶜala هجم (i, hujuum, hajma); haajam هاجم (hujuum, muhaajama)
attempt *v* ḥaawal حاول (muḥaawala)
attend ḥaḍar حضر (a, ḥuḍuur)
attendance ḥuḍuur حضور
attention intibaah إنتباه ; **to pay attention** intabah انتبه (intibaah); **to attract attention** lafat an-naẓar; **to stand at attention** tammam تمّم (tamaam)
attorney naayib نايب (*pl* nuwwaab); naa'ib نائب (*pl* nuwwaab); **the attorney general** an-naayib al-ᶜaamm; an-naa'ib al-ᶜaamm; **public attorney** (*m*) wakiil niyaaba; (*f*) wakiilat niyaaba
attract jazab جزب (i, jazib); **to be attracted** itjazab اتجزب (jazba) **to attract attention** lafat an-naẓar
attraction jaazibiyya جازبيّة
attractive jazzaab جزّاب ; jaazib جازب ; fattaan فتّان ; mughri مغري ; (**females**) faatna فاتنة
attribute *n* ṣifa صفة
aubergine aswad أسود ; baazinjaan بازنجان
auction dilaala دلالة ; mazaad مزاد (*pl* -aat)
auctioneer dallaal دلال
audience jamhuur جمهور (*pl* jamaahiir); mutfarrijiin متفرّجين
audit *n* muraajaᶜa مراجعة
August shahri tamaanya; aghosṭos أغسطس
aunt **paternal aunt** ᶜamma عمّة ; **maternal aunt** khaala خالة
Australia usturaaliyya أستراليا
Australian *adj/n* usturaali أسترالي (*pl* -yyiin)
Austria an-nimsa
Austrian *adj/n* nimsaawi نمساوي (*pl* -yyiin)
authenticate wassaq وسّق (tawsiiq)
author (*m*) mu'allif مؤلّف ; (*f*) mu'allifa مؤلّفة
authoritarian sulṭawi سلطوي (*pl* -yyiin); mutghaṭris متغطرس
authority sulṭa سلطة

authorization tafwiiḍ تفويض
authorize fawwaḍ فوّض (tafwiiḍ)
autumn al-khariif
available (**unoccupied**) faaḍi فاضي (*pl* -yyiin)
avarice fasaala فسالة
avaricious fasil فسل (*pl* fusala)
avenge intaqam (le-, min) انتقم (intiqaam); itsadda le- (min) اتسدّ (sadda, siddeey); **he avenged his brother's death on the murderer** intaqam/itsadda le-akhuu-ho min al-kaatil
average *adj* mutwassiṭ متوسّط; **Mr Average (the man in the street)** maḥammad aḥmad
aviation ṭayaraan طيران; **military aviation** aṭ-ṭayaraan al-ḥarbi
avoid itjannab اتجنّب (tajannub); (**place or person**) ḥawwad min حوّد (ḥiwweed, taḥwiid)
avoidance tajannub تجنّب
awake ṣaaḥi صاحي (*pl* ṣaaḥiin)
award *n* jaayza جايزة (*pl* jawaayiz)
aware waaᶜi واعي; **to make aware (of)** waᶜᶜa (be-) وعى (-i, tawᶜiya); **to be(come) aware of** ḥassa be- حسّ (i, iḥsaas)
awareness raising tawᶜiya توعية
awful faẓiiᶜ فظيع
awl ishfa إشفة (*pl* ishaf); mukhraz مخرز (*pl* makhaariz)
awning ṣeewaan صيوان (*pl* -aat)
axe faas فاس (*pl* fu'uus); (**small**) farraar فرّار (*pl* -aat, faraariir)
axis miḥwar محور (*pl* maḥaawir)
axle dingil دنقل (*pl* danaagil)

B - b

baboon tigil تقل (*pl* tuguul)
baby jana جنا (*pl* jinyaat, jannuun)
bachelor ᶜazzaabi عزّابي (*pl* ᶜazzaaba); aᶜzab اعزب (*pl* ᶜazzaaba)
back *n* ḍahar ضهر (*pl* ḍuhuur) • *adj* warraani ورّاني; **at the back** wara ورا
backbite gaṭaᶜ fi قطع (a, gaṭiiᶜa)
backbone ᶜaḍum aḍ-ḍahar
backside mu'akhkhira مؤخّرة; ṣulub صلب (*pl* -aat, ṣulubba, aṣlaab, ṣalabeen); gaᶜar قعر (*pl* guᶜuur)
backwards be-l-khalf
bad kaᶜab كعب; baṭṭaal بطال; sayyi' سيّئ
badness kuᶜuubiyya كعوبيّة
bag (**case, handbag**) shanṭa شنطة (*pl* shinaṭ); (**of cloth, plastic, paper**) kiis كيس (*pl* akyaas)
baggage ᶜafash عفش
bail *n* ḍamaana ضمانة; kafaala كفالة • *v* ḍaman ضمن (a, ḍamaan, ḍamaana)
bailor ḍaamin ضامن
bait ṭuᶜum طعم
bake khabaz خبز (i, khabiiz)
baker farraan فرّان; (**of pastry, biscuits/cookies**) khabbaaz خبّاز; ḥalawaani حلواني (*pl* -yyiin)
bakery (**bread**) furun فرن (*pl* afraan); ṭaabuuna طابونة (*pl* ṭawaabiin); (**pastries**) ḥalawaani حلواني (*pl* -yyiin)
balance *n* (**equilibrium**) tawaazun توازن (*pl* -aat); (**scales**) miizaan ميزان (*pl* mawaaziin); (**of an account**) baagi باقي (*pl* bawaagi) • v itᶜaadal اتعادل

(taᶜaadul); itwaazan اتوازن (tawaazun)
balcony balakoona بلكونة
bald muṣalliᶜ مصلّع ; **the bald guy** abu ṣalᶜa; **to become bald** ṣallaᶜ صلّع (ṣilleeᶜ)
baldness ṣalᶜa صلعة (*pl* ṣilaᶜ)
ball kuura كورة (*pl* kuwar); kura كرة (*pl* kuwar)
ball bearings balaali بلالي (*unit n* biliyya)
ballcock ᶜawwaama عوّامة
balloon ḥambuuka حمبوكة (*pl* ḥanaabiik); baaloona بالونة
bamboo gana قنا ; kheezaraan خيزران ; **bamboo cane** ganaaya قناية
banana(s) mooz موز
band (**music**) firga فرقة (*pl* firag)
bandage *n* rubaaṭ رباط (-aat, arbiṭa) • v laffa be-shaash, laffa be-gumaash
bandit hambaati همباتي (*pl* hambaata); rabbaaṭi ربّاطي (*pl* rabbaaṭiyya, rabaabiiṭ)
bang *v* khabaṭ خبط (i, khabiṭ, khabaṭaan)
banish nafa نفى (-i, nafi); ṭarad طرد (u, ṭarid)
bank (**financial**) bank بنك (*pl* bunuuk); maṣraf مصرف (*pl* maṣaarif)
bank (**river**) geef قيف ; (**cultivated**) jarif جرف (*pl* juruuf)
bankrupt mufallis مفلّس ; muflis مفلس ; **to be**(**come**) **bankrupt** fallas فلّس (tafliis)
bankruptcy falas فلس ; tafliis تفليس ; tafliisa تفليسة
banner ᶜalam علم (*pl* aᶜlaam); beerag بيرق (*pl* bayaarig); raaya راية
banquet waliima وليمة (*pl* walaayim)
baobab(s) (**tree**) tabaldi تبلدي (*unit n* tabaldiyya); (**fruit**) gongolees قنقليس (*unit n* gongoleesaaya)
baptism maᶜmuudiyya معموديّة
baptize ᶜammad عمّد (taᶜmiid)
bar *n* (**iron**) siikha سيخة (*pl* siyagh)
bar *n* (**drinking**) andaaya أنداية (*pl* anaadi)
barber ḥallaag حلاق
bare ᶜaryaan عريان
barefoot ḥafyaan حفيان
bareheaded kaashif كاشف
bargain *n* (**deal**) ṣafaga; صفقة ; (**cheap buy**) ḥaaja majaaniyya; ḥaaja balaash; **I bought it as a bargain** ligeet-o lagiya • *v* ᶜamal ṣafaga; (**haggle**) faaṣal فاصل (mufaaṣala, fiṣaal)
barge ṣandal صندل (*pl* ṣanaadil)
bark *n* (**of a tree**) liḥa لحا ; girif قرف (*unit n* girfa)
bark *v* nabaḥ (fi/foog) نبح (a, nabiiḥ, nabaḥaan); (**dogs only**) hawhaw (fi/foog) هوهو (hawhawa)
barley shaᶜiir شعير
barracks ishlaag إشلاق (*pl* -aat)
barrel barmiil برميل (*pl* baraamiil); (**gun**) maasuurat al-bundugiyya
barrier ḥaajiz حاجز (*pl* ḥawaajiz); sadd سد (*pl* suduud)
barter *v* baddal بدّل (biddeel, tabdiil)
base *adj* radi ردي ; munḥaṭṭ منحط ; dani دني • *n* (**stand**) qaaᶜida قاعدة (*pl* qawaaᶜid)
baseless saay ساي ; saakit ساكت
bashful khajuul خجول ; maksuuf مكسوف ; mukhtashi مختشى ; **to be bashful** khijil خجل (a,

khajal); itkasaf اتكسف (kasif, kasfa); ikhtasha اختشى (-i, ikhtisha)
basic asaasi أساسي
basil (plant) riiḥaan ريحان (*pl* rayaaḥiin)
basin ḥooḍ حوض (*pl* ḥeeḍaan, aḥwaaḍ)
basis asaas أساس (*pl* usus)
basket guffa قفّة (*pl* gufaf); sabat سبت (*pl* subaata); salla سلّة (*pl* -aat, silaal); **food basket** man-doola مندولة
basketball kuurat as-salla; kurat as-salla
bastard (son) wadd ḥaraam; wad zina; **(daughter)** bitt ḥaraam; bitt zina
bat (*zool*) abu riggeeᶜ; waṭwaaṭ وطواط (*pl* waṭaawiiṭ)
bat (instrument) maḍrab مضرب (*pl* maḍaarib)
batch irsaaliyya إرساليّة
bath ḥammaam حمام (*pl* -aat); **(tub)** banyo بنديو (*pl* -haat)
bathe (o.s.) istaḥamma استحمّ (a, ḥammaam); itbarrad اتبرّد (birreed); **(another)** ḥamma حمّى (-i, ḥimmeey); barrad برّد (birreed, tabriid)
bathroom ḥammaam حمام (*pl* -aat); baruud برود
bathtub banyo بنديو (*pl* -haat); ḥooḍ al-banyo
battalion katiiba كتيبة (*pl* kata-ayib); oorṭa اورطة (*pl* uraṭ)
batter ᶜajiina عجينة
battery baṭṭaariyya بطاريّة ; **dry battery** ḥajar حجر (aḥjaar); **small battery** ḥajar ṣubaaᶜ
battle kitaal كتال ; katla كتلة ; maᶜraka معركة (*pl* maᶜaarik)
bayonet soonki سونكي (*pl* sawaanki)
be kaan كان (u, koon)
beach shaaṭi شاطي (*pl* shawaaṭi)
beacon manaara منارة
bead(s) suksuk سكسك (*unit n* suk-suka, suksukaaya)
beak mungaar منقار (*pl* manaagiir)
beam *n* biim بيم (*pl* abyaam); **(lengthways)** maddaad مدّاد (*pl* -aat); **(transverse)** ᶜarraaḍ عرّاض (*pl* -aat); **(roof support)** mirig مرق (*pl* muruug); mariina مرينة (*pl* maraayin)
bean ḥabbat faaṣuulya; **beans** faaṣuulya فاصوليا ; **adzuki beans** baliila بليلة ; **black-eyed beans** luuba لوبا ; luubya لوبيا ; **fava/broad beans** fuul فول (*unit n* fuulaaya, fuula); **green beans** faaṣuulya khaḍra; **white beans** faaṣuulya beeḍa
bear *n* dubb دب (*pl* dababa)
bear *v* **(endure)** itḥammal اتحمّل (taḥammul); istaḥmal استحمل (istiḥmaal); **(carry)** shaal شال (i, sheel, shayalaan)
beard digin دقن (*pl* duguun)
beardless adruuj أدروج (*pl* adaariij)
beat *v* dagga دقّ (u, dagg); ḍarab ضرب (a, ḍarib); **to be beaten** iddagga ادقّ (dagg); iḍḍarab اضّرب (ḍarib); **to beat a drum** naggar نقّر (niggeer, nagir)
beautification tajmiil تجميل
beautiful samiḥ سمح ; ḥilu حلو (*f* ḥilwa); jamiil جميل
beauty samaaḥa سماحة ; samaaḥ سماح ; ḥalaawa حلاوة ; jamaal جمال
because ᶜashaan عشان ; la'ann-لأن ; la'anno لأنو ; **because**

of ʿashaan عشان ; ʿala shaan; be-sabab
become biga بقى (-a, bagayaan)
bed sariir سرير (*pl* saraayir); (**with bedding**) furaash فراش (*pl* -aat); **rope bed** ʿangareeb عنقريب (*pl* ʿanaagriib); **bed linen** milaaya ملاية
bedbug(s) maragoot مرقوت ; bagg بق
bedding (**mattress and sheet**) farish فرش
bedroom ooṭṭ an-noom
bee(s) naḥal نحل (*unit n* naḥla)
beef laḥam bagari; laḥam bagar
beefsteak bufteek بفتيك
beehive beet an-naḥal; khaliyya خليّة (*pl* khalaaya)
beer biira بيرة ; **millet beer** mariisa مريسة (*pl* maraayis)
beetle(s) khunfus خنفس (*unit n* khunfusaana, *pl* khanaafis); **dung beetle(s)** abu d-dardaag; **black beetle** juʿraan جعران (*pl* jaʿaariin); abu j-juʿraan
beetroot(s) banjar بنجر (*unit n* banjaraaya)
before *prep* gabul/gabil قبل ; gabli قبلى ; gubbaal قبّال • *adv* gibeel قبيل ; gabli kida; gubbaal kida • *conj* gabli ma; gubbaal ma; gabul/gabil ma
befriend ṣaaḥab صاحب (muṣaaḥaba); khaawa خاوى (-i, mukhaawaa); ṣaadag صادق (ṣadaaga)
beg (**for alms**) shaḥad شحد (a, shaḥda, shiḥda); (**implore**) raja رجا (-u, raja); itrajja اترجّا (-a, raja, tarjiya)
beggar shaḥḥaad شحّاد
begin *vi* bada (be-) بدا (-a, bidaaya); ibtada إبتدا (-i, bidaaya, ibtida) • *vt* bada بدا (-a, bidaaya)
beginning bidaaya بداية
behave itṣarraf اتصرّف (taṣarruf); salak سلك (u, suluuk)
behaviour taṣarruf تصرّف (*pl* -aat); suluuk سلوك (*pl* -iyaat)
behind *prep* wara ورا ; be-gafa; khalf خلف • *adv* wara ورا ; be-wara
beige beeji بيجي ; samni سمني
belch *n* karʿa كرعة ; tarʿa ترعة • *v* iddashshaʿ ادّشّع (dishsheeʿ); itkarraʿ اتكرّع (kirreeʿ, karʿa); ittarraʿ اتّرّع (tirreeʿ, tarʿa); tarraʿ ترّع (tirreeʿ, tarʿa)
Belgian *adj/n* baljiiki بلجيكي (*pl* -yyiin)
Belgium baljiika بلجيكا
belief iimaan إيمان ; ʿaqiida عقيدة (*pl* ʿaqaayid)
believe aaman be- آمن (yu'min, iimaan); (**think**) iftakar افتكر (iftikaar); ẓanna ظنّ (u, ẓann); (**trust**) ṣaddag صدّق (taṣdiig); **to be believed** itṣaddag اتصدّق (ṣiddeeg)
believer muu'min مؤمن
bell jaras جرس (*pl* ajraas)
bellows kuur كور ; kiir كير (*pl* kiiraan)
belly baṭun بطن (*pl* buṭuun); **pot-belly** karish كرش (*pl* kuruush)
belong ḥagg حق (*f* ḥaggat); bitaaʿ بتاع (*f* bitaaʿat)
beloved maḥbuub محبوب ; ḥabiib حبيب (*pl* aḥibba, ḥabaab); ʿaziiz عزيز (*pl* aʿizzaa)
belt ḥizaam حزام (*pl* -aat, aḥzima); **money belt** kamar كمر ; **safety belt** ḥizaam al-amaan; **transmission belt** **seer** سير (*pl* siyuur)

bench kanaba كنبة (*pl* -aat, kanab)
bend *n* ḥaniya حنية ; (**materials, road**) ʿawja عوجة ; (**materials**) lawiya لوية • *vi* inḥana انحنى (-i, ḥaniya); (**road**) itʿarraj اتعرّج (ʿirreej, taʿriij, taʿarruj); (**humans**) dangar دنقر (dingeer, dangara); dangas دنقر (dingees, dangasa) • *vt* ḥana حنى (-i, ḥaniya, ḥanayaan); lawa لوى (-i, lawi, lawiya, lawayaan); tana تنى (-i, tani, taniya); **to be bent** itlawa اتلوى (-i, lawiya); ittana اتّنى (-i, taniya)
benefit *n* faayda فايدة (*pl* fawaayid); istifaada إستفادة • *v* istafaad استفاد (i, istifaada)
Berber *adj/n* barbari بربري (*pl* baraabra)
berserk **to go berserk** haaj هاج (i, hayajaan)
besiege ḥaaṣar حاصر (ḥiṣaar, muḥaaṣara)
best al-aḥsan; al-afḍal
bet *n* shuraaṭ شراط (*pl* shuraaṭ); rihaan رهان (*pl* -aat) • *vt* shaaraṭ شارط (mushaaraṭa, shuraaṭ); raahan راهن (muraahana, rihaan) • *vi* itraahan اتراهن (muraahana, rihaan)
betray khaan خان (u, khiyaana); (**secret**) fasha فشى (-i, fashiya, fashayaan); kashaf كشف (i, kashif)
betrayal khiyaana خيانة
better aḥsan (min) أحسن ; akheer (min) أخير ; afḍal (min) أفضل ; **to get better** (**recover**) ṭaab طاب (i, ṭayabaan); shifa شفى (-a, shifaa); bira برى (-a, bariya, barayaan)
between been بين ; beenaat بينات
beware *interj* khalli baal-ak (min); khallii-k ḥariiṣ! • *v* iḥtaras احترس (iḥtiraas); **beware of the dog** iḥtaras min al-kalib!
bewilder ḥayyar حيّر (ḥiira, ḥiyyeer); maḥḥan محّن (miḥḥeen); **to be(come) bewildered** itḥayyar اتحيّر (ḥiira); itmaḥḥan اتمحّن (miḥna)
bewildered ḥayraan حيران ; mamaḥḥan ممحّن
bewilderment ḥiira حيرة ; miḥna محنة (*pl* miḥan)
bewitch saḥar سحر (a, siḥir)
biased munḥaaz منحاز ; mutḥayyiz متحيّز
bib maryala مريلة (*pl* -aat, maraayil)
Bible al-kitaab al-muqaddas
bicycle ʿajala عجلة
bid *n* ʿaṭaa عطا (*pl* ʿaṭaa'aat) • *v* (**for**) zaawad (ʿala) زاود (muzaawada)
bier ʿangareeb aj-jinaaza
big kabiir كبير (*pl* kubaar)
bile mirr مر
bilharzia *n* bilhaarsiya بلهارسيا
bill faatuura فاتورة (*pl* fawaatiir); ḥisaab حساب (*pl* -aat); **bill of exchange** kambiyaala كمبيالة ; **bill of lading** booliiṣat shaḥan
billboard looḥa iʿlaaniyya
billiards bilyaardo بلياردو
billion bilyoon بليون (*pl* balaayiin)
bind rabaṭ ربط (u, rabiṭ); rabbaṭ ربّط (ribbeeṭ); (**book**) jallad جلّد (tajliid)
binding (**book**) tajliid تجليد (*pl* -aat)
binoculars minẓaar منظار (*pl* manaaẓiir)
bird(s) ṭeer طير (*pl* ṭiyuur); **small bird(s)** ʿaṣfuur عصفور (*pl*

ʿaṣaafiir); **bird of prey** ṣagur صقر (*pl* ṣuguur)

birth miilaad ميلاد ; **to give birth (to)** waḍaʿ وضع (yaḍaʿ, wuḍuuʿ); wilid ولد (i, wilaada)

birth control (pills) ḥubuub manʿ al-ḥimil

birthday ʿiid miilaad

biscuit baskoota بسكوتة (*pl* baskawi-it); **shortbread biscuits** kaʿak كعك

bishop muṭraan مطران (*pl* maṭaarina); usquf أسقف (*pl* asaaqifa)

bit (mouthpiece of bridle) ḥadiid al-lijaam

bit (little) ḥabba حبّة ; shwayya شويّة ; **bit by bit** ḥabba ḥabba; shwayya shwayya

bitch kalba كلبة

bite *n* ʿaḍḍa عضّة ; **(by an insect)** garṣa قرصة ; **(by a snake)** ladgha لدغة ; **(of food)** garma قرمة (*pl* -aat, guram) • *v* ʿaḍḍa عضّ (u, ʿaḍḍ, ʿaḍḍa); **(of insects)** garaṣ قرص (u, gariṣ); garraṣ قرّص (girreeṣ, tagriiṣ); ladagh لدغ (a, ladigh, ladaghaan); **(of snake)** ladagh لدغ (a, ladigh, ladaghaan); **to be bitten** itʿaḍḍa اتعضّ (ʿaḍḍ, ʿaḍḍa); ingaraṣ انقرص (garṣa); itgarraṣ اتقرّص (garṣa); itladagh اتلدغ (ladgha)

bitter murr مر

black aswad أسود (*f* soda, *pl* suud); azrag أزرق (*f* zarga, zargaa, *pl* zurug)

blackboard sabbuura سبّورة (*pl* -aat, sabaabiir); takhta تختة (*pl* tikhat)

blackmail *n* ibtizaaz ابتزاز • *v* ibtazza ابتزّ (ibtizaaz)

blacksmith ḥaddaad حدّاد (*pl* -iin, ḥadaadiid)

bladder masaana مسانة

blade (of knife) sikkiin سكّين (*pl* sakaakiin); sikkiina سكّينة (*pl* sakaakiin); **razor blade** muus موس (*pl* amwaas)

blame *n* malaama ملامة ; loom لوم • *v* laam لام (u, loom); lawwam لوّم (liwweem); ʿayyab (ʿala) عيّب (ʿeeb); **to be blamed** itlawwam اتلوّم (loom, liwweem)

blank faaḍi فاضي

blanket baṭṭaaniyya بطانيّة (*pl* -aat, baṭaaṭiin); ghaṭa غطا (*pl* aghṭiya)

blaspheme kafar كفر (u, kufur)

blasphemer kaafir كافر (kuffaar, kafara)

blasphemy kufur كفر

bleach *n* bayaaḍ بياض • *v* bayyaḍ بيّض (biyyeeḍ, tabyiiḍ)

bleed *vi* nazaf نزف (i, naziif) • *vt* ḥajjam حجّم (ḥijjeem, ḥijaama)

bleeding naziif نزيف

blender khallaaṭ خلاط ; khallaaṭa خلاطة

bless baarak fi بارك (mubaaraka)

blessing baraka بركة ; **to seek a blessing** itbarrak اتبرّك (baraka, tabarruk)

blind *adj* ʿamyaan عميان ; kafiif كفيف ; ḍariir ضرير ; **to go blind** ʿima عمى (-a, ʿama); itʿama اتعمى (-i, ʿama); **half-blind** aʿmash أعمش (*f* ʿamsha, ʿamshaana, *pl* ʿumush) • *v* aʿma أعمى (-i, ʿamiya, ʿama); **(of light)** zaghlal زغلل (zighleel, zaghlala)

blindness ʿama عما ; **night blindness** ʿasha layli; **suffering from**

night blindness aʿmash أعمش (*f* ʿamsha, ʿamshaana, *pl* ʿumush)
blink ramash رمش (i, ramashaan)
blister *v* itbaggag اتبقّق (biggeeg); **to cause to blister** baggag بقّق (biggeeg)
blister(s) *n* bugaag بقاق
block *n* blok بلوك (*pl* -aat); (**of wood**) kutla كتلة (*pl* -aat, kutal); (**row of houses**) blok بلوك (*pl* -aat) • *v* sadda سدّ (i, sadd); **to be blocked** insadda انسدّ (sadd, insidaad); itsadda اتسدّ (sadd)
blockage sadd سد (*pl* suduud)
blog *n* mudawwana مدوّنة • *v* dawwan دوّن (tadwiin)
blood damm دم ; **blood clot** jalṭa جلطة ; **blood pressure** ḍaght ad-damm; **blood money** diyya ديّة
bloodshed *n* safk ad-damm
blood-vessel ʿirig عرق (*pl* ʿuruug)
bloody damawi دموي
blouse buluuza بلوزة
blow *n* dagga دقّة ; ḍarba ضربة ; khabṭa خبطة ; (**with fist**) bunya بنية
blow *v* (**wind**) habba هبّ (i, habba, habuub); (**with mouth**) nafakh نفخ (u, nafikh, nafakhaan); (**blow nose**) itmakhkhaṭ اتمخّط (mikhkheeṭ)
blue azrag أزرق (*f* zarga, *pl* zurug); ẓahri ظهري ; **dark blue** kuḥli كحلي ; **light blue** labani لبني ; **laundry blue** ẓahara ظهرة
blunt mayyit ميّت
blur shawwash ʿala شوّش (tashwiish); **to be blurred** itshawwash اتشوّش (shiwweesh)
board *n* (**wooden**) looḥ لوح (*pl* alwaaḥ, leeḥaan); looḥa لوحة ; (**of corporation**) hay'a هيئة ; **board of directors** majlis al-idaara; **board of trustees** majlis al-umana
board *v* rikib ركب (a, rukuub); **to cause to board** rakkab ركّب (rikkeeb, tarkiib)
boast fashshar (be-) فشّر (fishsheer, fashar); itfashshar (be-) فشّر (fishsheer, fashar)
boat murkab مركب (*pl* maraakib); **small sailing boat** (**river**) falluuka فلّوكة (*pl* fallaayik)
boatman maraakbi مراكبي (*pl* -yya)
body jisim جسم (*pl* ajsaam); jitta جتّة (*pl* jitat); jasad جسد (*pl* ajsaad)
boil *n* ḥabba حبّة (*pl* ḥubuub); ḥibin حبن (*pl* aḥbaan)
boil *vi* ghila غلى (-i, ghalayaan); faar فار (u, foora, fawaraan); itfawwar اتفوّر (foora); itghala اتغلى (-i, ghaliya, ghalayaan) • *vt* ghala غلى (-i, ghaliya); (**food**) salag سلق (i, salig, salga)
boldly be-shajaaʿa
boldness shajaaʿa شجاعة
bolt *n* (**fastening**) tarbaas ترباس (taraabiis); sidaada سدادة (*pl* -aat, sadaadiid); (**metal pin**) musmaar مسمار (*pl* masaamiir) • *v* (**fasten**) tarbas تربس (tirbees, tarbasa); **to be bolted** ittarbas اتّربس (tirbees)
bomb gumbula قمبلة (*pl* ganaabil)
bone ʿaḍum عضم (*pl* ʿuḍaam)
bonnet (**of car**) kabbuut كبّوت (*pl* kabaabiit)
bonus mukaafaa مكافاة (*pl* mukaafa'aat)
book *n* kitaab كتاب (*pl* kutub); **book fair** maʿraḍ al-kitaab; **book**

jacket jilaad جلاد (*pl* -aat); **exercise book** karraas كرّاس (*pl* -aat, karaariis)
book *v* ḥajaz حجز (i, ḥajiz)
bookcase maktaba مكتبة
booking ḥajiz حجز; **booking office** maktab al-ḥajiz
book-keeping muḥaasaba محاسبة
bookshop maktaba مكتبة
boomerang safaroog سفروق (*pl* safaariig)
boot (**footwear**) buut بوت (*pl* abwaat); **football boots** kaddaara كدّارة; (**of car**) shanṭa شنطة (*pl* shinaṭ)
border ḥuduud حدود
bore *v* (**hole**) kharam خرم (i, kharim); kharram خرّم (khirreem, takhriim); gadda قدّ (i, gadda, gadd); (**holes**) gaddad قدّد (giddeed); gadgad قدقد (gadgada, gidgeed)
bore *n* saqiil سقيل (*pl* suqala); **he is a bore** damm-o tagiil • *v* (**tire**) zahhaj زهّج (zihheej, tazhiij); **to get bored** zihij زهج (a, zahaj); **to feel bored** ḥassa be-malal
bored *adj* zahjaan زهجان
boredom malal ملل; zahaj زهج
boring mumill ممل
born mawluud مولود; **to be born** itwalad اتولد (miilaad, wilaada)
borrow istalaf استلف (sulfa, salaf, istilaaf); itsallaf اتسلّف (tasliif); (**money**) iddayyan ادّيّن (deen)
boss rayyis ريّس (*pl* ruwasa); (*m*) mudiir مدير; (*f*) mudiira مديرة; (**of craftsmen**) muʿallim معلّم; usṭa أسطى (*pl* usṭawaat)
both al-itneen
bother *vt* (**annoy**) ḍaayag ضايق (muḍaayaga); (**worry**) gallag قلّق (gilleeg); **don't bother** ma tatʿab nafs-ak
bottle gazaaza قزازة (*pl* gazaayiz); (**small**) fatiil فتيل (*pl* fataayil); **baby's bottle** bizza بزّة (*pl* bizzaz); **bottle cap** fulla فلّة (*pl* -aat, fulal)
bottle opener fattaaḥa فتّاحة; muftaaḥ مفتاح (*pl* mafaatiiḥ)
bottom gaʿar قعر (*pl* guʿuur); (**body only**) mu'akhkhira مؤخّرة; ṣulub صلب (*pl* -aat, ṣulubba, aṣlaab, ṣalabeen)
bougainvillea jahannamiyya جهنّميّة
bounce naṭṭaṭ نطّط (niṭṭeeṭ)
boundary ḥuduud حدود
bow *n* (**weapon**) goos قوس (*pl* agwaas)
bow *n* (**of respect**) ḥaniya حنية; (**also in prayer**) rakʿa ركعة • *v* inḥana انحنى (-i, ḥaniya); (**in prayer**) rakaʿ ركع (a, rakiʿ, rakʿa)
bowels maṣaariin مصارين (*sg* muṣraan)
bowl koora كورة (*pl* kuwar); kooriyya كوريّة (*pl* kawaari, kuwar); (**wooden**) gadaḥ قدح (*pl* gudaaḥa, agdaaḥ); **washbowl** ṭashit طشت (*pl* ṭushaata)
box *n* (**small**) ʿilba علبة (*pl* ʿilab); (**case**) ṣanduug صندوق (*pl* ṣanaadiig); (**of cardboard**) kartoona كرتونة (*pl* -aat, karaatiin); (**for perfumes**) ḥugg حق (*pl* ḥagaga)
box *v* (**sports**) laakam لاكم (mulaakama)
box office shubbaak at-tazaakir
boy wad ود (wadd, *pl* awlaad); walad ولد (*pl* awlaad); shaafiʿ

شافع (*pl* shuffaᶜ); wileed وليد (*pl* -aat); ṣabi صبي (*pl* ṣubyaan)

boycott *v* gaṭaᶜ قطع (a, gaṭiᶜ)

bra sityaan ستيان (*pl* -aat); ḥammaala حمّالة

brace ḥaamil حامل (*pl* ḥawaamil)

bracelet ghiweesha غويشة (*pl* -aat, ghawaayish); suwaar سوار (*pl* aswira, asaawir)

braces ḥammaala حمّالة

bracket (**punctuation**) goos قوس (*pl* agwaas); **in brackets** beengooseen

brag fashshar (be-) فشّر (fishsheer, fashar); itfashshar (be-) فشّر (fishsheer, fashar)

braid *n* ḍafiira ضفيرة (*pl* ḍafaayir) • *v* ḍafar ضفر (u, ḍafir); ḍaffar ضفّر (ḍiffeer)

braiding mushaaṭ مشاط

brain mukhkh مخ (*pl* amkhaakh)

brake *n* farmala فرملة (*pl* faraamil); **brake lining** gumaash قماش (*pl* -aat, agmisha) • *v* farmal فرمل (farmala)

bran nikhaala نخالة

branch *n* fariᶜ فرع (*pl* furuuᶜ) • *v* itfarraᶜ اتفرّع (tafarruᶜ)

branching tafarruᶜ تفرّع (*pl* -aat)

brand *n* (**mark**) wasim وسم (*pl* awsaam); (**trade name**) maarka ماركة • *v* kawa كوى (-i, kawi, kay, kawayaan); wassam وسّم (wisseem)

brass ṣifir صفر ; niḥaas aṣfar

brave jarii' جريء ; shujaaᶜ شجاع (*pl* shijᶜaan, shujᶜaan); jaasir جاسر ; **be brave!** shidd ḥeel-ak!

bravely be-shajaaᶜa

bravery shajaaᶜa شجاعة ; jur'a جرءة

bray hannag هنّق (hinneeg)

brazier kaanuun كانون (*pl* kawaaniin); mangad منقد (*pl* manaagid)

Brazil al-baraziil

Brazilian *adj/n* baraziili برازيلي (*pl* -yyiin)

bread ᶜeesh عيش (*pl* ᶜiyuush); **loaf of bread** ᶜeesha عيشة ; raghiifa رغيفة (*pl* raghiif); **dry/dried bread** gargoosh قرقوش (*pl* garaagiish)

breadth ᶜariḍ عرض (*pl* ᶜuruuḍ); ᶜuruḍ عرض

break *n* (**rest**) raaḥa راحة ; istiraaḥa إستراحة ; **to take a break** akhad raaḥa

break *vi* itkasar اتكسر (kasra); (**snap**) itgaṭaᶜ اتقطع (gaṭiᶜ); ingaṭaᶜ انقطع (ingiṭaaᶜ); **to break into pieces** itkassar اتكسّر (kisseer); **to break off** ittaram اتّرم (taram, tarma); itgalam (galma); **to break down** khisir خسر (a, khasaara); itᶜaṭṭal اتعطّل (ᶜuṭul); baṭṭal بطّل (biṭṭeel) • *vt* kasar كسر (i, kasir); **to break off** taram ترّم (u, tarim); galam قلم (i, galim); **to break into pieces** dashdash دشدش (dishdeesh, dashdasha); kassar كسّر (kisseer, taksiir); **to break a promise** nagaḍ waᶜad; khaalaf waᶜad; (**rules**) khaalaf خالف (mukhaalafa); kharag خرق (i, kharig)

breakdown inhiyaar انهيار ; (**of car**) ᶜuṭul عطل ; **nervous breakdown** inhiyaar ᶜaṣabi

breakfast *n* faṭuur فطور ; ifṭaar إفطار (*pl* -aat) • *v* faṭar فطر (u, faṭuur)

breast shaṭur شطر (*pl* shuṭuur); ṣadur صدر (*pl* ṣuduur); (**woman's**)

nahd نهد (*pl* nuhuud); (**chest**) ṣadur صدر (*pl* ṣuduur)
breastfeed raḍḍaᶜ رضع (a, riḍḍeeᶜ, riḍaaᶜa); **to be breastfed** riḍiᶜ رضع (a, riḍaaᶜa)
breath nafas نفس (*pl* anfaas); **out of breath** nafas gaayim; **to hold one's breath** katam nafas-o
breathe itnaffas اتنفّس (tanaffus)
breathlessness ḍiig an-nafas; nafas gaayim
breed rabba ربّى (-i, tarbiya)
breeze nasiim نسيم (*pl* nasaayim); nasma نسمة (*pl* nasamaat)
bribe *n* rashwa رشوة (*pl* -aat, rashaawi) • *v* rasha رشى (-i, rashwa)
brick(s) ṭuub طوب; (**fired**) ṭuub aḥmar; (**unfired**) ṭuub akhḍar; ṭuub nayy
bride ᶜaruus عروس (*pl* ᶜaraayis)
bridegroom ᶜariis عريس (*pl* ᶜirsaan)
bridesmaid waziira وزيرة
bridge kubri كبري (*pl* kabaari); jisir جسر (*pl* jusuur)
bridle lijaam لجام (*pl* -aat); **to put a bridle on** lajjam لجّم (lijjeem, taljiim); **to have a bridle put on** itlajjam اتلجّم (lijjeem)
briefcase shanṭa شنطة (*pl* shinaṭ)
briefing tanwiir تنوير (*pl* -aat)
brigade liwa لوا (*pl* alwiya)
brigadier liwa لوا (*pl* -'aat)
bright (**of light**) mushrig مشرق; (**of colours**) faatiḥ فاتح
bring jaab جاب (i, jeeba, jayabaan); **to bring back** rajjaᶜ رجّع (rijjeeᶜ); **to bring down** nazzal نزّل (nizzeel); **to bring out** marrag مرق mirreeg); ṭallaᶜ طلّع (tilleeᶜ); **to bring together** jamaᶜ جمع (a, jamiᶜ); jammaᶜ جمّع (jimmeeᶜ, tajmiiᶜ); **to bring s.o/sth. to (a place)** waṣṣal وصّل (wiṣṣeel) **to bring up** rabba ربّى (-i, tarbiya); **to be brought up** itrabba اتربّى (-a, tarbiya)
Britain biriṭaaniya بريطانيا
British biriṭaani بريطاني (*pl* -yyiin)
brittle fakhkh فخ
broad ᶜariiḍ عريض; **to be(come) broad** wisiᶜ وسع (a, wasaaᶜ)
broadcast *n* izaaᶜa إزاعة • *v* zaaᶜ زاع (i, izaaᶜa); **broadcasting station** izaaᶜa إزاعة; maḥaṭṭat izaaᶜa
broaden wassaᶜ وسّع (wisseeᶜ, tawsiiᶜ); ᶜarraḍ عرّض (taᶜriiḍ)
brochure manshuur منشور (*pl* -aat, manaashiir)
broken maksuur مكسور; **broken down** khasraan خسران; ᶜaṭlaan عطلان; kharbaan خربان
broker samsaar سمسار (*pl* samaasra)
bronchitis iltihaab shuᶜabi; nazla shuᶜabiyya
bronze ṣifir صفر
broom mugshaasha مقشاشة (*pl* magaashiish); maknasa مكنسة (*pl* makaanis); **ceiling broom** zaᶜᶜaafa زعّافة
broth saliiga سليقة; maraga مرقة
brother akhu أخو (*pl* akhwaan); **full brother** shagiig شقيق (*pl* ashigga); **brother-in-law** nasiib نسيب (*pl* nasaaba, nasaayib)
brown bunni بنّي; (**of skin**) asmar أسمر (*f* samra, *pl* sumur); **light brown** (**also of skin**) gamḥi قمحي; (**dark brown, of skin**)

akhḍar أخضر (*f* khaḍra, *pl* khuḍur)
bruise *n* aḍḍ رض *pl* ruḍuuḍ) • *v* raḍraḍ ر ضرض (riḍreeḍ, raḍraḍa); **to be bruised** itraḍraḍ اتر ضرض (riḍreeḍ, raḍraḍa)
brush *n* fursha فرشة (*pl* furash) • *v* naḍḍaf be-fursha; **to brush teeth** itsawwak اتسوّك (siw-week, taswiik)
brutal gaasi قاسي ; waḥish وحش
bubble *n* fuggaaᶜ فقّاع (*pl* fagaagiiᶜ)
bucket jardal جردل (*pl* jaraadil)
bud burᶜum برعم (*pl* baraaᶜim)
budget miizaaniyya ميزانيّة
buffalo jaamuus جاموس (*pl* jawaamiis)
buffet boofeeh بوفيه (*pl* -aat)
buffoon bahlawaan بهلوان (*pl* -aat); balyaatshu بلياتشو (*pl* -waat)
bugle buuri بوري (*pl* bawaari)
build *v* bana بنى (-i, buna); ᶜammar عمّر (taᶜmiir); **to be built** itbana اتبنى (-i, buna)
builder banna بنا (*pl* bannaayiin)
building mabna مبنى (*pl* ma-baani); binaaya بناية ; (**of sev-eral storeys**) ᶜamaara عمارة
bulb lamba لمبة (*pl* -aat, limaḍ); (**of bayonet type**) lambat ibra; (**screw-in**) lambat galawooẓ
bull toor تور (*pl* teeraan)
bulldozer karraaka كرّاكة ; buldoo-zar بلدوزر (*pl* -aat)
bullet raṣṣaaṣa رصّاصة ; ṭalga طلقة (*pl* -aat, ṭilag)
bullock toor makhṣi
bully faatiyya فاتّية
bullying fatwana فتونة
bump *n* ṣadma صدمة ; dagsha دقشة ; (**swelling**) kurdumma كردمّة (*pl* karaadiim) • *v* dagash دقش (u, dagish, dagsha); ṣadam صدم (u, ṣadma); ṣaadam maᶜa صادم (ṣadma, muṣaadama)
bumper (**car**) rafraf رفرف (*pl* ra-faarif); taṣaadum تصادم (*no pl*)
bundle rubṭa ربطة (*pl* rubaṭ); ḥizma حزمة (ḥizam); rizma رزمة (*pl* rizam); (**of cloth**) ṣurra صرة
bungle *n* kharmaja خرمجة ; khas-taka خستكة ; karwata كروتة • *v* kharmaj خستك (khirmeej, kharmaja); khastak خستك (kh-isteek, khastaka); karwat كروت (kirweet, karwata)
bungler jarabandi جربندي (*pl* -yya)
buoy ᶜawwaama عوّامة
burial dafin دفن ; janaaza جنازة (*pl* janaayiz)
burn *vt* ḥarag حرق (i, ḥarig, ḥariig, ḥariiga); ḥarrag حرّق (ḥirreeg); **to be burnt** ḥirig حرق (a, ḥarig); inḥarag انحرق (ḥarig); itḥarag اتحرق (ḥarig)
burrow juḥur جحر (*pl* juḥuur, jaḥḥaar)
burst *v* (**open**) iṭṭarshag اطّرشق (ṭirsheeg, ṭarshaga); itfargaᶜ اتفرقع (firgeeᶜ, fargaᶜa); **to cause to burst** (**open**) ṭarshag طرشق (ṭirsheeg, ṭarshaga); fargaᶜ فرقع (firgeeᶜ, fargaᶜa)
bury dafan دفن (a, dafin); (**person only**) satar ستر (u, sutra)
bus (**large**) baaṣṣ باص (*pl* baṣṣaat); **mini-bus** ḥaafla حافلة ; **circular bus** baaṣṣ daa'iri; (**long distance**) baaṣṣ safari; **bus stop** maḥaṭṭa محطة ; **bus station** mawgif al-ᶜarabaat/al-ḥaaflaat/al-baaṣṣaat

bush(**es**) shadar شدر ; shajar شجر ; **bush** shideera شديرة
business aʿmaal أعمال ; biznis بزنس ; shughul شغل (*pl* ashghaal); **that's none of your business** ma lee-k daʿwa; da ma yahimm-ak
businessman raajil aʿmaal
bustard(**s**) ḥubaar حبار
busy mashghuul مشغول ; mazḥuum مزحوم ; **to be busy** inshaghal انشغل (inshighaal); itshaghal (be-) اتشغل (shaghala)
busybody ḥushari حشري (*pl* -yyiin); mutḥashshir متحشّر
but laakin لاكن
butcher *n* jazzaar جزّار ; **butcher's shop** jizaara جزارة • *v* ḍabaḥ ضبح (a, ḍabiḥ)
butter zibda زبدة ; **clarified butter** samin سمن
butterfly (**butterflies**) faraash فراش
buttermilk roob روب
buttock jaʿba جعبة
button *n* ziraara زرارة (*pl* zaraayir); zuraar زرار (*pl* zaraayir); (**mechanical**) zirr زر (*pl* azraar); zuraar زرار (*pl* azirra) • *v* (**up**) zarrar زرّر (zirreer)
buttonhole *n* ʿirwa عروة (*pl* ʿaraawi, ʿarraaw)
buy ishtara اشترى (-i, shira); akhad أخد (biyaakhud, akhid); (**clothes**) inkasa انكس (-i, kiswa); (**goods**) itbaḍḍaʿ اتبدّع (biḍḍeeʿ); **to buy a ticket** gaṭaʿ tazkara
buzz *v* zanna زنّ (i, zann); (**of voices**) harjal هرجل (hirjeel, harjala)
by be- بـ ; (**in swearing an oath**) wa و

C - c

cabbage karnab كرنب (*pl* karaanib)
cabinet doolaab دولاب (*pl* dawaaliib)
cactus ṣabbaar صبّار
cage gafaṣ قفص (*pl* agfaaṣ)
cake keek كيك
calabash bukhsa بخسة (*pl* bukhas)
calamity muṣiiba مصيبة (*pl* maṣaayib)
calculate ḥasab حسب (i, ḥisaab); ḍarrab ضرّب (ḍirreeb, taḍriib); to be ʿalʿulated inḥasab انحسب (ḥisaab)
calendar natiija نتيجة (*pl* nataayij)
calf ʿijil عجل (*pl* ʿujuul); ʿijla عجلة ; (**of leg**) faara فارة
call *v* naada نادى (-i, munaada); nadah نده (a, nadiiha); **to call out** koorak كورك (kooraak); ṣarrakh صرّخ (ṣuraakh, ṣariikh); **to call in at** ghisha غشى (-a, ghashwa, ghashayaan); marra ʿala مرّ (u, muruur)
call *v* (**to prayer**) azzan أزّن (ta'ziin, azzaan) • *n* azzaan أزان (*pl* -aat)
calligrapher khaṭṭaaṭ خطّاط
calm *adj* haadi هادي (*f* hadiyya); raayig رايق ; **to be**(**come**) **calm** hida هدا (-a, huduu); raag راق (u, rooga, ruwaaga, rawagaan); itrawwa اتروّى (-a, riwweey) • *n* rooga روقة • *vt* hadda هدّى (-i, hiddeey, tahdiya)

camel jamal جمل (*pl* jumaal, jimaal); **camels** ibil إبل ; **she-camel** naaga ناقة (*pl* niyaag)
camera kamira كمرا (*pl* kamiraat)
camomile baabuunj بابونج
camp muʿaskar معسكر (*pl* -aat)
campaign ḥamla حملة
camphor kaafuur كافور
can *n* (**tin**) ʿilba علبة (*pl* ʿilab); (**large**) ṣafiiḥa صفيحة (*pl* ṣafaayiḥ)
can *v* gidir قدر (a, gudra); ʿirif عرف (a, maʿrifa)
canal qanaa قناة (*pl* qanawaat); **irrigation canal** majra مجرى (*pl* majaari); turʿa ترعة (*pl* turaʿ); (**small**) jadwal جدول (*pl* jadaawil)
cancel lagha لغى (-i, laghi); **to be cancelled** itlagha اتلغى (-i, laghayaan)
cancer saraṭaan سرطان
candidate murashshaḥ مرشّح
candle shamʿa شمعة (*pl* -aat, shumuuʿ)
candlestick shamʿadaan شمعدان (*pl* -aat)
candy giṭʿat ḥalaawa (*pl* ḥalaawa); ḥalawaaya حلواية (*pl* ḥalawiyyaat)
cane *n* (**for beating**) basṭoona بسطونة (*pl* -aat, basaaṭiin); **cane**(**s**) gaṣab قصب (*unit n* gaṣabaaya); buuṣ بوص ; **bamboo cane** ganaaya; **sugar cane** gaṣab as-sukkar
cannabis ḥashiish حشيش
cannon mudfaʿ مدفع (*pl* madaafiʿ)
can opener fattaaḥa فتّاحة ; muftaaḥ مفتاح (*pl* mafaatiiḥ)
canvas kheesh خيش
cap kaab كاب (*pl* -aat); kiskitta كسكتّة

capable gaadir قادر
capacity (**ability**) gudra قدرة ; magdara/magdira مقدرة ; (**holding power**) ḥumuula حمولة ; (**volume**) siʿa سعة ; (**position**) ṣifa صفة
capers ṭundub طندب
capital *n* raasmaal راسمال ; **capital punishment** iʿdaam إعدام (*pl* -aat); **capital city** ʿaaṣima عاصمة (*pl* ʿawaaṣim)
capitalism raasmaaliyya راسماليّة
capitalist raasmaali راسمالي (*pl* -yyiin)
capsule kabsuula كبسولة
captain kabtin كبتن (kabaatin)
capture *n* gabiḍ قبض
car ʿarabiyya عربيّة (*pl* -aat, ʿarabaat); sayyaara سيّارة ; **hired car** ʿarabiyyat ujra; **private car** ʿarabiyya mallaaki
carat (**gold**) giraaṭ قرا ط ; ʿiyaar عيار
carburettor karbareetar كربريتر (*pl* -aat)
carcass faṭiisa فطيسة (*pl* faṭaayis); rimma رمّة (rimam); jiifa جيفة (*pl* jiyaf)
card *n* buṭaaqa بطاقة ; karit كرت (*pl* kuruut); **identity card** buṭaaqa shakhṣiyya; **SIM card** shariiḥa (*pl* sharaayiḥ); **pack of cards** kushteena كشتينة
card *v* (**wool**) nafash نفش (u, nafashaan, nafish)
cardamom ḥabbahaan حبّهان
cardboard kartoon كرتون ; **cardboard box** kartoona كرتونة (*pl* -aat, karaatiin)
care *n* ʿinaaya عناية ; riʿaaya رعاية ; **intensive care** ʿinaaya mukassafa/murakkaza; **to take**

care of (**look after**) iʿtana be- اعتنى (-i, iʿtina); (**a matter**) ʿamal عمل (a/i, ʿamal); ihtamma be- اهتمّ (ihtimaam) • *v* (**about**) ihtamma (be-) اهتمّ (ihtimaam)
careful ḥariiṣ (ʿala) حريص
carefully be-raaḥa
careless muhmil مهمل; **to be careless** ithawwar اتهوّر (tahawwur)
carelessness ihmaal إهمال; ʿadam ihtimaam; ghafla غفلة
caretaker ghafiir غفير (*pl* ghufara)
cargo shuḥna شحنة (*pl* -aat, shuḥan)
caricature karikateer كركتير (*pl* -aat)
car park mawgif al-ʿarabaat
carpenter najjaar نجّار
carpentry nijaara نجارة; **to do carpentry** najar نجر (u, najir)
carpet busaaṭ بساط (-aat, absiṭa); sijjaada سجّادة (*pl* -aat, sajaajiid)
carrion faṭiisa فطيسة (*pl* faṭaayis); rimma رمّة (rimam); jiifa جيفة (*pl* jiyaf)
carrot(s) jazar جزر (*unit n* jazara, jazaraaya)
carry shaal شال (i, sheela, shayalaan); **to make s.o. carry sth.** shayyal شيّل (shiyyeel, shayalaan); **to carry out** (**implement**) adda أدّى (ya'addi, adaa); naffaz نفّز (tanfiiz)
cart kaarro كارو (*pl* kaarroohaat, karroowaat, kawaarro); **cart driver** ʿarbaji عربجي (*pl* -iyya)
cartilage ghaḍruuf غضروف (*pl* ghaḍaariif)
carton kartoona كرتونة (*pl* -aat, karaatiin)
cartoon kariikateer كريكتير (*pl* -aat); (**animated**) kartoon كرتون (*pl* -aat)
cartridge (**of gun**) kharṭuush خرطوش (*pl* kharaaṭiish)
carve kharaṭ خرط (i, khiraaṭa)
case (**box**) ṣanduug صندوق (*pl* ṣanaadiig); (**legal**) gaḍiyya قضيّة (*pl* gaḍaayaa); **in any case** ʿala kulli ḥaal, fi kull al-aḥwaal
cash *n* nagdiyya نقديّة • *v* ṣaraf صرف (u, ṣarif)
cashier ṣarraaf صرّاف
cassava bafra بفرة
casserole ṭawwa طوّة (*pl* ṭiwaw)
cassette shariiṭ شريط (*pl* sharaayiṭ, ashriṭa)
castle gaṣur قصر (*pl* guṣuur); galʿa قلعة (*pl* gilaaʿ)
castor oil plant(s) khirwiʿ خروع; **castor oil** zeet khirwiʿ
castrate khaṣa خصى (-i, khaṣayaan)
castrated makhṣi مخصي (*pl* -yyiin)
cat (*m*) kadiis كديس (*pl* kadaayis); (*f*) kadiisa كديسة (*pl* -aat, kadaayis)
catapult nibla نبلة (*pl* nibal)
cataract (**water**) shallaal شلال (*pl* -aat); (**in eye**) al-mooya al-beeḍa
catarrh nazla نزلة; zukma زكمة; zukaam زكام
catastrophe muṣiiba مصيبة (*pl* maṣaayib); kaarsa كارسة (*pl* kawaaris)
catch *v* masak مسك (i, masik, maska, masakaan); (**thieves**) ẓabaṭ ظبط (u, ẓabiṭ); **to catch up with** liḥig لحق (a, laḥagaan, laḥig); ḥaṣṣal حصّل (ḥiṣṣeel); **to help s.o. to catch up** laḥḥag لحّق (liḥḥeeg)
catechist mubashshir مبشّر
categorisation taṣniif تصنيف (*pl* -aat)

categorize ṣannaf صنّف (taṣniif)
category ṣanf صنف (*pl* aṣnaaf)
caterpillar duudat faraasha
catfish bayaaḍ بياض ; **eel catfish** garmuuṭ قرموط (*pl* garaamiiṭ)
cathedral katidraa'iyya كتدرائيّة ; kaniisa katidraa'iyya
catheter gasṭara قسطرة
cattle bagar بقر ; **cattle plague** abu dimeeʿaat; ṭaaʿuun bagari
cauliflower(s) garnabiiṭ قرنبيط
cause *n* sabab سبب (*pl* asbaab); (**of a quarrel**) sibba سبّة (*pl* as-baab) • *v* sabbab سبّب (sabab, tasbiib)
cauterize kawa كوى (-i, kawi, kay, kawayaan)
caution ḥirṣ حرص
cautious ḥariiṣ حريص
cavalry khayyaala خيّالة ; sawaari سواري
cave karkuur كركور (*pl* karaakiir); kahaf كهف (*pl* kuhuuf); ghaar غار (*pl* gheeraan)
CD usṭuwaana أسطوانة
ceasefire waqf iṭlaaq an-naar
ceiling ʿarish عرش (*pl* ʿuruush); sagif سقف (*pl* suguuf)
celebrate iḥtafal be- احتفل (iḥtifaal); (**a feast**) ʿayyad (ʿala) عيّد (ʿiid)
celebration iḥtifaal إحتفال (*pl* -aat)
celery karfas كرفس
cell khaliyya خليّة (*pl* khalaaya); **prison cell** zinzaana زنزانة
cement asmant أسمنت
cemetery maqaabir
cense bakhkhar بخّر (bikhkheer, bakhra); **to be censed** itbakhkhar اتبخّر (bakhra)
censorship raqaaba رقابة
census tiʿdaad تعداد
centimetre santi سنت ; santimitir سنتمتر (*pl* santimitraat)
central markazi مركزي
centralize santar سنتر (santara)
centre (**middle**) nuṣṣ نص ; wasaṭ وسط (*pl* awsaaṭ); **town centre** nuṣṣ al-balad; (**of attention**) santar سنتر (*pl* -aat); (**health, cultural**) markaz مركز (*pl* maraakiz)
century qarn قرن (*pl* quruun)
ceremony iḥtifaal إحتفال (*pl* -aat)
certain mu'akkad مؤكّد ; mut'akkid متأكّد ; akiid أكيد ; **a certain person** shakhiṣ muʿayyan
certainly ḥagiigi حقيقي ; akiid أكيد ; be-t-ta'kiid; **certainly not** abadan أبدا ; nihaa'i نهائي
certainty yagiin يقين
certificate shihaada شهادة (*pl* -aat, shahaayid); **medical certificate** igraar ṭibbi; **wedding certificate** gasiima قسيمة
cervix ʿunq ar-riḥim
Chad tashaad تشاد
Chadian *adj/n* tashaadi تشادي (*pl* -yyiin)
chaff gishir قشر (*unit n* gishra)
chain *n* silsila سلسلة (*pl* salaasil); **iron chain** jinziir جنزير (*pl* janaaziir); **timing chain** (**car**) katiina كتينة (*pl* kataayin)
chair kursi كرسي (*pl* karaasi)
chairperson (*m*) ra'iis aj-jalsa/al-ijtimaaʿ/al-majlis; (*f*) ra'iisat aj-jalsa/al-ijtimaaʿ/al-majlis
chalk (**for blackboard**) ṭabaashiir طباشير ; **piece or stick of chalk** ṭabaashiira طباشيرة
challenge *n* taḥaddi تحدّي (*pl* -yaat) • *v* itḥadda اتحدّى (-a, taḥaddi)

chameleon ḥirbooya حربوية
champion baṭal بطل (*pl* abṭaal)
championship buṭuula بطولة
chance furṣa فرصة (*pl* furaṣ); **by chance** ṣudfa صدفة ; be-ṣudfa ; **to happen by chance** ṣadaf صدف (u, ṣudfa)
change *n* (**alteration**) taghyiir تغيير (*pl* -aat); taḥawwul تحوّل (*pl* -aat); taghayyur تغيّر (*pl* -aat) • *vt* ghayyar غيّر (ghiyy-eer, taghyiir); (**into**) ḥawwal (le-) حوّل (taḥwiil) • *vi* itghayyar اتغيّر (ghiyyeer, taghayyur); (**into**) itḥawwal (le-) اتحوّل (taḥawwul)
change *n* (**from a payment**) baagi باقي (*pl* bawaagi); **small change** fakka فكّة • *vt* (**money**) ḥawwal حوّل (taḥwiil); fakka فكّ (i, fakka)
channel majra مجرى (*pl* majaari); qanaa قناة (*pl* qanawaat); **irrigation channel** turʿa ترعة (*pl* turaʿ); (**small**) jadwal جدول (*pl* jadaawil)
chaos fawḍa فوضى
chapter baab باب (*pl* abwaab); faṣil فصل (*pl* fuṣuul); (**of the Koran**) suura سورة (*pl* suwar)
character shakhṣiyya شخصيّة ; ṭabiʿ طبع ; ṭabiiʿa طبيعة
charcoal faḥam فحم ; **charcoal stove** kaanuun كانون ; mangad منقد (*pl* manaagid)
chard (**Swiss**) salij سلج
charge *n* taman تمن (*pl* atmaan); **in charge of** mas'uul min; **to put in charge of** kallaf be- كلّف (takliif)
charge *v* (**with electricity**) shaḥan شحن (a, shaḥin); **to be charged** itshaḥan شحن (shaḥin, shaḥna);
charger (**for battery**) shaaḥin شاحن (*pl* -aat)
charitable khayri خيري
charity ʿamal kheer; ʿamal khayri
charm *n* (**amulet**) ḥijaab حجاب (*pl* ḥijbaat, aḥjiba) • *v* fatan فتن (i, fitna)
charming fattaan فتّان ; (**females**) faatna فاتنة
chart jadwal جدول (*pl* jadaawil); (**map**) khariiṭa خريطة (*pl* kharaayiṭ); kharṭa خرطة (*pl* khuraṭ)
chase *v* sakka سكّ (u, sakk, sakakaan); ṭaarad طارد (muṭaarada)
chassis shaaseeh شاسيه (*pl* -aat); ḥammaalat al-ʿarabiyya
chat *n* wanasa ونسة • *v* wannas ونّس (wanasa); itwannas اتونّس (wanasa); dardash دردش (dardasha)
chatter *v* rajja رجّ (u, rajj)
cheap rakhiiṣ رخيص ; rakhi رخي
cheat *n* ghashshaash غشّاش ; naṣṣaab نصّاب ; dajjaal دجّال • *v* ghashsha غشّ (u, ghishsh, ghashsh); daggas دقّس (dagsa); khadaʿ خدع (a, khidaʿ); **to be cheated** inghashsha انغشّ (ghashsh, ghashashaan); itghashsha اتغشّ (ghashsh, ghashashaan); dagas دقس (u, dagis); iddaggas ادّقس (diggees)
check *v* (**mechanics**) faḥaṣ فحص (a, faḥiṣ); (**medical**) kashaf كشف (i, kashif); (**revise**) raajaʿ راجع (muraajaʿa)
checkup (**mechanics**) faḥiṣ فحص (*pl* fuḥuuṣaat); (**medical**) kashif كشف (*pl* kushuufaat)
cheek khadd خد (*pl* khuduud); juḍum جضم (*pl* juḍuum); shidig شدق (*pl* shuduug)

cheer *v* hataf هتف (u, hutaaf); **to cheer up** farfash فرفش (firfeesh, farfasha)
cheese jibna جبنة (*pl* ajbaan); (**white**) jibna beeḍa; (**European**) jibna ruumiyya; (**rope**) jibna muḍaffara
chemical kiimaawi كيماوي (*pl*-yyaat)
chemist kiimaawi كيماوي (*pl* -yyiin)
chemistry kiimiya كيميا
cheque sheek شيك (*pl* -aat)
chess shaṭaranj شطرنج
chest (**part of the body**) ṣadur صدر (*pl* ṣuduur)
chest (**box**) ṣanduug صندوق (*pl* ṣanaadiig); **chest of drawers** doolaab دولاب (*pl* dawaaliib)
chew garash قرش (u, garish, garashaan); laak لاك (u, looka, lawakaan); (**tobacco**) saffa سفّ (i, saff); (**the cud**) gaṣaᶜ aj-jirra
chic gaashir قاشر ; shiik شيك
chick siiwsiiw سيوسيو (*pl* sawaa-siiw); katkuut كتكوت (*pl* kataakiit)
chicken(**s**) jidaad جداد ; firaakh فراخ ; **young chicken** farruuja فرّوجة (*pl* faraariij)
chickenpox burjum برجم ; jadari kaazib
chickpeas kabkabee كبكبي
chief ra'iis رئيس (*pl* ruwasa, ru'asaa); (**of a tribe**) naaẓir ناظر (*pl* nuẓẓaar); sulṭaan سلطان (*pl* salaaṭiin); makk مك (*pl* mukuuk); (**of a village or district**) sheekh شيخ (*pl* shiyuukh, mashaayikh); ᶜumda عمدة (*pl* ᶜumad)
chieftaincy salṭana سلطنة
child shaafiᶜ شافع (*pl* shuffaᶜ); jaahil جاهل (*pl* juhhaal); jana جنا (*pl* jinyaat, jannuun); ṭifil طفل (*pl* aṭfaal); **children** shuffaᶜ شفع ; awlaad أولاد ; ᶜiyaal عيال
childbirth wilaada ولادة
chimney madkhana مدخنة (*pl* madaakhin)
chin digin دقن (*pl* duguun)
china ṣiini صيني ; boorsiliin بورسلين
China aṣ-ṣiin
Chinese *adj/n* ṣiini صيني (*pl* -yyiin)
chip *n* (**in china, glass**) kasra كسرة ; (**token, counter, in games**) fiisha فيشة (*pl* -aat, fiish)
chips (**fried potatoes**) shibsi شبسي ; (**homemade**) baṭaaṭis muḥammara
chisel (**stone**) izmiil إزميل (*pl* azaamiil); (**wood**) gadduum قدّوم (*pl* gadaadiim)
chocolate shokolaata شوكولاتة ; shiikoolaata شيكولاتة
choice ikhtiyaar إختيار (*pl* -aat); khiyaar خيار (*pl* -aat)
choir koras كورس
choke *vt* khanag خنق (i, khanig) • *vi* itkhanag اتخنق (khanga); inkhanag انخنق (khanig, khanga)
cholera kolira كلرا
choose ᶜazal عزل (i, ᶜazil); ikhtaar اختار (ikhtiyaar)
chop ḥashsha حشّ (i, ḥashsh); gaṭaᶜ قطع (a, gaṭiᶜ)
chopper saaṭuur ساطور (*pl* sawaaṭiir)
Christ al-masiiḥ
Christian masiiḥi مسيحي (*pl* -yyiin); naṣraani نصراني (*pl* naṣaara)

Christmas ʿiid miilaad al-masiiḥ
chronic muzmin مزمن
church kaniisa كنيسة (*pl* kanaayis)
churn v (**milk**) makhaḍ al-laban
cigarette sijaara سجارة (*pl* sajaayir)
cinema sinama سينما
cinnamon girfa قرفة
circle daayra دايرة (*pl* dawaayir)
circular *adj* mudawwar مدوّر; mudardam مدردم
circular *n* manshuur منشور (*pl* -aat, manaashiir)
circumcise ṭahhar طهّر (ṭahaara, ṭahuur)
circumcision khitaan ختان; ṭahuur طهور (*pl* -aat); **female circumcision** khifaaḍ خفاض; **pharaonic circumcision** khifaaḍ firʿooni; khitaan firʿooni
circumstance *n* ẓarf ظرف (*pl* ẓuruuf)
circus sirk سرك
cirrhosis talayyuf تليّف
cistern ḥooḍ حوض (*pl* ḥeeḍaan, aḥwaaḍ); khazzaan خزّان (*pl* -aat); ḥafiir حفير (*pl* ḥafaayir); (**of lavatory**) saayfun سايفون (*pl* -aat)
citizen muwaaṭin مواطن
citizenship muwaaṭana مواطنة
city madiina مدينة (*pl* mudun)
civic madani مدني
civil madani مدني; (**as opposed to military**) malaki ملكي (*pl* -yyiin); **civil servant** muwaẓẓaf موظّف; **civil society** al-mujtamaʿ al-madani
civilization ḥaḍaara حضارة
civilized mutḥaḍḍir متحضّر; **civilized world** madaniyya مدنيّة; **to be(come) civilized** itḥaḍḍar اتحضّر (taḥaḍḍur); itmaddan اتمدّن (tamaddun)
claim *n* (**demand**) ṭalab طلب (*pl* -aat) • *v* (**demand**) ṭalab طلب (u, ṭalab); (**allege**) iddaʿa ادّعى (-i, iddiʿa); gaal inn-/inno
clan khashm al-beet; ʿashiira عشيرة (*pl* ʿashaayir)
clap *v* ṣaffag صفّق (ṣiffeeg, ṣafga, taṣfiig)
clarification tawḍiiḥ توضيح (*pl* -aat)
clash *n* (**scuffle**) ishtibaak إشتباك (*pl* -aat) • *v* ishtabak (maʿa) اشتبك (ishtibaak); ṣaadam (maʿa) صادم (ṣidaam); itṣaadam (maʿa) اتصادم (muṣaadama); (**e.g. cars**) iddagash ادّقش (dagsha); ṣaadam (maʿa) صادم (ṣidaam); itṣaadam (maʿa) اتصادم (muṣaadama)
class (**year grade**) ṣaff صف (*pl* ṣufuuf); (**social**) ṭabaqa طبقة; (**quality**) daraja درجة; **first class** daraja uula
classification taṣniif تصنيف (*pl* -aat)
classify ṣannaf صنّف (taṣniif)
classroom faṣil فصل (*pl* fuṣuul)
clause band بند (*pl* bunuud)
claw makhlab مخلب (*pl* makhaalib)
clay *n* ṭiin طين (*pl* aṭyaan); **river clay** ṭami طمي • *adj* fukhkhaar فخّار
clean *adj* naḍiif نضيف; (**ritually**) ṭaahir طاهر • *v* naḍḍaf نضّف (niḍḍeef, naḍaafa, tanḍiif); (**rice, beans**) laggaṭ لقّط (liggeeṭ, talgiiṭ); nagga نقّى (-i, niggeey)
cleaner (*m*) farraash فرّاش; (*f*) farraasha فرّاشة
cleanliness naḍaafa نضافة

clear *adj* waaḍiḥ واضح ; baayin باين ; ẓaahir ظاهر ; **to be(come) clear** waḍaḥ وضح (yooḍaḥ, waḍḥa, wuḍuuḥ); wiḍiḥ وضح (yooḍaḥ, waḍḥa, wuḍuuḥ); **to make clear** waḍḍaḥ وضّح (wiḍḍeeḥ, tawḍiiḥ); bayyan بيّن (biyyeen) • *v* (**from customs**) khallaṣ خلّص (takhliiṣ); (**field**) kabar كبر (u, kabir); (**pipes**) sallak سلّك (silleek)

clearance (**from customs**) takhliiṣ تخليص (*pl* takhaaliiṣ); **to obtain clearance for** khallaṣ خلّص (khilleeṣ, takhliiṣ)

clergyman gassiis قسّيس (*pl* gasaawsa, gusus); giss قس (*pl* gasaawsa, gusus)

clerk kaatib كاتب (*pl* kataba); **head clerk** baashkaatib باشكاتب

clever najiiḍ نجيض (*pl* nujaaḍ); shaaṭir شاطر (*pl* shaaṭriin, shuṭṭaar); nabiih نبيه (*pl* nubaha)

cleverness najaaḍa نجاضة ; shaṭaara شطارة ; nabaaha نباهة

click *v* (**fingers**) ṭargaʿ طرقع (ṭargaʿa, ṭirgeeʿ); (**on a button**) daas داس (u, doosa)

climate manaakh مناخ (*pl* -aat); jaw جو (*pl* ajwaa)

climb *v* ṭalaʿ fi طلع (a, ṭuluuʿ); itshaʿbaṭ fi إتشعبط (shiʿbeeṭ, shaʿbaṭa)

cling masak مسك (i, masik, maska, masakaan)

clinic ʿiyaada عيادة ; **specialized clinic** maṣaḥḥa مصحّة

clitoris jana جنا ; bizr بزر

cloak ʿibaaya عباية

clock saaʿa ساعة

close *v* gafal قفل (i, gafil); sadda سدّ (i, sadd); **to be closed** itgafal اتقفّل (gafil); itgaffal اتقفّل (giffeel); itsadda اتسدّ (sadd, insidaad); insadda انسدّ (sadd, insidaad); **to close one's eyes** ghamaḍ al-ʿiyuun (i, ghamiḍ, ghimeeḍa); **to close one's mouth** ṣamma khashm-o

close *adj* gariib (min/le-) قريب (*pl* -iin, guraab)

closeness garaaba قرابة

cloth gumaash قماش (*pl* -aat, agmisha); (**for cleaning**) dulgaan دلقان (*pl* dalaagiin); dalguun دلقون (*pl* dalaagiin); fuuṭa فوطة (*pl* fuwaṭ)

clothe labbas لبّس (libbees); kasa كسا (i, kiswa)

clothes huduum هدوم ; malaabis ملابس ; libis لبس ; **new clothes** kasaawi كساوي ; **clothes horse** shammaaʿa شمّاعة

clothes hanger shammaaʿa شمّاعة

clothes peg mashbak مشبك (*pl* mashaabik)

cloud(s) saḥaab سحاب ; ghamaam غمام ; gheem غيم (*pl* ghiyuum)

clouded **to be clouded** ghayyam غيّم (gheem)

cloudy mughayyim مغيّم

clove (**of garlic**) faṣṣ tuum

cloves gurunful قرنفل (*unit n* gurunfulaaya)

club (**social centre**) naadi نادي (*pl* andiya, nawaadi)

club (**weapon**) kaaluut كالوت (*pl* kawaaliit); ʿukkaaz عكاز (*pl* ʿakaakiiz)

clumsy ashtar أشتر (*f* shatra, *pl* shutur)

clutch (**of vehicle**) kalatsh كلتش (*pl* -aat)

coal faḥam فحم ; **hot coals** jamur جمر (*unit n* jamra)

coarse khishin خشن ; **coarse ground** duraash دراش
coast saaḥil ساحل (*pl* sawaaḥil); shaaṭi شاطي (*pl* shawaaṭi)
coat balṭo بلطو (*pl* -haat)
coat hanger shammaaᶜa شمّاعة
cobbler nugulti نقلتي ; jazmaji جزمجي (*pl* -iyya); ṣarmaati صرماتي (*pl* -yya)
cock diik ديك (*pl* diyuuk, dayaka); abu taaj
cockroach(**es**) ṣarṣaar صرصار (*pl* ṣaraaṣiir); ṣarṣuur صرصور (*pl* ṣaraaṣiir); gurumbuᶜ قرمبع
cockscomb ᶜurf عرف (*pl* aᶜraaf); taaj ad-diik
cocoa kakaaw كاكاو
code shafra شفرة ; **criminal code** qaanuun aj-jinaa'iyyaat; **penal code** qaanuun al-ᶜuguubaat; **Islamic penal code** ḥuduud حدود
coercion ghaṣib غصب ; ikraah إكراه
coffee (**drink**) gahwa قهوة (*pl* gahaawi); (**beans**) bunn بن ; **coffee pot** jabana جبنة
coffin taabuut تابوت (*pl* tawaabiit)
cog *n* sinna سنّة
cogwheel tiris ترس (*pl* turuus)
coil *vt* laffa لفّ (i, laff); ṭawa طوى (-i, ṭawi) • *n* (intrauterine device) lawlab لولب (*pl* lawaalib)
coincidence ṣudfa صدفة (*pl* ṣudaf); **by coincidence** ṣudfa صدفة ; be-ṣudfa بصدفة ; **to happen by coincidence** ṣadaf صدف (u, ṣudfa)
coins fakka فكّة ; fakka ḥadiid
cold *adj* (**of things**) saagiṭ ساقط ; baarid بارد ; (**of persons**) bardaan بردان ; **cold weather** barid برد ; gurr قر ; **to become cold** birid برد (a, barid); **to make cold** barrad برّد (birreed, tabriid) • *n* sagaṭ سقط ; buruuda برودة ; **common cold** nazla نزلة ; zukma زكمة ; zukaam زكام
collaborate itshaarak (maᶜa) اتشارك (mushaaraka); itᶜaawanmaᶜa اتعاون (muᶜaawana, taᶜaawun)
collapse *n* inhiyaar انهيار • *v* inhaar انهار (inhiyaar); (**house**) inhadda انهدّ (hadd); ithadda اتهدّ (hadd)
collar liyaaga لياقة
colleague (*m*) zamiil زميل (*pl* zumlaan, zumala); (*f*) zamiila
collect lamma لمّ (i, lamm); jamaᶜ جمع (a, jamiᶜ); jammaᶜ جمّع (jimmeeᶜ, tajmiiᶜ); (**things only**) lamlam لملم (limleem, lamlama); **to be collected** itlamma اتلمّ (lamma, lamamaan); itjamaᶜ اتجمع (jamᶜa); itjammaᶜ اتجمّع (jimmeeᶜ, tajmiiᶜ); (**things only**) itlamlam اتلملم (lamlama, tilimlim)
collection majmuuᶜa مجموعة
collective *adj* jamaaᶜi جماعي • *n* mujammaᶜ مجمّع (*pl* -aat); majmaᶜ مجمع (*pl* -aat)
collide dagash دقش (u, dagish, dagsha); ṣadam صدم (u, ṣadma); ṣaadam maᶜa صادم (ṣadma, muṣaadama)
collision ṣadma صدمة ; taṣaadum تصادم (*pl* -aat)
colloquial **the colloquial language** al-lugha ad-daarija; al-lugha ad-daarijiyya; ad-daariji; al-lugha al-ᶜaammiyya; al-ᶜaammiyya
colonel ᶜagiid عقيد (*pl* ᶜugada)
colour *n* loon لون (*pl* alwaan) • *v* lawwan لوّن (talwiin); (**hair or**

clothes) ṣabagh صبغ (i, ṣabigh); ṣabbagh صبّغ (ṣibbeegh, taṣbiigh)
colt muhr مهر (*pl* muhuur)
column ʿamuud عمود (*pl* ʿawaamiid, aʿmida); **the spinal column** al-ʿamuud al-faqri
coma ghaybuuba غيبوبة ; kooma كوما ; **in a coma** mughayyib مغيّب ; **to go into a coma** ghabba غبّى (-i, ghaybuuba)
comb *n* mushuṭ مشط (*pl* amshaaṭ) • *v* sarraḥ سرّح (sirreeḥ, tasriiḥ)
combination (**compound**) tarkiib تركيب (*pl* -aat); (**arrangement**) tartiib تركيب (*pl* -aat)
combine (**compound**) rakkab ركّب (rikkeeb, tarkiib)
come ja جا (-i, jayya) • *imp* **come!** taʿaal تعال ; **come on!** yalla يللا ; **to come back** rajaʿ رجع (a, rujuuʿ); gabbal raajiʿ; ṣadda raajiʿ; **to come in** khashsha خشّ (u, khashsh); dakhal دخل (u, dukhuul); **to come near** (**to**) garrab (min/le-) قرّب (girreeb, tagriib); **to come out** ṭalaʿ طلع (a, ṭuluuʿ)
comfort *n* (**ease**) raaḥa راحة • *v* (console) waasa واسى (-i, muwaasaa)
comfortable muriiḥ مريح ; **feeling comfortable** murtaaḥ مرتاح
comic adj muḍḥik مضحك ; fukaahi فكاهي
comma kooma كوما ; shawla شولة
command *n* amr أمر (*pl* awaamir) • *v* amar (be-) أمر (u, amr)
commander qaa'id قائد (*pl* quwwaad); qaayid قايد (*pl* quwwaad)
comment *n* taʿliiq تعليق (-aat); mulaaḥaẓa ملاحظة • *v* ʿallaq (ʿala) علّق (taʿliiq)
commerce tijaara تجارة ; beeʿ wa shira
commercial tijaari تجاري
commission (**payment**) ʿumuula عمولة ; (**committee**) lajna لجنة (*pl* lijaan)
commissioner muʿtamad معتمد ; (**member of commission**) mufawwaḍ مفوّض
commit (**crime**) irtakab ارتكب (irtikaab); **to commit perjury** ḥalaf be-l-kiḍib; **to commit suicide** intaḥar انتحر (intiḥaar)
commitment iltizaam إلتزام (*pl* -aat); (**obligation**) irtibaaṭ إرتباط (*pl* -aat)
committee lajna لجنة (*pl* lijaan)
common ʿaadi عادي ; ʿaamm عامّ ; (**shared**) mushtarak مشترك
commotion dawsha دوشة ; jooṭa جوطة ; ḍajja ضجّة ; jaḍḍa جضّة
communicate itwaaṣal maʿa اتواصل (muwaaṣala, tawaaṣul)
communication muwaaṣala مواصلة ; tawaaṣul تواصل (*pl* -aat)
communism shuyuuʿiyya شيوعيّة
communist shuyuuʿi شيوعي (*pl* -yyiin)
community mujtamaʿ مجتمع (*pl* -aat); **community-based organization** jamʿiyya qaaʿidiyya
companion rafiig رفيق (*pl* rafaaga)
companionship rifga رفقة
company sharika شركة ; (**theatre**) firga فرقة (*pl* firag)
compare qaaran been قارن (muqaarana)
comparison muqaarana مقارنة
compass bawṣala بوصلة
compasses barjal برجل (*pl* baraajil)

compassion maḥanna محنّة ; ḥinniyya حنّيّة ; ḥanaan حنان ; raḥma رحمة
compassionate ḥaniin حنين ; raḥiim رحيم (*pl* ruḥama)
compel ghaṣab غصب (i, ghaṣib); jabar (ʿala) جبر (i, jabur)
compensate ʿawwaḍ عوّض (taʿwiiḍ)
compensation taʿwiiḍ تعويض (*pl* -aat); **without compensation** be-duun mugaabil
compete naafas نافس (munaafasa)
competent mukhtaṣṣ مختص
competition munaafasa منافسة
complain shaka (min) شكى (-i, shakwa, shakiyya); ishtaka (min) اشتكى (-i, shakwa, shakiyya)
complaint shakwa شكوى (*pl* shakaawi); shakiyya شكيّة ; **official complaint** balaagh بلاغ (*pl* -aat)
complete *adj* kaamil كامل ; shaamil شامل ; taamm تام • v kammal كمّل (kamaal, kamla); tamma تمّ (i, tamm); **to be completed** kimil كمل (a, kamla); ittamma اتّمّ (tamm, tamamaan)
completely (**with an adjective**) tabb تب ; tjatt تجت ; (**with a verb**) be-l-kaamil
complex *adj* muʿaggad معقّد • *n* majmuuʿa مجموعة ; (**psychological**) ʿugda عقدة (*pl* ʿugad)
complicate ʿaggad عقّد (taʿgiid)
component mukawwin مكوّن (*pl* -aat)
compose (**e.g. a song, a poem**) allaf ألّف (ya'allif, ta'liif)
composer mu'allif مؤلّف
compress *n* kammaada كمّادة ; mukammada مكمّدة
compulsion ghaṣib غصب ; jabur جبر
compulsory ijbaari اجباري
computer kombyuutar كمبيوتر (*pl* -aat); ḥaasuub حاسوب *n* (*pl* ḥawaasiib)
comrade rafiig رفيق (*pl* rifaag, rafaaga); zamiil زميل (*pl* zumala)
conceal dassa دسّ (i, dassa, dasasaan); labbad لبّد (libbeed); khabba خبّى (-i, khibbeey)
conceited mutkabbir متكبّر ; maghruur مغرور ; manfuukh منفوخ ; **to be**(**come**) **conceited** itkabbar اتكبّر (takabbur)
conceive ḥimil حمل (a, ḥimil)
concentrate *vi* (**on**) rakkaz (fi) ركّز (tarkiiz) • *vt* rakkaz ركّز (tarkiiz)
concentrated (**focussed**) murakkiz مركّز ; (**of solution, etc.**) murakkaz مركّز
concentration tarkiiz تركيز
concept mafhuum مفهوم (*pl* mafaahiim); taṣawwur تصوّر (*pl* -aat)
concern *n* (**interest**) ihtimaam إهتمام (*pl* -aat) • *v* khaṣṣa خصّ (u, khuṣuuṣ); (**care for**) hamma be- همّ (i, hamm)
concerned (**worried**) mahmuum (be) مهموم
concerning be-khuṣuuṣ; be-n-nisba le-
concession (**license**) imtiyaaz إمتياز (*pl* -aat); (**yielding**) tanaazul تنازل (*pl* -aat)
conciliate ṣaalaḥ صالح (i, muṣaalaḥa)
concise mukhtaṣar مختصر ; **to be concise** ikhtaṣar اختصر (ikhtiṣaar)

conclude khatam ختم (i, khatim)
conclusion khulaaṣa خلاصة ; (**out-come**) natiija نتيجة (*pl* nataayij)
concrete kharaṣaana خرصانة ; **reinforced concrete, ferrocon-crete** asmant musallaḥ
condemn adaan أدان (i, idaana)
condense ikhtaṣar اختصر (ikhtiṣaar)
condition (**requirement**) sharṭ شرط (*pl* shuruuṭ); (**state**) ḥaal حال (*pl* aḥwaal); ḥaala حالة (*pl* -aat, aḥwaal); **on the condition that** ʿala sharṭ, be-sharṭ
condole ʿazza fi عزّى (-i, ʿaza, taʿziya)
condolences taʿziya تعزية
condom kondoom كندوم (*pl* -aat)
conduct *n* suluuk سلوك (*pl* -iyaat)
conductor (**bus or train**) kumsaari كمساري (*pl* kamaasra)
conference mu'tamar مؤتمر (-aat); **press conference** mu'tamar ṣaḥafi; **summit conference** qimma قمّة (*pl* qimam)
confess iʿtaraf (be-) إعترف (iʿtiraaf); garra (be-) قرّ (i, igraar)
confession iʿtiraaf إعتراف (*pl* -aat)
confidence siqa سقة
confident waasiq واسق
confidential sirri سرّي
confine ḥabas حبس (i, ḥabis, ḥabsa)
confinement *n* ḥabis حبس
confirm akkad اكّد (ya'akkid, ta'kiid); asbat أسبت (i, isbaat)
confirmation ta'kiid تأكيد ; isbaat إسبات (*pl* -aat)
confiscate ṣaadar صادر (muṣaadara); **to be confiscated** itṣaadar اتصادر (muṣaadara)
confiscation muṣaadara مصادرة
conflict ṣiraaʿ صراع (*pl* -aat)
confront waajah واجه (muwaajaha)
confrontation muwaajaha مواجهة
confuse rabak ربك (i, rabka); lakham لخم (a, lakhma); lakhbaṭ لخبط (likhbeeṭ, lakhbaṭa); **to be(come) confused** itrabak اتربك (rabka); itlakham اتلخم (lakhma); itlakhbaṭ اتلخبط (likhbeeṭ, lakhbaṭa)
confused marbuuk مربوك ; mal-khuum ملخوم ; mutlakhim متلخم ; mutlakhbaṭ/mutlakhbiṭ متلخبط
confusion rabka ربكة ; lakhma لخمة ; lakhbaṭa لخبطة
congestion iḥtigaan إحتقان
congratulate baarak le- بارك (mubaaraka); hanna (be-) هنّى (-i, tahniya); baakhat باخت (mubaakhata)
congratulations *interj* mabruuk مبروك
congregation shaʿb شعب (*pl* shuʿuub)
congress mu'tamar مؤتمر (-aat)
conjurer ḥaawi حاوي (*pl* ḥuwaa); saaḥir ساحر (*pl* saḥara)
connect waṣṣal وصّل (wiṣṣeel); ittaṣṣal be- اتّصل (ittiṣaal)
connection ṣila صلة ; ʿalaaga (be-) علاقة ; (**telephone**) ittiṣaal إتّصال (*pl* -aat)
conquer ghalab غلب (i, ghulub)
conscience ḍamiir ضمير (*pl* ḍamaayiir); zimma زمّة (*pl* zimam)
conscious waaʿi واعي ; **to make s.o. conscious of sth.** waʿʿa (be-) وعى (-i, tawʿiya)
consecration takriis تكريس
consent *n* riḍa رضا • *v* riḍa (be-) رضى (-a, riḍa)

consequence natiija نتيجة (*pl* nataayij); **negative consequence** ʿaagiba عاقبة (*pl* ʿawaagib)
consequently ghaayto غايتو
consider iʿtabar إعتبر (iʿtibaar); ḥasab حسب (i, ḥisaab)
consideration iʿtibaar إعتبار (*pl* -aat); **to take into consideration** naẓar fi نظر (u, naẓir); akhad fi iʿtibaar-o
consignment (**of goods**) irsaaliyya إرساليّة
console waasa واسى (-i, muwaasaa)
conspiracy mu'aamara مؤامرة
conspire it'aamar (ʿala/ḍidd) اتآمر (mu'aamara, ta'aamur)
constant daayim دايم ; mustamirr مستمر
constipation imsaak إمساك ; yaabuusa يابوسة
constitution dastuur دستور (*pl* dasaatiir)
consult *v* istashaar استشار (istishaara); shaawar شاور (mushaawara)
consultant mustashaar مستشار
consultation istishaara استشارة ; shuura شورة ; **to hold a consultation** itfaakar اتفاكر (mufaakara); faakar فاكر (mufaakara)
consume istahlak استهلك (istihlaak)
consumer mustahlik مستهلك
consumption istihlaak إستهلاك (*pl* -aat)
contact *n* ittiṣaal إتّصال (*pl* -aat); **in contact with** ʿala ittiṣaal be- • *v* ittaṣṣal be- اتّصل (ittiṣaal)
contagious muʿdi معدي
contain ḥawa حوى (-i, ḥawiya); iḥtawa ʿala احتوى (iḥtiwa)
contemporary muʿaaṣir معاصر
contempt ḥagaara حقارة ; ḥugra حقرة ; **to treat with contempt** istakhaffa استخفّ (istikhfaaf); ḥagar حقر (i, ḥagaara); iḥtagar احتقر (ḥagaara, iḥtigaar)
contemptible ḥagiir حقير
contemptuous ḥaggaar حقّار
content *adj* qanuuʿ قنوع ; **to be content** iktafa (be-) إكتفى (iktifa)
content *n* maḍmuun مضمون (*pl* maḍaamiin)
contentment iktifa إكتفا ; qanaaʿa قناعة
contest *n* musaabaqa مسابقة ; sibaaq سباق
continent *n* qaarra قارة
continuation istimraar إستمرار ; istimraariyya إستمراريّة
continue istamarra استمرّ (istimraar, istimraariyya); waaṣal واصل (muwaaṣala); daawam داوم (mudaawama)
continuous mustamirr مستمر
continuously ṭawwaali طوّالى ; b-istimraar
contraband buḍaaʿa muharraba
contract *n* ʿagid عقد (*pl* ʿuguud); kontraato كنتراتو (*no pl*); **to make up a contract** ʿagad عقد (i, ʿagid) • *v* gaawal قاول (mugaawala); itgaawal maʿa اتقاول (mugaawala)
contract *v* (**shrink**) inkamash انكمش (inkimaash); (**from cold**) itkarfas اتكرفس (kirfees, karfasa)
contractor mugaawil مقاول ; (**contracted to supply**) mutʿahhid متعهّد
contradict ghaalaṭ غالط (mughaalaṭa); ʿaakas عاكس (muʿaakasa); ʿaariḍ (muʿaaraḍa);

khaalaf خالف (khilaaf, mukhaalafa)
contradiction tanaaquḍ تناقض (*pl* -aat)
contrary muᶜaakis معاكس ; mukhaalif مخالف ; **on the contrary** be-l-ᶜaks
contribute (**to**) saaham be- (fi) ساهم (musaahama); shaarak be- (fi) شارك (mushaaraka)
control *n* taḥakkum تحكّم • *v* itḥakkam fi اتحكّم (taḥakkum); sayṭar ᶜala سيطر (sayṭara); itsayṭar ᶜala اتسيطر (sayṭara)
convenient munaasib مناسب
convention (**treaty**) muᶜaahada معاهدة
conversation kalaam كلام ; (**formal**) muḥaadasa محادس
convert **to convert to Islam** aslam أسلم (i, islaam)
convey wadda ودّى (-i, widdeey); waṣṣal وصّل (wiṣṣeel)
convict *v* adaan أدان (i, idaana)
conviction (**belief**) ᶜaqiida عقيدة (*pl* ᶜaqaayid); (**verdict**) idaana إدانة ; **previous criminal conviction** saabiqa سابقة (*pl* sawaabiq)
convince aqnaᶜ أقنع (yuqniᶜ, iqnaaᶜ); **to be convinced** iqtanaᶜ إقتنع (iqtinaaᶜ)
convoy konfooy كنفوي (*pl* -aat); gaafilat ᶜarabaat; ṭaabuur ᶜarabaat
convulsion farfara فرفرة ; tashannuj تشنّج (*pl* -aat)
cook *n* ṭabbaakh طبّاخ • *v* ṭabakh طبخ (u, ṭabiikh); (**till done**) najjaḍ نجّض (nijjeeḍ, tanjiiḍ); **to be cooked** iṭṭabakh اطّبخ (ṭabikh); (**done**) nijiḍ نجض (najaaḍ); istawa استوى (-i, istiwa)
cooker **gas cooker** butajaaz بوتجاز (*pl* -aat)
cookies khabiiz خبيز
cool *adj* baarid بارد ; muraṭṭib مرطّب • *vt* barrad برّد (birreed, tabriid) • *vi* birid برد (a, barid)
cooler *n* ḥaffaaẓa حفّاظة
coolness (**of air**) ruṭuuba رطوبة ; ṭaraawa طراوة
cooperate itᶜaawan(maᶜa) اتعاون (muᶜaawana, taᶜaawun)
cooperation taᶜaawun تعاون
cooperative *n* mujammaᶜ مجمّع (*pl* -aat); majmaᶜ مجمع (*pl* -aat)
coordinate *v* nassaq نسّق (tansiiq)
coordination tansiiq تنسيق
coordinator munassiq منسّق
cope itṣarraf fi (**things**), maᶜa (**persons**) اتصرّف (taṣarruf)
copper niḥaas نحاس
Coptic gibṭi قبطي (*pl* agbaaṭ, gibaṭ)
copy *n* nuskha نسخة (*pl* nusakh); **rough copy** muswadda مسودّة • *v* nasakh نسخ (a, nasikh); nagal نقل (u, nagil)
copybook karraas كرّاس (*pl* -aat, karaariis)
coral murjaan مرجان
cord ḥabil حبل (*pl* ḥibaal); **umbilical cord** ḥabl as-surra, ḥabl al-mashiima
coriander (**dried**) kasbara كسبرة ; kashbara كشبرة ; (**fresh**) kasbara khaḍra
cork fulla فلّة (*pl* -aat, fulal)
corn (**maize**) ᶜeesh riif; dura shaami; **corn oil** zeet dura; **corn weevils** ᶜantat al-ḥubuub
corn (**on foot**) ᶜeen as-samak

corner *n* rukun ركن (*pl* arkaan); zaawiya زاوية (*pl* zawaaya); (**football**) ḍarba rukniyya; **street corner** naaṣya ناصية (*pl* nawaaṣi)
corporal ʿariif عريف (*pl* ʿurafa)
corporation hay'a هيئة
corpse janaaza جنازة (*pl* janaayiz); jussa جسّة (*pl* jusas); jitta جتّة (*pl* jitat)
correct *adj* maẓbuuṭ مظبوط ; saliim سليم ; ṣaaḥḥ صاح ; ṣaḥiiḥ صحيح ; (**of conduct**) aṣiil أصيل • *v* ṣaḥḥaḥ صحّح (taṣḥiiḥ); (**draft of document**) bayyaḍ بيّض (tabyiiḍ); **to be corrected** itṣaḥḥaḥ اتصحّح (taṣḥiiḥ)
correctness ṣaḥḥa صحّة
correspondence muraasala مراسلة ; mukaataba مكاتبة
corridor mamarr ممر (*pl* -aat)
corrode it'aakal اتآكل (ta'aakul)
corrupt *adj* faasid فاسد ; **to be(come) corrupt** fasad فسد (i, fasaad) • *v* afsad أفسد (i, ifsaad); fassad فسّد (fasaad)
corruption fasaad فساد
cosmetics adawaat tajmiil; kabareet كبريت ; **cosmetics vendor** ʿaṭṭaar عطار
cost *n* taman تمن (*pl* atmaan); **basic cost** taklifa تكلفة ; **high cost** ghala غلا ; **cost of labour** maṣnaʿiyya مصنعيّة • *v* itkallaf اتكلّف (taklifa, kulfa); kallaf كلّف (takliif)
cotton guṭun قطن ; **unbleached cotton** dammuuriyya دمّوريّة
couch kanaba كنبة (*pl* -aat, kanab)
cough *n* guḥḥa قحّة ; **whooping cough** suʿaal diiki • *v* gaḥḥa قحّ (u, guḥḥa)
council majlis مجلس (*pl* majaalis); **council of elders** ajaawiid أجاويد ; **state council** majlis ash-shuura
count ʿadda عدّ (i, ʿadd); **to be counted** inḥasab انحسب (ḥisaab); itʿadda اتعدّ (ʿadd)
counter (**in shop, bank**) kawntar كونتر (-aat); bank بنك (*pl* bunukka); (**of post office**) shubbaak شبّاك (*pl* shabaabiik); (**token, chip, in games**) fiisha فيشة (*pl* -aat, fiish)
counterfeit *adj* muzawwar مزوّر ; muzayyaf مزيّف ; maghshuush مغشوش ; **to be counterfeit** itzawwar اتزوّر (tazwiir); itzayyaf اتزيّف (tazyiif) • *v* zawwar زوّر (tazwiir); zayyaf زيّف (tazyiif)
country balad بلد (*pl* bilaad, buldaan); **open country** khala خلا
countryside riif ريف (*pl* aryaaf); **from the countryside** iqliimi إقليمي ; riifi ريفي
coup d'etat ingilaab إنقلاب (-aat)
courage shajaaʿa شجاعة
courageous shujaaʿ شجاع (*pl* shijʿaan, shujʿaan); jarii' جريء ; **courageous and trustworthy** ḍakraan ضكران
courageously be-shajaaʿa
courgette(s) koosa كوسا (*unit n* koosa, koosaaya)
courier mursaal مرسال (*pl* maraasiil)
course koors كورس (*pl* -aat); dawra taḍriibiyya; **of course** ṭabʿan طبعاً ; be-ṭ-ṭabʿ
court *n* (**tribunal**) maḥkama محكمة (*pl* maḥaakim); **court of appeal** maḥkamat al-isti'naaf;

high court maḥkama ʿulya; Islamic court maḥkama sharʿiyya; military court majlis ʿaskari; constitutional court al-maḥkama al-dastuuriyya; criminal court maḥkama jinaa'iyya; summary court maḥkama juz'iyya; traditional tribal court maḥkamat al-mashaayikh

courtesy mujaamala مجاملة ; **empty courtesy** mujaamala saay; **to show courtesy** jaamal جامل (mujaamala)

courtyard ḥoosh حوش (*pl* ḥeeshaan)

cousin (**male on father's side**) wad ʿamm(a); (**female on father's side**) bitt ʿamm(a); (**male on mother's side**) wad khaal(a); (**female on mother's side**) bitt khaal(a)

cover *n* (**lid**) ghuṭaaya غطاية ; ghuṭa غطا (*pl* ghuṭaayaat); (**of a book**) ghilaaf غلاف (*pl* -aat, aghlifa); (**book wrapper**) jilaad جلاد (*pl* -aat); **traditional food cover** ṭabag طبق (*pl* ṭubaaga) • *v* ghaṭṭa غطّى (-i, taghṭiya); (**with a sheet or carpet**) farrash فرّش (firreesh, farish); (**protect**) satar ستر (u, sitir)

covet ṭimiʿ fi طمع (a, ṭamaʿ)

cow(s) bagar بقر

coward jabaan جبان (*pl* -iin, jubana)

cowardice jubun جبن

co-wife ḍarra ضرّة

crack *n* shagg شق (*pl* shuguug); sharkha شرخة *n* (*pl* shuruukh); sharikh شرخ *n* (*pl* shuruukh) • *vi* inshagga انشقّ (shagg, shagagaan); itshagga اتشقّ (shagg, shagga); itsharakh اتشرخ (sharkha) • *vt* shagga شقّ (i, shagg, shagagaan); shaggag شقّق (shiggeeg, tashgiig); sharakh شرخ (a, sharikh, sharkha)

craft (**trade**) ḥirfa حرفة (*pl* ḥiraf)

craftsman ṣinaaʿi صناعي (*pl* ṣanaayʿiyya); ḥirafi حرفي (*pl* -yyiin)

craftsmanship mahaara مهارة ; ḥarfana حرفنة ; jadaara جدارة

cramp (**muscle**) shadd ʿaḍali; (**bowels**) lawaaya لوايا

crank karanki كرنكي

crankcase ʿilbat al-karanki

crankshaft ʿamuud al-karanki

crane(s) (**bird**) rahaw رهو

crash *n* ṣadma صدمة ; taṣaadum تصادم (*pl* -aat); (**plane**) taḥaṭṭum تحطّم (*pl* -aat) • *v* (**plane**) itḥaṭṭam اتحطّم (ḥiṭṭeem, taḥṭiim); **to crash into** dagash دقش (u, dagish, dagsha); ṣadam صدم (u, ṣadma); ṣaadam maʿa صادم (ṣadma, muṣaadama)

crave *v* ishtaha اشتهى (-i, shahwa, ishtiha); (**during pregnancy**) itwaḥam اتوحم (waḥam)

crawl zaḥaf زحف (a, zaḥif, zaḥafaan); (**child**) ḥaba حبى (-u, ḥabayaan)

crazy majnuun مجنون (*pl* majaaniin); mushooṭin مشوطن ; **crazy about** (**e.g. a person**) mukassar fi; **he is crazy about** (**ice cream**) jinn-o fi (ayskriim)

cream (**milk**) gishṭa قشطة ; jummaada جمّادة ; furṣa فرصة ; (**for cosmetic use**) kreem كريم (*pl* -aat); dihaan دهان (-aat); (**salve**) marham مرهم (*pl* maraahim); **shaving cream** maʿjuun ḥilaaga

crease *vt* karfas كرفس (kirfees, karfasa); karmash كرمش (kirmeesh, karmasha) • *vi* itkarfas اتكرفس (kirfees, karfasa); itkarmash اتكرمش (kirmeesh, karmasha)
create (**God**) khalaq خلق (i, khaliq); (**humans**) abdaᶜ ابدع
creation (**divine**) khalq خلق ; (**human**) ibdaaᶜ إبداع (*pl* -aat)
creature makhluug مخلوق (*pl* makhaaliig)
credit raṣiid رصيد
creditor daayin داين ; mudayyin مديّن
creep zaḥaf زحف (a, zaḥif, zaḥafaan)
crescent (**moon**) hilaal هلال ; **the Red Crescent** al-hilaal al-aḥmar
cress jirjiir جرجير
crest ᶜurf عرف (*pl* aᶜraaf)
crew fariig فريق (*pl* firag); **ship's crew** baḥḥaara
cricket (**field**) ṣarṣaar صرصار (*pl* ṣaraaṣiir); (**house**) abu j-jindi; abu j-jindib
crime janiyya جنيّة ; jariima جريمة (*pl* jaraayim); (**felony**) jinaaya جناية
criminal *adj* jinaa'i جنائي • *n* mujrim مجرم
crippled mukassaḥ مكسّح ; aᶜraj أعرج (*f* ᶜarja, *pl* ᶜuruj); **to be(come) crippled** ᶜaraj عرج (i, ᶜaraj, ᶜarja)
crisis azma أزمة (*pl* -aat, izam)
criterion miᶜyaar معيار (*pl* maᶜaayiir); miqyaas مقياس (*pl* maqaayiis)
critical (**grave**) khaṭiir خطير
criticize naqad نقد (u, naqd)
crocodile tumsaaḥ تمساح (*pl* tamaasiiḥ)
crooked aᶜwaj أعوج (*f* ᶜawja, *pl* ᶜuwuj); malwi ملوي
crops zarᶜa زرعة ; maḥṣuul محصول (*pl* maḥaaṣiil)
cross *n* ṣaliib صليب (*pl* ṣulbaan); **the Red Cross** aṣ-ṣaliib al-aḥmar; **to make the sign of the cross** ṣallab صلّب (taṣliib); **to put a cross** (**for marking or deleting**) ṣallab صلّب (taṣliib) • *v* gaṭaᶜ قطع (a, gaṭiᶜ); ᶜabar (ᶜabra, ᶜubuur); ᶜadda عدّى (-i, ᶜiddeey); **to cross out** shaṭab شطب (u, shaṭib); **to be crossed out** itshaṭab اتشطب (shaṭib)
crossbar (**of goalpost**) ᶜarraaḍa عرّاضة (*pl* -aat)
crossbeam ᶜarraaḍ عرّاض (*pl* -aat); ᶜarraaḍa عرّاضة
cross-examination istijwaab إستجواب (*pl* -aat)
cross-examine istajwab استجوب (istijwaab)
cross-eyed aḥwal أحول (*f* ḥawla, *pl* ḥuwul); aḥwaṣ أحوص (*f* ḥawṣa, *pl* ḥuwuṣ)
crossroads tagaaṭuᶜ تقاطع
crow *n* ghuraab غراب (*pl* ghirbaan) • *v* ᶜooᶜa عوعى (-i, ᶜooᶜaay); (**of rooster**) koorak كورك (kooraak)
crowbar ᶜatala عتلة
crowd *n* ḥashid حشد (*pl* ḥushuud); lamma لمّة
crowded mazḥuum مزحوم ; zaḥma زحمة
crown taaj تاج (*pl* tiijaan)
cruel gaasi قاسي
cruelty gaswa قسوة
crumb fatfuuta فتفوتة (*pl* fataafiit)
crumple karfas كرفس (kirfees, karfasa); karmash كرمش (kirmeesh,

karmasha); **to be crumpled** itkarfas اتكرفس (kirfees, karfasa); itkarmash اتكرمش (kirmeesh, karmasha)

crush *v* haras هرس (i, hars, haris); raḍakh رضخ (a, raḍikh); (**with the foot**) fajaq فجق (a, fajiq)

crutch ʿukkaaz عكاز (*pl* ʿakaakiiz); **to walk with crutches** itʿakkaz اتعكّز (ʿikkeez)

cry *n* ṣarkha صرخة • *v* koorak كورك (kooraak); ṣarrakh صرّخ (ṣuraakh, ṣirreekh); (**weep**) baka (ʿala) بكى (-i, bika)

crystal balluur بلّور (*pl* -aat)

cub jireew جريو (*pl* jireewaat); jiru جرو (*pl* jireewaat)

cube mukaʿʿab مكعّب (*pl* -aat)

cubic mukaʿʿab مكعّب

cucumber(s) (**ridge**) ʿajjuur عجّور ; (**smooth variety**) khiyaar خيار ; (**round variety**) tibish تبش

cud jirra جرّة ; **to chew the cud** gaṣaʿ aj-jirra

cultivate zaraʿ زرع (a, zariʿ, ziraaʿa); **to be cultivated** itzaraʿ اتزرع (zariʿ, ziraaʿa)

cultivation ziraaʿa زراعة

cultural saqaafi سقافي

culture saqaafa سقافة

cumin (**black**) kammuun كمّون ; (**green**) shamaar شمار

cunning *adj* la'iim لئيم (*pl* lu'ama); makkaar مكّار ; khabiis خبيس (*pl* -iin, khubasa) • *n* mukur مكر ; khubs خبس

cup kubbaaya كبّاية (*pl* -aat, kabaabi); **coffee cup** finjaan فنجان (*pl* fanaajiin)

cupboard doolaab دولاب (*pl* dawaaliib)

curds roob روب

curdle rawwab روّب (roob); **to be(come) curdled** raab راب (u, roob)

cure *v* daawa داوى (-i, mudaawaa); ʿaalaj عالج (ʿilaaj, muʿaalaja); (**of God**) ʿaafa عافى (-i, muʿaafaa); shafa شفى (-i, shifa); **to be cured** iddaawa ادّاوى (-a, mudaawaa); itʿaalaj اتعالج (muʿaalaja, ʿilaaj); silim سلم (a, salaama)

curfew ḥaẓr at-tajawwul

curiosity fuḍuuliyya فضوليّة

curious fuḍuuli فضولي ; ḥushari حشري ; mutḥashshir متحشّر

curl *vi* itlawlaw اتولو (liwleew, lawlawa) • *vt* lawlaw لولو (liwleew, lawlawa)

curly mulawlaw ملولو ; mutlawliw متولو

currency ʿumla عملة ; **hard currency** ʿumla ṣaʿba

current *adj* jaari جاري • *n* jarayaan جريان ; tayyaar تيار (*pl* -aat)

curse *n* (**of God**) laʿna لعنة • *v* laʿan لعن (a, laʿin)

curtain sitaara ستارة (*pl* -aat, sataayir)

curve *n* ḥaniya حنية ; ʿawja عوجة • *v* inḥana انحنى (-i, ḥaniya)

curved maḥni محني ; malwi ملوي ; (**materials only**) matni متني

cushion jaddaaʿa جدّاعة

custard kastar كستر

custody (**detention**) ḥabis حبس ; ḥiraasa حراسة ; ḥajiz حجز ; (**guardianship**) ʿuhda عهدة (*pl* ʿuhad)

custom ʿaada عادة (*pl* -aat, ʿawaayid); ʿurf عرف

customary ʿaadi عادي ; ʿurfi عرفي
customer zabuun زبون (*pl* zabaayin)
customs jumruk جمرك (*pl* jamaarik); **customs declaration** igraar jumruki; **customs clearance agent** mukhalliṣ مخلّص
cut *n* giṭʿa قطعة (*pl* -aat, giṭaʿ); (**of a garment**) tafṣiil تفصيل (*pl* tafaaṣiil) • *v* gaṭaʿ قطع (a, gaṭiʿ); (**hair**) ḥalag حلق (i, ḥilaaga); (**nails**) ḍaffar ضفّر (ḍiffeer); (**grass**) jazza جزّ (i, jazz); (**with scissors**) gaṣṣa قصّ (u, gaṣṣ); **to cut in** (**of a car overtaking**) gaaṭaʿ قاطع (mugaaṭaʿa); **to cut out** (**a pattern**) faṣṣal فصّل (tafṣiil); **to be cut** itgaṭaʿ اتقطع (gaṭiʿ); ingaṭaʿ انقطع (ingiṭaaʿ)
cutting (**of a plant**) shatla شتلة (*pl* -aat, shutuul); **to take cuttings** shatal شتل (i, shatil)
cycle dawra دورة ; **training cycle** dawra tadriibiyya
cylinder ambuuba أمبوبة (*pl* anaabiib); anbuuba أنبوبة (*pl* anaabiib); **gas cylinder** ambuubat/anbuubat ghaaz

D - d

dagger khanjar خنجر (*pl* khanaajir)
daily *adj* yoomaati يوماتي ; yoomi يومي ; **daily wages** yoomiyya يوميّة • *adv* kullo yoom; yoomiyyan يوميّا
dam sadd سد (*pl* suduud); khazzaan خزّان (*pl* -aat)
damage *n* ḍarar ضرر (*pl* aḍraar) • *v* bawwaẓ بوّظ (biwweeẓ, bawaẓaan); ḍarra ضرّ (u, ḍurr, ḍarar); khassar خسّر (khisseer, takhsiir); **to be damaged** khisir خسر (a, khasaara, khusraan)
damp layyin ليّن ; **to become damp** itballa اتبلّ (balal, balla)
dampen raṭṭab رطّب (tarṭiib); layyan ليّن (liyyeen); balla بلّ (i, balla); (**sound**) katam كتم (u, katim)
dance *n* ragṣa رقصة • *v* ragaṣ رقص (u, ragiiṣ); saksak سكسك (saksaka)
dancer raggaaṣ رقّاص
dandruff gishir قشر
danger khaṭar خطر ; khuṭuura خطورة
dangerous khaṭiir خطير
dangle iṭṭooṭaḥ اطّوطح (ṭooṭeeḥ)
dare itjarra' ʿala اتجرّأ (-a', jur'a)
daring jarii' جريء
dark *adj* muḍallim مضلّم ; (**of colour**) ghaamig غامق ; **to become dark** ḍallam ضلّم (ḍilleem); fallal فلّل (filleel)
darkness ḍalaam ضلام ; ḍalma ضلمة ; ḍulumma ضلمّة
dash *v* itsarraʿ اتسرّع (surʿa)
data maʿluumaat معلومات
date *n* (**record**) taariikh تاريخ (*pl* tawaariikh) • *v* arrakh أرّخ (ya'arrikh, ta'riikh)
date(s) *n* (**fruit**) balaḥ بلح ; tamur تمر (*unit n* tamra); **desert date tree** hijliij هجليج ; **fruit of the desert date tree** laaloob لالوب
daughter bitt بت (*pl* banaat, bannuut)

dawn *n* fajur فجر ; dughush دغش ; dughshiyya دغشيّة • *v* aṣbaḥ أصبح (i, ṣabaaḥ)

day (24 hours) yoom يوم (*pl* ayyaam); (**daytime**) nahaar نهار

dazzle zaghlal زغلل (zaghlala, zighleel); jahar جهر (a, jahra)

dead mayyit ميّت

deaf aṭrash أطرش (*f* ṭarsha, *pl* ṭurush); **to become deaf** ṭirish طرش (a, ṭarash)

deafness ṭarash طرش

deal *n* (**conclusion of transaction**) ṣafaga صفقة • *v* **to deal with** itᶜaamal maᶜa اتعامل (muᶜaamala, taᶜaamul); (**things**) itᶜaamal be- اتعامل (muᶜaamala)

dean ᶜamiid عميد (*pl* ᶜumada)

dear *adj* (**loved**) ᶜaziiz عزيز (*pl* aᶜizzaa); ḥabiib حبيب (*pl* aḥibba, aḥbaab); (**expensive**) ghaali غالي

death moot موت ; wafa/wafaat وفاة (*pl* wafiyaat); miita ميتة ; (**accidental**) miita faj'a; **death penalty** iᶜdaam إعدام (*pl* -aat)

debt *n* deen دين (*pl* diyuun); **in debt** madyuun مديون ; **bad debts** diyuun haalka

debtor madyuun مديون

decay *n* bawaẓaan بوظان • *v* itᶜaffan اتعفّن (ᶜiffeen, taᶜaffun); ᶜaffan عفّن (ᶜiffeen); baaẓ باظ (u, bawaẓaan, booẓ); tilif تلف (a, talaf)

deceit ghishsh غش ; iḥtiyaal إحتيال

deceitful ghashshaash غشّاش ; muḥtaal محتال

deceive ghashsha غشّ (u, ghishsh, ghashsh); daggas دقس (dagsa); khadaᶜ خدع (a, khidaᶜ); **to be deceived** inghashsha انغشّ (ghashsh, ghashashaan); itghashsha اتغشّ (ghashsh, ghashashaan); dagas دقس (u, dagis); iddaggas ادّقس (diggees)

December shahri iṭnaashar; disembar ديسمبر

decency adab أدب ; tahziib تهزيب ; (**dress**) ḥishma حشمة

decent mu'addab مؤدّب ; muhazzab مهزّب ; (**females**) muḥtashim محتشم

deception khidᶜa خدعة (*pl* khidaᶜ)

decide qarrar قرّر (qaraar)

decision qaraar قرار (*pl* -aat)

deck (**of a boat**) ḍahr al-murkab

declaration bayaan بيان (*pl* -aat)

declare ṣarraḥ (be-) صرّح (taṣriiḥ)

decline rafaḍ رفض (u, rafiḍ, rafḍ)

decorate zakhraf زخرف (zakhrafa, zikhreef); zayyan زيّن (ziyyeen, tazyiin)

decoration ziina زينة

decrease *vi* galla قلّ (i, gilla) • *vt* gallal (min) قلّل (tagliil); naggaṣ min نقّص (niggeeṣ, tangiiṣ); nagaṣ min نقص (u, nagṣ, nugṣaan)

deduct khaṣam (min) خصم (i, khaṣim)

deed (**act**) ᶜamal عمل (*pl* aᶜmaal); fiᶜil فعل (*pl* fiᶜaal); **good deed** ḥasana حسنة

deep ᶜamiiq عميق ; ghawiiṭ غويط

deep-rooted ᶜariiq عريق

defeat *n* haziima هزيمة (*pl* hazaayim) • *v* ghalab غلب (i, ghulub); hazam هزم (i, haziima); **to be defeated** inhazam انهزم (haziima, inhizaam)

defence difaaᶜ دفاع ; ḥimaaya حماية

defend daafaᶜ دافع (difaaᶜ)
deficiency nagṣ نقص ; ᶜajz عجز
deficient naagiṣ ناقص
deficit nagṣ نقص ; **in deficit** muᶜajjiz معجّز
deflate *vt* naffas نفّس (niffees, tanfiis)
deformed (**person**) khaliiga خليقة (*pl* khalaayig)
defy itḥadda اتحدّى (-a, taḥaddi)
degree daraja درجة
delay *n* ta'khiir تأخير (*pl* -aat) • *v* akhkhar أخّر (ya'akhkhir, ta'khiir); **to be delayed** it'akhkhar اتأخّر (ta'khiir)
delegate *n* manduub مندوب (*pl* -iin, manaadiib) • *v* fawwaḍ فوّض (tafwiiḍ)
delete shaṭab شطب (u, shaṭib); **to be deleted** itshaṭab اتشطب (shaṭib)
delicate hashsh هش ; rafiiᶜ رفيع ; rahiif رهيف
delicious laziiz لزيز ; ḥilu حلو (*f* ḥilwa)
delight *n* faraḥ فرح (*pl* afraaḥ); bahja بهجة ; inbisaaṭ إنبساط • *v* ᶜajab عجب (i, ᶜajab); farraḥ فرّح (firreeḥ, tafriiḥ); **to be delighted** ibtahaj إبتهج (ibtihaaj)
delirious **to be delirious** haḍrab هضرب (haḍraba); hatrash هترش (hatrasha)
deliver (**sth.**) sallam سلّم (tasliim); (**a baby**) waḍaᶜ وضع *vt* (yaḍaᶜ, wuḍuuᶜ); wilid ولد (i, wilaada)
delivery tasliim تسليم (*pl* -aat); (**childbirth**) wilaada ولادة
demand *n* ṭalab طلب (-aat) • *v* ṭalab طلب (u, ṭalab)
democracy diimuqraaṭiyya ديمقراطيّة
democratic diimuqraaṭi ديمقراطي
demolish hadam هدم (i, hadim); haddam هدّم (hiddeem, tahdiim); **to be demolished** ithadam إتهدم (hiddeem); ithaddam إتهدّم (hiddeem, tihiddim)
demon(s) jinn جنّ (*unit n m* jinni, *unit n f* jinniyya); **desert demon** ghuul غول (*pl* ghiilaan)
demonstration (**rally**) masiira مسيرة ; muẓaahara مظاهرة
denial inkaar إنكار
dense shaabik شابك
dent *n* ᶜafṣa عفّصة ; ṭafga طفقة • *v* ᶜafaṣ عفص (a, ᶜafiṣ, ᶜafṣa); ᶜaffaṣ عفّص (ᶜiffeeṣ); ṭafag طفق (i, ṭafig, ṭafga); ṭaffag طّفق (ṭiffeeg)
dentist diktoor asnaan
deny ankar انكر (u, inkaar); nafa نفى (-i, nafi); nakar نكر (u, nakaraan)
deodorant muziil ᶜarag
depart saafar سافر (safar); gaam قام (u, giyaam); raḥal رحل (a, ruḥuul, raḥiil)
department gisim قسم (*pl* agsaam); (**of a school**) shuᶜba شعبة (*pl* shuᶜab); **government department** maṣlaḥa مصلحة (*pl* maṣaaliḥ)
departure giyaam قيام ; raḥiil رحيل ; mughaadara مغادرة
depend iᶜtamad ᶜala إعتمد (iᶜtimaad); (**on God**) ittakal ᶜala اتّكل (ittikaal)
dependence iᶜtimaad إعتماد (*pl* -aat)
deport raḥḥal رحّل (tarḥiil)
depose (**from office, function**) rafad رفد (i, rafid); faṣal فصل (i, faṣil)

deposit *n* (**with person for safekeeping**) amaana أمانة ; (**in bank**) wadiiʿa وديعة (*pl* wadaayiʿ); (**down payment**) mugaddam مقدم ; ʿarbuun عربون (*pl* ʿaraabiin)
depressed mudabris مدبرس ; mukta'ib مكتئب ; **to be depressed** dabras دبرس (dabrasa, dibrees); ikta'ab إكتأب (ikti'aab)
depression (**gloom**) dabrasa دبرسة ; ikti'aab إكتآب
deprive ḥaram (min) حرم (i, ḥirmaan); (**of food**) jawwaʿ جوّع (jiwweeʿ, tajwiiʿ)
depth ʿumq عمق
deputy naayib نايب (*pl* nuwwaab); naa'ib نائب (*pl* nuwwaab)
dermatologist diktoor jildiyya
dervish darwiish درويش (*pl* daraawish)
descend nazal (min) نزل (i, nuzuul); iddalla ادّلّى (-a, dilleey)
descendants ʿugub عقب ; ʿagaab عقاب ; zurriyya زرّيّة
descent nuzuul نزول ; (**origin**) aṣil أصل (*pl* uṣuul)
describe waṣaf وصف (i, waṣif); waṣṣaf وصّف (wiṣṣeef)
description waṣif وصف (*pl* awṣaaf)
desert *n* khala خلا ; ṣaḥraa صحرا (*pl* ṣaḥaari); **pertaining to the desert** khalawi خلوي ; ṣaḥraawi صحراوي
desert *v* sharad (min) شرد (u, sharid, sharadaan)
deserve istaahal استاهل (*no vn*); istaḥagga استحقّ (istiḥgaag)
design *n* taṣmiim تصميم (*pl* -aat) • *v* ṣammam صمّم (taṣmiim)
designer muṣammim مصمّم
desire *n* raghba رغبة (*pl* raghabaat); muraad مراد (*pl* -aat) • *v* righib fi رغب (a, raghba)
desk maktab مكتب (*pl* makaatib); school desk duruj درج (*pl* adraaj)
despair *n* ya's يأس • *v* yi'is يئس (a, ya's); giniʿ قنع (a, ganiʿ)
desperate yaa'is يائس ; ganʿaan قنعان
despise ḥagar حقر (i, ḥagaara); iḥtagar احتقر (ḥagaara, iḥtigaar)
despite be-raghmi min; **despite the fact that** raghma inn-/anno
despotic mustabidd مستبد ; taghyaan تغيان
despotism istibdaad استبداد
dessert taḥliya تحلية
destiny naṣiib نصيب (*pl* anṣiba); gisma قسمة (*pl* -aat, gisam); qadar قدر (*pl* agdaar); qaḍaa wa qadar
destroy dammar دمّر (tadmiir); hadam هدم (i, hadim); haddam هدّم (hiddeem, tahdiim); kharrab خرّب (khirreeb, takhriib); **to be destroyed** iddammar ادّمّر ; ithadam إتهدم (hiddeem); ithaddam إتهدّم (hiddeem); itkharrab اتخرّب (khirreeb, kharaab)
destruction damaar دمار ; kharaab خراب ; taḥtiim تحطيم
detail tafṣiil تفصيل (*pl* tafaaṣiil)
detain ḥabas حبس (i, ḥabsa, ḥabis); iʿtaqal اعتقل (iʿtiqaal); ḥajaz حجز (i, ḥajiz); **to be detained** itḥabas اتحبس (ḥabsa, ḥabis); itḥajaz اتحجز (ḥajiz)
detention ḥabis حبس ; ḥiraasa حراسة ; ḥajiz حجز
determine ḥaddad حدّد (taḥdiid)
determined muṣirr مصر ; **to be determined** ṣammam (ʿala) صمّم

(taṣmiim); ʿazam (ʿala) عزم (i, ʿaziima)
develop *vi* iṭṭawwar اطّوّر (taṭawwur) • *vt* ṭawwar طوّر (taṭwiir); (**a film**) ḥammaḍ حمّض (taḥmiiḍ)
development taṭawwur تطوّر (*pl* -aat); taṭwiir تطوير ; (**growth**) tanmiya تنمية ; numuu نمو
deviate ḥawwad حوّد (ḥiwweed, tahwiiḥ)
device jihaaz جهاز (*pl* ajhiza)
devil sheeṭaan شيطان (*pl* shayaaṭiin); waswaas وسواس (*pl* wasaawiis); ibliis إبليس (*pl* abaaliis, abaalisa)
devoted mukhliṣ مخلص ; **to be devoted** akhlaṣ أخلص (i, ikhlaaṣ)
dew nada ندى
diabetes maraḍ as-sukkari
diagnose shakhkhaṣ شخّص (tashkhiiṣ)
diagnosis tashkhiiṣ تشخيص
dialect lahja لهجة
dialogue ḥiwaar حوار (*pl* -aat)
diamond(s) maas ماس
diaper ḥifaaḍ حفاض (*pl* -aat)
diarrhoea ishaal إسهال ; ṣabiib صبيب
diary yoomiyyaat يوميات ; (**pocket**) ajinda أجندة ; mufakkira مفكّرة
dice zahar زهر (*no sg*)
dictate malla ملّى (-i, tamliya)
dictation imla إملا (*pl* imla'aat)
dictator diktaatoor دكتاتور (*pl* -iyyiin)
dictatorship diktaatooriyya دكتاتوريّة
dictionary qaamuus قاموس (*pl* qawaamiis)
die maat مات (u, moot); itwaffa اتوفّى (-a, wafa, wafaat); (**animals**) hilik هلك (a, halik, halakaan); fiṭis فطس (a, faṭsa); **to die down** (**fire**) hamad همد (a, hamadaan, humuud)
diesel (**fuel**) jaaz جاز ; jazoliin جازولين ; diizil ديزل
diet rijiim رجيم
differ farag فرق (i, farig); ikhtalaf اختلف (ikhtilaaf); **to differ in opinion** (**about, with**) ikhtalaf (maʿa, fi) اختلف (ikhtilaaf)
difference ikhtilaaf إختلاف (*pl* -aat); farig فرق (*pl* furuugaat); **that doesn't make a difference** da ma bifrig
different mukhtalif مختلف ; **to be different** ikhtalaf اختلف (ikhtilaaf)
differentiate farrag been فرّق (tafriig)
difficult ṣaʿab صعب
difficulty ṣuʿuuba صعوبة
dig ḥafar حفر (i, ḥafir); ḥaffar حفّر (ḥiffeer); (**with the hands**) ḥafat حفت (i, ḥafit)
digest (**of the stomach**) haḍam هضم (i, haḍm)
dignity karaama كرامة ; ʿizza عزّة
diligence ijtihaad إجتهاد
diligent hamiim هميم ; mujtahid مجتهد
dill shamaar akhḍar
dimension buʿud بعد (*pl* abʿaad)
diminish gallal (min) قلّل (gilleel, tagliil)
dimple (**in cheek**) nuuna نونة
din dawsha دوشة ; ḍajja ضجّة ; ḍajiij ضجيج ; karkaba كركبة ; **to make a din** dawash دوش (yidwish, dawsha); ḍajja ضجّ (i, ḍajj, ḍajja, ḍajiij); karkab كركب (karkaba)

dine (**evening meal**) itʿashsha اتعشّى (-a, ʿasha)
diocese abrashiyya أبرشيّة ; muṭraaniyya مطرانيّة
dip *v* ghammas غمّس (ghimmees)
diphtheria difteeriya دفتيريا
diplomat diblomaasi ديبلوماسي
direct *adj* mubaashir مباشر • *adv* ṭawwaali طوّالى
direct *v* wajjah وجّه (wijjeeh, tawjiih)
direction ittijaah إتّجاه (*pl* -aat); naaḥya ناحية (*pl* nawaaḥi); jiha جهة ; **in the direction of** minnaaḥya; **to give directions to** wajjah وجّه (wijjeeh, tawjiih)
director (*m*) mudiir مدير (*pl* -iin, mudara); (*f*) mudiira مديرة
dirt wasakh وسخ (*pl* awsaakh); wasaakha وساخة
dirty waskhaan وسخان ; wisikh وسخ ; **to be**(**come**) **dirty** itwassakh اتوسّخ (wisseekh); **to make dirty** wassakh وسّخ (wisseekh, wasaakha)
disabled muʿaag معاق ; muʿawwag معوّق
disagree (**about, with**) ikhtalaf (maʿa, fi) اختلف (ikhtilaaf)
disagreement khilaaf خلاف (*pl* -aat)
disappear ikhtafa اختفى (-i, ikhtifa)
disappoint gaham قهم (a, gaham); **to be disappointed** itkhazal اتخزل (khazil); itgaham اتقهم (gaham)
disappointment kheebat amal
disapprove istankar استنكر (istinkaar)
disaster muṣiiba مصيبة (*pl* maṣaayib); bala بلا (*pl* balaawi); balwa بلوى (*pl* balaawi); baliyya بليّة (*pl* -aat, balaawi)
discharge *v* (**cause to leave**) mashsha مشّى (-i, tamshiya); marrag مرّق (marga, mirreeg); kharraj خرّج (khirreej)
discipline *n* ḍabiṭ ضبط ; ḍabṭ ضبط • *v* addab أدّب (ta'diib); ḍabaṭ ضبط (u, ḍabit)
disconnect gaṭaʿ قطع (a, gaṭiʿ); faṣal فصل (i, faṣil); **to be disconnected** ingaṭaʿ انقطع (ingiṭaaʿ); itgaṭaʿ اتقطع (gaṭiʿ); (**of utilities**) gaṭaʿ قطع (a, gaṭiʿ)
discount takhfiiḍ تخفيض (*pl* -aat)
discover iktashaf اكتشف (iktishaaf)
discovery iktishaaf إكتشاف (*pl* -aat)
discrimination tamyiiz تمييز ; **racial discrimination** tamyiiz ʿunṣuri; tafriqa ʿunṣuriyya
discuss naaqash ناقش (niqaash, munaaqasha); itfaakar اتفاكر (mufaakara)
disease maraḍ مرض (*pl* amraaḍ)
disgrace *n* faḍiiḥa فضيحة (*pl* faḍaayiḥ) • *v* faḍaḥ فضح (a, faḍiḥ, faḍiiḥa)
disguise *n* **in disguise** mutnakkir متنكّر • *v* (**o.s.**) itnakkar اتنكّر (tanakkur)
disgust *v* garraf قرّف (girreef); **disgusted** garfaan قرفان ; **to be disgusted** girif قرف (a, garaf)
disgusting mugrif مقرف
dish ṣaḥan صحن (*pl* ṣuḥuun); (**large**) sulṭaaniyya سلطانيّة ; **dishes** ʿidda عدّة (*pl* ʿidad)
dishcloth fuuṭa فوطة (*pl* fuwaṭ)
dishonest ma ṣariiḥ; ma ṣaadig
disinfect ṭahhar طهّر (ṭihheer, taṭhiir)

disinfection taṭhiir تطهير
diskette usṭuwaana أسطوانة
dislike *v* kirih كره (a, karih)
dislocate malakh ملخ (a, malakhaan); **to be dislocated** itmalakh اتملخ (malikh, malakhaan)
dislocation malikh; malakhaan
dismantle fartak فرتك (fartaka, firteek); fakka فكّ (i, fakk, fakakaan); **to be dismantled** itfartak اتفرتك (firteek); itfakka اتفكّ (fakk, fakakaan)
dismiss ṭarad طرد (u, ṭarid); (**from office**) rafad رفد (i, rafid); faṣal فصل (i, faṣil); (**from military service**) ʿazal عزل (i, ʿazil); **to be dismissed** iṭṭarad اطّرد (ṭarid); itrafad اترفد (rafid); itfaṣal اتفصل (faṣil, faṣalaan); itʿazal اتعزل (ʿazil)
dismissal (from office) rafdiyya رفديّة
dismount nazal (min) نزل (i, nuzuul)
disobedience ʿiṣyaan عصيان (*pl* -aat)
disobedient ʿaaṣi عاصي (*pl* -yyiin); **he is disobedient** raas-o gawwi
disobey ʿaṣa عصى (-i, ʿiṣyaan)
disorder bahdala بهدلة ; fawḍa فوضى ; jooṭa جوطة ; rabka ربكة ; lakhbaṭa لخبطة ; barjala برجلة
disperse (**group**) fartak فرتك (fartaka, firteek); (**individuals**) farzaʿ فرزع (farzaʿa); shattat شتّت (shitteet, tashtiit); **to be dispersed** itfarrag اتفرّق (firreeg, tafarrug); itfarzaʿ اتفرزع (farzaʿa); itshattat اتشتّت (shitteet, tashattut)
displaced (**person**) naaziḥ نازح ; **to be displaced** nazaḥ نزح (a, nuzuuḥ)
display *n* ʿariḍ عرض (*pl* ʿuruuḍ) • *v* ʿaraḍ **distance** masaafa مسافة ; **long distance** jabda جبدة ; **to stay at a distance** biʿid بعد (i, buʿaad)
distant baʿiid بعيد (*pl* buʿaad); **to be(come) distant** biʿid بعد (i, buʿaad)
distension (**abdominal**) nufaakh نفاخ
distinction imtiyaaz إمتياز (*pl* -aat)
distinctive mumayyaz مميّز
distinguish farrag been فرّق (tafriig); mayyaz ميّز (tamyiiz); **to be distinguished by** itmayyaz be- اتميّز (tamayyuz)
distress *n* ḍiig ضيق
distribute gassam قسّم (gisseem, tagsiim); wazzaʿ وزّع (tawziiʿ); **to be distributed** itgassam اتقسّم (gisseem, tagsiim); itwazzaʿ اتوزّع (tawziiʿ)
distribution tawziiʿ توزيع (*pl* -aat); (**division**) tagsiim تقسيم (*pl* -aat)
district (**of a town**) madiina مدينة (*pl* mudun); ḥayy حي (*pl* aḥyaa); (**division of district**) murabbaʿ مربّع ; ḥaara حارة
disturb azʿaj أزعج (i, izʿaaj); **to be disturbed** inzaʿaj انزعج (inziʿaaj); itʿakkar اتعكّر (ʿikkeer)
disturbance izʿaaj إزعاج
ditch khandag خندق (*pl* khanaadig); khoor خور (*pl* kheeraan)
dive *v* ghaṭas غطس (i, ghaṭis)
diverse mutʿaddid متعدّد
diversify nawwaʿ نوّع (tanwiiʿ)

diversion ʿirreeja عرّيجة
diversity tanawwuʿ تنوّع; taʿaddud تعدّد
divide gasam قسم (i, gasim, gisma); gassam قسّم (gisseem, tagsiim); **to be divided** itgassam اتقسّم (gisseem, tagsiim)
diviner kujuur كجور (kajara)
division gisma قسمة (*pl* agsaam); tagsiim تقسيم (*pl* -aat)
divorce *n* ṭalaag طلاق • *v* ṭallag طلّق (ṭalaag)
divorced (**of a man**) muṭallig مطلّق; (**of a woman**) muṭallaga مطلّقة
dizziness dookha دوخة; doosha دوشة; **fit of dizziness** laffat raas
dizzy daayikh دايخ; daayish دايش; **to be(come) dizzy** daakh داخ (u, dawakhaan); daash داش (u, doosha)
do ʿamal عمل (a/i, ʿamal); **to be done** itʿamal اتعمل (ʿamal)
dock moorada موردة (*pl* mawaarid); mushraʿ مشرع (*pl* mashaariʿ)
doctor diktoor دكتور (*pl* dakaatra); ṭabiib طبيب (*pl* aṭibba); (**Ph.D.**) diktoor دكتور
document *n* mustanad مستند (*pl* -aat); sanad سند (*pl* -aat); wasiiqa وسيقة (*pl* wasaayiq) • *v* wassaq وسّق (tawsiiq)
dodge zaaq min زاق (u, zooqa, zawaqaan); zawwaq min زوّق (ziwweeq, zawaqaan)
dog kalib كلب (*pl* kilaab)
doll bitt umm laʿʿaab; ʿaruusa عروسة (*pl* ʿaraayis)
dollar doolaar دولار (*pl* -aat)
domain majaal مجال (*pl* -aat)
dome gubba قبّة (*pl* gubab)
domesticate wallaf ولّف (willeef, wilfa); **to be(come) domesticated** itwallaf اتولّف (willeef, wilfa)
domesticated *adj* aliif أليف
dominoes ḍumana ضمنة
donate itbarraʿ اتبرّع (tabarruʿ)
donation tabarruʿ تبرّع (*pl* -aat); ʿaṭiyya عطيّة (*pl* ʿaṭaaya)
donkey ḥumaar حمار (*pl* ḥamiir); **young donkey** daḥash دحش (*pl* duḥuush); diḥeesh دحيش
donkey engine doonki دونكي (*pl* dawaanki)
donor maaniḥ مانح
door baab باب (*pl* beebaan, abwaab); **front door** khashm al-beet; **small door between backyards of neighbours** naffaaj نفّاج; **door handle** ukra اكرة (*pl* ukar); iid/yadd al-ukra
doorkeeper ghafiir غفير (*pl* ghufara); ḥaaris حارس (*pl* ḥurraas); bawwaab بواب
doorstep ʿataba عتبة
dormitory (**student hostel**) daakhiliyya داخليّة
dose *n* jurʿa جرعة
dossier dosseeh دسّيه (*pl* -aat)
dot *n* nugṭa نقطة (*pl* nugaṭ); **to put dots on** naggaṭ نقّط (niggeeṭ)
double *adj* dabul دبل • *v* ḍaaʿaf ضاعف (muḍaaʿafa)
doubt *n* shakk شك (*pl* shukuuk) • *v* shakka (fi) شكّ (u, shakk)
dough ʿajiina عجينة
dove(s) gumri قمري (*unit n* gumriyya, *pl* gamaari)
down tiḥit تحت

dowry mahar مهر (*pl* muhuur); ṣudaag صداق (*pl* -aat); (**jewellery**) shabka شبكة
doze ghafa غفى (-u, ghafwa)
dozen dasta دستة (*pl* disat)
draft *n* (**army**) dufʿa دفعة (*pl* -aat, dufaʿ)
draft *n* (**rough copy**) muswadda مسودّة
draftsman rassaam رسّام
drag jarra جرّ (u, jarr); jarjar جرجر (jirjeer, jarjara)
drain *n* jadwal جدول (*pl* jadaawil); majra مجرى (*pl* majaari); maṣraf مصرف (*pl* maṣaarif) • *v* ṣarraf صرّف (ṣirreef, taṣriif); **to drain away** shafaṭ شفط (u, shafiṭ)
drainage taṣriif تصريف (*pl* -aat)
drama draama دراما
draughts (**game**) siija سيجة
draw (**a picture**) rasam رسم (u, rasim)
drawer duruj درج (*pl* adraaj)
drawing rasim رسم (*pl* rusuumaat)
drawing pin dabbuus ḍaghiṭ
dream *n* ḥilim حلم (*pl* aḥlaam) • *v* ḥilim حلم (a, ḥilim)
dredger karraaka كرّاكة
dregs (**of coffee, tea**) tifil تفل
dress *n* (**for women**) fustaan فستان (*pl* fasaatiin) • *v* labbas لبّس (libbees); **to get dressed** libis لبس (a, libis)
dressing table tawaleet تواليت
dribble *n* riyaala ريالة; luʿaab لعاب • *v* rayyal ريّل (riyaala)
drill *n* (**an exercise**) tamriin تمرين (*pl* -aat, tamaariin); **electric drill** darbakiin دربكين (*pl* -aat); **hand drill** barriima بريمة (*pl* -aat, baraariim, barraayim) • *v* kharam خرم (i, kharim); kharram خرّم (khirreem, takhriim); (**for oil, water**) ḥafar حفر (i, ḥafir)
drilling rig ḥaffaara حفّارة
drink *n* sharaab شراب (*pl* -aat, ashriba); (**alcoholic**) khamra خمرة (*pl* khumuur) • *v* shirib شرب (a, sharaab); (**from a bottle**) bawwaz بوّز (biwweez); **to give to drink** sharrab شرّب (shirreeb)
drip *vi* itnaggaṭ اتنقّط (niggeeṭ) • *vt* naggaṭ نقّط (niggeeṭ); gaṭṭar قطّر (giṭṭeer, tagṭiir) • *n* (**intravenous**) dirib درب (*pl* -aat)
drive *v* (**car, cattle**) saag ساق (u, suwaaga); **to drive away** ṭarad طرد (u, ṭarid)
driver sawwaag سوّاق; (**of cart**) ʿarbaji عربجي (*pl* -iyya)
drizzle *n* nagnaaga نقناقة; shakshaaka شكشاكة
drop *n* nugṭa نقطة (*pl* nugaṭ); (**medicinal**) gaṭra قطرة
drop *n* (**in level**) hubuuṭ هبوط • *v* waggaʿ وقّع (wiggeeʿ); **to drop in on** ghisha غشى (-a, ghashwa, ghashayaan); marra ʿala مرّ (u, muruur)
dropper (**for medicinal drops**) gaṭṭaara قطّارة
droppings (**of goats, rabbits**) baʿar بعر; (**of birds**) ẓagg ظق
drought jafaaf جفاف; ʿaṭash عطش
drown *vi* ghirig غرق (a, gharag) • *vt* gharrag غرّق (ghirreeg)
drowned ghargaan غرقان; **drowned person** ghariig غريق (*pl* gharga)
drowning ghargaan غرقان
drowsiness naʿaas نعاس
drowsy naʿsaan نعسان; **to be(come) drowsy** niʿis نعس (a, naʿaas)

drug *n* (**medicine**) dawa دوا (*pl* adwiya); mukhaddir مخدّر ; (illegal) mukhaddiraat مخدرات • *v* khaddar خدّر (takhdiir); **to be drugged** itkhaddar اتخدّر (khiddeer)

drum *n* bungus بنقس ; (**small**) ṭabla طبلة (*pl* ṭubuul); **triple drum** darabukka دربكّة ; (**women**) dalluuka دلّوكة (*pl* dalaaliik); (**tribal**) nuggaara نقّارة (*pl* nagaagiir) • *v* ṭabbal طبّل (ṭibbeel)

drummer ṭabbaal طبّال

drunk sakraan سكران (*pl* -iin, sakaara); ṭaashim طاشم ; **to be drunk** sikir سكر (a, sakar); ṭasham طشم (u, ṭashma)

drunkard sukurji سكرجي (*pl* -yya)

drunkenness sakar سكر

dry *adj* naashif ناشف ; yaabis يابس ; jaaff جاف ; **to become dry** nishif نشف (a, nashaaf); yibis يبس (a, yabaas, yabasaan); itjaffaf اتجفّف (jafaaf); jaffa جفّ (i, jaffa) • *v* nashshaf نشّف (nishsheef); jaffaf جفّف (jiffeef)

duck(s) baṭṭ بط

dumb abkam أبكم (*f* bakma, *pl* bukum, bukama)

dune dabba دبّة (*pl* -aat, dibab); gooz قوز (*pl* geezaan)

dung samaad سماد ; **dung beetle** abu d-dardaag

durable muʿammir معمّر

duration dawaam دوام

during khilaal خلال

dust turaab تراب ; ʿajaaj عجاج ; (**brought by the wind**) ghubaar غبار ; **dust storm** habuub هبوب (*pl* habaayib)

dusty mughabbar مغبّر ; muʿaffar معفّر

Dutch hulandi هولندي (*pl* -yyiin)

Dutchman hulandi هولندي (*pl* -yyiin)

duty waajib واجب (*pl* -aat); fariḍ فرض (*pl* furuuḍ); **customs duty** rasm رسم (*pl* rusuum); ḍariibat aj-jamaarik

duty-free maʿfi min aj-jamaarik; **duty-free shops** as-suug al-ḥurr(a)

DVD usṭuwaana أسطوانة

dwarf biʿeew بعيو (*pl* -aat)

dwelling manzil منزل (*pl* manaazil); maskan مسكن (*pl* masaakin)

dye *n* ṣibgha صبغة • *v* ṣabagh صبغ (i, ṣibaagha, ṣabigh); ṣabbagh صبّغ (ṣibbeegh, taṣbiigh)

dyke taras ترس (*pl* turuus); radmiyya ردميّة ; (**small**) ḥaajiz حاجز (*pl* ḥawaajiz); trotwaar تروتوار (*pl* -aat)

dysentery dusuntaarya دسنتاريا

E - e

eager (**for**) ḥariiṣ (ʿala) حريص

eagle ḥiddeeya حدّيية (*pl* ḥiddeey); ṣagur صقر (*pl* ṣuguur)

ear (**organ of hearing**) aḍaan أضان (*pl* iḍneen); (**head of grain**) ganduul قندول (*pl* ganaadiil)

eardrum ṭabla طبلة (*pl* ṭubuul)

early badri بدرى

earn kisib كسب (a, kasib)

earnings makaasib مكاسب

earphone sammaaʿa سمّاعة

earring ḥalag حلق (*pl* ḥulgaan)

earth ariḍ أرض (*pl* araaḍi); (**soil**) turaab تراب ; turba تربة (*pl* turab); (**ground**) waaṭa واطا ; (**world**) dunya دنيا
earthenware fukhkhaar فخّار
earthquake zalzaal زلزال (*pl* zalaazil)
earthworm(s) ṣaargeel صارقيل
ease *n* raaḥa راحة ; suhuula سهولة ; **to be at ease** irtaaḥ ارتاح (raaḥa, irtiyaaḥ) • *v* (**pain, pressure**) rayyaḥ ريّح (riyyeeḥ, taryiiḥ); khaffaf خفف (khiffeef, takhfiif)
easily be-suhuula
east sharig شرق ; **the Middle East** ash-sharq al-awsaṭ
Easter ʿiid al-giyaama; ʿiid al-fiṣḥ
eastern shargi شرقي
easterner shargi شرقي (*pl* -yyiin); (**of Sudan**) shargaawi شرقاوي (*pl* naas ash-sharig)
eastwards be-sh-sharig
easy saahil ساهل ; (**of life**) rakhi رخي ; **to make easy** sahhal سهّل (tashiil)
easy-going raḍi رضي ; hayyin هيّن
eat akal أكل (biyaakul, akil); **to be eaten** it'akal اتأكل (akla); it-taakal اتّآكل (ikkeel)
eavesdrop itṣannat اتصنّت (taṣannut)
ebony aabanuus آبنوس ; baaban-uus بآبنوس
echo *n* ṣada صدى
eclampsia kalabsh كلبش
eclipse (**of the moon**) khusuuf خسوف ; (**of the sun**) kusuuf كسوف ; **to be in eclipse** khannag خنّق (khinneeg)
economic iqtiṣaadi إقتصادي
economise iqtaṣad إقتصد (iqtiṣaad)
economy iqtiṣaad إقتصاد
eczema akziima اكزيما
edge ḥaaffa حافّة (*pl* ḥawaaff); ṭaraf طرف (*pl* aṭraaf)
educate ʿallam علّم (taʿliim); **educated person** mutʿallim متعلّم
education taʿliim تعليم ; tarbiya تربية ; **civic education** at-tasqiif al-madani
eel dabiib al-baḥar; umm dibeebu
effect ta'siir تأسير (*pl* -aat)
effort majhuud مجهود (*pl* -aat); jahd جهد (*pl* juhuud); **to make an effort** ʿamal majhuud
egg(s) beeḍ بيض ; **boiled eggs** beeḍ masluug; **fried eggs** beeḍ be-ṭ-ṭawwa; beeḍ magli
eggplant aswad أسود
egg-shaped beeḍaawi بيضاوي
eggshell(s) gishir al-beeḍ
egoism anaaniyya أنانيّة
egoist anaani أناني
egret **cattle egret** ṭeerat al-bagar
Egypt maṣir مصر
Egyptian *adj/n* maṣri مصري (*pl* -yyiin)
eight tamanya تمنية ; **eight hundred** tumnumiyya تمنميّة
eighteen tamanṭaashar تمنطاشر
eighth taamin تامن
eighty tamaaniin تمانين
either **either/or** imma إمّا ; ya-imma
elastic *adj* maṭṭaaṭi مطّاطي ; **elastic band** istik إستك (*pl* asaatik) • *n* (**piece of**) listika لستك (*pl* lasaatik)
elbow kuuʿ كوع (*pl* keeʿaan, kuuʿeen, akwaaʿ)
elder *n* sheekh شيخ (*pl* shiyuukh, mashaayikh)
elderly shaayib شايب (*pl* shiyaab)
elect intakhab انتخب (intikhaab)

elections intikhaabaat إنتخابات
electric *adj* kahrabaa'i كهربائي ; **electric power point** kobs كبس (*pl* -aat); kobsi كبسي (*pl* -yyaat)
electrician kahrabji كهربجي (*pl* -yya)
electricity kahraba كهربا
elegance giyaafa قيافة ; rashaaga رشاقة
elegant gaashir قاشر ; rashiig رشيق ; shiik شيك
element ᶜunṣur عنصر (*pl* ᶜanaaṣir)
elephant fiil فيل (*pl* afyaal)
elephantiasis daa' al-fiil
elevation irtifaaᶜ إرتفاع
eleven ḥidaashar حداشر
eliminate gaḍa ᶜala قضى (-i, gaḍaa)
eloquent faṣiiḥ فصيح ; baliigh بليغ
e-mail bariid iliktrooni
embankment taras ترس (*pl* turuus); radmiyya ردميّة ; **(small)** ḥaajiz حاجز (*pl* ḥawaajiz); trotwaar تروتوار (*pl* -aat)
embarrass aḥraj احرج (i, iḥraaj); kasaf كسف (i, kasif, kasafaan); **to be(come) embarrassed** itkasaf اتكسف (kasif, kasfa); inkasaf انكسف (kasfa); itḥaraj اتحرج (ḥaraj)
embarrassment ḥaraj حرج ; iḥraaj احراج (*pl* -aat)
embassy safaara سفارة
ember(s) jamur جمر (*unit n* jamra)
embezzle ikhtalas اختلس (ikhtilaas)
embezzlement ikhtilaas اختلاس (*pl* -aat)
embrace *n* ḥuḍun حضن • *v* ḥaḍan حضن (i, ḥuḍun); galad قلد (i, galda, galadaan)
embroider ṭarraz طرّز (ṭirreez, taṭriiz)
embroidery taṭriiz تطريز
emerald zumurrud زمرّد
emerge ṭalaᶜ طلع (a, ṭuluuᶜ); ẓahar ظهر (a, ẓuhuur)
emergency ṭaari طاري (*pl* ṭawaari); **state of emergency** ṭawaari طواري
emigrate haajar min هاجر (hijra)
emigration hijra هجرة
eminent wajiih وجيه (*pl* wujaha)
emotion ᶜaaṭifa عاطفة (*pl* ᶜawaaṭif)
emotional ᶜaaṭifi عاطفي ; **to be(come) emotional** infaᶜal انفعل (infiᶜaal)
employ shaghghal شغّل (shighgheel, tashghiil); waẓẓaf وظّف (tawẓiif); **to be employed** itwaẓẓaf اتوظّف (tawẓiif)
employee (*m*) ᶜaamil عامل ; (*f*) ᶜaamila عاملة ; **(in office)** (*m*) muwaẓẓaf موظّف ; (*f*) muwaẓẓafa موظّفة
empowerment tamkiin تمكين
emptiness faraagh فراغ (*pl* -aat)
empty *adj* faaḍi فاضي ; faarigh فارغ ; khaali خالي ; **to become empty** fiḍa فضى (-a, faḍayaan) • *v* faḍḍa فضّى (-i, fiḍḍeey, tafḍiya); farragh فرّغ (tafriigh); **to be emptied** itfaḍḍa اتفضّى ; itfarragh اتفرّغ (tafarrugh)
enamel ṭalis طلس
enclosure suur سور (*pl* aswaar); siyaaj سياج (*pl* asyija); ḥoosh حوش (*pl* ḥeeshaan); zariiba زريبة (*pl* zaraayib); **(of reed or straw)** ṣariif صريف (*pl* ṣurfaan)
encounter *n* mugaabala مقابلة • *v* gaabal قابل (mugaabala)

encourage shajjaᶜ شجّع (shijjeeᶜ, tashjiiᶜ); **to be encouraged** itshajjaᶜ اتشجّع (tashajjuᶜ)
end *n* nihaaya نهاية ; khitaam ختام • *vi* intaha انتهى (-i, nihaaya); giḍa قضى (-a, gaḍayaan, gaḍiya) • *vt* naha نهى (-i, nihaaya, inhaa)
endorse ṣaadag ᶜala صادق (muṣaadaga); iᶜtamad إعتمد (iᶜtimaad); ṣaddag ᶜala صدّق (taṣdiig); **to be endorsed** itṣaddag ᶜala اتصدّق (taṣdiig)
endorsement iᶜtimaad إعتماد (*pl* -aat)
endure itḥammal اتحمّل (taḥammul); istaḥmal استحمل (istiḥmaal)
enemy ᶜadu عدو (*pl* aᶜdaa)
energetic nashiiṭ نشيط (*pl* -iin, nushaaṭ); hamiim هميم
energy ṭaaqa طاقة
engaged (**committed**) multazim ملتزم ; (**to marry, of men**) khaaṭib خاطب (*pl* -iin, khuṭṭaab); (**of women**) makhṭuuba مخطوبة ; **to get engaged** (**of men**) khaṭab خطب (u, khuṭuuba); shabak شبك (u, shabka); (**of women**) itkhaṭab اتخطب (khuṭuuba)
engaged (**telephone**) al-khaṭṭ mashghuul
engagement (**commitment**) iltizaam إلتزام (*pl* -aat); (**to marry**) khuṭuuba خطوبة
engine baabuur بابور (*pl* -aat, bawaabiir); waabuur وابور (*pl* -aat); makana مكنة ; motoor موتور (*pl* -aat); **railway engine** baabuur al-gaṭar بابور (*pl* -aat, bawaabiir); waabuur al-gaṭar وابور (*pl* -aat)
engineer muhandis مهندس ; **chief engineer** baashmuhandis باشمهندس
engineering handasa هندسة
England ingiltarra إنقلترا
English ingliizi إنقليزي (*pl* ingliiz)
Englishman ingliizi إنقليزي (*pl* ingliiz)
engrave nagash نقش (u, nigaasha)
engrossed **to be engrossed in** inghamas انغمس (inghimaas); inhamak fi انهمك (inhimaak)
enjoy istamtaᶜ be- استمتع (istimtaaᶜ); itmattaᶜ اتمتّع (tamattuᶜ)
enjoyable mumtiᶜ ممتع
enjoyment mutᶜa متعة ; istimtaaᶜ استمتاع
enlarge kabbar كبّر (kibbeer); **to be enlarged** itkabbar اتكبّر (kibbeer)
enlist dakhal al-khidma al-ᶜaskariyya
enormous ḍakham ضخم
enough *adj* kaafi كافي • *adv* kifaaya كفاية • *interj* bass بس ; khalaaṣ خلاص ; kifaaya كفاية ; **to be enough** kaffa كفّى (-i, kifaaya); kafa كفى (-i, kifaaya)
enrol sajjal سجّل (tasjiil)
enter khashsha خشّ (u, khashsh); dakhal دخل (u, dukhuul); **to cause to enter** dakhkhal دخّل (dikhkheel)
enterprise mashruuᶜ مشروع (*pl* -aat, mashaariiᶜ)
entertainment tasliya تسلية
enthusiasm ḥamaas حماس
enthusiastic mutḥammis متحمّس ; **to be(come) enthusiastic** itḥammas اتحمّس (ḥamaas)
entire kaamil كامل ; kull كل

entrance dukhuul دخول ; madkhal مدخل (*pl* madaakhil)
entrust amman أمّن (ya'ammin, amaana); (**bank**) awdaᶜ أودع (i, wadiiᶜa)
envelope ẓarif ظرف (*pl* ẓuruuf)
envious ḥaasid حاسد (*pl* ḥussaad)
environment bii'a بيئة
environmental bii'i بيئي
envy *v* ḥasad حسد (i, ḥasaada, ḥasad)
epidemic waba وبا (*pl* awbiya)
epilepsy ṣarᶜa صرعة
Epiphany ᶜiid aẓ-ẓuhuur
episcopal usqufi أسقفي
episode (**of a series**) ḥalaga حلقة
equal *adj* mutsaawi متساوي ; **to be(come) equal** itwaasa اتواسى (-i, muwaasaa); itsaawa اتساوى (-a, musaawaa); **to make equal** waasa واسى (-i, muwaasaa) • *v* saawa ساوى (-i, musaawaa)
equality musaawaa مساواة
equator khaṭṭ al-istiwa
equatorial istiwaa'i إستوائي
equilibrium tawaazun توازن (*pl* -aat)
equipment ᶜidda عدّة (*pl* ᶜidad); jihaaz جهاز (*pl* ajhiza)
era zaman زمن (*pl* azmina)
erase masaḥ مسح (a, masiḥ, masaḥaan); shaṭab شطب (u, shaṭib); **to be erased** itmasaḥ اتمسح (masiḥ, masaḥaan); itshaṭab اتشطب (shaṭib)
eraser istiika إستيكة
erect *v* ghazza غزّ (u, ghazz); naṣab نصب (u, naṣb); **to be erected** intaṣab إنتصب (intiṣaab) • *adj* gaayim قايم ; **to be(come) erect** gaam قام (u, gooma, giyaam)
erection intiṣaab إنتصاب (*pl* -aat)
Eritrea iriitriya إريتريا
Eritrean *adj/n* iriitri إريتري (*pl* -yyiin)
err ghiliṭ غلط (a, ghalaṭ); khita ختا (-i, khata, khatiya); khiṭa خطا (-i, khaṭa, khaṭiya)
errand mushwaar مشوار (*pl* mashaawiir)
error ghalaṭ غلط (*pl* -aat, ghalṭaaṭ); ghalṭa غلطة (*pl* ghalaṭaat); khata ختا (*pl* akhtaa)
escape *n* huruub هروب ; shuruud شرود • *v* harab (min) هرب (a, huruub, harabaan); sharad شرد (u, sharid, sharadaan)
escort *n* ḥaras حرس (*pl* ḥurraas)
especially be-z-zaat; khuṣuuṣan خصوصا ; khaaṣṣatan خاصّة ; **especially for** makhṣuuṣ le- مخصوص
estate agent samsaar سمسار (*pl* samaasra)
estimate *n* taqdiir تقدير ; takhmiin تخمين (*pl* -aat) • *v* qaddar قدّر (taqdiir); khamman خمّن (takhmiin)
eternal abadi أبدي
eternity al-abadiyya
Ethiopia isiyuubiya إسيوبيا ; al-ḥabasha
Ethiopian *adj/n* isiyuubi إسيوبي (*pl* -yyiin); ḥabashi حبشي (*pl* ḥabash)
ethnic ᶜirgi عرقي
ethnicity ᶜirig عرق
euro yuuro يورو (*pl* -haat)
Europe urubba أوروبّا
European *adj/n* urubbi اوروبّي (*pl* -yyiin); urubbaawi اوروبّاي (*pl* -yyiin); afranji افرنجي (*pl* -yya)
evade zaaq min زاق (u, zooqa, zawaqaan); zawwaq min زوّغ (ziwweeq, zawaqaan)

evaluate qayyam قيّم (taqyiim)
evaluation taqyiim تقييم (*pl* -aat)
evangelise bashshar (be-) بشّر (tabshiir)
evangelist mubashshir مبشّر
evaporate itbakhkhar اتبخّر (bakhra)
eve (**of a feast**) wagfa وقفة
even *adj* (**equal**) mutsaawi متساوي; (**ground**) mustawi مستوي; **to make even** waasa واسى (-i, muwaasaa); saawa ساوى (-i, musaawaa); (**of numbers**) zawji زوجي • *adv* **even if** ḥatta law; ḥatta wa law
evening masa/misa مسا; ʿashiyya عشيّة; **in the evening** be-l-leel; fi l-masa; masaa'an مساء; **good evening** masaa l-kheer, masaa n-nuur
event ḥadas حدس (*pl* aḥdaas)
every kullo كلّو
everybody an-naas kull-um; kullo n-naas
everyone kullo waaḥid
evidence bayyina بيّنة; daliil دليل (*pl* adilla); burhaan برهان (*pl* baraahiin); **to give evidence** gaddam shihaada; shihid شهد (a, shihaada)
evident baayin باين; ẓaahir ظاهر
evil *adj* sharraani شرّاني (*pl* –yyiin); shirriir شرّير (*pl* ashraar) • *n* sharr شر (*pl* shuruur)
ewe ḍaanaaya ضانااية; naʿja نعجة (*pl* niʿaaj)
exactly be-ḍ-ḍabt; be-ẓ-ẓabṭ; tamaam تمام
exaggerate baalagh بالغ (mubaalagha)
examination imtiḥaan إمتحان (*pl* -aat); **to sit for an examination** imtaḥan امتحن (imtiḥaan); **medical examination** kashif كشف (*pl* kushuufaat)
examine imtaḥan امتحن (imtiḥaan); **to examine medically** kashaf كشف (i, kashif)
example (**illustration**) masal مسل (*pl* amsaal); misaal مسال (*pl* amsila); **for example** masalan مسلا; (**model**) namuuzaj نموزج (*pl* namaazij); (**to be followed**) qudwa قدوة; (**warning**) ʿibra عبرة (*pl* ʿibar)
excavate ḥafar حفر (i, ḥafir)
exceed zaad ʿan زاد (i, zeeda, ziyaada); itjaawaz اتجاوز (tajaawuz); itʿadda اتعدّى (-a, taʿaddi)
excel itfawwag اتفوّق (tafawwug)
excellence imtiyaaz إمتياز (*pl* -aat)
excellent mumtaaz ممتاز; tamaam تمام; tamaam at-tamaam; miyya miyya
except bass بس; illa إلا; ma ʿada
exchange *n* badal بدل (*pl* badalaat); mubaadala مبادلة; mugaayaḍa مقايضة; **bill of exchange** kambiyaala كمبيالة • *v* baadal بادل (mubaadala, tabaadul); gaayaḍ قايض (mugaayaḍa)
excite hayyaj هيّج (hiyyeej, tahyiij); **to be excited** infaʿal انفعل (infiʿaal); ithayyaj اتهيّج
excitement hayajaan هيجان
exclamation mark ʿalaamat taʿajjub
excuse *n* ʿuzur عزر (*pl* aʿzaar); (**justification**) mubarrir مبرّر (*pl* -aat) • *v* ʿazar عزر (i, ʿuzur); **excuse me** ʿanizn-ak; law samaḥta

execute (**put to death**) aʿdam أعدم (iʿdaam); (**orders**) naffaz نفّز (tanfiiz)
execution (**death penalty**) iʿdaam إعدام (*pl* -aat); (**orders**) tanfiiz تنفيز (*pl* -aat)
exercise *n* (**drill**) tamriin تمرين (*pl* -aat, tamaariin); (**physical**) riyaaḍa رياضة **exercise book** karraas كرّاس (*pl* -aat, karaariis)
exhausted murhaq مرهق ; fatraan فتران ; najḍaan نجضان
exhaustion irhaaq إرهاق
exhaust pipe *n* ʿaadim عادم (*pl* ʿawaadim)
exhibit *v* ʿaraḍ عرض (a, ʿariḍ)
exhibition *n* (**fair**) maʿraḍ معرض (*pl* maʿaariḍ)
exile *n* manfa منفى (*pl* ma-naafi) • *v* nafa نفى (-i, nafi)
existence wujuud وجود
exit *n* khuruuj خروج
expand *vi* itwassaʿ اتوسّع (wisseeʿ, tawsiiʿ) • *vt* wassaʿ وسّع (wisseeʿ, tawsiiʿ); maddad مدّد (middeed, tamdiid)
expect itwaggaʿ اتوقّع (tawagguʿ)
expectation tawagguʿ توقّع (*pl* -aat)
expel ṭarad طرد (u, ṭarid); karash كرش (u, karish)
expenditure maṣaariif مصاريف
expenses takaaliif تكاليف ; maṣaariif مصاريف ; maṣruuf مصروف
expensive ghaali غالي ; **to be(come) expensive** ghila غلى (-a, ghala)
experience *n* tajruba تجربة (*pl* tajaarib); khibra خبرة ; **to gain/ have experience** akhad tajruba
experienced mujarrib مجرّب
experiment *n* tajruba تجربة (*pl* tajaarub)
expert *n* khabiir خبير (*pl* khu-bara) • *adj* jaʿiiṣ جعيص (*pl* -iin, juʿaṣa)
explain sharaḥ شرح (-a, shariḥ); waḍḍaḥ وضّح (tawḍiiḥ); fahham فهّم (fihheem, faham)
explanation shariḥ شرح (*pl* shuruuḥaat); tawḍiiḥ توضيح (*pl* -aat)
explode *vi* itfargaʿ اتفرقع (firgeeʿ, fargaʿa); fargaʿ فرقع (firgeeʿ, fargaʿa); itfajjar اتفجّر (fajra); in-fajjar انفجّر (infijaar) • *vt* fargaʿ فرقع (firgeeʿ, fargaʿa); fajjar فجّر (fijjeer, tafjiir)
exploit istaghalla استغلّ (istighlaal)
exploitation istighlaal إستغلال
explore istakshaf استكشف (istikshaaf)
explosion fargaʿa فرقعة ; infijaar إنفجار (*pl* -aat)
explosives mufargaʿaat مفرقعات ; mutfajjiraat متفجّرات
export *n* taṣdiir تصدير (*pl* -aat); **export license** izin taṣdiir/taṣriiḥ taṣdiir • *v* ṣaddar صدّر (taṣdiir)
exports ṣaadiraat صادرات
expose ʿarraḍ عرّض (ʿariḍ)
expression taʿbiir تعبير (*pl* -aat); (**phrase**) ʿibaara عبارة ; lafẓa لفظة (*pl* alfaaẓ)
extend (**e.g. a hand**) madda مدّ (i, madd); (**expand**) wassaʿ وسّع (wisseeʿ, tawsiiʿ); maddad مدّد (middeed, tamdiid); (**prolong**) madda (fi) مدّ (i, madda); mad-dad مدّد (middeed, tamdiid); **to be extended** itmadda اتمدّ (middeed); itwassaʿ (wisseeʿ, tawsiiʿ); itmaddad اتمدّد (mid-deed, tamdiid)

extension imtidaad إمتداد (*pl* -aat); **extension lead** waṣla وصلة ; tawṣiila توصيلة
extent mada مدى ; **to the extent** le-d-daraja
external khaariji خارجي
extinguish ṭafa طفى (-i, ṭafi); **to be extinguished** iṭṭafa اطّفى (-i, ṭafi); khamad خمد (i, khamid)
extra ziyaada زيادة
extract *v* salla سلّ (i, sall); sarat سرت (u, sarit); (**minerals**) is-takhraj استخرج (istikhraaj)
extreme muṭṭarrif مطرّف ; agṣa أقصى
extremely jiddan جداً ; shadiid شديد ; khaaliṣ خالص
extremism taṭarruf تطرّف
extremist muṭṭarrif مطرّف
eye ᶜeen عين (*pl* ᶜiyuun); **the evil eye** al-ᶜeen
eyebrow ḥaajib حاجب (*pl* ḥawaajib)
eyelash rimish رمش (*pl* rumuush); rushrush رشرش (*pl* rashaarish)
eyelid jifin جفن (*pl* jufuun)
eyesight shoof شوف ; naẓar نظر ; baṣar بصر ; **having poor eye-sight** ṭashaash طشاش

F - f

fable khuraafa خرافة
fabric gumaash قماش (*pl* -aat, ag-misha); nasiij نسيج (*pl* ansija)
face *n* washsh وش (*pl* wushuush); wajh وجه (*pl* wujuuh) • *v* waa-jah واجه (muwaajaha)
facilitate sahhal سهّل (tashiil); yassar يسّر (taysiir)
facilitation tashiil تسهيل (*pl* -aat)
facilitator muyassir ميسّر
facility tashiil تسهيل (*pl* -aat)
facing guṣaad قصاد
fact ḥagiiga حقيقة (*pl* ḥagaayig); waaqiᶜ واقع (*pl* waqaaᶜi); **in fact** aṣlo أصلو ; ghaayto غايتو ; aṣlan أصلا ; al-ḥagiiga
faction faṣiila فصيلة (*pl* faṣaayil)
factory maṣnaᶜ مصنع (*pl* maṣaaniᶜ)
faculty (**of university**) kulliyya كلّيّة
fade bihit بهت (a, bahta, bahata-an); bahat بهت (a, bahta, ba-hataan); inṭamas انطمس (ṭamsa)
faded baahit باهت
faeces faḍalaat فضلات ; buraaz براز huraar هرار ; khara خرا ; (**animal**) zibaala زبالة
fail fashal فشل (a, fashal); (**in ex-ams**) sagaṭ سقط (u, suguuṭ)
failure fashal فشل ; kheeba خيبة
faint *v* daakh داخ (u, dawakhaan); ghimir غمر (a, ghamra)
fair *adj* (**just**) dughri دغري ; ᶜaadil عادل ; naziih نزيه
fair *n* maᶜraḍ معرض (*pl* maᶜaariḍ)
faith iimaan إيمان
faithful amiin أمين ; mukhliṣ مخلص ; **to be faithful** wafa وفى (yuufi, wafaa); akhlaṣ أخلص (i, ikhlaaṣ)
faithfulness ikhlaaṣ إخلاص
faithless ghaddaar غدّار
fake *adj* faalso فالسو
falcon ṣagur صقر (*pl* ṣuguur)
fall *n* wagᶜa وقعة • *v* wagaᶜ وقع (yoogaᶜ, wuguuᶜ); (**a house**) inhadda انهدّ (hadd); **to fall apart** itfartak اتفرتك (firteek);

to make s.o. fall waggaᶜ وقّع (wiggeeᶜ)

fallow buur بور ; **to be fallow** baar بار (u, boora); **to leave fallow** bawwar بوّر (tabwiir)

false muzayyaf مزيّف ; kaaḍib كاضب ; kaazib كازب

fame shuhra شهرة ; ṣiit صيت

familiar ma'luuf مألوف

family usra أسرة (*pl* usar); (**nuclear**) ahal أهل (*pl* ahaali); **extended family** ᶜeela عيلة (*pl* ᶜaayilaat, ᶜawaayil)

famine majaaᶜa مجاعة

famous mashhuur (be-) مشهور ; shahiir شهير ; **to be famous for** ishtahar be- اشتهر (shuhra)

fan *n* (**hand**) habbaaba هبّابة ; (**electric**) marwaḥa مروحة (*pl* maraawiḥ) • *v* habbab هبّب (hibbeeb); (**o.s.**) ithabbab اتهبّب (hibbeeb)

fanatical mutᶜaṣṣib متعصّب ; **to be(come) fanatical** itᶜaṣṣab اتعصّب (taᶜaṣṣub)

fanaticism taᶜaṣṣub تعصّب

fantasy khayaal خيال

far baᶜiid بعيد (*pl* buᶜaad); **to be far away** biᶜid بعد (i, buᶜaad)

fare ujra أجرة (*pl* ujuur)

farewell wadaaᶜ وداع ; **to bid farewell** waddaᶜ ودّع (wadaaᶜ, wideeᶜ)

farm *n* mazraᶜa مزرعة (*pl* mazaariᶜ); **farm labourer** tarbaal تربال (*pl* taraabla)

farmer muzaariᶜ مزارع

fart *n* fasya فسية ; faswa فسوة ; ẓarṭa ظرطة (*pl* -aat, ẓuraaṭ) • *v* fasa فسى (-i, fasu); ẓaraṭ ظرط (u, ẓariṭ, ẓuraaṭ, ẓirreeṭ)

fast *adj* (**of colour**) saabit سابت ; (**speedy**) sariiᶜ سريع • *adv* be-surᶜa

fast *n* ṣiyaam صيام ; ṣoom صوم • *v* ṣaam صام (u, ṣiyaam, ṣoom); **to enable s.o. to fast** ṣawwam صوّم (ṣiyaam)

fasten rabbaṭ ربّط (rubaaṭ, ribbeeṭ)

fat *adj* (**obese**) samiin سمين (*pl* sumaan); shaḥmaan شحمان ; ghaliid غليد ; **to grow fat** simin سمن (a, sumun); shiḥim شحم (a, shaḥam) • *n* dihin دهن (*pl* duhuun); shaḥam شحم (*pl* shuḥuum); (**for cosmetic use**) dihaan دهان ; wadak ودك

fate naṣiib نصيب (*pl* anṣiba); qadar قدر (*pl* aqdaar); gisma قسمة (*pl* -aat, gisam); **by fate and divine decree** qaḍaa wa qadar

father abu أبو (*pl* abbahaat, abawaat); waalid والد ; (**priest**) abuu-na; **father-in-law** nasiib نسيب (*pl* nasaaba, nasaayib); ḥama حما (*pl* ḥimyaan); ḥamu حمو (*pl* ḥimyaan)

fatigue fatar فتر ; taᶜab تعب

fatten samman سمّن (tasmiin)

fault ghalaṭ غلط (*pl* -aat, aghlaaṭ); ghalṭa غلطة (*pl* ghalaṭaat); khata ختا (*pl* akhtaa)

fava beans fuul فول (*unit n* fuulaaya, fuula)

favour *n* maᶜruuf معروف ; khidma خدمة (*pl* khadamaat) • *v* faḍḍal فضّل (tafḍiil)

favourite mufaḍḍal مفضّل

fax *n* faaks فاكس (*pl* -aat)

fear *n* khoof خوف • *v* khaaf (min) خاف (a, khoof); itkhawwaf (min) اتخوّف (khoof)

feast *n* iḥtifaal احتفال (*pl* -aat); ᶜiid عيد (*pl* aᶜyaad); (**meal**) waliima وليمة (*pl* walaayim); **Feast of Breaking the Fast** ᶜiid

al-fiṭr; **Feast of the Sacrifice** ʿiid al-aḍḥa, ʿiid aḍ-ḍaḥiyya • *v* iḥtifal be- (iḥtifaal); ʿayyad (ʿala) عيّد (ʿiid)
feather(s) riish ريش (*pl* -aat, riyash)
feature miiza ميزة
February shahri itnee; fabraayir فبراير
fed up zahjaan زهجان ; ganʿaan قنعان ; **to be fed up (with)** zihij (min) زهج (a, zahaj); giniʿ (min) قنع (a, ganaʿ); **I am fed up with** baṭn-i ṭammat/ṭaamma min
feeble ḍaʿiif ضعيف (*pl* ḍuʿaaf); **to become feeble** ḍiʿif ضعف (a, ḍuʿuf)
feeble-minded kharfaan خرفان ; **to be(come) feeble-minded** kharraf خرّف (khirreef)
feed akkal أكّل (ya'akkil, ikkeel); **(animals)** ʿalaf علف (i, ʿalaf)
feel ḥassa حسّ (i, iḥsaas); shaʿar be- شعر (u, shuʿuur); **(touch)** lamas لمس (a, lamis)
feeling ḥiss حس (*no pl*); iḥsaas احساس (*pl* -aat, aḥaasiis); shuʿuur شعور
fees rusuum رسوم (*sg* rasm); **(for a lawyer)** atʿaab اتعاب ; **(taxes)** ḍaraayib ضرايب
fell *v* gaṭaʿ قطع (a, gaṭiʿ)
fellowship zamaala زمالة
female **(animals)** intaaya إنتاية
feminine mu'annas مؤنّس
fence *n* suur سور (*pl* aswaar); ḥoosh (*pl* ḥeeshaan); siyaaj سياج (*pl* -aat, asyija); **(of reed or metal)** darabziin درابزين (*pl* -aat); **(of reed or straw)** ṣariif صريف (*pl* ṣurfaan) • *v* sawwar سوّر (siwweer, taswiir); ḥawwash حوّش (ḥiwweesh); sayyaj سيّج (siyaaj, tasyiij)
fender **(of car)** rafraf رفرف (*pl* rafaarif)
fenugreek ḥilba حلبة
ferment *vi* khimir خمر (a, khamaraan); itkhammar اتخمّر (khimmeer) • *vt* khammar خمّر (khimmeer, takhmiir)
ferocious sharis شرس
ferroconcrete asmant musallaḥ
ferry banṭoon بنطون (*pl* -aat, banaaṭiin); maʿadiyya معديّة
fertile khiṣb خصب ; khaṣiib خصيب
fertility khuṣuuba خصوبة
fertilize **(plants)** laggaḥ لقّح (talgiiḥ); **(soil)** sammad سمّد (simmeed, tasmiid)
festival mahrajaan مهرجان (*pl* -aat); karnafaal كرنفال
fetch jaab جاب (i, jeeba, jayabaan)
feud taar تار (*pl* -aat)
fever ḥumma حمّى ; wirda وردة ; **to have a fever** wirid ورد (a, wirda)
feverish maḥmuum محموم ; mawruud موورود
few basiiṭ بسيط (*pl* -iin); galiil قليل (*pl* gulaal); shwayya شويّة
fiancé khaṭiib خطيب (*pl* khuṭṭaab)
fiancée khaṭiiba خطيبة
fibre liif ليف ; **palm fibre** saʿaf سعف (*unit n* saʿfa)
fibroids laḥmiyya لحميّة
field **(agricultural)** mazraʿa مزرعة (*pl* mazaariʿ); **(small)** ḥawwaasha حوّاشة ; **(fields)** bildaat بلدات ; **(domain)** majaal مجال (*pl* -aat)
fifteen khamasṭaashar خمسطاشر
fifth khaamis خامس
fifty khamsiin خمسين
fig(s) tiin تين ; **wild fig(s)** jummeez جمّيز

fight *n* kitaal كتال ; katla كتلة ; duwaas دواس • *v* ḍaarab ضارب (ḍarib, muḍaaraba); kaatal كاتل (kitaal, mukaatala); daawas داوس (duwaas, mudaawasa); (**in war**) ḥaarab حارب (ḥarib, muḥaaraba); kaatal كاتل (kitaal, mukaatala); **to fight with one another** iḍḍaarab اضّارب (muḍaaraba); itkaatal اتكاتل (mukaatala); iddaawas ادّاوس (mudaawasa)

fighter muḥaarib محارب ; **fighter in a holy war** mujaahid مجاهد

fighting kitaal كتال ; mukaatala مكتالة ; muḥaaraba محاربة ; mudaawasa مداوسة

figure (**number**) raqam رقم (*pl* arqaam)

file *n* (**of papers**) malaff ملف (*pl* -aat); dosseeh دسّيه (*pl* -aat); faayl فايل (*pl* -aat); (**paper/computer**) mustanad مستند (*pl* -aat)

file (**tool**) mubrad مبرد (*pl* mabaarid) • *v* barad برد (u, biraada)

filings (**metal**) biraada برادة

fill *v* mala ملى (-a, mali); ʿabba عبّى (-i, ʿibbeey, taʿbiya); **to fill to the brim** kabas كبس (i, kabis); kamad كمد (i, kamid); **to be filled** itmala اتملى (-i, mali, malayaan); **to be filled to the brim** itkabas اتكبس (kabsa)

filling (**for sandwich or tooth**) ḥashwa حشوة

film *n* filim فلم (*pl* aflaam) • *v* ṣawwar صوّر (taṣwiir)

film *n* (**over eyes**) bayaaḍ بياض ; ghashaawa غشاوة

filter *n* filtar فيلتر (*pl* -aat, falaatir); maṣfaa مصفاة (*pl* maṣaafi); **filter candle** shamʿa شمعة • *v* ṣaffa صفّى (-i, ṣiffeey)

filthy waskhaan وسخان ; **to be(come) filthy** itwassakh اتوسّخ (wisseekh)

fin zaʿnafa زعنفة (*pl* zaʿaanif)

final *adj* nihaa'i نهائي

finally akhiiran أخيرا

finance *v* mawwal موّل (tamwiil)

financial maali مالي

find *n* lagiya لقية • *v* liga لقى (-a, lagayaan); **to be found** itlaga اتلقى (-i, lagayaan); **to find out** iktashaf اكتشف (iktishaaf)

fine *adj* (**good**) samiḥ سمح ; (**delicate**) rafiiʿ رفيع ; (**thin**) rigeyyig رقيق (*f* rigeyga); (**powdery**) dugaag دقاق

fine *n* gharaama غرامة ; mukhaalafa مخالفة • *v* gharram غرّم (gharaama)

finger aṣbaʿ أصبع (*pl* aṣaabiʿ, aṣaabʿeen); muṣbaʿ مصبع ; **index finger** sabbaaba سبّابة

fingernail ḍufur ضفر (*pl* aḍaafir, aḍaafreen)

fingerprint baṣma بصمة (*pl* baṣamaat)

finish *n* (**sports**) meez ميز • *vi* khiliṣ خلص (a, khalaaṣ); intaha انتهى (-i, nihaaya); tamma تمّ (i, tamma) • *vt* khallaṣ (min) خلّص (khalaaṣ); kammal كمّل (kamaal, kamla); tamma تمّ (i, tamm); intaha min انتهى (-i, nihaaya); **to be finished** ittamma اتّمّ (tamm, tamamaan); (**of food, goods**) kimil كمل (a, kamla); (**with**) itkhallaṣ min اتخلّص (khilleeṣ); khiliṣ min خلص (a, khalaaṣ)

fire naar نار (*pl* niiraan); (**conflagration**) ḥariiga حريقة

(*pl* ḥaraayig); **fire brigade** al-maṭaafi; **fire extinguisher** ṭaffaaya طفّاية ; **to catch fire** ishtaᶜal اشتعل (ishtiᶜaal)
firearms silaaḥ سلاح (*pl* asliḥa)
fire engine ᶜarabiyyat al-maṭaafi
firefinch (**bird**) ṭeerat aj-janna
fireproof ma bitḥarig
firewood ḥaṭab حطب
fireworks alᶜaab naariyya
firm *adj* saabit سابت
firm *n* sharika شركة
first awwal أوّل (*f* uula); awwalaani أوّلاني
firstly be-l-awwal; fi l-awwal; awwalan أوّلا
fish *n* samak سمك (*pl* asmaak); ḥuut حوت (*unit n* ḥuutaaya, *pl* ḥeeṭaan); **fish bone**(**s**) shook شوك (*pl* -aat, ashwaak); **salt-cured fish** fasiikh فسيخ • *v* ṣaad samak
fisherman sammaaki سمّاكي (*pl* sammaaka); ṣayyaad samak; ḥawwaati حوّاتي (*pl* ḥawwaata, ḥawwaatiyya)
fishhook sinnaara سنّارة (*pl* -aat, sanaaniir)
fishing ṣeed as-samak; **fishing rod** jabbaada جبّادة
fist **a blow with the fist** bunya بنية (*pl* -aat, bunaj)
fistula naasuur ناسور (*pl* nawaasiir)
fit *adj* (**for use**) ṣaaliḥ صالح
fitter makaaniiki مكانيكي (*pl* -iyya)
five khamsa خمسة ; **five hundred** khumsumiyya خمسميّة
fix *v* (**repair**) ṣallaḥ صلّح (ṣilleeḥ, taṣliiḥ); ẓabaṭ ظبط (u, ẓabiṭ); (**determine**) ḥaddad حدّد (taḥdiid); (**a meeting**) ᶜagad عقد (i, ᶜagid); **to fix firmly** sabbat سبّت (sibbeet, tasbiit); ẓabbaṭ ظبّط ; barsham برشم (barshama)
flag ᶜalam علم (*pl* aᶜlaam); raaya راية ; beerag بيرق (*pl* bayaarig)
flail *n* mudgaag مدقاق (*pl* -aat)
flake *vi* **to flake off** itgashshar اتقشّر (gishsheer); (**of the skin**) itfasakh إتفسخ (faskha, fasakhaan)
flame(**s**) lahab لهب
flap *v* rafraf رفرف (rafrafa)
flash *v* shalaᶜ شلع (a, shaliᶜ); (**of lightning**) barag برق (i, barig)
flash(**es**) *n* shalaᶜ شلع
flashlight baṭṭaariyya بطاريّة
flask **vacuum flask** sirmus سيرمس (*pl* saraamis); tirmus تيرمس (*pl* taraamis); **water flask** ḥaafiẓa حافظة ; zamzamiyya زمزميّة
flat *adj* musaṭṭaḥ مسطّح ; mustawi مستوي
flat *n* (**apartment**) shagga شقّة (*pl* shugag)
flatter balbaṣ (ᶜala) بلبص (balbaṣa)
flavour ṭaᶜam طعم ; **flavoured** muᶜaṭṭar معطّر
flee fazza فزّ (i, fazza, fazazaan)
fleet (**navy**) usṭuul أسطول (*pl* asaaṭiil)
flesh laḥam لحم (*pl* luḥuum)
flexibility (**material**) liyuuna ليونة ; (**person**) muruuna مرونة
flexible (**material**) ṭayyiᶜ طيّع ; layyin ليّن ; ṭari طري ; (**person**) marin مرن
flight (**escape**) huruub هروب ; shuruud شرود ; fazza فزّة ; (**on plane**) riḥla رحلة (*pl* -aat, riḥal)
flinch gamaz قمز (i, gamiz)
flipflops safinja سفنجة
flirt *v* shaaghal شاغل (mushaaghala)

float *n* ᶜawwaama عوّامة • *v* ṭaffaḥ طفّح (ṭiffeeḥ)

flock gaṭiiᶜ قطيع (*pl* guṭᶜaan); muraaḥ مراح (-aat, murḥaat)

flog jalad جلد (i, jalid)

flood *n* (**from rain**) seel سيل (*pl* siyuul); (**from river**) fayaḍaan فيضان (*pl* -aat) • *v* saal سال (i, seel, sayalaan); faaḍ فاض (i, fayaḍaan)

floodlight kashshaafa كشّافة

floor waaṭa واطا ; (**storey**) door دور (*pl* adwaar); ṭaabig طابق (*pl* ṭawaabig); **the ground floor** ad-door al-arḍi

flour dagiig دقيق

flow *v* jara جرى (-i, jari, jarayaan)

flower(s) *n* zahar زهر (*unit n* zahra, *pl* zuhuur); ward ورد (*pl* wuruud); **flowerpot** zuhriyya زهريّة ; faaẓa فاظة ; aṣiiṣ أصيص (*pl* aṣaayiṣ)

flu influwanza إنفلونزا

fluff *n* nisaala نسالة

flute zumbaara زمبارة (*pl* zanaabi-ir); **to play the flute** zammar زمّر (zimmeer)

flutter *v* rafraf رفرف (rafrafa); (**birds**) habhab هبهب (habhaba, hibheeb)

fly *n* ḍubbaan ضبّان ; zubaab زباب ; **horsefly** ḍubbaanal-ḥamiir; **sand-fly** az-zubaaba ar-ramliyya; **tsetse fly** zubaabat at-tisii tisii

fly *v* ṭaar طار (i, ṭayaraan)

foal muhr مهر (*pl* muhuur)

foam *n* righwa رغوة ; (**sea**) zabad زبد • *v* (**of soap**) ragha رغى (-i, raghayaan); raghgha رغّى (-i, righgheey); **to foam at the mouth** zabbad زبّد (zibbeed)

focus *v* rakkaz ركّز (tarkiiz)

fodder ᶜalaf علف (*pl* aᶜlaaf); ᶜaliiga عليقة (*pl* ᶜalaayig)

foetus janiin جنين

fog ḍabaab ضباب

fold *v* ṭabbag طبّق (ṭibbeeg, taṭbiig); ṭabag طبق (u, ṭabig, ṭabagaan)

folder (**paper/computer**) malaff ملف (*pl* -aat)

folklore fulkluur فلكلور ; funuun shaᶜbiyya

folktale ḥujwa حجوة (*pl* aḥaaji, ḥuja); ḥajwa حجوة (*pl* aḥaaji, ḥuja); **to tell a folktale** ḥajja حجّى (-i, ḥuja)

follow tibiᶜ تبع (a, tabaᶜaan); taabaᶜ تابع (mutaabaᶜa); baara بارا (-i, mabaaraa); bira برا (-i, mabaaraa)

font (**printing/computer**) khaṭṭ خط (*pl* khuṭuuṭ)

food akil أكل ; **cooked food** ṭabiikh طبيخ (*pl* ṭabaayikh)

foodstuffs aghziya اغزية (*sg* ghiza)

fool *n* ᶜawiir عوير (*pl* ᶜuwara); ᶜabiiṭ عبيط (*pl* ᶜubaṭa); **to play the fool** istahbal استهبل (istihbaal)

foolish ᶜawiir عوير (*pl* ᶜuwara); ᶜabiiṭ عبيط (*pl* ᶜubaṭa); dilaaha دلاهة

foolishness ᶜawaara عوارة ; ᶜabaaṭa عباطة

foot kuraaᶜ كراع (*pl* kurᶜeen); rijil رجل (*pl* rijleen); gadam قدم (*pl* gadameen); (**of a camel**) khuff خفّ (*pl* akhfaaf); (**12 inches**) gadam قدم (*pl* agdaam); **on foot** kaddaari كدّاري

football (**soccer**) kuurat al-gadam; kurat al-gadam; al-kuura; al-kura

footprint asar أسر (*pl* aasaar); atar أتر

footstep khaṭwa خطوة (khaṭawaat)
for *conj* ᶜashaan عشان • *prep* le- ل
forbid manaᶜ منع (a, maniᶜ); ḥarram حرّم (taḥriim)
force *n* guwwa قوّة ; zindiyya زندية ; **by force** be-l-ᶜaafya; be-l-ghaṣib; be-j-jabur; be-z-zindiyya; **the armed forces** al-quwwaat al-musallaḥa; **the air force** al-quwwaat aj-jawwiyya • *v* ghaṣab غصب (i, ghaṣib); jabar (ᶜala) جبر (i, jabur)
ford makhaaḍa مخاضة (makhaayiḍ)
forehead jabha جبهة
foreign ajnabi أجنبى (*pl* ajaanib)
foreigner ajnabi أجنبى (*pl* ajaanib); **white foreigner** khawaaja خواجة (*f* khawaajiyya, *pl* -aat)
foreman rayyis ريّس (*pl* ruwasa)
foreskin ghalafa غلفة ; jilda جلدة
forest ghaaba غابة
forever le-l-abad
forge (**money, etc.**) zawwar زوّر (tazwiir); zayyaf زيّف (tazyiif); **to be forged** itzawwar اتزوّر (tazwiir); itzayyaf اتزيّف (tazyiif)
forgery tazwiir تزوير
forget nisa نسى (-a, nasayaan)
forgive ᶜafa le-/ᶜan عفى (-i, ᶜafu); saamaḥ سامح (musaamaḥa); ghafar (le-) غفر (i, ghufraan)
forgiveness ᶜafu عفو ; samaaḥ سماح ; musaamaḥa مسامحة
fork *n* shooka شوكة (*pl* shuwak) • *v* itfarraᶜ اتفرّع (tafarruᶜ)
form (**document**) foorm فورم (*pl* -aat); orneek ارنيك (*pl* araaniik); istimaara إستمارة
form *n* (**shape**) shakil شكل (*pl* ashkaal) • *v* shakkal شكّل ; kawwan كوّن (takwiin); **to be formed** it-shakkal اتشكّل ; itkawwan اتكوّن
formal rasmi رسمي
fortunately le-ḥasan al-ḥaẓẓ
fortune-teller (*f*) sitt al-wadiᶜ
forty arbaᶜiin أربعين
forum minbar منبر ; nadwa ندوة (*pl* nadawaat)
foster **foster child** raḍiiᶜ رضيع (*pl* ruḍḍaᶜ); **foster brother** akhu fi r-riḍaaᶜa
found *v* assas أسّس (ya'assis, ta'siis)
foundation (**basis**) asaas أساس (*pl* usus); (**of a building**) saas ساس ; (**institution**) mu'assasa مؤسّسة
fountain naafuura نافورة
four arbaᶜa أربعة ; **four hundred** urbuᶜmiyya أربعميّة
fourteen arbaᶜṭaashar أربعطاشر
fourth raabiᶜ رابع ; **one fourth** rubuᶜ ربع (*pl* arbaaᶜ)
fox saᶜlab سعلب (*pl* saᶜaalib); abu l-ḥiṣeen
fraction kasir كسر (*pl* kusuur)
fracture kasir كسر (*pl* kusuur)
fragile hashsh هش ; gaabil le-l-kasir
fragment giṭᶜa قطعة (*pl* -aat, giṭaᶜ); (**of broken glass, china**) kasra كسرة (*pl* kussaar)
frame *n* iṭaar إطار (*pl* -aat); **any round frame** ṭaara طارة ; (**of spectacles**) freem فريم (*pl* -aat); (**for picture**) burwaaz برواز (*pl* baraawiiz) • *v* (**a picture**) barwaz برْوز (barwaza, burwaaz)
France firansa فرنسا
franchise imtiyaaz إمتياز (*pl* -aat)
frank ṣariiḥ صريح
frankly be-ṣaraaḥa; **to speak out frankly** ṣaaraḥ صارح (ṣaraaḥa)
frankness ṣaraaḥa صراحة

fraud ghishsh غش ; (**swindler**) naṣṣaab نصّاب ; ghashshaash غشّاش
free *adj* ḥurr حر (*pl* aḥraar); (**unoccupied**) faaḍi فاضي (*pl* -yyiin); **free of charge** majjaan مجّان ; be-balaash; **free time** faḍwa فضوة • *v* fakka فكّ (i, fakk, fakka)
freedom ḥurriya حريّة
freely be-ḥurriya
freeze jammad جمّد (jimmeed, tajmiid); tallaj تلّج (tilleej); **to be frozen** itjammad اتجمّد (jimmeed); ittallaj اتّلّج (tilleej)
freight shuḥna شحنة (*pl* -aat, shuḥan)
French firansi فرنسي (*pl* -yyiin); firansaawi فرنساوي (*pl* -yyiin)
Frenchman firansi فرنسي (*pl* -yyiin); firansaawi فرنساوي (*pl* -yyiin)
frequently katiir كتير ; marraat katiira
fresh ṭaaza طازة ; ṭaazij طازج ; (**i.e. not dried, of vegetables, bread**) ṭari طري
Friday yoom aj-jumʿa
fridge tallaaja تلاجة
friend (*m*) ṣaaḥib صاحب (*pl* aṣḥaab); ṣadiig صديق (*pl* aṣdigaa); (*f*) ṣaaḥba صاحبة ; ṣadiiga صديقة ;
friendly ʿaṭuuf عطوف ; bashuush بشوش ; laṭiif لطيف (*pl* -iin, luṭaaf)
friendship ṣadaaga صداقة ; ṣuḥba صحبة
frighten khawwaf خوّف (takhwiif)
frightened marʿuub مرعوب ; **to be frightened** khaaf خاف (a, khoof)
frightening mukhiif مخيف ; murʿib مرعب
fringe ḥaaffa حافّة (*pl* ḥawaaff); (**hair**) guṣṣa قصّة
frog(s) goʿoonj قعونج
from min من
front *adj* giddaami قدّامي • *n* (**of building**) waajiha واجهة ; (**political organisation**) jabha جبهة ; **in front (of)** guddaam/giddaam قدّام ; be-guddaam/giddaam
frontier ḥuduud حدود
frown *v* kashshar كشّر (kishsheer, takshiir); ṣarṣar washsh-o; ṣarra washsh-o
fruit faakha فاكهة (*pl* fawaakih)
frustrate aḥbaṭ احبط (i, iḥbaaṭ)
frustration iḥbaaṭ إحباط
fry gala قلى (-i, galayaan); ḥammar حمّر (taḥmiir); **to be fried** itgala اتقلى ; itḥammar اتحمّر (taḥmiir)
fuel wuquud وقود ; banziin بنزين
fulfil waffa be- وفّى (-i, wafayaan)
full malyaan مليان
fumigate bakhkhar بخّر (bikhkheer); **to be fumigated** itbakhkhar اتبخّر (bikhkheer)
fun fukaaha فكاهة ; (**joking**) hiẓaar هظار
function *n* waẓiifa وظيفة (*pl* waẓaayif); (**rank**) martaba مرتبة (*pl* maraatib)
fund *n* ṣanduug صندوق (*pl* ṣanaadiig) • *v* mawwal موّل (tamwiil)
fundamental asaasi أساسي ; mabdaʾi مبدئي
fundamentalist uṣuuli أصولي
funding tamwiil تمويل
funeral jinaaza جنازة (*pl* janaayiz)
funfair malaahi ملاهي
funnel ṣabbaaba صبّابة

funny muḍḥik مضحك ; damm-o khafiif
fur farwa فروة
furious maghyuus مغيوز ; zaᶜlaan زعلان
furnace furun فرن (*pl* afraan)
furnish ᶜaffash عفّش (ᶜiffeesh, taᶜfiish)
furnishing farish فرش
furniture ᶜafash عفش ; asaas أساس (*pl* -aat)
fuse *n* fiyuus فيوس (*pl* -aat)
fuss *n* dawsha دوشة ; jooṭa جوطة
future mustaqbal مستقبل

G - g

gain *n* maksab مكسب (*pl* makaasib) • *v* iktasab اكتسب (iktisaab); kisib كسب (a, kasib); ribiḥ ربح (a, ribiḥ)
gall maraara مرارة
gallery (**art**) galiri قالري (*pl* -yaat); (**in stadium**) mudarrajaat مدرّجات
gallon jaaluun جالون (*pl* jawaaliin)
gallows mashnaga مشنقة (*pl* mashaanig)
gamble gaamar قامر (mugaamara, gumaar)
gambler gumurti قمرتي (*pl* -yya)
gambling gumaar قمار
game (**play**) laᶜba لعبة (*pl* -aat, alᶜaab)
game (**animals**) ganiiṣ قنيص ; ṣeed صيد
gang ᶜaṣaaba عصابة ; rabbaaṭa ربّاطة
gangrene ghargharina غرغرينا
gangway sigaala سقالة (*pl* -aat, sagaayil)
garage garraash قرّاش (*pl* -aat)
garbage wasaakha وساخة ; nafayaat نفايات ; **garbage collector** ᶜaamil naḍaafa; **garbage heap** kuusha كوشة (*pl* kuwash)
garden ḥadiiga حديقة (*pl* ḥadaayig); jineena جنينة (*pl* janaayin)
gardener janaayni جنايني (*pl* -yya)
garlic tuum توم ; baṣal makaada
garment hidim هدم (*pl* huduum); hidma هدمة (*pl* huduum); labsa لبسة (*pl* -aat, libis); **new garment** kiswa كسوة (*pl* kasaawi)
garrison ḥaamya حامية
gas ghaaz غاز (*pl* -aat); **gas cooker** butajaaz بوتجاز (*pl* -aat); **gas station** ṭurumba طرمبة
gasoline banziin بنزين
gastritis iltihaab miᶜda
gate baab باب (*pl* beebaan, abwaab); (**large**) bawwaaba بوابة
gatecrash inzagham انزغم (inzighaam)
gather *vt* jamaᶜ جمع (a, jamiᶜ); lamma لمّ (i, lamm); jammaᶜ جمّع (jimmeeᶜ, tajmiiᶜ); (**things only**) lamlam لملم (limleem, lamlama); **to gather with the hands** khamma خمّ (u, khamm); **to be gathered** itjamaᶜ اتجمع (jamᶜa); itjammaᶜ اتجمّع (jimmeeᶜ, tajmiiᶜ); itlamma اتلمّ (lamma, lamamaan); (**things only**) itlamlam اتلملم (lamlama, tilimlim)
gathering tajammuᶜ تجمّع ; **informal gathering** gaᶜda قعدة
gauge *n* miᶜyaar معيار (*pl* maᶜaayiir); miqyaas مقياس (*pl* maqaayiis)

gauze shaash شاش
gazelle(s) ghazaal غزال (*pl* ghuzlaan)
gearbox jaraboks جربكس (*pl* -aat); ʿilbat at-turuus
gear lever taʿshiiga تعشيقة (*pl* -aat, taʿaashiig)
gears tiris ترس (*pl* turuus)
gecko ḍabb ضب (*pl* ḍababa, ḍububba)
gender jandar جندر ; nooʿ نوع (*pl* anwaaʿ); jinis جنس (*pl* ajnaas)
genealogy nasab نسب (*pl* ansaab)
general *adj* ʿaamm عامّ ; ʿumuumi عمومي ; **in general** ʿala l-ʿumuum; ʿumuuman عموما
general *n* fariiq فريق (*pl* furaqa); jiniraal جنرال (*pl* -aat)
generalize ʿammam عمّم (taʿmiim)
generally ʿala l-ʿumuum; ʿumuuman عموما
generation jiil جيل (*pl* ajyaal)
generator janareetar جنريتر (*pl* -aat); baabuur بابور (*pl* -aat, bawaabiir); waabuur وابور (*pl* -aat)
generosity karam كرم ; juud جود
generous kariim كريم (*pl* -iin, kurama); faaḍil فاضل ; ajwaad أجواد (*pl* ahl juud); **to be generous to** akram أكرم (i, karam, ikraam)
gentle laṭiif لطيف (*pl* -iin, luṭaaf); raqiiq رقيق ; raaqi راقي
gentleness luṭf لطف
genuine aṣli أصلي ; ḥagiigi حقيقي
geographic jughraafi جغرافي
geography jughraafiya جغرافية
geometry handasa هندسة
German *adj/n* almaani الماني (*pl* almaan)
Germany almaanya المانيا
get jaab (maʿa) جاب (i, jeeba, jayabaan); **to get into** rikib ركب (a, rukuub); **to get off** nazal (min) نزل (i, nuzuul); **to get up** gaam قام (u, giyaam)
ghee samin سمن
ghost ʿafriit عفريت (*pl* ʿafaariit); shabaḥ شبح (*pl* ashbaaḥ)
ghoul ghuul غول (*pl* ghiilaan)
giardia gaardiya قارديا
giddiness dookha دوخة ; doosha دوشة ; **fit of giddiness** laffat raas
giddy daayikh دايخ ; daayish دايش
gift ʿaṭiyya عطيّة (*pl* ʿaṭaaya); (**present**) hadiyya هديّة (*pl* hadaayaa)
giggle ḍiḥik ضحك (a, ḍaḥik, daḥka)
gin *v* (**cotton**) ḥalaj حلج (i, ḥalij); **to be ginned** (**cotton**) itḥalaj اتحلج (ḥalij)
ginger janzabiil جنزبيل ; ʿirig abyaḍ; janjabiira جنجبيرة
gipsy ḥalabi حلبي (*pl* ḥalab, ḥalaba)
giraffe(s) zaraaf زراف
girder *n* kamara كمرة (*pl* kamiraat)
girl bitt بت (*pl* banaat, bannuut); bineyya بنيّة ; bint بنت (*pl* banaat, bannuut); fataa فتاة (*pl* fatawaat)
give adda أدّى (-i, iddeey); naawal ناول (munaawala); **to give back** rajjaʿ رجّع (rijjeeʿ)
glad farḥaan فرحان ; mabsuuṭ (be-, min) مبسوط ; masruur مسرور ; saʿiid سعيد (*pl* -iin, suʿada); **to be glad about** inbasaṭ (min) انبسط (inbisaaṭ); firiḥ (be-) فرح (a, faraḥ)
gladness faraḥ فرح (*pl* afraaḥ); bahja بهجة ; saʿaada سعادة

glance *n* lamḥa لمحة • *v* **to glance at** lamaḥ لمح (a, lamaḥaan)
gland ghudda غدّة (*pl* ghudad); **swollen glands** ishgaddi اشقدّي
glare ḥaddar حدّر (ḥiddeer); ḥammar حمّر (ḥimmeer)
glass (**drinking**) kubbaaya كبّاية (*pl* -aat, kabaabi); kaas كاس (*pl* -aat)
glass (**material**) gazaaz قزاز
glasses naḍḍaara نضّارة
glaucoma al-mooya as-sooda
gleam *v* lamaᶜ لمع (a, lamᶜaan)
glide inzalag انزلق (inzilaag); itzalag اتزلق (zalig, zalga)
glitter *v* ragash رقش (i, ragasha)
globalisation ᶜawlama عولمة
gloom ikti'aab إكتئآب
gloomy mukta'ib مكتئب
glove (**pair of**) jiwanti جونتي (*pl* -yyaat)
glue *n* ṣamugh صمغ ; ghira غرا ; **glue pot or bottle** ṣammaagha صمّاغة • *v* lazag لزق (i, lazig, lazga); lazzag لزّق (lizzeeg, talziig); laṣag لصق (i, laṣig, laṣga); laṣṣag لصّق (liṣṣeeg, talṣiig); ṣammagh صمّغ (taṣmiigh); **to be glued** itlazag اتلزق (lazga); itlazzag اتلزّق (lizzeeg, tilizzig); itlaṣag اتلصق (laṣga); itlaṣṣag اتلصّق (liṣṣeeg, tiliṣṣig); itṣammagh اتصمّغ (ṣamugh, ṣimmeegh)
gnaw garaḍ قرض (u, gariḍ); garraḍ قرّض (girreeḍ)
go masha مشى (-i, mashi); (**leave**) raaḥ راح (-u, no vn); rawwaḥ روّح (*no vn*); faat فات (u, foota, fawataan); **to go against** khaalaf خالف (khilaaf, mukhaalafa); **to go down** nazal نزل (i, nuzuul); iddalla ادلّى (-a, dilleey); **to go out** marag مرق (u, muruug); ṭalaᶜ طلع (a, ṭuluuᶜ); **to go up** (**ascend**) ṭalaᶜ طلع (a, ṭuluuᶜ); (**prices, temperature**) irtafaᶜ ارتفع (irtifaaᶜ)
goal hadaf هدف (*pl* ahdaaf); gaṣid قصد (*pl* agṣaad); gharaḍ غرض (*pl* aghraaḍ); (**score**) goon قون (*pl* agwaan); hadaf هدف (*pl* ahdaaf); (**net**) goon قون (*pl* agwaan); marma مرمى
goalkeeper ḥaaris al-marma
goat miᶜza (*pl* maaᶜiz, maᶜiiz); **goat(s)** ghanam غنم (*unit n* ghanamaaya); **he-goat** tees تيس (*pl* tiyuus); **she-goat** ghanamaaya غنماية ; **young goat(s)** sakhal سخل (*pl* sukhlaan); **young he-goat** ᶜatuud عتود (*pl* ᶜittaan); ᶜambalook عمبلوك (*pl* -aat); **young she-goat** sakhala سخلة
God **Allah** الل ; rabba-na
god ilaah إله (*pl* aaliha)
gold dahab دهب
golden dahabi دهبي
goldsmith ṣaayigh صايغ (*pl* ṣuyyaagh)
gonorrhea sayalaan سيلان
good kwayyis كويس ; ṭayyib طيّب ; jayyid جيّد ; samiḥ سمح
goodbye maᶜa s-salaama
good-for-nothing sajmaan سجمان ; khaayib خايب ; khaybaan خيبان
good-looking wajiih وجيه (*pl* wujaha)
goodness ṭiiba طيبة ; kheer خير (*pl* -aat); **my goodness!** ya salaam!
goods buḍaaᶜa بضاعة (*pl* baḍaayiᶜ); **unsold goods** buḍaaᶜa baayra
goose (**geese**) wizziin وزين

gospel injiil إنجيل (*pl* anaajiil)
gossip *n* (**person**) gawwaal قوّال ; nammaam نمّام ; (**talk**) namiima نميمة ; gaṭiiʿa قطيعة • *v* gaṭaʿ fi قطع (a, gaṭiiʿa)
gourd garaʿ قرع (*unit n* garʿa)
gout gaawt قاوت
govern ḥakam حكم (i, ḥukum)
governance ḥukum حكم (*pl* aḥkaam); **good governance** al-ḥukum ar-rashiid
government ḥakuuma حكومة
governor ḥaakim حاكم (ḥukkaam); (**of a district**) muḥaafiẓ محافظ ; (**of a state**) waali والي (*pl* wulaa)
governorate (**district**) maḥalliyya محلّيّة ; (**state**) wilaaya ولاية
gown (**for women**) fustaan فستان (*pl* fasaatiin)
grace faḍul فضل ; (**of God**) niʿma نعمة (*pl* niʿam); baraka بركة
grade daraja درجة ; (**in school**) ṣaff صف (*pl* ṣufuuf)
gradually shwayya shwayya; ḥabba ḥabba
graduate *v* itkharraj اتخرّج (takharruj)
graduation takhriij تخريج
grain ḥabb حب (*unit n* ḥabbaaya, *pl* -aat, ḥabbaat, ḥubuub); **grain market** zariibat al-ʿeesh; shuuna شونة
grammar qawaaʿid قواعد ; naḥu نحو
granary maṭmuura مطمورة (*pl* maṭaamiir); jurun جرن (*pl* ajraan); suweeba سويبة
grand ʿaẓiim عظيم (*pl* ʿuẓamaa)
granddaughter ḥafiida حفيدة
grandfather jidd جدّ (*pl* juduud, ajdaad)
grandmother ḥabbooba حبّوبة
grandson ḥafiid حفيد (*pl* aḥfaad)
granite garaaneet قرانيت ; ṣawwaan صوّان
grant *n* minḥa منحة (*pl* minaḥ) • *v* manaḥ منح (a, minḥa)
grape(s) ʿinab عنب
grapefruit(s) greeb قريب ; green قرين
grass gashsh قش ; ḥashiish حشيش (*pl* ḥashaayish); **to cut grass** ḥashsha حشّ (i, ḥashsh)
grasshopper(s) jaraad جراد
grate *v* bashar بشّر (u, bashir)
grateful shaakir شاكر ; **to be grateful** (**to**) shakar (fi/le-) شكر (u,shukur)
grater mabshara مبشرة
gratitude shukur شكر
grave *n* gabur قبر (*pl* gubuur); maqbara مقبرة (*pl* maqaabir); turba تربة (*pl* turab)
grave *adj* khaṭiir خطير
gravel ḥaṣḥaaṣ حصحاص ; (**for building**) kharaṣaana خرصانة
graveyard maqaabir مقابر
gravity jaazibiyya جازبيّة
graze *vt* (**feed**) raʿa رعى (-a, raʿi); sarah سرح (a, sarḥa)
graze *n* (**abrasion**) ẓalṭa ظلطة • *v* ẓalaṭ ظلط (u, ẓaliṭ)
grease *n* shaḥam شحم (*pl* shuḥuum); dihin دهن (*pl* duhuun) • *v* shaḥḥam شحّم (shiḥḥeem, tashḥiim)
great ʿaẓiim عظيم (*pl* ʿuẓamaa)
greatness ʿaẓama عظمة
greed ṭamaʿ طمع ; jaḥam جحم
greedy ṭammaaʿ طمّاع ; jaḥmaan جحمان ; nahim نهم ; **very greedy** jashiʿ جشع ; **to be greedy** ṭimiʿ fi طمع (a, ṭamaʿ); jiḥim جحم (a, jaḥam)

Greece al-yunaan
Greek *adj/n* yunaani يوناني (*pl* -yyiin)
green akhḍar أخضر (*f* khaḍra, *pl* khuḍur)
greengrocer khuḍurji خضرجي (*pl* -yya)
greet sallam ʿala سلّم (salaam); saalam سالم (musaalama); ḥayya حيّى (-i, taḥiya); **to greet each other** itsaalam اتسالم (musaalama)
greeting salaam سلام (*pl* -aat); taḥiyya تحيّة (*pl* -aat, taḥaaya)
grey ramaadi رمادي; raṣṣaaṣi رصّاصي
grid shabaka شبكة (*pl* -aat)
griddle ṣaaj صاج (*pl* ṣiijaan)
grief ḥuzun حزن (*pl* aḥzaan); kamad كمد; **deep grief** ghamm غم
grill *v* shawa شوى (-i, shawi)
grilled *adj* mashwi مشوي; **grilled meat** sheyya شية
grille (**car**) shabaka شبكة (*pl* -aat)
grind (**e.g. grain**) saḥan سحن (a, saḥin); ṭaḥan طحن (a, ṭaḥin); (**sharpen**) sanna سنّ *vt* (i, sann)
gristle ghaḍruuf غضروف (*pl* ghaḍaariif)
groan *v* ganat قنت (i, ganataan, ganit)
grocer baqqaal بقّال
grocery baqqaala بقّالة
ground (**earth**) waaṭa واطا; ariḍ أرض (*pl* araaḍi); jaabra جابرة
ground (**reason**) sabab سبب (*pl* asbaab)
groundnut(**s**) fuul suudaani (*unit n* fuulaaya, fuula); **groundnut paste** dakwa دكوة
group majmuuʿa مجموعة; **group of people** jamaaʿa جماعة
grow *vi* (**of plants**) gaam قام (u, giyaam); (**increase in size**) kibir كبر (a, kubur); **to grow up** riba ربى (-a, ribaaya); **to grow old** kibir كبر (a, kubur) • *vt* (cultivate) zaraʿ زرع (a, zariʿ, ziraaʿa)
growth numuu نمو; (**development**) tanmiya تنمية
grudge ghabiina غبينة (*pl* ghabaayin); maghaṣa مغصة; ghubun غبن (*pl* ghabaayin); **to bear a grudge** (**against**) itghaban (min) اتغبن (ghabiina); itmaghaṣ (min) اتمغص (maghaṣa)
gruel nasha/nisha نشا
grumble *v* nagga نقّ (i, nigga); nagnag نقنق (nagnaga)
grumbler naggaag نقّاق; shakkaay شكّاي
guarantee *n* ḍamaan ضمان; kafaala كفالة • *v* ḍaman ضمن (a, ḍamaan, ḍamaana)
guaranteed maḍmuun مضمون
guarantor ḍaamin ضامن
guard *n* ghafiir غفير (*pl* ghufara); ḥaras حرس (*pl* ḥurraas); ḥaaris حارس (*pl* ḥurraas) • *v* ḥaras (min) حرس (i, ḥaris, ḥiraasa)
guardian (**of a child**) wali l-amr; waṣi وصي (*pl* awṣiya)
guardianship wiṣaaya وصاية
guava jawwaafa جوّافة
guess *n* takhmiin تخمين (*pl* -aat) • *v* khamman خمّن (takhmiin)
guest ḍeef ضيف (*pl* ḍiyuuf); **uninvited guest** muṭṭaffil مطّفّل; mutaṭaffil متطفّل
guidance irshaad إرشاد (*pl* -aat); **to offer guidance to** wajjah وجّه (wijjeeh, tawjiih)
guide *n* (**person**) daliil دليل (*pl* adilla); murshid مرشد • *v* dalla

دلّ (i, dalla); arshad أرشد (i, irshaad); gaad قاد (u, giyaada); hada هدى (-i, hadayaan)
guilt zanib زنب (*pl* zunuub)
guilty muznib مزنب ; jaani جاني (*pl* junaat); **to find guilty** ḥakam ʿala حكم (i, ḥukum)
guinea fowl jidaad al-waadi
guinea worm(s) duud ghinya; farandiit فرنديت
gulf khaliij خليج (*pl* khiljaan)
gulp *n* jughma جغمة • *v* jagham جغم (u, jaghim); (**loudly**) garṭaʿ قرطع (girṭeeʿ, garṭaʿa)
gum ṣamugh صمغ ; **gum arabic** ṣamugh صمغ ; **chewing gum** lubaan لبان ; **mastic gum** mistika مستكا
gums lissa لسّة
gun bundugiyya بندقيّة (*pl* banaadig); **double-barrelled gun** umm ruuḥeen
gunpowder baaruud بارود
gut muṣraan مصران (*pl* maṣaariin)
gutter (**of roof**) sabalooga سبلوقة (sabaaliig); (**street**) khoor خور (*pl* kheeraan)
gymnastics jumbaaz جمباز ; riyaaḍa رياضة
gynaecologist diktoor amraaḍ nisa
gypsum jibis جبس ; **to plaster with gypsum** jabbas جبّس (jibbees)

H - h

habit ʿaada عادة (*pl* -aat, ʿawaayid)
haemorrhage naziif نزيف
haemorrhoids bawaasiir بواسير
haggle faaṣal فاصل (mufaaṣala, fiṣaal)
hail barad برد
hair shaʿar شعر (*unit n* shaʿara, shaʿaraaya, *pl* shuʿuur)
haircut ḥilaaga حلاقة ; **to have a haircut** (**men**) ḥalag حلق (i, ḥalga, ḥilaaga)
hairdresser kawaafeer كوافير ; (**traditional**) mashshaaṭa مشّاطة
hairpin dabbuus دبّوس (*pl* dabaabiis)
half nuṣṣ نص ; (**in football match etc.**) shooṭ شوط (*pl* ashwaaṭ)
hall qaaʿa قاعة ; ṣaala صالة
halt wagaf وقف (yagiif, wuguuf); itwaggaf اتوقّف (wagafaan, tawagguf)
hammer shaakuush شاكوش (*pl* shawaakiish)
hand *n* iid إيد (*pl* iideen, ayaadi); yadd يد (*pl* yaddeen, ayaadi); (**of a clock**) shooka شوكة (*pl* shuwak) • *v* adda أدّى (-i, iddeey); (**out**) wazzaʿ وزّع (tawziiʿ); (**over**) sallam سلّم (tasliim)
handbag shanṭa شنطة (*pl* shinaṭ)
handcuffs *n* kalabsh كلبش (*pl* -aat) • *v* kalbash كلبش (kalbasha)
handful khamsha خمشة ; kabsha كبشة ; gabḍa قبضة ; gabḍat yadd/iid; malyat yadd/iid; **to take a handful of** khamash خمش (i, khamish)
handicap iʿaaqa إعاقة
handicapped muʿaag معاق muʿawwag معوّق ; ʿaḍiir عضير
handkerchief mindiil منديل (*pl* manaadiil); mindiil warag
handle *n* iid إيد (*pl* iideen, ayaadi); yadd يد (*pl* yaddeen, ayaadi); **door handle** ukra اكرة (*pl* ukar);

iid/yadd al-ukra • *vt* itᶜaamal (be-) اتعامل (muᶜaamala)
handsome jamiil جميل ; wasiim وسيم ; samiḥ سمح
handwriting khaṭṭ خط (*pl* khuṭuuṭ)
handy najiiḍ نجيض (*pl* nujaaḍ)
hang *vi* itᶜallag اتعلّق (ᶜilleeg) • *vt* ᶜallag علّق (ᶜilleeg, taᶜliig); (**clothes to dry**) sharra شرّ (u, sharr); nashar نشر (u, nashir); (**as capital punishment**) shanag شنق (i, shanig)
hangar hangar هنقر (*pl* hanaagir); jamaloon جملون (*pl* -aat)
haphazard ᶜashwaa'i عشوائي
happen ḥaṣal حصل (a, ḥuṣuul); ḥadas حدس (u, ḥadas); **what's happened?** al-biga shinu?
happiness faraḥ فرح (*pl* afraaḥ); saᶜaada سعادة ; inbisaaṭ إنبساط
happy mabsuuṭ (be-, min) مبسوط ; farḥaan فرحان ; saᶜiid سعيد (*pl* -iin, suᶜada); **to be(come) happy (about)** firiḥ (be-) فرح (a, faraḥ); inbasaṭ انبسط (inbisaaṭ); **to make s.o. happy** farraḥ فرّح (firreeḥ, tafriiḥ); basaṭ بسط (i, basiṭ)
harass ḍaayag ضايق (muḍaayaga)
harassment muḍaayaga مضايقة
harbour miina مينا (*pl* mawaani); **small harbour** marsa مرسى (*pl* maraasi); mawrid مورد (*pl* mawaarid)
hard (**difficult**) ṣaᶜab صعب ; (**inflexible**) jaamid جامد ; (**solid**) ṣalb/ṣulb صلب ; (**tough**) gaasi قاسي ; ᶜaniif عنيف
hardship shagaawa شقاوة
hare arnab أرنب (*pl* araanib)
harm *n* aziyya أزيّة ; maḍarra مضرّة • *v* aza أزى (ya'zi, aziyya, aza); ḍarra ضرّ (maḍarra); (**a reputation**) shawwah شوّه (tashwiih)
harmful ḍaarr ضار ; mu'zi مؤزي
harvest *n* ḥaṣaad حصاد (*pl* -aat) • *v* ḥaṣad حصد (i, ḥaṣaad); (**fruit**) jana جنى (-i, jani)
haste ᶜajala عجلة ; surᶜa سرعة ; tasarruᶜ تسرّع
hasten *vt* ᶜajjal عجّل (ᶜijjeel, ᶜajala); sarraᶜ سرّع (sirreeᶜ)
hat ṭaagiyya طاقيّة (*pl* -aat, ṭawaagi); barniiṭa برنيطة (baraaniiṭ)
hatch *v* ḥaḍan حضن (i, ḥuḍun)
hatchet faas فاس (*pl* fu'uus); farraar فرّار (*pl* -aat, faraariir)
hate kirih كره (a, karih); katjtjan كتجّن (kitjtjeen); **to cause to hate** karrah (fi) كرّه (kirreeh)
hatred karaahiyya كراهيّة
haughty mutkabbir متكبّر ; **to be haughty** itkabbar اتكبّر (takabbur)
have ᶜind عند ; **she has a car** ᶜind-a ᶜarabiyya; **to have with** maᶜa مع ; **she has a car with her** maᶜaa-ha ᶜarabiyya; **to have to** laazim لازم ; ᶜala على ; **you have to go** laazim tamshi; **you have to finish this work** ᶜalee-k takhalliṣ ash-shughul da
hawk *n* (**generic**) ṣagur صقر (*pl* ṣuguur)
hawk *v* jalab جلب (i, jalib)
hawker sabbaabi سبّابي (*pl* sabbaaba); tashshaashi تشّاشي (tashshaasha)
hay gashsh قش ; tibin تبن ; **hay fever** ḥummat al- gashsh
hazy mughayyim مغيّم
he hu هو ; huwa هو

head raas راس (*pl* ruus, ru'uus, ruuseen, reeseen); dumaagh دماغ (*pl* admigha); **top of the head** ṣanguur صنقور (*pl* ṣanaagiir)
headache ṣudaaᶜ صداع ; wajaᶜ raas
headband ᶜugaal عقال (*pl* -aat)
headmaster naaẓir ناظر (*pl* nuẓẓaar); mudiir madrasa
headmistress mudiirat madrasa
headquarters ar-ri'aasa; markaz ar-ri'aasa
headscarf ṭarḥa طرحة (*pl* -aat, ṭiraḥ); (*Isl*) ḥijaab حجاب (*pl* -aat)
heal *vt* daawa داوى (-i, mudaawaa); ᶜaalaj عالج (ᶜilaaj, muᶜaalaja); **(of God)** shafa شفى (-i, shifa); ᶜaafa عافى (-i, muᶜaafaa); **(by incantation)** ᶜazam عزم (i, ᶜaziima) • *vi* bira برى (-a, bariya, barayaan); iddaawa اداّوى (-a, mudaawaa); itᶜaalaj اتعالج (muᶜaalaja, ᶜilaaj); silim سلم (a, salaama)
healing shifa شفا
health ṣaḥḥa صحّة ; **good health** ᶜaafya عافية (*pl* ᶜawaafi); **having poor health** muḍablin مضبلن ; ḍablaan ضبلان ; **health centre** markaz ṣiḥḥi
healthy ṣiḥḥi صحّي
heap *n* koom كوم (*pl* keemaan, akwaam); **to make a heap of sth.** kawwam كوّم (kiwweem, takwiim)
hear simiᶜ سمع (a, samaᶜ); **to cause to hear** sammaᶜ سمّع (simmeeᶜ, tasmiiᶜ); **to be heard** itsamaᶜ اتسمع (samaᶜ)
hearing **(sense of)** samaᶜ سمع
hearsay guwaala قوالة
heart galib قلب (*pl* guluub); **heart attack, heart failure** azma galbiyya
heartburn ḥeeragaan حيرقان
heat *n* sakhaana سخانة ; ḥarr حر ; ḥaraara حرارة ; **heat wave** moojat ḥarr • *v* sakhkhan سخّن (sikhkheen, taskhiin); **to be heated** itsakhkhan اتسخّن (sikhkheen, taskhiin)
heater sakhkhaan سخّان (*pl* -aat)
heaven sama سما (*pl* samawaat); **good heavens!** ya salaam!
heavy tagiil تقيل (*pl* tugaal)
hedgehog gunfud قنفد (*pl* ganaafid); abu gunfud
heel kaᶜab كعب (*pl* kuᶜuub)
heifer ᶜijil عجل (*pl* ᶜujuul)
height ṭuul طول (*pl* aṭwaal); (altitude) irtifaaᶜ إرتفاع
heir waaris وارس (*pl* wurraas, warasa); wariis وريس (wurraas, warasa)
helicopter marwaḥiyya مروحيّة
hell jahannam جهنّم ; jaḥiim جحيم ; an-naar
helmet khooza خوزة (-aat, khuwaz)
help *n* musaaᶜada مساعدة ; ᶜoon عون • *v* saaᶜad (fi) ساعد (musaaᶜada); ᶜaawan عاون (muᶜaawana); **to help one another** itsaaᶜad اتساعد (musaaᶜada)
helpful hamiim هميم ; khaduum خدوم
helpfulness muruwwa مروّة
hem *n* kaffa كفّة • *v* kaffa كفّ (i, kaff); ṭagga طقّ (u, ṭagg); **to be hemmed** itkaffa اتكفّ (kaff)
hemiplegia shalal niṣfi
hemp tiil تيل
hen(s) jidaad جداد ; firaakh فرخة (*unit n* farkha)
henna ḥinna حنة ; **to apply henna** ḥannan حنّن (ḥinneen); **to be decorated with henna** itḥannan اتحنّن (ḥinneen)

hepatitis yaraqaan يرقان ; eeraqaan ايرقان ; abu ṣuffeer; aṣ-ṣafra
herbs aʿshaab أعشاب
herd *n* gaṭiiʿ قطيع (*pl* guṭʿaan); muraaḥ مراح (-aat, murḥaat) • *v* raʿa رعى (-a, raʿi); saraḥ be- سرح (a, sariḥ)
herdsman raaʿi راعي (*pl* rawaaʿiyya, ruʿʿaa)
here hina هنا ; hini هني
hernia ghaḍruuf غضروف (*pl* ghaḍaariif)
hero baṭal بطل (*pl* abṭaal)
heroism buṭuula بطولة
heron abu girdaan; ḥabiib حبيب
herpes zoster ḥizaam naari
hesitate itraddad اتردّد (taraddud)
hesitation taraddud تردّد
hibiscus karkadee كركدي
hiccup *n* abu sh-shihheeg • *v* shahag شهق (a, shahig, shahagaan)
hide *n* jilid جلد (*pl* juluud); farwa فروة
hide *vi* iddassa ادّس (dass, dassa); labad لبد (i, labda, labadaan); itlabbad اتلبّد (libbeed, tilibbid) • *vt* dassa دسّ (i, dassa, dasasaan); labbad لبّد (libbeed); khabba خبّى (-i, khibbeey); **to be hidden** iddassa ادّس (dass, dassa); itlabbad اتلبّد (libbeed, tilibbid)
hide-and-seek ḥamad labad
high ʿaali عالي ; murtafiʿ مرتفع
hill jabal جبل (*pl* jibaal)
hinder ʿaṭṭal عطّل (taʿṭiil); ʿargal عرقل (ʿargala)
hinge *n* mufaṣṣala مفصّلة ; ʿaashig maʿshuug
hip makhruuga مخروقة (*pl* makhaarig)
hippopotamus(es) girinti قرنتي (*unit n* girintiyya)
hire ajjar أجّر (taʾjiir)
history taariikh تاريخ (*pl* tawaariikh)
hit *v* dagga دقّ (u, dagg); ḍarab ضرب (a, ḍarib); khabaṭ (i, khabiṭ, khabaṭaan); **(of a weapon)** naash ناش (i, neesha); **to be hit** iddagga ادّق (dagg); indagga اندقّ (dagg); inḍarab انضرب (ḍarib); inkhabaṭ (khabṭa); itkhabaṭ (khibbeeṭ)
hoarse mabḥuuḥ مبحوح
hobble *n* geed قيد (*pl* giyuud); **(on a camel)** ʿugaal عقال (*pl* -aat) • *v* gayyad قيّد (geed, giyyeed)
hobby hiwaaya هواية
hoe *n* **(for digging)** ṭuuriyya طوريّة (*pl* -aat, ṭawaari); **(types for weeding)** ḥashshaasha حشّاشة ; malooda ملودة ; kadanka كدنكة
hold *v* masak مسك (i, masik, masakaan); **to hold hands** itmaasak اتماسك (tamaasuk); **to hold on firmly to** itʿankash fi اتعنكش (ʿankasha); kankash fi كنكش (kankasha); **to hold up (hinder)** ʿaṭṭal عطّل (taʿṭiil); **(support)** sanad سند (i, sanad); **to hold up high** rafaʿ رفع (a, rafiʿ)
hole **(in wall, wood, cloth)** khurum خرم (*pl* akhraam); **(in cloth)** gadd قد (*pl* guduud); **(in ground)** ḥufra حفرة (*pl* ḥufar); **to make a hole** kharam خرم (i, kharim); gadda قدّ (i, giddeed); **to have a hole** itkharam اتخرم ; ingadda انقدّ (gadd)
holiday ijaaza إجازة ; ʿuṭla عطلة
hollow *adj* ajwaf أجوف (*f* jawfaa); mujawwaf مجوّف ; mugargar مقرقر
holy muqaddas مقدّس

home beet بيت (*pl* biyuut); daar دار (*pl* diyaar); **at home** fi l-beet
homeland daar دار (*pl* diyaar, duur); waṭan وطن (*pl* awṭaan); **absence from the homeland** ghurba غربة
homeless mutsharrid متشرد
homework waajib واجب (*pl* -aat)
homosexual (**dominant partner**) khawwal خوّل (*pl* -aat); ṣagur صقر (*pl* ṣuguur); (**submissive partner**) luuṭi لوطي (*pl* lawaayṭa)
homosexuality luwaaṭa لواطة
honest ṣariiḥ صريح; **to be honest** ṣaaraḥ صارح (ṣaraaḥa)
honestly be-ṣaraaḥa; **honestly?** be-zimmat-ak?
honesty ṣaraaḥa صراحة
honey ʿasal عسل; ʿasal an-naḥal
honour *n* sharaf شرف; ʿirḍ عرض • *v* karram كرّم (takriim); **to be honoured** itsharraf اتشرّف (sharaf)
honourable shariif شريف (*pl* ashraaf, shurafa); aṣiil أصيل (*pl* -iin, uṣala)
hoof ḍuluf ضلف (*pl* ḍalafeen, ḍuluuf); kudur كدر (*pl* kadaareen)
hook *n* (**for lifting, pulling**) shankal شنكل (*pl* shanaakil); (**for hanging**) ʿallaaga علاقة • *v* shankal شنكل (shinkeel, shankala)
hookah (**waterpipe**) shiisha شيشة (*pl* -aat, shiyash); **bowl of a hookah** ḥajar حجر (*pl* ḥujaara)
hoopoe hudhud هدهد (*pl* hadaahid)
hop *v* naṭṭaṭ نطّط (u, niṭṭeeṭ)
hope *n* amal أمل (*pl* aamaal); ʿasham عشم; raja رجا • *v* ammal (fi) أمّل (ya'ammil, amal); itmanna اتمنّى (-a, muna, tamanni); ʿishim عشم (a, ʿasham)
hopeful mu'ammil مؤمّل; ʿashmaan عشمان
hopper(s) (**of locust**) ʿattaab عتّاب; saari l-leel
hopscotch ḥijla
horizon ufuq أفق (*pl* aafaaq)
horizontal ufuqi أفقي
horn (**of animal**) garin قرن (*pl* guruun); (**of car**) buuri بوري (*pl* bawaari); (**musical instrument**) buug بوق (*pl* abwaag)
horror ruʿb رعب
horse ḥuṣaan حصان (*pl* ḥaṣiin); jawwaad جوّاد (*pl* jiyaad); **horsepower** guwwat ḥuṣaan
horseshoe ḥidwa حدوة (*pl* ḥidaw)
hose(pipe) kharṭuush خرطوش (*pl* kharaaṭiish)
hospitable miḍyaaf مضياف; kariim كريم (*pl* -iin, kurama)
hospital mustashfa مستشفى (*pl* -yaat); isbitaalya إسبتالية
hospitality ḍiyaafa ضيافة
host muḍiif مضيف
hostage rahiina رهينة (*pl* rahaayin)
hostess muḍiifa مضيفة
hostile ʿudwaani عدواني (*pl* -yyiin); **to be hostile** ʿaada عادى (-i, muʿaadaa); (**to one another**) itʿaada اتعادى (-a, ʿadaawa, muʿaadaa)
hostility ʿadaawa عداوة
hot sukhun سخن; ḥaarr حار; **feeling hot** musakhkhin مسخّن; ḥarraan حرّان
hotel funduq فندق (*pl* fanaadiq); (**basic**) lakonda لكوندة

hour saaᶜa ساعة
house *n* beet بيت (*pl* biyuut); manzil منزل (*pl* manaazil); daar دار (*pl* diyaar) • *v* sakkan سكّن (taskiin, iskaan)
housing iskaan إسكان
how keef كيف ; keefin كيفن ; izzay إزي ; **how many/how much?** kam كم ; gadur shinu? **how much (price)?** be-kam?
however laakin لاكن ; **however much** gadur ma
howl *v* ᶜawwa عوّى (-i, ᶜiwweey, ᶜawwa)
hub (**of wheel**) ᶜamuud al-ᶜajala
hubbub dawsha دوشة ; jooṭa جوطة ; ḍajja ضجّة ; rajja رجّة
hug *v* ḥaḍan حضن (i, ḥuḍun)
huge ḍakham ضخم ; ᶜaati عاتي (*pl* ᶜaatiin); maakin ماكن
hum *v* hamham همهم (himheem, hamhama)
human *adj* insaani انساني • *n* insaan إنسان (*pl* naas)
humanitarian insaani انساني
humble mutwaadiᶜ متواضع ; **to be humble** itwaaḍaᶜ اتواضع (tawaaḍuᶜ)
humid raṭib رطب
humidity ruṭuuba رطوبة
humiliate ahaan أهان (i, ihaana); haan هان (i, ihaana)
humiliation ihaana إهانة ; mahaa-na مهانة
humility tawaaḍuᶜ تواضع
hunchbacked aḥdab أحدب (*f* ḥadba, *pl* ḥudub)
hundred miyya ميّة
Hungarian *adj/n* majaraawi مجراي (*pl* -yyiin) majari مجري (*pl* -yyiin)
Hungary al-majar
hunger juuᶜ جوع
hungry jiᶜaan جعان ; **to be(come) hungry** jaaᶜ جاع (u, juuᶜ); **to make s.o. hungry** jawwaᶜ جوّع (jiwweeᶜ, tajwiiᶜ)
hunt *v* ṣaad صاد (i, ṣeed); iṣṭaad اصطاد (ṣeed, iṣṭiyaad); ganaṣ (le-) قنص (u, ganiiṣ)
hunter ṣayyaad صيّاد ; gannaaṣ قناص
hunting *n* ṣeed صيد
hurricane ᶜuṣaar عصار (*pl* -aat)
hurry *n* **in a hurry** mustaᶜjil مستعجل • *vi* istaᶜjal استعجل (istiᶜjaal); itᶜajjal اتعجّل (ᶜajala); itsarraᶜ اتسرّع (surᶜa); **hurry up!** gawwaam قوّام
hurt *vi* ḥarag حرق (i, ḥarig); wajaᶜ وجع (yuujiᶜ/yuujaᶜ, wajiᶜ, wajᶜa) • *vt* ḥarag حرق (i, ḥarig); ḥarrag حرّق (ḥirreeg); wajaᶜ وجع (yuujiᶜ/ yuujaᶜ, wajiᶜ, wajᶜa); wajjaᶜ وجّع (wijjeeᶜ, wajᶜa)
husband raajil راجل (*pl* rujaal, rijaal); zooj زوج (*pl* azwaaj)
husk *v* gashshar قشّر (gishsheer, tagshiir) • *n* **husk(s)** gishir قشر (*unit n* gishra)
hut ᶜishsha عشّة (*pl* ᶜishash); **thatched hut, round hut** guṭṭiyya قطّيّة (*pl* gaṭaaṭi)
hyena marfaᶜiin مرفعين (*pl* maraafiᶜiin)
hygiene naḍaafa نضافة
hygienic ṣiḥḥi صحّي
hymen ghishaa' al-bakaara
hyphen sharṭa شرطة
hypocrisy nifaaq نفاق ; munaafaqa منافقة
hypocrite munaafiq منافق

I - i

I ana أنا
ice jaliid جليد ; talij تلج
ice cream ayskriim أيسكريم ; **homemade ice cream** dandurma دندرمة
idea fikra فكرة (*pl* afkaar)
ideal *adj* misaali مسالي
identity huwiyya هويّة ; **identity card** buṭaaqa shakhṣiyya
idiot ablah أبله (*f* balha, *pl* buluh)
idle gaaʿid saay; ʿaaṭil عاطل
if law لو ; kaan كان ; law kaan; inkaan; in إن ; iza إزا ; **even if** ḥatta law; ḥatta wa law
ignite *vt* wallaʿ ولّع (willeeʿ); oogad أوقد (yoogid, wuguud) • *vi* itwallaʿ اتولّع (walʿa, willeeʿ)
ignoble dani دني (*pl* -yyiin); khasiis خسيس ; mutadanni متدنّي (*pl* -yyiin)
ignorance jahl جهل
ignorant jaahil جاهل (*pl* -iin, juhala); **to be ignorant of** jahal be- جهل (a, jahl); **to keep s.o. ignorant** jahhal جهّل (tajhiil)
ignore ṭannash طنّش (ṭanaash, ṭinneesh); itjaahal اتجاهل (tajaahul)
ill ʿayyaan عيّان ; marḍaan مرضان ; mariiḍ مريض (*pl* marḍa); **to be(come) ill** ʿiya عيى (-a, ʿaya); miriḍ مرض (a, maraḍ)
illegal ma qaanuuni; gheer qaanuuni
illegitimate **illegitimate daughter** bitt ḥaraam, bitt zina; **illegitimate son** wad ḥaraam, wad zina
illiteracy ummiyya أمّيّة
illiterate ummi أمي
illness ʿaya عيا
illuminate nawwar نوّر (tanwiir); ḍawwa (-i, ḍiwweey); **to be illuminated** itnawwar اتنوّر (tanwiir); iḍḍawwa (-a, ḍawayaan)
illusion waham وهم (*pl* awhaam)
image ṣuura صورة (*pl* ṣuwar)
imagination khayaal خيال
imagine itkhayyal اتخيّل (takhayyul); itṣawwar اتصوّر (taṣawwur)
imam imaam إمام (*pl* a'imma)
imitate ḥaaka حاكى (-i, muḥaakaa); gallad (fi) قلّد tagliid)
imitation tagliid تقليد
immediately ṭawwaali طوّالى ; ḥaalan حالا ; fi l-ḥaal
immigrant muhaajir مهاجر
immoral faajir فاجر ; raziil رزيل (*pl* ruzala); munḥall منحل ; safiih سفيه (sufaha); **immoral act** raziila رزيلة (*pl* razaayil); **immoral person** ṣaʿluuk صعلوك (*pl* ṣaʿaaliik)
immorality razaala رزالة ; akhlaag faasda
immorally **to behave immorally** itsaafah اتسافه (safaaha)
impartial naziih نزيه
impatience shafaga شفقة
impatient shafgaan شفقان ; **to be impatient** shifig شفق (a, shafaga)
impede ʿargal عرقل (ʿargala)
impediment maaniʿ مانع (*pl* mawaaniʿ)
impertinent ma mu'addab; galiil al-ḥaya

implement *v* ṭabbag طبّق (taṭbiig)
implore itrajja اترجّا (-a, raja, tarjiya); raja رجا (-u, raja)
impolite ma mu'addab; galiil al-adab
import *n* istiiraad إستيراد ; **import licence** taṣriiḥ istiiraad • *v* istawrad استورد (istiiraad)
important haamm هام ; muhimm مهم ; **to be important to s.o.** hamma همّ (i, hamm)
importation istiiraad إستيراد (*pl* -aat)
imports waaridaat واردات ; mustawradaat مستوردات
impose faraḍ (ʿala) فرض (i, fariḍ); **to be imposed on** itfaraḍ ʿala اتفرض (fariḍ)
impossible mustaḥiil مستحيل ; muḥaal محال
impostor dajjaal دجّال ; naṣṣaab نصّاب
impotent ʿaajiz عاجز (*pl* ʿaajziin)
impression inṭibaaʿ انطباع (*pl* -aat)
imprison ḥabas حبس (i, ḥabis, ḥabsa); sajan سجن (i, sajna, sijin); **to be imprisoned** itḥabas اتحبس (ḥabis, ḥabsa); itsajan اتسجن (sajna, sijin)
improper gheer laayig
improve ṣallaḥ صلّح (ṣilleeḥ, taṣliiḥ); **to be improved** itṣallaḥ إتصلّح (ṣilleeḥ, taṣliiḥ); itḥassan اتحسّن (taḥassun)
improvement taḥassun تحسّن (*pl* -aat)
impudent galiil al-ḥaya; ma mu'addab
in fi في ; foog فوق ; be- بـ
inappropriate ma munaasib
inattentive sarḥaan سرحان ; saariḥ سارح
incapable ʿaajiz عاجز (*pl* ʿaajziin)
incarnation tajassud تجسّد
incense bakhuur بخور ; **incense sticks** nadd ندّ ; **incense burner** mubkhar مبخر (*pl* mabaakhir)
incentive ḥaafiz حافز (*pl* ḥawaafiz)
inch buuṣa بوصة
incite ḥarrash (ʿala) حرّش (ḥirreesh, taḥriish); ḥarraḍ (ʿala) حرّض (ḥirreeḍ, taḥriiḍ)
inclination meel ميل
include ḍamma ضمّ (u, ḍamm); iḥtawa ʿala احتوى (iḥtiwa)
incognito mutnakkir متنكّر ; **to be incognito** itnakkar اتنكّر (tanakkur)
income dakhl دخل ; (**earnings**) ʿaayid عايد (*pl* ʿawaayid); (**revenue**) iiraad إيراد (*pl* -aat)
inconvenient ma munaasib
incorrect ma maẓbuuṭ; ma saliim; ma ṣaaḥḥ; ma ṣaḥiiḥ
increase *vi* zaad زاد (i, zeeda, ziyaada); kitir كتر (a, katara) • *vt* zaad زاد (i, zeeda, ziyaada); kattar كتّر (kitteer)
incubate ḥaḍan حضن (i, ḥuḍun)
incubator ḥaḍḍaana حضّانة
indecency gillat al-ḥaya
indecent galiil al-ḥaya
independence istiqlaal إستقلال
independent mustaqill مستقل
index *n* fihrist فهرست (*pl* fahaaris); fahrasa فهرسة (*pl* fahaaris); **index finger** sabbaaba سبّابة • *v* fahras فهرس (fahrasa)
India al-hind
Indian *adj/n* hindi هندي (*pl* hunuud)
indicate ashshar (ʿala/le-) أشّر (ya'ashshir, ishsheer, ta'shiir)

indication raas kheeṭ; raas mawḍuuʿ; fikra فكرة
indicator mu'ashshir مؤشّر (*pl* -aat)
indigenous maḥalli محلّي
indigestion tukhma تخمة; **suffering from indigestion** mutkham متخم
individual *adj* fardi فردي • *n* farid فرد (*pl* afraad)
industrial ṣinaaʿi صناعي
industrious mujtahid مجتهد; **to be industrious** ijtahad اجتهد (ijtihaad)
industry (**manufacture**) ṣinaaʿa صناعة
inevitable it is inevitable la budda
infant jana جنا (*pl* jinyaat, jannuun); jaahil جاهل (*pl* juhhaal)
infantry mushaa مشاة; quwwaat al-mushaa
infect ʿaada عادى (-i, ʿadwa)
infection iltihaab إلتهاب (*pl* -aat)
infectious muʿdi معدي
inferior adna أدنى (*f* dunya); agalla اقل
infiltrate itsallal اتسلّل (tasallul)
inflammable gaabil le-l-ishtiʿaal
inflammation iltihaab إلتهاب (*pl* -aat); **inflammation of the eye** ramad رمد
inflate nafakh نفخ (u, nafikh); **to be inflated** itnafakh اتنفخ (nafikh)
inflexible jaamid جامد
influence *n* ta'siir تأسير (*pl* -aat); (**power**) nufuuz نفوز • *v* assar ʿala/fi أسّر (ya'assir, ta'siir); **to be influenced (by)** it'assar (be-) اتأسّر (ta'assur)
influenza influwanza إنفلونزا; nazla نزلة

inform khabbar خبّر (khibbeer); ballagh بلّغ (billeegh); ʿarraf عرّف (taʿriif); (**on/against**) ballagh ʿan بلّغ (balaagh, tabliigh)
information maʿluumaat معلومات
informer mukhbir مخبر
ingratitude juḥuud جحود
ingredient mukawwin مكوّن (*pl* -aat)
inhabitant saakin ساكن (*pl* sukkaan)
inhale itnashshag اتنشّق (nishsheeg); shahag شهق (a, shahiig)
inherit waras ورس (i, wiraasa); wiris ورس (a, waris, wiraasa)
inheritance miiraas ميراس (*pl* mawaariis); warisa ورسة; wiraasa وراسة
initial mabda'i مبدئي
inject ṭaʿan طعن (a, ṭaʿin)
injection ḥugna حقنة (*pl* ḥugan)
injure jaraḥ جرح (a, jariḥ); jarraḥ جرّح (jirreeḥ, tajriiḥ); ʿawwar عوّر (ʿiwweer, taʿwiir); ʿawwag عوّق (ʿiwweeg, taʿwiig); **to be injured** itjaraḥ اتجرح (jariḥ); itjarraḥ اتجرّح (jirreeḥ); itʿawwar اتعوّر (ʿiwweer); itʿawwag اتعوّق (ʿiwweeg, taʿwiig)
injury jariḥ جرح (*pl* juruuḥ)
injustice ẓulum ظلم (*pl* maẓaalim)
ink ḥibir حبر (*pl* aḥbaar)
inner juwwaani جواني; daakhili داخلي
innocence baraa'a براءة
innocent barii' بريء (*pl* -iin, abriyaa)
innovation *n* bidʿa بدعة (*pl* bidaʿ)
inquire istafsar (ʿan) استفسر (istifsaar)
inquiry istifsaar استفسار; **inquiry office** maktab al-istiʿlaamaat

insane majnuun مجنون (*pl* majaaniin); mushooṭin مشوطن ; **to be(come) insane** itjannan اتجنّن (jinn, junuun); shooṭan شوطن (shawṭana)

insanity junuun جنون ; jinn جن

insect ḥashara حشرة

insensitive baarid بارد

insensitivity buruud برود

inside *prep* daakhil داخل ; juwwa جوّا • *adv* juwwa جوّا ; be-juwwa

inside out magluub مقلوب ; be-l-galaba; **to turn inside out** galab قلب (i, galib, galba); **to be turned inside out** itgalab اتقلب (galba); ingalab انقلب (galba)

insignificant taafih تافه

insist aṣarra أصرّ (i, iṣraar)

insolence *n* safaaha سفاهة

insolent safiih سفيه (sufaha); **to be insolent** itsaafah اتسافه (safaaha)

inspect fattash فتّش (taftiish)

inspection taftiish تفتيش (*pl* -aat); **on-the-spot inspection** muʿaayana معاينة

inspector mufattish مفتّش

installment gasiṭ قسط (*pl* agsaaṭ)

instead (of) *prep* badal min/ʿan/ma; ʿawaḍ ʿan

instinct ghariiza غريزة (*pl* gharaayiz)

institute maʿhad معهد (*pl* maʿaahid)

institution mu'assasa مؤسّسة ; munaẓẓama منظّمة

instruct ʿallam علّم (taʿliim)

instructions taʿliimaat تعليمات

instrument aala آلة ; jihaaz جهاز (*pl* ajhiza)

insufficient ma kaafi; **to be insufficient** gaṣṣar قصّر (giṣṣeer, tagṣiir)

insulator ʿaazil عازل (*pl* ʿawaazil)

insult *n* nabza نبزة ; shatiima شتيمة (*pl* shataayim) • *v* nabbaz نبّز (nibbeez, nabaz); shatam شتم (u, shatiima); **(a religion)** sabba سبّ (i, sabb)

insurance ta'miin تأمين (*pl* -aat)

insure amman أمّن (ya'ammin, ta'miin)

intact saalim سالم ; saliim سليم ; naṣiiḥ نصيح

integrity zimma زمّة (*pl* zimam)

intellectual musaqqaf مسقّف

intelligence zakaa زكا ; nabaaha نباهة ; **intelligence services** mukhaabaraat مخابرات

intelligent zaki زكي (*pl* azkiya); shaaṭir شاطر (*pl* shaaṭriin, shuṭṭaar)

intend nawa نوى (-i, niyya); gaṣad قصد (u, gaṣid)

intensity kasaafa كسافة

intensive mukassaf مكسّف

intention niyya نيّة ; gaṣid قصد (*pl* agṣaad); **bad intention** suu' niyya

interest *n* **(profit)** ribiḥ ربح (*pl* arbaaḥ); faayda فايدة (*pl* fawaayid); **(stake)** maṣlaḥa مصلحة (*pl* maṣaaliḥ)

interesting mumtiʿ ممتع ; musiir مسير

interfere iddakhkhal ادّخّل (tadakhkhul); itḥashshar اتحشّر (ḥishsheer, taḥashshur)

interference tadakhkhul تدخّل (*pl* -aat); taḥashshur تحشّر (*pl* -aat); **(by sound)** tashwiish تشويش

interior daakhil داخل

intermediary waasṭa واسطة

internal daakhili داخلي ; **internal medicine** ṭibb baaṭini

international duwali دولي ; ʿaalami عالمي
internet intirnet إنترنت ; shabakat al-intirnet
interpret (**explain**) fassar فسّر (tafsiir)
interpreter (**translator**) mutarjim fawri
interrogate istajwab استجوب (istijwaab)
interrogation istijwaab استجواب (*pl* -aat)
interrupt gaaṭaʿ قاطع (mugaaṭaʿa)
interruption mugaaṭaʿa مقاطعة
intersection tagaaṭuʿ تقاطع
interval faaṣil فاصل (*pl* fawaaṣil)
intervene iddakhkhal ادّخّل (tadakhkhul)
interview *n* mugaabala مقابلة ; **job interview** muʿaayana معاينة
intestine muṣraan مصران (*pl* maṣaariin)
intimidation takhwiif تخويف
intoxicant *n* khamr خمر (*pl* khumuur); khamra خمرة (*pl* khumuur)
intoxicate sakkar سكّر (sikkeer, taskiir)
intoxicated sakraan سكران (*pl* -iin, sakaara)
intrigue *n* dasiisa دسيسة (*pl* dasaayis); makiida مكيدة (*pl* makaayid) • *v* dassa دسّ (i, dasiisa); kaad كاد (i, keed)
introduce gaddam قدّم (tagdiim); (**a person**) **to** (**another**) ʿarraf be- عرّف (taʿriif)
introduction muqaddima مقدّمة
intrude iṭṭaffal (ʿala) اطّفّل (taṭafful)
inundation fayaḍaan فيضان (*pl* -aat)
invalid (**void**) laaghi لاغي ; malghi ملغي ; **to declare** (**a contract**) **invalid** fasakh فسخ (a, fasikh)
invent ikhtaraʿ اخترع (ikhtiraaʿ); ibtakar إبتكر (ibtikaar)
invention ikhtiraaʿ إختراع (*pl* -aat); ibtikaar إبتكار (*pl* -aat)
inventory jarid جرد ; **to take an inventory** jarad جرد (u, jarid)
investigate ḥaggag حقّق (taḥgiig); itḥaggag fi اتحقّق (taḥgiig); kashshaf كشّف (kishsheef)
investigation taḥgiig تحقيق (*pl* -aat)
invitation ʿazuuma عزومة (*pl* -aat, ʿawaaziim); daʿwa دعوة
invite ʿazam عزم (i, ʿazuuma); daʿa دعا (-u, daʿwa)
invoice faatuura فاتورة (*pl* fawaatiir); **final invoice** faatuura nihaa'iyya; **pro forma invoice** faatuura mabda'iyya
invoke (**God, a saint**) nadah نده (a, nadih, nadiiha); nadar ندر (u, nadir); **to invoke a blessing upon** daʿa (Allah) be-baraka le-; **to invoke a curse upon** daʿa (Allah) be-laʿna ʿala
Iraq al-ʿiraaq
Iraqi *adj/n* ʿiraaqi عراقي (*pl* -yyiin)
iron *n* (**metal**) ḥadiid حديد ; **galvanised iron** zink زنك ; tuutya توتيا
iron *n* (**for pressing clothes**) makwa مكوة (*pl* makaawi) • *v* kawa كوى (-i, kawi, kay, kawayaan); **to be ironed** itkawa اتكوى (kawi, kay)
irrigate rawa روى (-i, rayy); saga سقى (-i, sagi)
irrigation rayy ري ; sigaaya سقاية ; **irrigation channel** turʿa ترعة (*pl* turaʿ); majra مجرى (*pl* majaari); (**small**) jadwal جدول (*pl* jadaawil)

irritate zahhaj زهّج (zihheej, tazhiij); ghaaẓ غاظ (i, ighaaẓa, gheeẓ); narfaz نرفز (narfaza); **to be irritated (by)** itghaaẓ اتغاظ (gheeẓ); itnarfaz (min) اتنرفز (narfaza)
irritating muzᶜij مزعج
Islam islaam إسلام ; **to convert to Islam** aslam أسلم (i, islaam)
Islamic islaami إسلامي
island jaziira جزيرة (*pl* juzur, jazaayir)
isolate ᶜazal عزل (i, ᶜazil); **to be isolated** it ᶜazal اتعزل (ᶜuzla)
isolation ᶜuzla عزلة
issue *n* **(matter)** mas'ala مسألة (*pl* masaa'il); amr أمر (*pl* umuur); mawḍuuᶜ موضوع (*pl* -aat, mawaaḍiiᶜ) • *v* **(a permit)** rakhkhaṣ رخّص (tarkhiiṣ); **(a visa or travel permit)** ash-shar أشّر (ya'ashshir, ishsheer, ta'shiir); **(a book)** aṣdar أصدر (i, iṣdaar); **to be issued** ṣadar صدر (u, ṣuduur)
Italian *adj/n* iiṭaali إيطالي (*pl* -yyiin); ṭilyaani طلياني (*pl* ṭilyaan, ṭalaayna)
Italy iiṭaalya إيطاليا
itch *n* akuula اكولة ; kaaruusha كاروشة ; ḥakka حكّة ; akiila أكيلة • *v* akal أكل (biyaakul, akalaan, akuula)
ivory sinn al-fiil; ᶜaaj عاج

J - j

jack *n* **(for car)** ᶜafriita عفريتة (*pl* -aat, ᶜafaariit) • *v* **(up)** ᶜafrat عفرت (ᶜifreet, ᶜafrata)
jackal baᶜshoom بعشوم (baᶜaashiim)
jacket **(of suit)** jakitta جكتّة ; **(with zipper)** siwiitar سويتر (*pl* -aat); siyuutar سيوتر (*pl* -aat); **(sleeveless)** ṣideeri صديري (*pl* -yyaat)
jail *n* sijin سجن (*pl* sujuun)
jailer (*m*) sajjaan سجّان ; (*f*) saj-jaana سجّانة
jam marabba مربّى
January shahri waaḥid; yanaayir يناير
Japan al-yabaan
Japanese *adj/n* yabaani ياباني (*pl* -yyiin)
jar **(earthenware, large)** ziir زير (*pl* azyaar); **(small)** gulla قلّة (*pl* gulal); **(with lid)** burṭumaaniyya برطمانّية
jaundice yaraqaan يرقان ; eeraqaan ايرقان ; abu ṣuffeer; aṣ-ṣafra
jaw **(animals)** fakk فك (*pl* fukuuk, afkaak); **(human)** ḥanak حنك (*pl* aḥnaak)
jealous ghayraan غيران ; ghayuur غيور ; **to be jealous (about)** ghaar (min/ᶜala) غار (i, ghiira)
jealousy ghiira غيرة
jellabia jallaabiyya جلابيّة (*pl* -aat, jalaaliib)
jelly jali جلي
jerrycan baagha باغة ; jarikaana جركانة
jest *v* haẓẓar هظّر (hiẓaar)
jet **jet aircraft** ṭayyaara naffaasa
Jew yahuudi يهودي (*pl* yahuud)
jewel jawhara جوهرة (*pl* jawaahir)
jeweller ṣaayigh صايغ (*pl* ṣuyyaagh); jawaahirji جواهرجي (-iyya)
jewellery jawaahir جواهر

Jewish yahuudi يهودي (*pl* yahuud)
jingle *v* kashkash كشكش (kishkeesh)
job shughul شغل (*pl* ashghaal); shaghala شغلة ; waẓiifa وظيفة (*pl* waẓaayif); **job vacancy** waẓiifa faaḍya; waẓiifa khaalya
jobless ʿaaṭil عاطل ; mutbaṭṭil متبطّل
jog *v* jakka جكّ (u, jakk)
join shaarak شارك (mushaaraka); (**officially**) inḍamma le- انضمّ (inḍimaam)
joint (**of the body**) mafṣal مفصل (*pl* mafaaṣil)
joke *n* nukta نكتة (*pl* nukat, nikaat) • *v* hazzar هظّر (hizaar)
joker hazzaar هظّار ; laʿbanji لعبنجي (*pl* -yya); (**cards**) jookar جوكر (*pl* jawaakir)
jolt *n* hazza هزّة • *v* hazza هزّ (i, hazz)
Jordan al-urdun; **the Jordan river** nahar al-urdun
Jordanian *adj/n* urduni أردني (*pl* -yyiin)
journalism ṣaḥaafa صحافة
journalist *n* ṣaḥafi صحفي (*pl* –yyiin)
journey riḥla رحلة (*pl* -aat, riḥal); safar سفر (*pl* asfaar); safariyya سفريّة ; safra سفرة (*pl* safariyyaat)
joy faraḥ فرح (*pl* afraaḥ); inbisaaṭ إنبساط ; inbisaaṭa إنبساطة
joyful farḥaan فرحان ; masruur مسرور
judge *n* gaaḍi قاضي (*pl* guḍaa); **religious judge** gaaḍi sharʿi • *v* ḥakam حكم (i, ḥukum)
judgment ḥukum حكم (*pl* aḥkaam); gaḍaa قضا ; **the Day of Judgment** yoom al-qiyaama
jug jakk جك (*pl* jukukka, jukuuk); (**for ablutions**) ibriig إبريق (*pl* abaariig)
juggler ḥaawi حاوي (*pl* ḥuwaa)
juice ʿaṣiir عصير (*pl* ʿaṣaayir)
juicer ʿaṣṣaara عصّارة
jujube (**tree(s)**) sidir سدر (*unit n* sidra); shajar an-nabag; (**fruit**) nabag نبق
July shahri sabʿa; yuulyo يوليو
jump *n* naṭṭa نطّة • *v* naṭṭa نطّ (u, naṭṭ, naṭaṭaan); **to jump over** naṭṭa be- نطّ (u, naṭṭ); **to jump from** tallab تلب (tilleeb)
June shahri sitta; yuunyo يونيو
junior aṣ-ṣaghiir
junk karoor كرور ; hatash هتش ; hakar هكر
jurisprudence gaḍaa قضا ; (*Isl*) fiqh فقه
just *adj* dughri دغري ; ʿaadil عادل ; naziih نزيه • *adv* (**only**) bass بس ; (**just now**) yaadoob يادوب
justice ʿadaala عدالة ; ʿadl عدل
justification (**excuse**) mubarrir مبرّر (*pl* -aat)
justify barrar برّر (tabriir)
jute *n* kheesh خيش

K - k

kala azar kalazaar كلزار
karate karateeh كرتيه
keep ḥafaẓ حفظ (a, ḥafiẓ); iḥtafaẓ be- احتفظ (iḥtifaaẓ); ṣaan صان (u, ṣoon)
Kenya kiiniya كينيا
Kenyan *adj/n* kiini كيني (*pl* -yyiin)
kerosene jaaz جاز
kettle kafateera كفتيرة (*pl* -aat, kafaatiir)

key muftaaḥ مفتاح (*pl* mafaatiiḥ)
key ring ʿallaaga علاقة
kick *n* shalluut شلّوت (*pl* shalaaliit); rafsa رفسة ; lafkha لفخة ; **free kick** ḍarba ḥurra • *v* shallat شلّت (shilleet); rafas رفس (i, rafis); lafakh لفخ (a, lafikh)
kid(s) (**of goat**) sakhal سخل (*f* sakhala, *pl* sukhlaan); **male kid** ʿatuud عتود (*pl* ʿittaan); ʿambalook عمبلوك (*pl* -aat)
kidnap khaṭaf خطف (i, khaṭif)
kidney kilwa كلوة (*pl* kila, kilaw); **kidneys** (**as meat**) kalaawi كلاوي (*sg* kilwa); **kidney failure** fashal kilawi
kill katal كتل (u, katil); mawwat موّت (miwweet); **to be killed** itkatal اتكتل (katil)
killer kaatil كاتل
kiln kamiina كمينة (*pl* kamaayin)
kilogram kiilo كيلو (*pl* kiilohaat)
kilometre kiilo كيلو (*pl* kiilomitraat); kiilomitir كيلومتر (*pl* kiilomitraat)
kin (**group**) ahal أهل (*pl* ahaali); ʿeela عيلة (*pl* ʿaaylaat, ʿawaayil)
kind *adj* ṭayyib طيّب ; ʿaṭuuf عطوف ; ḥaniin حنين ; **to be kind to** ʿaṭaf ʿala عطف (i, ʿaṭf); ḥanna ʿala حنّ (i, ḥinn)
kind *n* nooʿ نوع (*pl* anwaaʿ); ṣanf صنف (*pl* aṣnaaf); (**species**) jinis جنس (*pl* ajnaas)
kindergarten rawḍa روضة ; (**toddlers**) ḥaḍaana حضانة
kindness ṭiiba طيبة ; ḥinniyya حنّيّة ; maḥanna محنّة
king malik ملك (*pl* muluuk)
kingdom mamlaka مملكة (*pl* mamaalik); salṭana سلطنة ; **the Kingdom of Saudi Arabia** al-mamlaka al-ʿarabiyya aṣ-ṣaʿuudiyya; **the United Kingdom** al-mamlaka al-muttaḥida
kinship garaaba قرابة ; **kinship ties** ʿaṣabiyya عصبيّة
kiosk kushuk كشك (*pl* akshaak)
kiss *n* boosa بوسة ; gadduum قدّوم (*pl* gadaadiim) • *v* baas باس (u, boos); maṣmaṣ مصمص (maṣmaṣa)
kitchen maṭbakh مطبخ (*pl* maṭaabikh); tukul تكل (*pl* takkaal)
kite (**toy**) ṣaaruukh صاروخ (*pl* ṣawaariikh); ṭayyaarat warag
kite(s) (**bird**) ḥiddeey حدّيي
knapsack bugja بقجة (*pl* bugaj); ṣurra صرة
knead ʿajan عجن (i, ʿajin); ʿajjan عجّن (ʿijjeen); **to be kneaded** itʿajan اتعجن (ʿajna); itʿajjan اتعجّن (ʿijjeen, tiʿijjin)
knee rukba ركبة (*pl* rukab, rakaabeen)
kneel barak برك (u, barik); (**in praying**) rakaʿ ركع (a, rukuuʿ)
knickers niksi نكسي (*pl* ankisa); nikis نكس (*pl* ankisa)
knife sikkiin سكّين (*pl* sakaakiin); sikkiina سكّينة (*pl* sakaakiin); **pocket knife** maṭwa مطوى (*pl* maṭaawi); **butcher's knife** saaṭuur ساطور (*pl* sawaaṭiir)
knight faaris فارس (*pl* fursaan)
knit ishtaghal triiko
knitting triiko تريكو
knock *v* dagga دقّ (u, dagg); ḍarab ضرب (a, ḍarib); (**on**) khabaṭ (ʿala) خبط (i, khabiṭ, khabaṭaan); khabbaṭ (ʿala) خبّط (khibbeeṭ, takhbiiṭ); nagar نقر (u, nagir); **to knock down** baṭaḥ بطح (a, baṭiḥ)

knot **(in rope, thread)** ʿugda عقدة (*pl* ʿugad); **(in wood)** ʿeen عين (*pl* ʿiyuun)
know ʿirif عرف (a, maʿrifa); ʿilim be- علم (a, ʿilim); **to know by heart** ḥafaẓ حفظ (a, ḥifiẓ)
knowledge ʿilim علم (*pl* ʿuluum); ʿirfa عرفة ; maʿrifa معرفة
kohl kuḥul كحل ; **kohl container** makḥala مكحلة (*pl* makaaḥil)
Koran al-qur'aan; **a copy of the Koran** muṣḥaf مصحف (*pl* maṣaaḥif)
Koranic qur'aani قرآني ; **Koranic school** khalwa خلوة (*pl* khalaawi); masiid مسيد (*pl* masaayid)

L - l

laboratory maʿmal معمل (*pl* maʿaamil); **laboratory test** faḥiṣ فحص (*pl* fuḥuuṣaat); **to do a laboratory test** faḥaṣ فحص (a, faḥiṣ)
labour *n* ʿamal عمل (*pl* aʿmaal); shughul شغل (*pl* ashghaal); **hard labour (punishment)** ashghaal shaaqqa; **cost of labour** maṣnaʿiyya مصنعيّة ; **labour pains** ṭalig طلق
labourer ʿaamil عامل (*pl* ʿummaal); **day labourer (construction)** ṭulba طلبة (*pl* ṭulab)
labyrinth mataaha متاهة
lace dantilla دنتلة
lack *n* nugṣaan نقصان
lacking naagiṣ ناقص
lactate darra درّ (u, darr, dararaan)
ladder sillim سلّم (*pl* salaalim)
ladle *n* kumsha/kamsha كمشة ; gharraafa غرّافة ; kabsha كبشة ; **slotted ladle** magṣuuṣa مقصوصة (*pl* magaaṣiiṣ)
lady sayyida سيّدة ; sitt ست (*pl* -aat); madaam مدام
lake buḥeera بحيرة ; **small lake** birka بركة (*pl* birak)
lamb ḥamal حمل (*pl* ḥimlaan)
lame aʿraj أعرج (*f* ʿarja, *pl* ʿuruj); **to be(come) lame** ʿaraj عرج (i, ʿaraj, ʿarja)
lament *v* baka (ʿala) بكى (-i, bika); koorak (ʿala) كورك (kooraak)
lamp lamba لمبة (*pl* -aat, limaḍ); **oil lamp, paraffin lamp** faanuus فانوس (*pl* fawaaniis); ratiina رتينة (*pl* rataayin); **table lamp** shamʿadaan شمعدان (*pl* -aat); abajuura أبجورة
lamp post ʿamuud an-nuur
lance ḥarba حربة (*pl* ḥuraab)
land *n* ariḍ أرض (*pl* araaḍi); waaṭa واطا ; turba تربة (*pl* turab); **(as opposed to sea and air)** barr بر ; **piece of land** arḍiyya أرضيّة (*pl* araaḍi); **land surveyor** massaaḥ مسّاح • *v* nazal نزل (i, nuzuul)
landing stage moorada موردة (*pl* mawaarid); mushraʿ مشرع (*pl* -aat, mashaariʿ)
landlady sitt al-beet; ṣaaḥbat al-beet
landlord siid al-beet; ṣaaḥib al-beet
land mine lagham لغم (*pl* alghaam)
language lugha لغة ; **local non-Arabic language** ruṭaana رطانة

lantern faanuus فانوس (*pl* fawaa-niis); ratiina رتينة (*pl* rataayin)
lap ḥijir حجر (*pl* ḥujuur)
large kabiir كبير (*pl* kubaar)
laryngoscope minẓaar منظار (*pl* manaaẓiir)
lash *n* ḍarba ضربة ; **(with whip)** jalda جلدة • *v* **(with whip)** jalad جلد (i, jalid)
last *adj* akhiir أخير ; akhraani أخراني ; (*before indef n*) aakhir آخر ; **the last one in a race, game or class** ṭiish طيش
last *n* **(for shoes)** gaalib قالب (*pl* gawaalib)
last *v* daam دام (u, dooma); **(stay in good condition)** ʿammar عمّر (taʿmiir)
lasting daayim دايم ; **(durable)** muʿammir معمّر
late **to be late** it'akhkhar اتأخّر (ta'khiir); **to make late** akhkhar أخّر (ya'akhkhir, ta'khiir)
late **the late (said of a deceased person)** al-marḥuum
later baʿdeen بعدين
lathe *n* makhraṭa مخرطة (*pl* makhaariṭ); **lathe turner** kharraaṭ خراط
latrine adbakhaana أدبخانة ; beet al-adab
laugh *n* ḍaḥka ضحكة • *v* ḍiḥik ضحك (a, ḍaḥik, daḥka)
laughing stock mahzala مهزلة (*pl* mahaazil); maskhara مسخرة (*pl* masaakhir)
laughter ḍaḥik ضحك
launder ghasal غسل (i, ghasiil); ghassal غسّل (ghisseel); **to be laundered** itghasal اتغسل (gha-siil); itghassal اتغسّل (ghisseel, ghasiil)
laundress ghassaala غسّالة
laundry ghasiil غسيل ; **laundry blue** ẓahara ظهرة
laundryman ghassaal غسّال ; makwaji مكوجي (*pl* -iyya)
lavatory adbakhaana أدبخانة ; ḥammaam حمام ; dubbilyuusii دبليوسي ; beet al-adab; **lavatory cistern** sayfon سيفون
law qaanuun قانون (*pl* qawaa-niin); **Islamic law** ash-shariiʿa; **(study)** ḥuguug حقوق
lawn **(grass)** najiila نجيلة
lawsuit gaḍiyya قضيّة (*pl* gaḍaayaa); daʿwa دعوى (daʿaawi); **to bring a lawsuit against** rafaʿ gaḍiyya ʿala
lawyer muḥaami محامي (*pl* -yyiin)
lax sabahlal سبهلل
laxative mulayyin مليّن (*pl* -aat); musahhil مسهّل (*pl* -aat)
laxity sabahlaliyya سبهلليّة
lay **(put)** khatta ختّ (u, khatt); **to lay eggs** bayyaḍ بيّض (biyyeeḍ, beeḍa)
layer shariiḥa شريحة (*pl* sharaayiḥ); ṭabaqa طبقة ; **layer of bricks** mudmaak مدماك (*pl* madaamiik); **layer of sand or earth** radmiyya ردميّة
laziness kasal كسل
lazy kaslaan كسلان
lead *v* qaad قاد (u, qiyaada); **(head)** ra'as رأس (a, riyaasa, ri'aasa); **to lead away** saag ساق (u, suwaaga)
lead *n* **(metal)** raṣṣaaṣ رصّاص
leader qaayid قايد (*pl* qi-yaadaat); qaa'id قائد (*pl* qiyaadaat); zaʿiim زعيم (*pl* zuʿama); **tribal/clan leader** sulṭaan سلطان (*pl* salaaṭiin);

ʿumda عمدة (*pl* cumad); sheekh شيخ (*pl* shiyuukh)
leadership qiyaada قيادة
leading (**main**) ra'iisi رئيسي
leaf (**leaves**) ṣafag صفق ; warag ورق
leaflet manshuur منشور (*pl* -aat, manaashiir)
leak *n* tasriib تسريب (*pl* -aat) • *v* (**liquid**) kharra خرّ (u, kharr, kharra, khararaan); naggaṭ نقّط (niggeeṭ); (**liquid, gas**) itsarrab اتسرّب (tasarrub); **the roof is leaking** al-beet bidaffig; **to cause to leak** sarrab سرّب (sirreeb)
lean *v* **to lean on** irtakaz ʿala ارتكز (irtikaaz); itrakkaz ʿala اتركّز (rikkeez, tarkiiz, tirikkiz); ittaka ʿala اتّكى (-i, ittika, takiya); **to lean over** mayyal ميّل (meel, mayalaan); **to lean towards** maal le- مال (i, mayalaan, meel); mayyal ميّل (meel, mayalaan)
leap *n* ṭafra طفرة • *v* ṭaffar طفّر (ṭiffeer); **leap year** sana kabiisa
learn itʿallam اتعلّم (taʿallum)
learned ʿaalim عالم (*pl* ʿulama)
lease *n* iijaar إيجار (*pl* -aat) • *v* ajjar أجّر (ta'jiir)
leather jilid جلد
leave *vi* (**go**) masha مشى (-i, mashi); faat فات (u, foota, fawataan); raaḥ راح (-u, no vn); rawwaḥ روّح (*no vn*); (**depart**) raḥal رحل (a, ruḥuul, raḥiil) • *vt* khalla خلّى (-i, kh-illeey); saab ساب (i, sayabaan)
leave *n* (**holiday**) ijaaza إجازة ; (**permission**) izin إزن (*pl* uzuunaat)
leaven *n* (**sourdough**) ḥaamuḍ حامض ; khammaar خمّار ; ʿajiin khammaar; (**of curds**) ruwaaba رواية ; (**yeast**) khamiira خميرة • *v* khammar خمّر (khimmeer, takhmiir); ḥammaḍ حمّض (ḥimmeeḍ); **to be leavened** itḥammaḍ اتحمّض (ḥimmeeḍ); khimir خمر (a, khamaraan); itkhammar اتخمّر (khimmeer)
leavened mukhammar مخمّر
Lebanese *adj/n* lubnaani لبناني (*pl* -yyiin)
Lebanon lubnaan لبنان
lecture muḥaaḍara محاضرة
left shimaal شمال ; **the Left** al-yasaar
left-handed ashwal أشول (*f* shawla, *pl* shuwul); aʿsar أعسر (*f* ʿasra, *pl* ʿusur)
leftovers faḍalaat فضلات ; (**in cooking pot**) ḥutrub حترب
leg kuraaʿ كراع (*pl* kurʿeen); rijil رجل (*pl* rijleen); (**humans only**) saag ساق (*pl* seegaan); (**of meat**) fakhda فخدة (*pl* fikhad)
legacy miiraas ميراس (*pl* mawaariis)
legal qaanuuni قانوني ; sharʿi شرعي ; **Islamic legal opinion** fatwa فتوى (*pl* fataawi)
legend usṭuura اسطورة (*pl* asaaṭiir)
legendary khuraafi خرافي
legislate qannan قنن (taqniin); sharraʿ شرّع (tashriiʿ)
legitimate sharʿi شرعي
lemon(s) leemuun ليمون
lemon-squeezer ʿaṣṣaara عصّارة
lend dayyan ديّن (deen); sallaf سلّف (tasliif)
length ṭuul طول (aṭwaal); (**of time**) mudda مدّة (*pl* -aat, mudad)
lengthen ṭawwal طوّل (ṭiwweel, taṭwiil); **to be lengthened** iṭṭawwal اطّوّل (ṭiwweel)

lens ʿadasa عدسة
Lent az-zaman al-arbaʿiini
lentil(s) ʿadas عدس (*unit n* ʿadasa, ʿadasaaya)
leopard nimir نمر (*pl* numuur)
leprosy juzaam جزام
lesbian ḍakariyya ضكريّة
less agalla (min); **to become less** galla قلّ (i, gilla)
lessen gallal (min) قلّل (gilleel, tagliil); naggaṣ min نقّص (niggeeṣ, tangiiṣ); nagaṣ min نقص (u, nagṣ, nugṣaan)
lesson daris درس (*pl* duruus); ḥiṣṣa حصّة (*pl* ḥiṣaṣ); (**warning**) ʿibra عبرة (*pl* ʿibar)
let *v* (**permit**) khalla خلّى (-i, khilleey)
let *v* (**lease**) ajjar أجّر (ta'jiir)
letter (**message**) jawwaab جوّاب (*pl* -aat); khiṭaab خطاب (*pl* -aat); risaala رسالة (*pl* rasaayil)
letter (**of alphabet**) ḥarif حرف (*pl* ḥuruuf)
lettuce khass خس
leukemia saraṭaan ad-damm
level mustawa مستوى (*pl* -yaat); **to make level** saawa ساوى (-i, musaawaa)
lever raafʿa رافعة (*pl* rawaafiʿ)
liability mas'uuliyya مسؤوليّة
liable mas'uul مسؤول
liar kaḍḍaab كضّاب
liberation taḥriir تحرير
librarian (*m*) amiin maktaba; (*f*) amiinat maktaba
library maktaba مكتبة
Libya liibiya ليبيا
Libyan *adj/n* liibi ليبي (*pl* -yyiin)
licence rukhṣa رخصة (*pl* rukhaṣ); **driving licence** rukhṣat qiyaada; (**franchise**) imtiyaaz إمتياز (*pl* -aat)
license plate looḥa لوحة
lick *n* laḥsa لحسة • *v* laḥas لحس (a, laḥasaan, laḥis); liḥis لحس (a, laḥasaan, laḥis); **to be licked** itlaḥas اتلحس (laḥis, laḥasaan)
lid ghuṭaaya غطاية ; ghuṭa غطا (*pl* ghuṭayaat)
lie *v* (**down**) ragad رقد (u, rugaad, ragda); itmaddad اتمدّد (mid-deed); itmadda اتمدّ (madda); **to lie on one's stomach** inbaṭaḥ انبطح (inbiṭaaḥ); **to make s.o. lie down** raggad رقّد (riggeed, rugaad, ragda)
lie *n* (**untruth**) kaḍba كضبة (*pl* -aat, kiḍib); kazba/kizba كزبة (*pl* -aat, akaaziib) • *v* (**to/about**) kaḍab (ʿala/fi) كضب (i, kaḍba); kaḍḍab كضّب (kiḍib); kazab كزب (kazba, kizba); kazzab كزّب (kizib)
lieutenant mulaazim ملازم
lieutenant colonel mugaddam مقدّم
life ḥayaa حياة
lift *v* rafaʿ رفع (a, rafiʿ); galla قلّ (i, gall)
light *adj* (**of weight**) khafiif خفيف (*pl* -iin, khufaaf); **to be(come) light** khaffa خفّ (i, khiffa)
light *n* nuur نور (*pl* anwaar); ḍaw ضو (*pl* aḍwaa); **traffic lights** istob استوب (*pl* -aat); al-ishaara; ishaarat al-muruur • *v* (**give light**) nawwar نوّر (tanwiir); ḍawwa ضوّى (-i, ḍiwweey); (ignite) oogad أوقد (yuugid, wuguud); wallaʿ ولّع (willeeʿ)
lighten (**of weight**) khaffaf خفّف (khiffeef, takhfiif)
lighter *n* **cigarette lighter** wallaaʿa ولاعة ; zinaad زناد (*pl* -aat)

lighthouse manaara منارة
lightning barraag برّاق ; **(flash of)** barig برق (*pl* buruug); **lightning strike** ṣaagᶜa صاقعة (*pl* ṣawaagiᶜ)
like *prep* zayy زي ; mitil متل ; misl مسل ; **like this** kida كدا ; kadi كدي
like *v* raad راد (i, reeda); ḥabba حبّ (i, ḥubb); **I liked your speech** ᶜajab-ni kalaam-ak; **I like your dress** ᶜana muᶜjab be-fustaan-ik
limb *n* ᶜaḍu عضو (*pl* aᶜḍaa)
lime **(chemical)** jiir جير
lime(s) **(fruit)** leemuun ليمون
limestone ḥajar jiir
limit *n* ḥadd حد (*pl* ḥuduud) • *v* ḥaddad حدّد (taḥdiid); **limited** maḥduud محدود
limp *v* ᶜaraj عرج (i, ᶜaraj, ᶜarja); ᶜatab عتب (i, ᶜatib)
line *n* khaṭṭ خط (*pl* khuṭuuṭ); **(of writing)** saṭur سطر (*pl* suṭuur); **(queue)** ṣaff صف (*pl* ṣufuuf); ṭaabuur طابور (*pl* ṭawaabiir); **to rule a line** saṭṭar سطّر (tasṭiir); **to mark with lines** khaṭṭaṭ خطّط (takhṭiiṭ)
line *v* **(a garment)** baṭṭan بطّن (tabṭiin)
linen tiil تيل ; **bed linen** milaaya ملاية
lining **(of a garment)** buṭaana بطانة
link *n* ttiṣaal إتّصال (*pl* -aat); ṣila صلة
linoleum mashammaᶜ مشمّع (*pl* -aat)
lintel ᶜatab عتب
lion asad أسد (*pl* usuud); duud دود (*no pl*)
lioness labwa لبوة
lip shalluufa شلّوفة (*pl* shalaaliif); shiffa شفّة (*pl* shafaayif)
lipoma kiis duhni
lipstick aḥmar shafaayif; rooj روج
liquid *adj* maayiᶜ مايع • *n* saayil سايل (*pl* sawaayil)
liquidation **(financial)** taṣfiya تصفية ; tasyiil تسييل (*pl* -aat); **(murder)** taṣfiya تصفية
liquidity siyuula سيولة
liquor khamr خمر (*pl* khumuur); khamra خمرة (*pl* khumuur)
liquorice ᶜirig suus
list *n* lista لستة (*pl* lisat); kashif كشف (*pl* kushuufaat); qaayma قايمة (qawaayim) • *v* fahras فهرس (fahrasa)
listen simiᶜ سمع (a, samaᶜ)
literal **(e.g. translation)** ḥarfi حرفي
literally ḥarfiyyan حرفيا
literature adab أدب (*pl* aadaab)
litter wisaakha وساخة
little basiiṭ بسيط (*pl* -iin); galiil قليل (*pl* gulaal); **a little** shwayya شويّة ; ḥabba حبّة
live *v* **(exist)** ᶜaash عاش (i, ᶜeesh, ᶜeesha); **(dwell)** sakan سكن (u, sakan)
live *adj* **(electricity)** fii-ho maas; **(of broadcast)** mubaashir مباشر
livelihood maᶜiisha معيشة (*pl* maᶜaayish); ᶜiisha عيشة
lively ḥayawi حيوي
liver kabid كبد ; **(as meat)** kabda كبدة (*pl* kibad)
livestock bahaayim بهايم (*sg* bahiima); maashiyya ماشيّة (*pl* mawaashi); saᶜiyya سعيّة
lizard siḥliyya سحليّة (*pl* saḥaali); **house lizard** ḍabb ضب (*pl*

ḍababa, ḍububba); **monitor lizard**(**s**) waral ورل (*pl* -aat, wurulla)

load *n* sheel شيل ; (**cargo**) shuḥna شحنة (*pl* -aat, shuḥan) • *v* shaḥan شحن (a, shaḥin); ḥammal حمّل (taḥmiil); (**a gun**) ʿammar عمّر (taʿmiir); **to be loaded** itshaḥan شحن (shaḥin, shaḥna); (**of a gun**) itʿammar اتعمّر (taʿmiir)

loaf ʿeesha عيشة ; raghiifa رغيفة (*pl* arghifa, raghiif)

loan salafiyya سلفيّة ; sulfa سلفة (*pl* sulaf); salaf سلف (*pl* -iyyaat)

loathe ʿaaf عاف (i, ʿuwaafa); kirih كره (a, kurh, karaahiya)

local baladi بلدي ; maḥalli محلّي

lock *n* gifil قفل (*pl* agfaal); kayluun كيلون (*pl* kawaaliin) • *v* gafal قفل (i, gafil); gaffal قفّل (giffeel, tagfiil); (**with a padlock**) ṭabal طبل (u, ṭabil)

locomotive gaaṭira قاطرة

locust(**s**) jaraad جراد ; **young locust**(**s**) ʿattaab عتّاب

log kutla كتلة (*pl* -aat, kutal)

logic manṭig منطق

logical manṭigi منطقي

logistical lojisti لوجستي

logistics imdaadaat إمدادات

logo shiʿaar شعار (*pl* -aat)

loneliness waḥsha وحشة ; wiḥda وحدة

lonely waḥiid وحيد

long *adj* ṭawiil طويل (*pl* ṭuwaal); **to be**(**come**) **long** ṭaal طال (u, ṭuul); **to take a long time** ṭawwal طوّل (ṭiwweel, taṭwiil)

long *v* ishtaag le- اشتاق (shoog, ishtiyaag); girim le- قرم (a, garam)

loofah liifa ليفة

look *v* ʿaayan (le-) عاين (ʿiyyeen, muʿaayana); (**watch**) itfarraj (ʿala) اتفرّج (tafarruj); **to look for** fattash (le-/ʿala) فتّش (fitteesh, taftiish); kaas le- كاس (u, kuwaasa); **to look after** iʿtana be- اعتنى (-i, iʿtina); raaʿa راعى (-i, muraaʿaa); **to look upwards** ṣangaʿ صنقع (ṣingeeʿ)

loom mansaj منسج (*pl* manaasij)

loose markhi مرخي ; maḥluul محلول ; **to be**(**come**) **loose** (**belt, shoes, rope**) itrakha اترخى (-i, rakhia); (**screw, rope**) itfakka اتفكّ (fakk, fakakaan); (**tooth, pole**) itkhalkhal اتخلخل (khilkheel, khalkhala); itlakhlakh اتلخلخ (likhleekh, lakhlakha)

loosen (**belt, shoes, rope**) rakha أرخى (-i, rakhiya, rakhayaan); (**screw, rope**) fakka اتفكّ (fakk, fakakaan); (**tooth, pole**) khalkhal خلخل (khilkheel, khalkhala); lakhlakh لخلخ (likhleekh, lakhlakha)

loot *v* nahab نهب (a, nahib)

lorry loori لوري (*pl* lawaari)

lose rawwaḥ روّح (rooḥa, rawaḥaan, riwweeḥ); waddar ودّر (widdeer); ḍayyaʿ ضيّع (ḍiyyeeʿ, ḍeeʿa); (**also a person**) fagad فقد (i, fagid, fugdaan); (**in a game**) khisir خسر (a, khasaara, khusraan); itghalab اتغلب (ghulub)

loser khasraan خسران

loss khasaara خسارة ; (**bereavement**) fugdaan فقدان ; (**waste**) ḍayaaʿ ضياع ; **to sell at a loss** baaʿ be-khasaara; **to be at a loss** itmaḥḥan اتمحّن (miḥna)

lost raayiḥ رايح ; ḍaayiʿ ضايع ; ḍahbaan ضهبان ; **to be lost**

(**things**) raaḥ راح (u, rooḥa, rawaḥaan); ḍaaᶜ ضاع (i, ḍeeᶜa); itfagad اتفقد (fug-daan); **to get lost** raaḥ راح (u, rooḥa, rawaḥaan); ḍaaᶜ ضاع (i, ḍeeᶜa); widir ودر (yawaddir, wadaar); waddar ودّر (wid-deer, wadaar); ṭashsha طشّ (i, ṭashsh, ṭashsha); taah تاه (u, tooha, tawahaan)

lot naṣiib نصيب (*pl* anṣiba); **drawing of lots** gurᶜa قرعة

lottery ya-naṣiib

loud ᶜaali عالي

loudspeaker sammaaᶜa سمّاعة

lounge ṣaaloon صالون (*pl* ṣawaaliin); diiwaan ديوان (*pl* dawaawiin)

louse (**lice**) gamul قمل (*unit n* gamla); **to be infested with lice** gammal قمّل (tagmiil)

love *n* ḥubb حب ; maḥabba محبّة ; reeda ريدة ; **ardent love** ᶜishig عشق • *v* ḥabba حبّ (i, ḥubb); raad راد (i, reeda); **to be loved** inḥabba انحبّ (ḥubb); itḥabba اتحبّ (ḥubb)

lover ᶜaashig عاشق ; ḥabiib حبيب (*pl* aḥibba, aḥbaab)

low *adj* (**of level**) munkhafiḍ منخفض ; muddanni مدنّي ; (*also fig*) waaṭi واطي ; mutadanni متدنّي (*pl* -yyiin)

low *v* (**of cattle**) jaᶜar جعر (a, jaᶜir, jiᶜᶜeer)

lower *v* (**things**) dalla دلّى (-i, dilleey); (**sound**) waṭṭa وطّى (-i, wiṭṭeey)

loyal mukhliṣ مخلص ; wafi وفي (*pl* awfiya); **to be loyal** akhlaṣ أخلص (i, ikhlaaṣ)

loyalty ikhlaaṣ إخلاص

lubricate zayyat زيّت (ziyyeet, tazyiit)

luck bakhit بخت ; ḥaẓẓ حظ ; **bad luck** naḥs نحس ; **to bring bad luck on** naḥas نحس (a, naḥis, naḥasaan)

lucky maḥẓuuẓ محظوظ ; **you lucky one!** ya bakht-ak!

luggage ᶜafash عفش ; ᶜidda عدّة (*pl* ᶜidad)

lump kurdumma كردمّة (*pl* karaa-diim); (**in throat**) (*also fig*) ghuṣṣa غصة (*pl* ghuṣaṣ); ᶜabra عبرة

lunatic majnuun مجنون (*pl* majaa-niin); mushooṭin مشوطن

lunch *n* ghada غدا ; **to give lunch to s.o.** ghadda غدّى (-i, ghada) • *v* itghadda اتغدّى (-a, ghada)

lung ri'a رئة ; (**as meat**) fashfaash فشفاش

lust shahwa شهوة

lute ᶜuud عود (*pl* aᶜwaad)

luxurious faakhir فاخر

luxury rafaahiyya رفاهية

M - m

macaroni makaroona مكرونة

machete saaṭuur ساطور (*pl* sawaaṭiir)

machine makana مكنة ; **sewing machine** makanat khiyaaṭa

machine gun rashshaash رشّاش (*pl* -aat)

mad majnuun مجنون (*pl* majaani-in); mushooṭin مشوطن ; tarallalli ترلّلي ; **to be(come) mad** itjannan

اتجنّن (jinn); ithawas اتهوس (hawas); **to drive s.o. mad** jan-nan جنّن (jinneen)
madam (**term of respect**) sayyida سيّدة; sitt ست (*pl* -aat); madaam مدام
madden jannan جنّن (jinneen)
madness junuun جنون; jinn جن; hawas هوس
magazine (**periodical**) majalla مجلّة; (**of a gun**) ẓarif ظرف (*pl* ẓuruuf)
magic siḥir سحر; (**black**) ʿamal عمل
magician ḥaawi حاوي (*pl* ḥuwaa); saaḥir ساحر (*pl* saḥara)
magistrate gaaḍi قاضي (*pl* guḍaa); **magistrate of a village or district** ʿumda عمدة (*pl* ʿumad)
magnet maghnaṭiis مغنطيس
magnetic maghnaṭiisi مغنطيسي
magnificent ʿaẓiim عظيم (*pl* ʿuẓama)
mahogany mahoogani مهوقني
maid khaddaama خدّامة; shagh-ghaala شغّالة
mail *n* bariid بريد; busṭa بسطة; **express mail** bariid sariiʿ
main *adj* ra'iisi رئيسي
maintain (**repair**) ṣaan صان (i, ṣiyaana); (**provide for**) ʿaal عال (u, iʿaala)
maintenance ṣiyaana صيانة; (**to a divorced wife and children**) nafaga نفقة
maize ʿeesh riif; dura shaami; **maize oil** zeet dura
major *n* (**army rank**) raa'id رائد (*pl* ruwwaad)
majority aghlabiyya أغلبيّة; **the majority of** muʿẓam معظم
make ʿamal عمل (a/i, ʿamal); (**e.g. tea, food**) sawwa سوّى (-i, siwweey, suwaa); (**manufacture**) ṣanaʿ صنع (a, ṣinaaʿa); (**an appointment**) gaṭaʿ miʿaad; **to be made** itʿamal اتعمل (ʿamla); itsawwa اتسوّى (-a, siwweey, suwaa); (**manufactured**) itṣanaʿ اتصنع (ṣinaaʿa, sinaʿ); **made (of)** maʿmuul (min) معمول; maṣnuuʿ (min) مصنوع
makeup mikyaaj مكياج; **to put on makeup** itzayyan اتزيّن (ziina, tazayyun)
malaria milaarya ملاريا
male ḍakar ضكر (*pl* ḍukuur)
malice ḥigid حقد; ḥasad حسد
malicious ḥaguud حقود; ḥaagid حاقد; shaamit شامت; (**causing the evil eye**) ḥasuud حسود; **malicious joy** shamaata شماتة; **to take malicious pleasure in** shamat fi شمت (a, shamaata)
malnutrition suu' taghziya
man raajil راجل (*pl* rujaal, rijaal); **the man in the street** maḥammad aḥmad
manage adaar أدار (yudiir, idaara); (**cope**) itṣarraf اتصرّف (taṣarruf); (**on a domestic level**) dabbar دبّر (dibbeer, tadbiir); **to manage without** istaghna min استغنى (istighna)
management idaara إدارة
manager (*m*) mudiir مدير (*pl* -iin, mudara); (*f*) mudiira مديرة
mandatory ilzaami الزامي
mange jarab جرب
mango(es) manga منقة
manhole manihool منهول (*pl* -aat)
mankind bashar بشر
manliness rujuula رجولة
manner ṭariiga طريقة; usluub أسلوب

manners suluuk سلوك (*pl* -iyaat); **good manners** adab أدب (*pl* aadaab); **having good manners** mu'addab مؤدّب ; muhazzab مهزّب ; **having bad manners** mamsuukh ممسوخ ; **to teach manners** addab أدّب (ta'diib)
manual *adj* yaddawi يدّوي
manufacture *v* ṣanaᶜ صنع (a, ṣinaaᶜa); **to be manufactured** itṣanaᶜ اتصنع (ṣinaaᶜa)
manure samaad سماد
many katiir كتير (*pl* kutaar); **to be(come) many** kitir كتر (a, katara); **how many** kam كم
map *n* khariiṭa خريطة (*pl* kharaayiṭ); kharṭa خرطة (*pl* khuraṭ)
marabou stork(s) abu siᶜin
marble (stone) rikhaam رخام
marble(s) billi بلي (*unit n* biliyya)
March shahri talaata; maaris مارس
march *n* masiira مسيرة
margin haamish هامش (*pl* hawaamish)
marginalize hammash همّش (tahmiish)
marijuana bango بنقو ; ḥashiish حشيش ; **to be(come) high on marijuana** saṭal سطل (u, saṭil); saṭṭal سطّل (siṭṭeel)
mark *n* ᶜalaama علامة ; **trademark** ᶜalaama tujaariyya; **school mark** daraja درجة ; nimra نمرة (*pl* nimar) • *v* ᶜallam علّم (taᶜliim); **(brand)** wassam وسّم (wisseem)
market suug سوق (*pl* aswaag); **charcoal, wood and earthenware market** zariiba زريبة (*pl* zara-ayib); **grain market** zariibat al-ᶜeesh • *v* sawwag سوّق (taswiig)
marketing taswiig تسويق
marquee ṣeewaan صيوان (*pl* -aat)
marriage zawaaj زواج (*pl* ziijaat)
marrow (of bone) mukhkh al-ᶜaḍum
marry ᶜarras عرّس (ᶜiris); izzaw-waj ازّوّج (zawaaj); itzawwaj اتزوّج (zawaaj); **to marry into (a family)** naasab ناسب (nasab)
Mars al-mirriikh المرّيخ
marsh mustangaᶜ مستنقع (*pl* -aat)
marshal field marshal mushiir مشير
martial ḥarbi حربي ; ᶜaskari عسكري
martyr shahiid شهيد (*pl* shu-hada); **to be martyred** istashhad إستشهد (istishhaad)
martyrdom istishhaad إستشهاد
masculine muzakkar مزكّر
mash *v* haras هرس (i, haris)
mask *n* qinaaᶜ قناع (*pl* -aat, aqniᶜa); **(against dust, pollu-tion)** kammaama كمّامة (*pl* -aat, kamaayim)
mass kutla كتلة (*pl* -aat, kutal); **mass production** al-intaaj be-j-jumla
mass (in church) quddaas قدّاس (*pl* -aat)
massacre majzara مجزرة (*pl* majaazir); mazbaḥa مزبحة (*pl* mazaabiḥ)
massage *n* dalik دلك ; tadliik تدليك ; masaaj (*pl* -aat) • *v* dalak دلك (i, dalik); dallak دلّك (dilleek, tadliik); ᶜaṣṣar عصّر (ᶜiṣṣeer)
mast saari ساري (*pl* saariya)
master sayyid سيّد (*pl* saada); **(schoolteacher)** ustaaz أستاز (*pl* asaatza, asaatiza)
mastitis iltihaab sadi

mat birish برش (*pl* buruush); ḥaṣiira حصيرة (*pl* ḥasaayir); sabaata سباتة

match *v* itnaasab اتناسب (nasab); naasab ناسب (nasab)

match *n* (**in sport**) mubaara مباراة (*pl* -yaat); matsh ماتش (*pl* -aat); **informal football match** daafuuri دافوري

match(es) *n* kibriit كبريت (*pl* kabaariit); kibriita كبريتة (*pl* kabaariit

matchstick ᶜuud kibriit

mate *v* ᶜashshar عشّر (ᶜishsheer)

material *adj* maaddi مادّي • *n* maadda مادّة (*pl* mawaadd); **raw material** maadda khaam; (**cloth**) gumaash قماش (*pl* -aat, agmisha)

materialistic maaddi مادّي

matter *n* (**material**) maadda مادّة (*pl* mawaadd); (**affair**) gaḍiyya قضيّة (*pl* gaḍaayaa); mas'ala مسألة (*pl* masaa'il); (**topic**) mawḍuuᶜ موضوع (*pl* -aat, mawaaḍiiᶜ) • *v* hamma همّ (i, hamm); **it doesn't matter** maᶜleesh معليش

mattress martaba مرتبة (*pl* maraatib); **thin mattress** liḥaaf لحاف (*pl* -aat)

mature baaligh بالغ

maximum aqṣa ḥaaja; aqṣa shi; al-ḥadd al-aqṣa

May shahri khamsa; maayo مايو

maybe jaayiz جايز; yajuuz يجوز; yimkin يمكن

meal wajba وجبة; akla أكلة

mean *adj* (**malicious**) ḥaagid حاقد; ḥaasid حاسد (*pl* ḥussaad); (**ignoble**) dani دني (*pl* -yyiin); khasiis خسيس; (**stingy**) bakhiil بخيل (*pl* bukhala)

mean *v* ᶜana عنى (-i, ᶜanayaan); gaṣad قصد (u, gaṣid)

meaning maᶜna معنى (*pl* maᶜaani)

means wasiila وسيلة (*pl* wasaayil); **by all means** be-ayyi ṭariiga; **by means of** be-waasṭat

measles ḥiṣba حصبة

measure *n* (**standard**) miᶜyaar معيار (*pl* maᶜaayiir); migyaas مقياس (*pl* magaayiis) • *v* gaas قاس (i, giyaas); (**length**) mattar متّر (mitteer); (**cloth**) ḍarraᶜ ضرّع (ḍirreeᶜ, taḍriiᶜ); (**grain**) kaal كال (i, keela); kayyal كيّل (kiyyeel); ᶜabar عبر (i, ᶜabir)

measurement giyaas قياس (*pl* -aat); (**cloth**) taḍriiᶜ تضريع (*pl* -aat)

meat laḥam لحم (*pl* luḥuum); laḥma لحمة (*pl* luḥuum); **meat without bones or fat** laḥam ṣaafi; **minced/ground meat** laḥma mafruuma; **dried meat** sharmuuṭ شرموط; **fried meat** kabaab كباب; **grilled or roasted meat** sheyya شية; **stewed meat** kabaab ḥalla; **meat cleaver** farraar فرّار (*pl* -aat, faraariir); **meat grinder** maframa مفرمة

meatball(s) kufta كفتة

mechanic makaaniiki مكانيكي (*pl* -iyya); miikaaniiki ميكانيكي (*pl* -iyya)

mechanism aaliyya آليّة

medal miidaaliyya ميداليّة; niishaan نيشان (*pl* -aat, nayaashiin)

meddle itḥashshar اتحشّر (ḥishsheer, taḥashshur); iddakhkhal اتدخّل (tadakhkhul)

mediate itwassaṭ اتوسّط (tawassuṭ)

mediator wasiiṭ وسيط (*pl* wusaṭa)

medical ṭibbi طبّي
medicine dawa دوا (*pl* adwiya); **study of medicine** ṭibb طب
medium (**size**) mutwassiṭ متوسّط; (**of height**) marbuuᶜ مربوع
meet gaabal قابل (mugaabala); laaga لاقى (-i, mulaagaa); itgaabal maᶜa اتقابل (mugaabala); itlaaga maᶜa اتلاقى (-a, mulaagaa)
meeting ijtimaaᶜ إجتماع (*pl* -aat); **to fix a meeting** ᶜagad ijtimaaᶜ; **to have a meeting** ijtamaᶜ اجتمع (ijtimaaᶜ)
melody laḥn لحن (*pl* alḥaan); nagham نغم (*pl* anghaam); naghama نغمة (*pl* anghaam)
melon(s) (**sweet**) shammaam شمّام; **watermelon(s)** baṭṭiikh بطّيخ
melt *vi* daab داب (u, dawabaan); saaḥ ساح (i, sayaḥaan) • *vt* dawwab دوّب (diwweeb, tadwiib); sayyaḥ سيّح (siyyeeḥ, tasyiiḥ)
member ᶜaḍu عضو (*pl* aᶜḍaa)
membership ᶜuḍwiyya عضويّة
memoirs zikrayaat زكريات; muzakkiraat مزكّرات
memorandum muzakkira مزكّرة
memory zaakira زاكرة
mend ᶜadal عدل (i, ᶜadil); ṣallaḥ صلّح (ṣilleeḥ, taṣliiḥ)
meningitis suḥaa'i سحائي; abu farraar
menopause sinn al-ya's; **having passed the menopause** gaaṭiᶜa قاطعة
menstruate ḥaaḍ حاض (i, ḥeeḍ)
menstruation al-ᶜaada; ad-dawra
mental ᶜagli عقلي; (**as opposed to material**) maᶜnawi معنوي
mention *n* zikir زكر (*pl* azkaar) • *v* zakar زكر (u, zikir)
menu lista لستة (*pl* lisat)
merchandise buḍaaᶜa بضاعة (*pl* baḍaayiᶜ)
merchant taajir تاجر (*pl* tujjaar); **builder's merchant** maghlag مغلق (maghaalig)
merciful ḥaniin حنين; raḥiim رحيم (*pl* ruḥama); (**of God**) raḥmaan رحمن
merciless gaasi قاسي; jabbaar جبّار; be-duun raḥma
mercury zeebag زيبق
mercy raḥma رحمة
mermaid ḥuur حور (*unit n* ḥuuriyya)
mess fawḍa فوضى; jooṭa جوطة; rabka ربكة; lakhbaṭa لخبطة; barjala برجلة; **to make a mess of** jaaṭ جاط (u, jooṭa); rabak ربك (i, rabka); lakhbaṭ لخبط (lakhbaṭa); barjal برجل (birjeel, barjala); **to be(come) messed up** ijjaaṭ اجّاط (jooṭa); itrabak اتربك (rabka); itlakhbaṭ اتلخبط (lakhbaṭa); itbarjal اتبرجل (birjeel, barjala)
message risaala رسالة (*pl* rasaayil); waṣiyya وصيّة (*pl* waṣaaya); khabar خبر (*pl* akhbaar)
messenger mursaal مرسال (*pl* maraasiil)
meter (**e.g. for electricity**) ᶜaddaad عدّاد (*pl* -aat)
method manhaj منهج (*pl* manaahij); ṭariiga طريقة (*pl* ṭurug)
metre mitir متر (*pl* amtaar)
microphone makrafoon مكرفون (*pl* -aat)
midday ḍuhur ضهر
middle *n* nuṣṣ نص; wasaṭ وسط (*pl* awsaaṭ) • *adj* wasṭaani وسطاني; **the middle class**

aṭ-ṭabaga al-wusṭa; **the Middle East** ash-sharq al-awsaṭ
middleman samsaar سمسار (*pl* samaasra)
midnight nuṣṣ al-leel
midwife daaya داية ; naffaasa نفّاسة
migraine ṣudaaᶜ niṣfi
migrate haajar le-/ila هاجر (hijra)
migration hijra هجرة
mile miil ميل (*pl* amyaal)
military ᶜaskari عسكري (*pl* ᶜasaakir)
milk *n* laban لبن (*pl* albaan); **fresh milk** ḥaliib حليب ; **curdled milk** roob روب • *v* ḥalab حلب (i, ḥalib)
mill ṭaaḥuuna طاحونة (*pl* ṭawaaḥiin); masḥana مسحنة (*pl* masaaḥin)
millet ᶜeesh عيش (*pl* ᶜiyuush); **pearl millet** dukhun دخن
millimetre milli ملّي
million milyoon مليون (*pl* malaayiin)
millstone murḥaaka مرحاكة (*pl* maraaḥiik)
minaret meyḍana ميضنة (*pl* mayaaḍin); mi'zana مئزنة (*pl* ma'aazin)
mince *n* mafruuma • *v* faram فرم (u, farim)
mincer maframa مفرمة
mind *n* ᶜagul عقل (*pl* ᶜuguul) • *v* **never mind** maᶜleesh معليش
mine *n* (**e.g. coal, iron**) manjam منجم (*pl* manaajim); (**explosive**) lagham لغم (*pl* alghaam)
mineral *n* maᶜdan معدن (*pl* maᶜaadin) • *adj* maᶜdani معدني
minibus amjaad أمجاد (*pl* -aat)
minimal ᶜala l-agall; agall-; agalla shi/ḥaaja
minimum al-ḥadd al-adna
minister waziir وزير (*pl* wuzara); **prime minister** ra'iis wuzara
ministry wazaara وزارة
minor gaaṣir قاصر (*pl* guṣṣar); ṣaghiir صغير (*pl* ṣughaar)
minority agalliyya أقلّيّة
mint (**plant**) naᶜnaaᶜ نعناع
minus naagiṣ ناقص
minute *n* dagiiga دقيقة (*pl* dagaayig)
minutes (**of a meeting**) maḥḍar محضر (*pl* maḥaaḍir)
miracle muᶜjiza معجزة
mirage rihaab رهاب (*pl* -aat); saraab سراب
mirror miraaya مراية
misappropriate ikhtalas اختلس (ikhtilaas)
misappropriation ikhtilaas اختلاس (*pl* -aat)
miscarriage dufaag دفاق (*pl* -aat); ijhaaḍ اجهاض (*pl* -aat); (**of animals**) ṭaraḥaan طرحان
miscarry (**humans**) daafag دافق (dufaag); asgaṭ أسقط (yusgiṭ, isgaaṭ); **the foetus miscarried** aj-janiin sagaṭ; (**animals**) ṭaraḥ طرح (a, ṭaraḥaan)
misdemeanour junḥa جنحة (*pl* junaḥ)
miser *n* bakhiil بخيل (*pl* bukhala)
miserable miskiin مسكين (*pl* masaakiin); shagyaan شقيان ; shagi شقي ; baa'is بائس (*pl* -iin, bu'asa)
misery shagaawa شقاوة ; bu's بؤس
misfortune ᶜaariḍ عارض (*pl* ᶜawaariḍ); suu' ḥaẓẓ
mislead jahjah جهجه (jahjaha); (**maliciously**) khamma خمّ (u, khamm)

mismanagement suu' idaara
miss *v* (**in throwing, shooting**) jalla جلّى (-i, jilleey); (**long for**) ishtaag le- اشتاق (shoog, ishtiyaag); girim le- قرم (a, garam)
mission (**delegation**) bi^csa بعسة ; (**objective**) muhimma مهمة ; risaala رسالة (*pl* rasaayil); (*Chr*) irsaaliyya إرساليّة
missionary mubashshir مبشّر
mist ḍabaab ضباب ; shabbuura شبّورة
mistake *n* ghalṭa غلطة (*pl* ghalaṭaat); ghalaṭ غلط (*pl* -aat); khata ختا (*pl* akhtaa); **to make a mistake** ghiliṭ (fi) غلط (a, ghalaṭ); khita ختا (-i, khata, khatiya); khiṭa خطا (-i, khaṭa, khaṭiya)
mistaken ghalṭaan غلطان ; khaati خاتي ; **to be mistaken** ghiliṭ (fi) غلط (a, ghalaṭ); khita ختا (-i, khata, khatiya)
mister sayyid سيّد (*pl* saada)
mistreatment suu' mu^caamala
misunderstanding suu' faham; (**mutual**) suu' tafaahum
mix *v* khalaṭ خلط (i, khaliṭ); **to mix up** lakhbaṭ لخبط (likhbeeṭ, lakhbaṭa)
mixed (**fruits, sweets**) mushakkal مشكّل ; (**e.g. boys and girls**) mukhtalaṭ; **mixed salad** salaṭa ḥamra
mixer khallaaṭ خلاط ; khallaaṭa خلاطة
mixture khaliiṭ خليط ; (**e.g. food**) khalṭa خلطة ; (**compound**) tarkiiba تركيبة (*pl* -aat, taraakiib)
moan *v* ganat قنت (i, ganataan, ganit)
mobile mutḥarrik متحرّك ; **mobile telephone** moobaayl موبايل (*pl* -aat); jawwaal جوّال (*pl* -aat)
mobilization ta^cbiya تعبية
mobilize ^cabba عبّا (-i, ta^cbiya)
mock sikhir min سخر (a, sukhriyya); hazza هزّا (-i, tahziya)
mockery sukhriyya سخريّة
model *n* modeel موديل (*pl* -aat); (**example**) namuuzaj نموزج (*pl* namaazij) • *adj* namuuzaji نموزجي
modern ^caṣri عصري ; ḥadiis حديس
modest ^cafiif عفيف
modesty ^ciffa عفة ; ḥaya حيا
moist raṭib رطب
moisten raṭṭab رطّب (tarṭiib); layyan ليّن (liyyeen); balla بلّ (i, balla)
moisture ruṭuuba رطوبة ; balal بلل ; liin لين
molar ḍiris/ḍurus ضرس (*pl* ḍuruus, aḍraas)
molasses muulaaṣ مولاص ; ^casal gaṣab
mole (**spot on skin**) shaama شامة
moment laḥẓa لحظة ; **wait a moment** antaẓir dagiiga
monastery deer دير (*pl* adiira)
Monday yoom al-itneen
money guruush قروش ; nuquud نقود ; (**wealth**) maal مال (*pl* amwaal); **money order** ḥuwaala حوالة ; **money transfer** taḥwiil تحويل (*pl* -aat, taḥaawiil)
money box ḥaṣṣaala حصّالة
moneychanger ṣarraaf صرّاف
monitor *n* (**observer**) muraaqib مراقب • *v* raaqab راقب (muraaqaba)
monkey girid قرد (*pl* guruud)
monkey wrench muftaaḥ ingiliizi
monopolise iḥtakar احتكر (iḥtikaar)
monopoly iḥtikaar إحتكار (*pl* -aat)
month shahar شهر (*pl* shuhuur)

monthly *adj* shahri شهري • *adv* shahriyyan شهرياً
mood mazaaj مزاج (*pl* -aat); **a bad mood** mazaaj ʿakraan
moon gamar قمر (*pl* agmaar); **crescent moon** hilaal هلال ; **full moon** badur بدر (*pl* buduur); gamar arbaʿṭaashar
morale maʿnawiyyaat معنويّات
morals *n* akhlaaq أخلاق ; **bad morals** akhlaaq faasda; **of questionable morals** maṭluug مطلوق (*pl* maṭaaliig); **to lose one's morals** inṭamas انطمس (ṭamsa)
more ziyaada زيادة ; **more (than)** aktar (min) أكتر ; **once more** kamaan marra
moreover ziyaada ʿala zaalik
morgue mashraḥa مشرحة (*pl* mashaariḥ)
morning ṣabaaḥ صباح ; ṣubuḥ صبح ; ḍuḥa ضحا ; **early morning** dughush دغش ; baakriyya باكرية ; **late morning** ḍaḥwa ضحوة ; **in the morning** fi ṣ-ṣabaaḥ; ṣabaaḥan صباحاً ; **good morning** ṣabaaḥ al-kheer, ṣabaaḥ an-nuur
morsel lugma لقمة (*pl* lugam)
mortar **(for building)** muuna مونة ; **(for grinding)** funduk فندك (*pl* fanaadik); **(weapon)** mudfaʿ haawun
mortgage *n* rahn رهن (*pl* ruhuunaat) • *v* rahan رهن (a, rahin)
mortuary mashraḥa مشرحة (*pl* mashaariḥ)
mosque jaamiʿ جامع (*pl* jawaamiʿ); masjid مسجد (*pl* masaajid)
mosquito(es) baaʿuuḍ باعوض ; naamuus ناموس ; **mosquito net** naamuusiyya ناموسيّة ; **mosquito screening** namli نملي ; silik namli
most (of) muʿẓam معظم ; **the most** al-aktar
mother umm أم (*pl* -aat, ummahaat); waalda والدة ; **mother-in-law** nasiiba نسيبة ; ḥamaa حماة (*pl* ḥamawaat)
mother-of-pearl ṣadaf صدف
motion **(movement)** ḥaraka حركة
motive daafiʿ دافع (*pl* dawaafiʿ)
motorboat abu raffaas
motorcycle mootar موتر (*pl* mawaatir)
motto shiʿaar شعار (*pl* -aat)
mould gaalib قالب (*pl* gawaalib)
mount *v* rikib ركب (a, rukuub); **to be mounted** itrakab اتركب (rukuub)
mountain jabal جبل (*pl* jibaal)
mourn ḥadda حدّ (-i, ḥidaad)
mourning ḥadaad حداد ; ḥidd حد ; **(woman) in mourning** ḥaadda حادّة
mouse umm siisi; faar فار (*pl* fiiraan)
moustache shanab شنب (*pl* ashnaab, shunubba)
mouth khashum خشم (*pl* khushuum); gadduum قدّوم (*pl* gadaadiim)
mouthful lugma لقمة (*pl* lugam)
move *vi* itḥarrak اتحرّك (ḥaraka); **to move away** raḥal رحل (a, ruḥuul, raḥiil); **to move from place to place** itjawwal اتجوّل (tajawwul) • *vt* ḥarrak حرّك (ḥirreek, taḥriik); **to move aside** zaḥḥa زحّ (i, zaḥḥa, zaḥaḥaan); **to be moved aside** itzaḥḥa اتزحّ (zaḥḥa)

movement ḥaraka حركة
movie filim فيلم (*pl* aflaam)
much katiir كتير (*pl* kutaar); **how much** be-kam كم ; **much as** gadur ma
mucus mukhkhaata مخاتة (*pl* makhaakhiit)
mud ṭiin طين (*pl* aṭyaan)
muddle *n* fawḍa فوضى ; jooṭa جوطة ; rabka ربكة ; lakhbaṭa لخبطة ; barjala برجلة • *v* (**disorder**) jaaṭ جاط (u, jooṭa); rabak ربك (i, rabka); lakhbaṭ لخبط (lakhbaṭa); barjal برجل (barjala); **to be muddled up** ijjaaṭ اجّاط (jooṭa); itrabak اتربك (rabka); itlakhbaṭ اتلخبط (lakhbaṭa); itbarjal اتبرجل (birjeel, barjala)
muddy *adj* ʿakraan عكران ; muʿakkar معكّر ; **to get muddy** itʿakkar اتعكّر (ʿikkeer) • *v* ʿakkar عكّر (ʿikkeer, taʿkiir)
mudguard rafraf رفرف (*pl* rafaarif)
muezzin mu'azzin مأزّن
mug mag مق (*pl* -aat); (**tin/steel**) kooz كوز (*pl* keezaan)
mule *n* baghal بغل (*pl* bighaal)
multicoloured mutʿaddid al-alwaan
multicultural mutʿaddid as-saqaafaat
multiple mutʿaddid متعدّد
multiply *vi* kitir كتر (a, katara) • *vt* (arithmetic) ḍarab ضرب (a, ḍarib)
multitude katara كترة
mumps abu ʿideelaat
municipality maḥalliyya محلّيّة ; baladiyya بلديّة
murder *n* katil كتل ; (**as revenge**) taṣfiya تصفية ; **premeditated murder** katil ʿamd • *v* katal كتل (u, katil); mawwat موّت (miwweet)
murderer kaatil كاتل
muscle ʿaḍala عضلة ; **muscle cramp** shadd fi l-ʿaḍala; shadd ʿaḍali
museum mathaf متحف (*pl* mataaḥif)
music muusiiqa موسيقا ; mizziiga مزّيقا (*pl* mazaaziig)
musician musiiqaar موسيقار ; musiiqi موسيقي (*pl* -yyiin)
musk misik مسك
Muslim muslim مسلم
muslin muusiliin موسلين
must laazim لازم ; lazam لزم (a, luzuum); ʿala على ; **you must go** laazim tamshi; yalzam tamshi; yalzam-ak tamshi; **you must finish this work** ʿalee-k takhalliṣ ash-shughul da
mustard (**ready**) mustarda مستردة ; (**seeds**) khardal خردل
mute *adj* abkam أبكم (*f* bakma, *pl* bukum, bukama)
mutineer mutmarrid متمرّد
mutiny tamarrud تمرّد
mutter (**in anger**) ṭanṭan طنطن (ṭanṭana)
mutton ḍaani ضاني ; laḥam ḍaani
mysterious ghaamiḍ غامض
mystic ṣuufi صوفي ; fagiir فقير (*pl* fugara)

N - n

nag *v* nagga نقّ (i, nigga); nagnag نقنق (nagnaga)
nail *n* (**metal**) musmaar مسمار (*pl* masaamiir); (**finger, toe**) ḍufur ضفر (*pl* aḍaafir, aḍaafreen) • *v* sammar سمّر (simmeer, tasmiir)
nail clipper ḍaffaara ضفّارة

naive saazij سازج
naivety sazaaja سزاجة
naked ʿaryaan عريان
name *n* isim إسم (*pl* asaami, asmaa) • *v* samma سمّى (-i, simaaya)
nameplate laafta لافتة (*pl* -aat, li-fat); yaafṭa يافطة (*pl* -aat, yifaṭ)
naming ceremony simaaya سماية
nap *n* ghafwa غفوة ; ghamḍa غمضة
napkin fuuṭa فوطة (*pl* fuwaṭ)
nappy ḥifaaḍ حفاض (*pl* -aat)
narcotic mukhaddir مخدّر (*pl* -aat)
narrow *adj* ḍayyig ضيّق
nastiness ghataata غتاتة
nasty ghatiit غتيت (*pl* ghutata); (**smell**) ʿafi
nation umma أمة (*pl* umam); (**populace**) shaʿb شعب (*pl* shuʿuub); **the United Nations** al-umam al-muttaḥida
national waṭani وطني ; qawmi قومي ; ahli أهلي
nationalism waṭaniyya وطنيّة
nationalistic waṭani وطني
nationality jinsiyya جنسيّة
native *adj* baladi بلدي ; maḥalli محلّي
natron ʿaṭruun عطرون
natural ṭabiiʿi طبيعي
naturally ṭabʿan طبعاً ; be-ṭ-ṭabʿ
nature (**natural world**) ṭabiiʿa طبيعة ; (**character**) ṭabiʿ طبع ; ṭabiiʿa طبيعة
naughtiness shagaawa شقاوة
naughty shagi شقي ; **a naughty child** sheeṭaan شيطان (*pl* shayaaṭiin); **to be(come) naughty** itshayṭan اتشيطن (shayṭana)
nausea ṭumaam طمام
nauseated I am nauseated baṭn-i ṭaamma

navel ṣurra صرة ; **navel orange(s)** burtukaan abu ṣ-ṣurra
navy al-quwwaat al-baḥriyya
near gariib (min/le-) قريب (*pl* -iin, guraab)
nearly *adv* gariib قريب ; **I have nearly finished** garrabta akhalliṣ
neat naḍiif نضيف
necessary ḍaruuri ضروري ; **it is necessary** laazim لازم ; **to be necessary** lazam لزم (a, luzuum)
necessity ḍaruura ضرورة ; luzuum لزوم ; **necessities** ḍaruuriyyaat ضروريّات ; lawaazim لوازم
neck ragaba رقبة (*pl* rugaab); **back of the neck** gafa قفا (*pl* agfiya)
neckband ṭoog طوق (*pl* aṭwaag)
necklace ʿigid عقد (*pl* ʿuguud); silsila سلسلة (*pl* salaasil)
necktie karafitta كرفتّة
need *n* ḥawja حوجة ; iḥtiyaaj إحتياج (*pl* -aat) • *v* iḥtaaj le- إحتاج (iḥtiyaaj)
needle ibra إبرة (*pl* ibar); **large needle** masalla مسلّة ; ishfa إشفة (*pl* ishaf); **knitting needle** ishfa إشفة (*pl* ishaf)
needy muḥtaaj محتاج ; ṣarmaan صرمان
neem (**tree**) niim نيم
negative *adj* salbi سلبي • *n* nafi نفي ; (**of a film**) ʿafriita عفريتة (*pl* -aat, ʿafaariit)
neglect *n* hamala هملة ; ihmaal إهمال • *v* hamal همل (i, ihmaal, hamala)
negligence hamla هملة ; ihmaal إهمال
negligent muhmil مهمل
neigh ṣahal صهل (a, ṣahiil)
neighbour jaar جار (*pl* jeeraan)

neighbourhood juwaar جوار ; (**district**) ḥayy حي (*pl* aḥyaa); **in the neighbourhood** fi j-juwaar
neighbourliness jiira جيرة
neither la لا ; **neither this...nor that** la da...la daak/la da...wa-la daak
neon naaylon نايلون ; niyoon نيون ; **neon light** lambat naaylon; lambat niyoon; **neon tube** shamᶜa شمعة
nephew (**son of brother**) wad akhu; (**son of sister**) wad ukhut
nerve ᶜaṣab عصب (*pl* aᶜṣaab)
nervous ᶜaṣabi عصبي ; **to be(come) nervous** itwattar اتوتّر (tawattur)
nervousness ᶜaṣabiyya عصبيّة
nest *n* ᶜushsh عش (*pl* ᶜashaash) • *v* ᶜashshash عشّش (ᶜishsheesh)
net *n* shabaka شبكة (*pl* -aat, shibak, shibaak) • *v* shabbak شبّك (shibbeek)
Netherlands the Netherlands hulanda هولندا ; al-araaḍi al-munkhafiḍa
netting shabak شبك ; (**mosquito**) silik namli; namli نملي ; (**chicken wire**) silik araanib
network *n* (**group of people, computer**) shabaka شبكة (*pl* -aat) • *v* shabbak شبّك (tashbiik)
networking tashbiik تشبيك (*pl* -aat)
neutral muḥaayid محايد
never abadan أبدا
nevertheless maᶜa zaalik
new jadiid جديد (*pl* judaad); ḥadiis حديس
news khabar خبر (*pl* akhbaar); **news broadcast** nashra نشرة (*pl* -aat, nasharaat); **the news** (**in the media**) al-akhbaar; **good news** bushaara بشارة (*pl* -aat, bashaayir); bushra saara; **to give good news to** bashshar be- بشّر (bushaara)
newspaper jariida جريدة (*pl* jaraayid); ṣaḥiifa صحيفة (*pl* ṣuḥuf)
next (**in time**) jaay جاي ; (**in space**) jamb جمب ; janb جنب
nibble *v* garam قرم (u, garim); garaḍ قرض (u, gariḍ); garraḍ قرّض (girreeḍ)
nice ẓariif ظريف (*pl* -iin, ẓuraaf, ẓurafa); (**humans**) laṭiif لطيف (*pl* -iin, luṭaaf); (**things**) ḥilu حلو (*f* ḥilwa)
nickname mushkaar مشكار ; laqab لقب (*pl* alqaab)
niece (**daughter of sister**) bitt ukhut; (**daughter of brother**) bitt akhu
night *adj* layli ليلي • *n* leela ليلة (*pl* -aat, layaali); **at night** be-l-leel; **to spend the night** baat بات (i, beeta, bayataan); bayyat بيّت (bayataan, mabiit)
nightgown gamiiṣ noom
nightingale(s) bulbul بلبل (*pl* balaabil)
nightjar (**bird**) ḥamad labad
nightmare kaabuus كابوس (*pl* kawaabiis); kabbaas كبّاس (*pl* kabaabiis); abu kabbaas
Nile al-baḥar; an-niil; **the Blue Nile** an-niil al-azrag; **the White Nile** an-niil al-abyaḍ
nine tisᶜa تسعة ; **nine hundred** tusᶜumiyya تسعميّة
nineteen tisᶜaṭaashar تسعطاشر
ninety tisᶜiin تسعين
ninth taasiᶜ تاسع

nipple ḥalamat shaṭur
nit(s) ṣawaab صواب
no la لا ; **no way** abadan أبدا ; ma fii ṭariiga
noble *adj* shariif شريف (*pl* ashraaf, shurafa)
nobody wala waaḥid
nod *v* hazza ar-raas (i, hazz)
noise ṣoot صوت (*pl* aṣwaat); **loud noise** ḍajja ضجّة ; ḍajiij ضجيج ; karkaba كركبة
noisy to be noisy ḍajja ضجّ (i, ḍajj, ḍajja, ḍajiij); jaḍḍa جضّ (i, jaḍḍ, jaḍḍa); karkab كركب (karkaba)
nomad ʿarabi عربي (*pl* ʿarab); **nomads** ruḥḥal رحّل ; ʿarab عرب ; ʿarab sayyaara
nominate rashshaḥ رشّح (tarshiiḥ, tarashshuḥ); **to be nominated** itrashshaḥ اترشّح (tarashshuḥ)
nominee murashshaḥ مرشّح
non-conductor ʿaazil عازل (*pl* ʿawaazil)
nonexistent maʿduum معدوم
non-governmental gheer ḥakuumi
nonsense kalaam faarigh; kalaam saakit; kalaam saay; kalaam faaḍi; kalaam khaarim baarim; **to talk nonsense** kharraf خرّف (khirreef)
noon ḍuhur ضهر
normal ʿaadi عادي
north shimaal شمال
northern shimaali شمالي
northerner (of Sudan) shimaali شمالي (*pl* -yyiin)
northwards be-sh-shimaal
Norway an-nirweej
Norwegian *adj/n* nirweeji نرويجي (*pl* -yyiin)
nose nakhara نخرة (*pl* -aat, nikhreen); nikhreen نخرين ; manaakhreen مناخرين
nosebag mukhlaaya مخلاية
nosebleed *n* riʿaaf رعاف
nostril nakhara نخرة (*pl* -aat, nikhreen)
not ma ما ; **certainly not** abadan أبدا ; **not even** wala ḥata
note *n* **(reminder)** muzakkira مزكّرة ; **musical note** noota musiiqiyya • *v* dawwan دوّن (tadwiin); sajjal سجّل (tasjiil); katab كتب (i, kitaaba)
notebook noota نوتة (*pl* nuwat); daftar دفتر (*pl* dafaatir)
nothing wa-la ḥaaja
notice *n* iʿlaan إعلان (*pl* -aat); muzakkira مزكّرة ; bayaan بيان (*pl* -aat); ifaada إفادة • *v* laaḥaẓ لاحظ (mulaaḥaẓa)
notice-board looḥat iʿlaan
notification iʿlaan إعلان (*pl* -aat); bayaan بيان (*pl* -aat); ifaada إفادة
notify ballagh بلّغ (billeegh)
noun isim إسم ; **verbal noun** maṣdar مصدر
novel *n* riwaaya رواية
November shahri ḥidaashar; nofembar نوفمبر
now hassaʿ هسّع ; hassi هسّي ; ḥassa حسّا ; ḥassi حسّي
numb khadraan خدران ; **to be(come) numb** khidir خدر (a, khadar, khadaraan)
number nimra نمرة (*pl* nimar); raqam رقم (*pl* arqaam); **(amount)** ʿadad عدد (*pl* aʿdaad)
number plate nimra نمرة (*pl* nimar)
numbness khadar خدر
nun raahba راهبة (*pl* raahibaat)
nurse *n* (*m*) mumarriḍ ممرّض ; (*f*) mumarriḍa ممرّضة ; **(for children)** daada دادة

nurse *v* (**breastfeed**) raḍḍaᶜ رضع (a, riḍḍeeᶜ, riḍaaᶜa)
nursery (**for plants**) mashtal مشتل (*pl* mashaatil); (**for toddlers**) ḥaḍaana حضانة ; **nursery school** rawḍa روضة
nut (**of a bolt**) ṣaamuula صامولة (*pl* ṣawaamiil)
nutmeg jooz aṭ-ṭiib
nutrition ghiza غزا (*pl* aghziya); taghziya تغزية
nutritious ghizaaʾi غزائي
nylon naaylon نايلون

O - o

oar mijdaaf مجداف (*pl* majaadiif)
oasis waaḥa واحة
oath ḥaliifa حليفة (*pl* ḥalaayif); qasam قسم ; yamiin يمين (*pl* -aat); **to take an oath** ḥalaf حلف (i, ḥalafaan); qasam قسم (i, qasam); aqsam أقسم (i, qasam)
oats shoofaan شوفان
obedient muṭiiᶜ مطيع ; ṭaayiᶜ طايع
obese samiin سمين (*pl* sumaan); shaḥmaan شحمان
obesity sumun سمن
obey simiᶜ al-kalaam; ṭaaᶜ طاع (i, ṭaaᶜa); ṭaawaᶜ طاوع (muṭaawaᶜa)
object *n* ḥaaja حاجة ; shii شي (*pl* ashyaa)
object *v* iᶜtaraḍ (ᶜala) إعترض (iᶜtiraaḍ)
objection iᶜtiraaḍ إعتراض (*pl* -aat); **there is no objection** ma fii maaniᶜ
objective *n* hadaf هدف (*pl* ahdaaf); gaṣid قصد (*pl* agṣaad); gharaḍ غرض (*pl* aghraaḍ)
obligation waajib واجب (*pl* -aat); fariḍ فرض (*pl* furuuḍ); **under obligation** mulzim ملزم ; **he has obligations** ᶜind-o irtibaaṭaat
obligatory ilzaami الزامي
obscure *adj* ghaamiḍ غامض
observation (**comment**) mulaaḥaẓa ملاحظة ; (**watching**) muraaqaba مراقبة ; (**meteorological**) irṣaad jawwiyya
observe raaqab راقب (muraaqaba)
observer muraaqib مراقب
obstacle ᶜaariḍ عارض (*pl* ᶜawaariḍ); maaniᶜ مانع (*pl* mawaaniᶜ)
obstinacy guwwat raas; mukaajara مكاجرة ; ᶜinaad عناد
obstinate ghashiim غشيم ; mukaajir مكاجر ; ᶜaniid عنيد ; **he is obstinate** raas-o gawwi; **to be obstinate** kaajar كاجر (mukaajara); ᶜaanad عاند (muᶜaanada)
obstruction ᶜaariḍ عارض (*pl* ᶜawaariḍ); maaniᶜ مانع (*pl* mawaaniᶜ)
obtain ḥaṣal ᶜala حصل (a, ḥuṣuul); ḥaṣṣal ᶜala حصّل (ḥiṣṣeel, taḥṣiil)
occasion furṣa فرصة (*pl* furaṣ); (**special**) munaasaba مناسبة
occasionally marraat مرّات ; saaᶜaat ساعات ; aḥyaanan أحيانا
occupation (**of a country**) iḥtilaal إحتلال
occupation (**job**) waẓiifa وظيفة (*pl* waẓaayif); (**professional**) mihna مهنة (*pl* mihan); shughul شغل (*pl* ashghaal)
occupy (**a country**) iḥtalla احتلّ (iḥtilaal)
occupy (**of work, mind**) shaghal شغل (a, shaghala); (**of space**)

shaghal شغل (a, shaghil); **to be occupied (by)** itshaghal (be-) اتشغل (shaghala)

occupied mashghuul مشغول

occur ḥaṣal حصل (a, ḥuṣuul); ḥadas حدس (u, ḥadas)

ocean muḥiiṭ محيط (*pl* -aat); **the Pacific Ocean** al-muḥiiṭ al-haadi; **the Atlantic Ocean** al-muḥiiṭ al-aṭlanṭi; **the Indian Ocean** al-muḥiiṭ al-hindi

October shahri ᶜashara; uktoobar أكتوبر

odd (of numbers) fardi فردي; **(different)** mukhtalif مختلف; **(weird)** ᶜajiib عجيب; ghariib غريب

oedema zulaali زلالي

oesophagus balᶜuum بلعوم; al-marii'

offence (affront) isaa'a اساءة; **(verbally or physically)** taᶜaddi تعدّي (*pl* -yyaat); **(crime)** janiyya جنيّة; jariima جريمة (*pl* jara-ayim); **capital offence** jinaaya جناية; **to commit an offence** irtakab janiyya/jariima/jinaaya

offend (affront) asaa le- اسا (yu-sii, isaa'a); **(verbally or physically)** khita ᶜala ختا (-i, khata, khatiya); khiṭa خطا (-i, khaṭa, khaṭiya); ghiliṭ fi/ᶜala غلط (a, ghalaṭ); itᶜadda ᶜala اتعدّى (-a, taᶜaddi); jana ᶜala جنى (-i, jani-yya, jinaaya, tajanni)

offer *n* ᶜariḍ عرض (*pl* ᶜuruuḍ) • *v* gaddam قدّم (tagdiim); ᶜaraḍ le- عرض (i, ᶜariḍ)

office maktab مكتب (*pl* makaatib)

officer ḍaabiṭ ضابط (*pl* ḍubbaaṭ); ẓaabiṭ ظابط (*pl* ẓubbaaṭ)

official *adj* rasmi رسمي • *n* muwaẓẓaf

often katiir كتير; marraat katiira

oil *n* zeet زيت (*pl* ziyuut); **corn/maize oil** zeet dura; **cotton-seed oil** zeet bizra; zeet fahad; **groundnut oil** zeet fuul; **crude oil** nafṭi نفطي; nafṭ نفط; bitrool khaam; **oil lamp** ratiina رتينة (*pl* rataayin); faanuus فانوس (*pl* fawaaniis) • *v* zayyat زيّت (ziyyeet, tazyiit)

oilcloth mashammaᶜ مشمّع (*pl* -aat)

ointment marham مرهم (*pl* maraahim); masḥa مسحة

okay ṭayyib طيّب; samiḥ سمح

okra baamya بامية; **dried okra powder** weeka ويكة

old (humans) ᶜajuuz عجوز (*pl* ᶜajaayiz); kabiir كبير (*pl* kubaar); **(of inanimate things)** gadiim قديم (*pl* gudaam); **old age** kubur كبر; sheykhuukha شيخوخة; **to grow old** ᶜajjaz عجّز (ᶜijjeez); kibir كبر (a, kubur); **to be(come) old (of things)** gidim قدم (a, gudum)

olive(s) zeetuun زيتون; **olive oil** zeet zeetuun

omen ishaara إشارة; **bad omen** shuum شوم; **good omen** faal فال

on (place) foog فوق; ᶜala على; **(time)** fi في

once marra waaḥda; **once more** marra taanya; marra taani; ka-maan marra; **once upon a time** marra min al-marraat; gadiim az-zamaan

one waaḥid واحد; waaḥda واحدة; **one by one** ḥabba ḥabba; **one of a pair** farda فردة (*pl* -aat, firad)

one-eyed aᶜwar أعور (*f* ᶜawra, *pl* ᶜuwur)

onion(**s**) baṣal بصل (*unit n* baṣala, baṣalaaya)
only *adj* waḥiid وحيد • *adv* bass بس
ooze nazza نزّ (i, nazz)
open *adj* faatiḥ فاتح ; maftuuḥ مفتوح • *v* fataḥ فتح (a, fatiḥ); (**a ceremony**) iftataḥ افتتح (iftitaaḥ); **to be opened** infataḥ انفتح (infitaaḥ, fatiḥ); itfataḥ اتفتح (fatiḥ)
opening (**aperture**) fatḥa فتحة ; (**of ceremony**) iftitaaḥ افتتاح (*pl* -aat)
open-minded mutfattiḥ متفتّح
operation ʿamaliyya عمليّة
operational saari ساري
opinion raay راي (*pl* aaraa); ra'y رأي (*pl* araa'); ruu'ya رؤية
opium afyuun أفيون
opponent khaṣiim خصيم (*pl* khuṣama); khiṣm خصم (*pl* khuṣuum); khaṣim خصم (*pl* khuṣuum)
opportunity furṣa فرصة (*pl* furaṣ); **to take the opportunity** intahaz al-furṣa
oppose ʿaaraḍ عارض (muʿaaraḍa); daaḍḍa داضّ (-i, mudaaḍḍa); ʿaakas عاكس (muʿaakasa)
opposite *prep* guṣaad قصاد ; muwaajih مواجه • *adj* muʿaakis معاكس ; muwaajih مواجه • *n* ʿaks عكس
opposition muʿaaraḍa معارضة
oppress ẓalam ظلم (u, ẓulum)
oppressor ẓaalim ظالم (*pl* -iin, ẓalama)
optician diktoor ʿiyuun
optimist mutfaa'il متفائل
optimistic mutfaa'il متفائل
or wa-la ولا
orange *adj* burtukaani برتكاني
orange(**s**) *n* burtukaan برتكان ; **navel orange**(**s**) burtukaan abu ṣ-ṣurra
orchard jineena جنينة (*pl* janaayin)
order *n* (**arrangement**) tartiib ترتيب (*pl* -aat); (**system**) niẓaam نظام (*pl* nuẓum); (**regularity**) intiẓaam إنتظام ; **to put in order** naẓẓam نظّم (niẓẓeem, tanẓiim); rattab رتّب (ritteeb, tartiib); ḍaayar ضاير (muḍaayara); waḍḍab وضّب (wiḍḍeeb, tawḍiib); **to be put in order** itnaẓẓam اتنظّم (niẓẓeem, tanẓiim); itrattab اترتّب (ritteeb, tartiib); iḍḍaayar إضّاير (muḍaayara); itwaḍḍab اتوضّب (wiḍḍeeb, tawḍiib); (**items**) raṣṣa رصّ (u, raṣṣ); **out of order** baayiẓ بايظ ; khasraan خسران ; muʿaṭṭal معطّل ; ʿaṭlaan عطّلان ; kharbaan خربان • *conj* **in order to** ʿashaan عشان
order *n* (**command**) amr أمر (*pl* awaamir); (**in a restaurant**) ṭalab طلب (*pl* -aat); ṭalabiyya طلبيّة • *v* (**command**) amar (be-) أمر (ya'mur, amr); (**in a restaurant**) ṭalab طلب (u, ṭalab)
orderly *adj* munaẓẓam منظّم ; murattab مرتّب • *n* nabatshi نبتشي (*pl* -yya)
ordinary ʿaadi عادي
organization tanẓiim تنظيم (*pl* -aat); (**corporation**) hay'a هيئة ; (**institution**) munaẓẓama منظّمة ; **non-governmental organization** munaẓẓama gheer ḥakuumiyya; **non-profit organization** munaẓẓama gheer ribḥiyya; (**society**) jamʿiyya جمعيّة ; **community-based organization** jamʿiyya qaaʿidiyya

organize naẓẓam نظّم (niẓẓeem, tanẓiim); **to be organized** itnaẓẓam إتنظّم (niẓẓeem, tanẓiim)
origin aṣil أصل (*pl* uṣuul); (**ethnicity**) jinis جنس (*pl* ajnaas); ʿirig عرق (*pl* ʿuruug)
original *adj* aṣli أصلي ; aṣiil أصيل • *n* nuskha aṣliyya
ornament ziina زينة
orphan yatiim يتيم (*pl* yutama)
orphanage malja yutama
oryx(es) bagar al-waḥsh
ostrich(es) naʿaam نعام
other taani تاني ; **other than** gheer- غير ; khilaaf- خلاف
ounce wagiyya وقيّة
outcome natiija نتيجة (*pl* nataay-ij); ḥaṣiila حصيلة (*pl* ḥaṣaayil); **negative outcome** ʿaagiba عاقبة (*pl* ʿawaagib)
outing fusḥa فسحة (*pl* fusaḥ); riḥla رحلة (*pl* -aat, riḥal); **to go on an outing** itfassaḥ اتفسّح (fusḥa, fisseeḥ)
outlaw balṭaji بلطجي (*pl* -yya); ʿaṣbaji عصبجي (*pl* -yya)
output ḥaṣiila حصيلة (*pl* ḥaṣaayil)
outside barra برا ; khaarij خارج
ovary mabyaḍ مبيض (*pl* mabaayiḍ)
oven furun فرن (*pl* afraan)
over foog فوق ; **over here** be-jaay; **over there** be-ghaadi
overalls abarool ابرول (*pl* -aat); ʿafriita عفريتة (*pl* -aat, ʿafaariit)
overcoat balṭo بالطو (*pl* -haat)
overcome ghalab غلب (i, ghulub); intaṣar (ʿala) انتصر (intiṣaar)
overflow (**e.g. of a vessel**) daffag دفّق (diffeeg); (**e.g. of a drain**) ṭafaḥ طفح (a, tafiḥ); (**river**) faaḍ فاض (i, fayaḍaan)
overseer mulaaḥiẓ ملاحظ ; mu-raaqib مراقب
overtake ʿadda عدّى (-i, ʿiddeey); faat فات (u, foota, fawataan); itkhaṭṭa اتخطّى (-a, takhaṭṭi)
overthrow *n* ingilaab إنقلاب (*pl* -aat) • *v* **to be overthrown** ingalab انقلب (ingilaab)
overtime zaman iḍaafi
overturn shaglab شقلب (shigleeb, shaglabaan); shangal شنقل (shingeel, shangala); **to be over-turned** itshaglab اتشقلب (shi-gleeb, shaglaba)
owe **I owe him** ana madyuun lee-ho; hu mudayyin-ni; hu ṭaalib-ni
owl(s) buum بوم
own *v* imtalak امتلك (imtilaak); malak ملك (i, milik)
owner (**male**) maalik مالك (*pl* mul-laak); siid سيد (*pl* asyaad); ṣaaḥib صاحب (*pl* aṣḥaab); (**female**) sitt ست (*pl* -aat); ṣaaḥba صاحبة
ownership milkiyya ملكيّة ; (**of land**) ḥikir حكر (*pl* aḥkaar)
ox toor تور (*pl* teeraan)
oxidize ṣaggar صقّر (ṣiggeer); itṣadda اتصدّى (-a, ṣiddeey, ṣadiya); ṣadda صدّى (-i, ṣiddeey, ṣadiya)
oxygen uksijiin أكسجين

P - p

pace (**step**) shabḥa شبحة ; (**tempo**) surʿa سرعة
pacify hadda هدّى (-i, hiddeey, tahdiya); sakkat سكّت (sikkeet)

pack *n* (**knapsack**) bugja بقجة (*pl* bugaj) • *v* sattaf ستّف (sitteef, tastiif)
package *n* ṭarid طرد (*pl* ṭuruud)
packaging taghliif تغليف
packet *n* baako باكو (*pl* baakwaat, bawaaki)
pact ḥilf حلف (*pl* aḥlaaf)
padlock ṭabla طبلة (*pl* ṭibal)
paediatrician diktoor aṭfaal
page *n* (**of book**) ṣafḥa صفحة (*pl* ṣafaḥaat)
pail jardal جردل (*pl* jaraadil)
pain waj^c^a وجعة *n* (*pl* -aat, awjaa^c^); alam ألم (*pl* aalaam); **abdominal pain** maghaṣ مغص; waja^c^ baṭun; **pain in the back** gaṭii^c^a fi ḍ-ḍahar; **to have pain** it'allam اتألّم (alam); **having generalised pain** maraḍraḍ مرضرض
painful ḥaarr حار; mu'lim مؤلم
painkiller musakkin مسكّن (*pl* -aat)
paint *n* buuhya بوهية; dihaan دهان • *v* (**a picture**) rasam رسم (u, rasim); (**building**) nagash نقش (u, nigaasha); ḍarab buuhya
painter rassaam رسّام; **house painter** naggaash نقّاش
painting (**picture**) looḥa لوحة; (**of house**) nigaasha نقاشة
pair *n* jooz جوز (*pl* ajwaaz); **one of a pair** farda فردة (*pl* -aat, firad)
palace gaṣur قصر (*pl* guṣuur); saraaya سرايا (*pl* -aat)
pale baahit باهت; (**of skin**) shaaḥib شاحب; makhtuuf al-loon
pallor shuḥuub شحوب
palm (**of hand**) kaff كفّ (*pl* kufuuf); raaḥat al-yadd/al-iid
palm(s) **date palm(s)** nakhal نخل (*unit n* nakhla); nakhiil نخيل (*unit n* nakhla); **doleib palm(s)** daleeb دليب; **doum palm(s)** doom دوم (*unit n* dooma, doomaaya); **palm branch(es)** jariid جريد; **palm fibre** sa^c^af سعف (*unit n* sa^c^fa); liif ليف
palpitation ziyaada fi ḍarbaat al-galib
pamper dalla^c^ دلّع (dala^c^); dallal دلّل (dalaal); **to be pampered** iddalla^c^ ادّلّع (dala^c^)
pamphlet manshuur منشور (*pl* -aat, manaashiir)
pan ḥalla حلّة (*pl* ḥilal); burma برمة (*pl* buraam); **cake pan** gaalib قالب (*pl* gawaalib); **frying pan** ṭawwa طوّة (*pl* ṭiwaw)
pant lahas لهس (a, lahis, lahasaan); nahad نهد (a, nahid)
papaya baabaay باباي
paper warag ورق; **sheet of paper** waraga ورقة (*pl* -aat, awraag); (**a written paper**) waraga ورقة (*pl* -aat, awraag)
paperclip dabbuus mashbak
parachute barashoot برشوت (*pl* -aat); maẓalla مظلّة
parade isti^c^raaḍ إستعراض (*pl* -aat); (**military**) ṭaabuur طابور (*pl* ṭawaabiir)
paradise janna جنّة; firdoos فردوس
paraffin jaaz جاز; jaaz abyaḍ; **paraffin lamp** ratiina رتينة (*pl* rataayin); faanuus فانوس (*pl* fawaaniis)
paragraph faqra فقرة
parallel muḥaazi محازي; muwaazi موازي; **to run parallel to** ḥaaza حازى (-i, muḥaazaa, ḥiza); waaza وازى (-i, muwaazaa)
paralysis shalal شلل

paralyse shalla شلّ (i, shalal); **paralysed** mashluul مشلول ; **to be(come) paralysed** itshalla اتشلّ (shalal)

parasite ṭufayli طفيلي (*pl* -yyaat)

parasol shamsiyya شمسيّة (*pl* shamaasi); maẓalla مظلّة

parcel ṭarid طرد (*pl* ṭuruud)

pardon *n* ᶜafu عفو ; iᶜfaa إعفاء ; samaaḥ سماح ; **I beg your pardon?** naᶜam نعم ; **I beg your pardon** al-ᶜafu • *v* ᶜafa le- عفى (-i, ᶜafu); saamaḥ سامح (musaamaḥa)

parenthesis qoos قوس (*pl* aqwaas); **in parentheses** beenqooseen

parents waalideen والدين

park *n* ḥadiiga حديقة (*pl* ḥadaayig); **amusement park** malaahi ملاهي

park *v* rakan ركن (i, rakin)

parliament barlamaan برلمان (*pl* -aat); majlis ash-shaᶜb; **member of parliament** naa'ib نائب (*pl* nuwwaab); naayib نايب (*pl* nuwwaab)

parrot baghbaghaan بغبغان (*pl* -aat)

parsley bagduunis بقدونس

part *n* juzu جزو (*pl* azjaa); (**side**) jaanib جانب (*pl* jawaanib, aj-naab) • *v* faarag فارق (furaag, mufaaraga); (**disjoin**) fakka فكّ (i, fakk, fakakaan)

partial juz'i جزئي ; (**prejudiced**) mutḥayyiz متحيّز ; munḥaaz منحاز

participant mushaarik مشارك

participate shaarak fi شارك (mush-aaraka)

participation mushaaraka مشاركة

particular muᶜayyan معيّن ; **in particular** be-z-zaat; be-ṣifa khaaṣṣa; khaaṣṣatan خاصّة

particularly be-z-zaat; khaaṣṣatan خاصّة ; khuṣuuṣan خصوصاً

particulars tafaaṣiil تفاصيل (*sg* tafṣiil)

partition faaṣil فاصل (*pl* fawaaṣil)

partner shariik شريك (*pl* shuraka)

partnership sharaaka شراكة ; **to enter into partnership** itshaarak maᶜa اتشارك (mushaaraka)

partridge(s) ḥijil حجل

party (**celebration**) ḥafla حفلة ; (**in dispute, contract**) ṭaraf طرف (*pl* aṭraaf); (**in a lawsuit**) khaṣim خصم (*pl* khuṣuum); khiṣm خصم (*pl* khuṣuum); **political party** ḥizib حزب (*pl* aḥzaab)

pass *vt* (**an exam**) marra (fi) مرّ (u, muruur); (**an object**) adda أدّى (-i, iddeey); (**a ball**) marrar مرّر (tamriir); (**approve**) waafag ᶜala وافق (muwaafaga); ṣaadag ᶜala صادق (muṣaadaga); (**overtake**) ᶜadda عدّى (-i, ᶜiddeey); faat فات (u, foota, fawataan); itkhaṭṭa اتخطّى (-a, takhaṭṭi) • *vi* marra مرّ (u, muruur); **to pass away** itwaffa اتوفّى (-a, wafa, wafaa); **to pass by** (**go past**) marra be-/ᶜala مرّ (u, muruur); **to pass by at** ghi-sha غشى (-a, ghashwa, ghashay-aan); marra ᶜala مرّ (u, muruur); **to pass over** faṭṭa فطّ (u, faṭṭ); fawwat فوّت (fiwweet, tafwiit)

passage mamarr ممر (*pl* -aat)

passenger raakib راكب (*pl* ruk-kaab); musaafir مسافر

passion ᶜishig عشق ; lawᶜa لوعة

passport jawaaz جواز (*pl* -aat); jawaaz as-safar; basboor بسبور (*pl* -taat, basaabiir)

past (**the past**) al-maaḍi; **past tense** al-maaḍi

pasta makaroona مكرونة
pastor raa^ci راعي (*pl* ru^{cc}aa)
pastry (**sweet**) baaṣta باسطة ; (**varieties of**) faṭiira فطيرة (*pl* faṭaayir); basbuusa بسبوسة ; kunaafa كنافة ; **pastry shop** ḥalawaani حلواني
pastry cook ḥalawaani حلواني (*pl* -yyiin)
pasture marᶜa مرعى (*pl* maraaᶜi)
pat *v* ṭabṭab ᶜala طبطب (ṭabṭaba, ṭibṭeeb)
patch *n* rugᶜa رقعة (*pl* rugaᶜ); (**on shoe**) nugla نقلة (*pl* nugal) • *v* raggaᶜ رقّع (riggeeᶜ); ragaᶜ رقع (a, ragiᶜ)
patent *n* baraa'at ikhtiraaᶜ
path darib درب (*pl* duruub); shaariᶜ شارع (*pl* shawaariᶜ)
patience ṣabur صبر
patient *adj* ṣabuur صبور ; ṣaabir صابر ; **to be patient** ṣabar صبر (u, ṣabur)
patient *n* mariiḍ مريض (*pl* marḍa)
patrol *n* dawriyya دوريّة ; ṭoof طوف (*pl* aṭwaaf)
pattern (**style**) namaṭ نمط (*pl* anmaaṭ)
paunch karish كرش (*pl* kuruush)
pause *n* wagfa وقفة ; (**break, rest**) raaḥa راحة ; istiraaḥa إستراحة • *v* wagaf وقف (yagiif, wuguuf)
pavement (**sidewalk**) raṣiif رصيف (*pl* arṣifa)
pavilion ṣeewaan صيوان (*pl* -aat)
paw kuraaᶜ كراع (*pl* kurᶜeen); rijil رجل (*pl* rijleen)
pawn *v* rahan رهن (a, rahin)
pawpaw baabaay باباي
pay *n* maahiyya ماهيّة (*pl* mawaahi); murattab مرتّب (*pl* -aat); raatib راتب (*pl* rawaatib); **pay rise** ᶜalaawa علاوة • *v* dafaᶜ دفع (a, dafiᶜ); **to be paid** iddafaᶜ ادّفع (dafiᶜ); (**of debt**) itsaddad اتسدّد (sadaad); **to make s.o. pay** daffaᶜ دفّع (diffeeᶜ)
payment dafiᶜ دفع (*pl* dafᶜiyyaat); **down payment** mugaddam مقدم ; ᶜarbuun عربون (*pl* ᶜaraabiin)
payroll kashf al-ujuur
peace salaam سلام ; **peace of mind** raaḥt al-baal; **to make peace between** ṣaalaḥ صالح (muṣaalaḥa); aṣlaḥ been اصلح (yuṣliḥ, ṣuluḥ)
peaceful silmi سلمي ; (**person**) musaalim مسالم
peacemaker muṣliḥ مصلح
peanut(s) fuul suudaani; **peanut butter** dakwa دكوة
pearl(s) luuli لولي (*unit n* luuliyya)
peas bisilla بسلّة
pebble(s) ḥaṣḥaaṣ حصحاص (*unit n* ḥaṣaaya, ḥaṣḥaaṣaaya)
peck *v* (**of a bird**) nagad نقد (u, nagid)
pedal baddaal بدّال (*pl* -aat)
pedestrians mushaa مشاة
pedigree nasab نسب (*pl* ansaab); shajarat an-nasab
pedlar sabbaabi سبّابي (*pl* sabbaaba); tashshaashi تشّاشي (tashshaasha)
peel *n* gishra قشرة (*pl* gushuur) • *vt* gashshar قشّر (gishsheer, tagshiir) • *vi* itgashshar اتقشّر (gishsheer); (**skin**) itfasakh إتفسخ (faskha, fasakhaan)
peer *n* (**same age**) nadiid نديد (*pl* andaad, nadada)
peg barabandi بربندي (*pl* -yyaat); (**hook**) ᶜallaaga علاقة ; (**in**

ground) witid وتد (*pl* awtaad); (**of stringed instrument**) ṣubaaᶜ صباع (*pl* -aat)
pelican(**s**) bajaᶜ بجع (*unit n* bajᶜa)
pelvis ḥooḍ حوض
pen *n* (**for writing**) galam قلم (*pl* aglaam)
pen *n* (**for animals**) zariiba زريبة (*pl* zaraayib) • *v* (**animals**) ḥaash حاش (u, ḥayashaan, ḥoosha)
penalty ᶜuquuba عقوبة ; ᶜiqaab عقاب ; **the death penalty** al-ḥukum be-l-iᶜdaam; (**in football**) bilenti بلنتي (*pl* -iyyaat)
penance takfiir تكفير ; kaffaara كفّارة ; **to do penance** kaffar كفّر (takfiir, kaffaara)
pencil galam raṣṣaaṣ; **pencil sharpener** barraaya براية
penetrate ikhtarag اخترق (ikhtiraag)
penis ḍakar ضكر (*pl* ḍukuur)
penknife maṭwa مطوى (*pl* maṭaawi)
penniless mufallis مفلّس ; muflis مفلس ; **to be**(**come**) **penniless** fallas فلّس (tafliis)
penny girish قرش (*pl* guruush)
pension (**after retirement**) maᶜaash معاش (*pl* -aat); (**guesthouse**) lakonda لكوندة
Pentecost ᶜiid al-ᶜansara; ᶜiid al-khamsiin
people naas ناس (*sg* insaan); (**populace**) shaᶜb شعب (*pl* shuᶜuub); **country people** naas al-balad; ahl al-balad
pepper **black pepper** filfil aswad; **sweet pepper**(**s**) filfil فلفل (*unit n* filfiliyya); **hot pepper**(**s**) shaṭṭa شطّة
perch **Nile perch** ᶜijil عجل (*unit n* ᶜijla)
perfect tamaam تمام ; miyya miyya; tamaam at-tamaam
perforate gadda قدّ (i, giddeed); kharam خرم (u, kharim); kharram خرّم (khirreem, takhriim); gadgad قدقد (gadgada)
perform (**in job**) adda أدّى (ya'addi, adaa); (**on stage**) massal مسّل (tamsiil)
performance (**in job**) adaa ادا ; (**show**) ᶜariḍ عرض (*pl* ᶜuruuḍ); (**theatrical**) tamsiiliyya تمسيليّة ; masraḥiyya مسرحيّة
perfume *n* riiḥa ريحة (*pl* aryaaḥ, rawaayiḥ); ᶜiṭir عطر (*pl* ᶜuṭuur); (**homemade**) khumra خمرة • *v* rayyaḥ ريّح (riiḥa); ᶜaṭṭar عطّر (ᶜiṭṭeer, taᶜṭiir); **to perfume o.s.** itrayyaḥ اتريّح (riiḥa); itᶜaṭṭar اتعطّر (ᶜiṭṭeer, taᶜṭiir)
perhaps jaayiz جايز ; yajuuz يجوز ; yimkin يمكن
period mudda مدّة (*pl* -aat, mudad); fatra فترة (*pl* -aat, fataraat)
periodical *adj* dawri دوري • *n* dawriyya دوريّة ; majalla dawriyya
perjury ḥalafaan be-l-kiḍib; shihaadat zuur; yamiin zuur
permanent daayim دايم
permission izin إزن (*pl* uzuunaat); **to ask permission** ista'zan(min) استأزن (izin, isti'zaan)
permit *n* taṣriiḥ تصريح (*pl* taṣaariiḥ); rukhṣa رخصة (*pl* rukhaṣ); taṣdiig تصديق (*pl* -aat); **stay permit** taṣriiḥ iqaama; **to issue a permit** rakhkhaṣ رخّص (tarkhiiṣ) • *v* azan le- أزن (ya'zin, izin); samaḥ le- سمح (a, samaaḥ); ṣarraḥ le- صرّح (taṣriiḥ)

permitted (**by Islamic law**) ḥalaal حلال ; **to declare permitted under Islamic law** ḥallal حلّل (taḥliil)
persist aṣarra أصرّ (yuṣirr, iṣraar)
persistence ilḥaaḥ الحاح
persistent muliḥḥ ملح ; muṣirr مصر
person shakhṣ شخص (*pl* ashkhaaṣ); zool زول (*no pl*); (**when counting**) nafar نفر (*pl* anfaar); (**individual**) fard فرد (*pl* afraad)
personal shakhṣi شخصي
personality shakhṣiyya شخصيّة
personally shakhṣiyyan شخصيّاً
perspiration ʿarag عرق
persuade aqnaʿ أقنع (yuqniʿ, iqnaaʿ); **to be persuaded** iqtanaʿ إقتنع (iqtinaaʿ)
pessimist mutshaa'im متشائم
pessimistic mutshaa'im متشائم
pestle iid/yadd al-funduk; madagg مدق (*pl* -aat)
petition ʿariiḍa عريضة (*pl* ʿaraayiḍ)
petrol banziin بنزين ; **petrol station** ṭurumba طرمبة
petroleum bitrool بترول ; nafṭi نفطي ; nafṭ نفط
petticoat ginilla قنلّة
pharaoh farʿoon فرعون (*pl* faraaʿna)
pharaonic farʿooni فرعوني
pharmacist ṣaydali صيدلي (*pl* ṣayaadla)
pharmacy ajzakhaana أجزخانة ; ṣaydaliyya صيدليّة
phlegm balgham بلغم
phone *n* talafoon تلفون (*pl* -aat); **mobile phone** moobaayl موبايل (*pl* -aat); jawwaal جوّال (*pl* -aat); **phone booth** kabiina كبينة (kabaayin) • *v* ḍarab talafoon; ittaṣṣal be- اتّصل (ittiṣaal)
photocopier aalat taṣwiir
photocopy *n* nuskha نسخة (*pl* nusakh) • *v* nasakh نسخ (a, nasikh)
photograph *n* ṣuura صورة (*pl* ṣuwar) • *v* ṣawwar صوّر (taṣwiir); **to be photographed** itṣawwar اتصوّر (taṣwiir)
photographer muṣawwir مصوّر ; muṣawwiraati مصوّراتي
photography taṣwiir تصوير
physician diktoor دكتور (*pl* dakaatra); ṭabiib طبيب (*pl* aṭibba)
physics fiiziyya فيزيا
piastre girish قرش (*pl* guruush)
pick (**cotton, flowers**) laggaṭ لقّط (liggeeṭ, talgiiṭ); lagaṭ لقط (u, lagiṭ); **to pick up** shaal شال (i, sheel, sheela); (**a person**) akhad أخد (biyaakhud, akhid)
pickaxe ʿazma عزمة (*pl* izam); balṭa بلطة (*pl* -aat, balaaṭi); (**two-headed**) azma abu raaseen
pickle *n* mukhallal مخلّل (*pl* -aat) • *v* khallal خلّل (khilleel); **to be pickled** itkhallal اتخلّل (khilleel, takhallul)
pickpocket *n* nashshaal نشّال • *v* nashal نشل (i, nashil)
pickup (**truck**) boksi بكسي (*pl* bakaasi)
picnic *n* fusḥa فسحة (*pl* fusaḥ)
picture ṣuura صورة (*pl* ṣuwar); (**drawing**) rasim رسم (*pl* rusuumaat)
piebald argaṭ أرقط (*f* ragṭa, *pl* ruguṭ); muraggaṭ مرقّط
piece gitʿa قطعة (*pl* gitaʿ); juzu جزو (*pl* azjaa); ḥitta حتة (*pl* ḥitat);

(**item**) ḥabba حبّة ; ḥabbaaya حبّاية ; **to take to pieces** fakka فكّ (i, fakk, fakakaan); fartak فرتك (fartaka, firteek); **to be taken to pieces** itfakka اتفكّ (fakk, fakakaan); itfartak اتفرتك (firteek)
pierce gadda قدّ (i, giddeed); kharam خرم (i, kharim); kharram خرّم (khirreem, takhriim)
piety taqwa تقوة ; ṣalaaḥ صلاح
pig kadruuk كدروك (*pl* kadaariik); khanziir خنزير (*pl* khanaaziir)
pigeon(**s**) ḥamaam حمام ; **young pigeon** farikh al-ḥamaam
pile *n* koom كوم (*pl* kiimaan, akwaam) • *v* **to pile up** kawwam كوّم (kiwweem, takwiim); **to be piled up** itkawwam اتكوّم (kiwweem)
piles (**haemorrhoids**) bawaasiir بواسير
pilgrim (*m*) ḥaajj حاج ; (*f*) ḥaajja حاجّة
pilgrimage (**to Mecca**) ḥajj حج ; (**the minor pilgrimage to Mecca**) ʿumra عمرة
pill ḥabba حبّة (*pl* -aat, ḥubuub); ḥabbaaya حبّاية (*pl* -aat, ḥubuub)
pillar ʿamuud عمود (*pl* ʿawaamiid, aʿmida)
pillow makhadda مخدّة
pillowcase kiis makhadda
pilot ṭayyaar طيّار
pimp maʿarraṣ معرّص
pimple ḥabba حبّة (*pl* ḥubuub); (**acne**) ḥabb ash-shabaab
pin dabbuus دبّوس (*pl* dabaabiis)
pincers kammaasha كمّاشة
pinch *n* garṣa قرصة • *v* garaṣ قرص (u, gariṣ); garraṣ قرّص (girreeṣ, tagriiṣ); **to be pinched** itgaraṣ اتقرص (garṣa); itgarraṣ اتقرّص (garṣa)
pineapple ananaas اناناس
pink bambi بمبي ; wardi وردي
pious taqi تقي
pip(**s**) (**fruit**) bizir بزر (*unit n* bizra, *pl* buzuur)
pipe maasuura ماسورة (*pl* -aat, mawaasiir); (**for tobacco**) kadoos كدوس (*pl* -aat)
pipeline khaṭṭ anaabiib
pistol musaddas مسدّس (*pl* -aat); ṭabanja طبنجة
pit ḥufra حفرة (*pl* ḥufar)
pitch *n* zifit زفت
pitch *v* (**a tent**) naṣab نصب (u, naṣb)
pitcher jakk جك (*pl* jukukka, jukuuk); (**for ablutions**) ibriig إبريق (*pl* abaariig)
pitfall maglab مقلب (*pl* magaalib)
pity *n* shafaga شفقة ; **what a pity!** ya khasaara! • *v* shifig ʿala شفق (a, shafaga)
place makaan مكان (*pl* amaakin); maḥall محل (*pl* -aat); fijja فجّة (*pl* -aat, fijaj); ḥitta حتة (*pl* ḥitat); bakaan بكان (*pl* -aat); **place of origin** balad بلد (*pl* bilaad)
placenta tabiiʿa تبيعة ; mashiima مشيمة
plague ṭaaʿuun طاعون ; **cattle plague** abu dimeeʿaat
plain *adj* (**colour**) saada سادة ; (**clear**) waaḍiḥ واضح
plain *n* sahala سهلة (*pl* sahlaat); ṣagiiʿa صقيعة (*pl* ṣagaayiʿ)
plaintiff muddaʿi مدّعي (*pl* -yyiin)
plait *n* ḍafiira ضفيرة (*pl* ḍafaayir); **hair plait** ḍafiira ضفيرة (*pl* ḍafaayir); masiira مسيرة (*pl* masaayir) • *v* ḍaffar

ضفّر (ḍiffeer); (**hair**) mashshaṭ مشّط (mushaaṭ)
plan *n* khuṭṭa خطّة (*pl* khuṭaṭ) • *v* khaṭṭaṭ خطّط (takhṭiiṭ)
plane (**tool**) faara فارة • *v* masaḥ be-l-faara
planet kawkab كوكب (*pl* kawaakib)
plank looḥ لوح (*pl* alwaaḥ, leeḥaan)
planning takhṭiiṭ تخطيط (*pl* -aat)
plant *v* gharas غرس (i, gharis); zaraᶜ زرع (a, zariᶜ, ziraaᶜa)
plant(**s**) *n* shajar شجر (*pl* ashjaar); shadar شدر; nabaat نبات (*pl* -aat); **succulent plant**(**s**) ṣabbaar صبّار; **young plant** shatla شتلة (*pl* -aat, shutuul); **plant nursery** mashtal مشتل (*pl* mashaatil); **plant pot** zuhriyya زهريّة; faaẓa فاظة; aṣiiṣ أصيص (*pl* aṣaayiṣ)
plantation mazraᶜa مزرعة (*pl* mazaariᶜ)
plaster *n* **sticking plaster** lazga لزقة; lasga لصقة
plaster *n* bayaaḍ بياض • *v* (**basic layer**) labbakh لبّخ (talbiikh); layyas ليّس (liyyees, talyiis); (**top layer**) bayyaḍ بيّض (biyyeeḍ); ballaṭ بلّط (billeeṭ, tabliiṭ); (**with gypsum**) jabbas جبّس (jibbees); (**with mud mixture**) zabbal زبّل (zibbeel)
plasterer bayyaaḍ بيّاض; mubayyiḍ مبيّض; (**with mud mixture**) zabbaal زبّال
plastic blaastik بلاستيك
plate ṣaḥan صحن (*pl* ṣuḥuun); **large plate** sulṭaaniyya سلطانيّة; gadaḥ قدح (*pl* gudaaḥa, agdaaḥ); (**for salad**) sirwiis سرويس (*pl* saraawiis)
platform minbar منبر (*pl* manaabir); (**railway station**) raṣiif رصيف (*pl* arṣifa); trotwaar تروتوار (*pl* -aat)
play *n* masraḥiyya مسرحيّة; tamsiiliyya تمسيليّة • *v* (**game**) liᶜib لعب (a, liᶜib); (**musical instrument**) ḍarab ضرب (a, ḍarib); ᶜazaf عزف (i, ᶜazif); **to be played** (**a game**) itlaᶜab اتلعب (liᶜib)
player laaᶜib لاعب
playground malᶜab ملعب (*pl* malaaᶜib)
pleasant ẓariif ظريف (*pl* -iin, ẓuraaf, ẓurafa)
pleasantness ẓaraafa ظرافة
please *v* basaṭ بسط (i, basiṭ); ᶜajab عجب (i, ᶜajab); **as you please** ᶜala keef-ak; **to be pleased** inbasaṭ (min) انبسط (inbisaaṭ) • *interj* (**requesting**) ᶜalee-k Allah; min faḍl-ak; law samaḥta; (**offering**) tafaḍḍal تفضّل; itfaḍḍal اتفضّل
pleased mabsuuṭ (be-, min) مبسوط
pleasure inbisaaṭ إنبساط; inbisaaṭa إنبساطة
pledge *n* ᶜahd عهد (*pl* ᶜuhuud); taᶜahhud تعهّد (*pl* -aat) • *v* itᶜahhad (be-) اتعهّد (taᶜahhud)
plentiful katiir كتير; waafir وافر
pliable ṭaayiᶜ طايع
pliers (**pair of**) zarradiyya زرّديّة
plot *n* (**conspiracy**) mu'aamara مؤامرة • *v* (**against**) it'aamar (ᶜala/ḍidd) اتآمر (mu'aamara, ta'aamur)
plot *n* (**of land**) arḍiyya أرضيّة (*pl* araaḍi); gitᶜat/ḥittat ariḍ
plough *n* miḥraat محرات (*pl* maḥaariit) • *v* ḥarat حرت (i, ḥiraata)
pluck (**e.g. a chicken**) maᶜaṭ معط (a, maᶜiṭ)

plug *n* sidaada سدادة (*pl* -aat, sadaadiid); saddaada سدّادة (*pl* -aat, sadaadiid); (**electric**) kobs كبس (*pl* -aat); kobs ḍakar; kobsi كبسي (*pl* -yyaat); **spark plug** buuji بوجي (*pl* bawaaji) • *v* (**block**) sadda سدّ (i, sadd)
plumber sabbaak سبّاك
plump malyaan مليان
plunder *v* nahab نهب (a, nahib); **to be plundered** itnahab اتنهب (nahib, nahba)
plunge ghaṭas غطس (i, ghaṭis)
plural jamiᶜ جمع
plus zaayid زايد
pneumonia iltihaab ri'awi
pocket jeeb جيب (*pl* jiyuub)
podium manaṣṣa منصّة; khashaba خشبة
poem gaṣiida قصيدة (*pl* gaṣaayid); (**in praise of the prophet Mohammed**) madiiḥ مديح (*pl* madaayiḥ)
poet shaaᶜir شاعر (*pl* shuᶜara)
poetry shiᶜir شعر; **love poetry** ghazal غزل
point *n* nugṭa نقطة (*pl* nugaṭ); **point of view** wijhat naẓar • *v* ashshar ᶜala, le- أشّر (ya'ashshir, ishsheer, ta'shiir)
pointer mu'ashshir مؤشّر (*pl* -aat)
poison *n* simm سم (*pl* sumu-um) • *v* sammam سمّم (sim-meem, tasmiim); **to be poisoned** itsammam اتسمّم (tasammum)
poisoning tasammum تسمّم
poisonous musimm مسم
poke *v* hammaz همّز (himmeez); nakhas نخس *vt* (a, nakhis)
pole (**support**) gaayim قايم (*pl* gawaayim); ᶜamuud عمود (*pl* ᶜawaamiid, aᶜmida); **forked pole** shiᶜba شعبة (*pl* shiᶜaab); (*geog*) quṭb قطب (*pl* aqṭaab); **pole star** aj-jaddi
police booliis بوليس; shurṭa شرطة; (**for emergencies**) booliis an-najda; **traffic police** booliis al-ḥaraka; **riot police** ash-shurṭa al-amniyya; **police station** gisim al-booliis; ẓabṭiyya ظبطيّة; **police post** nugṭat al-booliiṣ; an-nugṭa; **police swoop** kashsha كشّة
policeman ᶜaskari عسكري (*pl* ᶜasaakir); shurṭi شرطي (*pl* shurṭa); raajil al-booliis
policy siyaasa سياسة; (**insurance**) booliiṣa بوليصة
polio shalal al-aṭfaal
polish *n* orneesh ارنيش • *v* lammaᶜ لمّع (limmeeᶜ, talmiiᶜ)
polite mu'addab مؤدّب; muhazzab مهزّب
political siyaasi سياسي
politician siyaasi سياسي (*pl* -yyiin)
politics siyaasa سياسة
poll (**opinion**) istibyaan إستبيان (*pl* -aat)
pollen liqaaḥ لقاح
pollute lawwas لوّس (talwiis, talawwus)
pollution talawwus تلوّس
polyester buulistar بولستر
polygamy taᶜaddud az-zoojaat
pomposity fakhfakha فخفخة
pompous manfuukh منفوخ
pond birka بركة (*pl* birak)
pontoon banṭoon بنطون (*pl* -aat, banaaṭiin)
pool birka بركة (*pl* birak); (**man-made**) ḥafiir حفير (*pl* ḥafaayir); (**of rain water**) fuula فولة (*pl* -aat, fuwal); **swimming pool** ḥammaam as-sibaaḥa; ḥooḍ as-sibaaḥa

poor fagraan فقران ; fagiir فقير (*pl* fugara); **extremely poor** ʿadmaan عدمان
popcorn fishaar فشار
pope al-baaba
pop star najma نجمة (*pl* nujuum)
popular shaʿbi شعبي
popularity shaʿbiyya شعبيّة
population as-sukkaan; ʿadad as-sukkaan
porcelain ṣiini صيني ; boorsiliin بورسلين
porcupine abu shook
pore masaam مسام (*pl* -aat)
pork laḥam khanziir
porridge (**stiff**) ʿaṣiida عصيدة ; (**thin**) madiida مديدة
port miina مينا (*pl* mawaani)
porter ʿattaali عتّالي (*pl* ʿattaaliin, ʿattaala); ḥammaal حمّال ; shayy-aal شيّال
portfolio malaff ملف (*pl* -aat)
portion juzu جزو (*pl* azjaa)
position waḍʿ وضع (*pl* awḍaaʿ); (**rank**) martaba مرتبة (*pl* maraatib); (**standpoint**) mawgif موقف (*pl* mawaagif)
positive iijaabi ايجابي
possess malak ملك (i, milik); imtalak امتلك (imtilaak)
possessed ʿind-o zaar; **to be possessed by spirits** dastar دستر (dastuur)
possession milkiyya ملكيّة ; ḥiyaaza حيازة ; **possessions** mumtalakaat ممتلكات
possibility imkaaniyya إمكانيّة
possible mumkin ممكن ; **if possible** iza amkan
possibly mumkin ممكن ; yimkin يمكن
post *n* (**support**) ʿamuud عمود (*pl* ʿawaamiid, aʿmida); rakiiza ركيزة (*pl* rakaayiz); gaayim قايم (*pl* gawaayim); **house post** amiina أمينة (*pl* amaayin)
post *n* (**mail**) bariid بريد ; busṭa بسطة ; **the Post office** al-busṭa
postcard karit كرت (*pl* kuruut)
poster boostar بوستر (*pl* -aat)
postman busṭaji بسطجي (*pl* -yya)
postpone ajjal أجل (ta'jiil); **to be postponed** it'ajjal اتأجّل (ta'jiil)
postponement ta'jiil تأجيل (*pl* -aat)
pot burma برمة (*pl* buraam); **cooking pot** gidir قدر (*pl* guduur); burma برمة (*pl* buraam); ḥalla حلّة (*pl* ḥilal); (**large**) gooz قوز (*pl* geezaan); **coffee pot** (**for boiling coffee**) shaghghaal شغّال ; (**for serving coffee**) jabana جبنة ; **chamber pot** gaṣriyya قصريّة ; **plant pot** zuhriyya زهريّة ; faaẓa فاظة ; aṣiiṣ أصيص (*pl* aṣaayiṣ)
potato(**es**) baṭaaṭis بطاطس (*sg* baṭaaṭsa, baṭaaṭsaaya); **sweet potato**(**es**) baambey بامبي
pot-hole ḥufra حفرة (*pl* ḥufar)
potsherd giḥif قحف (*pl* guḥuuf)
potter (*m*) siid al-buraam; daggaag al-buraam; (*f*) sitt al-buraam
pottery fukhkhaar فخّار
potty gaṣriyya قصريّة
pouch khurtaaya خرتاية ; khartooya خرتوية ; khariita خريتة (*pl* khartooyaat, khurtaayaat); (**of leather**) juraab جراب (*pl* -aat)
poultry dawaajin دواجن ; jidaad جداد
pound *n* (**money**) jineeh جنيه (*pl* -aat); (*unit* **of weight**) raṭul رطل (*pl* arṭaal)
pound *v* dagga دقّ (u, dagg)
pour kabba كبّ (u, kabb); ṣabba صبّ (u, ṣabb); **to be poured**

(**out**) itkabba اتكبّ (kabb); itṣabba اتصبّ (ṣabb)
pout bawwaz بوّز (biwweez)
poverty fagur فقر
powder budra بودرة ; mashuug مسحوق
power (**strength**) guwwa قوّة ; (**ability**) gudra قدرة ; magdara/ magdira مقدرة ; (**political**) sulṭa سلطة ; nufuuz نفوز ; (**over**) saṭwa (ʿala) سطوة
powerful gaadir قادر
powerless ḍaʿiif ضعيف (*pl* ḍuʿaaf); ʿaajiz عاجز (*pl* ʿaajziin); ʿajzaan عجزان
practical ʿamali عملي
practically ʿamaliyyan عمليّا
practice mumaarasa ممارسة ; (**custom**) ʿaada عادة (*pl* -aat, ʿawaayid); **medical practice** mujammaʿ ṭibbi; majmaʿ ṭibbi; **the Medical Corps** as-silaaḥ aṭ-ṭibbi
practise maaras مارس *vt* (mumaarasa); itmarran اتمرّن (tamriin)
praise *n* shukur شكر ; (**God**) ḥamid حمد • *v* madaḥ مدح (a, madiḥ); shakkar شكّر (shikkeer); ashaada be- أشادة (yushiid, ishaada); (**God**) ḥamad حمد (i, ḥamid)
pray ṣalla صلّى (-i, ṣalaa); (**with prayer beads**) sabbaḥ سبّح (sibbeeḥ, tasbiiḥ); **to pray for** daʿa le- دعا (-u, duʿaa)
prayer ṣalaa صلاة (*pl* ṣalawaat); **Ramadan prayers** taraawiiḥ تراويح ; **place of prayer** muṣalla مصلّى ; **prayer beads** sibḥa سبحة (*pl* sibaḥ); **prayer mat** muṣlaaya مصلاية (*pl* maṣaali); farwa فروة (*pl* faraaw); tabarooga تبروقة ;
prayer corner zaawiya زاوية (*pl* zawaaya)
preach khaṭab خطب (u, khuṭba); waʿaẓ وعظ (yooʿiẓ, waʿiẓ)
preacher khaṭiib خطيب (*pl* khuṭaba); waaʿiẓ واعظ (*pl* wuʿʿaaẓ)
precaution wiqaaya وقاية ; iḥtiyaaṭ إحتياط (*pl* -aat); **to take precautions** iḥtaaṭ احتاط (iḥtiyaaṭ); akhad ḥazar-o
precautionary iḥtiyaaṭi إحتياطي
precede sabag سبق (u, sabag); itgaddam ʿala اتقدّم (tagaddum)
precedent saabiqa سابقة (*pl* sawaabiq)
precious ghaali غالي
precise daqiiq دقيق
predicament warṭa ورطة
predict itnabba اتنبّا (-a, tanabbu)
prediction tanabbu تنبّو (*pl* -ʾaat)
prefer faḍḍal (ʿala) فضّل (tafḍiil)
pregnancy ḥimil حمل ; **ectopic pregnancy** ḥimil khaarij ar-riḥim
pregnant ḥaamil حامل (*pl* ḥummal); tagiila تقيلة
prejudiced mutḥayyiz متحيّز ; munḥaaz منحاز
prepaid madfuuʿ مدفوع
preparation taḥḍiir تحضير (*pl* -aat); tajhiiz تجهيز (*pl* -aat)
prepare ḥaḍḍar حضّر (ḥiḍḍeer, taḥḍiir); jahhaz جهّز (jihheez, tajhiiz); **to be prepared** itḥaḍḍar اتحضّر (ḥiḍḍeer, tiḥiḍḍir); **to prepare o.s.** istaʿadda استعدّ (istiʿdaad)
prepuce ghalafa غلفة ; jilda جلدة
prescribe waṣaf وصف (yooṣif, waṣif)
prescription rooshetta روشتّة
presence ḥuḍuur حضور ; wujuud وجود

present *adj* mawjuud موجود ; ḥaaḍir حاضر ; **to be present** ḥiḍir حضر (a, ḥuḍuur); ḥaḍar حضر (a, ḥuḍuur) • *n* **the present** al-ḥaaḍir; **the present tense** al-muḍaariʿ

present *n* (**gift**) hadiyya هديّة (*pl* hadaayaa); ʿaṭiyya عطيّة (*pl* ʿaṭaaya); **to give a present** hada هدى (-i, ihda)

present *v* gaddam قدّم (tagdiim)

presentation ʿariḍ عرض (*pl* ʿuruuḍ)

preserve ḥafaẓ حفظ (a, ḥafiẓ); iḥtafaẓ be- احتفظ (iḥtifaaẓ)

preside ra'as رأس (a, riyaasa, ri'aasa)

presidency riyaasa رياسة ; ri'aasa رئاسة

president ra'iis رئيس (*pl* ruwasa, ru'asa); rayyis ريّس (*pl* ruwasa)

press *n* (**e.g. for oil**) ʿaṣṣaara عصّارة • *v* daas داس (u, doosa, dawasaan); (**oil etc.**) ʿaṣar عصر (i, ʿaṣir)

press *n* (**journalism**) ṣaḥaafa صحافة ; **press conference** mu'tamar ṣaḥafi

pressure ḍaghiṭ ضغط ; **to put pressure on** ḍaghaṭ ضغط (a, ḍaghiṭ); **under pressure** maḍghuuṭ مضغوط

pretend itẓaahar be- اتظاهر (taẓaahur); itḥaayal be- اتحايل (taḥaayul); itḥayyal be- اتحيّل (ḥiyyeel, taḥayyul)

pretty samiḥ سمح ; jamiil جميل ; **very pretty** shariṭ le-l-ariḍ

prevaricate lawlaw لولو (liwleew, lawlawa); itlawlaw اتلولو (liwleew, lawlawa)

prevent manaʿ منع (a, maniʿ)

prevention wiqaaya وقاية

previously gibeel قبيل ; gabli kida

prey ṣeeda صيدة ; fariisa فريسة (*pl* faraayis)

price siʿir سعر (*pl* asʿaar); taman تمن (*pl* atmaan); **everything has its price** kullo shii be-taman-o

prick *v* nakhas نخس (a, nakhis)

prickle *v* nammal نمّل (nimmeel, tanmiil) • *n* shook شوك (*pl* -aat, ashwaak)

prickly heat ḥamu n-niil

pride fakhr فخر

priest gassiis قسّيس (*pl* gasaawsa, gasasa); giss قس (*pl* gasaawsa, gasasa); **parish priest** raaʿi راعي (*pl* ruʿʿaa)

primary ibtidaa'i ابتدائي ; **primary school** al-madrasa al-ibtidaa'iyya; madrasat al-asaas

primitive budaa'i بدائي (*pl* -yyiin)

prince amiir أمير (*pl* umara)

princess amiira أميرة

principal (**male**) mudiir madrasa; naaẓir ناظر (*pl* nuẓẓaar); (**female**) mudiirat madrasa

principle mabda مبدا (*pl* mabaadi); (**rule**) qaaʿida قاعدة (*pl* qawaaʿid)

print *v* ṭabaʿ طبع (a, ṭibaaʿa); **printed matter** maṭbuuʿa مطبوعة

printer (**printing machine**) ṭaabʿa طابعة (*pl* ṭaabiʿaat); aala ṭaabiʿa; makanat ṭibaaʿa

printing ṭibaaʿa طباعة ; **printing press** maṭbaʿa مطبعة (*pl* maṭaabiʿ)

priority awlawiyya أولويّة

prison sijin سجن (*pl* sujuun); **prison cell** zinzaana زنزانة

prisoner masjuun مسجون (*pl* masaajiin); sajiin سجين (*pl* sujana);

maḥbuus محبوس (*pl* maḥaabiis); (**of war**) asiir أسير (*pl* usara); ma'suur مأسور ; **to take prisoner** ḥabas حبس (i, ḥabis, ḥabsa); sajan سجن (i, sajna, sijin); (**in war**) asar أسر (i, asr)
privacy khuṣuuṣiyya خصوصيّة
private khaaṣṣ خاصّ ; khuṣuuṣi خصوصي ; (**privately owned**) mallaaki ملاكي • *n* (**soldier**) ʿaskari nafar; jundi nafar
privatization khaṣkhaṣa خصخصة
privatize khaṣkhaṣ خصخص (khaṣkhaṣa)
privilege imtiyaaz إمتياز (*pl* -aat)
prize *n* jaayza جايزة (*pl* jawaayiz)
probability iḥtimaal إحتمال (*pl* -aat)
probable muḥtamal محتمل ; **it's probable that** minal-muḥtamal
probably fi l-ghaalib; waarid وارد ; ghaaliban غالبا
problem mushkila مشكلة (*pl* mashaakil); ʿawaja عوجة ; shibka شبكة (*pl* shibak)
procedure ijraa إجرا (*pl* -'aat)
process ʿamaliyya عمليّة
proclamation iʿlaan إعلان (*pl* -aat)
procrastinate itmaaṭal اتماطل (tamaaṭul, mumaaṭala)
produce *v* antaj انتج (i, intaaj); (**yield**) nataj نتج (i, intaaj); jaab جاب (i, jeeba); (**bring forward**) ṭallaʿ طلّع (tilleeʿ)
produce *n* ḥaṣiila حصيلة (*pl* ḥaṣaayil); maḥṣuul محصول (*pl* maḥaaṣiil); mantuuj منتوج
producer muntij منتج
product muntaj منتج (*pl* -aat)
production intaaj إنتاج (*pl* -aat); intaajiyya انتاجيّة ; **mass production** al-intaaj be-j-jumla
profession mihna مهنة (*pl* mihan); **profession of faith** shihaada شهادة
professional muḥtarif محترف ; mihani مهني
proficiency mahaara مهارة ; jadaara جدارة ; ḥarfana حرفنة
proficient maahir ماهر (*pl* mahara); ḥariif حريف (*pl* -iin, ḥurafa); jadiir جدير (*pl* judara)
profit *n* faayda فايدة (*pl* fawaayid); ribiḥ ربح (*pl* arbaaḥ); maksab مكسب (*pl* makaasib); **to make a profit** ribiḥ ربح (a, ribiḥ) **making a profit** kasbaan كسبان
program *n* barnaamij برنامج (*pl* baraamij) • *v* barmaj برمج (barmaja); **to be programmed** itbarmaj اتبرمج (barmaja)
programme *n* barnaamij برنامج (*pl* baraamij); **to plan a programme** barmaj برمج (barmaja)
progress *n* taqaddum تقدّم • *v* itgaddam اتقدّم (tagaddum)
prohibit manaʿ منع (a, maniʿ); ḥaram حرم (ḥirmaan)
project *n* mashruuʿ مشروع (*pl* -aat, mashaariiʿ)
prolong madda fi مدّ (i, madd); maddad مدّد (middeed, tamdiid); **to be prolonged** itmaddad اتمدّد (middeed, timiddid)
promise *n* waʿad وعد (*pl* wuʿuud); **to keep a promise** wafa be-l-waʿad • *v* waʿad (be-) وعد (yuuʿid, waʿad)
promote (**in rank, grade**) ragga رقّى (-i, targiya); **to be promoted** itragga اترقّى (-a, targiya)
promotion (**in rank, grade**) targiya ترقية
prompt *adj* sariiʿ سريع

promptly be-surᶜa بسرعة
pronounce naṭag نطق (u, nuṭug)
pronunciation nuṭug نطق
proof daliil دليل (*pl* adilla); bayyina بيّنة ; isbaat إسبات (*pl* -aat); burhaan برهان (*pl* baraahiin)
propaganda daᶜaaya دعاية
proper munaasib مناسب ; laayig لايق
properties khaṣaa'iṣ خصائص
property milik ملك (*pl* amlaak)
prophecy nubuwwa نبوّة
prophet nabi نبي (*pl* anbiya); rasuul رسول (*pl* rusul)
proposal iqtiraaḥ إقتراح (*pl* -aat); muqtaraḥ مقترح (*pl* -aat)
propose iqtaraḥ إقترح (iqtiraaḥ)
prosecute gaaḍa قاضى (-i, mugaaḍaa)
prosecution mugaaḍaa مقاضاة
prosecutor muddaᶜi مدّعي (*pl* -yyiin); **public prosecutor** wakiil(at) niyaaba; al-muddaᶜi al-ᶜaamm
prosperity maysara ميسرة
prosperous maysuur ميسور
prostate *n* brustaata برستاتا
prostitute sharmuuṭa شرموطة (*pl* sharaamiiṭ, sharammaṭ)
prostrate **(o.s. in prayer)** sajad سجد (u, sajda, sujuud)
prostration **(in prayer)** sajda سجدة ; sujuud سجود
protect ḥama حمى (-i, ḥimaaya); ḥaras (min) حرس (i, ḥaris, ḥiraasa); **(of God)** kafa كفى (-i, kafiya)
protection ḥimaaya حماية ; ḥiraasa حراسة ; riᶜaaya رعاية
protest *n* iḥtijaaj إحتجاج (*pl* -aat) • *v* iḥtajja (ᶜala) احتجّ (iḥtijaaj)
protractor mangala منقلة (*pl* manaagil)
proud fakhuur (min, be-) فخور ; **to be proud (of)** fakhar (be-) فخر (a, fakhr); iftakhar (be-) افتخر (fakhr, iftikhaar)
prove asbat أسبت (yusbit, isbaat); barhan برهن (barhana, burhaan)
proverb masal مسل (*pl* amsaal)
provide (with) adda أدّى (ya'addi, iddeey); mawwan (be-) موّن (tamwiin); **(for)** ᶜaal عال (u, iᶜaala); anfaq ᶜala أنفق (yunfiq, infaaq); **(of God)** razag رزق (i, rizig)
provoke ḥarraḍ حرّض (ḥirreeḍ, taḥriiḍ); hayyaj هيّج (hiyyeej, tahyiij); itḥarrash be- اتحرّش (taḥriish)
prowl ḥaam ḥawaleen
proxy niyaaba نيابة
prudent ᶜaagil عاقل ; ᶜaglaani عقلاني
psoriasis ṣadafiyya صدفيّة
psychiatrist diktoor nafsi
psychological nafsi نفسي
psychologist diktoor nafsi
psychology ᶜilm an-nafs
public *adj* ᶜaamm عام ; ᶜumuumi عمومي ; **public relations** al-ᶜalaagaat al-ᶜaamma • *n* jamhuur جمهور (*pl* jamaahiir)
publish nashar نشر (u, nashir); aṣdar أصدر (i, iṣdaar); **to be published** itnashar اتنشر (nashir); ṣadar صدر (u, ṣuduur); **publishing house** daar an-nashir
puff nafakh نفخ (u, nafikh)
pull jabad جبد (i, jabid); jabbad جبّد (jibbeed); shadda شدّ (i, shadd); jarra جرّ (u, jarr); **to pull out (knife, thorn)** salla سلّ

(i, sall); (**hair, feathers**) maᶜaṭ معط (a, maᶜiṭ)
pulley bakra بكرة
pullover buluufar بلوفر (*pl* -aat); faniilat ṣuuf/ṣagaṭ
pulp umbaaz أمباز
pulpit minbar منبر (*pl* manaabir)
pulse nabiḍ نبض (*pl* nabaḍaat)
pump *n* ṭurumba طرمبة; baabuur بابور (*pl* -aat, bawaabiir); waabuur وابور (*pl* -aat); (**donkey engine**) doonki دونكي (*pl* dawaanki); **air pump** munfaakh منفاخ (*pl* manaafiikh); **hand pump** maḍakhkha مضخّة • *v* ḍakhkha ضخّ (u, ḍakhkh); **to pump up** (**e.g. a tyre**) nafakh نفخ (u, nafikh)
pumpkin(s) garaᶜ قرع (*unit n* garᶜa)
punch *n* bunya بنية (*pl* -aat, bunaj); **hole punch** kharraama خرّامة • *v* lakam لكم (u, lakamaan, lakim); dabal دبل (i, dabil); (**holes**) kharram خرّم (khirreem, takhriim)
punctual munḍabiṭ منضبط; fi wakt-o; fi mawaaᶜiid-o
puncture (**tyre**) al-lastik naazil; al-lastik munaffis
punish ᶜaaqab عاقب (ᶜiqaab, muᶜaaqaba)
punishment ᶜuquuba عقوبة; ᶜiqaab عقاب; (**military, civil service**) jiza جزا (*pl* jiza'aat); (**prescribed by Islamic law**) ḥadd حد (*pl* ḥuduud)
pupil (*m*) tilmiiz تلميز (*pl* talaamiiz); (*f*) tilmiiza تلميزة; (**of the eye**) wadd al-ᶜeen
puppet bitt umm laᶜᶜaab; ᶜaruusa عروسة (*pl* ᶜaraayis); **hand puppet** araajooz اراجوز; **puppet theatre** masraḥ al-ᶜaraayis
puppy jaru جرو (*pl* jireewaat); jireew جريو (*pl* jireewaat)
purchase *v* ishtara اشترى (-i, shira)
pure naqi نقي; ṣaafi صافي
purification tanqiya تنقية; taṭhiir تطهير; (**before prayer**) waḍu وضو
purify nagga نقّى (-i, tanqiya); ṭahhar طهّر (ṭihheer, taṭhiir); (**water, by letting the mud sink**) rawwag روّق (riwweeg); (**water, with a kind of clay**) rawwab روّب (riwweeb)
purple banafsaji بنفسجي
purpose gaṣid قصد; gharaḍ غرض (*pl* aghraaḍ); hadaf هدف (*pl* ahdaaf); **on purpose** gaaṣid قاصد; be gaṣd-o
purposely gaaṣid قاصد; be gaṣd-o
purse (**for women**) maḥfaẓa محفظة (*pl* maḥaafiẓ); maṭbaga مطبقة (*pl* maṭaabig); (**for men**) juzlaan جزلان (*pl* -aat, jazaaliin)
purslane rijla رجلة
pursue (**chase**) ṭaarad طارد (muṭaarada); (**continue**) waaṣal واصل (muwaaṣala)
pus midda مدّة; ṣadiid صديد (*pl* ṣadaayid)
push *n* dafᶜa دفعة; dafra دفرة; (**gentle**) lazza لزّة • *v* dafaᶜ دفع (a, dafiᶜ); dafar دفر (i, dafir); (**gently**) lazza لزّ (i, lazz); (**one another**) iddaafar ادّافر (mudaafara); **to push aside** zaḥḥa زحّ (i, zaḥḥa, zaḥaḥaan)
put khatta ختّ (u, khatt); **to put aside** rakan ركن (i, rakin); **to put in order** rattab رتّب (ritteeb,

tartiib); waḍḍab وضّب (wiḍḍeeb, tawḍiib); **to put inside** dakhkhal دخّل (dikhkheel); **to put off (delay)** ajjal أجّل (ta'jiil); **to put on clothes** libis لبس (a, libis); **to put out (e.g. a fire, a cigarette)** ṭafa طفى (-i, ṭafi, ṭafayaan)

putrid baayiẓ بايظ ; muʿaffin معفّن ; talfaan تلفان

putty maʿjuun معجون

puzzle *n* lughz لغز (*pl* alghaaz) • *v* ḥayyar حيّر (ḥiira, ḥiyyeer); **to be(come) puzzled** itḥayyar اتحيّر (ḥiira)

pyjamas bijaama بجامة

pyramid haram هرم (*pl* ahraam, ahraamaat)

python aṣala أصلة

Q - q

quadriplegia shalal kaamil

qualification mu'ahhil مؤهّل (*pl* -aat)

qualified mu'ahhal مؤهّل

qualify ahhal اهّل (yu'ahhil, ta'hiil)

quality nooʿiyya نوعيّة ; kayfiyya كيفيّة ; **(good quality)** jawda جودة ; **(characteristic)** ṣifa صفة

quantity kimmiyya كمّيّة ; migdaar مقدار (*pl* magaadiir)

quarantine kirintiina كرينتينا ; ḥajir ṣiḥḥi; **to put in quarantine** khatta fi kirintiina

quarrel *n* shakla شكلة ; shakal شكل (*pl* shaklaat); shibka شبكة (*pl* shibak); mushaajara مشاجرة • *v* shaakal شاكل (shakal); itshabak maʿa اتشبك (shabik); **(with one another)** itshaakal اتشاكل (shakal)

quarrelsome shabbaak شبّاك ; shakkaal شكّال ; sharraani شرّاني ; shibka شبكة

quarter *n* rubuʿ ربع (*pl* arbaaʿ)

quay raṣiif رصيف (*pl* arṣifa)

queen malka ملكة ; malika ملكة

question *n* su'aal سؤال (*pl* as'ila); **(issue)** mas'ala مسألة (*pl* masaa'il); **question mark** ʿalaamat istifhaam

questionnaire istibyaan إستبيان (*pl* -aat)

queue *n* ṣaff صف (*pl* ṣufuuf); ṭaabuur طابور (*pl* ṭawaabiir)

quick sariiʿ سريع

quickly be-surʿa بسرعة ; **to do things too quickly** itsarraʿ اتسرّع (tasarruʿ)

quiet haadi هادي ; raayig رايق ; **(person)** haadi هادي ; wadiiʿ وديع ; **(voice)** khaafiḍ خافض ; **to be quiet** raag راق (u, rooga, rawaag, ruwaaga, rawagaan); **to make quiet** sakkat سكّت (sikkeet)

quietly be-raaḥa; be-huduu

quietness huduu هدو ; rooga روقة

quinine kiina كينا

quit waggaf وقّف (wiggeef, tawgiif); baṭṭal بطّل (biṭṭeel); **(a job)** istaqaal استقال (a, istiqaala)

quotation istishhaad إستشهاد (*pl* -aat); **(of price)** faatuura mabda'iyya

quote *v* istashhad إستشهد (istishhaad)

R - r

rabbit arnab أرنب (*pl* araanib)
rabid jaḥmaan جحمان ; saᶜraan سعران
rabies jaḥam جحم ; saᶜar سعر ; **to suffer from rabies** jiḥim جحم (a, jaḥam); siᶜir سعر (a, saᶜar)
race *n* (**contest**) sabag سبق ; **race track** meedaanas-sabag • *v* saabag سابق (sabag, musaabaga); itsaabag إتسابق (sabag, musaabaga)
race *n* (**ethnicity**) jinis جنس (*pl* ajnaas); ᶜirig عرق (*pl* ᶜuruug)
racquet maḍrab مضرب (*pl* maḍaarib)
radiator ladeetar لديتر (*pl* -aat)
radio raadi رادي (*pl* raadyohaat, rawaadi)
radish(es) fijil فجل (*unit n* fijla)
raft ṭoof طوف (*pl* aṭwaaf)
rafter mirig مرق (*pl* muruug); maddaad مدّاد (*pl* -aat
rag (**for cleaning**) dalguun دلقون (*pl* dalaagiin); dulgaan دلقان (*pl* dalaagiin)
raid *n* ghaara غارة ; (**police**) kashsha كشّة • *v* ghaar غار (i, ghaara)
rail gaḍiib قضيب (*pl* guḍbaan); shariiṭ شريط (*pl* sharaayiṭ)
railing darabziin درابزين (*pl* -aat)
railway as-sikka ḥadiid
rain *n* maṭar مطر ; maṭara مطرة (*pl* amṭaar); **light rain** shak-shaaka شكشاكة ; nagnaaga نقناقة • *v* maṭṭar مطّر (miṭṭeer, maṭara); itmaṭṭar اتمطّر (maṭara)
rainbow qoos quzaḥ
raincoat kabbuut كبّوت (*pl* kabaabiit)
rainspout sabalooga سبلوقة (sabaaliig)
rainy mumṭir ممطر ; **the rainy season** al-khariif; **pertaining to the rainy season** khariifi خريفي
raise rafaᶜ رفع (a, rafiᶜ); ᶜalla علّى (-i, ᶜilleey, taᶜliya); (**cattle, chil-dren**) rabba ربّى (-i, tarbiya)
raisin(s) zabiib زبيب
rake *n* karak كرك (*pl* -aat); kan-naasa كنّاسة
rally *n* ḥashid jamaahiiri; liqaa jamaahiiri
ram *n* kabish كبش (*pl* kibaash); kharuuf خروف (*pl* khirfaan)
Ramadan ramaḍaan رمضان
range (**distance**) buᶜud بعد (*pl* abᶜaad); mada مدى ; (**of a gun**) marma مرمى
rank (**grade, position**) daraja درجة ; martaba مرتبة (*pl* mara-atib); (**military**) rutba رتبة (*pl* rutab)
ransom *n* fidiya فدية • *v* fada فدى (-i, fidiya)
rape *n* ightiṣaab إغتصاب (*pl* -aat) • *v* ightaṣab اغتصب (ightiṣaab)
rare naadir نادر
rat jigir جقر (*pl* juguur); faar فار (*pl* fiiraan)
ration jaraaya جراية; taᶜyiin تعيين (*pl* -aat)
rational ᶜaglaani عقلاني (*pl* -yyiin)
rattle *n* kashkoosh كشكوش (*pl* kashaakiish) • *v* kashkash كشكش (kishkeesh)

raw nayy نيّ; (**material**) khaam خام

ray shuᶜaaᶜ شعاع (*pl* ashiᶜᶜa)

raze masaḥ مسح (a, masiḥ)

razor (**blade**) muus موس (*pl* amwaas); **safety razor**; **electric razor** makanat ḥilaaga

reach *v* waṣal (le-) وصل (yaṣal/ yuuṣal, wuṣuul); (**of water, electricity**) itwaṣṣal le- اتوصّل (waṣla)

reaction radd fiᶜil

read gara (fi) قرا (-a, giraaya); **to be read** itgara اتقرى (-i, giraaya)

reader (**person**) qaari قاري (*pl* qurraa); (**book**) muṭaalaᶜa مطالعة

readiness istiᶜdaad إستعداد; jaa-hiziyya جاهزيّة

reading giraaya قراية

ready jaahiz جاهز; **to get ready** jihiz جهز (a, jahiz); istaᶜadda استعدّ (istiᶜdaad); itḥaḍḍar اتحضّر (taḥḍiir)

real ḥagiigi حقيقي

realistic waaqiᶜi واقعي

reality al-waaqiᶜ

really jadd جد; be-j-jadd; ḥagiigi حقيقي

reap ḥaṣad حصد (i, ḥaṣaad)

reaping hook munjal منجل (*pl* manaajil)

rear *adj* warraani ورّاني; **rear end** mu'akhkhira مؤخّرة

reason *n* (**cause**) sabab سبب (*pl* asbaab); sibba سبّة (*pl* asbaab); (**mind**) ᶜagul عقل (*pl* ᶜuguul); **without a reason** be-duunsabab; saakit ساكت; saay ساي

reasonable maᶜguul معقول

reassure ṭamman طمّن (ṭimmeen); **to be reassured** (**about**) iṭṭamman(ᶜala) اطّمّن (iṭmi'naan)

rebel *adj* mutmarrid متمرّد • *v* itmarrad اتمرّد (tamarrud)

rebellion tamarrud تمرّد

rebuke wabbakh وبّخ (wibbeekh, tawbiikh)

receipt iiṣaal إيصال (*pl* -aat); waṣil وصل (*pl* wuṣuulaat)

receive istalam استلم (istilaam); (**people**) istaqbal استقبل (is-tiqbaal); (**guests**) istaḍaaf استضاف (i, ḍiyaafa, istiḍaafa)

recently mu'akhkharan مؤخرا; gariib قريب; min wakit gariib

reception istiqbaal إستقبال (*pl* -aat); (**of guests**) istiḍaafa استضافة; (**party**) ḥaflat istiqbaal; **reception room** diiwaan ديوان (*pl* dawaawiin); ṣaaloon صالون (*pl* ṣawaaliin)

receptionist muwaẓẓaf al-istiqbaal

recipe waṣfa وصفة

reckless ṭaayish طايش; **to be reck-less** jaazaf جازف (mujaazafa)

recklessness mujaazafa مجازفة; ṭeesh طيش

recognize ᶜirif عرف (a, maᶜrifa)

recoil gamaz قمز (i, gamiz); **to recoil from** kashsha min كشّ (i, kashsh)

recommend waṣṣa ᶜala وصّى (-i, tawṣiya); zakka زكّى (-i, tazkiya)

recommendation tawṣiya توصية; tazkiya تزكية

reconcile ṣaalaḥ صالح (muṣaalaḥa); aṣlaḥ been اصلح (yuṣliḥ, ṣuluḥ); **to be(come) reconciled** itṣaalaḥ اتصالح (muṣaalaḥa)

reconciliation muṣaalaḥa مصالحة; ṣuluḥ صلح

reconsideration iᶜaadat naẓar

record *n* (**of a meeting**) maḥḍar محضر (*pl* mahaaḍir); (**register**) sijill سجل (*pl* -aat); (**archive**) arshiif أرشيف (*pl* -aat); (**music**) usṭuwaana أسطوانة • *v* sajjal سجّل (tasjiil); (**in register**) gayyad قيّد (geed, giyyeed)
recording tasjiil تسجيل (*pl* -aat)
recover (**from illness**) ṭaab طاب (i, ṭayabaan); shifa شفى (-a, shifaa); itʿaafa اتعافى (-a, muʿaafaa); bira min برى (-a, bariya, barayaan)
recovery shifa شفا
recruit *n* mustajidd مستجد • *v* (**military**) jannad جنّد (jinneed, tajniid)
recruitment (**military**) tajniid (*pl* -aat) تجنيد
red aḥmar أحمر (*f* ḥamra, *pl* ḥumur); **dark red** kabdi كبدي
red-handed mutlabbis متلبّس; **to catch a person red-handed** kabas كبس (i, kabis)
reduce gallal (min) قلّل (gilleel, tagliil); naggaṣ min نقّص (niggeeṣ, tangiiṣ); nagaṣ min نقص (u, nagṣ, nugṣaan); (**price**) rakhkhaṣ رخّص (rikhkheeṣ, tarkhiiṣ); khaffaḍ خفّض (khiffeeḍ, takhfiiḍ)
reduction takhfiiḍ تخفيض (*pl* -aat)
reed(s) buuṣ بوص; (**dry stems**) ḥaṣiir حصير; **reed matting** ḥaṣiir حصير; **reed pipe** zumbaara زمبارة (*pl* zanaabiir); **reed for beating** basṭoona بسطونة (*pl* -aat, basaaṭiin)
reel *n* bakra بكرة; (**for thread**) karooriyya كروريّة
referee ḥakam حكم (*pl* ḥukkaam)
referendum istiftaa استفتا (*pl* -'aat)
refine (**e.g. petrol, sugar**) karrar كرّر (takriir); ṣaffa صفّى (-i, taṣfiya); nagga نقّى (-i, tangiya)
refined (**manners**) raaqi راقي
refinement (**e.g. of petrol, sugar**) takriir تكرير; taṣfiya تصفية; tangiya تنقية
refinery maṣfaa مصفاة (*pl* maṣaafi)
reflect (**light**) ʿakas عكس (i, ʿakis); **to be reflected** inʿakas انعكس (ʿaksa)
reflector (**for car**) ʿaakis عاكس (*pl* ʿawaakis)
reform *n* iṣlaaḥ إصلاح (*pl* -aat)
refresh naʿnash (naʿnasha); **to refresh o.s.** itnaʿnash (naʿnasha)
refreshments (**light**) muraṭṭabaat مرطّبات
refrigerator tallaaja تلاجة
refuge lujuu لجو; (**place**) malja ملجا (*pl* malaaji); **to take refuge** laja لجا (-a, lujuu)
refugee laaji لاجي (*pl* -'iin)
refusal rafiḍ رفض
refuse *v* aba أبى (biyaaba, abayaan); rafaḍ رفض (u, rafiḍ, rafḍ)
regardless (**of**) be-ṣarf an-naẓar min
regime niẓaam نظام
regiment oorṭa اورطة (*pl* uraṭ)
region iqliim إقليم (*pl* aqaaliim)
regional iqliimi إقليمي
register *n* sijill سجل (*pl* -aat); (**book**) daftar دفتر (*pl* dafaatir) • *v* sajjal سجّل (tasjiil); gayyad قيّد (geed, giyyeed)
registrar musajjil مسجّل
registration tasjiil تسجيل (*pl* -aat)
regret *n* asaf أسف • *v* it'assaf ʿala اتأسّف (asaf, ta'assuf)
regular muntaẓim منتظم; **on a regular basis** be-intiẓaam; **to**

be(come) regular intaẓam انتظم (intiẓaam)
regularity intiẓaam إنتظام
regularly be-intiẓaam
regulations lawaayiḥ لوايح
rehearsal broofa بروفة
reign *n* ḥukum حكم (*pl* -aat) • *v* ḥakam حكم (i, ḥukum)
rein *v* (**in**) lajam لجم (-i, lajim); shadda al-lijaam
reins lijaam لجام (*pl* -aat)
reject rafaḍ رفض (u, rafiḍ, rafḍ)
rejection rafiḍ رفض
rejoice firiḥ (be-) فرح (a, faraḥ)
relate (**tell**) ḥaka (le-) حكى (-i, ḥaki)
relative *adj* nisbi نسبي • *n* gariib قريب (*pl* garaayib, agaarib); **relatives** ahal أهل (*pl* ahaali)
relatively nisbiyyan نسبيّاً
relax *vi* istarkha استرخ (istirkhaa); (**in a cool place**) raṭṭab رطّب (riṭṭeeb, tarṭiib) • *vt* rakha رخى (-i, rakhiya, rakhi)
relaxation istirkhaa إسترخا ; raaḥa راحة ; tarṭiiba ترطيبة
release *n* (**e.g. from prison**) iṭlaaq إطلاق ; ifraaj min إفراج ; (**from customs**) takhliiṣ تخليص (*pl* takhaaliiṣ); **press release** bayaanṣaḥafi • *v* (**e.g. from prison**) fakka فكّ (i, fakka); sarraḥ min سرّح (tasriiḥ); afraj (ʿala) أفرج (i, ifraaj); **to be released** (**e.g. from prison**) itfakka اتفكّ (fakka)
reliable maḍmuun مضمون ; mawsuuq fii-ho
relief raaḥa راحة ; faraj فرج ; (**aid**) ighaasa إغاسة
relieve (**of pain, pressure, etc.**) rayyaḥ ريّح (riyyeeḥ, taryiiḥ); khaffaf خفّف (khiffeef, takhfiif); (**one's feelings**) faḍfaḍ فضفض (faḍfaḍa); **to be relieved** itkhaffaf اتخفّف (khiffeef, takhfiif); itfakka اتفكّ (fakk)
religion diin دين (*pl* adyaan); diyaana ديانة
religious *adj* diini دينى ; (**person**) muddayyin مدّيّن ; **religious community** milla ملّة (*pl* milal); **to become religious** iddayyan ادّيّن (tadayyun)
reluctant mutraddid متردّد ; **to be reluctant** itraddad اتردّد (taraddud)
rely (**on**) iʿtamad ʿala إعتمد (iʿtimaad); istanad ʿala استند (istinaad)
remain (**be leftover**) fiḍil فضل (a, faḍla); (**stay**) gaʿad قعد (u, guʿaad)
remains bawaagi بواقي ; bagaaya بقايا
remainder baagi باقي (*pl* bawaagi); bagiyya بقيّة (*pl* bagaaya)
remark *n* mulaaḥaẓa ملاحظة ; malḥuuẓa ملحوظة
remedy dawa دوا (*pl* adwiya)
remember itzakkar اتزكّر (tazakkur)
remembrance zikra زكرى (*pl* zikrayaat)
remind zakkar زكّر (zikkeer, tazkiir)
reminder muzakkira مزكّرة
remnant baagi باقي (*pl* bawaagi); bagiyya بقيّة (*pl* bagaaya)
remorse nadaama ندامة ; **to feel remorse** nidim ʿala ندم (a, nadam)
remote baʿiid بعيد (*pl* buʿaad)
remoteness buʿud بعد
remove shaal شال (i, sheel, sheela); azaal ازال (yuziil,

izaala); **to be removed** itshaal اتشال (sheel, sheela); itzaal اتزال (zeela, izaala)
renal kalawi كلوي
renew jaddad جدّد (tajdiid)
renovate rammam رمّم (tarmiim)
renovation tarmiim ترميم (*pl* -aat)
rent *n* iijaar إيجار (*pl* -aat) • *v* ajjar أجّر (ta'jiir)
repair *n* taṣliiḥ تصليح (*pl* -aat); ṣiyaana صيانة; **repair shop** warsha ورشة (*pl* wirash); **tyre repair shop** banshar بنشر • *v* ṣallaḥ صلّح (ṣilleeḥ, taṣliiḥ); ṣaan صان (i, ṣiyaana); **to be repaired** itṣallaḥ إتصلّح (ṣilleeḥ, taṣliiḥ)
repeat karrar كرّر (tikraar); raddad ردّد (riddeed, tardiid)
repeatedly be-t-tikraar
repent taab تاب (u, tooba)
repentance tooba توبة
repetition tikraar تكرار; iʿaada إعادة
replace baddal بدّل (biddeel, tabdiil); (**parts, e.g. of an engine**) ʿammar عمّر (ʿamra); (**by a non-original spare part**) wallaf ولّف (tawliif)
replacement badiil بديل (*pl* badaayil)
reply *n* radd رد (*pl* ruduud); ijaaba إجابة • *v* radda (ʿala) ردّ (u, radd); jaawab جاوب (ijaaba)
report *n* tagriir تقرير (*pl* tagaariir); (**of problem**) balaagh بلاغ (*pl* -aat) • *v* gaddam tagriir; (**to the police**) ballagh بلّغ (balaagh, tabliigh)
reportage taḥgiig ṣaḥafi
reporter (*m*) muraasil مراسل; (*f*) muraasila مراسلة
represent massal مسّل (tamsiil)
representation tamsiil تمسيل
representative (*m*) mumassil ممسّل; (*f*) mumassila ممسّلة; **company representative** manduub sharika
reproach *n* malaama ملامة; loom لوم; ʿitaab عتاب • *v* lawwam لوّم (liwweem); laam لام (u, loom); ʿaatab عاتب (ʿitaab, muʿaataba); **to be reproached** itlawwam اتلوّم (loom, liwweem)
republic jamhuuriyya جمهوريّة; **the Central African Republic** jamhuuriyyat ifriiqiya al-wusṭa
republican *adj* jamhuuri جمهوري (*pl* -yyiin)
reputation sumʿa سمعة
request *n* ṭalab طلب (*pl* -aat); (**for a favour**) rajaa' رجاء (*pl* -aat) • *v* ṭalab طلب (u, ṭalab); ṭaalab طالب (muṭaalaba)
rescue *n* najda نجدة • *v* najad نجد (i, najda); **to be rescued** itnajad اتنجد (najda)
research *n* baḥs بحس (*pl* buḥuus) • *v* baḥas fi بحس (a, baḥis)
resemblance tashaabuh تشابه (*pl* -aat)
resemble shabah شبه (a, shabah)
resent itghaban min اتغبن (ghabiina); itmaghaṣ min اتمغص (maghaṣa)
resentment ghabiina غبينة (*pl* ghabaayin); maghaṣa مغصة; ghubun غبن (*pl* ghabaayin)
reservation (**booking**) ḥajiz حجز
reserve *n* (**caution**) iḥtiyaaṭ إحتياط (*pl* -aat); (**for wild animals**) ḥaẓiira حظيرة • *v* ḥajaz حجز (i, ḥajiz)

reservoir khazzaan خزّان (*pl* -aat)
resettlement iʿaadat tawṭiin
residence (**house**) manzil منزل (*pl* manaazil); maskan مسكن (*pl* masaakin); (**stay**) iqaama إقامة; **residence permit** taṣriiḥ iqaama
residue raasib راسب (*pl* rawaasib)
resign istaqaal استقال (a, istiqaala)
resignation istiqaala إستقالة
resin ṣamugh صمغ
resist qaawam قاوم (muqaawama)
resistance muqaawama مقاومة
resolve ḥalla حلّ (i, ḥall); **to be resolved** itḥalla اتحلّ (ḥall)
resource mawrid مورد (*pl* mawaarid); **human resources** al-mawaarid al-bashariyya
respect *n* iḥtiraam إحترام; **with respect to** be-n-nisba-le; be-khuṣuuṣ • *v* iḥtaram احترم (iḥtiraam)
respite mahla مهلة
responsibility mas'uuliyya مسؤوليّة
responsible mas'uul مسؤول
rest *n* raaḥa راحة; (**lying down**) ragda رقدة; madda مدّة
rest *n* (**remnant**) baagi باقي (*pl* bawaagi); bagiyya بقيّة (*pl* bagaaya)
restaurant maṭʿam مطعم (*pl* maṭaaʿim)
rest house istiraaḥa إستراحة
restless mutgalgil متقلقل; **to be restless** itgalgal اتقلقل (gilgeel, galgala)
restore (**e.g. electricity**) rajjaʿ رجّع (rijjeeʿ)
restrain lajam لجم (i, lajim); **to restrain o.s.** masak nafs-o; malak nafs-o
restrict ḥadda حدّ (i, ḥadd); gayyad قيّد (geed, giyyeed)
result *n* natiija نتيجة (*pl* nataayij); **negative result** ʿaaqiba عاقبة (*pl* ʿawaaqib) • *v* **to result from** nataj min/ʿan نتج (i, natiija)
resurrection giyaama قيامة; qiyaama قيامة
retail *adj* gaṭṭaaʿi قطّاعي
retch tawwaʿ توّع (tiwweeʿ, tatwiiʿ)
retire nazal al-maʿaash; itgaaʿad اتقاعد (*no vn*)
retirement maʿaash معاش
retreat *n* insiḥaab انسحاب (*pl* -aat); (**spiritual**) khalwa خلوة • *v* insaḥab انسحب (insiḥaab)
return *n* ʿawda عودة; **in return for** fi mugaabil • *vi* rajaʿ رجع (a, rujuuʿ); gabbal قبّل (gibbeel); gabbal raajiʿ; ṣadda raajiʿ • *vt* rajjaʿ رجّع (rijjeeʿ)
reveal kashaf كشف (i, kashif); bayyan بيّن (biyyeen)
revenge *n* intiqaam إنتقام (*pl* -aat); **to take revenge** (**on**) intaqam (min) انتقم (intiqaam); **revenge killing** taar تار (*pl* -aat); taṣfiya تصفية
revenue ʿaayid عايد (*pl* -aat, ʿaa'idaat); iiraad إيراد (*pl* -aat)
reverse *n* ʿaks عكس; (**of a piece of cloth**) galaba قلبة • *v* (**a car**) rajaʿ khalif
revise raajaʿ راجع (muraajaʿa)
revision muraajaʿa مراجعة
revolt *n* intifaaḍa انتفاضة
revolution sawra سورة
revolutionary sawri سوري
revolver musaddas مسدّس (*pl* -aat); ṭabanja طبنجة
reward *n* ajur أجر; mukaafaa مكافاة (*pl* mukaafa'aat) • *v* kaafa كافى (-i, mukaafaa); jaza جزى (-i, jiza); jaaza جازى (-i, mujaazaa)

rheumatism ruṭuuba رطوبة ; ruma-tizim روماتيزم
rhinoceros khirtiit خرتيت (*pl* kharaatiit); waḥiid al-garin
rhyme *n* qaafya قافية (*pl* gawaafi)
rhythm iigaaᶜ إيقاع (*pl* -aat)
rib ḍalᶜa ضلعة (*pl* ḍuluuᶜ)
ribbon shariiṭ شريط (*pl* sharaayiṭ)
rice ruzz رز
rich ghanyaan غنيان ; ghani غني (*pl* aghniya); murayyish مريّش ; **to be(come) rich** ghina غنى (-a, ghina); rawwag روّق (rooga)
rickets kisaaḥ كساح ; **suffering from rickets** kasiiḥ كسيح (*pl* kusaḥa)
rickshaw riksha ركشة ; **public rickshaw** riksha ṭarḥa
rid **to get rid of** itkhallaṣ min اتخلّص (khalaaṣ, takhalluṣ); khallaṣ min خلّص (khalaaṣ, khilleeṣ); khiliṣ min خلّص (a, khalaaṣ, khalṣa, khalaṣaan)
riddle ghuluuṭiyya غلوطيّة ; lughz لغز (*pl* alghaaz); fazuura فزورة (*pl* fawaaziir)
ride *v* rikib ركب (a, rukuub); (**on top of a train**) saṭṭaḥ سطّح (siṭṭeeḥ)
ridge (**roof**) sikkiina سكّينة (*pl* sakaakiin)
ridiculous sakhiif سخيف (*pl* -iin, sukhafa); **this/he is ridiculous** da/hu mahzala; da/hu maskhara
rifle bundugiyya بندقيّة (*pl* banaa-dig); **small-bore rifle** bundugi-yyat kharṭuush
right *adj* ṣaḥḥ صح ; ṣaaḥḥ صاح ; ṣaḥiiḥ صحيح ; maẓbuuṭ مظبوط ; **to put right** ẓabaṭ ظبط (u, ẓabiṭ); ẓabbaṭ ظبّط (taẓbiiṭ); **he's right** maᶜaa-ho/ᶜalee-ho/lee-ho/ᶜind-o ḥagg • *n* ḥagg حق (*pl* ḥuguug); **human rights** ḥuguug al-insaan; **to have the right to** istaḥagga استحقّ (istiḥgaag)
right *adj* (**right-hand side**) yamiin يمين ; • *n* **the Right** al-yamiin; **on the right** be-l-yamiin, ᶜala l-yamiin
righteous ṣaaliḥ صالح
righteousness ṣalaaḥ صلاح
rightness ṣaḥḥa صحّة
rim ḥaaffa حافّة (*pl* ḥawaaff)
rind girif قرف (*unit n* girfa); gishir قشر (*unit n* gishra, *pl* gushuur)
rinderpest ṭaaᶜuun bagari
ring *n* (circle) daayra دايرة (*pl* dawaayir); (**finger**) khaatim خاتم (*pl* khatam, khawaatim); **wed-ding ring** dibla دبلة (*pl* dibal)
ring *vi* ranna رنّ (i, raniin); dagga دقّ (u, dagg); **the bell is ring-ing** aj-jaras bidugg • *vt* dagga دقّ (u, dagg); **he rings the bell** bidugg aj-jaras
rinse shaṭaf شطف (u, shaṭif); shaṭṭaf شطّف (u, shiṭṭeef, tashṭiif); (**dish-es**) maṣmaṣ مصمص (maṣmaṣa); (**the mouth**) maḍmaḍ مضمض (maḍmaḍa); itmaḍmaḍ اتمضمض (maḍmaḍa)
riot shaghab شغب ; mushaaghaba مشاغبة
rip (**into pieces**) gaṭṭaᶜ قطّع (giṭṭeeᶜ, tagṭiiᶜ); **to rip open at the seams** fatag فتق (i, fa-tag); fattag فتّق (fitteeg); **to be ripped apart** itgaṭṭaᶜ اتقطّع (giṭṭeeᶜ); **to be ripped open at the seams** itfatag اتفتق (fatga)
ripe mustawi مستوي ; najiiḍ نجيض (*pl* nujaaḍ)
ripen istawa استوى (-i, istiwa); nijiḍ نجض (a, najaaḍ)

rise *n* irtifaaᶜ إرتفاع ; (**salary**) ᶜalaawa علاوة • *v* (**ascend**) ṭalaᶜ طلع (a, ṭuluuᶜ); (**of dough**) faar فار (u, fawaraan); (**of prices, temperature**) irtafaᶜ ارتفع (irtifaaᶜ)
rite ṭaqs طقس (*pl* ṭuquus)
river baḥar بحر (*pl* biḥaar, buḥuur); nahar نهر (*pl* anhaar); **riverbank** ḍiffa ضفة (*pl* ḍifaaf); shaaṭi شاطي (*pl* shawaaṭi); **riverbed** ḥooḍ حوض (*pl* ḥeeḍaan, aḥwaaḍ); (**dry**) waadi وادي (*pl* widyaan)
rivet *n* burshaam برشام (*pl* -aat, baraashiim) • *v* barsham برشم (barshama)
road ṭariig طريق (*pl* ṭurug); shaariᶜ شارع (*pl* shawaariᶜ); sikka سكّة (*pl* sikak); darib درب (*pl* duruub); **paved road** shaariᶜ ẓalaṭ; **unpaved road** shaariᶜ turaab; **road junction** tagaaṭuᶜ تقاطع
roadblock ḥabs ad-darib; ḥabs aṭ-ṭariig
roam ḥaam حام (u, ḥuwaama); saaḥ ساح (u, seeḥa, siyaaḥa); itjawwal اتجوّل (tajawwul)
roar *v* (**of a lion**) natar نتر (u, natir)
roast *adj* mashwi مشوي ; **roast meat** sheyya شية • *v* shawa شوى (-i, shawi); (**coffee beans**) ḥammaṣ حمّص (ḥimmeeṣ, taḥmiiṣ)
rob (**steal**) sarag سرق (i, sarig, sarga); (**plunder**) nahab نهب (a, nahib); **to be robbed** sirig سرق (a, sarga); itsarag اتسرق (sarga); itnahab اتنهب (nahib, nahba)
robber nahhaab نهّاب ; rabbaaṭi ربّاطى (*pl* rabaaṭiyya, rabaabiiṭ); gaṭṭaaᶜ aṭ-ṭurug
rock *n* ḥajar حجر (*pl* ḥujaara, aḥjaar)
rock *v* (**a child**) loola لولى (-i, loolaay)
rocket ṣaaruukh صاروخ (*pl* ṣawaariikh); (**cress**) jirjiir جرجير
rod (**wooden**) muṭrag مطرق (*pl* maṭaarig); (**metal**) siikha سيخة (*pl* siyagh)
role door دور (*pl* adwaar)
roll *n* **roll call** (**in school or army**) ṭaabuur طابور (*pl* ṭawaabiir) • *vi* iddardag ادّردق (dirdeeg) • *vt* dardag دردق (dardaga); **to roll up** ṭawa طوى (-i, ṭawi)
roof sagif سقف (*pl* suguuf); ᶜarish عرش (*pl* ᶜuruush); (**covered by cement**) ᶜagid عقد ; **top layer of roof** saṭiḥ سطح (*pl* suṭuuḥ) • *v* (**house**) sagaf سقف (i, sagif); ᶜarash عرش (i, ᶜarish)
room (**in house**) ooḍa أوضة (*pl* owaḍ); ghurfa غرفة (*pl* ghuraf); ḥujra حجرة (*pl* ḥujar)
rooster diik ديك (*pl* diyuuk, dayaka)
root (**of plant**) ᶜirig عرق (*pl* ᶜuruug); jazr جزر (*pl* juzuur); (**origin**) aṣil أصل (*pl* uṣuul)
rope ḥabil حبل (*pl* ḥibaal); **thick rope** ḥabil tiil; **thin rope** dubaara دبارة ; **to make a rope** fatal فتل (i, fatil)
rosary sibḥa سبحة (*pl* sibaḥ)
rose(s) ward ورد (*pl* wuruud)
rot *v* itᶜaffan اتعفن (ᶜiffeen, taᶜaffun); ᶜaffan عفّن (ᶜiffeen); baaẓ باظ (u, bawaẓaan, booẓ); tilif تلف (a, talaf); (**of wood**) it'aakal اتآكل (ta'aakul)
rotten baayiẓ بايظ ; muᶜaffin معفّن ; talfaan تلفان
rottenness bawaẓaan بوظان
rough khishin خشن ; (**person**) ᶜaniif عنيف

round *adj* mudawwar مدوّر ; mudardam مدردم • *prep* ḥawaleen حولين • *n* door دور (*pl* adwaar) • *v* **to round up** kashsha كشّ (u, kashsha); (**livestock**) kashkash كشكش (kashkasha)

roundabout ṣiiniyya صينيّة

rouse *vt* tawwar توّر (tiwweer); ṣaḥḥa صحّى (-i, ṣiḥḥeey, taṣḥiya)

route ṭariig طريق (*pl* ṭurug); (**e.g. of a bus**) khaṭṭ خط (*pl* khuṭuuṭ)

row *n* (**quarrel**) shakla شكلة ; shakal شكل (*pl* shaklaat); shaghab شغب

row *n* (**line**) ṣaff صف (*pl* ṣufuuf); ṭaabuur طابور (*pl* ṭawaabiir); (**in theatre, stadium**) ṣaff صف (*pl* ṣufuuf)

row *v* (**a boat**) gaddaf قدّف (giddeef, gadaf)

royal malaki ملكي

royalties fawaayid فوايد

rub farak فرك (i, farik); (**skin**) daʿak دعك (a, daʿik); **to rub out** masaḥ مسح (a, masiḥ, masaḥaan); **to be rubbed out** itmasaḥ اتمسح (masiḥ, masaḥaan)

rubber *adj* maṭṭaaṭi مطّاطي • *n* (**material**) maṭṭaaṭ مطّاط ; (**eraser**) istiika إستيكة ; **rubber band** lastik/listik لستك (*pl* lasaatik)

rubbish karoor كرور ; hatash هتش ; hakar هكر

rudder daffa دفّة

rude jilif جلف (*pl* ajlaaf); jaaff جاف ; galiil al-adab

rudeness jalaafa جلافة ; gillat al-adab

rug sajjaada سجّادة (*pl* -aat, sajaajiid); (**of wool or goatshair**) shamla شملة (*pl* shimal)

ruin *n* **ruins** kharaabaat خرابات ; ḥuṭaam حطام • *v* kharab خرب (i, kharib); kharrab خرّب (khirreeb, takhriib); **ruins of a house** kharaaba خرابة ; **to be ruined** itkharab اتخرب (kharaab, kharba); itkharrab اتخرّب (khirreeb, kharaab)

rule *n* (**principle**) qaaʿida قاعدة (*pl* qawaaʿid); (**reign**) ḥukum حكم (*pl* aat) • *v* ḥakam حكم (i, ḥukum)

ruler (**for lines**) masṭara مسطرة (*pl* masaaṭir); (**of a country**) ḥaakim حاكم (*pl* ḥukkaam)

rumour ishaaʿa إشاعة

run *v* jara جرى (-i, jari, jarayaan); (**slowly**) jakka جكّ (u, jakk); **to run after** sakka سكّ (u, sakk, sakakaan); ṭaarad طارد (muṭaarada); **to run away** harab هرب (a, huruub, harabaan); sharad شرد (u, sharid, sharadaan); **to run off** ṭafash طفش (u, ṭafsha, ṭafashaan)

runway mudarraj ṭayyaaraat

rupture fitaag فتاق

rural riifi ريفي

ruse ḥiila حيلة (*pl* ḥiyal)

rush *n* (**haste**) ʿajala عجلة ; **rush hour** saaʿat az-zarwa • *v* istaʿjal استعجل (istiʿjaal); itsarraʿ اتسرّع (surʿa)

rush(es) (**plant**) siʿid سعد (*unit n* siʿda)

Russia ruusiya روسيا

Russian *adj/n* ruusi روسي (*pl* ruus)

rust *n* ṣagar صقر ; ṣada صدا • *v* ṣaggar صقّر (ṣiggeer); ṣadda صدّى (-i, ṣiddeey, ṣadiya); itṣadda اتصدّى (-a, ṣiddeey, ṣadiya)

rustle *v* washwash وشوش (wishweesh)

rusty muṣaggir مصقّر ; muṣaddi مصدّي

ruthless jabbaar جبّار ; galb-o ḥajar

S - s

sack *n* shawwaal شوّال (*pl* -aat)
sack *v* (**dismiss**) ṭarad طرد (u, ṭarid); rafad رفد (i, rafid); **to be sacked** iṭṭarad اطّرد (ṭarid); itrafad اترفد (rafid)
sacrament (**Catholic**) sirr سر (*pl* asraar); (**protestant**) fariiḍa فريضة (*pl* faraayiḍ); **the Blessed Sacrament** al-qurbaan al-aqdas; al-qurbaan al-muqaddas
sacred muqaddas مقدّس
sacrifice *n* ḍaḥiyya ضحيّة (*pl* ḍaḥaaya) • *v* ḍaḥḥa ضحّى (-i, taḍḥiya)
sad ḥaziin حزين ; ḥaznaan حزنان
saddle *n* sarij سرج (*pl* suruuj); **saddle girth** buṭaan بطان (*pl* -aat, abṭina); **saddle pad** libda لبدة (*pl* libad) • *v* shadda as-sarij
sadness ḥuzun حزن (*pl* aḥzaan)
safe *adj* aamin آمن ; saalim سالم (*pl* saalmiin); **to keep safe** (**of God**) sallam (tasliim) • *n* khaziina خزينة (*pl* khazaayin, khizan); khazna خزنة (*pl* khizan)
safety salaama سلامة ; amaan أمان
saffron zaᶜfaraan زعفران
sail *n* shuraaᶜ شراع (*pl* -aat, ashriᶜa)
sailor baḥḥaar بحّار (*pl* baḥḥaara); nawwaati نوّاتي (*pl* nawwaatiyya)
saint (*Chr*) qiddiis قدّيس ; (*Isl*) wali ولي (*pl* awliya)
sake **for the sake of** ᶜashaan عشان ; le-ajl; minajl; ᶜashaankhaaṭir; fi shaan; ᶜala shaan
salad salaṭa سلطة ; **mixed salad** salaṭa ḥamra
salary murattab مرتّب (*pl* -aat); raatib راتب (*pl* rawaatib); (**monthly**) maahiyya ماهيّة (*pl* mawaahi)
sale beeᶜ بيع (*pl* -aat); beeᶜa بيعة ; **for sale** le-l-beeᶜ
saliva riig ريق
salt miliḥ ملح (*pl* amlaaḥ)
salty maaliḥ مالح
salute *v* ḥayya حيّى (-i, taḥiya)
salvation inqaaz إنقاز (*pl* -aat); khalaaṣ خلاص
salve marham مرهم (*pl* maraahim)
same nafs نفس ; zaat- زات- ; zaato زاتو ; (**the very self**) be-ᶜeen-
sample ᶜayna عينة
sanction *n* ᶜuguuba عقوبة
sand ramla رملة (*pl* rimaal); **hot sand** mallaala ملالة
sandal ṣandal صندل (*pl* ṣanaadil); shabaṭ شبط (*pl* shubaaṭa); shibshib شبشب (*pl* shabaashib); (**plastic**) shidda شدّة
sandalwood ṣandal صندل ; **essence of sandalwood** ṣandaliyya صندليّة
sandpaper ṣanfara صنفرة
sandstorm habuub هبوب (*pl* habaayib); ᶜajaaj عجاج ; kandaaka كنداكة
sandwich sandewiitsh سندويتش (*pl* -aat); **sandwich filling** ḥashwa حشوة
sandy ramli رملي
sanitary ṣiḥḥi صحي
sap labanash-shajara
Satan ibliis إبليس ; ash-sheeṭaan
satellite gamar ṣinaaᶜi; **satellite dish** dish دش (*pl* dashasha, dushuush); **satellite channel** qanaa faḍaa'iyya
satin seetaan سيتان

satisfaction iktifa إكتفا ; qanaaʿa قناعة
satisfy kaffa كفّى (-i, kifaaya); **to be satisfied** itkaffa اتكفّى (-a, kifaaya); iktafa (be-) إكتفى (-i, iktifa); (**with food**) shibiʿ شبع (a, shabaʿ)
satisfied *adj* muktafi مكتفي ; (**with food**) shabʿaan شبعان
saturate shabbaʿ شبّع (shibbeeʿ, tashbiiʿ); **to be(come) saturated** itshabbaʿ اتشبّع (tashabbuʿ); shibiʿ شبع (a, shabiʿ)
Saturday yoom as-sabat
sauce mulaaḥ ملاح ; (**thin**) damʿa دمعة
saucepan ṭawwa
saucer ṣaḥan صحن (*pl* ṣuḥuun)
Saudi *adj/n* ṣaʿuudi صعودي (*pl* -yyiin); **Saudi Arabia** aṣ-ṣaʿuudiyya
sausage giṭʿat sujuuk; **sausages** sujuuk سجوك
savage mutwaḥḥish متوحّش
savannah safanna سافنّا
save (**rescue**) najad نجد (i, najda); **to be saved** itnajad اتنجد (najda); **to save up** ḥawwash حوّش (taḥwiish); waffar وفّر (tawfiir)
saviour (**of Jesus Christ**) al-mukhalliṣ
saw *n* munshaar منشار (*pl* manaashiir) • *v* nashar نشر (u, nashir); **to be sawn** itnashar اتنشر (nashir)
sawdust nishaara نشارة
say gaal قال (u, gool); **that's to say** yaʿni يعني ; **to be said** itgaal اتقال (gool)
saying *n* masal مسل (*pl* amsaal); gool قول (*pl* agwaal)
scab gishra قشرة (*pl* gushuur)
scabies jarab جرب
scaffold mashnaga مشنقة (*pl* mashaanig)
scaffolding sigaala سقالة (*pl* -aat, sagaayil)
scald ḥarrag حرّق (ḥirreeg, taḥriig)
scale (**of a balance**) kaffat al-miizaan; **pair of scales** miizaan ميزان (*pl* mawaaziin)
scale(s) (**of fish**) gishir as-samak
scam ghishsh غش ; naṣb نصب
scandal faḍiiḥa فضيحة (*pl* faḍaayiḥ)
scandalize faḍaḥ فضح (a, faḍiḥ, faḍiiḥa)
scar *n* asar jariḥ; nagra نقرة (*pl* nugar); **tribal scar on face** shalikh شلخ (*pl* shuluukh)
scarcity nudra ندرة
scare khawwaf خوّف (takhwiif); **to scare away** (**birds**) ḥaaḥa حاحا (-i, ḥiḥeey, muḥaaḥaa); **to be scared** (**of**) khaaf (min) خاف (a, khoof)
scarecrow hambuul همبول (*pl* hamaabiil)
scarf (**women**) ṭarḥa طرحة (*pl* -aat, ṭiraḥ); ishaarb إشارب (*pl* -aat); (**men**) shaal شال (*pl* -aat); (**worn by bride or by girl to be circumcised**) garmaṣiiṣ قرمصيص
scarify shallakh شلّخ (shilleekh)
scatter (**group**) fartak فرتك (fartaka, firteek); (**individuals**) farzaʿ فرزع (farzaʿa); shattat شتّت (shitteet, tashtiit); **to be scattered** itfartak اتفرتك (firteek); itfarzaʿ اتفرزع (farzaʿa); itshattat اتشتّت (shitteet, tashattut)
scatterbrained mukashkish مكشكش ; marwuush مرووش
scene (**of a play**) mashhad مشهد (*pl* mashaahid)

scent riiḥa ريحة (*pl* aryaaḥ, rawaayiḥ)
schedule jadwal جدول (*pl* jadaawil)
scheme *n* (**plan**) khuṭṭa خطّة (*pl* khuṭaṭ); (**project**) mashruuᶜ مشروع (*pl* -aat, mashaariiᶜ); (**intrigue**) makiida مكيدة (*pl* makaayid) • *v* khaṭṭaṭ خطّط (takhṭiiṭ)
scholar ᶜaalim عالم (*pl* ᶜulama)
scholarship minḥa diraasiyya
school madrasa مدرسة (*pl* madaaris); **pertaining to school** madrasi مدرسي ; **Koranic school** khalwa خلوة (*pl* khalaawi)
schoolmate zamiil زميل (*pl* zumala)
science ᶜilim علم (*pl* ᶜuluum); **medical science** ṭibb طب
scientist ᶜaalim عالم (*pl* ᶜulama)
scissors magaṣṣ مقص (*pl* -aat)
scold nahar نهر (a, nahir); nahhar نهّر (nihheer); haraj (fi) هرج (i, harja)
scoop *v* gharaf غرف (i, gharif); (**water**) shaṭaf شطف (u, shaṭif); (**with the hands**) khamma خمّ (u, khamm)
scope (**domain**) majaal مجال (*pl* -aat)
scorch shalwaṭ شلوط (shalwaṭa)
score *v* (**a goal**) sajjal سجّل (tas-jiil); jaab جاب (i, jeeba)
scorn *n* ḥagaara حقارة ; ḥugra حقرة ; (**mockery**) sukhriyya سخريّة
scorpion ᶜagrab عقرب (*pl* ᶜagaarib)
scout *n* kashshaaf كشّاف (*pl* kash-shaafa)
scouting istikshaaf إستكشاف (*pl* -aat); (**children**) kashshaafa كشّافة
scowl *v* kashshar كشّر (kishsheer, takshiira)
scrape *v* karad كرد (u, karid); ḥakka حكّ (u, ḥakk); kashaṭ كشط (u, kashiṭ)
scraper (**workshop**) makshaṭa كمكشة
scrap metal khurad خرد (*unit n* khurda)
scratch *n* kharsha خرشة ; khad-sha خدش (*pl* khuduush) • *v* kharash خرش beesh, kharba-sha); khadash خدش (i, khad-ish); (**o.s.**) ḥakka حكّ (u, ḥakk); karash كرش (u, karish); **to be scratched** itkharash اتخرش (kharsha); itkharbash اتخربش (kharbasha); itkhadash اتخدش (khadish)
scream *n* ṣarkha صرخة • *v* koorak كورك (kooraak); ṣarrakh صرّخ (ṣuraakh, ṣirreekh)
screen *n* shaasha شاشة ; (**curtain**) sitaara ستارة (*pl* -aat, sataayir)
screw *n* musmaar galawooẓ; mus-maar burma; **thread of a screw** galawooẓ قلووظ • *v* galwaẓ قلوظ (galwaẓa); baram برم (u, barim)
screwdriver mafakk مفك (*pl* -aat)
scribble shakhbaṭ شخبط (shakhbaṭa)
scrub *v* ḥakka حكّ (u, ḥakk); (**clothes**) garaḍ قرض (u, gariḍ) • *n* (**homemade**) **skin scrub** dilka دلكة
scuffle *n* ishtibaak إشتباك (*pl* -aat)
scurf guub قوب
scythe munjal منجل (*pl* manaajil)
sea al-baḥar al-maaliḥ
seal *n* (**stamp**) khitim ختم (*pl* akhtaam) • *v* khatam ختم (i,

khatim); (**with wax**) shammaᶜ شمّع (tashmiiᶜ)
search *n* (**inspection**) taftiish تفتيش (*pl* -aat) • *v* (**for**) fattash (le-/ᶜala) فتّش (fitteesh, taftiish); kaas (le-) كاس (u, kuwaasa); (**inspect**) fattash فتّش (taftiish)
searchlight kashshaafa كشّافة
seashell(s) wadiᶜ ودع (*unit n* wadᶜa); ṣadaf صدف
season *n* faṣil فصل (*pl* fuṣuul); muusim موسم (*pl* mawaasim); **the rainy season** al-khariif
season *v* ṭaᶜᶜam طعم (ṭiᶜᶜeem)
seasonal faṣli فصلي ; muusimi موسمي
seat *n* magᶜad مقعد (*pl* magaaᶜid) • *v* gaᶜᶜad قعّد (giᶜᶜeed, gaᶜda)
second *adj* taani تاني • *n* (**in time**) saanya سانية (*pl* sawaani)
secondary saanawi سانوي ; **secondary school** al-madrasa as-saanawiyya
secondhand mustaᶜmal مستعمل ; **secondhand goods market** suug ad-dilaala
secondly taani تاني ; taaniyyan تانيّاً
secret *adj* sirri سرّي ; **to keep secret** katam as-sirr • *n* sirr سر (*pl* asraar)
secretary (*m*) sikirteer سكرتير ; (*f*) sikirteera سكرتيرة
secretly sirri سرّي ; be-sirr
section gisim قسم (*pl* agsaam); (**of a school**) shuᶜba شعبة (*pl* shuᶜab); (**of a branch**) fariᶜ فرع (*pl* furuuᶜ)
sector giṭaaᶜ قطاع (*pl* -aat); **the private sector** al-giṭaaᶜ al-khaaṣṣ; **the public sector** al-giṭaaᶜ al-ᶜaamm
secure *adj* aamin آمن • *v* amman أمّن (ya'ammin, ta'miin)
security amaan أمان ; amn أمن ; **the security services** al-amn
sedate *v* sakkan سكّن (sikkeen, taskiin); hadda هدّى (-i,tahdiya)
sedative musakkin مسكن (*pl* -aat); muhaddi مهدّي (*pl* -yaat)
sediment raasib راسب (*pl* rawaasib)
seduce fatan فتن (i, fitna)
see shaaf شاف (u, shoof); (**in a dream or vision**) ra'a رأى (yara, ruu'ya); **to see off** waddaᶜ ودّع (wadaaᶜ, widdeeᶜ)
seed(s) *n* ḥabb حبّ (*pl* -aat, ḥubuub); bizir بزر (*unit n* bizra, *pl* buzuur); (**for sowing**) tagaawi تقاوي ; **sprouted seeds** zirriiᶜa زريعة ; **roasted watermelon or pumpkin seeds** tasaali تسالي
seedling shatla شتلة (*pl* -aat, shutuul)
segment juzu جزو (*pl* azjaa); (**of fruit or vegetable**) faṣṣ فص (*pl* fuṣuuṣ)
seize masak مسك (i, masik, masakaan); (**arrest**) gabaḍ (ᶜala) قبض (u, gabiḍ); **to be seized** itmasak اتمسك (maska); itgabaḍ اتقبض (gabiḍ)
seizure (**convulsion**) tashannuj تشنّج (*pl* -aat)
seldom naadir نادر
select *v* nagga نقّى (-i, niggeey); ᶜazal عزل (i, ᶜazil); ikhtaar اختار (ikhtiyaar); **to be selected** itnagga اتنقّى (-a, tiniggi); itᶜazal اتعزل (ᶜazil)
self nafis نفس ; zaat- ذات- ; **she did it herself** hi ᶜamalat-o be-nafs-a/

be-zaat-a/baraa-ha; **he killed himself** katal nafs-o/ruuḥ-o
self-controlled raasi راسي (*pl* raasiin)
selfish anaani أناني (*pl* -yyiin)
selfishness anaaniyya أنانيّة
sell baaᶜ باع (i, beeᶜ); saam سام (u, soom); **to sell on credit** gassaṭ قسّط (gisseeṭ, tagsiiṭ); **to be sold** itbaaᶜ اتباع (beeᶜ)
seller baayiᶜ بايع ; bayyaaᶜ بيّاع
semifinal gabli n-nihaa'i
seminar nadwa ندوة *pl* nadawaat); siminaar سمينار (*pl* -aat)
senate majlis ash-shiyuukh
send rassal رسّل (risseel); **to be sent** itrassal اترسّل (risseel); **to send away** ṭarad طرد (u, ṭarid); mashsha مشّى (-i, mishsheey); **to be sent away** iṭṭarad اطّرد (ṭarid); **to send back** rajjaᶜ رجّع (rijjeeᶜ)
sender mursil مرسل
senile mukharrif مخرّف ; kharf-aan خرفان ; **to be**(**come**) **senile** kharraf خرّف (kharfa, khirreef); itkharraf اتخرّف (kharfa, khirreef)
senior al-kabiir
seniority agdamiyya أقدميّة
sense *n* (**meaning**) maᶜna معنى (*pl* maᶜaani); (**one of the five senses**) ḥaassa حاسّة (*pl* ḥawaass)
sensible ᶜaagil عاقل
sensitive ḥassaas حسّاس
sensitivity ḥasaasiyya حساسيّة
sentence *n* (**grammatical**) jumla جملة (*pl* jumal)
sentence *n* (**in court**) ḥukum حكم (*pl* aḥkaam) • *v* ḥakam ᶜala حكم (i, ḥukum); **to be sentenced** itḥakam be- اتحكم (ḥukum)
sentry deedabaan ديدبان (*pl* -aat)
separate *vt* faṣal فصل (i, faṣil); farrag فرّق (firreeg, tafriig); **to be**(**come**) **separated** itfaṣal اتفصل (faṣla); itfarrag اتفرّق (firreeg, furga, tifirrig) • *vi* infaṣal انفصل (infiṣaal)
separation infiṣaal انفصال (*pl* -aat); (**parting**) furaag فراق
September shahri tisᶜa; sebtembar سبتمبر
sergeant raqiib رقيب (*pl* ruqaba); **sergeant major** ṣool صول ; **staff sergeant** shaawiish شاويش (*pl* -iyya)
series musalsal مسلسل (*pl* -aat)
serious (**grave**) khaṭiir خطير ; (**no fun**) jaadd جاد
seriously be-jadd; jadd jadd
seriousness (**danger**) khuṭuura خطورة ; (**no fun**) jadd جد
sermon waᶜiẓ وعظ (*pl* mawaaᶜiiẓ); khuṭba خطبة (*pl* khuṭab)
servant (*m*) khaddaam خدّام ; shaghghaal شغّال ; (*f*) khaddaa-ma خدّامة ; shaghghaala شغّالة ; **civil servant** (*m*) muwaẓẓaf موظّف ; (*f*) muwaẓẓafa موظّفة
serve khadam خدم (i, khidma)
service khidma خدمة (*pl* khad-amaat); (**of an engine**) ᶜamra عمرة ; **military service** al-khid-ma al-ᶜaskariyya; **at your service** ḥaaḍir حاضر ; tiḥit amr-ak • *v* (**an engine**) ᶜammar عمّر (ᶜamra); **to be serviced** itᶜammar اتعمّر (ᶜamra)
serviette fuuṭa فوطة (*pl* fuwaṭ)
sesame simsim سمسم ; **sesame paste** ṭaḥiina طحينة ; (**sweet**) ṭaḥniyya طحنيّة ; **sesame oil** zeet simsim

session jalsa جلسة
set *n* **set (of jewels, clothes, etc.)** ṭagim طقم (*pl* ṭuguum); **(of tools)** ʿidda عدّة *n* (*pl* ʿidad); **set square** zaawiya زاوية (*pl* zawaaya) • *v* **(down)** khatta ختّ (u, khatt); **(sun)** ghaab غاب (i, ghiyaab) غرب ; **to set bones** jabar جبر (i, jabur, jabir); jabbar جبّر (jibbeer); **to set free** fakka فكّ (i, fakka); **to be set free** itfakka اتفكّ (fakk, fakka); **to set up** kawwan كوّن (takwiin)
settle *vi* istaqarra استقرّ (istiqraar) • *vt* **(an account)** ḥaasab حاسب (muḥaasaba); **(a debt)** saddad سدّد (siddeed); **(reach an agreement on)** saawa ساوى (-i, taswiya)
settlement **(of accounts)** taswiya تسوية
seven sabʿa سبعة ; **seven hundred** subʿumiyya سبعميّة
seventeen sabʿṭaashar سبعطاشر
seventh saabiʿ سابع
seventy sabʿiin سبعين
several ʿidda عدّة ; **several people** ʿiddat naas
severe shadiid شديد (*pl* shudaad); **(stern)** gaasi قاسي
sew khayyaṭ خيّط (khiyaaṭa); **(with sewing machine)** ṭagga طقّ (u, ṭagg)
sewing khiyaaṭa خياطة
sewer **(drain)** majaari مجاري (*sg* majra)
sex **(intercourse)** jins جنس ; **(gender)** jinis جنس (*pl* ajnaas); **to have sex with** ragad maʿa
sexual jinsi جنسي
shade ḍull ضل (*pl* ḍalala)
shadow ḍull ضل (*pl* ḍalala)
shake hazza هزّ (i, hazz); **(liquid)** rajja رجّ (u, rajja); **to be shaken** ithazza اتهزّ (hazz); **(liquid)** itrajja اترجّ (rajj); **to shake s.o.'s hand** shadda ʿala iid-o
shallow ḍaḥil ضحل ; **(of well)** guṣayyir قصيّر
shame ʿeeb عيب ; **shame on you!** ʿeeb ʿalee-k!; ḥaraam ʿalee-k!; yikhṣ ʿalee-k!; yakhṣi ʿalee-k!
shampoo shamboo شامبو (*pl* -haat)
shanty towns aḥyaa ʿashwaa'iyya
shape *n* shakil شكل (*pl* ashkaal); **(of a person)** khilga خلقة (*pl* khilag)
share *n* naṣiib نصيب (*pl* anṣiba); gisma قسمة (*pl* agsaam); **(of company stock)** saham سهم (*pl* ashum); **(of inheritance)** ʿuud عود (*pl* aʿwaad) • *v* itgaasam اتقاسم (mugaasama); itshaarak (fi) اتشارك (mushaaraka); **(a single item)** khammas خمّس (khimmees, takhmiis); **(expenses)** itshaarak fi اتشارك (mushaaraka); shaarak fi شارك (mushaaraka); **(costs of food)** mayyaz ميّز (meez)
sharp ḥaadd حاد ; saniin سنين ; maaḍi ماضي ; ṭariin طرين
sharpen sanna سنّ (i, sann); ṭarran طرّن (ṭirreen); **(pencil)** bara برى (-i, bariya, bari)
shave *n* ḥilaaga حلاقة • *v* ḥalag حلق (i, ḥalga, ḥilaaga); **(head)** zayyan زيّن (ziyyeen)
shawl shaal شال (*pl* -aat); **(worn by men)** malfaḥa ملفحة (*pl* malaafiḥ)
she hi هى ; hiya هي
shear jazza جزّ (i, jazz)

sheep *n* (*m*) kharuuf خروف (*pl* khurfaan, khirfaan); kabish كبش (*pl* kibaash); (*f*) ḍaanaaya ضانايه; naʿja نعجة (*pl* niʿaaj) • *n pl* ḍaan ضان

sheepfold zariiba زريبة (*pl* zaraayib)

sheet (**bed linen**) milaaya ملاية; (**of paper**) waraga ورقة (*pl* -aat, awraag); **sheet iron** ṣafiiḥ صفيح

shelf raff رف (*pl* rufuuf)

shell(s) (**of mollusc**) wadiʿ ودع (*unit n* wadʿa); ṣadaf صدف

shell (**projectile**) qumbula قمبلة (*pl* qanaabil)

shelter *n* (**sun**) raakuuba راكوبة (*pl* rawaakiib); (**refuge**) malja ملجا (*pl* malaaji) • *vi* iḍḍaara اضّار (-a, muḍaaraa); (**from rain**) itmaṭṭar اتمطّر (miṭṭeer); maṭṭar مطّر (miṭṭeer)

shepherd *n* raaʿi راعي (*pl* rawaaʿiyya, ruʿʿaa) • v raʿa رعى (-a, raʿi)

shield *n* daraga درقة (*pl* -aat, dirag) • *v* ḥaras (min) حرس (i, ḥiraasa); (**from scandal**) satar ستر (u, sitr); itsattar ʿala اتستّر (tasattur)

shift *n* (**at work**) wardiyya ورديّة; dawwaam دوّام (*pl* -aat)

shift *v* ḥawwal حوّل (taḥwiil); **to be shifted** itḥawwal اتحوّل (taḥwiil)

shine *v* lamaʿ لمع (a, lamaʿaan); ragash رقش (i, ragish)

shingles ḥizaam naari

ship safiina سفينة (*pl* sufun)

shipment (**of goods**) irsaaliyya إرساليّة

shirt gamiiṣ قميص (*pl* gumṣaan)

shit (**faeces**) khara خرا

shiver *n* rajfa رجفة • *v* rajaf رجف (i, rajif, rajafaan); irtajaf ارتجف (rajafaan)

shock *n* ṣadma صدمة; **psychological shock** ṣadma nafsiyya • *v* ṣadam صدم (u, ṣadma); **to be shocked** (**by**) itṣadam (fi) اتصدم (ṣadma)

shoe jazma جزمة (*pl* -aat, jizam); (**traditional Sudanese**) markuub مركوب (*pl* maraakiib); **sports shoes** kaddaara كدّارة; kabak كبك (*pl* kubaaka)

shoelace rubaaṭ رباط (*pl* -aat, arbiṭa)

shoemaker nugulti نقلتي (*pl* -yya); jazmaji جزمجي (*pl* -iyya); ṣarmaati صرماتي (*pl* -yya); iskaafi اسكافي (*pl* -yyiin)

shoe mender nugulti نقلتي (*pl* -yya); jazmaji جزمجي (*pl* -iyya); ṣarmaati صرماتي (*pl* -yya); iskaafi اسكافي (*pl* -yyiin)

shoot (**with gun**) ḍarab naar; ḍarab be-r-raṣṣaaṣ; (**goal**) shaat شات (u, shoot)

shooting iṭlaaq an-naar

shop *n* dukkaan دكّان (*pl* dakaakiin) • *v* itsawwag اتسوّق (siwweeg)

shopkeeper siid ad-dukkaan

shopping area suug سوق (*pl* aswaag)

shore shaaṭi شاطي (*pl* shawaaṭi); geef قيف

short guṣayyir قصيّر (*pl* guṣayriin, guṣaar); gaṣiir قصير (*pl* guṣaar); (**lacking**) naagiṣ ناقص; **in short** be-ikhtiṣaar; **to be caught short** itzanag اتزنق (i, zanig); **to take a shortcut** ikhtaṣar aṭ-ṭariig

shortage ʿajz عجز ; nagṣ نقص ; nugṣaan نقصان ; **(in market)** azma أزمة
shortcoming *n* nagiiṣa نقيصة (*pl* nagaayiṣ)
shorten gaṣṣar قصّر (giṣṣeer, tagṣiir)
shortness guṣur قصر
shorts short شورت (*pl* -aat); rida ردا (*pl* ardiya)
shortsighted muʿammish معمّش
shortsightedness taʿmiish تعميش
shot *n* ṭalga طلقة (*pl* -aat, ṭilag); ḍarba be-n-naar
shoulder katif كتف (*pl* katfeen, kutuuf, aktaaf)
shoulder blade looḥat al-katif
shout *n* ṣarkha صرخة • *v* **(at)** koorak (fi) كورك (kooraak); ṣarrakh صرّخ (ṣuraakh, ṣirreekh); ṣarakh صرخ (a, ṣariikh)
shovel *n* kooreek كوريك (*pl* kawaariik)
show *v* warra ورّى (-i, wirreey); ʿaraḍ عرض (a, ʿariḍ); **to show out in leave-taking** gaddam قدّم (giddeem); **to show off** itfalham اتفلهم (falhama); itbaṭṭar اتبطّر (tabaṭṭur)
shower *n* dush دش (*pl* dushuush); **(of rain)** maṭara مطرة (*pl* amṭaar); **to take a shower** akhad dush
showy bitaaʿ al-maẓaahir; **(appearance)** ḥankuush حنكوش ; mutḥankish متحنكش
shred gaṭaʿ قطع (a, gaṭiʿ)
shredder gaṭṭaaʿa قطاعة
shrewd khabiis خبيس (*pl* -iin, khubasa); makkaar مكّار
shrewdness khubs خبس ; mukur مكر
shrimps jambari جمبري
shrink inkamash انكمش (inkimaash); kashsha كشّ (i, kashsh); **to shrink from** kashsha min كشّ (i, kashsh)
shroud kafan كفن (*pl* akfaan)
shut *v* gafal قفل (i, gafil); gaffal قفّل (giffeel); sadda سدّ (i, sadd)
shutter(s) shiish شيش
shuttle (loom) murkab مركب (*pl* maraakib)
shy *adj* khajuul خجول ; maksuuf مكسوف ; mukhtashi مختشى ; **to be(come) shy** khijil خجل (a, khajal); ikhtasha اختشى (-i, ikhtisha)
shyness khajal خجل
sick ʿayyaan عيّان ; marḍaan مرضان ; mariiḍ مريض (*pl* marḍa); **to be(come) sick** ʿiya عيى (-a, ʿaya); miriḍ مرض (a, maraḍ); **to feel sick (from)** ṭamma (min) طمّ (u, ṭumaam); **to make s.o. feel sick** ṭammam (min) طمّم (ṭimmeem)
sickle munjal منجل (*pl* manaajil)
sickness maraḍ مرض (*pl* amraaḍ)
side *n* jaanib جانب (*pl* jawaanib, ajnaab); naaḥya ناحية (*pl* nawaaḥi); **(of the body)** jamba جمبة ; **(direction)** naaḥya ناحية (*pl* nawaaḥi); jiha جهة ; **(on) that side** be-ghaadi; **(on) this side** be-jaay; **side turning** laffa لفّة
side effects muḍaaʿafaat مضاعفات
siege ḥiṣaar حصار (*pl* -aat)
sieve maṣfa مصفى (*pl* maṣaafi); ghurbaal غربال (*pl* gharaabiil)
sift gharbal غربل (gharbala); ṣaffa صفّى (-i, ṣiffeey)
sigh *n* nihheeda نهّيدة • *v* itnahhad اتنهّد (nihheed, tanhiid)

sight (**of eyes**) shoof شوف ; naẓar نظر ; baṣar بصر ; ruu'ya رؤية ; (**view**) manẓar منظر (*pl* manaaẓir)

sign *n* ishaara إشارة ; ʿalaama علامة ; **traffic sign** al-ishaara; ishaarat al-ḥaraka; ishaaratal-muruur • v maḍa مضا (-i, imḍa); waqqaʿ وقّع (tawqiiʿ)

signal *n* ishaara إشارة • *v* ash-shar أشّر (ya'ashshir, ishsheer, ta'shiir)

signature imḍa إمضا (*pl* imḍaa'aat); tawqiiʿ توقيع (*pl* -aat)

signboard laafta لافتة (*pl* -aat, li-fat); yaafṭa يافطة (*pl* -aat, yifaṭ)

silence sakta سكتة ; sukuut سكوت ; ṣamt صمت • *v* sakkat سكّت (sikkeet)

silencer (**of a gun**) kaatim ṣoot

silent saakit ساكت ; ṣaamit صامت ; ṣaanni صانّ (*pl* ṣaanniin); **to be silent** sakat سكت (u, sukuut); ṣamat صمت (u, ṣamt)

silk *adj* ḥariiri حريري • *n* ḥariir حرير (*pl* ḥaraayir)

silly (**stupid**) ahbal أهبل (*f* habla, *pl* hubul); maṭmuus مطموس (*pl* maṭaamiis); (**ridiculous**) sakhiif سخيف (*pl* -iin, sukhafa)

silt ṭami طمي

silver *adj* faḍḍi فضّي • *n* faḍḍa فضّة

silversmith ṣaayigh صايغ (*pl* ṣuyyaagh)

similar shabiih le- شبيه

simple basiiṭ بسيط (*pl* busaṭa)

simulate itẓaahar be- اتظاهر (taẓaahur); itṣannaʿ اتصنّع (taṣannuʿ)

simultaneously fi nafs al-wakit

sin *n* zanib/zanb زنب (*pl* zunuub); khaṭiya خطية (khaṭaaya); (*Chr*) khaṭii'a خطيئة (*pl* khaṭaaya); (*Isl*) sayyi'a سيّئة ; **to commit a sin** irtakab zanib/zanb

since (**from when**) min من ; min-wakit; (**as**) kawn- كون- ; ma daam

sincere ṣaadig صادق ; mukhliṣ مخلص

sincerity ṣaraaḥa صراحة ; ṣidig صدق

sinew watar وتر (*pl* awtaar)

sing ghanna غنّى (-i, ghuna); (**church songs**) rattal رتّل (tar-tiil); **to sing to sleep** loola لولى (-i, loolaay)

singe tashsha تشّ (i, tashsh, tashashaan); shalwaṭ شلوط (shalwaṭa); **to be singed** itshalwaṭ اتشلوط (shalwaṭa)

singer (*m*) mughanni مغنّي (*pl* -yyiin); (*f*) mughanniyya مغنّية ; **an accomplished singer** (*m*) muṭrib مطرب ; (*f*) muṭriba مطربة

single *adj* waḥiid وحيد

singular mufrad مفرد

sink *v* ghirig غرق (a, gharag)

sinusitis iltihaab aj-jiyuub al-anfiyya

sip *n* bugga بقّة • *v* bagga بقّ (u, bagga)

sir sayyid سيّد (*pl* saada)

sister ukhut أخت (*pl* akhawaat); **full sister** shagiiga شقيقة ; **sister-in-law** nasiiba نسيبة

sit gaʿad قعد (u, guʿaad); gannab قنب (ginneeb); ṣangar صنقر (ṣingeer); jalas جلس (i, juluus); **to sit cross-legged** itrabbaʿ اتربّع (ribbeeʿ); gaʿad mutrabbiʿ; **to make s.o. sit down** gaʿʿad قعّد (giʿʿeed, gaʿda)

situation ḥaal حال (*pl* aḥwaal, aḥaawiil); ḥaala حالة (*pl* -aat, aḥwaal); waḍᶜ وضع (*pl* awḍaaᶜ)
six sitta ستّة; **six hundred** suttumiyya ستّميّة
sixteen siṭṭaashar سطّاشر
sixth saadis سادس
sixty sittiin ستّين
size ḥajim حجم (*pl* aḥjaam); (**of clothes, shoes**) magaas مقاس (*pl* -aat)
skewer(s) siikh سيخ (*pl* siyakh)
skilful maahir ماهر (*pl* mahara); ḥariif حريف (*pl* -iin, ḥurafa); jadiir جدير (*pl* judara)
skill mahaara مهارة; ḥarfana حرفنة; jadaara جدارة
skin *n* jilid جلد; (**of fruit, nuts, etc.**) gishra قشرة (*pl* gushuur); **water skin** girba قربة (*pl* girab) • *v* salakh سلخ (a, salikh)
skip (**hop**) naṭṭaṭ نطّط (niṭṭeeṭ); (**miss out**) faṭṭa فطّ (u, faṭṭ); fawwat فوّت (fiwweet, tafwiit)
skirt iskeert إسكيرت (*pl* -aat); jiiba جيبة
skull jumjumma جمجمّة (*pl* jamaajim)
skullcap ṭaagiyya طاقيّة (*pl* -aat, ṭawaagi)
sky sama سما (*pl* samawaat)
slack (**negligent**) sajmaan سجمان; muhmil مهمل; (**loose**) markhi مرخي
slacken (**e.g. a rope**) rakha رخى (-i, rakhi, rakhiya)
slander *n* qazif قزف • *v* qazaf قزف (i, qazif)
slant (**toward**) maal مال (i, mayalaan, meel)
slap *n* kaff كفّ (*pl* kufuuf); laṭma لطمة • *v* (**on the face**) kaffat كفّت (kiffeet); ṣafaᶜ صفع (a, ṣafᶜaan); **he slapped him** addaaho kaff/ḍarab-o kaff; (**on the body**) raṣaᶜ رصع (a, raṣiᶜ); laṭam لطم (u, laṭim)
slaughter *v* (**animals**) ḍabaḥ ضبح (a, ḍabiḥ)
slaughterhouse salakhaana سلخانة
slave (*m*) ᶜabid عبد (*pl* ᶜabiid); (*f*) ᶜabda عبدة; **slaves** ragiig رقيق
slavery riqq رق
sledgehammer marazabba مرزبّة
sleep *n* noom نوم • *v* naam نام (u, noom); **to make s.o. sleep** nawwam نوّم (niwweem); **sleeping sickness** maraḍ an-noom
sleepy naᶜsaan نعسان; **to be(come) sleepy** niᶜis نعس (a, naᶜaas); rakhkham رخّم (rikhkheem)
sleeve kumm كم (*pl* akmaam); (**for tightening or attaching sth. e.g. water hose to tap, padlock to door**) gafiis قفيس (*pl* gafaayis)
slice shariiḥa شريحة (*pl* sharaayiḥ)
slide *v* inzalag انزلق (inzilaag); itzalag اتزلق (zalig, zalga)
slimy (*also fig*) laayuug لايوق
sling (**for throwing stones**) nibla نبلة (*pl* nibal)
slink iddabba ادّبّ (dabba, dibbeey)
slip *v* inzalag انزلق (inzilaag); itzalag اتزلق (zalig, zalga); **to slip away** zaaq زاق (u, zooqa, zawaqaan); **to slip out, to slip down** itmalaṣ اتملص (malṣa); **to cause to slip** zalag زلق (i, zalig); zallag زلّق (zilleeg)
slipper **pair of slippers** shibshib شبشب (*pl* shabaashib); **plastic or rubber slipper(s)** safinja سفنجة

slippery a slippery spot or place zalageeba زلقيبة ; **it is slippery** bi-yazlig

slither (**in mud**) khaaḍ خاض (u, khuwaaḍa)

slobber *n* riyaala ريالة ; luʿaab لعاب • *v* rayyal ريّل (riyaala)

slogan shiʿaar شعار (*pl* -aat); **crowd recruited for shouting slogans** hittiifa هتّيفة ; **to shout slogans** hataf be-shiʿaaraat

slope *n* inḥidaar إنحدار (*pl* -aat); meel ميل • *v* inḥadar انحدر (inḥidaar); **to slope** (**to/toward**) maal (le-/ ila) مال (i, mayalaan, meel)

slovenly mubashtan مبشتن ; **to produce slovenly work** karwat كروت (karwata)

slow baṭii بطي (*pl* -ʾiin); **he is slow** ḥarakt-o tagiila • *v* **to slow down** hadda as-surʿa

slowly *adv* be-raaḥa; ḥabba ḥabba; shwayya shwayya; be-shweesh

slurp shafaṭ شفط (u, shafiṭ)

sly la'iim لئيم (*pl* lu'ama); makkaar مكّار

smack *v* kaffat كفّت (kiffeet); ṣafaʿ صفع (a, ṣafʿaan); **he smacked him** addaa-ho kaff; **to smack one's lips** itmaṭṭag اتمطّق (miṭṭeeg)

small ṣughayyir صغير (*pl* -iin, ṣughaar); ṣaghiir صغير (*pl* ṣughaar); **to make sth. small(er)** ṣaghghar صغّر (taṣghiir, ṣighgheer)

smallness ṣughur صغر

smallpox jadari جدري

smart (**stylish**) gaashir قاشر ; (**clever**) najiiḍ نجيض (*pl* nujaaḍ); shaaṭir شاطر (*pl* shaaṭriin, shuṭṭaar); nabiih نبيه (*pl* nubaha)

smartness (**cleverness**) najaaḍa نجاضة ; shaṭaara شطارة ; nabaaha نباهة

smash *v* dashdash دشدش (dishdeesh, dashdasha); kassar كسّر (kisseer, taksiir)

smell *n* riiḥa ريحة (*pl* aryaaḥ, rawaayiḥ); **bad smell** ʿafaana عفانة ; (**of body**) ṣunaan صنان • *vt* shamma شمّ (i, shamm) • *vi* ṭallaʿ riiḥa

smile *n* basma بسمة ; ibtisaama إبتسامة (*pl* -aat) • *v* basam بسم (basma); ibtasam إبتسم (ibtisaam); itbassam اتبسّم (tibissim)

smith ḥaddaad حدّاد (*pl* -iin, ḥadaadiid)

smoke *n* dukhaan دخّان (*pl* dakhaakhiin) • *vi* dakhkhan دخّن (tadkhiin) • *vt* shirib شرب (a, sharaab); dakhkhan دخّن (tadkhiin)

smoke bath dukhaan دخّان

smooth naaʿim ناعم ; amlas أملس (*f* malsa, *pl* mulus)

smoothe (**the surface**) mallas ملّس (millees, tamliis)

smuggle harrab هرّب (hirreeb, tahriib)

smuggler muharrib مهرّب

smuggling tahriib تهريب

smutty (**of jokes**) baayikh بايخ

snack *n* wajba ṣughayra; mazza مزّة (*pl* mizzaz); (**nuts, popcorn, etc.**) mukassaraat مكسّرات ; (**to kill hunger before a meal**) taṣbiira تصبيرة

snail(**s**) garguur قرقور (*pl* garaagiir)

snake daabi دابى (*pl* dawaabi); dabiib دبيب (*pl* dabaayib); suʿbaan سعبان (*pl* saʿaabiin)

snap (**break**) ingaṭaᶜ انقطع (ingiṭaaᶜ); itgaṭaᶜ اتقطع (gaṭiᶜ); **to snap one's fingers** ṭargaᶜ طرقع (ṭargaᶜa, ṭirgeeᶜ)
snare *n* sharak شرك (*pl* ashraak) • *v* sharrak le- شرّك (shirreek, tashriik)
snatch *v* khaṭaf خطف (i, khaṭif)
sneeze *n* ᶜaṭas عطس • *v* ᶜaṭas عطس (a, ᶜiṭṭees)
sniff *v* (**glue, cocaine**) shamma شمّ (i, shamm); (**perfume, incense**) karaf كرف (u, karif)
snooze *n* ghamḍa غمضة ; ghafwa غفوة
snore *v* shakhar شخر (u, shakhiir); shakhkhar شخّر (shikhkheer)
snuff *n* (**tobacco**) ṣaᶜuuṭ صعوط ; tumbaak تمباك
so kida كدي ; **he said so** gaal kida; (**thus**) ghaayto غايتو ; **so then...** kade كدي ; **is that so?** hagiigi حقيقي ; be jadd?; **so that** ᶜashaan عشان ; **so-and-so** filaan فلان ; filaan al-filaani
soak ᶜaṭan عطن (i, ᶜaṭin); **to be soaked** inᶜaṭan انعطن (ᶜaṭin, inᶜiṭaan); itᶜaṭan اتعطن (ᶜaṭin)
soakaway biir بير (*pl* abyaar, aabaar)
soap ṣaabuun صابون ; **a piece of soap** ṣaabuuna صابونة ; **laundry soap** ṣaabuunghasiil; **toilet soap** ṣaabuunḥammaam
sober ṣaaḥi صاحي ; **to become sober** faag فاق (u, fooga)
soccer al-kuura; al-kura; kuurat al-gadam; kurat al-gadam
socialist ishtiraaki اشتراكي
society mujtamaᶜ مجتمع (*pl* -aat); (**organization**) jamᶜiyya جمعيّة
sociology ᶜilim al-ijtimaaᶜ
sock shurraab شرّاب (*pl* -aat)
socket (**electric**) balak بلك (*pl* bal-akkaat); kobs كبس (*pl* -aat); kobs intaaya; kobsi كبسي (*pl* -yyaat)
sofa kanaba كنبة (*pl* -aat, kanab)
soft naaᶜim ناعم ; amlas أملس (*f* malsa, *pl* mulus); **soft drink** ḥaaja baarda
soften naᶜᶜam نعّم (niᶜᶜeem)
soil ariḍ أرض (*pl* araaḍi); turaab تراب ; turba تربة (*pl* turab); ṭiin طين (*pl* aṭyaan); **preparation of the soil for sowing** koodeeb كوديب • *v* wassakh وسّخ (wis-seekh, wasaakha)
solder *n* liḥaam لحام ; giṣdiir قصدير (*pl* gaṣaadiir) • *v* laḥam لحم (a, laḥim); **soldering iron** kawwaaya كواية
soldier ᶜaskari عسكري (*pl* ᶜasaakir); jayyaashi جيّاشي (*pl* jayyaasha); jundi جندي (*pl* junuud); **private soldier** ᶜaskari nafar
sole *adj* waḥiid وحيد
sole *n* (**of foot**) waṭṭaaya وطاية ; baṭnal-kuraaᶜ; (**of shoe**) waṭṭaaya وطاية ; naᶜal نعل (*pl* niᶜlaat, niᶜleen)
solid *adj* matiin متين ; jaamid جامد ; ṣalb/ṣulb صلب
solidarity taḍaamun تضامن
solidly jaamid جامد
solution (**of a problem**) ḥall حل (*pl* ḥuluul); (**chemical**) maḥluul محلول (*pl* maḥaaliil); **wetting solution** ballaal بلال
solve ḥalla حلّ (i, ḥall); **to be solved** inḥalla انحلّ (a, inḥilaal, ḥall); itḥalla اتحلّ (ḥall)
some baᶜaḍ بعض ; **some people** waaḥdiin واحدين ; **some women** waaḥdaat واحدات

somebody waaḥid واحد (*pl* waaḥdiin)
someone (*m*) waaḥid واحد (*pl* waaḥdiin); (*f*) waaḥda واحدة (*pl* waaḥdaat)
somersault *n* galba قلبة • *v* ingalab انقلب (galba); galab al-huuba
something ḥaaja حاجة
sometimes marra marra; marraat مرّات ; saaʿaat ساعات ; aḥyaanan أحيانا
somewhat shwayya شويّة
somewhere makaan muʿayyan
son walad ولد (*pl* awlaad); wad ود (wadd *pl* awlaad); ibin ابن (*pl* abnaa)
song ghanwa غنوة (*pl* aghaani, ghunwaat); ghunya غنية (*pl* aghaani); ughniya أغنية (*pl* -aat, aghaani); **song in church** tarniima ترنيمة (*pl* taraaniim)
soon gariib قريب ; **as soon as** awwal ma; yaadoob ma
soot sakan سكن ; sajam سجم
soporific munawwim منوّم (*pl* -aat)
sorcerer saḥḥaar سحّار (*pl* saḥaaḥiir)
sorcery siḥir سحر
sore *n* ʿuwwaara عوّارة (*pl* -aat, ʿawaawiir)
sorghum ʿeesh عيش (*pl* ʿiyuush); zura زرة ; dura درة ; **varieties of sorghum** fatariita فتريتة ; maareeg ماريق ; ṣafra صفرة ; ʿankooliib عنكوليب
sorrow ghamm غم
sorry aasif آسف ; maʿleesh معليش ; **to be sorry for** it'assaf ʿala اتأسّف (asaf, ta'assuf)
sort *n* nooʿ نوع (*pl* anwaaʿ); (**species**) jinis جنس (*pl* ajnaas) • *v* **to sort out** faraz فرز (i, fariz); farraz فرّز (firreez)
so-so yaʿni يعني
soul nafis نفس (*pl* nufuus); ruuḥ روح (*pl* arwaaḥ)
sound *adj* saalim سالم • *n* ṣoot صوت (*pl* aṣwaat)
soup shoorba شوربة ; **soup made from sheep or cow's foot** kawaariʿ كوارع
sour ḥaamiḍ حامض ; **to be(come) sour** itḥammaḍ اتحمّض (ḥimmeeḍ); ḥammaḍ حمّض (ḥimmeeḍ)
source mawrid مورد (*pl* mawaarid); (**of information**) maṣdar مصدر (*pl* maṣaadir); (**of a river**) manbaʿ منبع (*pl* manaabiʿ); (**origin**) aṣil أصل (*pl* uṣuul)
south januub جنوب
southern januubi جنوبي
southerner (**of Sudan**) januubi جنوبي (*pl* -yyiin)
southwards be-j-januub
sow zaraʿ زرع (a, zariʿ, ziraaʿa); teerab تيرب (teeraab); **to be sown** itzaraʿ اتزرع (zariʿ, ziraaʿa)
space *adj* faḍaa'i فضائي • *n* (cosmic) faḍaa فضا ; (**room**) makaan مكان (*pl* amaakin); **open space** fasaḥa فسحة ; faḍaaya فضاية ; saaḥa ساحة ; (**town square**) meedaan/miidaan ميدان (*pl* mayaadiin); **little space** faraga فرقة
spacious waasiʿ واسع ; wasiiʿ وسيع ; (**e.g. house**) ḥaddaadi maddaadi
spade kooreek كوريك (*pl* kawaariik)
Spain asbaanya اسبانيا
Spaniard asbaani اسباني (*pl* asbaan)

Spanish asbaani اسباني (*pl* asbaan)
spanner muftaaḥ مفتاح (*pl* mafaatiiḥ); muftaaḥ ṣaamuula
spare *adj* iḥtiyaaṭi إحتياطي ; **spare part** isbeer إسبير (*pl* -aat); **spare tyre** ʿajala isbeer; lastik isbeer; **spare clothes (e.g. when travelling)** ghiyaar غيار
spark sharaara شرارة (*pl* -aat, sharar); **spark plug** buuji بوجي (*pl* bawaaji)
sparkle *v* barag برق (u, barig); ragash رقش (i, ragasha)
sparrow wad abrag; **sparrow(s)** ʿaṣfuur عصفور (*pl* ʿaṣaafiir)
spatial faḍaa'i فضائي
speak kallam كلّم (kalaam); itkallam اتكلّم (kalaam); naḍam نضم (u, naḍim)
spear *n* ḥarba حربة (*pl* ḥuraab); kookaab كوكاب (*pl* -aat)
special khaaṣṣ خاصّ
specialist ikhtiṣaaṣi إختصاصي (*pl* -yyiin); **medical specialist** akhiṣṣaa'i أخصّائي (*pl* -yyiin)
specialization takhaṣṣuṣ تخصّص (*pl* -aat)
specialize khaṣṣaṣ خصّص (takhṣiiṣ)
specially be-z-zaat; khuṣuuṣan خصوصا ; khaaṣṣatan خاصّة ; **specially for** makhṣuuṣ le- مخصوص
species nooʿ نوع (*pl* anwaaʿ); jinis جنس (*pl* ajnaas); ṣanf صنف (*pl* aṣnaaf)
specifically be-ṣifa khaaṣṣa
specifications muwaaṣafaat مواصفات
specify ḥaddad حدّد (taḥdiid)
specimen ʿayna عينة
spectacles naḍḍaara نضّارة
spectator mutfarrij متفرّج
speech **(public address)** khuṭba خطبة (*pl* khuṭab); **to give a speech** khaṭab خطب (u, khuṭba)
speed surʿa سرعة
spell *v* ithajja اتهجّى (-a, tahjiya)
spend **(money)** ṣaraf صرف (u, ṣarif); **(time)** gaḍḍa قضّى (giḍḍeey); **to spend all (e.g. money)** kammal كمّل (kimmeel); **to spend the afternoon** gayyal قيّل (giyyeel, magiil); **to spend the night** baat بات (i, beeta, bayataan); bayyat بيّت (bayataan, mabiit); **to spend the night without having had supper** baat al-gawa
spices dawa دوا (*pl* diwyaat); buhaaraat بهارات
spider umm shabatu; abu shabatu; ʿankabuut عنكبوت (*pl* ʿanaakib)
spill daffag دفّق (diffeeg); **to be spilled** iddaffag ادّفّق (diffeeg)
spin *v* **(yarn)** tarra ترّ (u, tarr); ghazal غزل (i, ghazil)
spinal faqri فقري ; **the spinal column** al-ʿamuud al-faqri
spindle mutraar مترار (*pl* -aat, mataariir)
spine ʿaḍum aḍ-ḍahar
spineless ḍaʿiif ضعيف (*pl* ḍuʿaaf); iḍeena إضينة
spirit ruuḥ روح (*pl* arwaaḥ); **(chemical)** isbirit اسبيرت ; **(supernatural being)** jinn جنّ (*unit n m* jinni, *f* jinniyya)
spiritual **(as opposed to material)** ruuḥi روحي
spit taffa تفّ (u, taff); bazag بزق (u, bazig, buzaag)
spite *n* ḥasad حسد ; ḥasaada حسادة ; ḥigid حقد ; **in spite of**

be-raghmi min • *v* ḥasad حسد (i, ḥasaada, ḥasad)

spiteful ḥasuud حسود ; ḥaasid حاسد (*pl* ḥussaad); ḥaagid حاقد ; ḥaguud حقود ; **to be spiteful** ḥasad حسد (i, ḥasaada, ḥasad); ḥagad حقد (i, ḥagid)

spittle tufaaf تفاف ; buzaag بزاق

spleen abu dammaam

splendid raa'iᶜ رائع

splint *n* jabiira جبيرة (*pl* jabaayir) • *v* jabar جبر (i, jabur); jabbar جبّر (jibbeer)

splinter kasra كسرة (*pl* kussaar); (**in skin**) sariiḥa سريحة (*pl* saraayiḥ)

split *n* shagg شق (*pl* shuguug) • *v* shagga شقّ (i, shagg, shagga); shaggag شقّق (shiggeeg); **to be split** inshagga انشقّ (shagg, shagagaan); **to split up** itfarrag اتفرّق (firreeg, tafarrug); (**separate**) infaṣal انفصل (infiṣaal)

spoil bawwaẓ بوّظ (biwweeẓ, tabwiiẓ); (**damage**) khassar خسّر (khisseer, takhsiir); (**pamper**) dallaᶜ دلّع (dilleeᶜ, dalaᶜ); dallal دلّل (dalaal, tadliil); **to be(come) spoiled** (**damaged**) khisir خسر (a, khasaara, khusraan); (**rotten**) baaẓ باظ (u, bawaẓaan, booẓ); tilif تلف (a, talaf); (**pampered**) iddallaᶜ ادّلّع (dalaᶜ, tidilliᶜ)

spoke (**e.g. of a bike**) silik سلك (*pl* aslaak)

spokesperson naaṭig ناطق

sponge(s) isfinja اسفنجة

sponger maẓalli مظلّي (*pl* -yyiin); muṭṭaffil مطّفّل

sponsor *n* mumawwil ممّوّل • *v* mawwal موّل (tamwiil)

spoon maᶜalaga ملعقة (*pl* maᶜaalig); malᶜaga ملعقة (*pl* malaaᶜig)

sports riyaaḍa رياضة ; **sports shoes** kaddaara كدّارة ; kabak كبك (*pl* kubaaka); **sports track** miidaan ميدان (*pl* mayaadiin); **to practise sports** itrayyaḍ اتريّض (riyaaḍa)

spot *n* (**dot**) nugṭa نقطة (*pl* nugaṭ); (**place**) bugᶜa بقعة (*pl* bugaᶜ); (**stain**) laṭkha لطخة (*pl* luṭakh)

spotted (**e.g. hide**) abrag أبرق (*f* barga, *pl* burug, buraga)

sprain *v* malakh ملخ (a, malakhaan); **to be sprained** itmalakh اتملخ (malikh, malakhaan)

spray *n* (**can**) bakhkhaakh بخّاخ (*pl* -aat); bakhkhaakha بخّاخة • *v* bakhkha بخّ (u, bakhkh); **to be sprayed** itbakhkha اتبخّ (bakhkh)

spread *vi* intashar انتشر (intishaar) • *vt* nashar نشر (u, nashir); **to spread a cover over** farrash فرّش (firreesh, farish)

spring *n* (**metal**) yaay يايى (*pl* -aat); zambalak زمبلك (*pl* -aat)

spring *n* (**well**) ᶜeen عين (*pl* ᶜiyuun)

spring *n* (**season**) rabiiᶜ ربيع

sprinkle rashsha رشّ (u, rashsh)

sprout *v* itzarraᶜ اتزرّع (zirriiᶜa); gaam قام (u, giyaam); nabat نبت (i, nabataan)

spur *n* mihmaaz مهماز (*pl* mahaamiiz); **to use spurs** (**on a horse**) lakaᶜ لكع (a, lakiᶜ) • *v* (**prod**) hamaz همز (i, hamiz)

spy *n* jaasuus جاسوس (*pl* jawaasiis) • *v* itjassas (ᶜala) اتجسّس (tajassus)

squab farikh al-ḥamaam

squad sariyya سريّة

squander baᶜzag بعزق (baᶜzaga)

squanderer baᶜzaag بعزاق (*pl* baᶜaaziig)
square *adj* murabbaᶜ مربّع; **square metre** mitir murabbaᶜ • *n* murabbaᶜ مربّع (*pl* -aat); marbuuᶜ مربوع (*pl* maraabiiᶜ); **public square** meedaan ميدان (*pl* mayaadiin); miidaan ميدان (*pl* mayaadiin)
squash *n* garaᶜ قرع (*unit n* garᶜa); (**zucchini**) koosa كوسا
squash *v* haras هرس (i, haris)
squat *v* gaᶜad umm galalo; gaᶜad mutgangin
squeak ṣarra صرّ (u, ṣariir); ṣarṣar صرصر (ṣarṣara)
squeeze ᶜaṣar عصر (i, ᶜaṣir); **to be squeezed** itᶜaṣar اتعصر (ᶜaṣir)
squint-eyed aḥwal أحول (*f* ḥawla, *pl* ḥuwul); aḥwaṣ أحوص (*f* ḥawṣa, *pl* ḥuwuṣ)
squirrel(**s**) ṣabar صبر
stab *v* ṭaᶜan طعن (a, ṭaᶜin); **to be stabbed** iṭṭaᶜan اطّعن (ṭaᶜin)
stability istiqraar استقرار
stable *adj* mustaqirr مستقر
stable *n* isṭabil إسطبل (*pl* isṭablaat); zariiba زريبة (*pl* zaraayib)
stack *n* raṣṣa رصّة • *v* raṣṣa رصّ (u, raṣṣ)
stadium istaad استاد (*pl* -aat)
staff **the staff** al-muwaẓẓafiin
stage (**theatre**) khashaba خشبة; masraḥ مسرح (*pl* masaariḥ); (**period**) marḥala مرحلة (*pl* maraaḥil); **cyclic stage** dawra دورة
stagger ittartaḥ اتّرتح (tirteeḥ, tartaḥa)
stain *n* laṭkha لطخة (*pl* luṭakh); bugᶜa بقعة (*pl* bugaᶜ) • *v* laṭṭakh لطّخ (liṭṭeekh); laṭakh لطخ (a, laṭikh); **to be**(**come**) **stained** itlaṭṭakh اتلطّخ (liṭṭeekh)
stairs sillim سلّم (*pl* salaalim)
stake maṣlaḥa مصلحة (*pl* maṣaaliḥ)
stale baayit بايت
stalk *n* saag ساق (*pl* seegaan)
stalk *v* iddabba wara; ṭaarad طارد (muṭaarada)
stammer tamtam تمتم (tamtama, timteem)
stamp *n* khitim ختم (*pl* akhtaam); **duty stamp** damgha دمغة; **postage stamp** ṭaabᶜa طابعة (*pl* ṭawaabiᶜ) • *v* khatam ختم (i, khatim)
stand *n* (**pedestal**) qaaᶜida قاعدة (*pl* qawaaᶜid); (**e.g. for a black-board, flip chart**) ḥaamil حامل (*pl* ḥawaamil); (**e.g. for a jar**) ḥammaala حمّالة; (**for a coffee pot**) wigaaya وقاية • *v* wagaf وقف (yagiif, wuguuf); **to stand up** gaam قام (u, giyaam); **to make s.o. stand up** gawwam قوّم (tagwiim)
standard (**criterion**) miᶜyaar معيار (*pl* maᶜaayiir); migyaas مقياس (*pl* magaayiis)
standpoint mawgif موقف (*pl* mawaagif)
staple dabbuus دبّوس (*pl* dabaabiis)
stapler dabbaasa دبّاسة
star najma نجمة (*pl* -aat, nujuum); kawkab كوكب (*pl* kawaakib); **pole star** aj-jaddi; **star**(**s**) najim نجم; (**badge of rank**) dabbuura دبّورة (*pl* dabaabiir); (**celebrity**) najma نجمة (*pl* nujuum)
stare *v* ḥaddag (fi/le-) حدّق (ḥiddeeg); rannag (le-) رنّق (rinneeg)

start *n* bidaaya بداية • *vi* bada (be) بدا (-a, bidaaya); ibtada إبتدا (-i, bidaaya, ibtida) • *vt* bada بدا (-a, bidaaya); (**engine, car**) daw-war دوّر (tadwiir); shaghghal شغّل (shighgheel, tashghiil)
startle khalaᶜ خلع (a, khaliᶜ); **to be startled** (**by**) itkhalaᶜ (min) اتخلع (khulᶜa)
starve maat be-j-juuᶜ
state *n* (**condition**) ḥaala حالة (*pl* -aat); (**nation**) dawla دولة (*pl* duwal); (**political entity**) wilaaya ولاية (*pl* wilaayaat); **the United States** al-wilaayaat al-muttaḥida
statement bayaan بيان (*pl* -aat)
station maḥaṭṭa محطّة; **railway station** maḥaṭṭat as-sikka ḥadiid; **bus station** mawgif al-ᶜarabaat; mawgif al-baaṣṣaat; mawgif al-ḥaaflaat; **petrol station, gas station** maḥaṭṭat al-banziin; **station master** naaẓir ناظر (*pl* nuẓẓaar)
stationery adawaat maktabiyya; ghurṭaaṣiyya غرطاصيّة; **stationery shop** maktaba مكتبة
statistical iḥṣaa'i إحصائي
statistics iḥṣa'aat إحصاءات; iḥṣaa'iyyaat إحصائيّات
statue timsaal تمسال (*pl* tamaasiil)
stature qaama قامة
statutes lawaayiḥ لوايح (*sg* laayḥa)
stay *n* iqaama إقامة; **stay permit** taṣriiḥ iqaama • *v* gaᶜad قعد (u, guᶜaad); **to cause to stay** gaᶜᶜad قعّد (giᶜᶜeed, gaᶜda)
steady (**regular**) muntaẓim منتظم; (**stable**) mustaqirr مستقر
steal sarag سرق (i, sarig, sarga); **to be stolen** itsarag اتسرق (sarga); insarag انسرق (sarga); sirig سرق (a, sarga)
steam *n* bukhaar بخار
steamboat baabuur baḥar; waabuur baḥar
steamer baabuur baḥar بابور بحر; waabuur baḥar وابور بحر
steel ṣulb صلب; ḥadiid ṣulb; **steel wool** silik سلك (*pl* aslaak)
steer *v* saag ساق (u, suwaaga)
stem *n* saag ساق (*pl* seegaan)
stench ᶜafan عفن; ᶜufuuna عفونة; (**of body**) ṣunaan صنان; ṣunaaḥ صناح
step *n* shabḥa شبحة; (*also fig*) khaṭwa خطوة (khaṭawaat); **step of stairs or ladder** daraja درجة • *v* **to step aside** zaḥḥa زحّ (i, zaḥaḥaan); **to step down** (**renounce**) itnaazal (min/ᶜan) اتنازل (tanaazul); **to step on** daas داس (u, doosa); wiṭa وطى (yowṭa, waṭi)
stepdaughter **my stepdaughter** bitt marat-i; bitt raajil-i
stepfather **my stepfather** raajil umm-i
stepmother **my stepmother** marat abuu-y
stepson **my stepson** walad marat-i; walad raajil-i
stereotype namaṭ نمط (*pl* anmaaṭ)
stereotypical namaṭi نمطي
sterile muᶜaqqam معقّم; (**woman**) ᶜaagir عاقر
sterilize ᶜaqqam عقّم (taᶜqiim)
stern *adj* ṣaarim صارم
stern *n* mu'akhkhirat al-murkab
stethoscope sammaaᶜa سمّاعة
stew *n* mulaaḥ ملاح; **thin meat stew** damᶜa دمعة; **thin vegetable stew** sakhiina سخينة
steward muḍiif مضيف
stewardess muḍiifa مضيفة

stick *n* ᶜaṣaaya عصاية (*pl* ᶜiṣi); ᶜaṣa عصا (*pl* ᶜiṣi); ᶜuud عود (*pl* ᶜeedaan, aᶜwaad); **forked stick** shiᶜba شعبة (*pl* shiᶜab, shiᶜaab); **stirring stick** mufraaka مفراكة (*pl* mafaariik); muswaaṭ مسواط (*pl* masaawiiṭ)

stick *vi* itlazag لزق (lazga, lazagaan); itlaṣag لصق (laṣga, laṣagaan) • *vt* (**glue**) lazag لزق (i, lazig, lazga); lazzag لزّق (lizzeeg, talziig); laṣag لصق (i, laṣig, laṣga); laṣṣag لصّق (liṣṣeeg, talṣiig); **to stick to** kankash fi كنكش (kankasha); **to be stuck (glued)** itlazag اتلزق (lazga); itlazzag اتلزّق (lizzeeg, tilizzig); itlaṣag اتلصق (laṣga); itlaṣṣag اتلصّق (liṣṣeeg, tiliṣṣig); (**of car in sand or mud**) wiḥil وحل (yooḥal, waḥla); (**e.g. of key in lock**) lizig لزق (a, lazga); liṣig لصق (a,laṣga); (**e.g. of paper in photocopier**) shabak شبك (u, shabak, shabka)

sticky lazij لزج

stiff gawwi قوّي (*pl* -yyiin); jaamid جامد ; naashif ناشف

stifle khanag خنق (i, khanig); (**suppress**) katam كتم (u, katim, katamaan); **to be stifled** itkhanag اتخنق (khanig); itkatam اتكتم (katma)

still *adv* lissaᶜ لسّع ; le-l-leela; **it's still early** lissaᶜ badri

sting *n* (**of a bee, scorpion**) ibra إبرة (*pl* ibar); (**wound, by bee**) ladgha لدغة ; (**by scorpion**) ᶜaḍḍa عضّة • *vt* (**bees**) ladagh لدغ (a, ladigh, ladaghaan); (**scorpions**) ᶜaḍḍa عضّ (u, ᶜaḍḍ, ᶜaḍḍa); **to be stung** itladagh اتلدغ (ladgha); itᶜaḍḍa اتعضّ (ᶜaḍḍa)

stinginess bukhul بخل ; fasaala فسالة

stingy bakhiil بخيل (*pl* bukhala)

stink ᶜaffan عفّن (ᶜiffeen); itᶜaffan اتعفّن (ᶜiffeen, taᶜaffun)

stinking ᶜafin عفن ; muᶜaffin معفّن

stipulate sharraṭ شرّط (sharṭ); **to be stipulated** itsharraṭ إتشرّط (sharṭ)

stipulation sharṭ شرط (*pl* shuruuṭ)

stir vi itḥarrak اتحرّك (ḥirreek, taḥriik) • *vt* (**move**) ḥarrak حرّك (ḥirreek, taḥriik); hayyaj هيّج (hiyyeej, tahyiij); (**e.g. tea**) saaṭ ساط (u, suwaaṭa); **to stir with a stick** farak فرك (i, farik)

stirrup rikaab ركاب (*pl* -aat)

stitch *n* ghurza غرزة (*pl* ghuraz) • *v* gharaz غرز (i, ghariz); khayyaṭ خيّط (khiyaaṭa)

stock *n* istok استوك (*pl* -aat); **stock market** buurṣa بورصة ; **stock certificate** saham سهم (*pl* ashum)

stocking shurraab شرّاب (*pl* -aat)

stocky marbuuᶜ مربوع

stomach baṭun بطن (*pl* buṭuun); miᶜda معدة ; **on an empty stomach** ᶜala r-riig

stone ḥajar حجر (*pl* ḥujaara, aḥjaar); (**in kidney**) ḥaṣwa حصوة ; (**of fruit**) ᶜaḍum عضم

stool (**chair**) bambar بمبر (*pl* banaabir); (**faeces**) fusḥa فسحة

stoop dangar دنقر (dangara)

stop *vi* wagaf وقف (yagiif, wuguuf) • *vt* waggaf وقّف (wiggeef, tawgiif); (**doing sth.**) waggaf وقّف (wiggeef, tawgiif); baṭṭal بطّل (biṭṭeel)

store *n* (**stock**) istok استوك (*pl* -aat); (**shop**) dukkaan دكّان (*pl* dakaakiin); (**storeroom**) makhzan مخزن (*pl* makhaazin); (**for grain**) shuuna شونة ; jurun جرن (*pl* ajraan); (**for building materials**) maghlag مغلق (maghaalig) • *v* khazzan خزّن (khizzeen, takhziin); (**for future use**) iddakhar ادّخر (iddikhaar); **to be stored** itkhazzan اتخزّن (takhziin)

storekeeper makhzanji مخزنجي (*pl* -yya)

storeroom makhzan مخزن (*pl* makhaazin)

storey door دور (*pl* adwaar); ṭaabig طابق (*pl* ṭawaabig)

stork(s) **Abdim's stork(s)** simbir سمبر (*unit n* simbiriyya); **marabou stork(s)** abu siᶜin; **shoebill stork(s)** abu markuub

storm *n* ᶜaaṣifa عاصفة (*pl* ᶜawaaṣif); **dust storm** habuub هبوب (*pl* habaayib); **rainstorm** nawwa نوّة

story giṣṣa قصّة (*pl* giṣaṣ); ḥikaaya حكاية ; **to make up a story** allaf ألّف (ya'allif, ta'liif)

stove (**gas**) butajaaz بوتجاز (*pl* -aat); **charcoal stove** kaanuun كانون (*pl* kawaaniin); mangad منقد (*pl* manaagid)

straight ᶜadiil عديل ; **straight ahead** ṭawwaali طوّالي ; ᶜala ṭuul

straighten ᶜaddal عدّل (taᶜdiil)

straightforward dughri دغري

strain *v* ṣaffa صفّى (-i, ṣiffeey)

strainer maṣfa مصفى (*pl* maṣaafi); ghurbaal غربال (*pl* gharaabiil)

strange (**unknown**) ghariib غريب (*pl* -iin); (**unusual**) ᶜajiib عجيب ; **a strange thing** ᶜajiiba عجيبة (*pl* ᶜajaayib)

stranger ghariib غريب (*pl* ghuraba)

strangle khanag خنق (i, khanig); **to be strangled** itkhanag اتخنق (khanig)

strap *n* seer سير (*pl* siyuur)

straw (**dried stems**) gaṣab قصب (*unit n* gaṣabaaya); gashsh قش ; **drinking straw** shafaaṭa شفّاطة

strawberry (**strawberries**) faraawla فراولة

stream *n* (**current**) tayyaar تيّار (*pl* -aat); (**seasonal**) waadi وادي (*pl* widyaan); khoor خور (*pl* kheeraan)

streambed majra مجرى (*pl* majaari); **seasonal streambed** waadi وادي (*pl* widyaan); khoor خور (*pl* kheeraan)

street shaariᶜ شارع (*pl* shawaariᶜ); **street sweeper, street cleaner** kannaas كنّاس

streetkid shammaasi شمّاسى (*pl* shammaasa); shammaashi شمّاشى (*pl* shammaasha)

streetwise mufattiḥ مفتّح ; taftiiḥa تفتيحة

strength guwwa قوّة ; ḥeel حيل ; shidda شدّة (*pl* shadaayid)

strengthen gawwa قوّى (-i, tagwiya); (**enhance**) ᶜazzaz عزّز (taᶜziiz)

stretch *vt* maṭṭa مطّ (i, maṭṭ) • *vi* itmaṭṭa اتمطّ (miṭṭeeṭ); **to be stretched** itmaṭṭa اتمطّ (miṭṭeeṭ)

stretchable maṭṭaaṭi مطّاطي

stretcher (**for carrying the sick**) naggaala نقّالة

strike *n* (**labour stoppage**) iḍraab إضراب (*pl* -aat); **to go on strike** aḍrab أضرب (i, iḍraab) • *v* dagga دقّ (u, dagg); ḍarab ضرب

(a, ḍarib); khabaṭ (i, khabiṭ, khabaṭaan); **to strike on the head** ṣagaᶜ صقع (a, ṣagiᶜ); **to strike out** shaṭab شطب (u, shaṭib)

string (**thin**) kheeṭ خيط (*pl* khiyuuṭ); (**thick**) ḥabil حبل (*pl* ḥibaal); (**of jute**) dubaara دبارة ; (**of instrument**) watar وتر (*pl* awtaar) • *v* (**beads**) laḍam لضم (u, laḍim)

strip *n* shariiṭ شريط (*pl* sharaayiṭ); **strip light** lambat naylon • *v* (**a branch of its leaves**) kharaṭ خرط (i, khariṭ); (**a branch of its thorns**) barbaḥ بربح (barbaḥa); (**of rank or weapons**) jarrad جرّد (tajriid)

stripe khaṭṭ خط (*pl* khuṭuuṭ); **to mark with stripes** khaṭṭaṭ خطّط (takhṭiiṭ)

stroke *n* (**blow**) dagga دقّة ; ḍarba ضربة ; (**in brain**) jalṭa جلطة ; (**line**) sharṭa شرطة

stroke *v* masaḥ ᶜala مسح (a, masiḥ, masaḥaan)

stroll *n* gadla قدلة ; mashiya مشية • *v* gadal قدل (i, gadil); itmashsha اتمشّى (-a, mashi, mashiya)

strong gawwi قوّي (*pl* -yyiin); shadiid شديد (*pl* shudaad); jaamid جامد (**of beverages**) tagiil تقيل ; **very strong** (**person**) maaniᶜ مانع ; **be strong!** shidd ḥeel-ak!

strongly shadiid شديد (*pl* shudaad); be-l-ḥeel

strut *n* (**laid lengthways**) maddaad مدّاد (*pl* -aat); **transverse strut** ᶜarraaḍ عرّاض (*pl* -aat)

strut *v* itbakhtar اتبختر (bakhtara, tabakhtur)

stubborn ᶜaniid عنيد ; mukaajir مكاجر ; **he is stubborn** raas-o gawwi; raas-o naashif; **to be stubborn** ᶜaanad عاند (muᶜaanada); kaajar كاجر (mukaajara)

stuck **to get stuck** (*see* **stick**)

student (*m*) ṭaalib طالب (*pl* ṭalaba, ṭullaab); (*f*) ṭaaliba طالبة

study *n* giraaya قراية ; diraasa دراسة • *v* (**lessons**) zaakar زاكر (muzaakara); (**a subject**) gara قرا (a, giraaya); daras درس (u, daris, diraasa); **to be studied** itgara اتقرى (-i, giraaya)

stuff *v* ḥasha حشى (-i, ḥashi); (**mattresses**) najjad نجّد (nijjeed, tanjiid); **to be stuffed** itḥasha اتحشى (-i, ḥashi); itnajjad اتنجّد (tanjiid, tinijjid); **stuffed vegetables** maḥshi محشي

stuffing (**for mattresses**) ḥashiya حشية

stumble (**at/over**) ᶜitir (fi) عتر (a, ᶜatir, ᶜatra); itᶜattar (fi) عتّر (ᶜataraan); (**across/on**) ᶜitir (ᶜala) عتر (a, ᶜatir, ᶜatra)

stump (**of tree**) dugul دقل (*pl* duguul)

stupid ᶜawiir عوير (*pl* ᶜuwara); baliid بليد (*pl* bulada); ᶜabiiṭ عبيط (*pl* ᶜubaṭa); ahbal أهبل (*f* habla, *pl* hubul); ghabi غبي (*pl* aghbiya)

stupidity ᶜawaara عوارة ; balaada بلادة ; ghabaawa غباوة

stutter tamtam تمتم (tamtama, timteem)

style (**fashion**) istaayl استايل (*pl* -aat); (**behaviour**) usluub أسلوب (*pl* asaaliib); (**calligraphic**) khaṭṭ خط (*pl* khuṭuuṭ)

subject *n* mawḍuuʿ موضوع (*pl* -aat, mawaaḍiiʿ); **school or university subject** maadda مادّة (*pl* mawaadd)
submit sallam سلّم (tasliim); gaddam قدّم (tagdiim)
subscribe ishtarak fi اشترك (ishtiraak); sajjal سجّل (tasjiil)
subscription ishtiraak اشتراك (*pl* -aat); tasjiil تسجيل (*pl* -aat)
subsidize daʿam دعم (a, daʿam)
subsidy daʿam دعم; daʿam maali
substance maadda مادّة (*pl* mawaadd)
substitute *n* badiil بديل (*pl* badaayil) • *v* baddal بدّل (biddeel)
subtract khaṣam (min) خصم (i, khaṣim); (*arith*) ṭaraḥ طرح (a, ṭariḥ)
suburbs ḍawaaḥi l-madiina
succeed (**prosper**) najaḥ (fi) نجح (a, najaaḥ); falaḥ فلح (a, falaaḥa); (**come after**) khalaf خلف (i, khilaafa); ʿagab عقب (i, ʿagib)
success najaaḥ نجاح; falaaḥa فلاحة; **success!** be-t-tawfiiq!; muwaffaq, in shaa Allah!
successful naajiḥ ناجح; faaliḥ فالح
succulent (**plant**(**s**)) ṣabbaar صبّار
such zayy/mitil/misl da/di/deel; **such people** naas zayy/mitil/misl deel; **such as** zayy زي; mitil متل; misl مسل
suck maṣṣa مصّ (u, maṣṣ); **to suck in** shafaṭ شفط (u, shafiṭ); **to suck up to** itmallaq اتملّق (tamalluq); balbaṣ ʿala بلبص (balbaṣa)
suckle raḍḍaʿ رضع (a, riḍḍeeʿ, riḍaaʿa)
Sudan as-suudaan
Sudanese *adj/n* suudaani سوداني (*pl* -yyiin)
sudden mufaaji مفاجي
suddenly faj'a فجأة; faj'atan فجأة; ʿala ghafla
suds raghwa رغوة
sue rafaʿ gaḍiyya/daʿwa ʿala; gaaḍa قاضى (-i, mugaaḍaa)
suffer gaasa قاسى (-i, mugaasaa); ʿaana عانى (-i, muʿaanaa); itʿazzab اتعزّب (ʿazaab); tiʿib تعب (a, taʿab); (**from pain**) it'allam اتألّم (alam); (**from withdrawal symptoms**) khirim خرم (a, kharam); **to make s.o. suffer** ʿazzab عزّب (ʿazaab); taʿʿab تعّب (tiʿʿeeb)
suffice kaffa كفّى (-i, kifaaya)
sufficiency kifaaya كفاية
sufficient kaafi كافي; kifaaya كفاية
suffocate *vi* itkhanag اتخنق (khanig) • *vt* khanag خنق (i, khanig)
Sufi (**adherent of mystical Islam**) ṣuufi صوفي; **Sufi order** ṭariiga طريقة (*pl* ṭurug)
Sufism aṣ-ṣuufiyya
sugar sukkar سكّر; **sugar cane** gaṣab sukkar; **sugar syrup** ʿasal sukkar
suggest iqtaraḥ إقترح (iqtiraaḥ)
suggestion iqtiraaḥ إقتراح (*pl* -aat); muqtaraḥ مقترح (*pl* -aat)
suicide intiḥaar إنتحار; **to commit suicide** intaḥar انتحر (intiḥaar)
suit *n* (**outfit**) badla بدلة (*pl* bidal); **full suit** badla kaamla
suit *v* naasab ناسب (munaasaba)
suitable laayig لايق; munaasib مناسب; **to be suitable** naasab ناسب (munaasaba)
suitcase shanṭa شنطة (*pl* shinaṭ)

sulphur kibriit كبريت
sultan sulṭaan سلطان (*pl* salaaṭiin)
sultanate salṭana سلطنة
sum (**amount of money**) mablagh مبلغ (*pl* mabaaligh); (**total**) jumla جملة (*no pl*); **total sum** majmuuᶜ مجموع
summarize lakhkhaṣ لخّص (talkhiiṣ); ikhtaṣar اختصر (ikhtiṣaar)
summary mulakhkhaṣ ملخّص (*pl* -aat); talkhiiṣ تلخيص
summer ṣeef صيف; **pertaining to the summer** ṣeefi صيفي
summit qimma قمّة (*pl* qimam)
summon kallaf be-l-ḥuḍuur
summons istidᶜaa استدعا; takliif be-l- ḥuḍuur
sun shamis شمس (*pl* shumuus); **sun shelter** raakuuba راكوبة (*pl* rawaakiib); kashshaasha كشّاشة; **makeshift sun shelter** ḍullaala ضلالة
Sunday yoom al-aḥad
sunflower(s) ᶜabbaad ash-shamis
sunglasses naḍḍaara shamsiyya
Sunna **the Sunna** as-sunna; **those who live according to the Sunna** anṣaar as-sunna
Sunni sunni سنّي
sunrise shuruug ash-shamis; ṭuluuᶜ ash-shamis
sunset mughrib مغرب; ghuruub ash-shamis
sunshade shamsiyya شمسيّة (*pl* shamaasi); maẓalla مظلّة
sunstroke ḍarbat shamis
superficial saṭḥi سطحي
superintendent mulaaḥiẓ ملاحظ
superior *adj* aᶜla أعلى (*f* ᶜulya) • *n* ra'iis رئيس (*pl* ruwasa, ru'asaa)
supermarket siyuubar maarkit
supervise ashraf (ᶜala) اشرف (i, ishraaf)
supervision ishraaf اشراف
supervisor mushrif مشرف
supper ᶜasha عشا; **to have supper** (**evening meal**) itᶜashsha اتعشّى (-a, ᶜasha); **to give supper to s.o.** ᶜashsha عشّى (i, ᶜasha)
supple layyin ليّن; ṭari طري; ṭaayiᶜ طايع
supplement mulḥag ملحق (*pl* malaaḥig)
supply *n* tawriid توريد (*pl* -aat); (*mil*) imdaad إمداد (*pl* -aat) • *v* mawwan (be-) موّن (tamwiin); warrad ورّد (wir-reed, tawriid); **he supplied them with the goods** warrad lee-hum al-buḍaaᶜa
support *n* daᶜam دعم; **moral support** daᶜam maᶜnawi; **financial support** daᶜam maali • *v* daᶜam دعم (a, daᶜam); (**hold up**) sanad سند (i, sanad); (**help**) ᶜaawan عاون (muᶜaawana); ayyad أيّد (ya'ayyid, ta'yiid); (**provide for**) ᶜaal عال (u, iᶜaala); ᶜayyash عيّش (iᶜaasha); anfaq ᶜala أنفق (yunfiq, infaaq)
suppose iftaraḍ افترض (iftiraaḍ); ẓanna ظنّ (i, ẓann, ẓunuun)
suppress katam كتم (u, katim, katamaan); (**emotions**) ḥagan حقن (i, ḥagin)
sure akiid أكيد; mu'akkad مؤكّد; **being sure** mut'akkid متأكّد; waasiq واسق
surely akiid أكيد; be-t-ta'kiid
surface saṭiḥ سطح (*pl* suṭuuḥ); washsh وش (*pl* wushuush)
surgeon jarraaḥ جرّاح
surgery jiraaḥa جراحة

surprise *n* mufaaja'a مفاجأة ; **by surprise** faj'a فجأة ; **to take by surprise** ghaffal غفل (ghiffeel) • *v* faaja' فاجأ (mufaaja'a); **to be surprised** istaghrab استغرب (istighraab); indahash اندهش (dahsha, indihaash); itᶜajjab اتعجّب (ᶜijjeeb, taᶜajjub)

surrender istaslam استسلم (istislaam)

surround ḥaaṭ حاط (i, ḥeeṭa)

surroundings ḍawaaḥi ضواحي

survey *n* masiḥ مسح (*pl* musuuḥaat) • *v* masaḥ مسح (a, masiḥ)

surveyor baaḥis باحس ; **land surveyor** massaaḥ مسّاح

survive naja (min) نجا (-u, najaa, najaat); nija (min) نجا (-u, najaa, najaat)

susceptible gaabil قابل

suspect *adj* mashbuuh مشبوه • *v* ishtabah fi اشتبه (ishtibaah)

suspend ajjal أجل (ta'jiil); ᶜallag علّق (ᶜilleeg, taᶜliig)

suspenders ḥammaala حمّالة

suspension ta'jiil تأجيل (*pl* -aat); taᶜliiq تعليق

suspicion ishtibaah إشتباه ; shubha شبهة (*pl* shubuuhaat)

suspicious (**doubting**) shaakki شاكّي *m* (*f* shaakka) fi; (**suspect**) mashbuuh مشبوه ; **to be suspicious of** shakka fi شكّ (u, shakk); shakkak fi شكّك (shikkeek, tashkiik)

sustain ᶜaal عال (u, iᶜaala); ᶜayyash عيّش (iᶜaasha); anfaq ᶜala أنفق (yunfiq, infaaq)

sustainable mustadaam مستدام

swallow *v* balaᶜ بلع (a, baliᶜ); **to swallow the wrong way** itsharag اتشرق (sharga, sharagaan); shirig شرق (a, sharga)

swallow(s) *n* ᶜaṣfuur aj-janna

swamp mustangaᶜ مستنقع (*pl* -aat)

swank *n* boobaar بوبار • *v* itboobar اتبوبر (boobaar)

swap *n* badal بدل (*pl* -aat) • *v* baddal بدّل (biddeel, tabdiil)

sway itmaayal اتمايل (mayalaan); (**to and fro**) itzaḥzaḥ إتزحزح (zaḥzaḥa, ziḥzeeḥ)

swear (**on/by**) qasam (be-) قسم (i, qasam); aqsam (be-) أقسم (i, qasam); **to swear an oath** ḥalaf (be-) حلف (i, ḥalafaan); **to make s.o. swear** ḥallaf حلّف (ḥilleef); **to swear at** nabbaz نبّز (nibbeez, nabaz); itlaffaẓ اتلفّظ (liffeeẓ, tiliffiẓ); shatam شتم (u, shatiima)

sweat *n* ᶜarag عرق • *v* ᶜirig عرق (a, ᶜarag)

sweating ᶜargaan عرقان

sweater siwiitar سويتر (*pl* -aat); siyuutar سيوتر (*pl* -aat)

Sweden as-siweed

Swede siweedi سويدي (*pl* -yyiin)

Swedish siweedi سويدي (*pl* -yyiin)

sweep *v* gashsha قشّ (u, gashsh); kanas كنس (u, kanis)

sweeper (*m*) farraash فرّاش ; (*f*) farraasha فرّاشة

sweepings kinaasa كناسة ; wasaakha وساخة

sweet ḥilu حلو (*f* ḥilwa)

sweeten (**with sugar**) sakkar سكر (sukkar); ḥalla حلّى (-i, taḥliya); ṭaᶜᶜam طعم (ṭiᶜᶜeem)

sweetness ḥalaawa حلاوة

sweets ḥalaawa حلاوة ; ḥalawiyyaat حلويّات

swell wirim ورم (a, waram); **to swell up** itwarram اتورّم (ta-warrum); **to cause to swell** war-ram ورّم (wirreem)
swelling waram ورم (*pl* awraam)
swim *n* ʿooma عومة • *v* ʿaam عام (u, ʿoom, ʿuwaama); sabaḥ سبح (a, sibaaḥa); **swimming pool** ḥammaam as-sibaaḥa; ḥooḍ as-sibaaḥa
swindle naṣab ʿala نصب (u, naṣb)
swindler naṣṣaab نصّاب ; dajjaal دجّال ; ghashshaash غشّاش
swing *n* murjeeḥa مرجيحة (*pl* maraajiiḥ); ṭooṭaḥaaniyya طوطحانيّة • *vi* iṭṭooṭaḥ اطّوطح (ṭooṭeeḥ); itloolaḥ اتلولح (loolaaḥ) • *vt* loolaḥ لولح (looleeḥ)
swish *n* shakhshakh شخشخ (shakhshakha)
Swiss *adj/n* siwisri سويسري (*pl* -yyiin)
switch *n* muftaaḥ مفتاح (*pl* mafaatiiḥ) • *v* **to switch on** (**light, gas**) fataḥ فتح (a, fatiḥ); wallaʿ ولّع (willeeʿ); (**engine**) dawwar دوّر (diwweer, tadwiir); shaghghal شغّل (shighgheel, tashghiil); **to switch off** (**light, gas**) gafal قفل (i, gafil); ṭafa طفى (-i, ṭafi, ṭafayaan); (**light**) katal كتل (u, katil); (**engine**) gafal قفل (i, gafil); waggaf وقّف (wiggeef, tawgiif); **to be switched on** (**light, gas**) itwallaʿ اتولّع (walʿa, willeeʿ); (**engine**) iddawwar دوّر (diwweer); **to be switched off** (**light, gas**) iṭṭafa اطّفى (-i, ṭafiya); (**engine**) itgafal اتقفل (gafla, gafalaan)
switchboard baddaala بدّالة ; kub-baaniyya كّبّانيّة
Switzerland siwisra سويسرا
sword seef سيف (*pl* siyuuf)
symbol *n* ramz رمز (rumuuz)
sympathy ḥinniyya حنّيّة ; maḥanna محنّة ; **to arouse sympathy** ḥannan حنّن (ḥinneen, taḥniin)
syndicate naqaaba نقابة
synopsis mukhtaṣar مختصر (*pl* -aat)
syphilis zuhri زهري
syringe siirinj سيرنج (*pl* -aat)
syrup ʿasal عسل ; ʿasal sukkar; (**medical**) dawa sharaab
system niẓaam نظام (*pl* nuẓum, anẓima)
systematic munaẓẓam منظّم
systematically be-n-niẓaam; be-shakil munaẓẓam
systematize naẓẓam نظّم (tanẓiim); **to be(come) system-atized** itnaẓẓam إتنظّم (tanẓiim)

T - t

table tarabeeza تربيزة (*pl* -aat, taraabiiz); ṭarabeeza طربيزة (*pl* -aat, ṭaraabiiz); **tablecloth** mafrash مفرش (*pl* mafaarish); **table tennis** tinis aṭ ṭawla; **bedside table** ko-midiino كمدينو (*pl* komidiinaat); (**chart**) jadwal جدول (*pl* jadaawil)
tablet ḥabba حبّة (*pl* ḥubuub); ḥabbaaya حبّاية (*pl* -aat, ḥubuub)
taboo *adj* muḥarram محرّم
tag *n* (**game**) ḥarreena حرّينة ; ḥarrat حرّت
tail ḍanab ضنب (*pl* ḍunuub, ḍunubba)

tailor tarzi ترزي (*pl* -yya); khayyaaṭ خيّاط

take shaal شال (i, sheel, sheela); akhad أخد (biyaakhud, akhid); itnaawal اتناول (munaawala); **to take away** shaal شال (i, sheel, sheela); **to take away by force** galaᶜ قلع (a, galiᶜ); **to take down** nazzal نزّل (nizzeel); **to takeoff** (**depart**) gaam قام (u, giyaam); (**clothes, jewellery**) malaṣ ملص (u, maliṣ); mallaṣ ملّص (milleeṣ, tamliiṣ); galaᶜ قلع (a, galiᶜ); gallaᶜ قلّع (gilleeᶜ); **to take out** marrag مرّق (mir-reeg); ṭallaᶜ طلّع (tilleeᶜ); **to take s.o. around** fassaḥ فسّح (fisseeḥ, fusḥa); ḥawwam حوّم (ḥuwaama); **to take s.o./sth. to** (**a place**) wadda le- ودّى (-i, widdeey); waṣṣal le- وصّل (wiṣṣeel); **take care!** khalli baal-ak!; aᶜmal ḥisaab-ak!; **to be taken** (**away**) itshaal اتشال (sheela)

takeaway (**food**) safari سفري

takeoff giyaam قيام

tale giṣṣa قصّة (*pl* giṣaṣ); ḥikaaya حكاية

talent mawhiba موهبة (*pl* mawaahib)

talented mawhuub موهوب

talk *n* kalaam كلام; gool قول; (**formal**) ḥadiis حديس (*pl* aḥaadiis) • *v* (**about**) itkallam (fi/ᶜan) اتكلّم (kalaam); naḍam (fi/ᶜan) نضم (u, naḍim); (**in one's sleep**) haḍrab هضرب (haḍraba); **to talk to** kallam كلّم (kalaam)

talkative kallaam كلام; naḍḍaam نضّام; barraay برّاي; rabraab ربراب; **to be talkative** rabrab ربرب (rabraba)

tall ṭawiil طويل (*pl* ṭuwaal); **to be(come) tall** ṭaal طال (u, ṭuul)

tamarind ᶜaradeeb عرديب

tambourine *n* (*sg & pl*) rigg رق; (**large, without jingles**) ṭaar طار (*pl* -aat)

tame *adj* aliif أليف • *v* wallaf ولّف (willeef, wilfa); **to be(come) tame** itwallaf اتولّف (willeef)

tan *v* (**leather**) dabagh دبغ (u, dibaagha)

tangerine(s) yuusif effendi

tangled mutbashik متبشك; mutlaf-lif متلفلف

tank *n* (**for fuel, water**) tank تنك (*pl* -aat, tunukka); (**for water**) fanṭaaẓ فنطاظ (*pl* fanaaṭiiẓ); ṣihriij صهريج (*pl* ṣahaariij); (**military**) dabbaaba دبّابة

tanker (**lorry**) tankar تنكر (*pl* tanaakir); (**for water**) fanṭaaẓ فنطاظ (*pl* fanaaṭiiẓ)

tanner dabbaagh دبّاغ

tannery madbagha مدبغة (*pl* madaabigh)

tap *n* maasuura ماسورة; ḥanafiyya حنفيّة

tap *v* khabaṭ (ᶜala) خبط (i, khabiṭ, khabaṭaan); khabbaṭ (ᶜala) خبّط (khibbeeṭ, takhbiiṭ); (**on shoulder**) rabbat (ᶜala) ربّت (ribbeet); (**with a stick**) nagar نقر (u, nagir); (**a gum tree**) ṭagga طقّ (u, ṭagg)

tape *n* shariiṭ شريط (*pl* sharaayiṭ); **tape measure** mitir متر; **tape recorder** musajjil مسجّل (*pl* -aat)

tapeworm duuda shariiṭiyya

tar *n* zifit زفت; guṭraan قطران

target hadaf هدف (*pl* ahdaaf); **target group** majmuuʿa mustahdafa
tariff taʿriifa تعريفة (taʿaariif)
tarmac ẓalaṭ ظلط ; **to cover with tarmac** saflat سفلت (saflata)
tarpaulin mashammaʿ مشمّع (*pl* -aat)
task waajib واجب (*pl* -aat)
tassel dantilla دنتلة
taste *n* (**sense of**) zoog زوق ; (**flavour**) ṭaʿam طعم • *v* ḍaag ضاق (u, ḍuwaaga, ḍooga); **to let s.o. taste sth.** ḍawwag ضوّق (ḍiwweeg)
tasteless masiikh مسيخ
tasty ṭaaʿim طاعم ; laziiz لزيز
tattoo *n* washim وشم (*pl* washmaat, awshaam) • *v* washam وشم (i, washim); dagga l-washam; (**the lips**) dagga sh-shalluufa
tax *n* ḍariiba ضريبة (*pl* ḍaraayib); rasm رسم (*pl* rusuum); **property taxes** ʿawaayid عوايد
taxation jibaaya جباية
taxi taksi تاكسي (*pl* takaasi); **taxi rank** mawgif at-taksi
tea shaay شاي ; shaahi شاهي ; **hibiscus tea** karkadee كركدي ; **tea lady** sitt ash-shaay
tea strainer maṣfa مصفى (*pl* maṣaafi); maṣfat shaay
teach garra قرّا (-i, giraaya); darras درّس (tadriis); ʿallam علّم (taʿliim); (**manners**) addab أدّب (ta'diib)
teacher (*m*) ustaaz أستاز (*pl* asaatza, asaatiza); mudarris مدرّس ; muʿallim معلّم ; (*f*) ustaaza أستازة ; mudarrisa مدرّسة ; muʿallima معلّمة ; **religious teacher** fakii فكي (*pl* fukaya)
teacup kubbaaya كبّاية (*pl* -aat, kabaabi)
teak khashab tiik
team fariiq فريق (*pl* firaq); tiim تيم (*pl* atyaam)
teapot *n* barraad براد (*pl* -aat, baraariid)
tear *n* (**rip**) shariṭ شرط ; sharṭa شرطة • *vt* sharaṭ شرط (u, shariṭ); sharraṭ شرّط (shirreeṭ, tashriiṭ); gaṭṭaʿ قطّع (giṭṭeeʿ, tagṭiiʿ); **to tear to pieces** mazzag مزّق (mizzeeg); (**of an animal**) nahash نهش (a, nahsha); **to be torn** itsharraṭ إتشرّط (shirreeṭ, tasharruṭ); insharaṭ انشرط (shariṭ); itgaṭṭaʿ اتقطّع (giṭṭeeʿ)
tear *n* (**in eye**) damʿa دمعة (*pl* dumuuʿ)
tease haẓẓar maʿa هظّر (hiẓaar); kaawa كاوى (-i, mukaawaa); shaaghal (fi) شاغل (mushaaghala)
tease (**wool, cotton**) nafash نفش (u, nafish)
teat (**of bottle**) bizza بزّة
technical fanni فنّي ; taqni تقنّي
tedious baayikh بايخ ; mumill ممل
telephone *n* talafoon تلفون (*pl* -aat); tilifoon تلفون (*pl* -aat); haatif هاتف (*pl* hawaatif); **mobile telephone** moobaayl موبايل (*pl* -aat); jawwaal جوّال (*pl* -aat); **satelite telephone** surayya سريّا ; **telephone call** mukaalama مكالمة ; **telephone receiver** sammaaʿa سمّاعة • *v* ḍarab talafoon; ittaṣṣal be- اتّصل (ittiṣaal)
television tilifizyoon تلفزيون (*pl* -aat)
tell ḥaka le- حكى (-i, ḥaki); gaal (le-) قال (u, gool); ḥaddas حدّس (ḥadiis); khabbar خبّر

(khibbeer); (**a story**) ḥaka le- حكى (-i, ḥikaaya); gaṣṣa قصّ (u, gaṣṣ); (**a folktale**) ḥajja حجّى (-i, ḥuja)

temperature ḥaraara حرارة ; (**degree of**) darajat al-ḥaraara

temple (**of worship**) maʿbad معبد (*pl* maʿaabid); (**head**) maḍaagha مضاغة

temporary muwaqqat موقّت

tempt fatan فتن (i, fitna); aghra أغرى (-i, ighraa); (**of devil**) waswas le- وسوس (waswasa, wiswees)

tempting mughri مغري

ten ʿashara عشرة

tenant mu'ajjir مؤجّر

tender *adj* (**person**) ḥinayyin حنيّن ; (**meat**) ṭari طري

tender *n* ʿaṭaa عطا (*pl* ʿaṭaa'aat)

tendon watar وتر (*pl* awtaar)

tennis tinis تنس

tense *n* **past tense** (**perfect**) al-maaḍi; **present tense** (**imperfect**) al-muḍaariʿ

tense *adj* mutwattir متوتّر ; **to be(come) tense** itwattar اتوتّر (tawattur)

tension tawattur توتّر (*pl* -aat)

tent kheema خيمة (*pl* khiyaam, khiyam); (**of camel hair**) beet shaʿar; (**of matting**) beet birish

tenth ʿaashir عاشر

tenure ḥiyaaza حيازة

term (**period**) fatra فترة (*pl* -aat, fataraat); (**stipulation**) sharṭ شرط (*pl* shuruuṭ); (**technical**) musṭalaḥ مصطلح (*pl* -aat)

terminate naha نهى (-i, inhaa); gaḍa ʿala قضى (-i, gaḍaa)

termite(s) arḍa أرضة

terrace (**in front of house**) baranda برندة ; (**agricultural**) teras ترس

terrible faẓiiʿ فظيع

terrified marʿuub مرعوب

terrify khawwaf خوّف (takhwiif)

terrifying murʿib مرعب

terror ruʿb رعب

terrorism irhaab إرهاب

terrorist irhaabi إرهابي (*pl* -yyiin)

terrorize arhab أرهب (i, irhaab)

test *n* ikhtibaar إختبار (*pl* -aat); tajruba تجربة (*pl* tajaarub); (**exam**) imtiḥaan إمتحان (*pl* -aat); (**of a car**) testa تستة ; (**in laboratory**) faḥiṣ فحص (*pl* fuḥuuṣaat) • *v* ikhtabar اختبر (ikhtibaar); jarrab جرّب (jirreeb, tajriib); imtaḥan امتحن (imtiḥaan); (**in laboratory**) faḥaṣ فحص (a, faḥiṣ)

testament **the New Testament** al-ʿahd al-jadiid; **the Old Testament** al-ʿahd al-gadiim

testicle beeḍa بيضة ; khiṣya خصية ; (**of animals**) galaga قلقة

testify gaddam shihaada; shihid شهد (a, shihaada)

testimony shihaada شهادة ; **false testimony** shihaadat zuur

tetanus tataanuus تتانوس

tether gayyad قيّد (giyyeed)

text (**wording**) naṣṣ نص (*pl* nuṣuuṣ)

textile nasiij نسيج (*pl* ansija)

than min من

thank (**for**) shakar (ʿala) شكر (u, shukur); **thank you** shukran شكرا ; Allah yabaarik fii-k; kattar kheer-ak; **thank you very much** shukran jaziilan; **thank God!** al-ḥamdu le-llaah!

that *adj* (*m*) daak داك ; (*f*) diik ديك • *conj* inn- إنـ ; inno إنو ; ann- أنـ ; anno أنو

thatch *v* ʿarash عرش (i, ʿarish); sagaf سقف (i, sagif); **thatched hut** guṭṭiyya قطّيّة (*pl* gaṭaaṭi)
the al- ال.
theatre masraḥ مسرح (*pl* masaariḥ)
theatrical masraḥi مسرحي
theft sarga سرقة (*pl* sarigaat)
then (**at that time**) saaʿt-a; saaʿaat-a; (**after that**) baʿd kida; baʿdaak بعداك ; baʿdeen بعدين ; **by then** saaʿt-a; saaʿaat-a; **till then** le-ghaayat daak; **every now and then** marra marra; marraat مرّات ; saaʿaat ساعات
theoretical naẓari نظري
theoretically naẓariyyan نظريّاً
theory naẓariyya نظريّة
there hinaak هناك ; **over there** be-ghaadi; **there is/are** fii في
therefore ʿashaankida; ʿashaankadi; fi shaankida; fi shaankadi
thermometer termomitir ترمومتر (*pl* -aat)
thermos sirmus سرمس (*pl* saraamis); tirmus ترمس (*pl* taraamis); turmusa ترمسة (*pl* taraamis)
these deel ديل ; hadeel هديل
they (*m/f*) hum هم ; (*f*) hin هن
thick takhiin تخين (*pl* tukhaan); (**hair, forest**) ghaziir غزير
thief ḥaraami حرامي (*pl* -yya); **thieves** naas tullub
thigh wirik ورك (*pl* awraak); (**meat**) laḥam fakhda
thin ḍaʿiif ضعيف (*pl* ḍuʿaaf); rigeyyig رقيق (*f* rigeyga); rafiiʿ رفيع ; (**transparent**) rahiif رهيف ; **to become thin** ḍiʿif ضعف (a, ḍuʿuf)
thing ḥaaja حاجة ; shii شي (*pl* ashyaa)
think (**believe**) iftakar افتكر (iftikaar); (**assume**) ẓanna ظنّ (u, ẓann, ẓunuun); (**about**) fakkar (fi) فكّر (tafkiir)
thinner *n* sinner سنر
third *adj* taalit تالت ; tiltaawi تلتاوي • *n* tilit تلت
thirst ʿaṭash عطش
thirsty ʿaṭshaan عطشان ; **to be(come) thirsty** ʿiṭish عطش (a, ʿaṭash)
thirteen talaṭṭaashar تلطّاشر
thirty talaatiin تلاتين
this (*m*) da دا ; (*f*) di دي
thistle(s) shook شوك (*pl* -aat, ashwaak)
thorn(s) shook شوك (*pl* -aat, ashwaak)
thorough shaamil شامل
those deelak ديلك ; deelaak ديلاك ; hadeek هديك
though maʿa inno/inn-; maʿa kawn; even though ḥatta law; ḥatta wa law; wa law
thought fikra فكرة (*pl* afkaar)
thousand *num* alif ألف (*pl* aalaaf; uuluuf)
thread *n* kheeṭ خيط (*pl* khiyuuṭ) • *v* laḍam لضم (u, laḍim)
threat tahdiid تهديد (*pl* -aat)
threaten haddad هدّد (hiddeed, tahdiid)
three talaata تلاتة ; **three hundred** tultumiyya تلتميّة
thresh dagga دقّ (u, dagg); gashshar قشّر (gishsheer, tagshiir)
threshing floor taga تقة
threshold ʿataba عتبة
thrifty iqtiṣaadi إقتصادي ; mudabbir مدبّر
throat ḥalig حلق (*pl* ḥuluug); ḥalguum حلقوم (*pl* ḥalaagiim); ḥanjara حنجرة (*pl* ḥanaajir); **I have a sore throat** ḥalg-i biyuujaʿ-ni

thrombosis jalṭa جلطة
throb **(heart)** ḍarab ضرب (a, ḍarib); **(pulse)** nataḥ نتح (a, natiḥ)
throne ʿarsh عرش (*pl* ʿuruush); **(for bride and bridegroom)** koosha كوشة
through be- بـ ; ʿan ṭariig; **(by means of)** be-waasṭat
throw **(at)** jadaʿ جدع (a, jadiʿ); rama رمى (-i, ramiya, ramayaan); **to throw away** jadaʿ جدع (a, jadiʿ); rama رمى (-i, ramiya, ramayaan); zagal زقل (u, zagil); **to throw up (vomit)** ṭarash طرش (u, ṭuraash); istafragh استفرغ (istifraagh); **to be thrown** itjadaʿ اتجدع (jadʿa); itrama اترمى (-i, ramiya); **to be thrown away** itjadaʿ اتجدع (jadʿa); itrama اترمى (-i, ramiya); itzagal اتزقل (zagla)
thumb mabṣam مبصم ; al-muṣbaʿ al-kabiir; al-aṣbaʿ al-kabiir
thunder *n* raʿad رعد (*pl* ruʿuud)
Thursday yoom al-khamiis
tick *v* **(sound)** taktak تكتك (taktaka); **(mark)** ʿallam علّم (ʿalaama)
tick(s) *n* guraad قراد ; **to be infested with ticks** garrad قرّد (girreed)
ticket tazkira تزكرة (*pl* tazaakir); **ticket collector** kumsaari كمساري (*pl* kamaasra); **ticket office** shubbaak at-tazaakir
tickle *v* kalkal كلكل (kilkeel, kalkala)
tide **high tide** madd مد ; **low tide** jazr جزر
tidy *adj* murattab مرتّب ; munaẓẓam منظّم • *v* waḍḍab وضّب (wiḍḍeeb, tawḍiib); rattab رتّب (ritteeb, tartiib)
tie *n* karafitta كرفتّة
tie *v* rabaṭ ربط (u, rabiṭ); rabbaṭ ربّط (ribbeeṭ); karab كرب (u, karib); karrab كرّب (kirreeb); **to tie up** gayyad قيّد (giyyeed); **(in a cloth)** ṣarra صرّ (u, ṣarra, ṣararaan); **(by hands and feet)** kattaf كتّف (kitteef, taktiif)
tiffin tin bastilla بستلّة
tight ḍayyig ضيّق ; **to become tight** ḍaag ضاق (i, ḍiig)
tighten shadda شدّ (i, shadd)
tilapia bulṭi بلطي
tile(s) *n* bulaaṭ بلاط ; **tiles** seeraamiik سيراميك • *v* ballaṭ بلّط (billeeṭ, tabliiṭ)
tiler ballaaṭ بلاط ; muballiṭ مبلّط
till *conj* le- لـ ; ḥatta حتّى ; le-ghaayat (ma); le-ḥaddi (ma); **till now** le-hassaʿ; le-l-leela
tilt *vi* iddankas ادّنكس (dinkees, dankasa) • *vt* dankas دنكس (dinkees, dankasa)
time wakit وكت (*pl* awkaat); zaman زمن (*pl* azmina, azmaan); **(period of time)** fatra فترة (*pl* -aat, fataraat); mudda مدّة (*pl* -aat, muddad); zaman زمن (*pl* azmina); **(occasion)** marra مرّة ; **a long time ago** min zamaan; min zaman baʿiid; **all the time** ṭawwaali طوّالي ; **for a long time** min zamaan; **what's the time?** as-saaʿa kam?; **take your time** ʿala mahl-ak
timetable jadwal جدول (*pl* jadaawil)
tin **(material)** giṣdiir قصدير (*pl* gaṣaadiir); **(can)** ʿilba علبة (*pl* ʿilab); **tin plate** ṣafiiḥ صفيح
tin opener fattaaḥa فتّاحة ; muftaaḥ مفتاح (*pl* mafaatiiḥ)

tingle nammal نمّل (nimmeel, tanmiil)
tinkle ranna رنّ (i, raniin)
tinsmith samkari سمكري (*pl* -yya)
tip *n* (**end**) raas راس (*pl* ruus, ru'uus, ruuseen, reeseen); (**of pen, knife**) sinna سنّة ; (**gratuity**) bakshiish بكشيش
tipper truck gallaab قلاب (*pl* -aat)
tipsy mabsuuṭ مبسوط ; ʿaamil sinna
tire *vi* fatar فتر (a, futuur, fatar); tiʿib تعب (a, taʿab) • *vt* fattar فتّر (fitteer); taʿʿab تعّب (tiʿʿeeb)
tired fatraan فتران ; taʿbaan تعبان ; **to get tired** fatar فتر (a, futuur, fatar); tiʿib تعب (a, taʿab)
tiring mutʿib متعب
tissue (**of body**) nasiij نسيج (*pl* ansija); (**handkerchief**) mindiil warag
title (**of book, film**) ʿunwaan عنوان (*pl* ʿanaawiin); (**of address**) laqab لقب (*pl* alqaab)
to le- لـ ; ila إلى ; (**towards**) ʿala على
tobacco tumbaak تمباك ; **chewing tobacco** ṣaʿuuṭ صعوط ; **quid of tobacco** saffa سفّة ; **to chew tobacco** saffa سفّ (i, saff)
today al-leela; al-yoom; al-yoom da; an-nahaar da
toe aṣbaʿ ar-rijil; muṣbaʿ ar-rijil; **on tiptoe** foog raas al-aṣaabiʿ
toecap buuz aj-jazma
together sawa سوى ; maʿa baʿaḍ; sawwiyyan سوّيًا
toilet ḥammaam حمام (*pl* -aat); adbakhaana أدبخانة ; dubbilyuusii دبليوسي ; mustaraaḥ مستراح ; **flush toilet** sayfon سايفون (*pl* -aat)
toiletries tawaleet تواليت
token (**chip, counter, in games**) fiisha فيشة (*pl* -aat, fiish); (**in restaurant**) maarka ماركة ; (**symbol**) daliil دليل (*pl* dalaayil); ramz رمز (rumuuz)
tolerance musaamaḥa مسامحة ; tasaamuḥ تسامح ; samaaḥ سماح
tomato ṭamaṭmaaya طمطماية (*pl* ṭamaaṭim); banaḍoora بنضورة ; **tomato sauce/paste** ṣalṣa صلصة
tomb gabur قبر (*pl* gubuur); maqbara مقبرة (*pl* maqaabir); **saint's tomb** ḍariiḥ ضريح (*pl* ḍaraayiḥ, aḍriḥa)
tomorrow bukra بكرة ; **the day after tomorrow** baʿad bukra
ton ṭann طن (*pl* aṭnaan)
tongs (**for hot coals**) maasha ماشة
tongue lisaan لسان (*pl* alsina)
tongue-twister ghuluuṭiyya غلوطيّة
tonsil looza لوزة (*pl* -aat, luwaz)
tonsilitis iltihaab al-luwaz
too (**also**) barḍ- برضـ ; barḍo برضو ; kamaan كمان ; zaat- زاتـ
tool adaa اداة (*pl* adawaat); **set of tools** ʿidda عدّة *n* (*pl* ʿidad)
tooth sinn سن (*pl* sunuun, asnaan); (**front**) naab ناب (*pl* nawaayib); (**molar**) ḍurus ضرس (*pl* ḍuruus, aḍraas); **wisdom tooth** ḍurs al-ʿagul; **to develop teeth** tawwar توّر (tatwiir); sannan سنّن (tasniin)
toothbrush furshat asnaan
toothpaste maʿjuunasnaan
tooth-stick muswaak مسواك (*pl* masaawiik)
top raas راس ; (**of pot, bottle**) ghuṭaaya غطاية ; ghuṭa غطا (*pl* ghuṭaayaat); (**summit**) qimma

قمّة (*pl* qimam); **on top of** foog فوق ; ʿala على
topic mawḍuuʿ موضوع (*pl* -aat, mawaaḍiiʿ); (**of an agenda**) jand جند (*pl* ajinda)
torch (**electric**) baṭṭaariyya بطاريّة ; kashshaafa كشّافة ; (**of fire**) shuʿla شعلة
tornado ʿuṣaar عصار (*pl* -aat)
tortoise abu l-gadaḥ
torture *n* taʿziib تعزيب (*pl* -aat) • *v* ʿazzab عزّب (taʿziib); **to be tortured** itʿazzab اتعزّب (taʿziib)
total *adj* kulli كلّي ; **total sum** majmuuʿ مجموع • *n* jumla جملة (*no pl*); (**amount of money**) al-mablagh al-kulli
totally nihaa'i نهائي ; tabb تب ; tjatt تجت
touch *v* habash هبش (i, habish); habbash هبّش (hibbeesh, tahbiish); lamas لمس (a, lamis)
tough (**person**) gaasi قاسي ; (**material**) khishin خشن ; yaabis يابس ; **a tough day** yoom ʿaniif
tour *n* riḥla رحلة ; laffa لفّة ; jawla جولة • *v* laffa لفّ (i, laff); itjawwal اتجوّل (tajawwul)
tourism siyaaḥa سياحة
tourist saayiḥ سايح (*pl* suyyaaḥ, suwwaaḥ); saa'iḥ سائح (*pl* suyyaaḥ, suwwaaḥ)
tow gaṭar قطر (u, gaṭir)
towards naaḥyat ناحية ; ʿala على
towel bishkiir بشكير (*pl* bashaakiir)
tower buruj برج (*pl* abraaj)
town madiina مدينة (*pl* mudun); **provincial town** bandar بندر (*pl* banaadir); **town hall** baladiyya بلديّة
toxic musimm مسم
toy laʿba لعبة (*pl* -aat, luʿab)
trace *n* asar أسر (*pl* aasaar); atar أتر
trachea al- gaṣaba al-hawa'iyya
track *n* darib درب (*pl* duruub); khaṭṭ خط (*pl* khuṭuuṭ); **to follow a track** baara d-darib; bira d-darib • *v* gaṣṣa al-atar
tracker gaṣṣaaṣ قصّاص
tractor taraktar تركتر (*pl* -aat)
trade *n* tijaara تجارة ; **trade union** naqaaba نقابة • *v* taajar تاجر (tijaara)
trademark maarka tijaariyya
trader taajir تاجر (*pl* tijjaar, tujjaar)
tradition ʿaada عادة (*pl* -aat, ʿawaayid); **traditions** taqaaliid تقاليد
traditional taqliidi تقليدي ; ʿurfi عرفي
traffic ḥarakat al-muruur; ḥaraka حركة ; muruur مرور ; **the traffic police** (booliis) al-ḥaraka; **traffic lights** istob استوب ; al-ishaara; ishaarat al-ḥaraka; ishaarat al-muruur; **traffic sign** ishaarat al-ḥaraka; ishaarat al-muruur
train *n* (**railway**) gaṭar قطر (*pl* giṭaaraat, guṭaara); **freight train** gaṭar al-buḍaaʿa
train *v* darrab درّب (dirreeb, tadriib); **to be trained** iddarrab ادّرّب (dirreeb, tadriib)
trainee (*m*) muddarrib مدّرّب ; mutadarrib متدرّب ; (*f*) muddarriba مدّرّبة ; mutadarriba متدرّبة
trainer (*m*) mudarrib مدرّب ; (*f*) mudarriba مدرّبة
training tadriib تدريب (*pl* -aat)
traitor khaayin خاين (*pl* -iin, khawana)

trample daas داس (u, doosa)
trance **in a trance** ghargaan غرقان ; mughayyib مغيّب ; **to go into a trance** ghayyab غيّب (ghiyyeeb)
tranquillize hadda هدّى (-i,tahdiya); sakkan سكّن (sikkeen, taskiin)
tranquillizer muhaddi مهدّي (*pl* -yaat); musakkin مسكّن (*pl* -aat)
transfer *n* taḥwiil تحويل (*pl* -aat, taḥaawiil); iḥaala احالة • *v* ḥawwal حوّل (taḥwiil); nagal نقل (u, nagil); **to be transferred** itḥawwal اتحوّل (taḥwiil); itnagal اتنقل (nagil)
transformer ummiyya أمّيّة
translate tarjam ترجم (tarjama)
translation tarjama ترجمة ; **simultaneous translation** tarjama fawriyya
translator (*m*) mutarjim مترجم ; (*f*) mutarjima مترجمة ; **simultaneous translator** (*m*) mutarjim fawri ; (*f*) mutarjima fawriyya
transmission nagil نقل ; **(radio, TV)** irsaal إرسال
transparency shaffaafiyya شفّافية
transparent shaffaaf شفّاف ; rahiif رهيف
transplant *v* zaraᶜ زرع (a, ziraaᶜa)
transport *n* nagil نقل ; **(public)** muwaaṣalaat مواصلات • *v* nagal نقل (u, nagil); **(people)** raḥḥal رحّل (tarḥiil)
transportation nagil نقل ; **(public)** muwaaṣalaat مواصلات ; **(persons)** tarḥiil ترحيل
trap *n* sharak شرك (*pl* ashraak); fakhkh فخ (*pl* afkhaakh); maḍabb مضبّ (*pl* -aat); **(ambush)** kamiin كمين (*pl* kamaayin); **bird trap** galluubiyya قلوبيّة ; **steel trap** kajjaama كجّامة ; kallaaba كلابة ; **to set a trap** sharrak le- شرّك (shirreek, tashriik); (*fig*) ḥafar le- حفر (i, ḥafir) • *v* zarra زرّ (u, zarra); **to be trapped** inzarra انزرّ (zarra); itzarra اتزرّ (zarra)
travel *n* safar سفر ; **travel permit** ta'shiira تأشيرة • *v* saafar سافر (safar); **(unexpectedly)** khaṭar خطر (i, khaṭra)
traveller musaafir مسافر
tray ṣiiniyya صينيّة (*pl* ṣawaani); **(of basketwork)** reeka ريكة
treacherous ghaddaar غدّار
tread daas داس (u, doosa)
treasure kanz كنز (*pl* kunuuz)
treasurer (*m*) amiin khazna; (*f*) amiinat khazna
treasury khaziina خزينة (*pl* khazaayin, khizan); khazna خزنة (*pl* khizan)
treat *v* **(behave towards)** ᶜaamal عامل (muᶜaamala); itᶜaamal maᶜa اتعامل (muᶜaamala, taᶜaamul); **(medically)** daawa داوى (-i, mudaawaa); ᶜaalaj عالج (ᶜilaaj, muᶜaalaja); **to be treated medically** iddaawa ادّاوى (a, mudaawaa); itᶜaalaj اتعالج (muᶜaalaja, ᶜilaaj)
treatment **(behaviour towards)** muᶜaamala معاملة ; **(medical)** ᶜilaaj علاج (*pl* -aat); muᶜaalaja معالجة
treaty muᶜaahada معاهدة
tree(s) shadar شدر ; shajar شجر (*pl* ashjaar); **small tree** shideera شديرة ; **genealogical tree** shajarat an-nasab
trellis taᶜriisha تعريشة (*pl* taᶜaariish)

tremble rajaf رجف (i, rajiif, rajafaan); irtajaf ارتجف (rajafaan)
tremor rajfa رجفة
trench khandag خندق (*pl* khanaadig)
trespass itʿadda اتعدّى (-a, taʿaddi)
trial (**in court**) muḥaakama محاكمة; **to put on trial** ḥaakam حاكم (muḥaakama); (**test**) tajruba تجربة (*pl* tajaarub); **on trial** (**at work**) tiḥt al-ikhtibaar
triangle musallas مسلّس
tribal qabali قبلي; **tribal leader** sulṭaan سلطان (*pl* salaaṭiin)
tribalism ʿaṣabiyya عصبيّة
tribe gabiila قبيلة (*pl* gabaayil); **to which tribe do you belong?** jins-ak shinu?; **section of a tribe** baṭun بطن (*pl* buṭuun)
tribunal maḥkama محكمة (*pl* maḥaakim)
trick *n* malʿuub ملعوب (*pl* malaaʿiib); ḥiila حيلة (*pl* ḥiyal) • *v* itḥaayal ʿala اتحايل (taḥaayul)
trickle *v* naggaṭ نقّط (niggeeṭ); nazza نزّ (i, nazz)
trigger *n* titik تتك (*pl* -aat); zinaad زناد (*pl* -aat); ghammaaz غماز (*pl* -aat)
trill *n* zaghruuda زغرودة (zaghaarid) • *v* zaghrad زغرد (zaghrada)
trinity saaluus سالوس; **the Blessed Trinity** as-saaluus al-aqdas
trip *n* (**outing**) fusḥa فسحة (*pl* fusaḥ); riḥla رحلة (*pl* -aat, riḥal); jawla جولة; **to go on a trip** itfassaḥ اتفسّح (tifissiḥ); **to take s.o. out on a trip** fassaḥ فسّح (fisseeḥ, fusḥa)
trip *vi* (**over**) ʿitir (fi) عتر (a, ʿatir, ʿatra); itʿattar (fi) عتّر (ʿataraan); itshankal (fi) اتشنكل (shinkeel, shankala) • *vt* shankal (le-) شنكل (shinkeel, shankala)
tripe karsha كرشة
trivial taafih تافه
trot *n* jakka جكّة • *v* jara fi j-jakka; jakka جكّ (u, jakk)
trouble *n* mashaakil; **big trouble** wagʿa sheena/sooda; **in trouble** fi warṭa; fi mushkila; **to make trouble** ʿamal mashaakil • *v* gallag قلّق (gilleeg); (**disturb**) azʿaj أزعج (i, izʿaaj)
troublemaker shakkaal شكّال; bitaaʿ shibak; sharraani شرّاني
trough ḥooḍ حوض (*pl* ḥeeḍaan, aḥwaaḍ)
troupe firqa فرقة (*pl* firaq)
trousers banṭaloon بنطلون (*pl* banaaṭliin); (**loose**) sirwaal سروال (*pl* saraawiil)
trowel (**cement**) masṭariina مسطرينة; (**for plaster**) muḥaara محارة
truant daakki داكّي; **to play truant** dakka دكّ (u, dakk, dakakaan)
truck loori لوري (*pl* lawaari); ʿarabiyyat nagil; (**large**) gunduraani قندراني (*pl* -yyaat); **tipper truck** gallaab قلاب (*pl* -aat)
true ṣaaḥḥ صاح; ṣaḥiiḥ صحيح; ṣaḥḥ صح; **is it true?** ṣaḥii صحي; hagiigi حقيقي; **to be true** ṣaḥḥa صحّ (i, ṣaḥḥa); to **make sth. come true** ḥaggag حقّق (taḥgiig)
trumpet ṭurumba رمبة; turumbeeta ترمبيتة
trunk (**chest**) ṣanduug صندوق (*pl* ṣanaadiig); (**of a tree**) saag ساق (*pl* seegaan); (**of an elephant**) zalluuma زلّومة (*pl* zalaaliim); kharṭuum خرطوم (*pl* kharaaṭiim)

trust n siqa سقة • *v* wasaq fi وسق (yasiq, siqa)
trustee amiin أمين (*pl* umana)
trustworthy maḍmuun مضمون; mawsuuq fii-ho
truth ḥagiiga حقيقة (*pl* ḥagaayig); **to tell the truth** ṣadag صدق (i, ṣidig)
truthful ṣaadig صادق
truthfulness ṣidig صدق
try *v* ḥaawal حاول (muḥaawala); jarrab جرّب (jirreeb, tajriib); (**put on trial**) ḥaakam حاكم (muḥaakama)
T-shirt tiishirt تيشرت (*pl* -aat)
tub ṭashit طشت (*pl* ṭushaata); (**bath**) banyo بنيو (*pl* -haat); ḥooḍ al-banyo
tube ambuuba أمبوبة (*pl* anaabiib); anbuuba أنبوبة (*pl* anaabiib); maasuura ماسورة (*pl* -aat, mawaasiir); (**of toothpaste**) ṣubaaᶜ صباع (*pl* -aat); **inner tube** listik juwwaani
tuberculosis daran درن; sull سل; tiibii تيبي
Tuesday yoom at-talaata
tumbler kubbaaya كبّاية (*pl* -aat, kabaabi)
tumor waram ورم (*pl* awraam)
tuna tuuna تونة
tune *n* laḥn لحن (*pl* alḥaan); nagham نغم (*pl* anghaam); naghama نغمة (*pl* anghaam)
turban ᶜimma عمّة (*pl* ᶜimam)
Turk turki تركي (*pl* atraak)
Turkey turkiya تركيا
turkey(s) diik ruumi; jidaad ar-ruum
Turkish turki تركي (*pl* atraak)
turmeric kurkum كركم
turn *n* (**turning**) laffa لفّة; (**in succession**) door دور (*pl* adwaar) • *vi* laffa لفّ (i, laff); **to turn** (**round**) daar دار (u, doora, dawaraan) • *vt* laffa لفّ (i, laff); **to turn one's head** itlaffat (le-) اتلفّت (liffeet, lafta); **to turn on** (**light, gas**) fataḥ فتح (a, fatiḥ); wallaᶜ ولّع (willeeᶜ); (**engine**) dawwar دوّر (diwweer, tadwiir); shaghghal شغّل (shighgheel, tashghiil); **to turn off** (**light, gas**) gafal قفل (i, gafil); ṭafa طفى (-i, ṭafi, ṭafayaan); (**light**) katal كتل (u, katil); (**engine**) gafal قفل (i, gafil)); **to turn over** gallab قلّب (galba); (**e.g. cakes in oil**) gallab قلّب (gilleeb); **to turn inside out/ upside down** galab قلّب (i, galib, galba); **to turn upside down** shaglab شقلب (shigleeb, shaglabaan); **to be turned on** (**light, gas**) itwallaᶜ اتولّع (walca, willeeᶜ); (**engine**) iddawwar ادّوّر (diwweer); **to be turned off** (**light, gas**) iṭṭafa اطّفى (-i, ṭafiya); (**engine**) itgafal اتقفل (gafla, gafalaan); **to be turned over** itgallab اتقلّب (galba); (**e.g. of cakes in oil**) itgallab اتقلّب (gilleeb); **to be turned inside out/upside down** itgalab اتقلب (galba); ingalab انقلب (galba)
turning *n* laffa لفّة
turpentine sinner سنر
turtle abu l-gadaḥ
tusk sinn al-fiil
tweezers mulgaaṭ ملقاط (*pl* malaagiiṭ)
twelve iṭnaashar اطناشر
twenty ᶜishriin عشرين
twice marrateen مرّتين
twin *n* toom توم (*pl* teemaan); taw'am توءم (*pl* teemaan)

twist laffa لفّ (i, laff, laffa); (**a rope**) baram برم (u, barim); fatal فتل (i, fatil); **a muscle** shadda ʿaḍala; **to be twisted** it-laffa اتلفّ (laffa, lafafaan); (**of a rope**) itbaram اتبرم (barma, baramaan); itfatal اتفتل (fat-la); (**of a muscle**) itshaddat ʿaḍala

twitter shaghshagh شغشغ (shaghshagha)

two itneen اتنين ; **two hundred** miiteen ميتين

type *n* (**kind**) nooʿ نوع (*pl* anwaaʿ); (**stereotype**) namaṭ نمط (*pl* anmaaṭ)

type *v* ṭabaʿ طبع (a, ṭibaaʿa)

typewriter aala kaatba

typhoid taayfooyd تايفويد

tyrannical mustabidd مستبد ; taghyaan تغيان

tyranny istibdaad استبداد

tyre ʿajala عجلة ; listik لستك (*pl* lasaatik); **spare tyre** ʿajala isbeer; listik isbeer; **tyre repair shop** banshar بنشر (*pl* banaashir)

U - u

udder ḍiriʿ ضرع (*pl* ḍuruuʿ); shaṭur شطر (*pl* shuṭuur)

Uganda yughanda اوغندا

Ugandan *adj/n* yughandi اوغندي (*pl* -yyiin)

ugliness shana شنا ; gabaaḥa قباحة

ugly sheen شين ; gabiiḥ قبيح (*pl* -iin, gubaaḥ); **he/it is ugly** shakl-o sheen

ulcer gurḥa قرحة (*pl* guraḥ)

umbilical cord ḥabl as-surra; ḥabl al-mashiima

umbrella shamsiyya شمسيّة (*pl* -aat, shamaasi); maẓalla مظلّة

unbelievable ma maʿguul

unbeliever kaafir كافر (*pl* kuffaar, kafara)

unblock (**pipes**) sallak سلّك (silleek)

unburden (**one's mind**) faḍfaḍ فضفض (faḍfaḍa)

uncircumcised aghlaf أغلف (*f* ghalfa, *pl* ghuluf)

uncivilized jilif/jilf جلف (*pl* ajlaaf); hamaji همجي (*pl* -yyiin, hamaj); baladi ashaw; **un-civilized behaviour** hamajiyya همجيّة

uncle (**paternal**) ʿamm عم (*pl* aʿmaam); (**maternal**) khaal خال (*pl* akhwaal, kheelaan)

unclear ma waadiḥ; ghaamiḍ غامض ; (**of sound**) mushawwash مشوّش

unconscious ghamraan غمران

unconsciousness ghamra غمرة

uncooked nayy ني

uncover kashaf كشف (i, kashif)

under tiḥit تحت ; asfal أسفل

underpants libaas لباس (*pl* -aat); niksi نكسي (*pl* ankisa)

undershirt faniila فنيلة (*pl* fanillaat, fanaayil); faniila be-ḥammaalaat; (**worn under a jellabia**) ʿarraagi عراقي (*pl* ʿaraariig)

understand fihim فهم (a, faham); **to make s.o. understand** fah-ham فهّم (fihheem, tafhiim)

understanding faham فهم ; **mu-tual understanding** tafaahum

تفاهم ; **to reach an understanding** itfaaham اتفاهم (tafaahum)
undertake itʿaagad اتعاقد (taʿaagud); (**construction**) gaawal قاول (mugaawala); itgaawal اتقاول (mugaawala)
underwear malaabis daakhiliyya
undo fakka فكّ (i, fakk, fakakaan); ḥalla حلّ (i, ḥalla); (**hair**) nakash نكش (u, nakish)
undress malaṣ ملص (u, maliṣ); mallaṣ ملّص (milleeṣ, tamliiṣ); galaʿ قلع (a, galiʿ); gallaʿ قلّع (gilleeʿ)
uneasiness galag قلق
unemployed ʿaaṭil عاطل ; mutbaṭṭil متبطّل
unemployment ʿaṭaala عطالة ; baṭaala بطالة
unexpectedly faj'a فجأة ; faj'atan فجأة ; ʿala ghafla
unfaithful khaayin خاين (*pl* -iin, khawana)
unfortunate (**person**) ma maḥẓuuẓ; manḥuus منحوس
unfortunately le-suu' al-ḥaẓẓ; le-l-lasaf
ungrateful naakir aj-jamiil; jaaḥid جاحد ; **to be ungrateful** jaḥad جحد (a, juḥuud)
unhappy ma mabsuuṭ; ḥaznaan حزنان
uniform *n* labsa rasmiyya; yuniforim يونيفورم (*pl* -aat)
unintentionally be-duun gaṣid; be-gheer gaṣid; min duun ʿinya; sahwan سهوا
union ittiḥaad إتّحاد (*pl* -aat)
unit wiḥda وحدة (*pl* waḥadaat)
unite ittaḥad اتّحد (ittiḥaad)
united muttaḥid متّحد
unity waḥda وحدة
universe koon كون
university jaamʿa جامعة
unjust ma ʿaadil; ẓaalim ظالم
unlawful gheer qaanuuni
unless illa iza; illa law; law ma; inma; imma إمّا
unload (**goods**) nazzal نزّل (nizzeel); (**e.g. lorry**) farragh فرّغ (tafriigh); faḍḍa فضّى (-i, fiḍḍeey, tafḍiya); **to be unloaded** itnazzal اتنزّل (nizzeel); itfarragh اتفرّغ (tafriigh); itfaḍḍa اتفضّى (-a, tifiḍḍi)
unlucky ma maḥẓuuẓ; manḥuus منحوس
unoccupied faaḍi فاضي (*pl* -yyiin)
unofficial ma rasmi; gheer rasmi
unofficially be-ṣifa ma/gheer rasmiyya
unpleasant kariih كريه
unreasonable ma maʿguul
unripe nayy ني
unscrew fakka فكّ (i, fakk, fakakaan); **to be unscrewed** itfakka اتفكّ (fakk)
unsold baayir باير ; **to be unsold** baar بار (u, boora); **to leave unsold** bawwar بوّر (tabwiir)
unsuitable ma munaasib
untidy mubashtan مبشتن ; **to be untidy** itbashtan اتبشتن (bashtana)
untie fakka فكّ (i, fakk, fakakaan); ḥalla حلّ (i, ḥalla); **to be(come) untied** itfakka اتفكّ (fakk, fakakaan); itḥalla اتحلّ (ḥalla); inḥalla انحلّ (a, inḥilaal)
until le- لـ ; ḥatta حتّى ; le-ghaayat (ma); le-ḥaddi ma; **until now** le-hassaʿ; le-l-leela
unveil kashaf كشف (i, kashif)
unwell taʿbaan تعبان

up foog فوق
upbringing tarbiya تربية
upholster najjad نجّد (nijjeed, tanjiid); **to be upholstered** itnajjad اتنجّد (nijjeed, tanjiid)
upholstery nijaada نجادة ; tanjiid تنجيد
upon foog فوق ; ʿala على
upper foogaani فوقاني ; aʿla أعلى (*f* ʿulya)
uproar shaghab شغب ; mushaaghaba مشغابة
upset *adj* zaʿlaan زعلان • *v* zaʿʿal زعّل (ziʿʿeel, zaʿal)
upside down magluub مقلوب ; **to turn upside down** *vt* galab قلب (i, galib, galba) • *vi* itshaglab اتشقلب (shigleeb, shaglaba, shaglabaan); **to be turned upside down** itgalab اتقلب (galba); ingalab انقلب (galba)
upstairs foog فوق
upstream ʿaks at-tayyaar; ḍidd at-tayyaar
ureter ḥaalib حالب (*pl* ḥawaalib)
urethra majra al-bool
urgent ʿaajil عاجل ; mustaʿjil مستعجل
urinal mabwala مبولة
urinate baal بال (u, bool)
urine bool بول ; **obstruction or retention of urine** ḥabs bool
use *n* istiʿmaal إستعمال (*pl* -aat); istikhdaam إستخدام (*pl* -aat); **it's no use** ma binfaʿ; **what's the use of it?** da faaydat-o shinu? • *v* istaʿmal استعمل (istiʿmaal); istakhdam استخدم (istikhdaam)
used (**secondhand**) mustaʿmal مستعمل ; **to be(come) used (to)** itʿawwad (ʿala) اتعوّد (taʿwiid)
useful mufiid مفيد ; naafiʿ نافع ; **to be useful** nafaʿ نفع (a, nafiʿ); faad فاد (i, faayda)
useless ma naafiʿ; ma mufiid; **to be(come) useless** baaẓ باظ (u, bawaẓaan, booẓ)
usual ʿaadi عادي
usually ʿaadatan عادة
utensils adawaat ادوات ; **set of utensils** ʿidda عدّة (*pl* ʿidad); **kitchen utensils** mawaaʿiin مواعين
uterus riḥim رحم (*pl* arḥaam)
utility (**use**) faayda فايدة (*pl* fawaayid)

V - v

vacancy waẓiifa faaḍya; waẓiifa khaalya
vacant faaḍi فاضي ; khaali خالي
vacation ijaaza إجازة
vaccinate ṭaʿʿam طعم (tatʿiim); **to be vaccinated** iṭṭaʿʿam اطّعّم (taṭʿiim)
vaccination taṭʿiim تطعيم
vaccine maṣil مصل (*pl* amṣaal)
vacuum faraagh فراغ (*pl* -aat); **vacuum cleaner** maknasa kahraba'iyya
vagina mihbal مهبل (*pl* mahaabil)
vain **he is vain** shaayif nafs-o; **in vain** be-la faayda; be-duunfaayda; min gheer faayda
valid ṣaaliḥ صالح ; (**in force**) saari ساري
validity ṣalaaḥiyya صلاحيّة
valley waadi وادي (*pl* widyaan)
valuable qayyim قيّم ; ghaali غالي
value *n* qiima قيمة (*pl* qiyam); taman تمن (*pl* atmaan) • *v* (**set a**

value on) qaddar قدّر (taqdiir); qayyam قيّم (taqyiim); tamman تمّن (timmeen)
valve balif بلف (*pl* -aat)
vampire maṣṣaaṣ damm
vapour bukhaar بخار
variety taᶜaddud تعدّد ; tanawwuᶜ تنوّع
various mutᶜaddid متعدّد ; mukhtalif مختلف ; mutnawwiᶜ متنوّع ; munawwaᶜ منوّع
vary ikhtalaf اختلف (ikhtilaaf); itnawwaᶜ اتنوّع (tanawwuᶜ)
vase faaẓa فاظة ; zuhriyya زهريّة
veal ᶜajjaali عجّالي ; laḥam ᶜajjaali
vegetable(s) khuḍaar خضار ; khuḍrawaat خضروات
vegetarian nabaati نباتي
vegetation khuḍra خضرة
vehement ᶜaniif عنيف
vehemently be-shidda
veil *n* niqaab نقاب ; **to make s.o. wear a veil** naqqab نقّب (tanqiib) • *v* (**o.s.**) itnaqqab اتنقّب (niqaab)
vein ᶜirig عرق (*pl* ᶜuruug); **jugular vein** shiryaan شريان (sharaayiin); **varicose veins** dawaali دوالي
velvet gaṭiifa قطيفة (*pl* gaṭaayif)
vendor baayiᶜ بايع ; bayyaaᶜ بيّاع ; (**of secondhand goods**) dallaal دلال
vengeance intiqaam إنتقام (*pl* -aat)
venom simm سم (*pl* sumuum)
vent ṭaaga طاقة
ventilate (**e.g. a room**) hawwa هوّى (-i, tahwiya)
ventilation tahwiya تهوية
veranda baranda برندة
verb fiᶜil فعل (*pl* afᶜaal)
verdict ḥukum حكم (*pl* aḥkaam); **guilty verdict** idaana إدانة ; **to pronounce a verdict** ḥakam حكم (i, ḥukum)
verify it'akkad min اتأكّد (ta'kiid); itḥaggag min اتحقّق (taḥgiig); ityaggan be- اتيقّن (tayaggun)
vermin ḥasharaat حشرات
vertical ra'si رأسي
vertigo dookha دوخة
very jiddan جداً ; khaaliṣ خالص ; khalaaṣ خلاص ; shadiid شديد ; be-l-ḥeel
vest faniila فنيلة (*pl* fanillaat, fanaayil); (**worn under a jellabia**) ᶜarraagi عراقي (*pl* ᶜaraariig); (**waistcoat**) ṣideeri صديري (*pl* -yyaat)
veterinarian baṭari بطري (*pl* bayaaṭra); diktoor baṭari
vex maghaṣ مغص (i, maghaṣ); **to be vexed** itmaghaṣ (min) اتمغص (maghaṣa)
vice (**moral**) razaala رزالة
vicious sharis شرس
victim ḍaḥiyya ضحيّة (*pl* ḍaḥaaya)
victory (**in a game**) fooz فوز ; ghulub غلب ; (**in battle**) intiṣaar إنتصار (*pl* -aat); naṣr نصر ; **to gain victory** (**over**) intaṣar (ᶜala) انتصر (intiṣaar)
video vidiyuu فديو (*pl* -haat)
view *n* (**sight, outlook**) manẓar منظر (*pl* manaaẓir); (**opinion**) raay راي (*pl* aaraa); ra'y رأي (*pl* araa'); ruu'ya رؤية ; **point of view** wijhat naẓar
village ḥilla حلّة (*pl* ḥilal, ḥallaal); qarya قرية (*pl* qura); balad بلد (*pl* buluud, bilaad, buldaan); **small village** ḥileela حليلة
vinegar khall خل
violate itᶜadda ᶜala اتعدّى (-a, taᶜaddi)

violation taᶜaddi تعدّي (*pl* -yyaat); intihaak انتهاك (*pl* -aat)
violence ᶜunf عنف
violent ᶜaniif عنيف
violin kamanja كمنجا (*pl* -aat)
virgin bikra بكرة; bikr بكر (*pl* -aat); ᶜazraa عزرا (*pl* ᶜazaara)
virginity bakaara بكارة
virtue faḍiila فضيلة (*pl* faḍaayil)
virus fayrus فيروس (*pl* -aat)
visa ta'shiira تأشيرة; viiza فيزا (*pl* -aat)
visible baayin باين; waaḍiḥ واضح; ẓaahir ظاهر; **to become visible** ẓahar ظهر (a, ẓuhuur); **to make visible** ẓahhar ظهّر (ẓihheer, taẓhiir)
vision (**eyesight**) shoof شوف; naẓar نظر; baṣar بصر; (**dream**) ruu'ya رؤيا
visit *n* ziyaara زيارة • *v* zaar زار (u, ziyaara); (**regularly**) waaṣal واصل (muwaaṣala)
visitor ḍeef ضيف (*pl* ḍiyuuf); zaayir زاير (*pl* zuwwaar)
vital ḥayawi حيوي
vitiligo baraṣ برص; bahag بهق; buhaag بهاق; **afflicted with vitiligo** abraṣ أبرص (*f* barṣa, *pl* buruṣ)
vocational mihani مهني
voice ṣoot صوت (*pl* aṣwaat); ḥiss حس
volleyball kuura ṭaayra; kura ṭaayra; vooli فولي
voluntary ṭawᶜi طوعي
volunteer *n* muṭṭawwiᶜ مطوّع • *v* iṭṭawwaᶜ اطّوّع (taṭawwuᶜ)
vomit *n* ṭuraash طراش; istifraagh استفراغ • *v* ṭarash طرش (u, ṭuraash); istafragh استفرغ (istifraagh)
vote *n* ṣoot صوت (*pl* aṣwaat) • *v* ṣawwat صوّت (taṣwiit)
voucher iiṣaal إيصال (*pl* -aat); waṣil وصل (*pl* wuṣuulaat)
vow *n* ᶜahd عهد (*pl* ᶜuhuud); taᶜahhud تعهّد (*pl* -aat) • *v* itᶜahhad (be-) اتعهّد (taᶜahhud)
vulture killding abu ṣalᶜa; **Egyptian vulture(s)** rakham رخم
vulva faraj فرج (*pl* furuuj)

W - w

wade khaaḍ خاض (u, khuwaaḍa)
wadi waadi وادي (*pl* widyaan)
wage ajr أجر (*pl* ujuur); murattab مرتّب (*pl* -aat); (**for piecework**) ujra أجرة (*pl* ujar)
wail *v* walwal ولول (wilweel, walwala); ᶜawwa عوّى (-i, ᶜiwweey, ᶜawwa); (**of men**) jaᶜar جعر (a, jaᶜir, jiᶜᶜeer); (**of women**) saklab سكلب (saklaba)
waist wasaṭ وسط (*pl* awsaaṭ); ḥasha حشا; khiṣr خصر (*pl* khuṣuur)
waistband kamar كمر
waistcoat faniilat ṣuuf; faniilat ṣagaṭ
wait istanna استنّ (*no vn*); intaẓar انتظر (intiẓaar)
waiting intiẓaar انتظار; **to keep s.o. waiting** sharra شرّ (u, sharr); laṭaᶜ لطع (a, laṭiᶜ); **waiting list** ᶜadad al-muntaẓiriin
waiter sufraji سفرجي (*pl* -yya); jarasoon جرسون (*pl* -aat)
waitress sufrajiyya سفرجية; jarasoona جرسونة

wake up *vi* ṣiḥa صحا (-a, ṣaḥayaan); (**in the morning**) aṣbaḥ أصبح (i, ṣabaaḥ) • *vt* ṣaḥḥa صحّى (-i, ṣiḥḥeey, taṣḥiya); tawwar توّر (tiwweer)

walk *n* mashiya مشية ; **to go for a walk** itfassaḥ اتفسّح (fusḥa, fisseeḥ); itmashsha اتمشّى (-a, mashi, mashiya) • *v* masha مشى (-i, mashi, mashiya); **to walk quickly** (**in a hurry**) kasaḥ كسح (a, kasiḥ); (**taking big steps**) shabaḥ شبح (a, shabiḥ)

wall ḥeeṭa حيطة (*pl* ḥeeṭaan, ḥiyaṭ); (**fence, enclosure**) suur سور (*pl* aswaar)

wallet (**for men**) juzlaan جزلان (*pl* -aat, jazaaliin); (**for women**) maḥfaẓa محفظة (*pl* maḥaafiẓ); maṭbaga مطبقة (*pl* maṭaabig)

wander ḥaam حام (u, ḥuwaama); itjawwal اتجوّل (tajawwul)

want *n* ḥawja حوجة • *v* daar دار (u, deera); ʿaaz عاز (u, ʿooza)

war ḥarib حرب (*pl* ḥuruub, ḥuruubaat); **civil war** ḥarib ahliyya; **to wage war** ḥaarab حارب (ḥarib, muḥaaraba); **Islamic holy war** jihaad جهاد ; **fighter in a holy war** mujaahid مجاهد

ward *n* (**of hospital, prison**) ʿanbar عنبر (*pl* ʿanaabir)

wardrobe doolaab دولاب (*pl* dawaaliib)

warehouse makhzan مخزن (*pl* makhaazin)

warm *adj* daafi دافي ; ḥaami حامي • *vt* sakhkhan سخّن (sikhkheen, taskhiin); **to warm up** (**a person**) daffa دفّى (-i, diffeey) • *vi* (**for sports**) sakhkhan سخّن (sikhkheen, taskhiin); **to be warmed up** itsakhkhan اتسخّن (sikhkheen, taskhiin); (**of a person**) iddaffa ادّفا (-a, diffeey)

warmth dafa دفا

warn ḥazzar (min) حزّر (taḥziir); nabbah نبّه (tanbiih); anzar (min) أنزر (yunzir, inzaar)

warning ḥazar حزر ; inzaar إنزار (*pl* -aat); taḥziir تحزير (*pl* -aat)

warp *vi* itlawa اتلوى (-i, lawiya) • *vt* lawa لوى (-i, lawi, lawiya, lawayaan)

warranty ḍamaan ضمان ; ḍamaana ضمانة

wart nakhla نخلة

warthog ḥalluuf حلّوف (*pl* ḥalaaliif)

wash *v* ghasal غسل (i, ghasiil); ghassal غسّل (ghisseel, ghasiil); **to wash away** jaraf جرف (i, jarif); **to be washed** itghasal اتغسل (ghasiil); itghassal اتغسّل (ghisseel, ghasiil)

washbasin ḥooḍ حوض (*pl* ḥeeḍaan, aḥwaaḍ)

washer (**for taps**) jilba جلبة ; jilda جلدة

washerman ghassaal غسّال

washerwoman ghassaala غسّالة

washing machine ghassaala غسّالة

wasp abu dannaan; abu zannaan

waste *v* bazzar بزّر (bizzeer, tabziir); (**money**) baʿzag بعزق (baʿzaga)

watch *n* (**timepiece**) saaʿa ساعة ; **seller or repairer of watches** saaʿaati ساعاتي (*pl* -iyya) • *v* itfarraj ʿala اتفرّج (tafarruj); (**monitor**) raaqab راقب (muraaqaba); (**witness**) shaahad شاهد (mushaahada); (**guard**) ḥaras (min) حرس (i/u, ḥaris,

ḥiraasa); **watch out!** ḥaasib حاسب ; khalli baal-ak!
watchman ghafiir غفير (*pl* ghufara)
water *n* mooya موية ; **fresh water** mooya ḥilwa; **brackish water** mooya murra; **distilled water** mooya magaṭṭara; **mineral water** mooya maʿdaniyya; **water outlet** maṣraf مصرف (*pl* maṣaarif); **water seller** bitaaʿ al-mooya; **water tower** ṣihriij صهريج (*pl* ṣahaariij) • *v* saga سقى (-i, sagi)
waterfall shallaal شلال (*pl* -aat)
watermelon(s) baṭṭiikh بطّيخ
water pipe (hookah) shiisha شيشة (*pl* -aat, shiyash)
water skin khuruj خرج (*pl* akhraaj)
water tank fanṭaaẓ فنطاظ (*pl* fanaaṭiiẓ); ṣihriij صهريج (*pl* ṣahaariij)
waterwheel saagiya ساقية (*pl* sawaagi)
wave(s) *n* mooj موج
wax *n* shamiʿ شمع
way (thoroughfare) ṭariig طريق (*pl* ṭurug); sikka سكّة (*pl* sikak); shaariʿ شارع (*pl* shawaariʿ); **(method/means)** ṭariiga طريقة (*pl* ṭurug); **way in** dukhuul دخول ; **way out** khuruuj خروج ; **(escape)** mafarr مفر ; **no way** ma fii ṭariiga; **to give way** zaḥḥa زح (i, zaḥḥa, zaḥaḥaan); **by the way** be-l-munaasaba; **in this way** kida كدا ; kadi كدي
we niḥna نحنا
weak ḍaʿiif ضعيف (*pl* ḍuʿaaf); **to become weak** ḍiʿif ضعف (a, ḍuʿuf)
weakness ḍuʿuf ضعف ; ʿajz عجز
weak-willed iḍeena إضينة
wealth sarwa سروة
wealthy ghani غني (*pl* aghniya); ghanyaan غنيان
wean faṭam فطم (i, faṭim, fiṭaam); **to be weaned** itfaṭam اتفطم (faṭim, fiṭaam)
weapon(s) silaaḥ سلاح (*pl* asliḥa); **(sharp)** asliḥa beeḍa; **automatic weapon** dooshka دوشكا (*pl* -aat)
wear libis لبس (a, libis)
weariness zahaj زهج
weary (tired) murhaq مرهق
weather jaw جو (*pl* ajwaa)
weave nasaj نسج (u, nasiij, nisaaja)
weaver nassaaj نساج ; **weaver bird(s)** nassaaj نساج ; dukhaan al-ʿazaba
weaving nisaaja نساجة
web (of spider) beet abu/umm shabatu; **(internet)** shabakat al-intirnet
wedding ʿiris عرس (*pl* aʿraas); faraḥ فرح (*pl* afraaḥ); **wedding certificate** gasiima قسيمة ; **wedding procession** zaffa زفّة
wedge *n* khaabuur خابور (*pl* khawaabiir) • *v* **to wedge in** zannag زنّق (zinneeg, zanga)
Wednesday yoom al-arbiʿa
weed *n* gashsh قش ; ḥashiish حشيش (*pl* ḥashaayish) • *v* ḥashsha حشّ (i, ḥashsh); kaddab كدّب kiddeeb)
week usbuuʿ أسبوع (*pl* asaabiiʿ)
weekly *adj* usbuuʿi أسبوعي • *adv* usbuuʿiyyan أسبوعيّاً
weep baka (ʿala) بكى (-i, bika)
weevil(s) suus سوس ; **weevils** ʿantat عنتت ; ʿitta عتّة ; **to be(come) infested with weevils**

sawwas سوّس (siwwees, taswiis); ʿattat عتّت (ʿitteet)
weevil-ridden musawwis مسوّس; muʿattit معتّت
weigh wazan وزن (yoozin, wazin, wazna); **to weigh one against another** waazan been وازن (muwaazana)
weight wazin وزن; (*fig*) tugul تقل; **weight of a balance** wazna وزنة (*pl* awzaan); **to gain weight** simin سمن (a, sumun); **to lose weight** khassa خسّ (i, khassa, khasasaan)
weird ʿajiib عجيب; ghariib غريب (*pl* -iin)
welcome *interj* ahlan أهلا; ahlan wa sahlan; marḥab مرحب; marḥaban مرحبا; **you're welcome (answer to thanks)** ʿafwan عفواً • *v* raḥḥab رحّب (tarḥiib)
well *n* ʿeen عين (*pl* ʿiyuun); biir بير (*pl* abyaar, aabaar) • *v* **to well up (of water)** nabaʿ نبع (u, nabʿ)
well *adj* kwayyis كويّس; ṭayyib طيّب • *adv* kwayyis كويّس; **to get well** ṭaab طاب (i, ṭayabaan); shifa شفى (-a, shifaa); itʿaafa اتعافى (-a, muʿaafaa); **to do sth. well** karrab كرّب (kirreeb)
well-being salaama سلامة
well-cooked najiiḍ نجيض (*pl* nujaaḍ); mustawi مستوي; **to be well-cooked** nijiḍ نجض (najaaḍ); istawa استوى (-i, istiwa)
well-known maʿruuf معروف; **to be well-known for** ishtahar be- اشتهر (shuhra)
well-mannered muhazzab مهزّب; mu'addab مؤدّب; khaluug خلوق
west gharib غرب
western gharbi غربي (*pl* -yyiin)
westerner gharbi غربي (*pl* -yyiin); **(of Sudan)** gharbaawi غرباوي (*pl* gharraaba); gharraabi غرّابي (*pl* gharraaba)
westward be-l-gharib
wet *adj* mabluul مبلول; layyin ليّن; **to be(come) wet** itballa اتبلّ (balal, ball); itballal اتبلّل (billeel, tibillil); itbalbal اتبلبل (bilbeel) • *v* balla بلّ (i, balla); ballal بلّل (billeel); balbal بلبل (bilbeel)
what *interrog* shinu شنو; shin شن; eeh ايه; **what for?** le-shinu?
whatever mahma مهما
wheat gamiḥ قمح
wheel ʿajala عجلة
wheelbarrow dardaaga درداقة
when *interrog* miteen متين; biteen بتين • *conj* lamman لمّن; lamma لما; wakit ma; mata ma; saaʿta ساعة
whenever wakit ma; kullo ma; miteenma; mata ma; saaʿat ma
where *interrog* ween وين
whether kaan كان; in kaan
whetstone ḥajar masann
which *interrog* yaat- ياتـ; yaato ياتو • *pron* al- أل
while *conj* lamman لمّن; lamma لما • *n* mudda مدّة; **for a while (past)** min mudda; le-mudda; **(future)** le-mudda
whinny *v* ḥamḥam حمحم (ḥamḥama)
whip *n* sooṭ سوط (*pl* seeṭaan); **(of rhinoceros hide)** kurbaaj كرباج (*pl* karaabiij) • *v* jalad جلد (i, jalid)
whirlpool dawwaama دوامة

whirlwind ʿuṣaar عصار (*pl* -aat)
whisper *n* hamsa همسة • *v* hamas همس (i, hams); waswas وسوس (waswasa, wiswees); washwash وشوش (washwasha)
whistle *n* ṣuffaara صفّارة (*pl* -aat, ṣafaafiir) • *v* ṣaffar صفّر (taṣfiir)
white abyaḍ أبيض (*f* beeḍa, *pl* buyuḍ); **white of egg** bayaaḍ بياض
whitewash *v* ḍarab be-j-jiir; bayyaḍ be-j-jiir
who *pron* al- ألـ • *interrog* minu منو
whole kaamil كامل; kull كل
wholesale jumla جملة (*no pl*)
whooping cough katkoota كتكوتة
why *interrog* leeh ليه; ʿashaan shinu; le-shinu
wick (**of candle**) fatiila فتيلة (fataayil); (**of kerosene lamp or stove**) shariiṭ شريط (*pl* sharaayiṭ)
wicked shirriir شرّير (*pl* ashraar); sharraani شرّاني
wickedness sharr شر; khasaasa خساسة
wide waasiʿ واسع; wasiiʿ وسيع; **to be(come) wide** wisiʿ وسع (a, wasaaʿ)
widen wassaʿ وسّع (wisseeʿ, tawsiiʿ); **to be widened** itwassaʿ اتوسّع (tawassuʿ)
widow armala أرملة
widower armal أرمل (*pl* araamil)
width ʿariḍ عرض (*pl* ʿuruuḍ); wusuʿ وسع; (**materials**) ʿuruḍ عرض
wife mara مرة (*pl* niswaan, nasaawiin); zooja زوجة; **my wife** umm awlaad-i
wig baaruuka باروكة
wild mutwaḥḥish متوحّش; waḥsh وحش (*pl* wuḥuush)
wilderness khala خلا; **pertaining to the wilderness** khalawi خلوي
will (**testament**) waṣiyya وصيّة (*pl* waṣaaya); (**desire**) iraada إرادة; **strong will** ʿaziima عزيمة (*pl* ʿazaayim)
willow(s) ṣafṣaaf صفصاف
wily khabiis خبيس (*pl* -iin, khubasa); la'iim لئيم (*pl* lu'ama); makkaar مكّار; khasiis خسيس
win *vi* ghalab غلب (i, ghulub); kisib كسب (a, kasib); (**in gambling**) kharat خرت (i, kharit); **to make s.o. win** fawwaz فوّز (fooz) • *vt* faaz (be-) فاز (u, fooz); ribiḥ ربح (a, ribiḥ)
winch (**machine**) winish ونش (*pl* awnaash)
wind *n* hawa هوا; **hot wind** sumuum سموم; **cold wind** ziifa زيفة; **winds** aryaaḥ ارياح
wind *vi* (**e.g. road**) inḥana انحنى (-i, ḥaniya) • *vt* laffa لفّ (i, laff); **to wind up** (**e.g. a clock**) mala ملى (-a, mali)
window shubbaak شبّاك (*pl* shabaabiik)
windpipe al-gaṣaba al-hawa'iyya
wing jinaaḥ جناح (*pl* ajniḥa)
wink *n* ghamza غمزة • *v* ghamaz غمز (i, ghamiz)
winner ghaalib غالب; faayiz فايز
winnow ḍarra ضرّى (-i, ḍirreey)
winnowing fork ḍarraaya ضرّاية
winter shita شتا; **pertaining to the winter** shitwi شتوي
wipe masaḥ مسح (a, masiḥ, masaḥaan); **to wipe off dust** nafaḍ نفض (u, nafiḍ)
wiper massaaḥa مسّاحة

wire *n* silik سلك (*pl* aslaak); **wire netting (fine)** silik namli; namli نملي ; **chicken wire** silik araanib

wisdom ḥikma حكمة (*pl* ḥikam); baṣaara بصارة ; dabaara دبارة

wise ḥakiim حكيم (*pl* -iin, ḥukama); **(sensible)** ʿaagil عاقل ; ʿaglaani عقلاني

wish *n* umniya أمنية (*pl* -aat, amaani); tamanni تمني (*pl* -yaat); muniya منية (*pl* amaani) • *v* itmanna اتمنّى (-a, muna, tamanni); **I wish** ya-reet

witchcraft siḥir سحر

with (person) maʿa مع ; **(thing)** be- بـ

withdraw *vt* saḥab سحب (a, saḥib) • *vi* insaḥab انسحب (insiḥaab); **(socially)** inkamash min انكمش (inkimaash)

wither ḍablan ضبلن (ḍablana); ṣaffar صفّر (ṣiffeer)

withered *adj* ḍablaan ضبلان

within (time) khilaal خلال ; **(place)** juwwa جوّا

without duun دون ; be-duun; min gheer; be-la

witness *n* shaahid شاهد (*pl* shuhuud); **false witness** shaahid zuur; **witness for the defence** shaahid nafi; **witness for the prosecution** shaahid isbaat; **to bear witness** shihid شهد (a, shihaada) • *v* shaahad شاهد (mushaahada)

wobble *v* **(in walking)** itmaayal اتمايل (gilgeel, galgala); **(seated)** itgalgal اتقلقل (gilgeel, galgala)

woman mara مرة (*pl* niswaan, nasaawiin); **married woman** ḥurma حرمة (*pl* ḥariim)

womb riḥim رحم (*pl* arḥaam)

women ʿawiin عوين ; ḥariim حريم

wonder *n* **(amazing thing)** ʿajiiba عجيبة (*pl* ʿajaayib); **(miracle)** muʿjiza معجزة • *v* **I wonder** ya tara

wonderful raayiʿ رايع

wood khashab خشب ; **(for fire)** ḥaṭab حطب ; **piece of wood** ʿuud عود (*pl* ʿeedaan, aʿwaad); khashaba خشبة (*pl* -aat, akshaab); **wood vendor** ḥaṭṭaabi حطّابي (*pl* ḥaṭṭaaba)

woodcutter ḥaṭṭaabi حطّابي (*pl* ḥaṭṭaaba)

woodland ghaaba غابة

woodworm suus سوس

wool ṣuuf صوف (*pl* aṣwaaf)

word kalma كلمة (*pl* kalimaat); kilma كلمة (*pl* kalimaat)

work *n* shughul شغل (*pl* ashghaal); ʿamal عمل (*pl* aʿmaal); **work per day** yoomiyya يوميّة • *v* ishtaghal اشتغل (shughul); **to make/give s.o. work** shaghghal شغّل (shighgheel, tashghiil)

working shaghghaal شغّال

worker ʿaamil عامل (*pl* ʿummaal)

workshop warshat ʿamal

world ʿaalam عالم (*pl* ʿawaalim); dunya دنيا

worm abu ḥurguṣ; **worm(s)** duud دود (*unit n* duuda, duudaaya, *pl* deedaan); **guinea worm(s)** duud ghiiniyya; **to get worms** dawwad دوّد (diwweed)

worm-eaten musawwis مسوّس

worry *n* galag قلق ; hamm هم (*pl* humuum) • *vt* gallag قلّق (gilleeg) • *vi* **(about)** gilig (ʿala/be-) قلق (a, galag); gallag (ʿala/be-) قلّق (gilleeg)

worried (**about**) galgaan (ʿala) قلقان ; mugallig (ʿala) مقلّق ; mahmuum (be-) مهموم
worse akʿab أكعب ; aswa أسوا
worship *n* ʿibaada عبادة • *v* ʿabad عبد (u, ʿibaada)
worth qiima قيمة (*pl* qiyam); **to be worth** saawa ساوى (-i, musaawaa)
worthless be-la qiima
wound *n* jariḥ جرح (*pl* juruuḥ); (**caused by a splinter**) nashra نشرة • *v* jaraḥ جرح (a, jariḥ); ʿawwar عوّر (ʿiwweer, taʿwiir); **to be wounded** injaraḥ انجرح (jariḥ); itʿawwar اتعوّر (ʿiwweer); itʿawwag اتعوّق (taʿwiig)
wrap *v* laffa لفّ (i, laff); ghallaf غلّف (ghilleef, taghliif); **to be wrapped** itlaffa اتلفّ (laff); it-ghallaf اتغلّف (ghilleef, taghliif)
wrapping taghliif تغليف (*pl* -aat, taghaaliif)
wreck *n* ḥuṭaam حطام • *v* kharrab خرّب (khirreeb, takhriib); ḥaṭṭam حطّم (ḥiṭṭeem, taḥṭiim); **to be wrecked** itkharrab اتخرّب (kh-irreeb, kharaab); itḥaṭṭam اتحطّم (ḥiṭṭeem, taḥṭiim)
wrench *n* muftaaḥ مفتاح (*pl* mafaatiiḥ); **monkey wrench** muftaaḥ ingiliizi
wrestle ṣaaraʿ صارع (muṣaaraʿa)
wrestler muṣaariʿ مصارع
wretched shagyaan شقيان ; shagi شقي ; taʿiis تعيس ; miskiin مسكين (*pl* masaakiin)
wriggle (**fidget**) itgalgal اتقلقل (gilgeel, galgala); itmalmal اتململ (milmeel, malmala); (**snake, worm**) itḥargaṣ اتحرقص (ḥirgeeṣ, ḥargaṣa); itlawlaw اتلولو (liwleew, lawlawa)
wring maṣar مصر (u, maṣir)
wrinkle *n/n pl* karmasha كرمشة • *v* karmash كرمش (kirmeesh, karmasha); karfas كرفس (kir-fees, karfasa)
wrinkled (**clothes, skin**) mukar-mash مكرمش ; (**clothes only**) mukarfas مكرفس
wrist buuʿ بوع (buuʿeen)
write katab كتب (i, kitaaba); **to write down** dawwan دوّن (tad-wiin); katab كتب (i, kitaaba)
writer kaatib كاتب (*pl* kuttaab); mu'allif مؤلّف
writing kitaaba كتابة
wrong *adj* ghalaṭ غلط ; ghalṭaan غلطان ; khaaṭi خاطي ; **to be wrong** ghiliṭ غلط (a, ghalaṭ); khiṭa خطى (-i, khaṭa, khaṭiya) • *n* khaṭiya خطية (*pl* khaṭaaya) • *v* asaa le- اسا (yusii, isaa'a); ghiliṭ fi/ʿala غلط (a, ghalaṭ); khiṭa ʿala خطى (-i, khaṭa, khaṭiya); ẓalam ظلم (u, ẓulum)
wrongdoer ẓaalim ظالم (*pl* -iin, ẓalama)

X - x

X-rays ashiʿʿa أشعة (*sg* shuʿaaʿ)

Y - y

yam baambey بامبي
yard (**measure**) yaarda ياردة ; (**courtyard**) ḥoosh حوش (*pl* ḥeeshaan)
yawn *v* itshahhag اتشهّق (shihheeg)
year sana سنة (*pl* sanawaat, siniin); ʿaam عام (*pl* aʿwaam); ḥool حول (*pl* -aat); **school year** ṣaff صف (*pl* ṣufuuf); **New Year** raas as-sana
yeast khamiira خميرة ; **brewer's yeast** khamiira biira
yell *n* ṣarkha صرخة • *v* koorak كورك (kooraak); ṣarakh (fi) صرخ (a, ṣariikh); ṣarrakh صرّخ (ṣuraakh, ṣirreekh)
yellow aṣfar أصفر (*f* ṣafra, *pl* ṣufur); **to be(come) yellow** ṣaffar صفّر (ṣiffeer)
yes aywa أيوا ; aay آي ; (**as conversation response**) naʿam نعم
yesterday umbaariḥ أمبارح ; amis أمس ; **the day before yesterday** awwal amis; awwal umbaariḥ
yet (**however**) laakin لاكن ; **not yet** lissaʿ لسّع
yield *n* maḥṣuul محصول (*pl* maḥaaṣiil) • *v* (**produce**) nataj نتج (i, intaaj); jaab جاب (i, jeeba); (**renounce**) itnaazal (min/ʿan) اتنازل (tanaazul)
yoghurt zabaadi زبادي
yoke jooz جوز (*pl* jeezaan)
yolk ṣafaar al-beeḍ
you (*m*) inta انت ; (*f*) inti انتي ; (*pl*) intu انتو
young ṣighayyir صغير ; ṣaghiir صغير (*pl* ṣughaar); **young people** shabaab شباب ; **young woman** shaabba شابّة ; **young man** shaabb شاب (*pl* shabaab)
youth shabaab شباب

Z - z

zeal himma همة ; ḥamaasa حماسة
zealous hamiim هميم ; mujtahid مجتهد ; **to be(come) zealous** itḥammas اتحمّس (ḥamaas)
zebra ḥumaar al-waḥsh; ḥumaar al-waadi
zero ṣifir صفر ; ziiro زيرو
zinc zink زنك
zipper susta سستة (*pl* susat)
zone manṭiga منطقة (*pl* manaaṭig)
zoo ḥadiigat al-ḥayawaanaat
zucchini koosa كوسا (*unit n* koosa, koosaaya)

References

Comboni Fathers. 2005. *Spoken Arabic of Khartoum,* rev. Khartoum: CLIK.

Dal Cason, Orlando, Muhammed Mabrouk, and Shahinaz Muhammed, eds. 1991. *Spoken Arabic of Khartoum.* Khartoum: CLIK.

Hillelson, S., comp. 1925. *Sudan Arabic: English-Arabic vocabulary.* London: The Sudan Government.

Persson, Andrew M., and Janet R. Persson, with Ahmed Hussein. 2003. *Sudanese colloquial Arabic for beginners.* Khartoum: SudMedia.

Qaasim, Awn ash-Shariif. 1972. *qaamuus al-lahja al-'aammiyya fi s-suudaan.* Khartoum: University of Khartoum Press.

SIL International Publications

Additional Releases in the **Publications in Linguistics** Series

149. **A Grammar of Digo, A Bantu language of Kenya and Tanzania**, by Steve Nicolle, 2013, 443 pp., ISBN 978-1-55671-281-4 *Coming in 2013.*
148. **A Grammar of Bora with Special Attention to Tone**, by Wesley Thiesen and David Weber, 2012, 585 pp., ISBN 978-1-55671-301-9
147. **The Kifuliiru Language, Volume 2: A descriptive grammar**, by Roger Van Otterloo, 2011, 612 pp., ISBN 978-1-55671-270-8
146. **The Kifuliiru language, Volume 1: Phonology, tone, and morphological derivation**, by Karen Van Otterloo, 2011, 512 pp., ISBN 978-1-55671-261-6
145. **Language death in Mesmes**, by Michael B. Ahland, 2010, 155 pp., ISBN 978-1-55671-227-2
144. **The phonology of two central Chadic languages**, by Tony Smith and Richard Gravina, 2010, 267 pp., ISBN 978-155671-231-9
143. **A grammar of Akoose: A northwest Bantu language**, by Robert Hedinger, 2008, 318 pp., ISBN 978-1-55671-222-7
142. **Word order in Toposa: An aspect of multiple feature-checking**, by Helga Schröder, 2008, 213 pp., ISBN 978-1-55671-181-7
141. **Aspects of the morphology and phonology of Kɔnni**, by Michael C. Cahill, 2007, 537 pp., ISBN 978-1-55671-184-8
140. **The phonology of Mono**, by Kenneth Olson, 2005, 311 pp., ISBN 978-1-55671-160-2
139. **Language and life: Essays in memory of Kenneth L. Pike**, edited by Wise, Headland, and Brend, 2003, 674 pp., ISBN 978-1-55671-140-4

SIL International Publications
7500 W. Camp Wisdom Road
Dallas, TX 75236-5629

Voice: 972-708-7404
Fax: 972-708-7363
publications_intl@sil.org
www.ethnologue.com/bookstore.asp